Traditions & Encounters

A Global Perspective on the Past

Volume C: From 1750 to the Present

FOURTH EDITION

Jerry H. Bentley

University of Hawai`i

Herbert F. Ziegler

University of Hawai`i

Boston   Burr Ridge, IL   Dubuque, IA   Madison, WI   New York   San Francisco   St. Louis
Bangkok   Bogotá   Caracas   Kuala Lumpur   Lisbon   London   Madrid   Mexico City
Milan   Montreal   New Delhi   Santiago   Seoul   Singapore   Sydney   Taipei   Toronto

McGraw-Hill
Higher Education

Published by McGraw-Hill, an imprint of The McGraw-Hill Companies, Inc., 1221 Avenue of the Americas, New York, NY 10020.
Copyright © 2008, 2006, 2003, 2000. All rights reserved. No part of this publication may be reproduced or distributed in any form
or by any means, or stored in a database or retrieval system, without the prior written consent of The McGraw-Hill Companies, Inc.,
including, but not limited to, in any network or other electronic storage or transmission, or broadcast for distance learning.

This book is printed on acid-free paper.

1 2 3 4 5 6 7 8 9 0 DOW/DOW 0 9 8 7

ISBN: 978-0-07-333066-2
MHID: 0-07-333066-3

Editor in Chief: *Michael Ryan*
Publisher: *Lisa Moore*
Sponsoring Editor: *Jon-David Hague*
Marketing Manager: *Pamela Cooper*
Media Producer: *Jessalyn Clark*
Developmental Editor: *Susan Gouijnstook*
Production Editor: *Brett Coker*
Manuscript Editor: *Carole Crouse*
Art Director: *Jeanne M. Schreiber*
Designers: *Lisa Devenish and Kim Menning*
Cover Designers: *Linda Beaupre and Cassandra Chu*
Art Manager: *Robin Mouat*
Manager, Photo Research: *Brian J. Pecko*
Production Supervisor: *Richard DeVitto*
Composition: *Thompson Type*
Printing: *45# Publishers Matte Plus by R.R. Donnelley & Sons*

Credits: The credits section for this book begins on page C-1 and is considered an extension of the copyright page.

Library of Congress Cataloging-in-Publication Data

Bentley, Jerry H., 1949–
    Traditions & encounters: a global perspective on the past / Jerry H. Bentley, Herbert F. Ziegler.—4th ed.
       p. cm.
    Includes bibliographical references and index.
    ISBN-13: 978-0-07-340693-0 (hbk. : alk. paper)
    MHID: 0-07-340693-7 (hbk. alk. paper)
    1. World history. 2. Intercultural communication—History. I. Ziegler, Herbert F., 1949–   II. Title.
III. Title: Traditions and encounters.
D20.B42 2009
909—dc22

                                                    2007007832

The Internet addresses listed in the text were accurate at the time of publication. The inclusion of a Web site does not indicate an
endorsement by the authors or McGraw-Hill, and McGraw-Hill does not guarantee the accuracy of the information presented at
these sites.

www.mhhe.com

Brief Contents

Maps   ix
Sources from the Past   x
Preface   xi
Acknowledgments   xxvi

PART VI **An Age of Revolution, Industry, and Empire, 1750 to 1914**   778
   29 Revolutions and National States in the Atlantic World   781
   30 The Making of Industrial Society   815
   31 The Americas in the Age of Independence   847
   32 Societies at Crossroads   879
   33 The Building of Global Empires   909

PART VII **Contemporary Global Realignments, 1914 to the Present**   942
   34 The Great War: The World in Upheaval   945
   35 An Age of Anxiety   977
   36 Nationalism and Political Identities in Asia, Africa, and Latin America   1005
   37 New Conflagrations: World War II   1031
   38 The Bipolar World   1063
   39 The End of Empire   1095
   40 A World without Borders   1131
   Glossary   G-1
   Credits   C-1
   Index   I-1

Detailed Contents

Maps ix | Sources from the Past x | Preface xi
A Brief Note on Usage xxiii | About the Authors xxv | Acknowledgments xxvi

PART VI   An Age of Revolution, Industry, and Empire, 1750 to 1914   778

CHAPTER 29

Revolutions and National States in the Atlantic World   781

Popular Sovereignty and Political Upheaval   782
  Enlightened and Revolutionary Ideas   783
  The American Revolution   784
  The French Revolution   787

SOURCES FROM THE PAST: The Declaration of the Rights of Man and the Citizen   789

  The Reign of Napoleon   792
The Influence of Revolution   794
  The Haitian Revolution   795
  Wars of Independence in Latin America   796
  The Emergence of Ideologies: Conservatism and Liberalism   800
  Testing the Limits of Revolutionary Ideals: Slavery   801
  Testing the Limits of Revolutionary Ideals: Women's Rights   802

SOURCES FROM THE PAST: Declaration of the Rights of Woman and the Female Citizen   804

The Consolidation of National States in Europe   805
  Nations and Nationalism   805
  The Emergence of National Communities   807
  The Unifications of Italy and Germany   809
Summary   811
Chronology   812
For Further Reading   813

CHAPTER 30

The Making of Industrial Society   815

Patterns of Industrialization   816
  Foundations of Industrialization   817
  The Factory System   820
  The Early Spread of Industrialization   821
  Industrial Capitalism   824
Industrial Society   825
  The Fruits of Industry   826
  Urbanization and Migration   829

SOURCES FROM THE PAST: Thomas Malthus on Population   830

iv

Industry and Society   832
The Socialist Challenge   834

SOURCES FROM THE PAST: Marx and Engels on Bourgeoisie and Proletarians   836

Global Effects of Industrialization   838
The Continuing Spread of Industrialization   838
The International Division of Labor   839
Summary   842
Chronology   843
For Further Reading   843

CHAPTER 31

The Americas in the Age of Independence   847
The Building of American States   848
The United States:
Westward Expansion and Civil War   849
The Canadian Dominion:
Independence without War   853
Latin America:
Fragmentation and Political Experimentation   854

SOURCES FROM THE PAST:
Ponciano Arriaga Calls for Land Reform   859

American Economic Development   860
Migration to the Americas   861
Economic Expansion in the United States   862
Canadian Prosperity   865
Latin American Investments   865
American Cultural and Social Diversity   867
Multicultural Society in the United States   868
Canadian Cultural Contrasts   870

SOURCES FROM THE PAST:
The Meaning of Freedom for an Ex-Slave   871

Ethnicity, Identity, and Gender in Latin America   872
Summary   875
Chronology   876
For Further Reading   876

CHAPTER 32

Societies at Crossroads   879
The Ottoman Empire in Decline   880
The Nature of Decline   881
Reform and Reorganization   883
The Young Turk Era   885

SOURCES FROM THE PAST:
Proclamation of the Young Turks   886

The Russian Empire under Pressure   886
Military Defeat and Social Reform   887
Industrialization   889
Repression and Revolution   890
The Chinese Empire under Siege   892
The Opium War and the Unequal Treaties   892

SOURCES FROM THE PAST:
Letter of Lin Zexu to Queen Victoria   894

The Taiping Rebellion   896
Reform Frustrated   898
The Transformation of Japan   899
From Tokugawa to Meiji   900
Meiji Reforms   902
Summary   904
Chronology   905
For Further Reading   905

CHAPTER 33

The Building of Global Empires   909
Foundations of Empire   910
Motives of Imperialism   910
Tools of Empire   912

SOURCES FROM THE PAST:
Rudyard Kipling on the White Man's Burden   913

European Imperialism   915
The British Empire in India   915
Imperialism in Central Asia and Southeast Asia   917
The Scramble for Africa   919

SOURCES FROM THE PAST: Lord Lugard Justifies Imperialism and Indirect Rule in Africa   924

European Imperialism in the Pacific   925
The Emergence of New Imperial Powers   927
U.S. Imperialism in Latin America and the Pacific   928
Imperial Japan   929
Legacies of Imperialism   930
Empire and Economy   931
Labor Migrations   932
Empire and Society   934
Nationalism and Anticolonial Movements   936
Summary   938
Chronology   939
For Further Reading   939

PART VII   Contemporary Global Realignments, 1914 to the Present   942

CHAPTER 34

The Great War: The World in Upheaval   945

The Drift toward War   946
  Nationalist Aspirations   947
  National Rivalries   947
  Understandings and Alliances   949
Global War   950
  The Guns of August   951
  Mutual Butchery   952
  Total War: The Home Front   956

SOURCES FROM THE PAST:
Dulce et decorum est   957

Conflict in East Asia and the Pacific   959
  Battles in Africa and Southwest Asia   960
The End of the War   962
  Revolution in Russia   963
  U.S. Intervention and the Collapse
    of the Central Powers   964

SOURCES FROM THE PAST:
The State and Revolution   965

  After the War   967
  Challenges to European Preeminence   972
Summary   974
Chronology   974
For Further Reading   975

CHAPTER 35

An Age of Anxiety   977

Probing Cultural Frontiers   979
  Postwar Pessimism   979
  Revolutions in Physics and Psychology   980
  Experimentation in Art and Architecture   982
Global Depression   985
  The Great Depression   985
  Despair and Government Action   987
  Economic Experimentation   988

SOURCES FROM THE PAST:
Franklin Delano Roosevelt: Nothing to Fear   990

Challenges to the Liberal Order   990
  Communism in Russia   991
  The Fascist Alternative   994
  Italian Fascism   995
  German National Socialism   997

SOURCES FROM THE PAST: Mein Kampf   998

Summary   1001
Chronology   1002
For Further Reading   1002

CHAPTER 36

Nationalism and Political Identities in Asia, Africa, and Latin America   1005

Asian Paths to Autonomy   1006
  India's Quest for Home Rule   1006
  China's Search for Order   1008

SOURCES FROM THE PAST:
"Self Rule Is My Birthright"   1009

  Imperial and Imperialist Japan   1012
Africa under Colonial Domination   1014
  Africa and the Great War   1014
  The Colonial Economy   1016
  African Nationalism   1018

SOURCES FROM THE PAST: Africa for Africans   1019

Latin American Struggles with Neocolonialism   1020
  The Impact of the Great War and the
    Great Depression   1021
  The Evolution of Economic Imperialism   1023
  Conflicts with a "Good Neighbor"   1025
Summary   1028
Chronology   1028
For Further Reading   1029

CHAPTER 37

New Conflagrations: World War II 1031

Origins of World War II 1032
  Japan's War in China 1032
  Italian and German Aggression 1035
Total War: The World under Fire 1037
  Blitzkrieg: Germany Conquers Europe 1037
  The German Invasion of the Soviet Union 1039
  Battles in Asia and the Pacific 1040
  Defeat of the Axis Powers 1043
SOURCES FROM THE PAST:
A Hiroshima Maiden's Tale 1045

Life during Wartime 1047
  Occupation, Collaboration, and Resistance 1048
  The Holocaust 1050
SOURCES FROM THE PAST:
"We Will Never Speak about It in Public" 1051

Women and the War 1053
Neither Peace nor War 1054
  Postwar Settlements and Cold War 1055
  Global Reconstruction and the United Nations 1057
Summary 1058
Chronology 1059
For Further Reading 1059

CHAPTER 38

The Bipolar World 1063

The Formation of a Bipolar World 1064
  The Cold War in Europe 1064
  Confrontations in Korea and Cuba 1067
  Cold War Societies 1070
SOURCES FROM THE PAST:
Nikita Khrushchev on the Capitalist Iron Curtain 1074

Challenges to Superpower Hegemony 1076
  Defiance, Dissent, and Intervention in Europe 1077
  The People's Republic of China 1079
  Détente and the Decline of Superpower Influence 1081
The End of the Cold War 1084
  Revolutions in Eastern and Central Europe 1085
  The Collapse of the Soviet Union 1087
  Toward an Uncertain Future 1088
Summary 1090
Chronology 1091
For Further Reading 1091

CHAPTER 39

The End of Empire 1095

Independence in Asia 1097
  India's Partitioned Independence 1097
SOURCES FROM THE PAST: Muhammad Ali Jinnah on
the Need for a Muslim Pakistan 1099

Nationalist Struggles in Vietnam 1101
Arab National States and the Problem of Palestine 1103
Decolonization in Africa 1106
  Forcing the French out of North Africa 1106
  Black African Nationalism and Independence 1108
  Freedom and Conflict in Sub-Saharan Africa 1109
SOURCES FROM THE PAST:
Kwame Nkrumah on African Unity 1111

After Independence:
  Long-Term Struggles in the Postcolonial Era 1112
  Communism and Democracy in Asia 1112
  Islamic Resurgence in
    Southwest Asia and North Africa 1115
  Politics and Economics in Latin America 1118
  War and Peace in Sub-Saharan Africa 1124
Summary 1127
Chronology 1128
For Further Reading 1128

CHAPTER 40

A World without Borders 1131

The Global Economy 1132
  Economic Globalization 1133
  Economic Growth in Asia 1135
  Trading Blocs 1137
Cross-Cultural Exchanges and
  Global Communications 1139
  Global Barbie 1140
  Consumption and Cultural Interaction 1141
  The Age of Access 1142
Global Problems 1143
  Population Pressures and
    Environmental Degradation 1143
SOURCES FROM THE PAST: Silent Spring 1146

Economic Inequities and Labor Servitude 1148
Global Diseases 1149
Global Terrorism 1151
Coping with Global Problems:
  International Organizations 1153

Crossing Boundaries 1156
    Women's Traditions and Feminist Challenges 1156
    Migration 1160
    Cross-Cultural Travelers 1163
Summary 1165

Chronology 1166
For Further Reading 1166
Glossary G-1
Credits C-1
Index I-1

Maps

MAP 29.1 The American revolution. 787

MAP 29.2 Napoleon's empire in 1812. 793

MAP 29.3 Latin America in 1830. 798

MAP 29.4 The unification of Italy and Germany. 809

MAP 30.1 Industrial Europe, ca. 1850. 823

MAP 31.1 Westward expansion of the United States during the nineteenth century. 850

MAP 31.2 The Dominion of Canada in the nineteenth century. 855

MAP 31.3 Latin America in the late nineteenth century. 856

MAP 32.1 Territorial losses of the Ottoman empire, 1800–1923. 882

MAP 32.2 The Russian empire, 1801–1914. 887

MAP 32.3 East Asia in the nineteenth century. 895

MAP 33.1 Imperialism in Asia, ca. 1914. 918

MAP 33.2 Imperialism in Africa, ca. 1914. 923

MAP 33.3 Imperialism in Oceania, ca. 1914. 926

MAP 33.4 Imperialism and migration during the nineteenth and early twentieth centuries. 933

MAP 34.1 The Great War in Europe and southwest Asia, 1914–1918. 953

MAP 34.2 Territorial changes in Europe after the Great War. 971

MAP 34.3 Territorial changes in southwest Asia after the Great War. 973

MAP 36.1 The struggle for control in China, 1927–1936. 1011

MAP 36.2 The United States in Latin America, 1895–1941. 1024

MAP 37.1 High tide of Axis expansion in Europe and north Africa, 1942–1943. 1043

MAP 37.2 World War II in Asia and the Pacific. 1046

MAP 37.3 The Holocaust in Europe, 1933–1945. 1052

MAP 38.1 Occupied Germany, 1945–1949. 1066

MAP 38.2 The cold war, 1949–1962. 1071

MAP 38.3 The collapse of the Soviet Union and European communist regimes, 1991. 1089

MAP 39.1 Decolonization in Asia. 1100

MAP 39.2 The Arab-Israeli conflict, 1949–1982. 1105

MAP 39.3 Decolonization in Africa. 1109

MAP 40.1 European Union membership, 2004. 1138

MAP 40.2 Global estimates of HIV/AIDS. 1150

Sources from the Past

CHAPTER 29

Declaration of the Rights of Man and the Citizen   789

Declaration of the Rights of Woman
and the Female Citizen   804

CHAPTER 30

Thomas Malthus on Population   830

Marx and Engels on Bourgeoisie and Proletarians   836

CHAPTER 31

Ponciano Arriaga Calls for Land Reform   859

The Meaning of Freedom for an Ex-Slave   871

CHAPTER 32

Proclamation of the Young Turks   886

Letter of Lin Zexu to Queen Victoria   894

CHAPTER 33

Rudyard Kipling on the White Man's Burden   913

Lord Lugard Justifies Imperialism
and Indirect Rule in Africa   924

CHAPTER 34

Dulce et decorum est   957

The State and Revolution   965

CHAPTER 35

Franklin Delano Roosevelt: Nothing to Fear   990

Mein Kampf   998

CHAPTER 36

"Self Rule Is My Birthright"   1009

Africa for Africans   1019

CHAPTER 37

A Hiroshima Maiden's Tale   1045

"We Will Never Speak about It in Public"   1051

CHAPTER 38

Nikita Khrushchev on the Capitalist Iron Curtain   1074

CHAPTER 39

Muhammad Ali Jinnah on
the Need for a Muslim Pakistan   1099

Kwame Nkrumah on African Unity   1111

CHAPTER 40

Silent Spring   1146

Preface

Since the early 1990s, journalists, politicians, scholars, and others have frequently resorted to the term *globalization* when commenting on the increasingly tight connections linking the world's lands and peoples. By the late twentieth century, global transportation and communication networks had become more intricate than ever before, and they promoted both economic integration and systematic interaction among peoples throughout the world. Trade goods and electronic currency flowed around the world while manufacturers restlessly sought new sites to produce consumer goods. Globalization brought tremendous wealth to some, and it facilitated both commercial and cultural exchanges that enriched the lives of many peoples. Alongside opportunities, the era of globalization also brought numerous problems: widespread pollution, global warming, cultural challenges, ethnic tensions, political conflicts, and weapons of mass destruction loomed as potential threats to peoples of all world regions.

Yet even though they are more prominent today than ever before, global interactions and global problems are by no means new features of world history. On the contrary, there is a long historical context for contemporary globalization, and only in light of past experience is it possible to understand the contemporary world.

A Global Perspective on the Past

Our purpose in *Traditions & Encounters* is to offer a global perspective on the past—a vision of history that is meaningful and appropriate for the interdependent world of contemporary times. During an era when peoples from all parts of the earth meet, mingle, interact, and do business with one another, a global perspective has become an essential tool for informed and responsible citizenship. Because global interactions profoundly influence the fortunes of peoples in all lands, it is impossible to understand the contemporary world by approaching it exclusively from the viewpoint of western Europe, the United States, Japan, or any other individual society. It is equally impossible to understand the world's history by viewing it exclusively through the lenses of any particular society's historical experience.

A global perspective on the past calls for analysis that respects the historical experiences of all the world's peoples—not just one or a few—and that examines the roles of all in the making of a world inhabited by all. A global perspective calls also for analysis that goes beyond the study of individual societies to examine their larger regional, continental, hemispheric, and global contexts. A global perspective calls further for exploration of the networks and structures that have promoted interactions between peoples of different societies. A global perspective calls finally for attention to the effects of interactions on the lands, peoples, and societies that have participated in large-scale historical processes. By bringing a global perspective to the study of world history, we seek to offer an understanding of the past that places the contemporary world in meaningful historical context.

On the basis of a superficial inspection, *Traditions & Encounters* might look similar to several other textbooks that survey the world's past. Like other books, for example, *Traditions & Encounters* examines the historical development of societies in Asia, Europe, Africa, the Americas, and Oceania. Yet *Traditions & Encounters* differs from other works in two particularly important ways. First, it relies on a pair of prominent themes to bring a global perspective to the study of world history: it traces the historical development of individual societies in all world regions, and it also focuses attention systematically on interactions between peoples of different societies. Second, it organizes the human past into seven eras that represent distinct and coherent periods of global historical development.

Themes: Tradition and Encounter

How is it possible to make sense of the entire human past? The study of world history is an exhilarating project that offers unparalleled opportunities to understand oneself and one's own society in relation to the larger world. Given the range of human diversity, however, world history also presents a daunting challenge. Human communities have adopted widely varying forms of political, social, and economic organization, and they have elaborated even more diverse cultural, religious, and philosophical legacies. Given the manifold diversity of human societies, it might seem that masses of unrelated detail threaten to swamp any effort to deal with all the world's history.

In this book we concentrate on two main themes—tradition and encounter—that help bring order to world history. These two themes bring focus to some of the most important features of human experience on the earth. In combination, they account for much of the historical development of human societies.

The theme of tradition draws attention to the formation, the maintenance, and sometimes also the collapse of individual societies. From their earliest days on earth, human groups have generated distinctive political, social, economic, and cultural traditions that have guided affairs in their own societies. Some of those traditions arose and disappeared relatively quickly, whereas others influenced human affairs over the centuries and millennia, sometimes down to the present day. Thus one of our principal concerns in this book is to examine the development of the diverse political, social, economic, and cultural traditions that have shaped the lives and experiences of the world's various peoples. Individual chapters explore the traditions that different peoples have relied on to organize and sustain societies in Asia, Europe, Africa, the Americas, and Oceania. Emphasis falls especially on the large, densely populated, complex, city-based societies that have most deeply influenced world affairs for the past six thousand years, but smaller and less powerful societies also receive their share of attention. This fourth edition of *Traditions & Encounters* draws on recent scholarship to offer updated and enhanced understanding of the world's individual societies.

While elaborating distinctive political, social, economic, and cultural traditions to organize their affairs, the world's peoples have also interacted regularly with one another since the earliest days of human history. The theme of encounter directs attention to communications, interactions, networks, and exchanges that have linked individual societies to their neighbors and others in the larger world. By systematically examining encounters among peoples of different societies, we draw attention to processes of cross-cultural interaction that have been some of the most effective agents of change in all of world history. In the form of mass migrations, campaigns of imperial expansion, long-distance trade, diffusions of food crops, the spread of infectious and contagious diseases, transfers of technological skills, and the spread of religious and cultural traditions, those interactions have profoundly influenced the experiences of individual societies and the development of the world as a whole. Thus, while presenting wide-ranging discussion of individual societies and their traditions, this book also devotes considerable attention to the many and varied forms of interaction that have linked the fortunes of peoples from different societies. Many of the book's chapters also examine the large-scale structures of transportation, communication, and exchange that supported interactions among the world's peoples. Just as it updates treatments of individual societies, this fourth edition of *Traditions & Encounters* also draws on recent scholarship to enhance discussions of encounters and focus attention more clearly than before on processes of cross-cultural interaction.

Organization: Seven Eras of Global History

While relying on the themes of tradition and encounter to bring the diversity of world history into focus, we also seek to bring about improved understanding of the world's development through time by organizing it into seven eras of global history. These eras, treated successively in the seven parts of this book, represent coherent epochs that form the larger architecture of world history as we see it. The seven eras do not reflect the particular experience of any single society so much as the common experiences of all societies participating in processes of cross-cultural interaction. Thus our seven eras of global history owe their coherence particularly to patterns in the networks of transportation, communication, and exchange that have linked peoples of different societies at different times in the past. Even in ancient times those networks supported interactions that shaped the experiences of peoples from different lands, and with the development of increasingly effective technologies of transportation and communication, interactions have grown more frequent, systematic, and intense over time. By studying the world's peoples in the framework of the seven eras of global history, we seek to offer meaningful comparisons between different societies and also to highlight the role of cross-cultural interactions in shaping the experiences of individual societies and influencing the development of the world as a whole.

Thus from the beginning to the end of this book we focus on the twin themes of tradition and encounter, which in combination go a long way toward accounting for the historical development of the human species on planet earth, and we situate the experiences of individual societies in their larger regional, continental, hemispheric, and global contexts. By bringing a global perspective to the study of humanity's common historical experience, we seek to offer a vision of the past that is both meaningful and appropriate for the interdependent world of contemporary times. We hope that *Traditions & Encounters* will enable readers to understand the development of human societies through time and also to place the contemporary world in relevant historical context.

Changes for the Fourth Edition

In preparing this fourth edition of *Traditions & Encounters,* we have paid close attention to recent scholarship that has transformed historians' understanding of the global past—sometimes dramatically so. That effort has resulted in revised, updated, and expanded treatments of societies in all world regions. In addition to reflecting the best recent scholarship, we have revised the book's maps so that they communicate the appropriate geographical information and complement the text more clearly. Quite apart from general updating of information and revision of the maps, almost every chapter of *Traditions & Encounters* reflects some kind of substantive change or revision, which we hope will promote improved understanding of the world and its development through time. Some of the more notable changes and revisions include the following:

Chapter 1   Revised discussions of human ancestors and early *Homo sapiens*

Chapter 2   Expanded discussion of Mesopotamian empires and revised discussion of Hebrews, Israelites, and Jews

Chapter 3   Expanded discussion of gender issues in ancient Egypt

Chapter 4   Revised discussion of social history in ancient India

Chapter 9   Revised discussion of Indian science and mathematics and expanded discussion of early Buddhism and its social role

Chapter 12   Expanded discussion of military threats to the late Roman empire and revised discussion of the early Christian church

Chapter 14   Revised discussions of Islam's relationships with Judaism and Christianity and of early Islamic conquests

Chapter 19   New discussion of relationships between Bantu and forest peoples

Chapter 20   Expanded discussions of Norman roles in European expansion and the fourth crusade

Chapter 26   Expanded discussion of African-American cultural traditions

Chapter 29   Expanded discussions of the political effects of democratic revolutions and Miguel de Hidalgo

Chapter 31   Expanded discussions of the Mexican-American War and of women in Latin America

Chapter 34   Revised discussion of Arab nationalism and new discussions of the Armenian massacre and the influenza pandemic of 1918

Chapter 39   New discussion of women in Latin America and revised discussion of Latin American economic history

Chapter 40   Revised and expanded discussion of HIV/AIDS, revised discussion of population movements, and new discussion of emerging economies

In addition to introducing revisions that reflect the best recent scholarship, we have revised the entire map program and added several new features to support student learning:

- **Revised Map Program** Fully revised and enhanced maps show more detail and include more topographical information. Maps now include newly written captions that draw attention to the geographical dimensions of historical developments.

- **New Running Pronunciation Guide** Newly added to the fourth edition, this guide appears along the bottom of pages and helps readers with unfamiliar names and terms.
- **New Chapter Opening Design** A fresh design highlights the vignettes that introduce each chapter's themes and illustrates the effects of large-scale historical developments on individual experiences.

Outstanding Features

As in the case of earlier editions, this fourth edition of *Traditions & Encounters* provides a carefully selected range of tools to enhance students' comprehension and interest.

- **Part Openers** Brief part openers explain the rationale behind each major era of human history, and all seven part openers combine to provide a cohesive summary of the seven-era scheme, the larger interpretive framework of the book.

- **Sources from the Past** Appearing in every chapter, these primary source excerpts illustrate fundamental ideas raised in the text and provide individual voices from the human past.

- **Chronology** Each chapter ends with a chronology box that lists the most important dates and events discussed in the chapter.

- **Summary** Clearly written chapter-ending summaries remind students of the highlights in each chapter.

- **For Further Reading** Fully updated in the fourth edition, these annotated lists of references that end each chapter provide readers with a starting point for research assignments or their own study.

- **Strong Visual Appeal** Images are seamlessly integrated into the narrative to enhance and support the stories of history that unfold through the themes of traditions and encounters.

As we strengthened the substantive content of *Traditions & Encounters,* we also worked to produce a book more accessible and useful for readers. **The entire map program has been revised** for clarity, greater detail, and more topographical information. Maps now include detailed captions with questions that encourage critical analysis of the map content.

Topographical treatment of maps aids students' understanding of the geographical impact on the development of societies.

Insets provide a closer look at key areas in the map.

New captions provide students with questions for deeper analysis of the relationship between geographic areas and conditions.

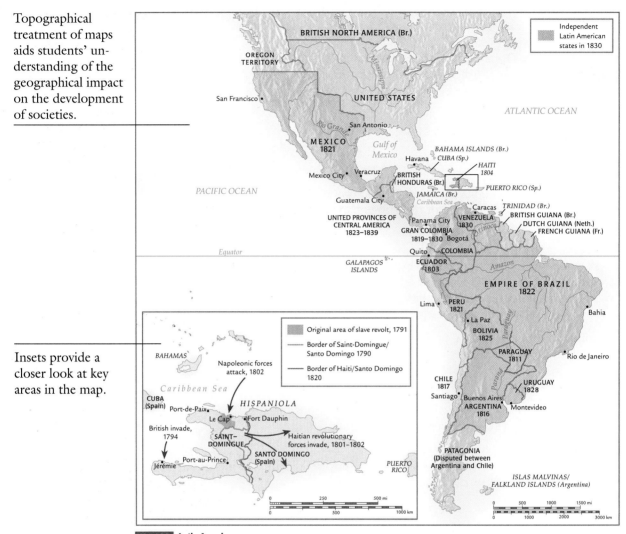

Map 29.3 **Latin America in 1830.** Note the dates each state won its independence. Since most states became independent in very close succession, what conditions prevented Latin American states from joining together in a federation like that in the United States?

IV

AN AGE OF CROSS-CULTURAL INTERACTION, 1000 TO 1500 C.E.

The half millennium from 1000 to 1500 C.E. differed markedly from earlier eras. During classical and postclassical times, large, regional societies situated in China, India, southwest Asia, and the Mediterranean basin dominated the eastern hemisphere. Peoples of these lands built extensive networks of trade and communication that spanned the eastern hemisphere and influenced the development of all its societies. From 1000 to 1500 C.E., however, nomadic Turkish and Mongol peoples overran settled societies and established vast transregional empires from China to eastern Europe.

Nomadic peoples toppled several postclassical states, most notably the Song empire in China and the Abbasid realm in southwest Asia. By building empires that transcended the boundaries of postclassical states, however, nomadic Turks and Mongols laid a political foundation for sharply increased trade and communication between peoples of different societies and cultural regions. Indeed, their empires prompted the peoples of the eastern hemisphere to forge closer links than ever before in history. By the mid-fourteenth century, merchants, diplomats, and missionaries traveled frequently between lands as far removed as Italy and China.

Increased trade in the Indian Ocean basin also promoted more intense cross-cultural communications. Mari-

time trade built on the political stability, economic expansion, and demographic growth of the postclassical era. By the fourteenth century, mariners called at ports throughout the Indian Ocean basin from southeast Asia to India, Ceylon, Arabia, and east Africa, while sea lanes through the South China Sea offered access to ports in the islands of southeast Asia, China, Japan, and Korea. Commercial goods traveled over the Indian Ocean in larger quantities than ever before. From the eleventh century forward, cargoes increasingly consisted of bulky commodities such as timber, coral, steel, building materials, grains, dates, and other foodstuffs. This trade in bulk goods indicated a movement toward economic integration as societies of the Indian Ocean basin concentrated increasingly on cultivating crops or producing goods for export while importing foods or goods that they could not produce very well themselves.

Demographic growth, increased agricultural production, and economic expansion helped to underwrite rapid political development in sub-Saharan Africa and western Europe. Powerful regional states and centralized empires emerged in west Africa and central Africa while a series of wealthy city-states dominated the east African coast. In western Europe the decentralized states of the early middle ages evolved into more tightly centralized regional states. Rulers in several of these states were able to organize networks of military retainers and political supporters who strengthened the claims

of central authorities against local challengers. Increasing volumes of trade favored this movement toward centralization in sub-Saharan Africa and western Europe, since taxes levied on trade helped to finance the professional bureaucrats and armed forces that centralized states required.

Although they did not participate in the demographic and economic expansion of the eastern hemisphere, the indigenous peoples of the Americas and Oceania also built larger and more centralized societies from 1000 to 1500 C.E. Centralized empires appeared in Mesoamerica and Andean South America while agricultural societies emerged in several regions of North America. Even in the absence of large domesticated animals, trade networks linked peoples as far distant as Mexico and the Great Lakes region. Pacific island societies also moved toward tighter political organization. Because they lived on small land bases distributed irregularly throughout a vast ocean, Pacific islanders had no realistic possibility of building large imperial states. Within their own agricultural and fishing societies, however, they established tightly centralized kingdoms that organized public affairs and sponsored distinctive cultural traditions.

During the fourteenth and fifteenth centuries C.E., much of the eastern hemisphere experienced difficulties not only because of warfare arising from the conquests of nomadic peoples but also because of epidemic bubonic plague and global climatic changes that brought cooler temperatures. In building their transregional empires, nomadic peoples sometimes devastated the lands that they conquered, throwing societies and economies into tur-

moil. While facilitating trade and travel, nomadic empires also made it possible for diseases to spread rapidly over long distances, and during the fourteenth century, epidemic bubonic plague became a hemispheric phenomenon. Meanwhile, cooler weather resulted in lower agricultural yields in many lands, and in some far northern lands, it made agriculture impractical. Together with military destruction and pandemic plague, reduced agricultural production led to political, social, and economic problems throughout much of the eastern hemisphere.

Nevertheless, by the mid-fifteenth century, peoples from China to western Europe were recovering from those difficulties and rebuilding prosperous societies. In their own quest for prosperity, western European peoples unwittingly laid the foundations of a new era in world history. While searching for sea routes to Asian markets, European mariners happened upon the continents of North and South America. They soon ventured into the Pacific Ocean, where they found their way to Australia and the Pacific islands. Their voyages brought the world's various peoples for the first time into permanent and sustained communication with one another, and their interactions triggered a series of consequences that profoundly influenced modern world history. The European voyages that gave rise to this interdependent and interconnected world took place precisely because of the movement toward increasing interaction in the eastern hemisphere during the centuries following 1000 C.E. The period from 1000 to 1500 C.E. set the stage for the modern era of world history.

The newly designed seven part openers begin with an introduction that outlines the themes running through all the chapters in that part. This information creates a strong framework for understanding the details of individual chapters.

Each newly designed chapter opener begins with a story of individual experiences that draws readers into the chapter and illustrates its main themes.

18

Nomadic Empires and Eurasian Integration

Turkish Migrations and Imperial Expansion
Nomadic Economy and Society
Turkish Empires in Persia, Anatolia, and India

The Mongol Empires
Chinggis Khan and the Making of the Mongol Empire
The Mongol Empires after Chinggis Khan
The Mongols and Eurasian Integration
Decline of the Mongols in Persia and China

After the Mongols
Tamerlane the Whirlwind
The Foundation of the Ottoman Empire

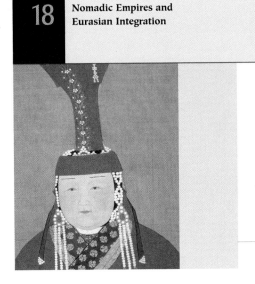

Guillaume Boucher was a goldsmith who lived during the early and middle decades of the thirteenth century. At some point, perhaps during the 1230s, he left his native Paris and went to Budapest, which was then a part of the kingdom of Hungary. There he was captured by Mongol warriors campaigning in Hungary. The Mongols noticed and appreciated Boucher's talents, and when they left Hungary in 1242, they took him along with other skilled captives to their central Asian homeland.

For at least the next fifteen years, Boucher lived at the Mongol capital at Karakorum. Though technically a slave, he enjoyed some prestige. He supervised fifty assistants in a workshop that produced decorative objects of gold and silver for the Mongol court. His most ingenious creation was a spectacular silver fountain in the form of a tree. Four pipes, concealed by the tree's trunk, carried wines and other intoxicating drinks to the top of the tree and then dispensed them into silver bowls from which courtiers and guests filled their cups. Apart from his famous fountain, Boucher also produced statues in gold and silver, built carriages, designed buildings, and even sewed ritual garments for Roman Catholic priests who conducted services for Christians living at Karakorum and sought converts in the Mongol empire.

Boucher was by no means the only European living at the Mongol court. His wife was a woman of French ancestry whom Boucher had met and married in Hungary. The Flemish missionary William of Rubruck visited Karakorum in 1254, and during his sojourn there he encountered a French woman named Paquette who was an attendant to a Mongol princess, an artisan from Russia (Paquette's husband), an unnamed nephew of a French bishop, a Greek soldier, and an Englishman named Basil. Other European visitors to the Mongol court found Germans, Slavs, and Hungarians as well as Chinese, Koreans, Turks, Persians, and Armenians, among others. Many thirteenth-century roads led to Karakorum.

Nomadic peoples had made their influence felt throughout much of Eurasia as early as classical times. The Xiongnu confederation dominated central Asia and posed a formidable threat to the Han dynasty in China from the third to the first century B.C.E. During the second and third centuries C.E., the Huns and other nomadic peoples from central Asia launched the migrations that helped bring down the western Roman empire, and later migrations of the White Huns destroyed the Gupta state in India. Turkish peoples ruled a large central Asian empire from the sixth through the ninth centuries, and the Uighur Turks even seized the capital cities of the Tang dynasty in the mid-seventh century.

Between the eleventh and fifteenth centuries, nomadic peoples became more prominent than ever before in Eurasian affairs. Turkish peoples migrated to Persia, Anatolia, and India, where they overcame existing authorities and established new states. During the thirteenth

OPPOSITE: A sixth-century icon depicting an enthroned Virgin Mary and infant Jesus attended by angels and saints.

461

Sources from the Past

The Quran on Allah and His Expectations of Humankind

The foundation of the Islamic faith is the understanding of Allah, his nature, and his plan for the world as outlined in the Quran. Through his visions Muhammad came to understand Allah as the one and only god, the creator and sustainer of the world in the manner of the Jews' Yahweh and the Christians' God. Those who rejected Allah and his message would suffer eternal punishment, but those who recognized and obeyed him would receive his mercy and secure his blessings.

In the name of Allah, most benevolent,
    ever-merciful.
All praise be to Allah,
Lord of all the worlds,
Most beneficent, ever-merciful,
King of the Day of Judgement.
You alone we worship, and to You
    alone turn for help.
Guide us (O Lord) to the path that is straight,
The path of those You have blessed,
Not of those who have earned Your anger,
    nor those who have gone astray. . . .

Verily men and women who have come to
    submission,
men and women who are believers,
men and women who are devout,
truthful men and women,
men and women with endurance,
men and women who are modest,
men and women who give alms,
men and women who observe fasting,
men and women who guard their private parts,
and those men and women who remember God
    a great deal,
for them God has forgiveness and a great reward.
No believing men and women have any choice in
    a matter
after God and His Apostle [i.e., Muhammad]
    have decided it.
Whoever disobeys God and His Apostle
has clearly lost the way and gone astray. . . .

O you who believe, remember God a great deal,
And sing His praises morning and evening.

It is He who sends His blessings on you,
    as (do) His angels, that He may lead you out
        of darkness into light,
for He is benevolent to the believers. . . .
I call to witness
the early hours of the morning,
And the night when dark and still,
Your Lord has neither left you,
    nor despises you.
What is to come is better for you
than what has gone before;
For your Lord will certainly give you,
and you will be content.
Did He not find you an orphan
and take care of you?
Did He not find you poor
and enrich you?
So do not oppress the orphan,
And do not drive
the beggar away,
And keep recounting the favours of your
    Lord. . . .

Say: "He is God
the one the most unique,
God the immanently indispensable.
He has begotten no one,
and is begotten of none.
There is no one comparable to Him."

FOR FURTHER REFLECTION

Compare the Quran's teachings on the relationship between Allah and human beings with the views of Zoroastrians, Jews, and Christians discussed in earlier chapters.

SOURCE: *Al-Qur'an: A Contemporary Translation.* Trans. by Ahmed Ali. Princeton: Princeton University Press, 1984, pp.11, 358, 359, 540, 559.

Sources from the Past boxes bring the past to life, spotlighting significant primary source documents relevant to the chapter, such as poems, journal accounts, religious writings, and letters. Introductions place the documents in context and explain their significance; new thought provoking questions prompt readers to contextualize and think critically about key issues raised in the document.

Muhammad's faith and his personal leadership decisively shaped the values and the development of the Islamic community. The foundation of the Islamic faith as elaborated by Muhammad consists of obligations known as the Five Pillars of Islam: (1) Muslims must acknowledge Allah as the only god and Muhammad as his prophet. (2) They must pray to Allah daily while facing Mecca. (3) They must observe a fast during the daylight hours of the month of Ramadan. (4) They must contribute alms for the relief of the weak and poor. (5) Finally, in honor of Muhammad's visits to Mecca in 629 and 632, those who are physically and financially able must undertake the hajj and make at least one pilgrimage to Mecca. During the centuries since its appearance, Islam has generated many schools and sects, each with its own particular legal, social, and doctrinal features. The Five Pillars of Islam, however, constitute a simple but powerful framework that has bound the *umma* as a whole into a cohesive community of faith.

The Five Pillars of Islam

Some Muslims, though by no means all, have taken *jihad* as an additional obligation for the faithful. The term *jihad* literally means "struggle," and Muslims have understood its imperatives in various ways. In one sense, *jihad* imposes spiritual and moral obligations on Muslims by requiring them to combat vice and evil. In another sense, *jihad* calls on Muslims to struggle against ignorance and unbelief by spreading the word of Islam and seeking converts to the faith. In some circumstances, *jihad* also involves physical struggle, obliging Muslims to take up the sword and wage war against unbelievers who threaten Islam.

Jihad

Beyond the general obligations prescribed by the Five Pillars, Islamic holy law, known as the *sharia*, emerged during the centuries after Muhammad and offered detailed guidance on proper behavior in almost every aspect of life. Elaborated by jurists and legal scholars, the *sharia* drew its inspiration especially from the Quran and the early historical accounts of Muhammad's life and teachings. It offered precise guidance

Islamic Law: The Sharia

shari'a (shah-REE-ah)

Marginal notes highlight key terms, events, and concepts as they appear within the narrative.

A running pronunciation guide appears along the bottom of pages to help readers with unfamiliar words and phrases.

As European mariners ventured into the Indian and Atlantic Ocean basins, they unwittingly inaugurated a new era in world history. For millennia, peoples of different societies had traded, communicated, and interacted. As technologies of transportation improved, they dealt with peoples at increasingly greater distances. By 1500 the Indian Ocean served as a highway linking peoples from China to east Africa, and overland traffic kept the silk roads busy from China to the Mediterranean Sea. Trade goods, diplomatic missions, religious faiths, technological skills, agricultural crops, and disease pathogens all moved readily over the sea lanes and the silk roads, and they profoundly influenced the development of societies throughout the eastern hemisphere. In the western hemisphere, trading networks linked lands as distant as Mexico and the Great Lakes region while Pacific islanders regularly traveled and traded between island groups.

Never before, however, had peoples of the eastern hemisphere, the western hemisphere, and Oceania dealt with one another on a regular and systematic basis. The voyages of European mariners during the fifteenth and following centuries initiated a long-term process—one that continues in the present day—that brought all regions and peoples of planet earth into permanent and sustained interaction. The formation and reconfiguration of global networks of power, communication, and exchange that followed from those interactions rank among the most prominent themes of modern world history.

A paragraph summary at the end of each chapter reinforces the chapter's key points.

CHRONOLOGY

1214	Creation of a Mongol artillery unit
1253–1324	Life of Marco Polo
1287–1288	Rabban Sauma's embassy to Europe
1291–1328	John of Montecorvino's mission to China
1304–1369	Life of Ibn Battuta
1304–1374	Life of Francesco Petrarca
1330s	First outbreaks of bubonic plague in China
1337–1453	Hundred Years' War
1347	Arrival of bubonic plague in the Mediterranean basin
1368–1644	Ming dynasty
1405–1433	Zheng He's expeditions in the Indian Ocean
1466–1536	Life of Desiderius Erasmus of Rotterdam
1488	Bartolomeu Dias's voyage around Africa
1492	Christopher Columbus's first voyage to the western hemisphere
1497–1498	Vasco da Gama's voyage to India

A concise chronological table summarizes the critical events covered in the chapter.

FOR FURTHER READING

Janet L. Abu-Lughod. *Before European Hegemony: The World System, A.D. 1250–1350*. New York, 1989. An important study of long-distance trade networks during the Mongol era.

Jerry H. Bentley. *Humanists and Holy Writ: New Testament Scholarship in the Renaissance*. Princeton, 1983. Examines Renaissance humanists' efforts to prepare accurate texts, translations, and commentaries on the New Testament.

———. *Old World Encounters: Cross-Cultural Contacts and Exchanges in Pre-Modern Times*. New York, 1993. Studies cultural and religious exchanges in the eastern hemisphere before 1500 C.E.

Jerry Brotton. *The Renaissance Bazaar: From the Silk Road to Michelangelo*. Oxford, 2002. A provocative and well-illustrated study arguing that encounters in the larger world deeply influenced Renaissance cultural development in Europe.

Kenneth Chase. *Firearms: A Global History to 1700*. Cambridge, 2003. Offers a fresh interpretation of the invention and early diffusion of gunpowder weapons.

Felipe Fernández-Armesto. *Before Columbus: Exploration and Colonisation from the Mediterranean to the Atlantic, 1229–1492*. London, 1987. Scholarly survey of early European ventures in the Atlantic Ocean.

Robert S. Gottfried. *The Black Death: Natural and Human Disaster in Medieval Europe*. New York, 1983. The best general study of bubonic plague and its effects in Europe.

Margaret L. King. *Women of the Renaissance*. Chicago, 1991. A lively and imaginative discussion of women's roles and experiences in Renaissance Europe.

John Larner. *Marco Polo and the Discovery of the World*. New Haven, 1999. Excellent study of Marco Polo and his significance, based on a thorough review of both textual evidence and recent scholarship.

Louise L. Levathes. *When China Ruled the Seas: The Treasure Fleet of the Dragon Throne, 1405–1433*. New York, 1994. Excellent popular account of Zheng He's voyages.

Lauro Martines. *Power and Imagination: City States in Renais-*

Each chapter concludes with a For Further Reading section that contains a list and brief description of the most important books available about topics discussed in the chapter. This list can help readers get started with research projects or follow up on subjects that they find especially interesting.

Supplements

Primary Source Investigator Online

McGraw-Hill's Primary Source Investigator (PSI), now available online at www.mhhe .com/psi, is designed to support and enrich the text discussion in *Traditions & Encounters: A Global Perspective on the Past.* PSI gives instructors and students access to more than 650 primary and secondary sources including documents, images, maps, and videos. Students can use these resources to formulate and defend their arguments as well as further their understanding of the topics discussed in each chapter. All assets are indexed alphabetically as well as by type, subject, place, and time period, allowing students and instructors to locate resources quickly and easily.

Student Resources in PSI

Primary Source Documents: Newly updated for *Traditions & Encounters,* this database includes items from a wide range of contemporary accounts. Each document is accompanied by a detailed description and a series of critical thinking questions that draw students into the content and engages them in thoughtful analysis.

Images: This extensive collection includes photographs of artifacts and buildings as well as contemporary paintings, engravings, and drawings. Each image is also accompanied by a description and critical thinking questions.

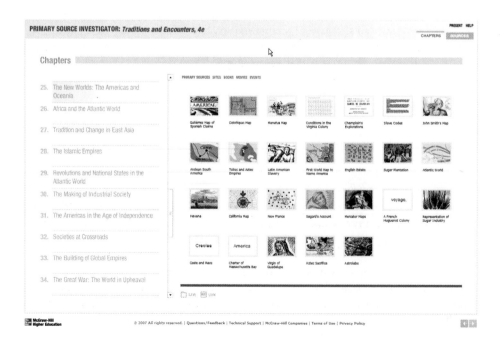

Interactive Maps: Each map's legend is interactive, allowing students to see historical change over time and compare various factors in the order of their choice.

Sites: Organized by chapter, this feature lists reliable Internet sites that provide further information on particular topics. These can be especially useful to students who are searching for dependable research sources.

Books: This list includes both standard texts as well as the most recent scholarship on topics within each chapter, another valuable resource for student researchers.

Movies: This list includes both educational and commercial films.

Events: More than simply a timeline, this feature includes annotated entries of important events in chronological order.

NEW! *Online Reader:* New for *Traditions & Encounters,* the Online Reader gives students an opportunity to try their hand at historical analysis. Based on sources found in PSI, the reader's modules ask students to evaluate sources and formulate their own interpretation of an historical event, providing valuable skills for their own research.

NEW! *Writing Guide:* New for *Traditions & Encounters,* the online Writing Guide offers both general assistance for writing college papers, as well as specific tips for history papers. Topics include research, paragraph and argument creation, a comparison of style guides, information on plagiarism and source citation, and much more.

Instructor Resources in PSI

Faculty Guide: The Faculty Guide provides easy reference to all learning assets, both in the text and on PSI, available to teachers and students. Each chapter is accompanied by a rich list of resources, including **PowerPoint slides, image bank, outline maps, book maps,** and **test bank questions,** all keyed to the chapter. Resources are organized within chapters by A-Heads to streamline lecture and assignment preparation. Icons allow users to quickly differentiate between text and PSI sources. Each asset is listed by title and includes a brief annotation.

In addition to assets, the Faculty Guide also includes a chapter overview, a list of themes, lecture strategies, discussion suggestions, suggestions for further reading, and chapter-specific film recommendations. These, too, are organized by chapter and A-Head to make classroom implementation simple.

Additional Resources for Instructors

- The **Online Learning Center for Instructors** at www.mhhe.com/bentley4 contains several instructor tools, including a link to the faculty guide on Primary Source Investigator (www.mhhe.com/psi) and PowerPoint presentations for each chapter. The instructor side of the OLC is password protected to prevent tampering. Please contact your local McGraw-Hill sales representative for details.
- A **Computerized Test Bank,** McGraw-Hill's **EZ Test** allows you to quickly create a customized test using the publishers supplied test banks or your own questions. You decide the number, type, and order of test questions with a few simple clicks. **EZ Test** runs on your computer without a connection to the Internet.
- **Videos** on topics in world history are available through the Films for Humanities and Sciences collection. Contact your local McGraw-Hill sales representative for further information.

- **Classroom Performance System (CPS).** The Classroom Performance System brings ultimate interactivity to *Traditions & Encounters*. CPS is a wireless response system that gives you immediate feedback from every student in the class. With CPS you can ask subjective and objective questions during your lecture, prompting every student to respond with their individual, wireless response pad, and providing you with instant results. A complete CPS Tutorial is available at www.einstruction.com.

Additional Resources for Students

- The **Online Learning Center for Students** at www.mhhe.com/bentley4 provides students with a wide range of tools that will help them test their understanding of the book. It includes chapter overviews, interactive maps, multiple choice and essay quizzes, matching and identification games, as well as primary source indexes for further research.
- Two **After the Fact Interactive** units are available for use with *Traditions & Encounters:* "After the Fact Interactive: Tracing the Silk Roads" for volume 1 (ISBN 0-07-281843-3) and "After the Fact Interactive: Envisioning the Atlantic World" for volume 2 (ISBN 0-07-281844-1). These rich, visually appealing modules on CD-ROM allow students to be apprentice historians, examining a variety of multimedia primary source material and constructing arguments based on their research.
- **Titles in the Exploration in World History Series:** This McGraw-Hill series conveys the results of recent research in world history in a form wholly accessible to beginning students. It also provides a pedagogical alternative to, or supplement for, the large and inclusive core textbooks. Each volume in the series focuses briefly on a particular theme, set in a global and comparative context. Each book in this series is "open-ended," raising questions and drawing students into the larger issues which animate world history.

  - Rainer Buschmann, *Oceans in World History,* ISBN 0-07-301903-8

  - Carl J. Guarneri, *America in the World: United States History in Global Context,* ISBN 0-07-254115-6

  - Donald Johnson & Jean Elliot Johnson, *Universal Religions in World History: Buddhism, Christianity, and Islam,* ISBN 0-07-295428-0

  - Xinru Liu & Lynda Shaffer, *Connections Across Eurasia: Transportation, Communication, and Cultural Exchange on the Silk Roads,* ISBN 0-07-284351-9

  - Lauren Ristvet, *In the Beginning: World History from Human Evolution to First Civilizations,* ISBN 0-07-284803-0

  - Robert Strayer, *Communist Experiment: Revolution, Socialism, and Global Conflict in the Twentieth Century,* ISBN 0-07-249744-0

  - Catherine Clay, Christine Senecal & Chandrika Paul, *Envisioning Women in World History: 1500–Present,* Volume 2, ISBN 0-07-351322-9

  - Pamela McVay, *Envisioning Women in World History: 1500–Present,* Volume 2, ISBN 0-07-353465-X

A Brief Note on Usage

This book qualifies dates as B.C.E. ("Before the Common Era") or C.E. ("Common Era"). In practice, B.C.E. refers to the same epoch as B.C. ("Before Christ"), and C.E. refers to the same epoch as A.D. (*Anno Domini,* a Latin term meaning "in the year of the Lord"). As historical study becomes a global, multicultural enterprise, however, scholars increasingly prefer terminology that does not apply the standards of one society to all the others. Thus reference in this book to B.C.E. and C.E. reflects emerging scholarly convention concerning the qualification of historical dates.

Measurements of length and distance appear here according to the metric system, followed by their English-system equivalents in parentheses.

The book transliterates Chinese names and terms into English according to the *pinyin* system, which has largely displaced the more cumbersome Wade-Giles system. Transliteration of names and terms from other languages follows contemporary scholarly conventions.

About the Authors

Jerry H. Bentley is professor of history at the University of Hawai`i and editor of the *Journal of World History*. He has written extensively on the cultural history of early modern Europe and on cross-cultural interactions in world history. His research on the religious, moral, and political writings of the Renaissance led to the publication of *Humanists and Holy Writ: New Testament Scholarship in the Renaissance* (1983) and *Politics and Culture in Renaissance Naples* (1987). His more recent research has concentrated on global history and particularly on processes of cross-cultural interaction. His book *Old World Encounters: Cross-Cultural Contacts and Exchanges in Pre-Modern Times* (1993) studies processes of cultural exchange and religious conversion before modern times, and his pamphlet *Shapes of World History in Twentieth-Century Scholarship* (1996) discusses the historiography of world history. His current interests include processes of cross-cultural interaction and cultural exchange in modern times.

Herbert F. Ziegler is an associate professor of history at the University of Hawai`i. He has taught world history since 1980 and currently serves as director of the world history program at the University of Hawai`i. He also serves as book review editor of the *Journal of World History*. His interest in twentieth-century European social and political history led to the publication of *Nazi Germany's New Aristocracy* (1990). He is at present working on a study that explores from a global point of view the demographic trends of the past ten thousand years, along with their concomitant technological, economic, and social developments. His other current research project focuses on the application of complexity theory to a comparative study of societies and their internal dynamics.

Acknowledgments

Many individuals have contributed to this book, and the authors take pleasure in recording deep thanks for all the comments, criticism, advice, and suggestions that helped to improve the work. The editorial team at McGraw-Hill did an outstanding job of keeping the authors focused on the project. Special thanks go to Lisa Moore, Jon-David Hague, Pamela Cooper, Susan Gouijnstook, Sora Kim, and Brett Coker, who provided crucial support by helping the authors work through difficult issues and solve the innumerable problems of content, style, and organization that arise in any project to produce a history of the world. Many colleagues at the University of Hawai`i and elsewhere aided and advised the authors on matters of organization and composition. Mimi Henriksen was especially generous with her time and advice. Finally, we would like to express our appreciation for the advice of the following individuals who read and commented on the original manuscript and previous editions of this text:

Heather J. Abdelnur
Blackburn College

Henry Abramson
Florida Atlantic University

Roger Adelson
Arizona State University

William Alexander
Norfolk State University

Alfred Andrea
University of Vermont

Ed Anson
University of Arkansas at Little Rock

Henry Antkiewicz
East Tennessee State University

Maria Arbelaez
University of Nebraska at Omaha

Peter Arnade
University of California—San Marcos

Karl Bahm
University of Wisconsin, Superior

Vaughan Baker
University of Louisiana at Lafayette

Beth Allison Barr
Baylor University

Ian Barrow
Middlebury College

Dixee Bartholomew-Feis
Buena Vista University

Guy Beckwith
Auburn University

Lynda Bell
University of California—Riverside

Norman Bennett
Boston University

Houri Berberian
California State University, Long Beach

Robert Blackey
*California State University—
    San Bernardino*

David Blaylock
Eastern Kentucky University

Wayne Bodle
Indiana University of Pennsylvania

Michael Brescia
State University of New York, Fredonia

Samuel Brunk
University of Texas, El Paso

Deborah Buffton
University of Wisconsin, La Crosse

Maureen Burgess
Colorado State University

Rainer Buschmann
Hawai`i Pacific University

Sharon L. Bush
LeMoyne-Owen College

Antonio Calabria
University of Texas, San Antonio

Lewis Call
*California Polytechnic State University,
San Luis Obispo*

Thomas Callahan, Jr.
Rider University

Alice-Catherine Carls
University of Tennessee at Martin

Kay Carr
Southern Illinois University

James Carroll
Iona College

Carol Carter
University of Central Arkansas

Tom Carty
Springfield College

Bruce Castleman
San Diego State University

Douglas Catterall
Cameron University

Douglas Chambers
*University of Southern Mississippi
Hattiesburg*

Choi Chatterjee
California State University, Los Angeles

Orazio Ciccarelli
University of Southern Mississippi

Andrew Clark
*University of North Carolina
at Wilmington*

Hugh R. Clark
Usrinus College

Harold Cline
Middle Georgia College

Tim Coates
College of Charleston

Joan Coffey
Sam Houston State University

Daniel Connerton
North Adams State

Keith Cox
California State University

Bruce Cruikshank
Hastings College

Graciella Cruz-Tara
Florida Atlantic University

Lynn Curtright
Tallahassee Community College

Richard Cusimano
University of Louisiana at Lafayette

Ken Czech
St. Cloud State University

Touraj Daryaee
California State University, Fullerton

Jon Davidann
Hawai`i Pacific University

Allen Davidson
Georgia Southern University

Denise Z. Davidson
Georgia State University

Brian Davies
University of Texas, San Antonio

John Davis
Radford University

Thomas Davis
Virginia Military Institute

Elisa Denlinger
University of Wisconsin, La Crosse

Stewart Dippel
University of the Ozarks

Ross Doughty
Ursinus College

Cathi Dunkle
Mid-Michigan Community College

Ross Dunn
San Diego State University

Peter Dykema,
Arkansas Tech University

Lane Earns
University of Wisconsin, Oshkosh

Christopher Ehret
University of California, Los Angeles

Laura Endicott
Southwestern Oklahoma State

Nancy Erickson
Erskine College

James Evans
Southeastern Community College

David Fahey
Miami University

Edward Farmer
University of Minnesota

James David Farthing
Oklahoma Baptist University

Lanny Fields
*California State University—
San Bernardino*

Robert Frankle
University of Memphis

Bonnie Frederick
Washington State University

Karl Friday
University of Georgia

Amy Froide
University of Tennessee, Chattanooga

James Fuller
University of Indianapolis

Jessie Ruth Gaston
California State University, Sacramento

Robert Gomez
San Antonio College

Paul Goodwin
University of Connecticut, Storrs

Matthew Gordon
Miami University of Ohio

Steve Gosch
University of Wisconsin, Eau Claire

Joseph Gowaskie
Rider University

Brian Gurian
Harrisburg Area Community College

John Haag
University of Georgia

Raymond J. Haberski, Jr.
Marian College

Jeffrey Hamilton
Baylor University

Michael Hamm
Centre College

Travis Hanes III
*University of North Carolina—
Wilmington*

Preston Hardy, Jr.
University of Tennessee, Martin

Stephen Harmon
Pittsburg State University

Russell Hart
Hawai`i Pacific University

John Hayden
Southwestern Oklahoma State

Randolph Head
University of California, Riverside

Mary Hedberg
Saginaw Valley State University

Gerald Herman
Northeastern University

David Hertzel
Southwestern Oklahoma State

Udo Heyn
California State University—Los Angeles

Kathryn Hodgkinson
The Hockaday School

Peter Hoffenberg
University of Hawai`i, Manoa

Blair Holmes
Brigham Young University

Mary Hovanec
Cuyahoga Community College

Scott Howlett
Saddleback Community College

Kailai Huang
Massachusetts College of Liberal Arts

J. Sanders Huguenin
*University of Science and Arts of
Oklahoma*

Richard Hume
Washington State University

Carol Sue Humphrey
Oklahoma Baptist University

Alfred Hunt
State University of New York

Raymond Hylton
J. Sergeant Reynolds Community College

Phyllis Jestice
*University of Southern Mississippi,
Hattiesburg*

Cheryl Johnson-Odim
Loyola University

Kimberley Jones-de Oliveira
Long Island University

Jonathan Judaken
University of Memphis

Theodore Kallman
Delta College

Alan Karras
University of California, Berkeley

Thomas Kay
Wheaton College

Charles Keller
Pittsburgh State University

David L. Kenley
Elizabethtown College

Winston Kinsey
Appalachian State University

Cengiz Kirli
Purdue University

Paul Knoll
University of Southern California

Keith Knuuti
University of Hawai`i, Hilo

Kenneth Koons
Virginia Military Institute

Cheryl Koos
California State University, Los Angeles

Cynthia Kosso
Northern Arizona University

Zoltan Kramer
Central Washington University

James Krokar
DePaul University

Glenn Lamar
University of Louisiana at Lafayette

Lisa Lane
Miracosta College

George Lankevich
Bronx Community College

Dennis Laumann
University of Memphis

Donald Layton
Indiana State University

Loyd Lee
SUNY-New Paltz

Jess LeVine
Brookdale Community College

Keith Lewinstein
Bridgewater State University

Richard Lewis
St. Cloud State University

Yi Li
Tacoma Community College

Tony Litherland
Oklahoma Baptist University

James Long
Colorado State University

David Longfellow
Baylor University

Ben Lowe
Florida Atlantic University

Jared Ludlow
Brigham Young University, Hawai`i

Herbert Luft
Pepperdine Univeristy

Lu Lui
University of Tennessee—Knoxville

Paul Madden
Hardin-Simmons University

Farid Mahdavi
San Diego State University

Dorothea A. L. Martin
Appalachian State University

Tracey Martin
Benedictine University

Ken Mason
Santa Monica College

Robert Mathews
Northshore Community College

Laura E. Mayhall
The Catholic University of America

William Maynard
Arkansas State University

Robert McCormick
*University of South Carolina—
  Spartanburg*

Jeff McEwen
Chattanooga State Technical College

Randall McGowen
University of Oregon

Adam McKeown
Columbia University

John McNeill
Georgetown University

James McSwain
Tuskegee University

Pamela McVay
Ursuline College

John Mears
Southern Methodist University

Daniel Miller
Calvin College

Monserrat Miller
Marshall University

Laura Mitchell
University of Texas, San Antonio

David Montgomery
Brigham Young University

Garth Montgomery
Radford University

George Moore
San Jose State University

Gloria Morrow
Morgan State University

David Mungello
Baylor University

Jeffrey Myers
Avila College

Peter Nayenga
Saint Cloud State University

Ruth Necheles-Jansyn
Long Island University

Marian Nelson
University of Nebraska

Janise Nuckols
Windward Community College

Deanne Nuwer
*University of Southern Mississippi,
   Hattiesburg*

Greg O'Brien
*University of Southern Mississippi,
   Hattiesburg*

Veena Talwar Oldenburg
Baruch College

Brian O'Neil
University of Southern Mississippi

Patricia O'Niell
Central Oregon Community College

Samuel Oppenheim
California State University, Stanislaus

John Oriji
*California Polytechnic State University,
   San Luis Obispo*

Anne Osborne
Rider University

James Overfield
University of Vermont

Keith Pacholl
State University of West Georgia

Melvin Page
East Tennessee State University

Loretta Pang
Kapiolani Community College

Jean Paquette
Lander University

Jotham Parsons
University of Delaware

Denis Paz
University of North Texas

Patrick Peebles
University of Missouri—Kansas City

Peter W. Petschauer
Appalachian State University

Phyllis Pobst
Arkansas State University

Jon Porter
Franklin College

Clifton Potter
Lynchburg College

David Price
Santa Fe Community College

Alfonso Quiroz
Bernard M. Baruch College, CUNY

Stephen Rapp
Georgia State University

Vera Reber
Shippensburg University

John Reid
Georgia Southern University

Thomas Renna
Saginaw Valley State University

Diana Reynolds
Point Loma Nazarene University

Douglas Reynolds
Georgia State University

Ira Rice
Ball State University

Cheryl Riggs
California State University—San Bernardino

John Ritter
Chemeketa Community College

Bill Rodner
Tidewater Community College, Virginia Beach

Lynn Rose
Truman State University

Aviel Roshwald
Georgetown University

Chad Ross
East Carolina University

Dan Russell
Springfield College

Eric Rust
Baylor University

John Ryan
Kansas City Kansas Community College

William Schell
Murray State University

Daryl Schuster
University of Central Florida

Jane Scimeca
Brookdale Community College

Gary Scudder
Georgia Perimiter College

Kimberly Sebold
University of Maine, Presque Isle

Tara Sethia
California State University, Pomona

Howard Shealy
Kennesaw State College

Nancy Shoemaker
University of Connecticut, Storrs

MaryAnn Sison
University of Southern Mississippi, Hattiesburg

Jonathan Skaff
Shippensburg University

David Smith
California State Polytechnic University, Pomona

Michael Smith
Purdue University

Roland Spickerman
University of Detroit—Mercy

Wendy St. Jean
Springfield College

Michelle Staley
East Mississippi Community College

Tracy Steele
Sam Houston State University

Richard Steigmann-Gall
Kent State University, Kent

John Steinberg
Georgia Southern University

Heather Streets
Washington State University

Laichen Sun
California State University, Fullerton

Roshanna Sylvester
California State University, Fullerton

Stephen Tallackson
Purdue University, Calumet

Lenette S. Taylor
Kent State University

John Thornton
Millersville University

Robert Tignor
Princeton University

James Tueller
Brigham Young University, Hawai`i

Kirk Tyvela
Ohio University

Deborah Vess
Georgia College and State University

Sandra Wagner-Wright
University of Hawai`i, Hilo

Mark Wasserman
Rutgers University

Jeff Wasserstrom
Indiana University—Bloomington

Watrous-Schlesinger
Washington State University, Pullman

Theodore Weeks
Southern Illinois University

Guy Wells
Kent State University

Robert Wenke
University of Washington

Sally West
Truman State University

Sherri West
Brookdale Community College

Scott Wheeler
West Point

Joe Whitehorne
Lord Fairfax Community College

S. Jonathan Wiesen
Southern Illinois University, Carbondale

Anne Will
Skagit Valley Community College

Richard Williams
Washington State University

Allen Wittenborn
San Diego State University

David Wittner
Utica College

William Wood
Point Loma Nazarene University

John Woods
University of Chicago

John Voll
Georgetown University

Anand Yang
University of Utah

Ping Yao
California State University, Los Angeles

C. K. Yoon
James Madison University

Herb Zettl
Springfield College

AN AGE OF REVOLUTION, INDUSTRY, AND EMPIRE, 1750 TO 1914

During the early modern era, from 1500 to 1800, peoples from all parts of the world entered into sustained interactions with one another for the first time in history. Commercial, biological, and cultural exchanges influenced the development of societies in all the world's regions. European peoples in particular benefited from increased global interactions because they established the principal maritime links between the world's regions. As a result, they realized enormous profits from interregional trade, and they were also able to establish large empires and flourishing settler colonies in the Americas.

During the period from about 1750 to 1914, European peoples parlayed their advantageous position into global hegemony: by the late nineteenth century, European powers controlled affairs in most of Asia and almost all of Africa, while their Euro-American cousins dominated the Americas. Even tiny Pacific islands fell under the rule of European and Euro-American peoples. Three historical developments—revolution, industrialization, and imperialism—help to explain how European and Euro-American peoples came to dominate so much of the world.

Revolution transformed European and American societies in the late eighteenth and early nineteenth centuries. Revolution broke out first in North America, where

thirteen British colonies rebelled and won their independence. These colonies joined together to form a new republic, the United States of America, which drew heavily on the Enlightenment values of freedom, equality, and popular sovereignty in justifying its existence as an independent land. The success of the American revolution inspired the people of France to undertake a thorough transformation of their own society: after abolishing the monarchy and the aristocracy, they established a republic based on freedom, equality, and popular sovereignty. Although turmoil soon brought down the French republic, Enlightenment values continued to influence public affairs in France after the revolution. From France, revolution moved back to the western hemisphere, where the French colony of Saint-Domingue (modern Haiti) and Iberian colonies in Mexico, Central America, and South America won their independence.

Revolutions had a profound effect on the organization of societies in the Atlantic Ocean basin. First in Europe and later in the Americas as well, revolutions and the conflicts that followed from them encouraged the formation of national identities. States seeking to pursue the interests of national communities were able to mobilize popular support on a scale never before achieved and often enjoyed success in conflicts with neighboring peoples who had not been able to organize effective national states. The idea of organizing states around national communities eventually influenced political development throughout the world.

While organizing themselves into national states, western European and North American peoples also embarked on processes of industrialization. By harnessing inanimate sources of energy and organizing production in factories, industrialists were able to produce high-quality goods at low cost. Because industrialization encouraged continuous innovation, industrial societies were also able to improve constantly on their economic performance. Industrialization caused a great deal of discomfort and dislocation as workers adjusted from the rhythms of agricultural society to the demands of factories, machines, and managers seeking efficiencies in production. Over time, however, industrial societies

became economically much stronger than agricultural societies, and industrial production brought about general improvement in material standards of living. After originating in Britain in the late eighteenth century, industrialization spread rapidly to western Europe and North America and, by the late nineteenth century, to Russia and Japan as well. Even the lands that did not undergo processes of industrialization until the twentieth century immediately felt the effects of industrialization as demand rose for agricultural products and natural resources needed by industrial societies.

Alongside increased material standards of living, industrialization also brought political, military, and economic strength. Particularly in western Europe and the United States, where it occurred alongside the formation of national communities, industrialization helped underwrite processes of imperialism and colonialism. Industrial lands developed powerful transportation, communication, and military technologies that agricultural societies could not match. Railroads, steamships, telegraphs, and lethal weapons enabled western European peoples to impose their rule in most of Asia and Africa in the nineteenth century, just as Euro-American settlers relied on industrial technologies to drive the indigenous peoples of North America and South America onto marginal lands. Toward the end of the nineteenth century, the United States and Japan each used their industrial technologies to increase their presence in the larger world and thus joined western European lands as global imperial and colonial powers.

Revolution, industrialization, and imperialism had effects that were felt around the world. Western European and North American lands vastly strengthened their position in the world by exercising political or economic influence over other societies. In some lands, particularly the Ottoman empire, Russia, China, and Japan, reformers worked to restructure their societies and increase their influence in global affairs by building national states that harnessed the energies of their populations. In doing so they studied the experience of western European societies and sought to adapt the principles of European political and social organization to their societies. In the absence of a revolution that toppled ruling elites, however, critics found it difficult to bring about meaningful reform, since privileged classes resisted change that threatened their position in their societies. Colonized peoples had even less opportunity to bring about political and social reform, but they frequently resisted imperial powers by mounting rebellions and organizing anticolonial movements. Revolution, industry, and empire fueled conflict throughout the world in the nineteenth century, and in combination they forced the world's peoples to deal with each other more systematically than ever before in history.

29 Revolutions and National States in the Atlantic World

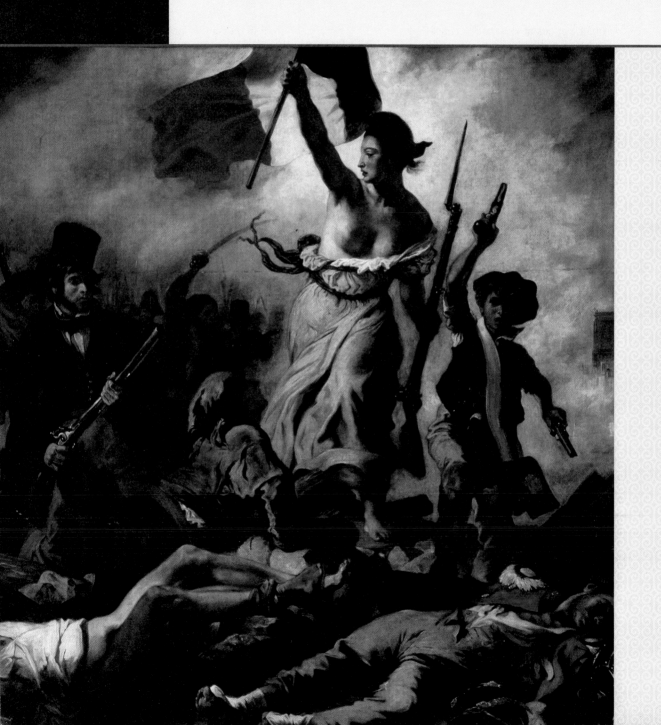

Popular Sovereignty and Political Upheaval
Enlightened and Revolutionary Ideas
The American Revolution
The French Revolution
The Reign of Napoleon

The Influence of Revolution
The Haitian Revolution
Wars of Independence in Latin America
The Emergence of Ideologies: Conservatism
and Liberalism

Testing the Limits of Revolutionary Ideals: Slavery
Testing the Limits of Revolutionary Ideals:
Women's Rights

The Consolidation of National States in Europe
Nations and Nationalism
The Emergence of National Communities
The Unifications of Italy and Germany

Marie Gouze was a French butcher's daughter who educated herself by reading books, moved to Paris, and married a junior army officer. Under the name Olympe de Gouges she won some fame as a journalist, actress, and playwright. Gouges was as flamboyant as she was talented, and news of her well-publicized love affairs scandalized Parisian society.

Gouges was also a revolutionary and a strong advocate of women's rights. She responded enthusiastically when the French revolution broke out in July 1789, and she applauded in August when revolutionary leaders proclaimed freedom and equality for all citizens in the *Declaration of the Rights of Man and the Citizen*. It soon became clear, however, that in the view of revolutionary leaders, freedom and equality pertained only to male citizens. They welcomed women's contributions to the revolution but withheld the right to vote and left women under the patriarchal authority of their fathers and husbands.

Gouges campaigned fervently to raise the standing of women in French society. She called for more education and demanded that women share equal rights in family property. She challenged patriarchal authority and appealed to Queen Marie Antoinette to use her influence to advance women's rights. In 1791 Gouges published a *Declaration of the Rights of Woman and the Female Citizen,* which claimed the same rights for women that revolutionary leaders had granted to men in August 1789. She asserted that freedom and equality were inalienable rights of women as well as men, and she insisted on the rights of women to vote, speak their minds freely, participate in the making of law, and hold public office.

Gouges's declaration attracted a great deal of attention but little support. Revolutionary leaders dismissed her appeal as a publicity stunt and refused to put women's rights on their political agenda. In 1793 they executed her because of her affection for Marie Antoinette and her persistent crusade for women's rights. Yet Gouges's campaign illustrated the power of the Enlightenment ideals of freedom and equality. Revolutionary leaders stilled her voice, but once they had proclaimed freedom and equality as universal human rights, they were unable to suppress demands to extend them to new constituencies.

Violence rocked lands throughout much of the Atlantic Ocean basin in the late eighteenth and early nineteenth centuries as a series of revolutions brought dramatic political and social change in the European and Euro-American world. Revolution broke out first in the British colonies of North America, where colonists asserted their independence and founded a new republic. A few years later, revolutionaries abolished the French monarchy and thoroughly reorganized French society. Revolutionary ideas soon spread to other lands. They inspired popular movements throughout Europe and prompted Latin American peoples

OPPOSITE: Liberty, personified as a woman, leads the French people in a famous painting by Eugène Delacroix.

to seek independence from Spanish and Portuguese colonial rule. In Saint-Domingue, revolution led to the abolition of slavery as well as independence from French rule. By the 1830s, peoples had reorganized political and social structures throughout western Europe and the Americas.

Apart from affecting individual lands, the revolutions of the late eighteenth and early nineteenth centuries had two results of deep global significance. First, they helped to spread a cluster of Enlightenment ideas concerning freedom, equality, and popular sovereignty. Revolutionary leaders argued that political authority arose from the people and worked to establish states in the interests of the people rather than the rulers. Usually they instituted republican forms of government, in which constituents selected delegates to represent their interests. In fact, early revolutionaries extended political rights to a privileged group of white men, but they justified their actions in general terms that invited new constituencies to seek enfranchisement. Ideas about freedom, equality, and popular sovereignty spread globally after the American and French revolutions as social reformers and revolutionaries struggled throughout the nineteenth and twentieth centuries to make freedom and equality a reality for oppressed groups and subject peoples throughout the world. By the mid-twentieth century, nearly every state in the world formally recognized the freedom and equality of all its citizens—even if they did not always honor their official positions—and claimed authority to rule on the basis of popular sovereignty.

While promoting Enlightenment values, revolutions also encouraged the consolidation of national states as the principal form of political organization. As peoples defended their states from enemies and sometimes mounted attacks on foreign lands, they developed a powerful sense of identity with their compatriots, and nationalist convictions inspired them to work toward the foundation of states that would advance the interests of the national community. During the nineteenth century, strong national identities and movements to build national states profoundly influenced the political experiences of European states. Strong nationalist sentiments created problems for multicultural states like the Austrian empire, which embraced several distinct linguistic and ethnic communities, but also fueled movements to unify lands like Italy and Germany, which previously had no national state. During the late nineteenth and twentieth centuries, efforts to harness nationalist sentiments and form states based on national identity became one of the most powerful and dynamic movements in world history.

Popular Sovereignty and Political Upheaval

Drawing on Enlightenment ideals, revolutionaries of the eighteenth and nineteenth centuries sought to fashion an equitable society by instituting governments that were responsive to the needs and interests of the peoples they governed. In justifying their policies, revolutionaries attacked monarchical and aristocratic regimes and argued for popular sovereignty—the notion that legitimate political authority resides not in kings but, rather, in the people who make up a society. In North America, colonists declared independence from British rule and instituted a new government founded on the principle of popular sovereignty. Soon thereafter, French revolutionaries abolished the monarchy and revamped the social order. Yet revolutionaries in France were unable to devise a stable alternative to the monarchy, and French society experienced turmoil for more than twenty years. In the early nineteenth century, Napoleon Bonaparte imposed military rule on France and helped spread revolutionary ideas to much of western Europe.

Enlightened and Revolutionary Ideas

Throughout history kings or emperors ruled almost all settled agricultural societies. Small societies occasionally instituted democratic governments, in which all citizens participated in political affairs, or republican governments, in which delegates represented the interests of various constituencies. Some societies, especially those with weak central leadership, also relied on aristocratic governments, in which privileged elites supervised public affairs. But hierarchical rule flowing from a king or an emperor was by far the most common form of government in settled agricultural societies.

In justifying their rule, kings and emperors throughout the world often identified themselves with deities or claimed divine sanction for their authority. Some rulers were priests, and most others cooperated closely with religious authorities. On the basis of their association with divine powers, kings and emperors claimed sovereignty—political supremacy and the authority to rule. In imperial China, for example, dynastic houses claimed to rule in accordance with the "mandate of heaven," and in early modern Europe centralizing monarchs often asserted a "divine right of kings" to rule as absolute monarchs.

Popular Sovereignty

During the seventeenth and eighteenth centuries, philosophes and other advocates of Enlightenment ideas (discussed in chapter 24) began to question long-standing notions of sovereignty. The philosophes rarely challenged monarchical rule, but sought instead to make kings responsible to the people they governed. They commonly regarded government as the result of a contract between rulers and ruled. The English philosopher John Locke (1632–1704) formulated one of the most influential theories of contractual government. In his *Second Treatise of Civil Government,* published in 1690, Locke held that government arose in the remote past when people decided to work together, form civil society, and appoint rulers to protect and promote their common interests. Individuals granted political rights to their rulers but retained personal rights to life, liberty, and property. Any ruler who violated those rights was subject to deposition. Furthermore, according to Locke, because individuals voluntarily formed society and established government, rulers derived their authority from the consent of those whom they governed. If subjects withdrew their consent, they had the right to replace their rulers. In effect, Locke's political thought relocated sovereignty, removing it from rulers as divine agents and vesting it in the people of a society.

Individual Freedom

Enlightenment thinkers addressed issues of freedom and equality as well as sovereignty. Philosophes such as Voltaire (1694–1778) resented the persecution of religious minorities and the censorship of royal officials, who had the power to prevent printers from publishing works that did not meet the approval of political and religious authorities. Philosophes called for religious toleration and freedom to express their views openly. When censors prohibited the publication of their writings in France, they often worked with French-speaking printers in Switzerland or the Netherlands who published their books and smuggled them across the border into France.

Political and Legal Equality

Many Enlightenment thinkers also called for equality. They condemned the legal and social privileges enjoyed by aristocrats, who in the philosophes' view made no more contribution to the larger society than a peasant, an artisan, or a crafts worker. They recommended the creation of a society in which all individuals would be equal before the law. The most prominent advocate of political equality was the French-Swiss thinker Jean-Jacques Rousseau (1712–1778), who identified with simple working people and deeply resented the privileges enjoyed by elite classes. In his influential book *The Social Contract* (1762), Rousseau argued that members of a society were collectively the sovereign. In an ideal society all individuals would participate directly in the formulation of policy and the creation of laws. In the absence of royalty, aristocrats, or other privileged elites, the general will of the people would carry the day.

Enlightenment thought on freedom, equality, and popular sovereignty reflected the interests of educated and talented men who sought to increase their influence and enhance their status in society. Most Enlightenment thinkers were of common birth but comfortable means. Although seeking to limit the prerogatives of ruling and aristocratic classes, they did not envision a society in which they would share political rights with women, children, peasants, laborers, slaves, or people of color.

Global Influence of Enlightenment Values

Nevertheless, Enlightenment thought constituted a serious challenge to long-established notions of political and social order. Revolutionary leaders in Europe and the Americas readily adopted Enlightenment ideas when justifying their efforts to overhaul the political and social structures they inherited. Over time, Enlightenment political thought influenced the organization of states and societies throughout the world. Enlightenment ideals did not spread naturally or inevitably. Rather, they spread when social reformers and revolutionaries claimed and fought for rights previously denied to them by ruling authorities and elite classes. Arguments for freedom, equality, and popular sovereignty originally served the interests of relatively privileged European and Euro-American men, but many other groups made effective use of them in seeking the extension of political rights.

The American Revolution

In the mid-eighteenth century there was no sign that North America might become a center of revolution. Residents of the thirteen British colonies there regarded themselves as British subjects: they recognized British law, read English-language books, and often braved the stormy waters of the North Atlantic Ocean to visit friends and family in England. They benefited handsomely from British rule. Trade brought prosperity to the colonies, and British military forces protected colonists' interests. From 1754 to 1763, for example, British forces waged an extremely expensive conflict in North America known as the French and Indian War. This conflict merged with a larger contest for imperial supremacy, the Seven Years' War (1756–1763), in which British and French forces battled each other in Europe and India as well as North America. Victory in the Seven Years' War ensured that Britain would dominate global trade and that British possessions, including the North American colonies, would prosper.

Tightened British Control of the Colonies

After the mid-1760s, however, North American colonists became increasingly disenchanted with British imperial rule. Faced with staggering financial difficulties arising from the Seven Years' War, the British Parliament passed legislation to levy new taxes and bring order to a far-flung trading empire. Parliament expected that the North American colonies would bear a fair share of the empire's tax burden and respect imperial trade policies. But parliamentary legislation proved extremely unpopular in North America. Colonists especially resented the imposition of taxes on molasses by the Sugar Act (1764), on publications and legal documents by the Stamp Act (1765), on a wide variety of imported items by the Townshend Act (1767), and on tea by the Tea Act (1773). They objected to strict enforcement of navigation laws—some of them a century old, but widely disregarded—that required cargoes to travel in British ships and clear British customs. Colonists also took offense at the Quartering Act (1765), which required them to provide housing and accommodations for British troops.

In responding to British policies, colonists argued that they should govern their affairs rather than follow instructions from London. They responded to new parliamentary levies with the slogan "no taxation without representation." They boycotted British products, physically attacked British officials, and mounted protests such as the Boston Tea Party (1773), in which colonists dumped a cargo of tea into Boston harbor rather than pay duties under the Tea Act. They also organized the Continental

In this painting by American artist John Trumbull, authors of the Declaration of Independence, including John Adams, Thomas Jefferson, and Benjamin Franklin, stand before a desk at the Continental Congress in Philadelphia.

Congress (1774), which coordinated the colonies' resistance to British policies. By 1775 tensions were so high that British troops and a colonial militia skirmished at the village of Lexington, near Boston. The war of American independence had begun.

On 4 July 1776 the Continental Congress adopted a document entitled "The unanimous Declaration of the thirteen united States of America." This Declaration of Independence drew deep inspiration from Enlightenment political thought in justifying the colonies' quest for independence. The document asserted "that all men are created equal, that they are endowed by their Creator with certain unalienable Rights, that among these are Life, Liberty, and the pursuit of Happiness." It echoed John Locke's contractual theory of government in arguing that individuals established governments to secure these rights and in holding that governments derive their power and authority from "the consent of the governed." When any government infringes upon individuals' rights, the document continued, "it is the Right of the People to alter or abolish it, and to institute new Government." The Declaration of Independence presented a long list of specific abuses charged to the British crown and concluded by proclaiming the colonies "Free and Independent States" with "full Power to levy War, conclude Peace, contract Alliances, establish Commerce, and to do all other Acts and Things which Independent States may of right do."

The Declaration of Independence

It was one thing to declare independence, but a different matter altogether to make independence a reality. At the beginning of the war for independence, Britain enjoyed many advantages over the rebels: a strong government with clear lines of authority, the most powerful navy in the world, a competent army, and a sizable population of loyalists in the colonies. But to wage war in a distant land full of opponents, Britain had to

Fighting in the American revolution ended when Cornwallis' troops were defeated at Yorktown.

ship supplies and reinforcements across a stormy ocean. Meanwhile, the rebels benefited from the military and economic support of European states that were eager to chip away at British hegemony in the Atlantic Ocean basin: France, Spain, the Netherlands, and several German principalities contributed to the American quest for independence. Moreover, George Washington (1732–1799) provided strong and imaginative military leadership for the colonial army while local militias employed guerrilla tactics effectively against British forces.

By 1780 all combatants were weary of the conflict. In the final military confrontation of the war, American and French forces under the command of George Washington surrounded the British forces of Charles Cornwallis at Yorktown, Virginia. After a twenty-day siege, the British forces surrendered in October 1781, and major military hostilities ceased from that point forward. In September 1783 diplomats concluded the Peace of Paris, by which the British government formally recognized American independence.

Building an Independent State

The leaders of the fledgling republic organized a state that reflected Enlightenment principles. In 1787 a constitutional convention drafted the blueprint for a new system of government—the Constitution of the United States—which emphasized the rights of individuals. American leaders based the federal government on popular sovereignty, and they agreed to follow this written constitution that guaranteed individual liberties such as freedom of speech, of the press, and of religion. They did not grant political and legal equality to all inhabitants of the newly independent land. They accorded full rights only to men of property, withholding them from landless men, women, slaves, and indigenous peoples. Over time, however, disenfranchised groups claimed and struggled for political and legal rights. Their campaigns involved considerable personal sacrifice and sometimes led to violence, since those in possession of rights did not always share them readily with others. With the extension of civil rights, American society broadened the implications of the Enlightenment values of freedom and equality as well as popular sovereignty.

The French Revolution

French revolutionaries also drew inspiration from Enlightenment political thought, but the French revolution was a more radical affair than its American counterpart. American revolutionary leaders sought independence from British imperial rule, but they were content to retain British law and much of their British social and cultural heritage. In contrast, French revolutionary leaders repudiated existing society, often referred to as the *ancien régime* ("old order"), and sought to replace it with new political, social, and cultural structures.

Serious fiscal problems put France on the road to revolution. In the 1780s approximately half of the French royal government's revenue went to pay off war debts—some of them arising from French support for colonists in the war of American independence—and another quarter went to French armed forces. King Louis XVI (reigned 1774–1793) was unable to raise more revenue from the overburdened peasantry, so he sought to increase taxes on the French nobility, which had long been exempt from many levies. Aristocrats protested that effort and forced Louis to summon the Estates General, an assembly that represented the entire French population through groups

The Estates General

Map 29.1 **The American revolution.** Note the location of both the major towns and cities in the colonies and the location of the major battles that occurred during the revolution. Why were both situated so close to the eastern coast?

Legend:
- Spanish Territory
- Thirteen British colonies in revolt
- Quebec under Quebec Act, 1774
- Other British possessions
- ✦ Major battles of the American Revolution

A contemporary print depicts the storming of the Bastille in 1789. The deeds of common people working in crowds became a favorite theme of artists after the outbreak of the French revolution.

known as estates. In the ancien régime there were three estates, or political classes. The first estate consisted of about one hundred thousand Roman Catholic clergy, and the second included some four hundred thousand nobles. The third estate embraced the rest of the population—about twenty-four million serfs, free peasants, and urban residents ranging from laborers, artisans, and shopkeepers to physicians, bankers, and attorneys. Though founded in 1303, the Estates General had not met since 1614. The third estate had as many delegates as the other two estates combined, but that numerical superiority offered no advantage when the assembly voted on issues, because voting took place by estate—one vote for each—not by individuals.

In May 1789 King Louis called the Estates General into session at the royal palace of Versailles in hopes that it would authorize new taxes. Louis never controlled the assembly. Representatives of the third estate arrived at Versailles demanding political and social reform. Although some members of the lower clergy and a few prominent nobles supported reform, the first and second estates stymied efforts to push measures through the Estates General.

The National Assembly

On 17 June 1789, after several weeks of fruitless debate, representatives of the third estate took the dramatic step of seceding from the Estates General and proclaiming themselves to be the National Assembly. Three days later, meeting in an indoor tennis court, members of the new Assembly swore not to disband until they had provided France with a new constitution. On 14 July 1789 a Parisian crowd, fearing that the king sought to undo events of the previous weeks, stormed the Bastille, a royal jail and arsenal, in search of weapons. The military garrison protecting the Bastille surrendered to the crowd but only after killing many of the attackers. To vent their rage, members of the crowd hacked the defenders to death. One assailant used his pocketknife to sever the garrison commander's head, which the victorious crowd mounted on a pike and paraded around the streets of Paris. News of the event soon spread, sparking insurrections in cities throughout France.

Emboldened by popular support, the National Assembly undertook a broad program of political and social reform. The *Declaration of the Rights of Man and the Citizen*, which the National Assembly promulgated in August 1789, articulated the

Sources from the Past

Declaration of the Rights of Man and the Citizen

While developing their program of reform, members of the National Assembly consulted closely with Thomas Jefferson, the principal author of the American Declaration of Independence, who was the U.S. ambassador to France in 1789. Thus it is not surprising that the Declaration of the Rights of Man and the Citizen *reflects the influence of American revolutionary ideas.*

First Article. Men are born and remain free and equal in rights. Social distinctions may be based only on common utility.

Article 2. The goal of every political association is the preservation of the natural and inalienable rights of man. These rights are liberty, property, security, and resistance to oppression.

Article 3. The principle of all sovereignty resides essentially in the nation. No body and no individual can exercise authority that does not flow directly from the nation.

Article 4. Liberty consists in the freedom to do anything that does not harm another. The exercise of natural rights of each man thus has no limits except those that assure other members of society their enjoyment of the same rights. These limits may be determined only by law.

Article 6. Law is the expression of the general will. All citizens have the right to participate either personally or through their representatives in the making of law. The law must be the same for all, whether it protects or punishes. Being equal in the eyes of the law, all citizens are equally eligible for all public honors, offices, and occupations, according to their abilities, without any distinction other than that of their virtues and talents.

Article 7. No person shall be accused, arrested, or imprisoned except in the cases and according to the forms prescribed by law. Any one soliciting, transmitting, executing, or causing to be executed, any arbitrary order, shall be punished. But any citizen summoned or arrested in virtue of the law shall submit without delay, as resistance constitutes an offense.

Article 9. As all persons are held innocent until they shall have been declared guilty, if arrest shall be deemed indispensable, all harshness not essential to the securing of the prisoner's person shall be severely repressed by law.

Article 11. The free communication of thoughts and opinions is one of the most precious rights of man: every citizen may thus speak, write, and publish freely, but will be responsible for abuse of this freedom in cases decided by the law.

Article 13. For the maintenance of public military force and for the expenses of administration, common taxation is necessary: it must be equally divided among all citizens according to their means.

Article 15. Society has the right to require from every public official an accounting of his administration.

Article 16. Any society in which guarantees of rights are not assured and separation of powers is not defined has no constitution at all.

Article 17. Property is an inviolable and sacred right. No one may be deprived of property except when public necessity, legally determined, clearly requires it, and on condition of just and prearranged compensation.

FOR FURTHER REFLECTION

In what ways do the principles established in the Declaration reflect the political transformations taking place throughout the age of Atlantic revolutions?

SOURCE: *Déclaration des droits de l'homme et du citoyen.* Translated by Jerry H. Bentley.

guiding principles of the program. Reflecting the influence of American revolutionary ideas, the *Declaration of the Rights of Man and the Citizen* proclaimed the equality of all men, declared that sovereignty resided in the people, and asserted individual rights to liberty, property, and security.

Between 1789 and 1791 the National Assembly reconfigured French society. Taking "liberty, equality, and fraternity" as its goals, the Assembly abolished the old social order along with the many fees and labor services that peasants owed to their

Liberty, Equality, and Fraternity

landlords. It dramatically altered the role of the church in French society by seizing church lands, abolishing the first estate, defining clergy as civilians, and requiring clergy to take an oath of loyalty to the state. It also promulgated a constitution that made the king the chief executive official but deprived him of legislative authority. France became a constitutional monarchy in which men of property—about half the adult male population—had the right to vote in elections to choose legislators. Thus far, the French revolution represented an effort to put Enlightenment political thought into practice.

The Convention

The revolution soon took a radical turn. Efforts by the French nobility to mobilize foreign powers in support of the king and the restoration of the ancien régime gave the Assembly the pretext to declare war against Austria and Prussia in April 1792. Adding to the military burden of France, revolutionary leaders declared war in the following year on Spain, Britain, and the Netherlands. Fearing military defeat and counterrevolution, revolutionary leaders created the Convention, a new legislative body elected by universal manhood suffrage, which abolished the monarchy and proclaimed France a republic. The Convention rallied the French population by instituting the *levée en masse*, ("mass levy"), or universal conscription that drafted people and resources for use in the war against invading forces. The Convention also rooted out enemies at home. It made frequent use of the guillotine, a recently invented machine that brought about supposedly humane executions by quickly severing a victim's head—whereas beheading with a sword or axe often led to needless suffering because executioners frequently needed several whacks to get the job done. In 1793 King Louis XVI and his wife, Queen Marie Antoinette, themselves went to the guillotine when the Convention found them guilty of treason. The king's prior reluctance to approve the constitution, his opposition to anticlerical legislation, and his family's unsuccessful flight from Paris branded the royals as traitors. Marie Antoinette's unpopularity—due to her Austrian heritage, her extravagance, and her influence over her husband—also helped undermine the credibility of the monarchy.

Revolutionary chaos reached its peak in 1793 and 1794 when Maximilien Robespierre (1758–1794) and the radical Jacobin party dominated the Convention. A lawyer by training, Robespierre had emerged during the revolution as a ruthless but popular radical known as "the Incorruptible," and he dominated the Committee of Public Safety, the executive authority of the Republic. The Jacobins believed passionately that France needed complete restructuring, and they unleashed a campaign of terror to promote their revolutionary agenda. They sought to eliminate the influence of Christianity in French society by closing churches and forcing priests to take wives. They promoted a new "cult of reason" as a secular alternative to Christianity. They reorganized the calendar, keeping months of thirty days but replacing seven-day weeks with ten-day units that recognized no day of religious observance. The Jacobins also proclaimed the inauguration of a new historical era with the Year I, which began with the declaration of the First Republic on 22 September 1792. They encouraged citizens to display their revolutionary zeal by wearing working-class clothes. They granted increased rights to women by permitting them to inherit property and divorce their husbands, although they did not allow women to vote or participate in political affairs. The Jacobins also made frequent use of the guillotine: between the summer of 1793 and the summer of 1794, they executed about forty thousand people and imprisoned three hundred thousand suspected enemies of the revolution. Even the feminist Olympe de Gouges (1748–1793) was a victim of the Jacobins, who did not appreciate her efforts to extend the rights of freedom and equality to women.

The Directory

Many victims of this reign of terror were fellow radicals who fell out of favor with Robespierre and the Jacobins. The instability of revolutionary leadership eventually

The guillotine was an efficient killing machine. In this contemporary print the executioner displays the just-severed head of King Louis XVI to the crowd assembled to witness his execution.

undermined confidence in the regime itself. In July 1794 the Convention arrested Robespierre and his allies, convicted them of tyranny, and sent them to the guillotine. A group of conservative men of property then seized power and ruled France under a new institution known as the Directory (1795–1799). Though more pragmatic than previous revolutionary leaders, members of the Directory were unable to resolve the economic and military problems that plagued revolutionary France. In seeking a middle way between the ancien régime and radical revolution, they lurched from one policy to another, and the Directory faced constant challenges to its authority. It came to an end in November 1799 when a young general named Napoleon Bonaparte staged a coup d'état and seized power.

Jacques-Louis David's *Napoleon on Horseback at the St. Bernard Pass* (1801) presents a famously heroic image of Napoleon's attack on Italy in 1800.

The Reign of Napoleon

Born to a minor noble family of Corsica, a Mediterranean island annexed by France in 1768, Napoleon Bonaparte (1769–1821) studied at French military schools and became an officer in the army of King Louis XVI. A brilliant military leader, he became a general at age twenty-four. He was a fervent supporter of the revolution and defended the Directory against a popular uprising in 1795. In a campaign of 1796–1797, he drove the Austrian army from northern Italy and established French rule there. In 1798 he mounted an invasion of Egypt to gain access to the Red Sea and threaten British control of the sea route to India, but the campaign ended in a complete British victory. Politically ambitious, Napoleon returned to France in 1799 and joined the Directory. When Austria, Russia, and Britain formed a coalition to attack France and end the revolution, he overthrew the Directory, imposed a new constitution, and named himself first consul with almost unchecked power to rule the French republic for ten years. In 1802 he became consul for life, and two years later he crowned himself emperor.

Napoleonic France   Napoleon brought political stability to a land torn by revolution and war. He made peace with the Roman Catholic church and in 1801 concluded an agreement with the pope. The pact, known as the Concordat, provided that the French state would retain church lands seized during the revolution, but the state agreed to pay clerics' salaries, recognize Roman Catholic Christianity as the preferred faith of France, and extend freedom of religion to Protestant Christians and Jews. This measure won Napoleon a

Map 29.2 **Napoleon's empire in 1812.** Observe the number of states dependent on or allied with Napoleon as opposed to those who were at war with him. Were there geographical conditions that allowed some states to resist Napoleon's efforts at conquest better than others?

great deal of support from people who supported the political and social goals of the revolution but balked at radicals' efforts to replace Christianity with a cult of reason.

In 1804 Napoleon promulgated the Civil Code, a revised body of civil law, which also helped stabilize French society. The Civil Code affirmed the political and legal equality of all adult men and established a merit-based society in which individuals qualified for education and employment because of talent rather than birth or social standing. The code protected private property, and Napoleon allowed aristocratic opponents of the revolution to return to France and reclaim some of their lost property. The Civil Code confirmed many of the moderate revolutionary policies of the National Assembly but retracted measures passed by the more radical Convention. The code restored patriarchal authority in the family, for example, by making women and children subservient to male heads of households. French civil law became the model for the civil codes of Québec Province, Canada, the Netherlands, Italy, Spain, some Latin American republics, and the state of Louisiana.

Although he approved the Enlightenment ideal of equality, Napoleon was no champion of intellectual freedom or representative government. He limited free speech and routinely censored newspapers and other publications. He established a secret police force that relied heavily on spies and detained suspected political opponents by the thousands. He made systematic use of propaganda to manipulate public opinion. He ignored elective bodies and surrounded himself with loyal military officers who ensured that representative assemblies did not restrict his authority. When he crowned himself emperor, he founded a dynasty that set his family above and apart from the people in whose name they ruled.

Napoleon's Empire

While working to stabilize France, Napoleon also sought to extend his authority throughout Europe. He was an imaginative tactician and strategist, the greatest general of his time. Full of revolutionary zeal and inspired by his leadership, Napoleon's armies conquered the Iberian and Italian peninsulas, occupied the Netherlands, and inflicted humiliating defeats on Austrian and Prussian forces. Napoleon sent his brothers and other relatives to rule the conquered and occupied lands, and he forced Austria, Prussia, and Russia to ally with him and respect French hegemony in Europe.

Napoleon's empire began to unravel in 1812, when he decided to invade Russia. Convinced that the tsar was conspiring with his British enemies, Napoleon led a Grand Army of six hundred thousand soldiers to Moscow. He captured the city, but the tsar withdrew and refused to surrender. Russians set Moscow ablaze, leaving Napoleon's massive army without adequate shelter or supplies. Napoleon ordered a retreat, but the bitter Russian winter destroyed his army. Napoleon had defied the combined forces of Britain, Austria, and Prussia, but he was no match for "General Winter." The Grand Army disintegrated, and a battered remnant of only thirty thousand soldiers limped back to France.

The Fall of Napoleon

Napoleon's disastrous Russian campaign emboldened his enemies. A coalition of British, Austrian, Prussian, and Russian armies converged on France and forced Napoleon to abdicate his throne in April 1814. The victors restored the French monarchy and exiled Napoleon to the tiny Mediterranean island of Elba, near Corsica. But Napoleon's adventure had not yet come to an end. In March 1815 he escaped from Elba, returned to France, and reconstituted his army. For a hundred days he ruled France again before a British army defeated him at Waterloo in Belgium. Unwilling to take further chances with the wily general, European powers banished Napoleon to the remote and isolated island of St. Helena in the South Atlantic Ocean, where he died of natural causes in 1821.

The Influence of Revolution

The Enlightenment ideals promoted by the American and French revolutions—freedom, equality, and popular sovereignty—appealed to peoples throughout Europe and the Americas. In the Caribbean and Latin America, they inspired revolutionary movements: slaves in the French colony of Saint-Domingue rose against their overlords and established the independent republic of Haiti, and Euro-American leaders mounted independence movements in Mexico, Central America, and South America. The ideals of the American and French revolutions also encouraged social reformers to organize broader programs of liberation. Whereas the American and French revolutions guaranteed political and legal rights to white men, social reformers sought to extend those rights to women and slaves of African ancestry. During the nineteenth century all European and Euro-American states abolished slavery, but former slaves and their descendants remained an underprivileged and often oppressed class in most of the Atlantic world. The quest for women's rights also proceeded slowly during the nineteenth century.

The Haitian Revolution

The only successful slave revolt in history took place on the Caribbean island of Hispaniola in the aftermath of the French revolution. By the eighteenth century, Hispaniola was a major center of sugar production with hundreds of prosperous plantations. The Spanish colony of Santo Domingo occupied the eastern part of the island (modern Dominican Republic), and the French colony of Saint-Domingue occupied the western part (modern Haiti). Saint-Domingue was one of the richest of all European colonies in the Caribbean: sugar, coffee, and cotton produced there accounted for almost one-third of France's foreign trade.

In 1790 the population of Saint-Domingue included about forty thousand white *Saint-Domingue* French settlers, thirty thousand *gens de couleur* (free people of color, including mulat-*Society* toes as well as freed slaves), and some five hundred thousand black slaves, most of whom were born in Africa. Led by wealthy planters, white residents stood at the top of society. *Gens de couleur* farmed small plots of land, sometimes with the aid of a few slaves, or worked as artisans in the island's towns. Most of the colony's slaves toiled in the fields under brutal conditions. Planters worked their slaves so hard and provided them with so little care that mortality was very high. Many slaves ran away into the mountains. By the late eighteenth century, Saint-Domingue had many large communities of maroons, who maintained their own societies and sometimes attacked plantations in search of food, weapons, tools, and additional recruits. As planters lost laborers, they imported new slaves from Africa and other Caribbean islands. This pattern continued throughout the eighteenth century, until prices of new slaves from Africa rose dramatically.

The American and French revolutions prepared the way for a violent political and social revolution in Saint-Domingue. Because French policy supported North American colonists against British rule, colonial governors in Saint-Domingue sent about five hundred *gens de couleur* to fight in the American war of independence. They returned to Saint-Domingue with the intention of reforming society there. When the French revolution broke out in 1789, white settlers in Saint-Domingue sought the right to govern themselves, but they opposed proposals to grant political and legal equality to the *gens de couleur.* By May 1791 civil war had broken out between white settlers and *gens de couleur.*

The conflict expanded dramatically when a charismatic Vodou priest named *Slave Revolt* Boukman organized a slave revolt. In August 1791 some twelve thousand slaves began killing white settlers, burning their homes, and destroying their plantations. Within a few weeks the rebels attracted almost one hundred thousand slaves into their ranks. Saint-Domingue quickly descended into chaos as white, *gens de couleur,* and slave factions battled one another. Many slaves were battle-tested veterans of wars in Africa, and they drew on their military experience to organize large armies. Slave leaders also found recruits and reinforcements in Saint-Domingue's maroon communities. Foreign armies soon complicated the situation: French troops arrived in 1792 to restore order, and British and Spanish forces intervened in 1793 in hopes of benefiting from France's difficulties.

Boukman died while fighting shortly after launching the revolt, but slave forces *Toussaint Louverture* eventually overcame white settlers, *gens de couleur,* and foreign armies. Their successes were due largely to the leadership of François-Dominique Toussaint (1744–1803), who after 1791 called himself Louverture—from the French *l'ouverture,* meaning "the

Former slave and effective military leader, Toussaint Louverture led the Haitian revolution.

opening," or the one who created an opening in enemy ranks. The son of slaves, Toussaint learned to read and write from a Roman Catholic priest. Because of his education and intelligence, he rose to the position of livestock overseer on the plantation and subsequently planted coffee on leased land with rented slaves. A free man since 1776, Toussaint was also an astute judge of human character. When the slave revolt broke out in 1791, Toussaint helped his masters escape to a safe place, then left the plantation and joined the rebels.

Toussaint was a skilled organizer, and by 1793 he had built a strong, disciplined army. He shrewdly played French, British, and Spanish forces against one another while also jockeying for power with other black and mulatto generals. By 1797 he led an army of twenty thousand that controlled most of Saint-Domingue. In 1801 he promulgated a constitution that granted equality and citizenship to all residents of Saint-Domingue. He stopped short of declaring independence from France, however, because he did not want to provoke Napoleon into attacking the island.

The Republic of Haiti

Nevertheless, in 1802 Napoleon dispatched forty thousand troops to restore French authority in Saint-Domingue. Toussaint attempted to negotiate a peaceful settlement, but the French commander arrested him and sent him to France, where he died in jail of maltreatment in 1803. By the time he died, however, yellow fever had ravaged the French army in Saint-Domingue, and the black generals who succeeded Toussaint had defeated the remaining troops and driven them out of the colony. Late in 1803 they declared independence, and on 1 January 1804 they proclaimed the establishment of Haiti, meaning "land of mountains," which became the second independent republic in the western hemisphere.

Wars of Independence in Latin America

Latin American Society

Revolutionary ideals traveled beyond Saint-Domingue to the Spanish and Portuguese colonies in the Americas. Though governed by *peninsulares* (colonial officials from Spain or Portugal), the Iberian colonies all had a large, wealthy, and powerful class of Euro-American criollos or creoles. In 1800 the *peninsulares* numbered about 30,000, and the creole population was 3.5 million. The Iberian colonies also had a large population—about 10 million in all—of less privileged classes. Black slaves formed a ma-

The slave rebellion in Saint-Domingue struck fear in the hearts of European and Euro-American peoples. This French print depicts out-numbered white settlers under attack on a plantation.

jority in Brazil, but elsewhere indigenous peoples and individuals of mixed ancestry such as mestizos and mulattoes were most numerous.

Creoles benefited greatly during the eighteenth century as they established planta-tions and ranches in the colonies and participated in rapidly expanding trade with Spain and Portugal. Yet the creoles also had grievances. Like British colonists in North America, the creoles resented administrative control and economic regulations im-posed by the Iberian powers. They drew inspiration from Enlightenment political thought and occasionally took part in tax revolts and popular uprisings. The creoles desired neither social reform like that promoted by Robespierre nor the establishment of an egalitarian society like Haiti. Basically they sought to displace the *peninsulares* but retain their privileged position in society: political independence on the model of the United States in North America struck them as an attractive alternative to colonial status. Between 1810 and 1825, creoles led movements that brought independence to all Spanish colonies in the Americas—except Cuba and Puerto Rico—and estab-lished creole-dominated republics.

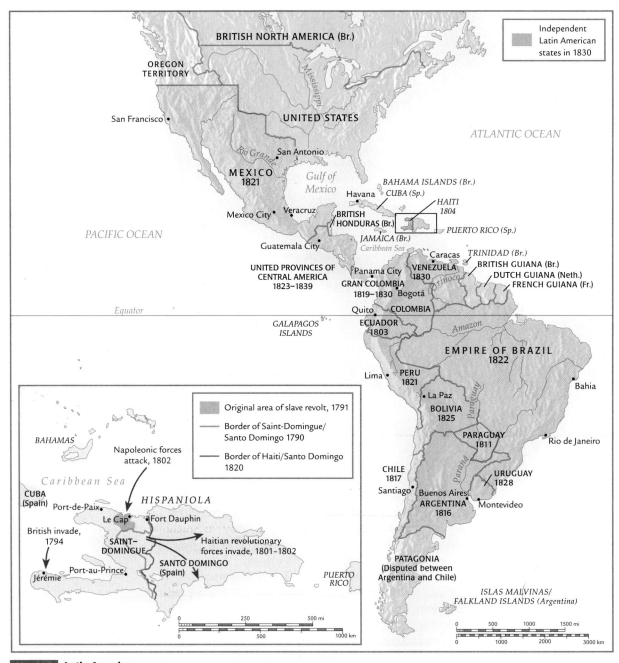

Map 29.3 **Latin America in 1830.** Note the dates each state won its independence. Since most states became independent in very close succession, what conditions prevented Latin American states from joining together in a federation like that in the United States?

Mexican Independence

The struggle for independence began in the wake of Napoleon's invasion of Spain and Portugal (1807), which weakened royal authority in the Iberian colonies. By 1810 revolts against Spanish rule had broken out in Argentina, Venezuela, and Mexico. The most serious was a peasant rebellion in Mexico led by a parish priest, Miguel Hidalgo y Costilla (1753–1811), who rallied indigenous peoples and mestizos against colonial rule. Many contemporaries viewed Hidalgo's movement for independence from Spanish rule as social and economic warfare by the masses against the elites of Mexican society, particularly since he rallied people to his cause by invoking the name of the popular and venerated Virgin of Guadalupe and by calling for the death of Spaniards. Conservative creoles soon captured Hidalgo and executed him, but his rebellion continued to flare for three years after his death. Hidalgo became the symbol of Mexican independence, and the day on which he proclaimed his revolt—16 September 1810—is Mexico's principal national holiday.

Colonial rule came to an end in 1821, when the creole general Augustín de Iturbide (1783–1824) declared independence from Spain. In the following year, he declared himself emperor of Mexico. Neither Iturbide nor his empire survived for long. Though an able general, Iturbide was an incompetent administrator, and in 1823 creole elites deposed him and established a republic. Two years later the southern re-

Simón Bolívar, creole leader of the independence movement in Latin America, was a favorite subject of painters in the nineteenth century. This portrait depicts him as a determined and farsighted leader.

gions of the Mexican empire declared their own independence. They formed a Central American Federation until 1838, when they split into the independent states of Guatemala, El Salvador, Honduras, Nicaragua, and Costa Rica.

In South America, creole elites such as Simón Bolívar (1783–1830) led the movement for independence. Born in Caracas (in modern Venezuela), Bolívar was a fervent republican steeped in Enlightenment ideas about popular sovereignty. Inspired by the example of George Washington, he took up arms against Spanish rule in 1811. In the early days of his struggle, Bolívar experienced many reversals and twice went into exile. In 1819, however, he assembled an army that surprised and crushed the Spanish army in Colombia. Later he campaigned in Venezuela, Ecuador, and Peru, coordinating his efforts with other creole leaders, such as José de San Martín (1778–1850) in Argentina and Bernardo O'Higgins (1778–1842) in Chile. By 1825 creole forces had overcome Spanish armies and deposed Spanish rulers throughout South America.

Simón Bolívar

Bolívar's goal was to weld the former Spanish colonies of South America into a great confederation like the United States in North America. During the 1820s independent Venezuela, Colombia, and Ecuador formed a republic called Gran Colombia, and Bolívar attempted to bring Peru and Bolivia (named for Bolívar himself) into the confederation. By 1830, however, strong political and regional differences had undermined Gran Colombia. As the confederation disintegrated, a bitterly disappointed Bolívar pronounced South America "ungovernable" and lamented that "those who have served the revolution have plowed the sea." Shortly after the breakup of Gran Colombia, Bolívar died of tuberculosis while en route to self-imposed exile in Europe.

Independence came to Portuguese Brazil at the same time as to Spanish colonies, but by a different process. When Napoleon invaded Portugal in 1807, the royal court fled Lisbon and established a government in exile in Rio de Janeiro. In 1821 the king returned to Portugal, leaving his son Pedro in Brazil as regent. The next year Brazilian creoles called for independence from Portugal, and Pedro agreed to their demands. When the Portuguese *Cortes* (parliament) tried to curtail his power, Pedro declared Brazil's independence and accepted appointment as Emperor Pedro I (reigned 1822–1834).

Brazilian Independence

Creole Dominance

Although Brazil achieved independence as a monarchy rather than a republic, creole elites dominated Brazilian society just as they did in former Spanish colonies. Indeed, independence brought little social change in Latin America. The *peninsulares* returned to Europe, but Latin American society remained as rigidly stratified as it had been in 1800. The newly independent states granted military authority to local charismatic strongmen, known as *caudillos,* allied with creole elites. The new states also permitted the continuation of slavery, confirmed the wealth and authority of the Roman Catholic church, and repressed the lower orders. The principal beneficiaries of independence in Latin America were the creole elites.

The Emergence of Ideologies: Conservatism and Liberalism

While inspiring revolutions and independence movements in other lands, the American and French revolutions also prompted political and social theorists to crystallize the modern ideologies of conservatism and liberalism. An *ideology* is a coherent vision of human nature, human society, and the larger world that proposes some particular form of political and social organization as ideal. Some ideologies seek to justify the current state of affairs, whereas others sharply criticize the status quo in arguing for movement toward an improved society. In all cases, ideologists seek to design a political and social order appropriate for their communities.

Conservatism

The modern ideology of conservatism arose as political and social theorists responded to the challenges of the American and especially the French revolutions. Conservatives viewed society as an organism that changed slowly over the generations. The English political philosopher Edmund Burke (1729–1797) held, for example, that society was a compact between a people's ancestors, the present generation, and their descendants as yet unborn. While admitting the need for gradual change that came about by general consensus, Burke condemned radical or revolutionary change, which in his view could only lead to anarchy. Thus Burke approved of the American revolution, which he took as an example of natural change in keeping with the historical development of North American society, but he denounced the French revolution as a chaotic and irresponsible assault on society.

Liberalism

In contrast to conservatives, liberals took change as normal and welcomed it as the agent of progress. They viewed conservatism as an effort to justify the status quo, maintain the privileges enjoyed by favored classes, and avoid dealing with injustice and inequality in society. For liberals the task of political and social theory was not to stifle change but, rather, to manage it in the best interests of society. Liberals championed the Enlightenment values of freedom and equality, which they believed would lead to higher standards of morality and increased prosperity for the whole society. They usually favored republican forms of government in which citizens elected representatives to legislative bodies, and they called for written constitutions that guaranteed freedom and equality for all citizens and that precisely defined the political structure and institutions of their societies. Although liberalism eventually became associated with the extension of democracy, leading to universal suffrage, many liberals during the nineteenth century considered democracy dangerous because it championed mass participation in politics.

The most prominent exponent of early liberalism was John Stuart Mill (1806–1873), an English philosopher, economist, and social reformer. Mill tirelessly promoted the freedom of individuals to pursue economic and intellectual interests. He tried to ensure that powerful minorities, such as wealthy businessmen, would not curb the freedoms of the poorly organized majority, but he also argued that it was improper for the majority to impose its will on minorities with different interests and values. He advocated universal suffrage as the most effective way to advance individual freedom, and he called for taxation of business profits and high personal incomes to forestall the or-

Caudillos (KAW-dee-ohs)

ganization of wealthy classes into groups that threatened individual liberties. Mill went further than most liberals in seeking to extend the rights of freedom and equality to women and working people as well as men of property.

As Mill recognized, the age of revolutions in the Atlantic world illustrated the centrality of suffrage in establishing a people's and a nation's sense of democratic legitimacy and political sovereignty. Defined as either the right or the privilege to vote, in order to elect public officials or to adopt laws, suffrage derived its revolutionary significance from Enlightenment notions about self-government and about governments deriving authority from the consent of the governed. Voting rights and restrictions evolved into powerful political concerns during and after the age of revolutions.

Voting Rights and Restrictions

The American and French revolutions championed the ideal of equality among all citizens, but tensions over the extension of the franchise nonetheless arose in the wake of those revolutions. Perhaps persuaded by the view that voting was more a privilege than a right, and therefore was legitimately subject to certain qualifications, early leaders restricted suffrage to white male citizens who possessed varying amounts of property. Limitations on the franchise thereafter long characterized suffrage in democratic nations, with residents being disenfranchised on the basis of citizenship, class, age, gender, and race, among other factors. Women in western Europe, North America, and South America actively sought and fought to gain suffrage rights, but their quests proved futile until the twentieth century. Whereas white men of all social and economic classes witnessed the removal of property restrictions on their voting rights so that during the nineteenth century almost all enjoyed the right to vote, black men in places such as the United States faced more obstacles. Their suffrage story suggested how long and contested the struggle over voting rights and restrictions could be.

Testing the Limits of Revolutionary Ideals: Slavery

The Enlightenment ideals of freedom and equality were watchwords of revolution in the Atlantic Ocean basin. Yet different revolutionaries understood the implications of freedom and equality in very different ways. In North America revolution led to political independence, a broad array of individual freedoms, and the legal equality of adult white men. In France it destroyed the hierarchical social order of the ancien régime and temporarily extended political and legal rights to all citizens, although Napoleon and later rulers effectively curbed some of those rights. In Haiti revolution brought independence from French rule and the end of slavery. In South America it led to independence from Iberian rule and societies dominated by creole elites. In the wake of the Atlantic revolutions, social activists in Europe and the Americas considered the possibility that the ideals of freedom and equality might have further implications as yet unexplored. They turned their attention especially to the issues of slavery and women's rights.

The campaign to end the slave trade and abolish slavery began in the eighteenth century. Freed slaves such as Olaudah Equiano (1745–1797) were among the earliest critics of slavery. Beginning in the 1780s European Christian moralists also voiced opposition to slavery.

Movements to End the Slave Trade

Only after the American, French, and Haitian revolutions, however, did the antislavery movement gain momentum. The leading spokesman of the movement was William Wilberforce (1759–1833), a prominent English philanthropist elected in 1780 to a seat in Parliament. There he tirelessly attacked slavery on moral and religious grounds. After the Haitian revolution he attracted supporters who feared that continued reliance on slave labor would result in more and larger slave revolts, and in 1807 Parliament passed Wilberforce's bill to end the slave trade. Under British pressure, other states also banned commerce in slaves: the United States in 1808, France in 1814, the Netherlands in 1817, and Spain in 1845. The British navy, which dominated the North Atlantic Ocean, patrolled the west coast of Africa to ensure compliance with the law. But the slave trade died slowly, as illegal trade in African slaves continued on a small scale: the last documented ship to carry slaves across the Atlantic Ocean arrived in Cuba in 1867.

Movements to Abolish Slavery

The abolition of slavery itself was a much bigger challenge than ending the slave trade because owners had property rights in their slaves. Planters and merchant elites strongly resisted efforts to alter the system that provided them with abundant supplies of inexpensive labor. Nevertheless, the end of the slave trade doomed the institution of slavery in the Americas. In Haiti the end of slavery came with the revolution. In much of South America, slavery ended with independence from Spanish rule, as Simón Bolívar freed slaves who joined his forces and provided constitutional guarantees of free status for all residents of Gran Colombia. In Mexico slavery was abolished in 1829, though not solely for humanitarian reasons. It served as a mechanism to stop the influx of residents from the southern United States coming in with their slaves to grow cotton.

Meanwhile, as they worked to ban traffic in human labor, Wilberforce and other moralists also launched a campaign to free slaves and abolish the institution of slavery itself. In 1833, one month after Wilberforce's death, Parliament provided twenty million pounds sterling as compensation to slave owners and abolished slavery throughout the British empire. Other states followed the British example: France abolished slavery in 1848, the United States in 1865, Cuba in 1886, and Brazil in 1888.

Freedom without Equality

Abolition brought legal freedom for African and African-American slaves, but it did not bring political equality. In most lands other than Haiti, African-American peoples had little influence in society. Property requirements, literacy tests, poll taxes, and campaigns of intimidation effectively prevented them from voting. Nor did emancipation bring social and economic improvements for former slaves and their descendants. White creole elites owned most of the property in the Americas, and they kept blacks in subordination by forcing them to accept low-paying work. A few African-Americans owned small plots of land, but they could not challenge the economic and political power of creole elites.

Testing the Limits of Revolutionary Ideals: Women's Rights

Women participated alongside men in the movement to abolish slavery, and their experience inspired feminist social reformers to seek equality with men. They pointed out that women suffered many of the same legal disabilities as slaves: they had little access to education, they could not enter professional occupations that required advanced education, and they were legally deprived of the right to vote. They drew on Enlightenment thought in making a case for women's rights, but in spite of support from prominent liberals such as John Stuart Mill, they had little success before the twentieth century.

Enlightenment Ideals and Women

Enlightenment thought called for the restructuring of government and society, but the philosophes mostly held conservative views on women and their roles in family and society. Rousseau, for example, advised that girls' education should prepare them to become devoted wives and mothers. Yet social reformers found Enlightenment thought extremely useful in arguing for women's rights. Drawing on the political thought of John Locke, for example, the English writer Mary Astell (1666–1731) suggested that absolute sovereignty was no more appropriate in a family than in a state. Astell also reflected Enlightenment influence in asking why, if all men were born free, all women were born slaves?

During the eighteenth century, advocates of women's rights were particularly active in Britain, France, and North America. Among the most prominent was the British writer Mary Wollstonecraft (1759–1797). Although she had little schooling,

Parisian women were the leaders of the crowd that marched to Versailles, protested high food prices, and forced the king and queen to return to Paris in October 1789.

Wollstonecraft avidly read books at home and gained an informal self-education. In 1792 she published an influential essay entitled *A Vindication of the Rights of Woman.* Like Astell, Wollstonecraft argued that women possessed all the rights that Locke had granted to men. She insisted on the right of women to education: it would make them better mothers and wives, she said, and would enable them to contribute to society by preparing them for professional occupations and participation in political life.

Women played crucial roles in the revolutions of the late eighteenth and early nineteenth centuries. Some women supported the efforts of men by sewing uniforms, rolling bandages, or managing farms, shops, and businesses. Others actively participated in revolutionary activities. In October 1789, for example, about six thousand Parisian women marched to Versailles to protest the high price of bread. Some of them forced their way into the royal apartments and demanded that the king and queen return with them to Paris—along with the palace's supply of flour. In the early 1790s, pistol-wielding members of the Republican Revolutionary Women patrolled the streets of Paris. The fate of Olympe de Gouges made it clear, however, that revolutionary women had little prospect of holding official positions or playing a formal role in public affairs.

Women and Revolution

Under the National Assembly and the Convention, the French revolution brought increased rights for women. The republican government provided free public education for girls as well as boys, granted wives a share of family property, and legalized divorce. Yet the revolution did not bring women the right to vote or to play major roles in public affairs. Under the Directory and Napoleon's rule, women lost even the rights that they had won in the early days of the revolution. In other lands, women never gained as much as they did in revolutionary France. In the United States and the independent states of Latin America, revolution brought legal equality and political rights only for adult white men, who retained patriarchal authority over their wives and families.

Nevertheless, throughout the nineteenth century social reformers pressed for women's rights as well as the abolition of slavery. The American feminist Elizabeth Cady Stanton (1815–1902) was an especially prominent figure in this movement. In 1840 Stanton went to London to attend an antislavery conference but found that the organizers barred women from participation. Infuriated, Stanton returned to the United States and began to build a movement for women's rights. She organized a

Women's Rights Movements

Sources from the Past

Declaration of the Rights of Woman and the Female Citizen

In 1791 Olympe de Gouges, a butcher's daughter and playwright of some note, wrote and published the Declaration of the Rights of Woman and the Female Citizen. *She directly challenged the inferiority presumed of women by the 1789* Declaration of the Rights of Man and the Citizen, *which limited citizenship to males. By publicly asserting the equality of women, Gouges breached barriers that most revolutionary leaders wanted to perpetuate. Charged with treason during the rule of the National Convention, Gouges went to the guillotine on 3 November 1793.*

Article 1. Woman is born free and lives equal to man in her rights. Social distinctions can be based only on the common utility.

Article 2. The purpose of any political association is the conservation of the natural and imprescriptible rights of woman and man; these rights are liberty, property, security, and especially resistance to oppression.

Article 3. The principle of all sovereignty rests essentially with the nation, which is nothing but the union of woman and man; no body and no individual can exercise any authority which does not come expressly from it (the nation).

Article 4. Liberty and justice consist of restoring all that belongs to others; thus, the only limits on the exercise of the natural rights of woman are perpetual male tyranny; these limits are to be reformed by the laws of nature and reason.

Article 6. The law must be the expression of the general will; all female and male citizens must contribute either personally or through their representatives to its formation; it must be the same for all: male and female citizens, being equal in the eyes of the law, must be equally admitted to all honors, positions, and public employment according to their capacity and without other distinctions besides those of their virtues and talents.

Article 7. No woman is an exception; she is accused, arrested, and detained in cases determined by law. Women, like men, obey this rigorous law.

Article 11. The free communication of thoughts and opinions is one of the most precious rights of woman, since that liberty assures recognition of children by their fathers. Any female citizen thus may say freely, I am the mother of a child which belongs to you, without being forced by a barbarous prejudice to hide the truth; (an exception may be made) to respond to the abuse of this liberty in cases determined by law.

Article 13. For the support of the public force and the expenses of administration, the contributions of woman and man are equal; she shares all the duties and all the painful tasks; therefore, we must have the same share in the distribution of positions, employment, offices, honors, and jobs.

Article 14. Female and male citizens have the right to verify, either by themselves or through their representatives, the necessity of the public contribution. This can only apply to women if they are granted an equal share, not only of wealth, but also of public administration, and in the determination of the proportion, the base, the collection, and the duration of the tax.

Article 17. Property belongs to both sexes whether united or separate; for each it is an inviolable and sacred right; no one can be deprived of it, since it is the true patrimony of nature, unless the legally determined public need obviously dictates it, and then only with a just and prior indemnity.

FOR FURTHER REFLECTION

How does Olympe de Gouges's feminist restatement of the Declaration of the Rights of Man and the Citizen intensify its radical precepts?

SOURCE: Darline Gay Levy, Harriet Branson Applewhite, and Mary Durham Johnson. *Women in Revolutionary Paris, 1789–1795.* Urbana: University of Illinois Press, 1979, pp. 90–92.

conference of feminists who met at Seneca Falls, New York, in 1848. The conference passed twelve resolutions demanding that lawmakers grant women rights equivalent to those enjoyed by men. The resolutions called specifically for women's rights to vote, attend public schools, enter professional occupations, and participate in public affairs.

The women's rights movement experienced limited success in the nineteenth century. More women received formal education than before the American and French revolutions, and women in Europe and North America participated in academic, literary, and civic organizations. Rarely did they enter the professions, however, and nowhere did they enjoy the right to vote. Yet, by seeking to extend the promises of Enlightenment political thought to blacks and women as well as white men, social reformers of the nineteenth century laid a foundation that would lead to large-scale social change in the twentieth century.

The Consolidation of National States in Europe

The Enlightenment ideals of freedom, equality, and popular sovereignty inspired political revolutions in much of the Atlantic Ocean basin, and the revolutions in turn helped spread Enlightenment values. The wars of the French revolution and the Napoleonic era also inspired the development of a particular type of community identity that had little to do with Enlightenment values—nationalism. Revolutionary wars involved millions of French citizens in the defense of their country against foreign armies and the extension of French influence to neighboring states. Wartime experiences encouraged peoples throughout Europe to think of themselves as members of distinctive national communities. Throughout the nineteenth century, European nationalist leaders worked to fashion states based on national identities and mobilized citizens to work in the interests of their own national communities, sometimes by fostering jealousy and suspicion of other national groups. By the late nineteenth century, national identities were so strong that peoples throughout Europe responded enthusiastically to ideologies of nationalism, which promised glory and prosperity to those who worked in the interests of their national communities.

Nations and Nationalism

One of the most influential concepts of modern political thought is the idea of the nation. The word *nation* refers to a type of community that became especially prominent in the nineteenth century. At various times and places in history, individuals have associated themselves primarily with families, clans, cities, regions, and religious faiths. During the nineteenth century, European peoples came to identify strongly with communities they called nations. Members of a nation considered themselves a distinctive people born into a unique community that spoke a common language, observed common customs, inherited common cultural traditions, held common values, and shared common historical experiences. Often they also honored common religious beliefs, although they sometimes overlooked differences of faith and construed the nation as a political, social, and cultural, rather than religious, unit.

Intense feelings of national identity fueled ideologies of nationalism. Advocates of nationalism insisted that the nation must be the focus of political loyalty. Zealous nationalist leaders maintained that members of their national communities had a common destiny that they could best advance by organizing independent national states and resolutely pursuing their national interests. Ideally, in their view, the boundaries of the national state embraced the territory occupied by the national community, and its government promoted the interests of the national group, sometimes through conflict with other peoples.

Early nationalist thought often sought to deepen appreciation for the historical experiences of the national community and foster pride in its cultural accomplishments. During the late eighteenth century, for example, Johann Gottfried von Herder (1744–1803) sang the praises of the German *Volk* ("people") and their powerful and expressive language. In reaction to Enlightenment thinkers and their quest for a

Cultural Nationalism

A portrait of the Italian nationalist leader Giuseppe Mazzini as a disappointed but determined idealist.

scientific, universally valid understanding of the world, early cultural nationalists such as Herder focused their attention on individual communities and relished their uniqueness. They emphasized historical scholarship, which they believed would illuminate the distinctive characteristics of their societies. They also valued the study of literature, which they considered the best guide to the *Volksgeist*, the popular soul or spirit or essence of their community. For that reason the German brothers Jakob and Wilhelm Grimm collected popular poetry, stories, songs, and tales as expressions of the German *Volk*.

Political Nationalism

During the nineteenth century, nationalist thought became much more strident than the cultural nationalism of Herder or the brothers Grimm. Advocates of nationalism demanded loyalty and solidarity from members of the national group. In lands where they were minorities or where they lived under foreign rule, they sought to establish independent states to protect and advance the interests of the national community.

In Italy, for example, the nationalist activist Giuseppe Mazzini (1805–1872) formed a group called Young Italy that promoted independence from Austrian and Spanish rule and the establishment of an Italian national state. Mazzini likened the nation to a family and the nation's territory to the family home. Austrian and Spanish authorities forced Mazzini to lead much of his life in exile, but he used the opportunity to encourage the organization of nationalist movements in new lands. By the mid-nineteenth century, Young Italy had inspired the development of nationalist movements in Ireland, Switzerland, and Hungary.

While it encouraged political leaders to work toward the establishment of national states for their communities, nationalism also had strong potential to stir up conflict between different groups of people. The more nationalists identified with their own national communities, the more they distinguished themselves both from peoples in other lands and from minority groups within their societies.

Nationalism and Anti-Semitism

This divisive potential of nationalism helps to explain the emergence of Zionism, a political movement that holds that the Jewish people constitute a nation and have the right to their own national homeland. Unlike Mazzini's Italian compatriots, Jews did not inhabit a well-defined territory but, rather, lived in states throughout Europe. As national communities tightened their bonds, nationalist leaders often became distrustful of minority populations. Suspicion of Jews fueled anti-Semitism in many parts of Europe. Whereas anti-Semitism was barely visible in countries such as Italy and the Netherlands, it operated openly in those such as Austria-Hungary and Germany. In eastern Europe, anti-Semitism often turned violent. In Russia and in the Russian-controlled areas of Poland, the persecution of Jews climaxed in a series of pogroms. Beginning in 1881 and lasting into the early twentieth century, these massacres claimed the lives and property of thousands of Jews.

During the late nineteenth and twentieth centuries, millions of Jews migrated to other European lands or to North America to escape persecution and violence. Anti-Semitism was not as severe in France as in central and eastern Europe, but it reached a fever pitch there after a military court convicted Alfred Dreyfus, a Jewish army officer, of spying for Germany in 1894. Although he was innocent of the charges and eventually had the verdict reversed on appeal, Dreyfus was the focus of bitter debates about the trustworthiness of Jews in French society. The trial also became a key event in the evolution of Zionism.

A determined Theodor Herzl founded the Zionist movement.

Zionism

Among the reporters at the Dreyfus trial was a Jewish journalist from Vienna, Theodor Herzl (1860–1904). As Herzl witnessed mobs shouting "Death to the Jews" in the land of enlightenment and liberty, he concluded that anti-Semitism was a persistent feature of human society that assimilation could not solve. In 1896 Herzl published the pamphlet *Judenstaat,* which argued that the only defense against anti-Semitism lay in the mass migration of Jews from all over the world to a land that they could call their own. In the following year, Herzl organized the first Zionist Congress in Basel, Switzerland, which founded the World Zionist Organization. The delegates at Basel formulated the basic platform of the Zionist movement, declaring that "Zionism seeks to establish a home for the Jewish people in Palestine," the location of the ancient Kingdom of Israel. During the next half century, Jewish migrants trickled into Palestine, and in 1948 they won recognition for the Jewish state of Israel. Although it arose in response to exclusive nationalism in Europe, Zionism in turn provoked a resentful nationalism among Palestinians displaced by Jewish settlers. Conflicts between Jews and Palestinians continue to the present day.

The Emergence of National Communities

The French revolution and the wars that followed it heightened feelings of national identity throughout Europe. In France the establishment of a republic based on liberty, equality, and fraternity inspired patriotism and encouraged citizens to rally to the defense of the revolution when foreign armies threatened it. Revolutionary leaders took the tricolored flag as a symbol of the French nation, and they adopted a rousing marching tune, the "Marseillaise," as an anthem that inspired pride in and identity with the national community. In Spain, the Netherlands, Austria, Prussia, and Russia, national consciousness surged in reaction to the arrival of revolutionary and Napoleonic armies. Opposition to Napoleon and his imperial designs also inspired national feeling in Britain.

The Congress of Vienna

After the fall of Napoleon, conservative political leaders feared that heightened national consciousness and ideas of popular sovereignty would encourage further experimentation with revolution and undermine European stability. Meeting as the Congress of Vienna (1814–1815), representatives of the "great powers" that defeated Napoleon—Britain, Austria, Prussia, and Russia—attempted to restore the prerevolutionary order. Under the guidance of the influential foreign minister of Austria, Prince

The charming and polished courtier Prince Klemens von Metternich (standing at left center) dominated the Congress of Vienna. Here delegates to the Congress are gathered at the Habsburg palace in Vienna.

Klemens von Metternich (1773–1859), the Congress dismantled Napoleon's empire, returned sovereignty to Europe's royal families, restored them to the thrones they had lost during the Napoleonic era, and created a diplomatic order based on a balance of power that prevented any one state from dominating the others. A central goal of Metternich himself was to suppress national consciousness, which he viewed as a serious threat to the multicultural Austrian empire that included Germans, Italians, Magyars, Czechs, Slovaks, Poles, Serbs, and Croats among its subjects.

The efforts of Metternich and the Congress of Vienna to restore the ancien régime had limited success. The European balance of power established at Vienna survived for almost a century, until the outbreak of a general continental and global war in 1914. Metternich and the conservative rulers installed by the Congress of Vienna took measures to forestall further revolution: they censored publications to prevent communication of seditious ideas and relied on spies to identify nationalist and republican activists. By 1815, however, it was impossible to suppress national consciousness and ideas of popular sovereignty.

Nationalist Rebellions

From the 1820s through the 1840s, a wave of rebellions inspired by nationalist sentiments swept through Europe. The first uprising occurred in 1821 in the Balkan peninsula, where the Greek people sought independence from the Ottoman Turks, who had ruled the region since the fifteenth century. Many western Europeans sympathized with the Greek cause. The English poet Lord Byron even joined the rebel army and in 1824 died (of a fever) while serving in Greece. With the aid of Britain, France, and Russia, the rebels overcame the Ottoman forces in the Balkans by 1827 and won formal recognition of Greek independence in 1830.

In 1830 rebellion showed its face throughout Europe. In France, Spain, Portugal, and some of the German principalities, revolutionaries inspired by liberalism called for constitutional government based on popular sovereignty. In Belgium, Italy, and Poland, they demanded independence and the formation of national states as well as popular sovereignty. Revolution in Paris drove Charles X from the throne, while uprisings in Belgium resulted in independence from the Netherlands. By the mid-1830s authorities had put down the uprisings elsewhere, but in 1848 a new round of rebellions shook European states. The uprisings of 1848 brought down the French monarchy and seriously threatened the Austrian empire, where subject peoples clamored for constitutions and independence. Prince Metternich resigned his office as Austrian for-

Map 29.4 **The unifi-cation of Italy and Germany.** The unification of Italy and Germany as national states in the nineteenth century fundamentally altered the balance of power in Europe. Why did unification result from diplomacy and war conducted by conservative statesmen rather than popular nationalist action?

eign minister and unceremoniously fled Vienna as rebels took control of the city. Uprisings also rocked cities in Italy, Prussia, and German states in the Rhineland.

By the summer of 1849, the veteran armies of conservative rulers had put down the last of the rebellions. Advocates of national independence and popular sovereignty remained active, however, and the potential of their ideals to mobilize popular support soon became dramatically apparent.

The Unifications of Italy and Germany

The most striking demonstration of the power that national sentiments could unleash involved the unification of Italy and Germany. Since the fall of the Roman empire, Italy and Germany had been disunited lands. A variety of regional kingdoms, city-states, and ecclesiastical states ruled the Italian peninsula for more than a thousand years, and princes divided Germany into more than three hundred semiautonomous jurisdictions. The Holy Roman Empire claimed authority over Germany and much of Italy, but the emperors were rarely strong enough to enforce their claims.

As they dismantled Napoleon's empire and sought to restore the ancien régime, delegates at the Congress of Vienna placed much of northern Italy under Austrian rule. Southern Italy was already under close Spanish supervision because of dynastic ties between the Kingdom of the Two Sicilies and the Spanish Bourbon monarchy. As national sentiment surged throughout nineteenth-century Europe, Italian political leaders worked to win independence from foreign rule and establish an Italian national state. Mazzini's Young Italy movement attracted discontented idealists throughout the peninsula. In 1820, 1830, and 1848, they mounted major uprisings that threatened but did not dislodge foreign rule in Italy.

Wearing a white jacket, Otto von Bismarck (center) witnesses the crowning of King Wilhelm I of Prussia as German emperor. The coronation followed the victory of Prussia over France in 1871, and it took place in the royal palace at Versailles.

Cavour and Garibaldi

The unification of Italy came about when practical political leaders such as Count Camillo di Cavour (1810–1861), prime minister to King Vittore Emmanuele II of Piedmont and Sardinia, combined forces with nationalist advocates of independence. Cavour was a cunning diplomat, and the kingdom of Piedmont and Sardinia was the most powerful of the Italian states. In alliance with France, Cavour expelled Austrian authorities from most of northern Italy in 1859. Then he turned his attention to southern Italy, where Giuseppe Garibaldi (1807–1882), a dashing soldier of fortune and a passionate nationalist, led the unification movement. With an army of about one thousand men outfitted in distinctive red shirts, Garibaldi swept through Sicily and southern Italy, outmaneuvering government forces and attracting enthusiastic recruits. In 1860 Garibaldi met King Vittore Emmanuele near Naples. Not ambitious to rule, Garibaldi delivered southern Italy into Vittore Emmanuele's hands, and the kingdom of Piedmont and Sardinia became the kingdom of Italy. During the next decade the new monarchy absorbed several additional territories, including Venice, Rome, and their surrounding regions.

In Germany as in Italy, unification came about when political leaders harnessed nationalist aspirations. The Congress of Vienna created a German Confederation composed of thirty-nine states dominated by Austria. Metternich and other conservative German rulers stifled nationalist movements, and the suppression of the rebellions of 1848 left German nationalists frustrated at their inability to found a national state.

Otto von Bismarck

In 1862 King Wilhelm I of Prussia appointed a wealthy landowner, Otto von Bismarck (1815–1898), as his prime minister. Bismarck was a master of *Realpolitik* ("the politics of reality"). He succinctly expressed his realistic approach in his first speech as prime minister: "The great questions of the day will not be settled by speeches or majority votes—that was the great mistake of 1848 and 1849—but by blood and iron."

It was indeed blood and iron that brought about the unification of Germany. As prime minister, Bismarck reformed and expanded the Prussian army. Between 1864 and 1870 he intentionally provoked three wars—with Denmark, Austria, and France—and whipped up German sentiment against the enemies. In all three conflicts Prussian forces quickly shattered their opponents, swelling German pride. In 1871 the Prussian king proclaimed himself emperor of the Second Reich—meaning the Second German Empire, following the Holy Roman Empire—which embraced almost all German-speaking peoples outside Austria and Switzerland in a powerful and dynamic national state.

The unification of Italy and Germany made it clear that when coupled with strong political, diplomatic, and military leadership, nationalism had enormous potential to mobilize people who felt a sense of national kinship. Italy, Germany, and other national states went to great lengths to foster a sense of national community. They adopted national flags to serve as symbols of unity, national anthems to inspire patriotism, and national holidays to focus public attention on individuals and events of special importance for the national community. They established bureaucracies that took censuses of national populations and tracked vital national statistics involving birth, marriage, and death. They built schools that instilled patriotic values in students, and they recruited young men into armies that defended national interests and sometimes went on the offensive to enhance national prestige. By the end of the nineteenth century, the national state had proven to be a powerful model of political organization in Europe. By the mid-twentieth century it had become well-nigh universal as political leaders adopted the national state as the principal form of political organization throughout the world.

———————————

The Enlightenment ideals of freedom, equality, and popular sovereignty inspired revolutionary movements throughout much of the Atlantic Ocean basin in the late eighteenth and early nineteenth centuries. In North America colonists threw off British rule and founded an independent federal republic. In France revolutionaries abolished the monarchy, established a republic, and refashioned the social order. In Saint-Domingue rebellious slaves threw off French rule, established an independent Haitian republic, and granted freedom and equality to all citizens. In Latin America creole elites led movements to expel Spanish and Portuguese colonial authorities and to found independent republics. During the nineteenth century, adult white men were the main beneficiaries of movements based on Enlightenment ideals, but social reformers launched campaigns to extend freedom and equality to Africans, African-Americans, and women.

Meanwhile, as they fought each other in wars sparked by the French revolution, European peoples developed strong feelings of national identity and worked to establish states that advanced the interests of national communities. Nationalist thought was often divisive: it pitted national groups against one another and fueled tensions especially in large multicultural states. But nationalism also had strong potential to contribute to state-building movements, and nationalist appeals played prominent roles in the unification of Italy and Germany. During the nineteenth and twentieth centuries, peoples throughout the world drew inspiration from Enlightenment ideals and national identities when seeking to build or restructure their societies.

CHRONOLOGY

1632–1704	Life of John Locke
1694–1778	Life of Voltaire
1712–1778	Life of Jean-Jacques Rousseau
1744–1803	Life of Toussaint Louverture
1748–1793	Life of Olympe de Gouges
1753–1811	Life of Miguel Hidalgo y Costilla
1769–1821	Life of Napoleon Bonaparte
1773–1859	Life of Klemens von Metternich
1774–1793	Reign of King Louis XVI
1775–1781	American revolution
1783–1830	Life of Simón Bolívar
1789–1799	French revolution
1791–1803	Haitian revolution
1799–1814	Reign of Napoleon
1805–1872	Life of Giuseppe Mazzini
1807–1882	Life of Giuseppe Garibaldi
1810–1825	Wars of independence in Latin America
1810–1861	Life of Camillo di Cavour
1814–1815	Congress of Vienna
1815–1898	Life of Otto von Bismarck
1821–1827	War of Greek independence
1859–1870	Unification of Italy
1864–1871	Unification of Germany

FOR FURTHER READING

Benedict Anderson. *Imagined Communities: Reflections on the Origin and Spread of Nationalism.* Rev. ed. London, 1991. A pioneering work that analyzes the means and the processes by which peoples came to view themselves as members of national communities.

David A. Bell. *The Cult of the Nation in France: Inventing Nationalism, 1680–1800.* Cambridge, Mass., 2001. Looks at how patriotism and national sentiment were grafted onto religious forms of community in the context of the eighteenth century and the French revolution.

———. *The First Total War: Napoleon's Europe and the Birth of Warfare as We Know It.* Boston, 2007. A fine work that argues that nearly every "modern" aspect of war was born in the Revolutionary and Napoleonic wars.

Bernard Bailyn. *The Ideological Origins of the American Revolution.* 2nd ed. Cambridge, Mass., 1992. A fundamental study of pamphlets and other publications that criticized British colonial policy in North America.

Keith M. Baker. *Inventing the French Revolution: Essays on French Political Culture in the Eighteenth Century.* Cambridge, 1990. Important exploration of the ideological origins of the French Revolution.

Reinhard Bendix. *Kings or People: Power and the Mandate to Rule.* Berkeley, 1978. A challenging but important comparative study of popular sovereignty and its displacement of monarchical authority.

Aviva Chomsky and Aldo Lauria-Santiago, eds. *Identity and Struggle at the Margins of the Nation-State: The Laboring Peoples of Central America and the Hispanic Caribbean.* Durham, 1998. Discusses the impact that peasant action had on political and cultural development in different societies.

Linda Colley. *Britons: Forging the Nation, 1707–1837.* New Haven, 1992. A detailed analysis of the emergence of British national identity.

Laureant Dubois. *Avengers of the New World: The Story of the Haitian Revolution.* Cambridge, Mass., 2005. Comprehensive study of how the French slave colony of Saint-Domingue became a unique example of a successful black revolution that challenged the boundaries of freedom, citizenship, and empire.

———. *A Colony of Citizens: Revolution and Slave Emancipation in the French Caribbean, 1787–1804.* Chapel Hill, 2006. Explores the contest over the meaning of words and symbols of the French Revolution in the context of one of France's slave colonies.

Susan Dunn. *Sister Revolutions: French Lightning, American Light.* New York, 1999. An accessible and stimulating work that traces the different legacies of the American and French revolutions of the eighteenth century.

Geoffrey Ellis. *Napoleon.* New York, 1997. An excellent biography of a pivotal figure in modern European history.

Carolyn Fick. *The Making of Haiti: The Saint Domingue Revolution from Below.* Knoxville, 1990. A valuable study focusing on the role of slaves in the Haitian revolution.

François Furet. *Revolutionary France, 1770–1880.* Trans. by A. Nevill. Oxford, 1992. An influential interpretation emphasizing the ideological dimension of the French revolution.

Eric Hobsbawm. *Nations and Nationalism Since 1780: Programme, Myth, and Reality.* 2nd ed. Cambridge, 1992. A brief interpretation of nationalism in Europe and the larger world.

——— and Terence Ranger, eds. *The Invention of Tradition.* Cambridge, 1983. A fascinating collection of essays examining the rituals and other traditions that modern states have relied on to enhance their authority.

Lynne Hunt. *Politics, Culture, and Class in the French Revolution.* Berkeley and Los Angeles, 1984. Continues to be a touchstone for the history of the French revolution's political culture and of the meanings of the revolution's symbols to the course of events.

Lester D. Langley. *The Americas in the Age of Revolution, 1750–1850.* New Haven, 1997. A comparative study of revolutions and wars of independence in the western hemisphere.

Mary Beth Norton. *Liberty's Daughters: The Revolutionary Experience of American Women, 1750–1800.* Boston, 1980. Focuses on the role of women in the American revolution and the early republic.

Robert Palmer. *The Age of the Democratic Revolution: A Political History of Europe and America, 1760–1800.* 2 vols. Princeton, 1959–64. A classic study of the American and French revolutions and their influence in Europe and the Americas.

David Parker, ed. *Revolutions and the Revolutionary Tradition in the West, 1560–1991.* London and New York, 2000. In this comparative survey of revolutions—from the English revolution of 1649 to the revolutions within Eastern Europe and the Soviet Union (1989–1991)—leading historians examine how a wider revolutionary tradition has shaped modern European history.

Otto Pflanze. *Bismarck and the Development of Germany.* Princeton, 1971. The product of a lifetime of scholarship, this masterful work remains a significant contribution to nineteenth-century German history.

Simon Schama. *Citizens: A Chronicle of the French Revolution.* New York, 1989. Detailed narrative of the French revolution focusing on the experiences and decisions made by individual actors.

Dale Van Kley. *The Religious Origins of the French Revolution: From Calvin to the Civil Constitution.* New Haven, 1996. Account of the important religious background of this "modern" revolution that is generally associated with secularization and dechristianization.

Eric Van Young. *The Other Rebellion: Popular Violence, Ideology, and the Mexican Struggle for Independence, 1810–1821.* Stanford, 2001. An exhaustive account of Mexico's movement toward independence from Spain that stresses the importance of domestic struggles that pitted classes and ethnic groups against one another.

Gordon S. Wood. *The Radicalism of the American Revolution.* New York, 1991. A comprehensive synthesis emphasizing the role of republican and democratic ideas in the overthrow of monarchical institutions.

30 The Making of Industrial Society

Patterns of Industrialization
Foundations of Industrialization
The Factory System
The Early Spread of Industrialization
Industrial Capitalism

Industrial Society
The Fruits of Industry
Urbanization and Migration

Industry and Society
The Socialist Challenge

Global Effects of Industrialization
The Continuing Spread of Industrialization
The International Division of Labor

In 1827, shortly after marrying at the age of twenty-three, Betty Harris took a job as a drawer in a coal pit near Manchester, England. A drawer's job involved crawling down narrow mine shafts and hauling loads of coal from the bottom of the pit, where miners chipped it from the earth, to the surface. From there the coal went to fuel the steam engines that powered the factories and the mills of early industrial society. Drawers performed unskilled labor for low wages, but their work was essential for the emergence of industrial production.

While working, Harris wore a heavy belt around her waist. Hitched to the belt was a chain that passed between her legs and attached to the coal cart that she pulled through the mine shafts, often while creeping along on hands and knees. The belt strained against her body, and the mine shafts were steep and slippery. Yet every work day, even when she was pregnant, Harris strapped on her belt and chain at 6:00 A.M., removing her bindings only at the end of the shift twelve hours later.

Work conditions for Betty Harris were less than ideal. She labored in the coal pit with six other women and six boys and girls. All members of the crew experienced hardships and exploitation. Harris reported that drawing coal was "very hard work for a woman," and she did not exaggerate. She and her companions often had to crawl through water that collected in the mine shafts during rainstorms, and the men who mined coal in the pits showed scant respect for the lowly, ill-paid drawers. The belts and chains worn by drawers often chafed their skin raw, and miners contributed to their physical discomfort by beating them for slow or clumsy work. The miners, many of whom shed their clothes and worked naked in the hot, oppressive coal pits, also took sexual liberties with the women and girl drawers: Harris personally knew several illegitimate children conceived during forced sexual encounters in the coal pits.

Betty Harris faced her own sexual problems once she arrived home. Exhausted from twelve hours of work, with only a one-hour break for a midday meal consisting of bread and butter, she often tried to discourage her husband's advances. Her husband had little patience, however, and Harris remarked that "my feller has beaten me many a time for not being ready." Harris's work schedule made comfortable family life impossible. A cousin had to care for her two children during the day, and Harris tended to them and her husband at night. The grinding demands of the coal pit took a toll: at age thirty-seven, after fourteen years in the mines, Harris admitted that "I am not so strong as I was, and cannot stand my work so well as I used to."

Not all industrial workers suffered the indignities that coal drawers endured, but Betty Harris's experience nonetheless illustrates some of the deep changes that industrialization wrought in patterns of work and family life. Beginning in the late eighteenth century, workers and their

---

OPPOSITE: **Young woman at work in a mechanized mill in the 1830s.**

815

families had to adjust to the sometimes harsh demands of the machine age. First in Britain, then in western Europe, North America, Russia, and Japan, machines and factories transformed agricultural societies into industrial societies. At the heart of this transformation were technological changes based on newly developed, inanimate sources of power that led to the extensive use of machinery in manufacturing. Machine production raised worker productivity, encouraged economic specialization, and promoted the growth of large-scale enterprise. Industrial machinery transformed economic production by turning out high-quality products quickly, cheaply, and efficiently. The process of industrialization encouraged rapid technological innovation and over the long term raised material standards of living in much of the world.

But the impact of industrialization went beyond economics, generating widespread and often unsettling social change as well. Early industrialists created a new work environment, the factory, which concentrated large numbers of workers under one roof to operate complicated machinery. The concentration of workers made it possible to rely on inanimate motive power such as waterwheels or steam engines. Factories also enabled managers to impose work discipline and closely supervise the quality of production at their plants. By moving work outside the home, however, factories drew fathers, mothers, and children in different directions, altered traditional patterns of domestic life, and strained family relations in the industrial era.

Industrialization encouraged rapid urbanization and migration. New cities mushroomed to house workers who left the countryside for jobs in factories. Millions of migrants traveled even farther, crossing the seas in search of opportunities in new lands. Often, however, early industrial workers found themselves living in squalor and laboring under dangerous conditions.

Social critics and reformers worked to alleviate the problems of early industrial society. Most scathing and influential of the critics were the German theorists Karl Marx and Friedrich Engels, who called for the destruction of capitalism and the establishment of a more just and equitable socialist society. Despite their appeals, capitalism and industrialization flourished and spread rapidly from Britain to continental Europe, North America, and Asia. Although industrialization spread unevenly around the globe, it profoundly influenced social and economic conditions throughout the world, since industrial societies created a new international division of labor that made most African, Asian, and American lands dependent on the export of raw materials.

Patterns of Industrialization

Industrialization refers to a process that transformed agrarian and handicraft-centered economies into economies distinguished by industry and machine manufacture. The principal features of this process were technological and organizational changes that transformed manufacturing and led to increased productivity. Critical to industrialization were technological developments that made it possible to produce goods by machines rather than by hand and that harnessed inanimate sources of energy such as coal and petroleum. Organizational changes accompanied technological developments. By the end of the nineteenth century, the factory had become the predominant site of industrial production in Europe, the United States, and Japan. Factory production strongly encouraged the emergence of new divisions of labor as interchangeable parts and belt-driven assembly lines made the mass production of goods a hallmark of industrialized societies. The need to invest in increasingly expensive equipment encouraged the formation of large businesses: by the mid-nineteenth century many giant corporations had joined together to control trade through trusts and cartels.

Foundations of Industrialization

By the mid-eighteenth century, several areas of the world—Great Britain in western Europe, the Yangzi Delta in China, Japan—exhibited growing and dynamic economies that shared many common features. High agricultural productivity in those regions resulted in significant population growth. High population densities in turn encouraged occupational specialization and permitted many individuals to work at tasks other than cultivation. Navigable rivers and networks of canals facilitated trade and transport, and cities and towns were home to sophisticated banking and financial institutions. At the same time, these commercially sophisticated economies ran up against difficult ecological obstacles—especially soil depletion and deforestation—that threatened continued population growth and consumption levels. First Great Britain and subsequently the other regions of western Europe transcended these ecological constraints by exploiting coal deposits fortuitously found at home and natural resources found abroad.

Coal and Colonies

Coal played a crucial role in the industrialization of Great Britain. Until the eighteenth century, wood had served as the primary source of fuel for iron production, home heating, and cooking. Prodigious uses of wood, however, had also hastened deforestation, causing serious wood shortages. Geographic luck had placed some of western Europe's largest coal deposits in Great Britain, within easy reach of water transport, centers of commerce, and pools of skilled labor. The fortunate conjunction of coal deposits and the skills necessary to extract this fuel encouraged the substitution of coal for wood, thus creating a promising framework for industrialization. In the absence of easily accessible coal deposits, it was unlikely that the economy could have supported an expanding iron production and the application of steam engines to mining and industry—both crucial to the industrial process in Great Britain. In this respect Britain's experience proved unique and differed from that of China, where the breakthrough to industrialization occurred at a later time. In China, geography conspired against an important early shift from wood to coal, because the main coal-producing regions of northwest China were too distant from the Yangzi Delta, economically China's most promising region.

The unique economic relationship between Europe and the Americas gave Great Britain additional ecological relief. The conquered and colonized lands of the Americas lifted European land constraints by supplying European societies with a growing volume of primary products. During the eighteenth century the slave-based plantations of northeastern Brazil, the Caribbean islands, and later the southern United States supplied Europe with huge amounts of sugar and cotton; the former increased available food calories while the latter kept emerging textile industries going. Neither of these products could have been grown in Europe. The plantation economies of the Caribbean islands in particular also created significant markets for manufactured imports from Europe, the poverty of slaves notwithstanding. Almost one-half of the proceeds from sugar exports paid for the importation of manufactured goods from Europe, including cheap cotton cloth for slaves to wear. The significance of valuable American resources grew after 1830, when large amounts of grain, timber, and beef traveled across the Atlantic to European destinations. All of these products grew on colonial acreage, which expanded Europe's land base. Later in the century, American lands also served as outlets for Europe's surplus population.

Access to coal deposits and the exploitation of overseas resources provided a context—one not yet available to societies such as China's—that increased the odds for an industrial breakthrough. This industrial expansion, in fact, started with Britain's textiles. Beginning about the mid-eighteenth century, consumer demand encouraged a transformation of the British cotton industry.

During the seventeenth century, English consumers had became fond of calicoes—inexpensive, brightly printed textiles imported from India. Cotton cloth came into demand because it was lighter, easier to wash, and quicker to dry than wool, which was the principal fabric of European clothes before the nineteenth century. Threatened by the popularity of cotton products, British wool producers persuaded Parliament to pass a series of laws to protect the domestic wool industry. The Calico Acts of 1720 and 1721 prohibited imports of printed cotton cloth and restricted the sale of calicoes at home. Parliament even passed a law requiring corpses to be buried in woolen shrouds, but legislation did not dampen consumers' enthusiasm for cotton. Consumer demand for cotton products drove the development of a British cotton textile industry.

Mechanization of the Cotton Industry

Demand for cotton was so strong that producers had to speed up spinning and weaving to supply growing domestic and foreign markets. To increase production they turned to inventions that rapidly mechanized the cotton textile industry. In the early 1730s, artisans began to develop labor-saving devices for spinning and weaving cotton, thereby moving away from hand-based techniques derived from the wool and linen industries. The first important technological breakthrough came in 1733 when Manchester mechanic John Kay invented the flying shuttle. This device speeded up the weaving process and stimulated demand for thread. Within a few years, competitions among inventors resulted in the creation of several mechanical spinning devices. The most important was Samuel Crompton's "mule," built in 1779. Adapted for steam power by 1790, the mule became the device of choice for spinning cotton. The mule turned out strong, fine thread, and it worked fast as well. A worker using a steam-driven mule could produce a hundred times more thread than a worker using a manual spinning wheel.

The new spinning machines created an imbalance in manufacturing because weavers could not keep up with the production of thread, so innovators turned their attention next to weaving. In 1785 Edmund Cartwright, a clergyman without training or experience in either mechanics or textiles, patented a water-driven power loom that inaugurated an era of mechanical weaving. Within two decades steam moved the power loom, and by the 1820s it had largely supplanted hand weavers in the cotton industry. A young boy working on two power looms could produce fifteen times more cloth than the fastest hand weaver. Collectively, these technological developments permitted the production of textile goods in great volume and variety and at low cost. By 1830 half a million people worked in the cotton business, Britain's leading industry, which accounted for 40 percent of exports.

Steam Power

The most crucial technological breakthrough of the early industrial era was the development of a general-purpose steam engine in 1765 by James Watt, an instrument maker at the University of Glasgow in Scotland. Steam engines burned coal to boil water and create steam, which drove mechanical devices that performed work. Even before Watt's time, primitive steam engines had powered pumps that drew water out of coal mines, but those devices consumed too much fuel to be useful for other purposes. Watt's version relied on steam to force a piston to turn a wheel, whose rotary motion converted a simple pump into an engine that had multiple uses. Watt's contemporaries used the term *horsepower* to measure the energy generated by his steam engine, which did the work of numerous animals. By 1800 more than a thousand of Watt's steam engines were in use in the British isles. They were especially prominent in the textile industry, where their application resulted in greater productivity for manufacturers and cheaper prices for consumers.

Iron and Steel

Innovation did not stop with cotton production and steam engines. The iron and steel industries also benefited from technological refinement, and the availability of

A woman working as a drawer in a British coal mine drags her coal cart with the aid of a belt and chain. Manually produced coal fueled the machines of early industrial society.

inexpensive, high-quality iron and steel reinforced the move toward mechanization. After 1709 British smelters began to use coke (a purified form of coal) rather than more expensive charcoal as a fuel to produce iron. Deforestation in England had made wood—the principal source of charcoal—scarce. Besides being cheaper than charcoal, coke made it possible for producers to build bigger blast furnaces and turn out larger lots of iron. As a result, British iron production skyrocketed during the eighteenth century, and prices to consumers fell. Inexpensive iron fittings and parts made industrial machinery stronger, and iron soon became common in bridges, buildings, and ships.

The nineteenth century was an age of steel rather than iron. Steel is much harder, stronger, and more resilient than iron, but until the nineteenth century it was very expensive to produce. Between 1740 and 1850 a series of improvements simplified the process. In 1856 Henry Bessemer built a refined blast furnace known as the Bessemer converter that made it possible to produce steel cheaply and in large quantities. Steel production rose sharply, and steel quickly began to replace iron in tools, machines, and structures that required high strength.

Steam engineering and metallurgical innovations both contributed to improvements in transportation technology. James Watt's steam engine did not adapt well to transportation uses because it consumed too much coal. After his patent expired, however, inventors devised high-pressure engines that required less fuel. In 1815 George Stephenson, a self-educated Englishman, built the first steam-powered locomotive. In 1829 his Rocket won a contest by reaching a speed of 45 kilometers (28 miles) per hour. Although they were more efficient than Watt's invention, Stephenson's engines still burned too much coal for use at sea. Sailing ships remained the most effective means of transport over the seas until the middle of the nineteenth century, when refined engines of high efficiency began to drive steamships.

Transportation

Because they had the capacity to carry huge cargoes, railroads and steamships dramatically lowered transportation costs. They also contributed to the creation of dense transportation networks that linked remote interior regions and distant shores more closely than ever before. Between 1830 and 1870, British entrepreneurs laid about 20,000 kilometers (13,000 miles) of railroads, which linked industrial centers, coalfields, iron deposits, and port cities throughout the land—and also carried some 322 million passengers as well as cargoes of raw materials and manufactured goods. Steamships proved their own versatility by advancing up rivers to points that sailboats

George Stephenson's North Star engine of 1837.

could not reach because of inconvenient twists, turns, or winds. Railroads and steamships benefited from the innovations that drove the industrialization process and in turn encouraged continuing industrialization by providing rapid and inexpensive transport.

The Factory System

In the emerging capitalist society of early modern Europe (discussed in chapter 24), most manufacturing took place under the putting-out system. To avoid guild restrictions on prices and wages, entrepreneurs in early modern Europe paid individuals to work on materials in their households. That protoindustrial system of production centered on the household and usually involved fewer than ten people. During the seventeenth and early eighteenth centuries, new and larger units of production supplemented the putting-out system. Rising demand for certain products such as textiles and the growing use of water and wind power led to the formation of protoindustrial factories, where workers performed specialized tasks under one roof. Nevertheless, the largest preindustrial workforces consisted of unskilled laborers in mines and slaves on plantations.

The Factory   The factory system replaced both the putting-out system and protoindustrial factories and became the characteristic method of production in industrial economies. It began to emerge in the late eighteenth century, when technological advances transformed the British textile industry, and by the mid-nineteenth century most cotton production took place in factories. Many of the newly developed machines were too large and expensive for home use, and it became necessary to move work to locations where entrepreneurs and engineers built complicated machinery for large-scale production. This centralization of production brought together more workers doing specialized tasks than ever before. Most industrial workers hailed from the countryside. A combination of factors provided a plentiful supply of cheap labor for the burgeoning factories, including rural overpopulation, declining job opportunities, and the financial difficulties of small farmers who had to sell their land to large landowners.

The factory system with its new machines demanded a rational organization of job functions that differed from earlier forms of industrial organization. The factory became associated with a new division of labor, one that called for a production process in which each worker performed a single task, rather than one in which a single worker completed the entire job, as was typical of handicraft traditions. In the first chapter of the *Wealth of Nations* (1776), Adam Smith used a pin factory to describe the new system of manufacture. "One man draws out the wire, another straights it, a third cuts it, a fourth points it, a fifth grinds it at the top for receiving the head; . . . and the important business of making a pin is, in this manner, divided into about eighteen distinct operations." Factories also enabled managers to impose strict work discipline and closely supervise employees. Thus Josiah Wedgwood (1730–1795), an Englishman with a wooden leg who owned a pottery plant, held his employees to high standards in an effort to produce the highest quality pottery. When he spotted inferior work, he frequently dumped it on the factory floor and crushed it with his peg leg saying, "This will not do for Josiah Wedgwood!"

Working Conditions   With its new divisions of labor, the factory system allowed managers to improve worker productivity and realize spectacular increases in the output of manufactured goods. But the new environment also had unsettling effects on the nature of work. The factory system led to the emergence of an owner class whose capital financed equipment and machinery that were too expensive for workers to acquire. Industrial workers themselves became mere wage earners who had only their labor services to offer and who depended on their employers for their livelihood. In addition, any broad-range skills that workers may have previously acquired as artisans often became obsolete in a work environment that rewarded narrowly defined skills. The repetitious and boring nature of many industrial jobs, moreover, left many workers alienated or estranged from their work and the products of their labor.

Equally disturbing was the new work discipline and the pace of work. Those accustomed to rural labor soon learned that the seasons, the rising and setting of the sun, and fluctuations in the weather no longer dictated work routines. Instead, clocks, machines, and shop rules established new rhythms of work. Industrial workers commonly labored six days a week for twelve to fourteen hours daily. The factory whistle sounded the beginning and the end of the working day, and throughout the day workers had to keep pace with the monotonous movements of machines. At the same time, they faced strict and immediate supervision, which made little allowance for a quick nap or socializing with friends. Floor managers pressured men, women, and children to speed up production and punished them when they did not meet expectations. Because neither the machines nor the methods of work took safety into account, early industrial workers constantly faced the possibility of maiming or fatal accidents.

In some instances, machine-centered factories sparked violent protest. Between 1811 and 1816, organized bands of English handicraft workers known as Luddites went on a rampage and destroyed textile machines that they blamed for their low wages and unemployment. They called their leader King Lud, after a legendary boy named Ludlam who broke a knitting frame to spite his father. The movement broke out in the hosiery and lace industries around Nottingham and then spread to the wool and cotton mills of Lancashire. The Luddites usually wore masks and operated at night. Because they avoided violence against people, they enjoyed considerable popular support. Nevertheless, by hanging fourteen Luddites in 1813, the government served notice that it was unwilling to tolerate violence even against machines, and the movement gradually died out.

Industrial Protest

The Early Spread of Industrialization

Industrialization and the technological, organizational, and social transformations that accompanied it might have originated in many parts of the world where abundant craft skills, agricultural production, and investment capital could support the industrialization process. For half a century, however, industrialization took place only in Great Britain. Aware of their head start, British entrepreneurs and government officials forbade the export of machinery, manufacturing techniques, and skilled workers.

Yet Britain's monopoly on industrialization did not last forever, because enterprising entrepreneurs recognized profitable opportunities in foreign lands and circumvented government regulations to sell machinery and technical know-how abroad. Moreover, European and North American businesspeople did their best to become acquainted with British industrial techniques and lure British experts to their lands. European and North American entrepreneurs did not hesitate to bribe or even kidnap British engineers, and they also smuggled advanced machinery out of the British isles. Sometimes they got poor value for their investments: they found that it was difficult to attract the best British experts to foreign lands and had to make do with drunkards or second-rate specialists who demanded high pay but made little contribution to industrialization.

■ **Workers tend to a massive steam hammer under dangerous conditions.**

Industrialization in Western Europe

Nevertheless, by the mid-nineteenth century industrialization had spread to France, Germany, Belgium, and the United States. The French revolution and the Napoleonic wars helped set the stage for industrialization in western Europe by abolishing internal trade barriers and dismantling guilds that discouraged technological innovation and restricted the movement of laborers. The earliest continental center of industrial production was Belgium, where coal, iron, textile, glass, and armaments production flourished in the early nineteenth century. About the same time, France also moved toward industrialization. By 1830 French firms employed about fifteen thousand skilled British workers who helped establish mechanized textile and metallurgical industries in France. By the mid-nineteenth century, French engineers and inventors were devising refinements and innovations that led to greater efficiencies especially in metallurgical industries. Later in the century a boom in railroad construction stimulated economic development while also leading to decreased transportation costs.

German industrialization proceeded more slowly than did Belgian and French, partly because of political instability resulting from competition between the many German states. After the 1840s, however, German coal and iron production soared, and by the 1850s an extensive railroad network was under construction. After unification in 1871, Bismarck's government sponsored rapid industrialization in Germany. In the interests of strengthening military capacity, Bismarck encouraged the development of heavy industry, and the formation of huge businesses became a hallmark of German industrialization. The giant Krupp firm, for example, dominated mining, metallurgy, armaments production, and shipbuilding.

Industrialization in North America

Industrialization transformed North America as well as western Europe in the nineteenth century. In 1800 the United States possessed abundant land and natural

written by Scottish economist & philospher Adam Smith (1776)
An account of economics at the dawn of IR, to educate individuals, advocating
free market economy as more productive and beneficial to society

Map 30.1 **Industrial Europe ca. 1850.** Locate the places marked as emerging industrial areas. Are there any features those areas have in common? If so, what are they?

resources but few laborers and little money to invest in business enterprises. Both labor and investment capital came largely from Europe: migrants crossed the Atlantic in large numbers throughout the nineteenth century, and European bankers and business-people eagerly sought opportunities to invest in businesses that made use of American natural resources. American industrialization began in the 1820s when entrepreneurs lured British crafts workers to New England and built a cotton textile industry. By midcentury well over a thousand mills were producing fabrics from raw cotton grown in the southern states, and New England had emerged as a site for the industrial production also of shoes, tools, and handguns. In the 1870s heavy iron and steel industries emerged in areas such as western Pennsylvania and central Alabama where there were abundant supplies of iron ore and coal. By 1900 the United States had become an economic powerhouse, and industrialization had begun to spill over into southern Canada.

The vast size of the United States was advantageous to industrialists because it made abundant natural resources available to them, but it also hindered travel and communication between the regions. To facilitate transportation and distribution, state governments built canals, and private investors established steamship lines and railroad networks. By 1860 rails linked the industrial northeast with the agricultural south and the midwestern cities of St. Louis and Chicago, where brokers funneled wheat and beef from the plains to the more densely populated eastern states. As in other lands, railroad construction in the United States spurred industrialization by providing cheap transportation and stimulating coal, iron, and steel industries.

Industrial Capitalism

Mass Production   Cotton textiles were the major factory-made products during the early phase of industrialization, but new machinery and techniques soon made it possible to extend the factory system to other industries. Furthermore, with refined manufacturing processes, factories could mass-produce standardized articles. An important contribution to the evolving factory system came from the American inventor Eli Whitney (1765–1825). Though best remembered as the inventor of the cotton gin (1793), Whitney also developed the technique of using machine tools to produce large quantities of interchangeable parts in the making of firearms. In conventional methods a skilled worker made a complete musket, forming and fitting each unique part; Whitney designed machine tools with which unskilled workers made only a particular part that fit every musket of the same model. Before long, entrepreneurs applied Whitney's method to the manufacture of everything from clocks and sewing machines to uniforms and shoes. By the middle of the nineteenth century, mass production of standardized articles was becoming the hallmark of industrial societies.

In 1913 Henry Ford improved manufacturing techniques further when he introduced the assembly line to automobile production. Instead of organizing production around a series of stations where teams of workers assembled each individual car using standardized parts, Ford designed a conveyor system that carried components past workers at the proper height and speed. Each worker performed a specialized task at a fixed point on the assembly line, which churned out a complete chassis every 93 minutes—a task that previously had taken 728 minutes. The subdivision of labor and the coordination of operations resulted in enormous productivity gains, enabling Ford Motor Company to produce half the world's automobiles in the early twentieth century. With gains in productivity, car prices plummeted, allowing millions of people to purchase automobiles. The age of the motor car had arrived.

Big Business   As the factory evolved, so too did the organization of business. Industrial machinery and factories were expensive investments, and they encouraged businesses to organize on a large scale. Thus industrialization spurred the continuing development of capitalist business organization. Entrepreneurs in early modern Europe formed private businesses in the hopes of profiting from market-oriented production and trade. Some businesses, such as the English East India Company and other commercial concerns, organized joint-stock companies in the interests of spreading risk, achieving efficiency, and maximizing profits. With industrialization, manufacturers followed the lead of merchants by organizing on a large scale.

The Corporation   During the 1850s and 1860s, government authorities in Britain and France laid the legal foundations for the modern corporation, which quickly became the most common form of business organization in industrial societies. A corporation was a private business owned by hundreds, thousands, or even millions of individual and institutional investors who financed the business through the purchase of stocks representing shares in the company. When a corporation flourished, investors received dividends in proportion to their stake in the company. But if a corporation went bankrupt, laws protected shareholders from any liability or financial loss beyond the extent of their investments. Thus corporate organization was extremely attractive to investors. By the late nineteenth century, corporations controlled most businesses requiring large investments in land, labor, or machinery, including railroads, shipping lines, and industrial concerns that produced iron, steel, and armaments. Meanwhile, an array of investment banks, brokerage firms, and other financial businesses arose to serve the needs of industrial capitalists organized in corporations.

Li Ruzhen — phonologist of Qing Dynasty; author of Jing Hua Yuan

To protect their investments, some big businesses of the late nineteenth century sought not only to outperform their competitors in the capitalist marketplace but also to eliminate competition. Business firms formed associations to restrict markets or establish monopolies in their industries. Large-scale business organizations formed trusts and cartels. The difference between the two was largely a technical one, and both shared a common goal: to control the supply of a product and hence its price in the marketplace. Some monopolists sought to control industries through vertical organization, by which they would dominate all facets of a single industry. The industrial empire of the American petroleum producer John D. Rockefeller, for example, which he ruled through Standard Oil Company and Trust, controlled almost all oil drilling, processing, refining, marketing, and distribution in the United States. Control over all aspects of the petroleum industry enabled Standard Oil to operate efficiently, cut costs, and undersell its competitors. Vertical organization of this kind offered large corporations great advantages over smaller companies.

Monopolies, Trusts, and Cartels

Other monopolists tried to eliminate competition by means of horizontal organization, which involved the consolidation or cooperation of independent companies in the same business. Thus cartels sought to ensure the prosperity of their members by absorbing competitors, fixing prices, regulating production, or dividing up markets. The German firm IG Farben, the world's largest chemical concern until the middle of the twentieth century, grew out of a complex merger of chemical and pharmaceutical manufacturers that controlled as much as 90 percent of production in chemical industries. By the end of the nineteenth century, some governments outlawed these combinations and broke them up. Yet, when governments proved unwilling to confront large businesses, or when the public remained ignorant or indifferent, monopolistic practices continued well into the twentieth century.

Industrial Society

Industrialization brought material benefits in its train: inexpensive manufactured products, rising standards of living, and population growth. Yet industrialization also unleashed dramatic and often unsettling social change. Massive internal and external migrations took place as millions of people moved from the countryside to work in new industrial cities, and European migrants crossed the Atlantic by the tens of millions to seek opportunities in the less densely populated lands of the western hemisphere. Industrialization encouraged the emergence of new social classes—especially the middle class and the working class—and forced men, women, and children to adjust to distinctly new patterns of family and work life. Reformers sought to alleviate the social and economic problems that accompanied industrialization. The most influential

Exhibitors from around the world displayed fine handicrafts and manufactured goods at the Crystal Palace exhibition of 1851 in London. Industrial products from Britain and the United States particularly attracted the attention of visitors to the enchanting and futuristic exhibition hall.

critics were the socialists, who did not object to industrialization per se but worked toward the building of a more equitable and just society.

The Fruits of Industry

Industrialization brought efficiencies in production that flooded markets with affordable manufactured goods. In 1851 the bounty of industry went on display in London at the Crystal Palace, a magnificent structure made of iron and glass that enclosed trees, gardens, fountains, and manufactured products from around the world. Viewers flocked to the exhibition to see industrial products such as British textiles, iron goods, and machine tools. Colt revolvers and sewing machines from the United States also attracted attention as representatives of the "American system of manufacture," which used interchangeable parts in producing large quantities of standardized goods at low prices. Observers marveled at the Crystal Palace exhibits and congratulated themselves on the achievements of industrial society.

In many ways, industrialization raised material standards of living. Industrial production led to dramatic reductions in the cost of clothing, for example, so individuals were able to add variety to their wardrobes. By the early nineteenth century, all but the desperately poor could afford several changes of clothes, and light, washable underwear came into widespread use with the availability of inexpensive manufactured cotton. Industrial factories turned out tools that facilitated agricultural work, while steam-powered locomotives delivered produce quickly and cheaply to distant markets, so industrialization contributed as well to a decline in the price of food. Consumers in early industrial Europe also filled their homes with more furniture, cabinets, porcelain, and decorative objects than any but the most wealthy of their ancestors.

The populations of European and Euro-American peoples rose sharply during the eighteenth and nineteenth centuries, and they reflected the rising prosperity and standards of living that came with industrialization. Between 1700 and 1800 the population of Europe increased from 105 to 180 million, and during the nineteenth century it more than doubled to 390 million. Demographic growth in the western hemisphere—fueled by migration from Europe—was even more remarkable. Between 1700 and 1800 the population of North America and South America rose from 13 million to 24 million and then surged to 145 million by 1900. Demographic growth was most spectacular in the temperate regions of the western hemisphere. In Argentina, for example, population expanded from 300,000 in 1800 to 4.75 million in 1900—a 1,583 percent increase. In temperate North America—what is now the United States—population rose from 6 million to 76 million (1,266 percent) during the 1800s.

Population Growth

The rapid population growth in Europe and the Americas reflected changing patterns of fertility and mortality. In most preindustrial societies fertility was high, but famines and epidemics resulted in high mortality, especially child mortality, which prevented explosive population growth.

Medical advances over time supplied the means to control disease and reduce mortality. A case in point was smallpox, an ancient, highly contagious, and often fatal viral disease that had killed more people than any other malady in world history. The experiments of the English physician Edward Jenner dealt an effective blow against smallpox. Knowing that milkmaids often contracted cowpox, in 1797 Jenner inoculated an eight-year-old boy with cowpox and followed it six weeks later with the smallpox virus. The boy became ill but soon recovered fully, leading Jenner to deduce that cowpox conferred immunity against smallpox. Later called vaccination (from *vacca*, the Latin word for "cow"), Jenner's procedure not only created a powerful weapon in the war against smallpox but also laid the foundation for scientific immunology. Over time, physicians developed vaccines that prevented sickness and death from polio, tetanus, typhoid, whooping cough, and many other diseases that once plagued humankind.

High birthrates were common also in early industrializing societies, but death rates fell markedly because better diets and improved disease control reduced child mortality. Because more infants survived to adulthood, the population of early industrializing societies grew rapidly. By the late nineteenth century, better diets and improved sanitation led to declining levels of adult as well as child mortality, so populations of industrial societies expanded even faster. Britain and Germany, the most active sites of early industrialization, experienced especially fast population growth. Between 1800 and 1900 the British population increased from 10.5 million to 37.5 million while German numbers rose from 18 million to 43 million.

Beginning in the nineteenth century, industrializing lands experienced a social change known as the *demographic transition,* which refers to shifting patterns of fertility and mortality. As industrialization transformed societies, fertility began a marked decline. In the short run, mortality fell even faster than fertility, so the populations of industrial societies continued to increase. Over time, however, declining birthrates led to

The Demographic Transition

A French newspaper sponsored free smallpox vaccinations in 1905; the serum of a cow infected with cowpox is being injected into awaiting Parisians.

Birth Control

lower population growth and relative demographic stability. The principal reason for declining fertility in industrial lands was voluntary birth control through contraception.

For thousands of years, people tried to find deliberate ways of preventing or reducing the probability of pregnancy resulting from sexual intercourse. Some of the methods, such as coitus interruptus, proved not to be particularly reliable, and others, such as sexual abstinence, turned out to be unrealistic. More ingenious methods of birth control such as vaginal depositories, cervical caps, or drinkable concoctions designed to prevent pregnancies or induce miscarriages usually carried serious health risks for women. Because none of those methods proved effective, people throughout the world had resorted to abortion or infanticide.

The first efficient means of contraception without negative side effects was the male condom. Initially made of animal intestines, it came into use in the seventeenth century. In reference to its place of origin, the Italian adventurer and womanizer Casanova called the condom an "English riding coat." The effectiveness and popularity of the condom soared in the mid-nineteenth century with the arrival of the latex condom, which served both as a contraceptive device and as a barrier against syphilis, a much-feared venereal disease. Since then, a plethora of contraceptive devices has become available.

Married couples might have chosen to have fewer offspring because raising them cost more in industrial than in agricultural societies or because declining child mortality meant that any children born were more likely to survive to adulthood. In any case the demographic transition accompanied industrialization in western Europe, the United States, Japan, and other industrializing lands as well.

Urbanization and Migration

Industrialization and population growth strongly encouraged migration and urbanization. Within industrial societies, migrants flocked from the countryside to urban centers in search of work. Industrial Britain led the world in urbanization. In 1800 about one-fifth of the British population lived in towns and cities of 10,000 or more inhabitants. During the following century a largely rural society became predominantly urban, with three-quarters of the population working and living in cities. That pattern repeated itself in continental Europe, the United States, Japan, and the rest of the industrialized world. By 1900 at least 50 percent of the population in industrialized lands lived in towns with populations of 2,000 or more. The increasing size of cities reflected this internal migration. In 1800 there were barely twenty cities in Europe with populations as high as 100,000, and there were none in the western hemisphere. By 1900 there were more than 150 large cities in Europe and North America combined. With a population of 6.5 million, London was the largest city in the world, followed by New York with 4.2 million, Paris with 3.3 million, and Berlin with 2.7 million.

With urbanization came intensified environmental pollution. Although cities have always been putrid and unsanitary places, the rapid increase in urban populations during the industrial age dramatically increased the magnitude and severity of water and air pollution. The widespread burning of fossil fuels, such as wood and coal, fouled the air with vast quantities of chemicals and particulate matter. This pollution led to typical occupational diseases among some trades. Chimney sweeps, for instance, contracted cancer of the scrotum from hydrocarbon deposits found in chimney soot. Effluents from factories and mills and an increasing amount of untreated sewage dirtied virtually every major river. No part of a city was immune to the constant stench coming from air and water pollution. Worse, tainted water supplies and unsanitary living conditions led to periodic epidemics of cholera and typhus, and dysentery and tuberculosis were also common maladies. Until the latter part of the nineteenth century, urban environments remained dangerous places in which death rates commonly exceeded birthrates, and only the constant stream of new arrivals from the country kept cities growing.

The Urban Environment

Income determined the degree of comfort and security offered by city life. The wealthy typically tried to insulate themselves the best they could from urban discomforts by retreating to their elegant homes in the newly growing suburbs. The working poor, in contrast, crowded into the centers of cities to live in shoddy housing constructed especially for them. The rapid influx of people to expanding industrial cities such as Liverpool and Manchester encouraged the quick but slipshod construction of dwellings close to the mills and factories. Industrial workers and their families occupied overcrowded tenements lacking in comfort and amenities. The cramped spaces in apartments obliged many to share the same bed, increasing the likelihood of incestuous relationships and the ease of disease transmission. The few open spaces outside the buildings were usually home to herds of pigs living in their own dung or were depositories for pools of stagnant water and human waste. Whenever possible, the inhabitants of such neighborhoods flocked to parks and public gardens.

By the later nineteenth century, though, government authorities were tending to the problems of the early industrial cities. They improved municipal water supplies, expanded sewage systems, and introduced building codes that outlawed the construction of rickety tenements to accommodate poorly paid workers. Those measures made city

Sources from the Past

Thomas Malthus on Population

The Reverend Thomas R. Malthus (1766–1834), English economist and pioneer of modern population study, generated controversy with his pessimistic predictions regarding the future of humanity. In his famous Essay on the Principle of Population *(1798, rev. ed. 1803), he insisted that poverty and distress are the inevitable consequences of unchecked population growth. Malthus argued that demand for food will invariably exceed the means of subsistence.*

The principal object of the present essay is to examine the effects of one great cause intimately united with the very nature of man; which, though it has been constantly and powerfully operating since the commencement of society, has been little noticed by the writers who have treated this subject. . . . The cause to which I allude is the constant tendency in all animated life to increase beyond the nourishment prepared for it.

This is incontrovertibly true. Through the animal and vegetable kingdoms Nature has scattered the seeds of life abroad with the most profuse and liberal hand; but has been comparatively sparing in the room and the nourishment necessary to rear them. The germs of existence contained in this earth, if they could freely develop themselves, would fill millions of worlds in the course of a few thousand years. Necessity, that imperious, all pervading law of nature, restrains them within the prescribed bounds. The race of plants and the race of animals shrink under this great restrictive law; and man cannot by any efforts of reason escape from it.

It may safely be pronounced, therefore, that population, when unchecked, goes on doubling itself every twenty-five years, or increases in a geometrical ratio. . . . It may fairly be pronounced, therefore, that considering the present average state of the earth, the means of subsistence, under circumstances the most favorable to human industry, could not possibly be made to increase faster than in an arithmetical ratio.

The ultimate check to population appears then to be want of food, arising necessarily from the different ratios according to which population and food increase. But this ultimate check is never the immediate check, except in the cases of actual famine.

The immediate check may be stated to consist in all those customs and diseases, which seem to be gener-

ated by a scarcity of the means of subsistence; and all those causes, independent of this scarcity, whether of a moral or physical nature, which tend prematurely to weaken and destroy the human frame.

These checks to population which are constantly operating with more or less force in every society, and keep down the number to the level of the means of subsistence, may be classed under two general heads—the preventative and positive checks.

The preventative check, as far as it is voluntary, is peculiar to man, and arises from that distinctive superiority in his reasoning faculties which enables him to calculate distant consequences. . . . These considerations are calculated to prevent, and certainly do prevent, a great number of persons in all civilised nations from pursuing the dictate of nature in an early attachment to one woman. . . . [T]he restraint from marriage which is not followed by irregular gratifications may properly be termed moral restraint.

The positive checks to population are extremely various, and include every cause, whether arising from vice or misery, which in any degree contributes to shorten the natural duration of human life. Under this head, therefore, may be enumerated all unwholesome occupations, severe labor and exposure to the seasons, extreme poverty, bad nursing of children, great towns, excesses of all kinds, the whole train of common diseases, and epidemics, wars, plague, and famine.

FOR FURTHER REFLECTION

Were Malthus's fears about a lack of food realized during the age of industrialization, or did aspects of the new industrial society in fact help to prevent those fears from being realized?

SOURCE: Thomas R. Malthus. *An Essay on Population.* London: J. M. Dent, 1914, pp. 6–15.

Handwritten margin notes:
Columbian exchange
1492
Large scale contact
between old & New words
disease, animal, culture, plant
Asia, Africa, Europe
Alfred Crosby
1972 Book

This landscape of cramped working-class housing was one of the many drawings of London that the French book illustrator Gustave Doré produced between 1869 and 1871.

life safer and brought improved sanitation that helped to eliminate epidemic disease. City authorities also built parks and recreational facilities to make cities more livable.

While workers moved from the countryside to urban centers, rapid population growth in Europe encouraged massive migration to the Americas, especially to the United States. During the nineteenth and early twentieth centuries, about fifty million Europeans migrated to the western hemisphere, and this flow of humanity accounts for much of the stunning demographic growth of the Americas. Many of the migrants intended to stay for only a few years and fully expected to return to their homelands with a modest fortune made in the Americas. Indeed, some did return to Europe: about one-third of Italian migrants to the Americas made the trip back across the Atlantic. The vast majority, however, remained in the western hemisphere. They and their descendants transformed the Americas into Euro-American lands.

Most of the migrants came from the British isles in the early nineteenth century, from Germany, Ireland, and Scandinavia in the middle decades, and from eastern and southern Europe in the late nineteenth century. Migration reflected difficult political, social, and economic circumstances in Europe: British migrants often sought to escape dangerous factories and the squalor of early industrial cities, most Irish migrants departed during the potato famines of the 1840s, and millions of Jews left the Russian empire in the 1890s because of the tsar's anti-Semitic policies. Many of those migrants entered the workforce of the United States, where they settled in new industrial centers such as New York, Pittsburgh, and Cleveland. Indeed, labor from abroad made it possible for the United States to undergo rapid industrialization in the late nineteenth century.

Transcontinental Migration

Industry and Society

As millions of people moved from the countryside to industrial centers, society underwent a dramatic transformation. Before industrialization, the vast majority of the world's peoples worked in rural areas as cultivators or herders. Rulers, aristocrats, priests, and a few others enjoyed privileged status, and small numbers of people worked in cities as artisans, crafts workers, bureaucrats, or professionals. Many societies also made use of slave labor, occasionally on a large scale.

Industrialization radically altered traditional social structures. It encouraged the disappearance of slavery in lands undergoing industrialization, partly because the economics of industrial society did not favor slave labor. Slaves were generally poor, so they did not consume the products of industrial manufacturers in large quantities. Industrialists preferred free wage laborers who spent their money on products that kept their factories busy.

New Social Classes

Industrialization also helped bring new social classes into being. Captains of industry and enterprising businesspeople became fabulously wealthy and powerful enough to overshadow the military aristocracy and other traditionally privileged classes. Less powerful than this new elite was the middle class, consisting of small business owners, factory managers, engineers, accountants, skilled employees of large corporations, and professionals such as teachers, physicians, and attorneys. Industrial production generated great wealth, and a large portion of it flowed to the middle class, which was a principal beneficiary of industrialization. Meanwhile, masses of laborers who toiled in factories and mines constituted a new working class. Less skilled than the artisans and crafts workers of earlier times, the new workers tended to machines or provided heavy labor for low wages. Concentrated in mining and industrial centers, the working class began to influence political affairs by the mid-nineteenth century.

Industrial Families

The most basic unit of social organization—the family—also underwent fundamental change during the industrial age. In preindustrial societies the family was the basic productive unit. Whether engaged in agriculture, domestic manufacturing, or commerce, family members worked together and contributed to the welfare of the larger group. Industrialization challenged the family economy and reshaped family life by moving economic production outside the home and introducing a sharp distinction between work and family life. During the early years of industrialization, family economies persisted as fathers, mothers, and children pooled their wages and sometimes even worked together in factories. Over time, however, it became less common for family members to work in groups. Workers left their homes each day to labor an average of fourteen hours in factories, and family members led increasingly separate lives.

Men at Work and Play

Men gained increased stature and responsibility in the industrial age as work dominated public life. When production moved outside the home, some men became owners or managers of factories, although the majority served as wageworkers. Industrial work seemed to be far more important than the domestic chores traditionally carried out by women, or even the agricultural and light industrial work performed by women and children. Men's wages also constituted the bulk of their families' income. Upper-class and middle-class men especially enjoyed increased prestige at home, since they usually were the sole providers who made their families' comfortable existence possible.

Internalizing the work ethic of the industrial age, professional men dedicated themselves to self-improvement even in their leisure hours. They avidly read books and attended lectures on business or cultural themes. They also strove to instill their values in the industrial workforce and to impose work discipline on the laborers under their supervision. Threats of fines, beatings, and dismissal coerced workers into accepting factory rules against absenteeism, tardiness, and swearing. Through their support for churches and Sunday schools, factory owners sought to persuade workers to adopt middle-class norms of respectability and morality.

For their part, industrial workers often resisted the work discipline and moral pressures they encountered at the factory. They frequently observed "Holy Monday" and stayed home to lengthen their weekly break from work on Sundays. In their leisure time they flocked to sporting events: European soccer and American baseball both became popular sports during the industrial era. They also gambled, socialized at bars and pubs, and staged fights between dogs or roosters. The middle and upper classes tried to suppress these activities and established urban police forces to control workers' public behavior. But efforts at regulation had limited success, and workers persistently pursued their own interests.

Women at Home and Work

Like men, women had worked long hours in preindustrial times. Agriculture and domestic manufacturing could easily accommodate women's dual role as mothers and workers, since the workplace was either at home or nearby. Industrialization dramatically changed the terms of work for women. When industry moved production from the home to the factory, married women were unable to work unless they left their homes and children in someone else's care. By the late nineteenth century industrial society neither expected nor wanted women to engage in labor but, instead, encouraged women to devote themselves to traditional pursuits such as the raising of children, the management of the home, and the preservation of traditional family values. Rather than thrusting women wholesale into the workplace, industrialization effectively seated middle-class women in the domestic sphere.

Middle-class women generally did not work outside the home. For them, industrialization brought stringent confinement to the domestic sphere and pressure to conform to new models of behavior revolving around their roles as mothers and wives. In a book entitled *Woman in Her Social and Domestic Character* (1833), Mrs. John Sandford—who referred to herself by her husband's name rather than her own—described the ideal British woman. "Domestic life is the chief source of her influence," Sandford proclaimed, adding that "there is, indeed, something unfeminine in independence." (By *independence* Sandford meant taking a job or "acting the Amazon.") The model woman "knows that she is the weaker vessel" and takes pride in her ability to make the home a happy place for her husband and children.

Industrialization increased the demand for domestic servants as the middle class grew in both numbers and wealth. One of every three European women became a domestic servant at some point in her life. Rural women sometimes had to move long distances to take positions in middle-class homes in cities, where they experienced adventure and independence from family control. Their employers replaced their parents as guardians, but high demand for servants ensured that women could switch jobs readily in search of more attractive positions. Young women servants often sent some of their earnings home, but many also saved wages for personal goals: amassing a dowry, for example, or building funds to start careers as clerks or secretaries.

Child Labor

Industrialization profoundly influenced the childhood experience. Like their elders, children in preindustrial societies had always worked in and around the family home. Industrial work, which took children away from home and parents for long hours with few breaks, made child labor seem especially pitiable and exploitative. Early reports from British textile mills described sensational abuses by overseers who forced children to work from dawn until dark and beat them to keep them awake. Yet many families needed their children's wages to survive, so they continued to send their offspring to the factories and mines. By the 1840s the British Parliament began to pass laws regulating child labor and ultimately restricted or removed children from the industrial workforce. In the long term, industrial society was responsible for removing

Unlike working-class children, offspring of middle-class and upper-class families enjoyed leisure and luxury. Here the children of U.S. railroad executive George Jay Gould ride in miniature cars in Paris.

children from the labor process altogether, even in the home. Whereas agricultural settings continued to demand that children make a contribution to the family income, urban industrial societies redefined the role of children. Motivated in part by moral concerns and in part by the recognition that modern society demanded a highly skilled and educated labor force, governments established the legal requirement that education, and not work for monetary gain, was the principal task of childhood. In England, for instance, education for children age five to ten became mandatory by 1881.

The Socialist Challenge

Among the most vocal and influential critics of early industrial society were the socialists, who worked to alleviate the social and economic problems generated by capitalism and industrialization. Socialists deplored economic inequalities, as represented by the vast difference in wealth between a captain of industry and a factory laborer, and they condemned the system that permitted the exploitation of laborers, especially women and children. Early socialists sought to expand the Enlightenment understanding of equality: they understood equality to have an economic as well as a political, legal, and social dimension, and they looked to the future establishment of a just and equitable society. Although most socialists shared this general vision, they held very different views on the best way to establish and maintain an ideal socialist society.

Utopian Socialists

The term *socialism* first appeared around 1830, when it referred to the thought of social critics such as Charles Fourier (1772–1837) and Robert Owen (1771–1858). Often called utopian socialists, Fourier, Owen, and their followers worked to establish ideal communities that would point the way to an equitable society. Fourier spent most of his life as a salesman, but he loathed the competition of the market system and called for social transformations that would better serve the needs of humankind. He painstakingly planned model communities held together by love rather than coercion in which everyone performed work in accordance with personal temperament and inclination. Owen, a successful businessman, transformed a squalid Scottish cotton mill town called New Lanark into a model industrial community. At New Lanark, Owen raised wages, reduced the workday from seventeen to ten hours, built spacious housing, and opened a store that sold goods at fair prices. Despite the costs of those reforms, the mills of New Lanark generated profits. Out of the two thousand residents of the community, five hundred were young children from the poorhouses of Glasgow and Edinburgh, and Owen devoted special attention to their education. He kept young children out of the factories and sent them to a school that he opened in 1816. Owen's indictment of competitive capitalism, his stress on cooperative control of industry, and his advocacy of improved educational standards for children left a lasting imprint on the socialist tradition.

The ideas of the utopian socialists resonated widely in the nineteenth century, and their disciples established experimental communities from the United States to Romania. Despite the enthusiasm of the founders, most of the communities soon encountered economic difficulties and political problems that forced them to fold. By the mid-nineteenth century, most socialists looked not to utopian communities but to large-scale organization of working people as the best means to bring about a just and equitable society.

Once held almost exclusively by men, clerical jobs increasingly went to women as industrial society matured. Men assumed positions as managers who supervised their female employees.

Most prominent of the nineteenth-century socialists were the German theorists Karl Marx (1818–1883) and Friedrich Engels (1820–1895). They scorned the utopian socialists as unrealistic dabblers whose ideal communities had no hope of resolving the problems of the early industrial era. Marx and Engels believed that social problems of the nineteenth century were inevitable results of a capitalist economy. They held that capitalism divided people into two main classes, each with its own economic interests and social status: the capitalists, who owned industrial machinery and factories (which Marx and Engels called the means of production), and the proletariat, consisting of wageworkers who had only their labor to sell. Intense competition between capitalists trying to realize a profit resulted in ruthless exploitation of the working class. To make matters worse, according to Marx and Engels, the state and its coercive institutions, such as police forces and courts of law, were agencies of the capitalist ruling class. Their function was to maintain capitalists in power and enable them to continue their exploitation of the proletariat. Even music, art, literature, and religion served the purposes of capitalists, according to Marx and Engels, since they amused the working classes and diverted attention from their misery. Marx once referred to religion as "the opiate of the masses" because it encouraged workers to focus on a hypothetical realm of existence beyond this world rather than trying to improve their lot in society.

Marx and Engels

Marx developed those views fully in a long, theoretical work called *Capital*. Together with Engels, Marx also wrote a short, spirited tract entitled *Manifesto of the Communist Party* (1848). In the *Manifesto* Marx and Engels aligned themselves with the communists, who worked toward the abolition of private property and the institution

The Communist Manifesto

Sources from the Past

Marx and Engels on Bourgeoisie and Proletarians

Karl Marx and Friedrich Engels were the most scathing critics of early industrial society. Indeed, their critique extended to industrial capitalism in general. In their view, contemporary society pitted capitalists (whom they called the bourgeoisie in their Manifesto of the Communist Party*) against proletarians. Marx and Engels argued that in the short term capitalists would exploit the proletarians, but that over the longer term proletarians would become aware of their misery, rise up, and destroy capitalist society.*

The history of all hitherto existing society is the history of class struggles.

Freeman and slave, patrician and plebeian, lord and serf, guild-master and journeyman, in a word, oppressor and oppressed, stood in constant opposition to one another, carried on an uninterrupted, now hidden, now open fight, a fight that each time ended, either in a revolutionary reconstitution of society at large, or in the common ruin of the contending classes. . . .

The modern bourgeois society that has sprouted from the ruins of feudal society has not done away with class antagonisms. It has but established new classes, new conditions of oppression, new forms of struggle in place of the old ones.

Our epoch, the epoch of the bourgeoisie, possesses, however, this distinctive feature: it has simplified the class antagonisms. Society as a whole is more and more splitting up into two great hostile camps, into two great classes directly facing each other: Bourgeoisie and Proletariat. . . .

The bourgeoisie has stripped of its halo every occupation hitherto honoured and looked up to with reverent awe. It has converted the physician, the lawyer, the priest, the poet, the man of science, into its paid wage-labourers. . . .

The need for a constantly expanding market for its products chases the bourgeoisie over the whole surface of the globe. It must nestle everywhere, settle everywhere, establish connexions everywhere. . . .

The weapons with which the bourgeoisie felled feudalism to the ground are now turned against the bourgeoisie itself.

But not only has the bourgeoisie forged the weapons that bring death to itself; it has also called into existence the men who are to wield those weapons—the modern working class—the proletarians.

In proportion as the bourgeoisie, i.e., capital, is developed, in the same proportion is the proletariat, the modern working class, developed—a class of labourers, who live only so long as they find work, and who find work only so long as their labour increases capital. These labourers, who must sell themselves piecemeal, are a commodity, like every other article of commerce, and are consequently exposed to all the vicissitudes of competition, to all the fluctuations of the market. . . .

The advance of industry, whose involuntary promoter is the bourgeoisie, replaces the isolation of the labourers, due to competition, by their revolutionary combination, due to association. The development of Modern Industry, therefore, cuts from under its feet the very foundation on which the bourgeoisie produces and appropriates products. What the bourgeoisie, therefore, produces, above all, is its own grave-diggers. Its fall and the victory of the proletariat are equally inevitable.

FOR FURTHER REFLECTION

How did Marx and Engels's historical embrace of the concept of class struggle shape their understanding of the great forces clashing during this industrial age?

SOURCE: Karl Marx and Friedrich Engels. *Manifesto of the Communist Party.* Trans. by Samuel Moore. London: W. Reeves, 1888.

of a radically egalitarian society. The *Manifesto* asserted that all human history has been the history of struggle between social classes. It argued that the future lay with the working class because the laws of history dictated that capitalism would inexorably grind to a halt. Crises of overproduction, underconsumption, and diminishing profits would shake the foundations of the capitalist order. Meanwhile, members of the constantly growing and thoroughly exploited proletariat would come to view the forcible overthrow of the existing system as the only alternative available to them. Marx and Engels believed that a socialist revolution would result in a "dictatorship of the proletariat," which would abolish private property and destroy the capitalist order. After the revolution was secure, the state would wither away. Coercive institutions would also disappear, since there would no longer be an exploiting class. Thus socialism would lead to a fair, just, and egalitarian society infinitely more humane than the capitalist order.

The doctrines of Marx and Engels came to dominate European and international socialism, and socialist parties grew rapidly throughout the nineteenth century. Political parties, trade unions, newspapers, and educational associations all worked to advance the socialist cause. Yet socialists disagreed strongly on the best means to reform society. Revolutionary socialists such as Marx, Engels, and other communists urged workers to seize control of the state, confiscate the means of production, and distribute wealth equitably throughout society. Doubting that a revolution could succeed, evolutionary socialists placed their hopes in representative governments and called for the election of legislators who supported socialist reforms.

Although socialists did not win control of any government until the Russian revolution of 1917, their critiques—along with those of conservatives and liberals—persuaded government authorities to attack the abuses of early industrialization and provide security for the working classes. Parliament prohibited underground employment for women, like the drawer Betty Harris, as well as for boys and girls under age ten and stipulated that children under age nine not work more than nine hours a day. In the wake of social reform came political reform. Beginning in 1832, a series of parliamentary acts expanded the franchise for men by reducing property qualifications, preparing the way for universal male suffrage. The same reform acts also removed the glaring inequalities in representation between rural areas and the growing cities of industrial society. For example, in the mid-nineteenth century, the sparsely populated rural county of Cornwall sent forty-four members to Parliament, whereas the city of London returned only four members. In the 1880s, under the leadership of Otto von Bismarck, Germany introduced medical insurance, unemployment compensation, and retirement pensions to provide social security for working people in industrial society.

Social Reform

Trade unions also sought to advance the quest for a just and equitable society. As governments regulated businesses and enhanced social security, trade unions struggled to eliminate abuses of early industrial society and improve workers' lives by seeking higher wages and better working conditions for their members. Through most of the nineteenth century, both employers and governments considered trade unions illegal associations whose purpose was to restrain trade. Tensions ran high when union members went on strike, especially when employers sought to keep their businesses going by hiring replacement workers. In those cases violence frequently broke out, prompting government authorities to send in police or military forces to maintain order. Over the longer run, though, trade unions gradually improved the lives of working people and reduced the likelihood that a disgruntled proletariat would mount a revolution to overthrow industrial capitalist society. Indeed, trade unions became an integral part of industrial society because they did not seek to destroy capitalism but rather to make employers more responsive to their employees' needs and interests.

Trade Unions

Global Effects of Industrialization

Early industrialization was a British, western European, and North American affair. By the late nineteenth century, Russia and Japan were beginning to industrialize. Quite apart from its spread beyond western Europe, industrialization had deep global implications because industrial powers used their tools, technologies, business organization, financial influence, and transportation networks to obtain raw materials from preindustrial societies around the world. Many lands that possessed natural resources became increasingly oriented to exporting raw materials but maintained little control over them because representatives of industrial countries dominated the commercial and financial institutions associated with the trade. Some societies saw their home markets flooded with inexpensive manufactured products from industrial lands, which devastated traditional industries and damaged local economies.

The Continuing Spread of Industrialization

By the mid-nineteenth century, industrialization processes were well under way in western Europe and North America as well as Britain. Industry brought economic and military power, and leaders in other lands began to seek paths to industrialization. After 1870 Russia and Japan embarked on campaigns of rapid industrialization. Government authorities took the lead in sponsoring industrialization in both lands, largely to strengthen their societies and enable them to resist military and economic pressures from western Europe and the United States.

Robert Koehler's painting *The Strike* depicts a situation verging toward violence as workers mill about in a confrontation with factory owners and one angry laborer crouches to pick up a stone.

In Russia the tsarist government promoted industrialization by encouraging the construction of railroads to link the distant regions of the far-flung empire. In 1860 Russia had less than 1,100 kilometers (700 miles) of railroads, but by 1900 there were more than 58,000 kilometers (36,000 miles). Most impressive of the Russian railroads was the trans-Siberian line, constructed between 1891 and 1904, which stretched more than 9,000 kilometers (5,600 miles) and linked Moscow with the port of Vladivostock on the Pacific Ocean. Apart from drawing the regions of the Russian empire together, railroads stimulated the development of coal, iron, and steel industries and enabled Russia to serve as a commercial link between western Europe and east Asia.

Industrialization in Russia

Russian industry experienced explosive growth when Count Sergei Witte served as finance minister (1892–1903). Witte oversaw construction of the trans-Siberian railroad, and he worked to push Russian industrialization by reforming commercial law, protecting infant industries, supporting steamship companies, and promoting nautical and engineering schools. He invited foreign investors to bring their capital and expertise to Russia, and he encouraged the establishment of savings banks to raise additional investment funds at home. By 1900 Russia produced half the world's oil, and Russian steel production ranked fourth in the world, behind the United States, Germany, and Britain. As a result of Witte's efforts, Russia also had enormous coal and iron industries, and government demand for weapons also supported a vast armaments industry.

In Japan, too, imperial authorities pushed industrialization. The government hired thousands of foreign experts to instruct Japanese workers and managers in the techniques of modern industry. The government also took the initiative by modernizing iron foundries and dockyards established during the Tokugawa shogunate, founding new businesses, and opening schools and universities specializing in scientific and technical fields. Government support was responsible for the construction of railroads, the opening of mines, the organization of a banking system, and the establishment of mechanized industries producing ships, armaments, silk, cotton, chemicals, and glass.

Industrialization in Japan

When businesses were able to operate on their own, the government sold them to private entrepreneurs, who often built huge industrial empires known as *zaibatsu* ("wealthy cliques"). Zaibatsu were similar to the trusts and cartels that emerged in nineteenth-century Europe and the United States but most commonly organized around a single family. Zaibatsu usually operated and controlled companies in several industries. The Mitsui combine, for example, owned or had large investments in a multitude of enterprises engaged in banking, trade, mining, food processing, and textile manufacturing. By 1900, as a result of active government encouragement and the organization of large-scale enterprises that operated efficiently, Japan was the most industrialized land in Asia, and it was poised for dramatic economic and industrial expansion in the twentieth century.

The International Division of Labor

Industrialization brought great economic and military strength to societies that reconfigured themselves and relied on mechanized production. Their power encouraged other societies to work toward industrialization. Before the mid-twentieth century, however, those efforts had limited results outside Europe, North America, and Japan. In India, for example, entrepreneurs established a thriving industry in the production of jute—a natural, hemplike fiber used for making carpets, upholstery, and burlap bags—as well as a small domestic steel industry. But fledgling Indian industries lacked government support, and private investment capital was insufficient to bankroll industrialization on a large scale.

Witte, Sergei (VIHT-tee, SAYR-gay)

zaibatsu (zeye-BAHT-soo)

The Tomioka silk factory, established in the 1870s, was one of the earliest mechanized textile factories in Japan. In this factory, as in many textile mills in Europe and North America, male managers oversaw female factory workers.

*Demand for
Raw Materials*

Nevertheless, industrialization had deep global ramifications. The industrialization process influenced the economic and social development of many societies because it promoted a new international division of labor. Industrial societies needed minerals, agricultural products, and other raw materials from sometimes distant regions of the world. Representatives of industrial societies searched the globe for raw materials to supply their factories.

Large-scale global trade in agricultural products was nothing new. From the sixteenth through the eighteenth centuries, European countries had imported sugar, spices, tobacco, tea, coffee, cotton, and other products grown mostly on plantations. In the nineteenth century, demand for these products increased sharply because of population growth. But industrial society fueled the demand for additional products as British, European, and U.S. industrialists sought the natural resources and agricultural products of Africa, the Americas, Asia, Australia, and eastern Europe. The mechanization of the textile industry, for example, produced a demand for large quantities of raw cotton, which came mostly from India, Egypt, and the southern rim of the United

States. Similarly, new industrial technologies increased demand for products such as rubber, the principal ingredient of belts and tires that were essential to industrial machinery, which came from Brazil, Malaya, and the Congo River basin.

In some lands, specialization in the production and export of primary goods paved the way for economic development and eventual industrialization. This pattern was especially noticeable in lands settled by European colonists, including Canada, Argentina, Uruguay, South Africa, Australia, and New Zealand, each of which experienced economic growth through the export of primary products and the infusion of foreign capital and labor. The same societies had an additional advantage in that they were high-wage economies. High incomes fostered economic development in two ways: they created flourishing markets, and they encouraged entrepreneurs to counteract high wages and labor scarcity by inventing labor-saving technologies.

Economic Development

Other lands were less fortunate. The peoples of Latin America, sub-Saharan Africa, south Asia, and southeast Asia also exported primary products but attracted little foreign investment and developed little mechanical industry. Export-oriented agriculture dominated these lands, where the major cash crops were sugar, cotton, and rubber. Foreign owners controlled the plantations that produced these crops, and most of the profits went abroad, depriving domestic economies of funds that might otherwise have contributed to the building of markets and industries. The low wages of plantation workers made the situation worse by dampening demand for manufactured goods. The result was a concentration of wealth in the hands of small groups that contributed little to economic development through consumption or investment. To compound the problem, the dominant financial interests adopted free-trade policies allowing unrestricted entry of foreign manufactures, which supported continuing industrialization in foreign lands but sharply limited opportunities for indigenous industrialization.

Economic Interdependence

An Eastern Steamboat, a watercolor by Pavel Petrovich Svinin, depicted Robert Fulton's steamboat the *Paragon*. Steamboats transported passengers and cargo and helped spread industrialization around the world.

The new geographic division of labor, in which some of the world's peoples provided raw materials while others processed and consumed them, increased the volume of world trade and led to increased transportation on both sea and land. Bigger ships, larger docks, and deeper canals facilitated trade and transport. The benefits of this new system flowed primarily to Europe, North America, and Japan. Other lands realized few benefits from the process of industrialization, but the process nevertheless increasingly linked the fortunes of all the world's peoples.

The process of industrialization involved the harnessing of inanimate sources of energy, the replacement of handicraft production with machine-based manufacturing, and the generation of new forms of business and labor organization. Along with industrialization came demographic growth, large-scale migration, and rapid urbanization, which increased the demand for manufactured goods by the masses of working people. Societies that underwent industrialization enjoyed sharp increases in economic productivity: they produced large quantities of high-quality goods at low prices, and their increased productivity translated into higher material standards of living. Yet industrialization brought costs, in the form of unsettling social problems, as well as benefits. Family life changed dramatically in the industrial age as men, women, and children increasingly left their homes to work in factories and mines, often under appalling conditions. Socialist critics sought to bring about a more just and equitable society, and government authorities curtailed the worst abuses of the early industrial era. Governments and labor unions both worked to raise living standards and provide security for working people. Meanwhile, industrialization increasingly touched the lives of peoples around the world. Western European, North American, and Japanese societies followed Britain's lead into industrialization, while many African, Asian, and Latin American lands became dependent on the export of raw materials to industrial societies.

CHRONOLOGY

1730–1795	Life of Josiah Wedgwood
1733	John Kay develops the flying shuttle
1765	James Watt patents an improved steam engine
1765–1825	Life of Eli Whitney
1779	Samuel Crompton develops the spinning mule
1785	Edmund Cartwright develops the power loom
1797	Eli Whitney introduces interchangeable parts to the manufacturing process
1829	George Stephenson's locomotive, the Rocket, attains a speed of 45 kilometers (28 miles) per hour
1832	Reform Bill expands electorate to House of Commons
1833	Factory Act restricts employment of women and children in textile factories
1842	Mines Act restricts employment of women and children in mines
1848	Karl Marx and Friedrich Engels publish *Manifesto of the Communist Party*
1849–1915	Life of Sergei Witte
1851	Crystal Palace exhibition in London
1856	Bessemer converter developed
1913	Henry Ford introduces the assembly line to the manufacture of automobiles

FOR FURTHER READING

Sean Patrick Adams. *Old Dominion, Industrial Commonwealth: Coal, Politics, and Economy in Antebellum America*. Baltimore, 2004. Shrewd and innovative analysis of the development of the coal industry in Virginia and Pennsylvania.

T. S. Ashton. *The Industrial Revolution, 1760–1830*. New York, 1968. A brief and readable survey of early industrialization in the British isles.

Jeffrey Auerbach. *The Great Exhibition of 1851: A Nation on Display*. New Haven, 1999. Analyzes the significance of the first world's fair and industrial exhibit held at London's Crystal Palace.

Rondo Cameron. *A Concise Economic History of the World from Paleolithic Times to the Present*. 3rd ed. New York, 1997. A comprehensive and useful work on economic development, concentrating on industrial Europe.

Daniel R. Headrick. *The Tentacles of Progress: Technology Transfer in the Age of Imperialism, 1850–1940*. New York, 1988. Concentrates on the political and cultural obstacles that hindered transfer of European technologies to colonial lands.

Tom Kemp. *Historical Patterns of Industrialization*. 2nd ed. London, 1993. Focuses on the relationship between industrialization and the peasantry, banking institutions, and the state.

A. G. Kenwood and A. L. Lougheed. *Technological Diffusion and Industrialisation before 1914*. London, 1982. A balanced interpretation drawing on different theoretical perspectives raised by industrialization worldwide.

David S. Landes. *The Unbound Prometheus: Technological Change and Industrial Development in Western Europe from 1750 to the Present*. Cambridge, 1969. A comprehensive study of industrialization concentrating on the role of technological innovation.

———. *The Wealth and Poverty of Nations: Why Some Are So Rich and Some So Poor*. New York, 1998. A wide-ranging analysis arguing that social and cultural attitudes serve as the foundation of economic development.

Penelope Lane, Neil Raven, and K. D. M. Snell, eds. *Women, Work and Wages in England, 1600–1850*. Rochester, N.Y., 2004. Study of women's contributions to British industrialization and how it was rewarded.

Karl Marx and Friedrich Engels. *The Communist Manifesto.* Trans. by Samuel Moore. Harmondsworth, 1967. English translation of the most important tract of nineteenth-century socialism, with an excellent introduction by historian A. J. P. Taylor.

David R. Meyer. *The Roots of American Industrialization.* Baltimore, 2003. Interdisciplinary study that ties America's industrialization to increasing agricultural productivity of the antebellum period.

Joel Mokyr. *The Lever of Riches: Technological Creativity and Economic Progress.* New York, 1990. Examines European technological development in a comparative context.

Lawrence A. Peskin. *Manufacturing Revolution: The Intellectual Origins of Early American Industry.* Baltimore, 2003. The intellectual foundations of industrialization and economic growth take center stage.

Kenneth Pomeranz. *The Great Divergence: China, Europe, and the Making of the Modern World Economy.* Princeton, 2000. Argues that the fortuitous location of coal deposits and access to the resources of the Americas created a uniquely advantageous framework for English industrialization.

Peter N. Stearns. *The Industrial Revolution in World History.* Boulder, 1993. An excellent overview of industrialization, its European origins, its spread, and its effects in the larger world.

——— and Herrick Chapman. *European Society in Upheaval: Social History since 1750.* 3rd ed. New York, 1992. Important synthetic study examining the social effects of industrialization in Europe.

Mikulas Teich and Roy Porter, eds. *The Industrial Revolution in National Context: Europe and the USA.* Cambridge, 1996. A collection of essays by leading scholars who reappraise industrialization and explore the new approaches that have emerged.

E. P. Thompson. *The Making of the English Working Class.* New York, 1966. A classic work that analyzes the formation of working-class consciousness in England from the 1790s to the 1830s.

Louise A. Tilly. *Industrialization and Gender Inequality.* Washington, D.C., 1993. A brief historiographical survey of debates on gender and industrialization in England, France, Germany, the United States, Japan, and China.

31

The Americas in the Age of Independence

The Building of American States
The United States: Westward Expansion and Civil War
The Canadian Dominion: Independence without War
Latin America: Fragmentation and Political Experimentation

American Economic Development
Migration to the Americas
Economic Expansion in the United States

Canadian Prosperity
Latin American Investments

American Cultural and Social Diversity
Multicultural Society in the United States
Canadian Cultural Contrasts
Ethnicity, Identity, and Gender in Latin America

A village fish peddler, Fatt Hing Chin often roamed the coast of southern China in search of fish to sell at market. One day at the wharves, he heard a tale of mysterious but enticing mountains of gold beckoning young Chinese to cross the ocean. At nineteen years of age, Chin felt restless, and he longed for the glittering mountains. He learned that he could purchase passage on a foreign ship, but he also needed to be cautious. He did not want to alarm his parents, nor did he want to draw the attention of the authorities, who were reportedly arresting individuals seeking to leave China. Eventually he reconciled his parents to his plans, and in 1849 he boarded a Spanish ship to sail to California and join the gold rush.

Chin felt some uncertainty once at sea. Surprised at the large number of young Chinese men crammed in with him in the ship's hold, he shared their dismay as they remained confined for weeks to the vomit-laden cargo areas of the ship. Ninety-five days and nights passed before the hills of San Francisco came into view. Upon arrival the travelers met Chinese veterans of life in the United States who explained the need to stick together if they were to survive and prosper.

Chin hired out as a gold miner and headed for the mountains of gold. After digging and sifting for two years, he had accumulated his own little pile of gold. He wrote to his brothers and cousins, urging them to join him, and thus helped fuel the large-scale overseas migration of workers. Having made his fortune, though, Chin decided to return to China. Wealthy, he traveled more comfortably this time around, with a bunk and other amenities—and temptations. He participated in the gambling that took place at sea and lost half his gold by the time the ship docked in Guangzhou. What remained still amounted to a small fortune. California gold provided him with the means to take a wife, build a house, and buy some land.

Although settled and prosperous, Chin remained restless and longed for the excitement of California. Leaving his pregnant wife, he sailed for California again after only a year in China. He returned to mining with his brother, but the gold was more difficult to find. Inspired by the luck of another migrant, Tong Ling, who managed to get one dollar for each meal he sold, Chin's cousins in San Francisco decided to open a restaurant. As one of them said, "If the foreign devils will eat his food, they will eat ours." Chin found the city much more comfortable than the mountains. "Let the others go after the gold in the hills," he said. "I'll wait for the gold to come to the city."

Fatt Hing Chin was one of the earliest Chinese migrants to settle in the Americas. His career path—from a miner in search of quick riches to an urban resident committed to a new homeland and hoping to profit from the service industry—was quite typical of Chinese migrants to

---

OPPOSITE: **Chinese migrants toil at various tasks, from sifting soil and panning to carrying water, in their search for wealth in the California gold mines.**

the United States. Some went from mining to railroad construction or agricultural labor, but all contributed to the transformation of the Americas. Along with millions of others from Europe and Asia, Chinese migrants increased the ethnic diversity of American populations and stimulated political, social, and economic development in the western hemisphere.

During the late eighteenth and early nineteenth centuries, almost all the lands of the western hemisphere won their independence from European colonial powers. American peoples then struggled throughout the nineteenth century to build states and societies that realized their potential in an age of independence. The United States built the most powerful state in the western hemisphere and embarked on a westward push that brought most of the temperate regions of North America under U.S. control. Canada built a federal state under British Canadian leadership. The varied lands of Latin America built smaller states that often fell under the sway of local military leaders. One issue that most American peoples wrestled with, regardless of their region, was the legacy of the Enlightenment. The effort to build societies based on freedom, equality, and constitutional government was a monumental challenge only partially realized in lands characterized by enormous social, economic, and cultural diversity. Both the institution of slavery and its ultimate abolition complicated the process of building societies in the Americas, particularly in regard to defining and diversifying a new type of workforce for free and increasingly industrial economies. Asian and European migrants joined freed slaves and native-born workers in labor systems—from plantations and factories to debt peonage—that often betrayed American promises of welcome and freedom.

The age of independence for the United States, Canada, and Latin America was a contentious era characterized by continuous mass migration and explosive economic growth, occasionally followed by deep economic stagnation, and punctuated with civil war, ethnic violence, class conflict, and battles for racial and sexual equality. Independence did not solve all the political and social problems of the western hemisphere but, rather, created a new context in which American peoples struggled to build effective states, enjoy economic prosperity, and attain cultural cohesion. Those goals were elusive throughout the nineteenth century and in many ways remain so even in the present day. Nevertheless, the histories of these first lands to win independence from colonial powers inspired other peoples who later sought freedom from imperial rule, but they also served as portents of the difficulties faced by newly free states.

The Building of American States

After winning independence from Britain, the United States fashioned a government and began to expand rapidly to the west. By midcentury the new republic had absorbed almost all the temperate lands of North America. Yet the United States was an unstable society composed of varied regions with diverse economic and social structures. Differences over slavery and the rights of individual states as opposed to the federal government sparked a devastating civil war in the 1860s. That conflict resulted in the abolition of slavery and the strengthening of the federal state. The experience of Canada was very different from that of the United States. Canada gained independence from Britain without fighting a war, and even though Canada also was a land of great diversity, it avoided falling into a civil war. Although intermittently nervous about the possibility that the United States might begin to expand to the north, Canada established a relatively weak federal government, which presided over provinces that had considerable power over local affairs. Latin American lands were even more diverse than their counterparts to the north, and there was never any real possibility that they could join together in a confederation. Throughout the nineteenth century Latin America was a politically fragmented region, and many individual states faced serious problems and divisions within their own societies.

The United States: Westward Expansion and Civil War

After gaining independence the United States faced the need to construct a machinery of government. During the 1780s leaders from the rebellious colonies drafted a constitution that entrusted responsibility for general issues to a federal government, reserved authority for local issues for individual states, and provided for the admission of new states and territories to the confederation. Although the Declaration of Independence had declared that "all men are created equal," most individual states limited the vote to men of property. But the Enlightenment ideal of equality encouraged political leaders to extend the franchise: by the late 1820s most property qualifications had disappeared, and by midcentury almost all adult white men were eligible to participate in the political affairs of the republic.

While working to settle constitutional issues, residents of the United States also began to expand rapidly to the west. After the American revolution, Britain ceded to the new republic all lands between the Appalachian Mountains and the Mississippi River, and the United States doubled in size. In 1803 Napoleon Bonaparte needed funds immediately to protect revolutionary France from its enemies, and he allowed the United States to purchase France's Louisiana Territory, which extended from the Mississippi River to the Rocky Mountains. Overnight the United States doubled in size again. Between 1804 and 1806 a geographic expedition led by Meriwether Lewis and William Clark mapped the territory and surveyed its resources. Settlers soon began to flock west in search of cheap land to cultivate. By the 1840s westward expansion was well under way, and many U.S. citizens spoke of a "manifest destiny" to occupy all of North America from the Atlantic to the Pacific Ocean.

Westward Expansion and Manifest Destiny

Westward expansion brought settlers and government forces into conflict with the indigenous peoples of North America, who resisted efforts to push them from their ancestral lands and hunting grounds. Native peoples forged alliances among themselves and also sought the backing of British colonial officials in Canada, but U.S. officials and military forces supported Euro-American settlers and gradually forced the continent open to white expansion. With the Indian Removal Act of 1830, the United States government determined to move all native Americans west of the Mississippi River into "Indian Territory" (Oklahoma). Among the tribes affected by this forced removal from the east were the Seminoles, some of whom managed to avoid capture and the long march to Oklahoma by resisting and retreating to Florida's swampy lowlands. The Cherokees also suffered a harrowing 800-mile migration from the eastern woodlands to Oklahoma on the Trail of Tears (1838–1839), so known because thousands died from disease, starvation, and the difficulties of relocation.

Conflict with Indigenous Peoples

After 1840 the site of conflict between Euro-American and indigenous peoples shifted to the plains region west of the Mississippi River. Settlers and ranchers in the trans-Mississippi west encountered peoples such as the Sioux, Comanche, Pawnee, and Apache, who possessed firearms and outstanding equestrian skills. The native peoples of the plains offered effective resistance to encroachment by white settlers and at times celebrated powerful victories over U.S. forces. In 1876, for example, thousands of Lakota Sioux and their allies annihilated an army under the command of Colonel George Armstrong Custer in the battle of Little Big Horn (in southern Montana). Despite occasional successes in battle, native Americans on the plains ultimately lost the war against the forces of U.S. expansionism. The technologically sophisticated weaponry employed against native peoples included cannons and deadly,

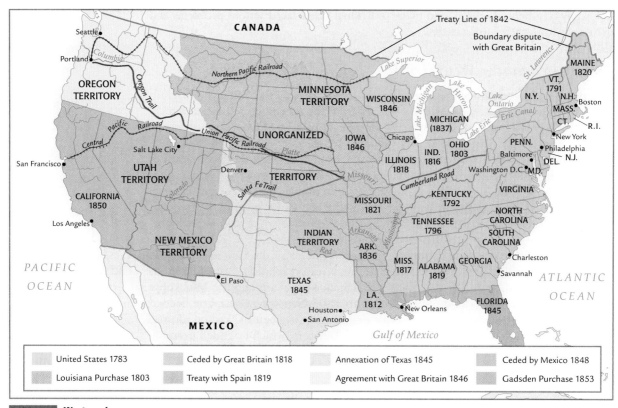

Map 31.1 **Westward expansion of the United States during the nineteenth century.** Note the large land claims ceded by Britain, France, and Mexico. Why were there no portions of North America purchased from or ceded by native Americans?

The Mexican-American War

rapid-fire Gatling guns. These weapons aided U.S. forces in breaking native resistance and opened the western plains to U.S. conquest.

One last forbidding and symbolic conflict took place in 1890 at Wounded Knee Creek in South Dakota. Frightened and threatened by the Sioux adoption of the Ghost Dance, an expression of religious beliefs that included a vision of an afterlife in which all white peoples disappeared, whites wanted these religious ceremonies suppressed. U.S. cavalry forces chased the Sioux who were fleeing to safety in the South Dakota Badlands. At Wounded Knee Creek, a Sioux man accidentally shot off a gun, and the cavalry overreacted badly, slaughtering more than two hundred men, women, and children with machine guns. Emblematic of harsh U.S. treatment of native peoples, Wounded Knee represented the place where "a people's dream died," as a later native leader put it.

Westward expansion also generated tension between the United States and Mexico, whose territories included Texas, California, and New Mexico (the territory that is now the American southwest). Texas declared independence from Mexico in 1836, largely because the many U.S. migrants who had settled there wanted to run their own affairs. In 1845 the United States accepted Texas as a new state—against vigorous Mexican protest—and moved to consolidate its hold on the territory. Those moves led to conflicts that rapidly escalated into the Mexican-American War (1846–1848), or, as it is known in Mexico, *la intervención norteamericano* (the North American Intervention) or *la guerra del 47* (the War of 1847). U.S. forces instigated the war and then inflicted a punishing defeat on the Mexican army. By the Treaty of Guadalupe Hidalgo (1848), the United States took possession of approximately one-half of Mexico's territory, paying a mere fifteen million dollars in exchange for Texas north of the Rio Grande, California, and New Mexico. Thousands of U.S. and Mexican soldiers died in

This photograph of an 1890s Plains Indian camp in South Dakota offers an idealized, pastoral, and peaceful image of the disappearing indigenous societies in the United States.

the conflict, and thousands of Mexican families found themselves stranded in the territories annexed by the United States. Some returned to Mexico, but most stayed put and attained U.S. citizenship. This conflict nonetheless fueled Mexican nationalism, as well as disdain for the United States.

While satisfying desires for the United States to realize its manifest destiny, westward expansion also created problems within the republic by aggravating tensions between regions. The most serious and divisive issue had to do with slavery, which had vexed American politics since independence. The Enlightenment ideal of equality clearly suggested that the appropriate policy was to abolish slavery, but the leaders of the American revolution and framers of the Constitution recognized the sanctity of private property, including slaves. U.S. independence initially promoted a surge of antislavery sentiment, as states from Delaware north abolished slavery within their jurisdictions. Abolition did not bring full equality for free blacks in northern states, but it hardened divisions between slave and free states. Westward expansion aggravated tensions further by raising the question of whether settlers could extend slavery to newly acquired territories.

Opponents of slavery had dreamed that the institution would die a natural death *Sectional Conflict* with the decline of tobacco cultivation. Their hopes faded, however, with the invigoration of the slave system by the rise of cotton as a cash crop in the early nineteenth century, followed by westward expansion. The U.S. slave population rose sharply, from five hundred thousand in 1770 to almost two million in 1820. As the numbers of slaves grew, antislavery forces fought to limit the spread of slavery to new territories. Beginning with the Missouri Compromise of 1820, a series of political compacts attempted to maintain a balance between slave and free states as the republic admitted new states carved out of western territories. Those compromises ultimately proved too brittle to endure, as proslavery and antislavery forces became more strident. Abraham Lincoln (1809–1865) predicted in 1858 that "a house divided against itself cannot stand," and he made the connection to slavery explicit: "I believe this government cannot endure permanently half *slave* and half *free*. . . . It will become *all* one thing, or *all* the other."

The U.S. Civil War

LINCOLN'S ADDRESS AT GETTYSBURG.

This early-twentieth-century postcard offered an idealized depiction of Abraham Lincoln delivering his Gettysburg Address, which commemorated the Union soldiers who fell in that crucial battle.

The election of Abraham Lincoln to the presidency in 1860 was the spark that ignited war between the states (1861–1865). Lincoln was an explicitly sectional candidate, was convinced that slavery was immoral, and was committed to free soil—territories without slavery. Although slavery stood at the center of the conflict, the Civil War also revolved around issues central to the United States as a society: the nature of the Union, states' rights as opposed to the federal government's authority, and the imperatives of a budding industrial-capitalist system against those of an export-oriented plantation economy.

Eleven southern states withdrew from the Union in 1860 and 1861, affirming their right to dissolve the Union and their support for states' rights. Slavery and the cultivation of cotton as a cash crop had isolated the southern states from economic developments in the rest of the United States. By the mid-nineteenth century, the southern states were the world's major source of cotton, and the bulk of the crop went to the British isles. Manufactured goods consumed in the southern states came mostly from Britain, and almost all food came from the region's farms. Southerners considered themselves self-sufficient and believed that they did not need the rest of the United States. Northerners saw the situation differently. They viewed secession as illegal insurrection and an act of betrayal. They fought not only against slavery but also against the concept of a state subject to blackmail by its constituent parts. They also fought for a way of life—their emerging industrial society—and an expansive western agricultural system based on free labor.

The first two years of the war ended in stalemate. The war changed character on 1 January 1863, however, when Abraham Lincoln signed the Emancipation Proclamation, making the abolition of slavery an explicit goal of the war. The Emancipation Proclamation struck at the heart of the southern war effort, since slaves constituted a sizable portion of the region's labor force. In practical terms the Emancipation Proclamation had little immediate effect on slaves' status, but its promise of abolition foreshadowed radical changes to come in southern life. The bloody battle of Gettysburg in July 1863 turned the military tide against southern forces.

Ultimately, the northern states prevailed. They brought considerable resources to the war effort—some 90 percent of the country's industrial capacity and approximately

The grotesquely twisted bodies of dead northern soldiers lay near a fence outside Antietam, Maryland, in 1862. The Civil War was the most costly in U.S. history in terms of lives lost.

two-thirds of its railroad lines—but still they fought four bitter years against a formidable enemy. The victory of the northern states ended slavery in the United States. Moreover, it ensured that the United States would remain politically united, and it enhanced the authority of the federal government in the republic. Thus, as European lands were building powerful states on the foundations of revolutionary ideals, liberalism, and nationalism, the United States also forged a strong central government to supervise westward expansion and deal with the political and social issues that divided the nation.

The Canadian Dominion: Independence without War

Canada did not fight a war for independence, and in spite of deep regional divisions, it did not experience bloody internal conflict. Instead, Canadian independence came gradually as Canadians and the British government agreed on general principles of autonomy. The distinctiveness of the two dominant ethnic groups, the British Canadians and the French Canadians, ensured that the process of building an independent society would not be smooth, but intermittent fears of U.S. expansion and concerns about the possibility of an invasion from the south helped submerge ethnic differences. By the late nineteenth century, Canada was a land in control of its own destiny, despite continuing ties to Britain and the looming presence of the United States to the south.

Autonomy and Division

Originally colonized by trappers and settlers from both Britain and France, the colony of New France passed into the British empire after the British victory in the Seven Years' War (1756–1763). Until the late eighteenth century, however, French Canadians outnumbered British Canadians, so imperial officials made large concessions to their subjects of French descent to forestall unnecessary strife. Officials recognized the Roman Catholic church and permitted continued observance of French civil law in Quebec and other areas of French Canadian settlement, which they governed through appointed councils staffed by local elites. British Canadians, in contrast, were Protestants who lived mostly in Ontario, followed British law, and governed themselves through elected representatives. After 1781 large numbers of British loyalists fled the newly formed United States to the south and sought refuge in Canada, thus greatly enlarging the size of the English-speaking community there.

Map 31.2 **The Dominion of Canada in the nineteenth century.** Note the provinces that make up the modern state of Canada and the dates in which they were incorporated into the Dominion. At what date were eastern and western Canada geographically united?

The War of 1812

Ethnic divisions and political differences could easily have splintered Canada, but the War of 1812 stimulated a sense of unity against an external threat. The United States declared war on Britain in retaliation for encroachments on U.S. rights during the Napoleonic wars, and the British colony of Canada formed one of the front lines of the conflict. U.S. military leaders assumed that they could easily invade and conquer Canada to pressure their foes. Despite the greater resources of the United States, however, Canadian forces repelled U.S. incursions. Their victories promoted a sense of Canadian pride, and anti-U.S. sentiments became a means for covering over differences among French Canadians and British Canadians.

After the War of 1812, Canada experienced an era of rapid growth. Expanded business opportunities drew English-speaking migrants, who swelled the population. That influx threatened the identity of Quebec, and discontent in Canada reached a critical point in the 1830s. The British imperial governors of Canada did not want a repeat of the American revolution, so between 1840 and 1867 they defused tensions by expanding home rule in Canada and permitting the provinces to govern their own internal affairs. Inspiring this imperial move toward Canadian autonomy was the Durham Report, issued in 1839 by John George Lambton (1782–1840), the first earl of Durham and the recent governor-general and lord high commissioner of Canada. He advocated a good deal of self-government for a united Canada, and his report became a model for British imperial policy and colonial self-rule in other states, including Australia and New Zealand.

Dominion

Westward expansion of the United States and the U.S. Civil War pushed Canada toward political autonomy. Fear of U.S. expansion helped stifle internal conflicts among Canadians and prompted Britain to grant independence to Canada. The

British North America Act of 1867 joined Quebec, Ontario, Nova Scotia, and New Brunswick and recognized them as the Dominion of Canada. Other provinces joined the Dominion later. Each province had its own seat of government, provincial legislature, and lieutenant governor representing the British crown. The act created a federal government headed by a governor-general who acted as the British representative. An elected House of Commons and appointed Senate rounded out the framework of governance. Provincial legislatures reserved certain political matters for themselves, whereas others fell within the purview of the federal government. Without waging war, the Dominion of Canada had won control over all Canadian internal affairs, and Britain retained jurisdiction over foreign affairs until 1931.

John A. Macdonald (1815–1891) became the first prime minister of Canada, and he moved to incorporate all of British North America into the Dominion. He negotiated the purchase of the huge Northwest Territories from the Hudson Bay Company in 1869, and he persuaded Manitoba, British Columbia, and Prince Edward Island to join the Dominion. Macdonald believed, however, that Canada's Dominion would remain symbolic—a mere "geographic expression," as he put it—until the government took concrete action to make Canadian unity and independence a reality. To strengthen the union, he oversaw construction of a transcontinental railroad, completed in 1885. The railroad facilitated transportation and communications throughout Canada and eventually helped bring new provinces into the Dominion: Alberta and Saskatchewan in 1905 and Newfoundland in 1949. Internal conflicts never disappeared, but the Dominion provided a foundation for Canadian independence and unity. Although maintaining ties to Britain and struggling to forge an identity distinct from that of its powerful neighbor to the south, Canada developed as a culturally diverse yet politically unified society.

Latin America: Fragmentation and Political Experimentation

Political unity was short-lived in Latin America. Simón Bolívar (1783–1830), hailed as South America's liberator, worked for the establishment of a large confederation that would provide Latin America with the political, military, and economic strength to resist encroachment by foreign powers. The wars of independence that he led encouraged a sense of solidarity in Latin America. But Bolívar once admitted that "I fear peace more than war," and after the defeat of the common colonial enemy, solidarity was impossible to sustain. Bolívar's Gran Colombia broke into its three constituent parts—Venezuela, Colombia, and Ecuador—and the rest of Latin America fragmented into numerous independent states.

Following the example of the United States, creole elites usually established republics with written constitutions for the newly independent states of Latin America. Yet constitutions were much more difficult to frame in Latin America than in the United States. Before gaining independence, Latin American leaders had less experience with self-government because Spanish and Portuguese colonial regimes were far more autocratic than was the British imperial government in North America. Creole elites responded enthusiastically to Enlightenment values and republican ideals, but they had little experience putting their principles into practice. As a result, several Latin American lands lurched from one constitution to another as leaders struggled to create a machinery of government that would lead to political and social stability.

Creole Elites and Political Instability

Creole elites also dominated the newly independent states and effectively prevented mass participation in public affairs. Less than 5 percent of the male population was active in Latin American politics in the nineteenth century, and millions of indigenous peoples lived entirely outside the political system. Without institutionalized means of expressing discontent or opposition, those disillusioned with the system had little choice beyond rebellion. Aggravating political instability were differences among

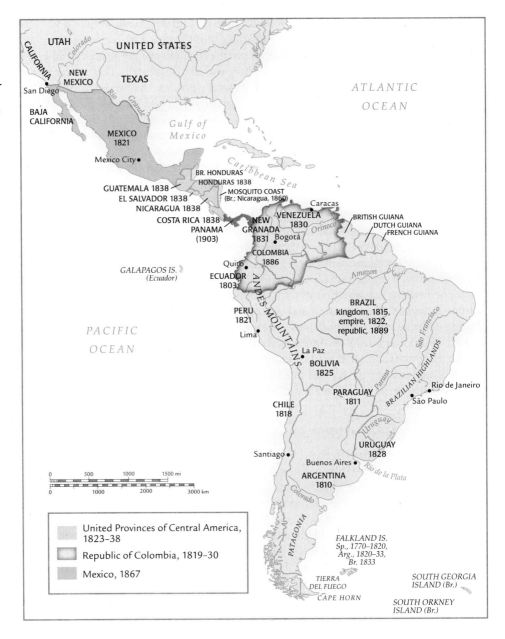

Map 31.3 **Latin America in the nineteenth century. Date is year of independence.** Note the many states that emerged from the independence movements early in the century. Why was it difficult for large, federated republics, such as the Republic of Colombia, founded by Simón Bolívar, to survive?

elites. Whether they were urban merchants or rural landowners, Latin American elites divided into different camps as liberals or conservatives, centralists or federalists, secularists or Roman Catholics.

Conflicts with Indigenous Peoples

One thing elites agreed on was the policy of claiming American land for agriculture and ranching. That meant pushing aside indigenous peoples and establishing Euro-American hegemony in Latin America. Conflict was most intense in Argentina and Chile, where cultivators and ranchers longed to take over the South American plains. During the mid-nineteenth century, as the United States was crushing native resistance to western expansion in North America, Argentine and Chilean forces brought modern weapons to bear in their campaign to conquer the indigenous peoples of South America. By the 1870s, they had pacified the most productive lands and forced indigenous peoples either to assimilate to Euro-American society or to retreat to marginal lands that were unattractive to cultivators and ranchers.

Although creole elites agreed on the policy of conquering native peoples, division and discord in the newly independent states helped caudillos, or regional military leaders, come to power in much of Latin America. The wars of independence had lasted well over a decade, and they provided Latin America with military rather than civilian heroes. After independence, military leaders took to the political stage, appealing to populist sentiments and exploiting the discontent of the masses. One of the most notable caudillos was Juan Manuel de Rosas, who from 1829 to 1852 ruled an Argentina badly divided between the cattle-herding and gaucho society of the pampas (the interior grasslands) and the urban elite of Buenos Aires. Rosas himself emerged from the world of cattle ranching, and he used his skills to subdue other caudillos and establish control in Buenos Aires. Rosas called for regional autonomy in an attempt to reconcile competing interests, but he worked to centralize the government he usurped. He quelled rebellions, but he did so in bloody fashion. Critics often likened Rosas to historically infamous figures, calling him "the Machiavelli of the pampas" and "the Argentine Nero," and they accused him of launching a reign of terror to stifle opposition. One writer exiled by the caudillo compiled a chart that counted the number of Rosas's victims and the violent ways they met their ends; of the 22,404 total victims killed, most met their end in armed clashes but others died by poisoning, hanging, and assassination.

Caudillos

Rosas did what caudillos did best: he restored order. In doing so, however, he made terror a tool of the government, and he ruled as a despot through his own personal army. Rosas also, however, embodied the winning personality traits most exemplified by caudillos. He attained great popularity through his identification with the people and with gauchos, and he demonstrated his physical strength and machismo. Although caudillo rule often limited freedom and undermined republican ideals, it sometimes also gave rise to an opposition that aimed to overthrow the caudillos and work for liberal reforms that would promote democratic forms of government.

Independent Mexico experienced a succession of governments, from monarchy to republic to caudillo rule, but it also generated a liberal reform movement. The Mexican-American War caused political turmoil in Mexico and helped the caudillo General Antonio López de Santa Anna (1797–1876) perpetuate his intermittent rule. After the defeat and disillusion of the war, however, a liberal reform movement attempted to reshape Mexican society. Led by President Benito Juárez (1806–1872), a Mexican of indigenous ancestry, La Reforma of the 1850s aimed to limit the power of the military and the Roman Catholic church in Mexican society. Juárez and his followers called for liberal reform, designed in part to create a rural middle class. The Constitution of 1857 set forth the ideals of La Reforma. It curtailed the prerogatives of priests and military elites, and it guaranteed universal male suffrage and other civil liberties, such as freedom of speech. Land reform efforts centered on dismantling corporate properties, which had the effect of parceling out communal Indian lands and villages as private property, much of which ended up in the hands of large landowners, not indigenous peoples.

Mexico: War and Reform

La Reforma challenged some of the fundamental conservatism of Mexican elites, who led spirited opposition to political, social, and economic reform. Liberals and conservatives in Mexico stayed bitterly divided, and conservatives forced the Juárez government out of Mexico City until 1861, when Juárez struggled to establish order in his country. To lessen Mexico's financial woes, Juárez chose to suspend loan payments to foreign powers, and that led to French, British, and Spanish intervention as Europeans sought to recover and protect their investments in Mexico. France's

Mexico: Revolution

Edouard Manet's painting depicts the execution by firing squad of Emperor Maximilian, whose death in 1867 ended attempted French rule in Mexico.

Napoleon III proved especially persistent and intrusive. His attempts to end Mexican disorder by re-creating a monarchy met unexpected resistance in Puebla, where Mexican forces beat back the French invaders on 5 May 1862, a date thereafter celebrated as Cinco de Mayo. Napoleon III then sent tens of thousands of troops and proclaimed a Mexican empire, although he had to withdraw those forces in 1867. A Mexican firing squad killed the man he had appointed emperor, the Austrian archduke Maximilian (1832–1867). Juárez managed to restore a semblance of liberal government, but Mexico remained beset by political divisions.

By the early twentieth century, Mexico was a divided land moving toward civil war. The Mexican revolution (1910–1920), a bitter and bloody conflict, broke out when middle-class Mexicans joined with peasants and workers to overthrow the powerful dictator Porfirio Díaz (1830–1915). The revolt in Mexico, which was the first major, violent effort in Latin America to attempt to topple the grossly unequal system of landed estates—whereby fully 95 percent of all peasants remained landless—turned increasingly radical as those denied land and representation armed themselves and engaged in guerrilla warfare against government forces. The lower classes took up weapons and followed the revolutionary leaders Emiliano Zapata (1879–1919) and Francisco (Pancho) Villa (1878–1923), charismatic agrarian rebels who organized massive armies fighting for *tierra y libertad* (land and liberty), which were Zapata's stated revolutionary goals. Zapata, the son of a mestizo peasant, and Villa, the son of a field worker, embodied the ideals and aspirations of the indigenous Mexican masses and enjoyed tremendous popular support. They discredited timid governmental efforts at reform and challenged governmental political control; Zapata confiscated hacienda

Sources from the Past

Ponciano Arriaga Calls for Land Reform

During the era of La Reforma in Mexico, the leftist liberal Ponciano Arriaga voiced demands for land reform on behalf of the Mexican masses, reflecting the broader problem of land control throughout Latin American societies. At the Constitutional Convention of 1856–1857, Arriaga spoke about the troubles resulting from an aristocratic monopoly on land and argued passionately for reform.

One of the most deeply rooted evils of our country—an evil that merits the close attention of legislators when they frame our fundamental law—is the monstrous division of landed property.

While a few individuals possess immense areas of uncultivated land that could support millions of people, the great majority of Mexicans languish in a terrible poverty and are denied property, homes, and work.

Such a people cannot be free, democratic, much less happy, no matter how many constitutions and laws proclaim abstract rights and beautiful but impracticable theories—impracticable by reason of an absurd economic system.

There are Mexican landowners who occupy (if one can give that name to a purely imaginary act) an extent of land greater than the area of some of our sovereign states, greater even than that of one or several European states.

In this vast area, much of which lies idle, deserted, abandoned, awaiting the arms and labor of men, live four or five million Mexicans who know no other industry than agriculture, yet are without land or the means to work it, and who cannot emigrate in the hope of bettering their fortunes. They must either vegetate in idleness, turn to banditry, or accept the yoke of a landed monopolist who subjects them to intolerable conditions of life. . . .

How can a hungry, naked, miserable people practice popular government? How can we proclaim the equal rights of men and leave the majority of the nation in conditions worse than those of helots or pariahs? How can we condemn slavery in words, while the lot of most of our fellow citizens is more grievous than that of the black slaves of Cuba or the United States? When will we begin to concern ourselves with the fate of the proletarians, the men we call Indians, the laborers and peons of the countryside, who drag the heavy chains of serfdom established not by Spanish laws—which were so often flouted and infringed—but by the arbitrary mandarins of the colonial regime? Would it not be more logical and honest to deny our four million poor Mexicans all share in political life and public offices, all electoral rights, and declare them to be things, not persons, establishing a system of government in which an aristocracy of wealth, or at most of talent, would form the basis of our institutions?

For one of two things is inevitable: either our political system will continue to be dominated for a long time to come by a *de facto* aristocracy—no matter what our fundamental laws may say—and the lords of the land, the privileged caste that monopolizes the soil and profits by the sweat of its serfs, will wield all power and influence in our civil and political life; or we will achieve a reform, shatter the trammels and bonds of feudal servitude, bring down all monopolies and despotisms, end all abuses, and allow the fruitful element of democratic equality, the powerful element of democratic sovereignty—to which alone authority rightfully belongs—to penetrate the heart and veins of our political institutions. The nation wills it, the people demand it; the struggle has begun, and sooner or later that just authority will recover its sway. The great word "reform" has been pronounced, and it is vain to erect dykes to contain those torrents of truth and light.

FOR FURTHER REFLECTION

In studies of life not just in Mexico but throughout the Americas, can the issue of land control help explain societies' economic and political power structures?

SOURCE: "A Mexican Radical: Ponciano Arriaga." In Benjamin Keen, ed., *Latin American Civilization History and Society, 1492 to the Present*, 6th ed., revised and updated. New York: Westview Press, 1996, pp. 273–74.

Zapata, hailing from the southern state of Morelos, was the very picture of a revolutionary leader, heavily armed and sporting his dashing, trademark moustache.

lands and began distributing the lands to the peasants, while Villa attacked and killed U.S. citizens in retaliation for U.S. support of Mexican government officials—and succeeded in eluding capture by either U.S. or Mexican forces.

Despite the power and popularity enjoyed by Zapata and Villa, they were unable to capture Mexico's major cities, and they did not command the resources and wealth to which government forces had access. The Mexican revolution came to an end soon after government forces ambushed and killed Zapata in 1919. Villa was killed a few years later, assassinated in 1923 while driving in the town of Hidalgo de Parral, his car and body riddled with bullets. Government forces regained control over Mexico, a land battered and devastated by long years of war and by the death of as many as two million Mexicans. Although radicals such as Zapata and Villa were ultimately defeated, the Mexican Constitution of 1917 had already addressed some of the concerns of the revolutionaries by providing for land redistribution, universal suffrage, state-supported education, minimum wages and maximum hours for workers, and restrictions on foreign ownership of Mexican property and mineral resources. Although these constitutional provisions were not soon implemented, they provided important guarantees for the future.

In the form of division, rebellion, caudillo rule, and civil war, instability and conflict plagued Latin America throughout the nineteenth century. Many Latin American peoples lacked education, profitable employment, and political representation. Simón Bolívar himself once said that "independence is the only blessing we have gained at the expense of all the rest."

American Economic Development

During the nineteenth and early twentieth centuries, two principal influences—mass migration and British investment—shaped economic development throughout the Americas. But American states reacted in different ways to migration and foreign investment. The United States and Canada absorbed waves of migrants, exploited British capital, built industrial societies, and established economic independence. The fragmented states of Latin America were unable to follow suit, however, as they struggled with the legacies of colonialism, slavery, and economic dependence on single export crops. Migrants to Latin America mostly worked not in factories but on plantations. The importation of migrant laborers for agricultural work in South America and the Caribbean indicated some of the major alterations in labor systems taking place throughout the Americas in the wake of slavery's abolition. Freedom for slaves did not necessarily bring about freer forms of labor, because many migrants arrived under contract or as indentured laborers. Although some freed slaves became small landowning farmers, more found themselves still subject to landowning elite control in the form of debt peonage or sharecropping. Life and labor in the Americas, whether for freedmen and freedwomen, migrants, or industrial workers, often proved arduous and at times heartbreaking, even as those American workers contributed to the economic development of the region.

Italian migrants construct a railway in New York. Italians were just one of many European groups coming to the Americas in the nineteenth century.

Migration to the Americas

Underpinning the economic development of the Americas was the mass migration of European and Asian peoples to the United States, Canada, and Latin America. Internal migration within the Americas also contributed to a new economic landscape, particularly as Latin Americans journeyed to the United States in search of work and financial well-being. Gold discoveries drew prospectors hoping to make a quick fortune: the California gold rush of 1849 drew the largest crowd, but Canadian gold also lured migrants by the tens of thousands. Outnumbering gold prospectors were millions of European and Asian migrants who made their way to the factories, railroad construction sites, and plantations of the Americas. Following them were others who offered the support services that made life for migrant workers more comfortable and at the same time transformed the ethnic and cultural landscape of the Americas. Fatt Hing Chin's restaurant in San Francisco's Chinatown fed Chinese migrants, but it also helped introduce Chinese cuisine to American society. Migrants from all over the world found similar comforts as their foods, religious beliefs, and cultural traditions migrated with them to the Americas.

After the mid-nineteenth century, European migrants flocked to North America, where they filled the factories of the growing industrial economy of the United States. Their lack of skills made them attractive to industrialists seeking workers to operate machinery or perform heavy labor at low wages. By keeping labor costs down, migrants helped increase the profitability and fuel the expansion of U.S. industry. *Industrial Migrants*

In the 1850s European migrants to the United States numbered 2.3 million— almost as many as had crossed the Atlantic during the half century from 1800 to

1850—and the volume of migration surged until the early twentieth century. Increasing rents and indebtedness drove cultivators from Ireland, Scotland, Germany, and Scandinavia to seek opportunities in North America. Some of them moved to the Ohio and Mississippi River valleys in search of cheap and abundant land, but many stayed in the eastern cities and contributed to the early industrialization of the United States. By the late nineteenth century, most European migrants were coming from southern and eastern Europe. Poles, Russian Jews, Slavs, Italians, Greeks, and Portuguese were most prominent among the later migrants, and they settled largely in the industrial cities of the eastern states. They dominated the textile industries of the northeast, and without their labor, the remarkable industrial expansion that the United States experienced in the late nineteenth century would have been inconceivable.

Asian migrants further swelled the U.S. labor force and contributed to the construction of an American transportation infrastructure. Chinese migration grew rapidly after the 1840s, when British gunboats opened China to foreign influences. Officials of the Qing government permitted foreigners to seek indentured laborers in China and approved their migration to distant lands. Between 1852 and 1875 some two hundred thousand Chinese migrated to California. Some, like Fatt Hing Chin, negotiated their own passage and sought to make their fortune in the gold rush, but most traveled on indentured labor contracts that required them to cultivate crops or work on the Central Pacific Railroad. An additional five thousand Chinese entered Canada to search for gold in British Columbia or work on the Canadian Pacific Railroad.

Plantation Migrants   Whereas migrants to the United States contributed to the development of an industrial society, those who went to Latin American lands mostly worked on agricultural plantations. Some Europeans figured among these migrants. About four million Italians sought opportunities in Argentina in the 1880s and 1890s, for example, and the Brazilian government paid Italian migrants to cross the Atlantic and work for coffee growers, who experienced a severe labor shortage after the abolition of slavery there (1888). Many Italian workers settled permanently in Latin America, especially Argentina, but some, popularly known as *golondrinas* ("swallows") because of their regular migrations, traveled back and forth annually between Europe and South America to take advantage of different growing seasons in the northern and southern hemispheres.

Other migrants who worked on plantations in the western hemisphere came from Asian lands. More than fifteen thousand indentured laborers from China worked in the sugarcane fields of Cuba during the nineteenth century, and Indian migrants traveled to Jamaica, Trinidad, Tobago, and Guyana. Laborers from both China and Japan migrated to Peru, where they worked on cotton plantations in coastal regions, mined guano deposits for fertilizer, and built railroad lines. After the middle of the nineteenth century, expanding U.S. influence in the Pacific islands also led to Chinese, Japanese, Filipino, and Korean migrations to Hawai`i, where planters sought indentured laborers to tend sugarcane. About twenty-five thousand Chinese went to Hawai`i during the 1850s and 1860s, and later 180,000 Japanese also made their way to island plantations.

Economic Expansion in the United States

British Capital   British investment capital in the United States proved crucial to the early stages of industrial development by helping businesspeople establish a textile industry. In the late nineteenth century, it also spurred a vast expansion of U.S. industry by funding entrepreneurs, who opened coal and iron ore mines, built iron and steel factories, and constructed railroad lines. The flow of investment monies was a consequence of Britain's own industrialization, which generated enormous wealth and created a need for investors to find profitable outlets for their funds. Stable, white-governed states and colonies were especially fertile grounds for British investment, which often provided the impetus for industrial expansion and economic independence in those regions. In the case of the United States, it helped create a rival industrial power that would eventually outperform Britain's economy.

After the 1860s, U.S. businesses made effective use of foreign investment capital as the reunited land recovered from the Civil War. The war determined that the United States would depend on wage labor rather than slavery, and entrepreneurs set about tapping American resources and building a continental economy.

Perhaps the most important economic development of the later nineteenth century was the construction of railroad lines that linked all U.S. regions and helped create an integrated national economy. Because of its enormous size and environmental diversity, the United States offered an abundance of natural resources for industrial exploitation. But vast distances made it difficult to maintain close economic ties between regions until a boom in railroad construction created a dense transportation, communication, and distribution network. Before the Civil War the United States had about 50,000 kilometers (31,000 miles) of railroad lines, most of them short routes east of the Mississippi River. By 1900 there were more than 320,000 kilometers (200,000 miles) of track, and the U.S. rail network stretched from coast to coast. Most prominent of the new lines was a transcontinental route, completed in 1869, running from Omaha, where connections provided access to eastern states, to San Francisco.

Railroads

Railroads decisively influenced U.S. economic development. They provided cheap transportation for agricultural commodities, manufactured goods, and individual travelers as well. Railroads hauled grain, beef, and hogs from the plains states, cotton and tobacco from the south, lumber from the northwest, iron and steel from the mills of Pittsburgh, and finished products from the eastern industrial cities. Quite apart from the transportation services they provided, railroads spurred the development of other industries: they required huge amounts of coal, wood, glass, and rubber, and by the 1880s some 75 percent of U.S. steel went to the railroad industry. Railroads also required the development of new managerial skills to operate large, complicated businesses. In 1850 few if any U.S. businesses had more than a thousand employees. By the early 1880s, however, the Pennsylvania Railroad alone employed almost fifty thousand people, and the size of the business called for organization and coordination on an unprecedented scale. Railroads were the testing grounds where managers developed the techniques they needed to run big businesses.

Railroads led to drastic changes in the ways people organized and controlled space and time. Railroads altered the landscape in often extreme fashion, and the transformations consequent to the building of railroads—in land control and development, the transportation of migrants and settlers to the west, and the exploitation of natural resources—only furthered the environmental impact of the railroad. The westward expansion driven by the railroad led to broadscale land clearing and the extension of farming and mining lands, and brought about both human suffering for indigenous peoples and environmental damage through soil erosion and pollution. Irrigation and the politics of water also sparked trouble, especially as settlers and farmers entered the drier plains and even desert regions. The dark smoke emanating from railroad engines undoubtedly represented progress to industrial promoters, but it also symbolized an ever-widening intrusion into the natural environment.

Space and Time

Railroads even shaped the sense of time in the United States. Until rapid and regular rail transportation became available, communities set their clocks by the sun. As a result, New York time was eleven minutes and forty-five seconds behind Boston time.

In this lithograph of Frances F. Palmer's well-known painting *American Express Train* (ca. 1864), the railroad demonstrates its domination of the natural landscape and its role as the harbinger of change and industry.

When the clock showed 12 noon in Chicago, it was 11:50 A.M. in St. Louis and 12:18 P.M. in Detroit. Those differences in local sun times created scheduling nightmares for railroad managers, who by the 1880s had to keep track of more than fifty time standards. Observance of local time also created hazards because a small miscalculation in scheduling could bring two massive trains hurtling unexpectedly toward each other on the same track. To simplify matters, in 1883 railroad companies divided the North American continent into four zones in which all railroad clocks read precisely the same time. The general public quickly adopted "railroad time" in place of local sun time, and in 1918 the U.S. government legally established the four time zones as the nation's official framework of time.

Economic Growth   Led by railroads, the U.S. economy expanded at a blistering pace between 1870 and 1900. Inventors designed new products and brought them to market: electric lights, telephones, typewriters, phonographs, film photography, motion picture cameras, and electric motors all made their appearance during this era. Strong consumer demand for those and other products fueled rapid industrial expansion and suggested to observers that the United States had found the road to continuous progress and prosperity.

Yet the march of U.S. industrialization did not go entirely unopposed: large-scale labor unions emerged alongside big business in the period from 1870 to 1900, and confrontations between business owners seeking profits and workers seeking higher wages or job security sometimes grew ugly. A nationwide, coordinated strike of rail workers in 1877 shut down two-thirds of the nation's railroads. Violence stemming from the strike took the lives of one hundred people and resulted in ten million dollars' worth of property damage. Nevertheless, big business prevailed in its disputes with workers during the nineteenth century, often with support from federal or state governments, and by the early twentieth century the United States had emerged as one of the world's major industrial powers.

Canadian Prosperity

British investment deeply influenced the development of the Canadian as well as the U.S. economy in the nineteenth and early twentieth centuries. Canadian leaders, like U.S. leaders, took advantage of British capital to industrialize without allowing their economy to fall under British control. During the early nineteenth century, Britain paid relatively high prices for Canadian agricultural products and minerals, partly to keep the colony stable and discourage the formation of separatist movements. As a result, white Canadians enjoyed a high standard of living even before industrialization.

After the establishment of the Dominion, politicians started a program of economic development known as the National Policy. The idea was to attract migrants, protect nascent industries through tariffs, and build national transportation systems. The centerpiece of the transportation network was the transcontinental Canadian Pacific Railroad, built largely with British investment capital and completed in 1885. The Canadian Pacific Railroad opened the western prairie lands to commerce, stimulated the development of other industries, and promoted the emergence of a Canadian national economy. The National Policy created some violent altercations with indigenous peoples who resisted encroachment on their lands and with trappers who resented disruption of their way of life, but it also promoted economic growth and independence. In Canada as in the United States, the ability to control and direct economic affairs was crucial to limiting the state's dependence on British capital.

The National Policy

As a result of the National Policy, Canada experienced booming agricultural, mineral, and industrial production in the late nineteenth and early twentieth centuries. Canadian population surged as a result of both migration and natural increase. Migrants flocked to Canada's shores from Asia and especially from Europe: between 1903 and 1914 some 2.7 million eastern European migrants settled in Canada. Fueled in part by this population growth, Canadian economic expansion took place on the foundation of rapidly increasing wheat production and the extraction of rich mineral resources, including gold, silver, copper, nickel, and asbestos. Industrialists also tapped Canadian rivers to produce the hydroelectric power necessary for manufacturing.

Canada remained wary of its powerful neighbor to the south but did not keep U.S. economic influence entirely at bay. British investment dwarfed U.S. investment throughout the nineteenth century: in 1914 British investment in Canada totaled $2.5 billion, compared with $700 million from the United States. Nevertheless, the U.S. presence in the Canadian economy grew. By 1918, Americans owned 30 percent of all Canadian industry, and thereafter the U.S. and Canadian economies became increasingly interdependent. Canada began to undergo rapid industrialization after the early twentieth century, as the province of Ontario benefited from the spillover of U.S. industry in the northeastern states.

U.S. Investment

Latin American Investments

Latin American states did not undergo industrialization or enjoy economic development like that of the United States and Canada. Colonial legacies help explain the different economic development in Latin American lands. Even when Spain and Portugal controlled the trade and investment policies of their American colonies, their home economies were unable to supply sufficient quantities of the manufactured goods that colonial markets demanded. As a result, they opened the colonies to European trade, which snuffed out local industries that could not compete with British, French, and German producers of inexpensive manufactured goods. Moreover, both in colonial times and after independence, Latin American elites—urban merchants and large landholders—retained control over local economies. Elites profited handsomely from European trade and investment and thus had little incentive to seek different economic policies or work toward economic diversification. Thus foreign investment and trade had more damaging effects in Latin America than in the United States or Canada.

British Investment

The relatively small size of Latin American markets limited foreign influence, which generally took the form of investment. British merchants had little desire to transform Latin American states into dependent trading partners for the simple reason that they offered no substantial market for British goods. Nevertheless, British investors took advantage of opportunities that brought them handsome profits and considerable control over Latin American economic affairs. In Argentina, for example, British investors encouraged the development of cattle and sheep ranching. After the 1860s and the invention of refrigerated cargo ships, meat became Argentina's largest export. British investors controlled the industry and reaped the profits, however, as Argentina became Britain's principal supplier of meat. Between 1880 and 1914, European migrants labored in the new export industries and contributed to the explosive growth of urban areas such as Buenos Aires: by 1914 the city's population exceeded 3.5 million. Although migrant laborers rarely shared in the profits controlled by elites, the domination of urban labor by European migrants represented yet another form of foreign influence in Latin American economic affairs.

Attempted Industrialization

In a few lands, ruling elites made attempts to encourage industrialization, but with only limited success. The most notable of those efforts came when the dictatorial general Porfirio Díaz ruled Mexico (1876–1911). Díaz represented the interests of large landowners, wealthy merchants, and foreign investors. Under his rule, railroad tracks and telegraph lines connected all parts of Mexico, and the production of mineral resources surged. A small steel industry produced railroad track and construction materials, and entrepreneurs also established glass, chemical, and textile industries. The capital, Mexico City, underwent a transformation during the Díaz years: it acquired paved streets, streetcar lines, and electric streetlights. But the profits from Mexican enterprises did not support continuing industrial development. Instead, they went into the pockets of the Mexican oligarchy and foreign investors who supported Díaz, while a growing and discontented urban working class seethed with resentment at low wages, long hours, and foreign managers. Even as agriculture, railroad construction, and mining were booming, the standard of living for average Mexicans had begun to decline by the early twentieth century. Frustration with that state of affairs helps explain the sudden outbreak of violent revolution in 1910.

Despite a large proportion of foreign and especially British control, Latin American economies expanded rapidly in the late nineteenth century. Exports drove that growth: copper and silver from Mexico, bananas and coffee from Central America, rubber and coffee from Brazil, beef and wheat from Argentina, copper from Chile, and tobacco and sugar from Cuba. Other areas in the world also developed many of those same products for export, however, and competition for markets often led to lower prices for those commodities. As in the United States and Canada, foreign investment in Latin America provided capital for development, but unlike the situation in the northern lands, control over industries and exports remained in foreign hands.

British and U.S. investors underwrote economic and industrial development in Latin America during the late nineteenth century, but most of the profits flowed outside the region. This copper mine in northwestern Mexico was built with U.S. investments.

Latin American economies were thus subject to decisions made in the interests of foreign investors, and unstable governments could do little in the face of strong foreign intervention. Controlled by the very elites who profited from foreign intervention at the expense of their citizens, Latin American governments helped account for the region's slower economic development, despite growth in industrial and export economies.

American Cultural and Social Diversity

In his "Song of Myself" (1855), a poetic celebration of himself as well as the vast diversity of his nation, U.S. poet Walt Whitman asked:

> Do I contradict myself?
> Very well then I contradict myself,
> (I am large, I contain multitudes.)

Much of the allure of the Americas derived from their vast spaces and diverse populations. The Americas were indeed large, and they contained multitudes. While diversity distinguished the Americas, it also provided abundant fuel for conflicts between ethnic groups, social classes, and those segregated into rigid castes based on race and gender. The social and cultural diversity of American societies challenged their ability to achieve cultural cohesion as well as political unity and democratically inclusive states. The lingering legacies of European conquest, slavery, migration, and patriarchy highlighted contradictions between the Enlightenment ideals of freedom and equality and the realities of life for native and African-American peoples as well as recent migrants and women. American societies experienced ample strife in the age of independence. In efforts to maintain their own position and preserve social stability, the dominant political forces in the Americas often repressed demands for recognition by dispossessed groups.

Multicultural Society in the United States

By the late nineteenth century, the United States had become a boisterous multicultural society—the most culturally diverse land of the western hemisphere—whose population included indigenous peoples, Euro-American settlers, African-American laborers, and growing numbers of migrants from Europe and Asia. Walt Whitman described the United States as "not merely a nation but a teeming nation of nations." Yet political and economic power rested almost exclusively with white male elites of European ancestry. The United States experienced tension and occasional conflict as members of various constituencies worked for dignity, prosperity, and a voice in society. During the nineteenth century, cultural and social tension swirled especially around indigenous peoples, African-American slaves and their descendants, women, and migrants.

Native Peoples   As they expanded to the west, Euro-American settlers and ranchers pushed indigenous peoples onto reservations. Although promising to respect those lands, the U.S. government permitted settlers and railroads to encroach on the reservations and force native peoples into increasingly cramped and marginal territories. Begrudging native Americans even these meager lands, the United States embarked in the latter half of

The Apache youths at the Carlisle Indian School offer stark faces to the camera, suggesting their discontent with reform efforts directed at assimilation through education.

the nineteenth century on a policy designed to reduce native autonomy even further through laws and reforms aimed at assimilating tribes to the white way of life. The U.S. government and private citizens acted to undermine or destroy outright the bases of native cultural traditions. Native tribes on the plains, for example, had developed material cultures largely centered on the hunting of bison, or buffalo, and the skillful exploitation of those animal resources. Beginning in 1850 but accelerating after the Civil War, white migrants, railroad employees, hunters, and "wild west" men such as Buffalo Bill Cody shot and killed hundreds of thousands of bison, effectively exterminating the buffalo and the economy of the plains Indians. Herds numbering at least 15 million had been reduced to a mere thousand by 1875.

Other U.S. actions also attempted to sever native Americans' ties to their communal traditions and cultural practices. The Dawes Severalty Act of 1887 shifted land policies away from collective tribal reservations and toward individual tracts of land meant to promote the family farms once common in white U.S. society and now becoming increasingly less competitive. Even more traumatically, government officials removed native children from their families and tribes and enrolled them in white-controlled boarding schools. These schools, such as the Carlisle Indian School and the Toledo Indian School, illustrated the extent to which white society sought to eliminate tribal influences and inculcate Christian,

A lithograph from *Harper's Weekly* after the Civil War. A black artisan, a middle-class African-American, and a black Union soldier are in the process of voting, perhaps for the first time in their lives.

U.S. values. Tribal languages as well as native dress and hair fashions were banned, further distancing the children from their cultures. Native Americans, however, resisted these forms of assimilation, often fleeing from boarding schools or refusing to agree to new governmental land policies. Native land control diminished as a result, but over the following decades tribes rebuilt and reaffirmed native identities.

The Civil War ended slavery, but it did not bring about instant equality for freed slaves and their African-American descendants. In an effort to establish a place for freed slaves in American society, northern forces sent armies of occupation to the southern states and forced them to undergo a program of social and political reconstruction (1867–1877). They extended civil rights to freed slaves and provided black men with voting rights. Black and white citizens in southern states elected biracial governments for the first time in U.S. history, and freed slaves participated actively in the political affairs of the republic.

Freed Slaves

After Reconstruction, however, the armies of occupation went back north, and a violent backlash soon dismantled the program's reforms. Freed slaves had not received land grants or any other means of economic support, so many had to work as sharecroppers for former slave owners. Under those circumstances it was relatively easy for white southerners to take away the political and civil liberties that former slaves had gained under Reconstruction. By the turn of the century, U.S. blacks faced violence and intimidation when they tried to vote. Southern states fashioned a rigidly segregated society that deprived the African-American population of educational, economic, and political opportunities. Although freedom was better than slavery, it was far different from the hopeful visions of the slaves who had won their emancipation.

Even before the Civil War, a small but growing women's movement had emerged in the United States. At the Seneca Falls Convention in 1848, feminists issued a "declaration of sentiments" modeled on the Declaration of Independence—"We hold

Women

these truths to be self-evident: that all men and women are created equal"—and they demanded equal political and economic rights for U.S. women:

> Now, in view of this entire disenfranchisement of one-half the people of this country, their social and religious degradation—in view of the unjust laws above mentioned, and because women do feel themselves aggrieved, oppressed, and fraudulently deprived of their most sacred rights, we insist that they have immediate admission to all the rights and privileges which belong to them as citizens of the United States.

Women fought for equal rights throughout the nineteenth century, and new opportunities for education and employment offered alternatives to marriage and domesticity. Women's colleges, reform activism, and professional industrial jobs allowed some women to pursue careers over marriage. Yet meaningful economic and political opportunities for women awaited the twentieth century.

Migrants

Between 1840 and 1914 some twenty-five million European migrants landed on American shores, and in the late nineteenth century most of them hailed from southern and eastern European countries. Migrants introduced new foods, music, dances, holidays, sports, and languages to U.S. society and contributed to the cultural diversity of the western hemisphere. Yet white, native-born citizens of the United States began to feel swamped by the arrival of so many migrants. Distaste for foreigners often resulted in hostility to the migrants who flooded into the expanding industrial cities. Migrants and their families tended to concentrate in certain districts, such as Little Italy and Chinatown—partly out of choice, since they preferred neighbors with familiar cultural traditions, but partly also because native-born citizens discouraged the migrants from moving into other neighborhoods. Concerns about growing numbers of migrants with different cultural and social traditions eventually led to the exclusion of new arrivals from Asian lands: the U.S. government ordered a complete halt to migration from China in 1882 and from Japan in 1907.

Canadian Cultural Contrasts

Ethnic Diversity

British and French settlers each viewed themselves as Canada's founding people. This cleavage, which profoundly influenced Canadian political development, masked much greater cultural and ethnic diversity in Canada. French and British settlers displaced the indigenous peoples, who remain a significant minority of Canada's population today. Slavery likewise left a mark on Canada. Slavery was legal in the British empire until 1833, and many early settlers brought their slaves to Canada. After the 1830s, escaped slaves from the United States also reached Canada by way of the Underground Railroad. Blacks in Canada were free but not equal, segregated and isolated from the political and cultural mainstream. Chinese migrants also came to Canada; lured by gold rushes such as the Fraser River rush of 1858 and by opportunities to work on the Canadian Pacific Railway in the 1880s, Chinese migrants lived mostly in segregated Chinatowns in the cities of British Columbia, and like blacks they had little voice in public affairs. In the late nineteenth and early twentieth centuries, waves of migrants brought even greater ethnic diversity to Canada. Between 1896 and 1914 three million migrants from Britain, the United States, and eastern Europe arrived in Canada.

Despite the heterogeneity of Canada's population, communities descended from British and French settlers dominated Canadian society, and conflict between the two communities was the most prominent source of ethnic tension throughout the nineteenth and twentieth centuries. After 1867, as British Canadians led the effort to settle the Northwest Territories and incorporate them into the Dominion, frictions between the two groups intensified. Westward expansion brought British Canadian settlers and cultivators into conflict with French Canadian fur traders and lumber-

Sources from the Past

The Meaning of Freedom for an Ex-Slave

Even before the conclusion of the Civil War brought slavery to an end in the United States, Jourdan Anderson had taken the opportunity to run away and claim his freedom. After the war his former master, Colonel P. H. Anderson, wrote a letter asking him to return to work on his Tennessee plantation. In responding from his new home in Dayton, Ohio, Anderson respectfully refers to the colonel as "my old master" and addresses him as "sir." Yet Anderson's letter makes it clear that his family's freedom and welfare were his principal concerns.

I want to know particularly what the good chance is you propose to give me. I am doing tolerably well here; I get $25 a month, with victuals and clothing; have a comfortable home for Mandy (the folks here call her Mrs. Anderson), and the children, Milly, Jane and Grundy, go to school and are learning well; the teacher says Grundy has a head for a preacher. They go to Sunday-School, and Mandy and me attend church regularly. We are kindly treated; sometimes we overhear others saying, "Them colored people were slaves" down in Tennessee. The children feel hurt when they hear such remarks, but I tell them it was no disgrace in Tennessee to belong to Col. Anderson. Many darkies would have been proud, as I used to was, to call you master. Now, if you will write and say what wages you will give me, I will be better able to decide whether it would be to my advantage to move back again.

As to my freedom, which you say I can have, there is nothing to be gained on that score, as I got my free-papers in 1864 from the Provost-Marshal-General of the Department at Nashville. Mandy says she would be afraid to go back without some proof that you are sincerely disposed to treat us justly and kindly—and we have concluded to test your sincerity by asking you to send us our wages for the time we served you. This will make us forget and forgive old scores, and rely on your justice and friendship in the future. I served you faithfully for thirty-two years and Mandy twenty years. At $25 a month for me, and $2 a week for Mandy, our earnings would amount to $11,680. Add to this the interest for the time our wages has been kept back and deduct what you paid

for our clothing and three doctor's visits to me, and pulling a tooth for Mandy, and the balance will show what we are in justice entitled to. Please send the money by Adams Express, in care of V. Winters, esq, Dayton, Ohio. If you fail to pay us for faithful labors in the past we can have little faith in your promises in the future. We trust the good Maker has opened your eyes to the wrongs which you and your fathers have done to me and my fathers, in making us toil for you for generations without recompense. Here I draw my wages every Saturday night, but in Tennessee there was never any pay day for the negroes any more than for the horses and cows. Surely there will be a day of reckoning for those who defraud the laborer of his hire.

In answering this letter please state if there would be any safety for my Milly and Jane, who are now grown up and both good-looking girls. You know how it was with poor Matilda and Catherine. I would rather stay here and starve and die if it comes to that than have my girls brought to shame by the violence and wickedness of their young masters. You will also please state if there has been any schools opened for the colored children in your neighborhood, the great desire of my life now is to give my children an education, and have them form virtuous habits.

FOR FURTHER REFLECTION

In what clever ways does Jourdan Anderson test the seriousness of his former owner's offer of employment, and what does his approach say about the meaning of black freedom?

SOURCE: Leon F. Litwack. *Been in the Storm So Long: The Aftermath of Slavery.* New York: Knopf, 1979, pp. 334–35.

jacks. The fur traders in particular often lived on the margins between European and indigenous societies. They frequently married or consorted with native women, giving rise to the métis, individuals of mixed European and indigenous ancestry.

A major outbreak of civil strife took place in the 1870s and 1880s. Native peoples and métis had moved west throughout the nineteenth century to preserve their land and trading rights, but the drive of British Canadians to the west threatened them.

The Métis and Louis Riel

This photograph from the late nineteenth century captures the busy street life in San Francisco's Chinatown. Migrants flocked to urban centers and created ethnic enclaves such as Chinatown for comfort and protection, transforming the urban landscapes of the Americas in the process.

Louis Riel (1844–1885) emerged as the leader of the métis and indigenous peoples of western Canada. A métis himself, Riel abandoned his studies for the priesthood in Montreal and returned to his home in the Red River Settlement (in the southern part of modern Manitoba). Sensitive to his community's concern that the Canadian government threatened local land rights, Riel assumed the presidency of a provisional government in 1870. He led his troops in capturing Fort Garry (modern Winnipeg) and negotiated the incorporation of the province of Manitoba into the Canadian Dominion. Canadian government officials and troops soon outlawed his government and forced Riel into years of exile, during which he wandered through the United States and Quebec, even suffering confinement in asylums.

Work on the Canadian Pacific Railroad in the 1880s renewed the threat of white settlement to indigenous and métis society. The métis asked Riel to lead resistance to the railroad and British Canadian settlement. In 1885 he organized a military force of métis and native peoples in the Saskatchewan river country and led an insurrection known as the Northwest Rebellion. Canadian forces quickly subdued the makeshift army, and government authorities executed Riel for treason.

Although the Northwest Rebellion never had a chance of success, the execution of Riel nonetheless reverberated throughout Canadian history. French Canadians took it as an indication of the state's readiness to subdue individuals who were culturally distinct and politically opposed to the drive for a nation dominated by British Canadian elites. In the very year when completion of the transcontinental railroad signified for some the beginnings of Canadian national unity, Riel's execution foreshadowed a long term of cultural conflict between Canadians of British, French, and indigenous ancestry.

Ethnicity, Identity, and Gender in Latin America

The heritage of Spanish and Portuguese colonialism and the legacy of slavery inclined Latin American societies toward the establishment of hierarchical distinctions based on ethnicity and color. At the top of society stood the creoles, individuals of European ancestry born in the Americas, while indigenous peoples, freed slaves, and their black descendants occupied the lowest rungs of the social ladder. In between were various groups of mixed ancestry, such as mestizos, mulattoes, zambos, and castizos. Although most Latin American states ended the legal recognition of these groups, the distinctions themselves persisted after independence and limited the opportunities available to peoples of indigenous, African, or mixed ancestry.

Migration and Cultural Diversity

Large-scale migration brought added cultural diversity to Latin America in the nineteenth century. Indentured laborers who went from Asian lands to Peru, Brazil, Cuba, and other Caribbean destinations carried with them many of their native cultural practices. When their numbers were relatively small, as in the case of Chinese migrants to Cuba, they mostly intermarried and assimilated into the working classes without leaving much foreign influence on the societies they joined. When they were relatively more numerous, however, as in the case of Indian migrants to Trinidad and Tobago, they formed distinctive communities in which they spoke their native languages, prepared foods from their homelands, and observed their inherited cultural and social traditions. Migration of European workers to Argentina brought a lively diversity to the capital of Buenos Aires, which was perhaps the most cosmopolitan city of nineteenth-century Latin America. With its broad avenues, smart boutiques, and handsome buildings graced with wrought iron, Buenos Aires enjoyed a reputation as "the Paris of the Americas."

Latin American intellectuals seeking cultural identity usually saw themselves either as heirs of Europe or as products of the American environment. One spokesperson who identified with Europe was the Argentine president Domingo Faustino Sarmiento (1811–1888). Sarmiento despised the rule of caudillos that had emerged after independence and worked for the development of the best society based on European values. In his widely read book *Facundo: Civilization and Barbarism* (1845), Sarmiento argued that it was necessary for Buenos Aires to bring discipline to the disorderly Argentine countryside. Deeply influenced by the Enlightenment, he characterized books, ideas, law, education, and art as products of cities, and he argued that only when cities dominated the countryside would social stability and genuine liberty be possible.

Gauchos

Sarmiento admired the bravery and independence of Argentina's gauchos (cowboys), but he considered it imperative that urban residents rather than ranchers make society's crucial decisions. Although the mystique of the gaucho did not extend throughout all of Latin America, observers did see gauchos as one symbol of Latin American identity. Most gauchos were mestizos or castizos, but there were also white and black gauchos. For all intents and purposes, anyone who adopted gaucho ways became a gaucho, and gaucho society acquired an ethnic egalitarianism rarely found elsewhere in Latin America. Gauchos were most prominent in the Argentine pampas, but their cultural practices linked them to the cowboys, or vaqueros, found throughout the Americas. As pastoralists herding cattle and horses on the pampas, gauchos stood apart from both the indigenous peoples and the growing urban and agricultural elites who gradually displaced them with large land holdings and cattle ranches that spread to the pampas.

The gauchos led independent and self-sufficient lives that appealed broadly in hierarchical Latin American society. Gauchos lived off their own skills and needed only their horses to survive. They dressed distinctively, with sashed trousers, ponchos, and boots. Countless songs and poems lauded their courage, skills, and lovemaking bravado. Yet independence and caudillo rule disrupted gaucho life as the cowboys increasingly entered armies, either voluntarily or under compulsion, and as settled agriculture and ranches surrounded by barbed wire enclosed the pampas. The gauchos did not leave the pampas without resistance. The poet José Hernandez offered a romanticized vision of the gaucho life and protested its decline in his epic poem *The Gaucho Martín Fierro* (1873). Hernandez conveyed the pride of gauchos, particularly those who resisted assimilation into Euro-American society, by having Martín Fierro proclaim his independence and assert his intention to stay that way:

I owe nothin' to nobody;
I don't ask for shelter, or give it;
and from now on, nobody
better try to lead me around by a rope.

Male Domination

Pedro Damian Alegre is an Argentinian gaucho, dressed traditionally and striking a solitary pose symbolic of gaucho individualism.

Nevertheless, by the late nineteenth century, gauchos were more echoes of the Latin American past than makers of a viable society.

Even more than in the United States and Canada, male domination was a central characteristic of Latin American society in the nineteenth century. Women could not vote or hold office, nor could they work or manage estates without permission from their male guardians. In rural areas, women were liable to rough treatment and assault by gauchos and other men steeped in the values of *machismo*—a social ethic that honored male strength, courage, aggressiveness, assertiveness, and cunning. A few women voiced their discontent with male domination and machismo. In her poem "To Be Born a Man" (1887), for example, the Bolivian poet Adela Zamudio lamented bitterly that talented women could not vote, but ignorant men could, just by learning how to sign their names. Although Latin American lands had not yet generated a strong women's movement, they did begin to expand educational opportunities for girls and young women after the mid-nineteenth century. In large cities most girls received some formal schooling, and women usually filled teaching positions in the public schools that proliferated throughout Latin America in the late nineteenth century.

Female Activism

Women did carve spaces for themselves outside or alongside the male world of machismo, and this was especially true in the home and in the marketplace, where Latin American women exerted great influence and control. In the early twentieth century, women served in conjunction with men in the Mexican revolution, most famously as Zapatistas, or followers of Emiliano Zapata. Many women supporting Zapata labored within the domestic realm to provide food for the soldiers, and others breached the domestic barrier to become soldiers and officers themselves. Although those women who became *soldaderas* (female soldiers or supporters of soldiers) demonstrated the most extreme forms of activism during the Mexican revolution, Mexican women on the whole made major contributions to the success of the revolution and shared in the radical spirit of change that characterized much of early-twentieth-century Latin America.

After gaining independence from European colonial powers, the states of the western hemisphere worked to build stable and prosperous societies. The independent American states faced difficult challenges—including vast territories, diverse populations, social tensions, and cultural differences—as they sought to construct viable societies on the Enlightenment principles of freedom, equality, and constitutional government. The United States and Canada built large federal societies in North America, whereas a series of smaller states governed affairs in Latin America. The United States in particular was an expansive society, absorbing Texas, California, and the northern territories of Mexico while extending its authority from the Atlantic to the Pacific Ocean. Throughout the hemisphere descendants of European settlers subdued indigenous American peoples and built societies dominated by Euro-American peoples. They established agricultural economies, exploited natural resources, and in some lands launched processes of industrialization. They accepted streams of European and Asian migrants, who contributed not only to American cultural diversity but also to the transformations in labor practices necessitated by the abolition of slavery and the rise of industry. All American lands experienced tensions arising from social, economic, cultural, and ethnic differences, which led occasionally to violent civil conflict and often to smoldering resentments and grievances. The making of independent American societies was not a smooth process, but it reflected the increasing interdependence of all the world's peoples.

CHRONOLOGY

1803	Louisiana Purchase
1804–1806	Lewis and Clark expedition
1812–1814	War of 1812
1829–1852	Rule of Juan Manuel de Rosas in Argentina
1838–1839	Trail of Tears
1846–1848	Mexican-American War
1848	Seneca Falls Convention
1849	California gold rush
1850s	La Reforma in Mexico
1861–1865	U.S. Civil War
1867	Establishment of the Dominion of Canada
1867	French troops withdraw from Mexico
1867–1877	Reconstruction in the United States
1869	Completion of the transcontinental railroad line in the United States
1876	Battle of Little Big Horn
1876–1911	Rule of Porfirio Díaz in Mexico
1885	Completion of the Canadian Pacific Railroad
1885	Northwest Rebellion
1890	Massacre at Wounded Knee
1910–1920	Mexican revolution

FOR FURTHER READING

Richard Buel Jr. *America on the Brink: How the Political Struggle over the War of 1812 Almost Destroyed the Young Republic.* New York, 2004. Scholarly examination of the conflicts between Federalists and Jeffersonians that culminated in the War of 1812.

Victor Bulmer-Thomas, John H. Coatsworth, and Robert Cortés Conde, eds. *The Cambridge Economic History of Latin America.* Vol. 1: *The Colonial Era and the Short Nineteenth Century.* Cambridge, 2006. Scholarly collection of essays that outlines the region's main economic trends and developments.

Colin G. Calloway. *First Peoples: A Documentary Survey of American Indian History.* Boston, 1999. A fine text on native American history, written by a knowledgeable scholar in the field.

Roderic Ai Camp. *Politics in Mexico: The Democratic Transformation.* 4th ed. New York, 2004. The best introduction to Mexican politics.

William Cronon. *Nature's Metropolis: Chicago and the Great West.* New York, 1991. A valuable study exploring the role of Chicago in the economic development of the American west.

Ellen C. DuBois. *Feminism and Suffrage: The Emergence of an Independent Women's Movement in America, 1848–1869.* Ithaca, 1984. Traces the rise and character of the U.S. women's movement in the nineteenth century.

David Barry Gaspar and Darlene Clark Hine, eds. *Beyond Bondage: Free Women of Color in the Americas.* Chicago, 2004. Collection of essays on free black women and their unique abilities to negotiate social and legal institutions in the era of slavery.

Tom Holm. *The Great Confusion in Indian Affairs: Native Americans and Whites in the Progressive Era.* Austin, 2005. Study of native American resistance to the American government's attempts at subjugation.

Joseph Kinsey Howard. *Strange Empire: A Narrative of the Northwest.* Westport, Conn., 1974. An in-depth and often moving account of Louis Riel, the métis, and their struggles with the Canadian government.

Alan Knight. *The Mexican Revolution.* Cambridge, 1986. An excellent analysis of the Mexican revolution.

Patricia Nelson Limerick. *The Legacy of Conquest: The Unbroken Past of the American West.* New York, 1987. A provocative work exploring the influences of race, class, and gender in the conquest of the American west.

Leon F. Litwack. *Been in the Storm So Long: The Aftermath of Slavery.* New York, 1979. The best study of the promises and perils of life for freed slaves after the U.S. Civil War.

James M. McPherson. *Battle Cry of Freedom: The Civil War Era.* New York, 1988. A balanced account of the Civil War by a renowned scholar.

J. R. Miller. *Skyscrapers Hide the Heavens: A History of Indian-White Relations in Canada.* Toronto, 1989. An important study of Canadian policies toward indigenous peoples.

Walter Nugent. *Crossings: The Great Transatlantic Migrations, 1870–1914.* Bloomington, 1992. Provides an overview and analysis of the mass migrations to North America in the nineteenth and twentieth centuries.

Marc Reisner. *Cadillac Desert: The American West and Its Disappearing Water.* Revised and updated ed. New York, 1993. An incisive analysis of water policies and politics from an engaging and environmentalist point of view.

Armstead L. Robinson. *Bitter Fruits of Bondage: The Demise of Slavery and the Collapse of the Confederacy, 1861–1865.* Charlottesville, Va., 2005. Controversial history of the Civil War arguing that class conflict impelled by slavery destroyed southern culture and ultimately caused the Confederacy's defeat.

Robert L. Scheina. *Latin American Wars.* Vol. 1: *The Age of the Caudillos, 1791–1899.* Washington, D.C., 2003. Definitive study of Latin American military history.

Ronald Takaki. *A Different Mirror: A History of Multicultural America.* Boston, 1993. A spirited account of the contributions made by peoples of European, African, Asian, and native American ancestry to the modern American society.

———. *Strangers from a Different Shore: A History of Asian Americans.* Boston, 1989. Fascinating survey of the experiences of Asian migrants who came to North America across the Pacific Ocean.

Richard White. *"It's Your Misfortune and None of My Own": A History of the American West.* Norman, Okla., 1991. Surveys the conquest, exploitation, and transformation of the American west.

Sean Wilentz. *The Rise of American Democracy: Jefferson to Lincoln.* New York, 2005. Dense political history of the birth and evolution of the democratic tradition in antebellum America by a prominent U.S. historian.

Ralph Lee Woodward. *Central America: A Nation Divided.* 3rd ed. New York, 1999. Simply the best survey available.

Donald Worster. *Rivers of Empire: Water, Aridity, and the Growth of the American West.* New York, 1985. Focuses on the role of irrigation in the establishment of a Euro-American agricultural society in the arid west.

Jean Fagan Yellin. *Harriet Jacobs: A Life.* New York, 2003. Scholarly biography of an important figure in the abolitionist movement.

32 Societies at Crossroads

The Ottoman Empire in Decline
The Nature of Decline
Reform and Reorganization
The Young Turk Era

The Russian Empire under Pressure
Military Defeat and Social Reform
Industrialization
Repression and Revolution

The Chinese Empire under Siege
The Opium War and the Unequal Treaties
The Taiping Rebellion
Reform Frustrated

The Transformation of Japan
From Tokugawa to Meiji
Meiji Reforms

Hong Xiuquan, the third son of a poor family, grew up in a farming village in southern China about 50 kilometers (31 miles) from Guangzhou. Although he was arrogant and irritable, he showed intellectual promise. His neighbors made him village teacher so that he could study and prepare for the civil service examinations, the principal avenue to government employment, since a position in the Qing bureaucracy would bring honor and wealth to both his family and his village. Between 1828 and 1837 Hong took the exams three times but failed to obtain even the lowest degree. This outcome was not surprising, since thousands of candidates competed for a degree, which only a few obtained. Yet the disappointment was too much for Hong. He suffered an emotional collapse, lapsed into a delirium that lasted about forty days, and experienced visions.

Upon recovering from his breakdown, Hong resumed his position as village teacher. After failing the civil service examinations a fourth time in 1843, he began studying the works of a Chinese missionary who explained the basic elements of Christianity. As he pondered the religious tracts, Hong came to believe that during his illness he had visited heaven and learned from God that he was the younger brother of Jesus Christ. He believed further that God had revealed to him that his destiny was to reform China and pave the way for the heavenly kingdom. Inspired by these convictions, Hong baptized himself and worked to build a community of disciples.

Hong's personal religious vision soon evolved into a political program: Hong believed that God had charged him with the establishment of a new order, one that necessitated the destruction of the Qing dynasty, which had ruled China since 1644. In 1847 he joined the Society of God Worshipers, a religious group recently founded by disgruntled peasants and miners. Hong soon emerged as the group's guiding force, and in the summer of 1850 he led about ten thousand followers in rebellion against the Qing dynasty. On his thirty-seventh birthday, 11 January 1851, he assumed the title of "Heavenly King" and proclaimed his own dynasty, the Taiping tianguo ("Heavenly Kingdom of Great Peace"). Hong's followers, known as the Taipings, quickly grew from a ragtag band to a disciplined and zealous army of over one million men and women who pushed the Qing dynasty to the brink of extinction.

China was not the only land that faced serious difficulties in the nineteenth century: the Ottoman empire, the Russian empire, and Tokugawa Japan experienced problems similar to those of China during the late Qing dynasty. One problem common to the four societies was military weakness that left them vulnerable to foreign threats. The Ottoman, Russian, Qing, and Tokugawa armies all fought wars or engaged in military confrontations with the industrial

Taiping (TEYE-pihng)

OPPOSITE: Japanese women wearing European-style clothes learn to play European musical instruments in the Meiji era.

lands of western Europe and the United States, and all discovered suddenly and unexpectedly that they were militarily much weaker than the industrial powers. European lands occasionally seized territories outright and either absorbed them into their own possessions or ruled them as colonies. More often, however, European and U.S. forces used their power to squeeze concessions out of militarily weak societies. They won rights for European and U.S. businesses to seek opportunities on favorable terms and enabled industrial capitalists to realize huge profits from trade and investment in militarily weak societies.

Another problem common to the four societies was internal weakness that was due to population pressure, declining agricultural productivity, famine, falling government revenue, and corruption at all levels of government. Ottoman, Russian, Chinese, and Japanese societies all experienced serious domestic turmoil, especially during the second half of the nineteenth century, as peasants mounted rebellions, dissidents struggled for reform, and political factions fought among themselves or conspired to organize coups. Military weakness often left leaders of the four societies unable to respond effectively to domestic strife, which sometimes provided western European powers and the United States with an excuse to intervene to protect their business interests.

Thus, by the late nineteenth century, the Ottoman empire, the Russian empire, Qing China, and Tokugawa Japan were societies at crossroads. Unless they undertook a program of thoroughgoing political, social, and economic reform, they would continue to experience domestic difficulties and would grow progressively weaker in relation to industrial lands. Reformers in all four societies promoted plans to introduce written constitutions, limit the authority of rulers, make governments responsive to the needs and desires of the people, guarantee equality before the law, restructure educational systems, and begin processes of industrialization. Many reformers had traveled in Europe and the United States, where they experienced constitutional government and industrial society firsthand, and they sought to remodel their own societies along the lines of the industrial lands.

Vigorous reform movements emerged in all four lands, but they had very different results. In the Ottoman empire, the Russian empire, and Qing China, ruling elites and wealthy classes viewed reform warily and opposed any changes that might threaten their status. Reform in those three lands was halting, tentative, and sometimes abortive, and by the early twentieth century, the Ottoman, Romanov, and Qing dynasties were on the verge of collapse. In Japan, however, the Tokugawa dynasty fell and so was unable to resist change. Reform there was much more thorough than in the other lands, and by the early twentieth century, Japan was an emerging industrial power poised to expand its influence in the larger world.

The Ottoman Empire in Decline

During the eighteenth century the Ottoman empire experienced military reverses and challenges to its rule. By the early nineteenth century, the Ottoman state could no longer ward off European economic penetration or prevent territorial dismemberment. As Ottoman officials launched reforms to regenerate imperial vigor, Egypt and other north African provinces declared their independence, and European states seized territories in the northern and western parts of the Ottoman empire. At the same time, pressure from ethnic, religious, and nationalist groups threatened to fragment the polyglot empire. The once-powerful realm slipped into decline, its sovereignty maintained largely by the same European powers that exploited its economy.

The Nature of Decline

By the late seventeenth century, the Ottoman empire had reached the limits of its expansion. Ottoman armies suffered humiliating defeats on the battlefield, especially at the hands of Austrian and Russian foes. Ottoman forces lagged behind European armies in strategy, tactics, weaponry, and training. Equally serious was a breakdown in the discipline of the elite Janissary corps, which had served as the backbone of the imperial armed forces since the fifteenth century. The Janissaries repeatedly masterminded palace coups during the seventeenth and eighteenth centuries and by the nineteenth century had become a powerful political force within the Ottoman state. The Janissaries neglected their military training and turned a blind eye to advances in weapons technology. As its military capacity declined, the Ottoman realm became vulnerable to its more powerful neighbors.

Military Decline

Loss of military power translated into declining effectiveness of the central government, which was losing power in the provinces to its own officials. By the early nineteenth century, semi-independent governors and local notables had formed private armies of mercenaries and slaves to support the sultan in Istanbul in return for recognition of autonomy. Increasingly these independent rulers also turned fiscal and administrative institutions to their own interests, collecting taxes for themselves and sending only nominal payments to the imperial treasury, thus depriving the central state of revenue.

The Ottoman government managed to maintain its authority in Anatolia, the heart of the empire, as well as in Iraq, but it suffered serious territorial losses elsewhere. Russian forces took over poorly defended territories in the Caucasus and in central Asia, and the Austrian empire nibbled away at the western frontiers. Nationalist uprisings forced Ottoman rulers to recognize the independence of Balkan provinces, notably Greece (1830) and Serbia (1867).

Territorial Losses

Most significant, however, was the loss of Egypt. In 1798 the ambitious French general Napoleon invaded Egypt in hopes of using it as a springboard for an attack on the British empire in India. His campaign was a miserable failure: Napoleon had to abandon his army and sneak back to France, where he proceeded to overthrow the Directory. But the invasion sparked turmoil in Egypt, as local elites battled to seize power after Napoleon's departure. The ultimate victor was the energetic general Muhammad Ali, who built a powerful army modeled on European forces and ruled Egypt from 1805 to 1848. He drafted peasants to serve as infantry, and he hired French and Italian officers to train his troops. He also launched a program of industrialization, concentrating on cotton textiles and armaments. Although he remained nominally subordinate to the Ottoman sultan, by 1820 he had established himself as the effective ruler of Egypt, which was the most powerful land in the Muslim world. He even invaded Syria and Anatolia, threatening to capture Istanbul and topple the Ottoman state. Indeed, the Ottoman dynasty survived only because British forces intervened out of fear that Ottoman collapse would result in a sudden and dangerous expansion of Russian influence. Nevertheless, Muhammad Ali made Egypt an essentially autonomous region within the Ottoman empire.

Economic ills aggravated the military and political problems of the Ottoman state. The volume of trade passing through the Ottoman empire declined throughout the later seventeenth and eighteenth centuries, as European merchants increasingly circumvented Ottoman intermediaries and traded directly with their counterparts in India and China. By the eighteenth century the focus of European trade had shifted to the Atlantic Ocean basin, where the Ottomans had no presence at all.

Map 32.1   **Territorial losses of the Ottoman empire, 1800–1923.** Compare the borders of the Ottoman empire in 1800 with what was left of the empire in 1914. What might have been the strategic value of the remaining Ottoman territories?

Economic Difficulties   Meanwhile, as European producers became more efficient in the eighteenth and nineteenth centuries, their textiles and manufactured goods began to flow into the Ottoman empire. Because those items were inexpensive and high-quality products, they placed considerable pressure on Ottoman artisans and crafts workers, who frequently led urban riots to protest foreign imports. Ottoman exports consisted largely of raw materials such as grain, cotton, hemp, indigo, and opium, but they did not offset the value of imported European manufactures. Gradually, the Ottoman empire moved toward fiscal insolvency and financial dependency. After the middle of the nineteenth century, economic development in the Ottoman empire depended heavily on foreign loans, as European capital financed the construction of railroads, utilities, and mining enterprises. Interest payments grew to the point that they consumed more than half of the empire's revenues. In 1882 the Ottoman state was unable to pay interest on its loans and had no choice but to accept foreign administration of its debts.

The Capitulations   Nothing symbolized foreign influence more than the capitulations, agreements that exempted European visitors from Ottoman law and provided European powers with extraterritoriality—the right to exercise jurisdiction over their own citizens according to their own laws. The practice dated back to the sixteenth century, when Ottoman sultans signed capitulation treaties to avoid the burden of administering justice for communities of foreign merchants. By the nineteenth century, however, Ottoman officials regarded the capitulations as humiliating intrusions on their sovereignty. Capitulations also served as instruments of economic penetration by European businesspeople who established tax-exempt banks and commercial enterprises in the Ottoman empire, and they permitted foreign governments to levy duties on goods sold in Ottoman ports.

By the early twentieth century, the Ottoman state lacked the resources to maintain its costly bureaucracy. Expenditures exceeded revenues, and the state experienced growing difficulty paying the salaries of its employees in the palace household, the military, and the religious hierarchy. Declining incomes led to reduced morale, recruitment difficulties, and a rise in corruption. Increased taxation designed to offset revenue losses only led to increased exploitation of the peasantry and a decline in agricultural production. The Ottoman empire was ailing, and it needed a major restructuring to survive.

Reform and Reorganization

In response to recurring and deepening crises, Ottoman leaders launched a series of reforms designed to strengthen and preserve the state. Reform efforts began as early as the seventeenth century, when sultans sought to limit taxation, increase agricultural production, and end official corruption. Reform continued in the eighteenth century, as Sultan Selim III (reigned 1789–1807) embarked on a program to remodel his army along the lines of European forces. But the establishment of a new crack fighting force, trained by European instructors and equipped with modern weapons, threatened the elite Janissary corps, which reacted violently by rising in revolt, killing the new troops, and locking up the sultan. When Selim's successor tried to revive the new military force, rampaging Janissaries killed all male members of the dynasty save one, Selim's cousin Mahmud II, who became sultan (reigned 1808–1839).

The encroachment of European powers and the separatist ambitions of local rulers persuaded Mahmud to launch his own reform program. Politically savvy, Mahmud ensured that his reforms were perceived not as dangerous infidel innovations but, rather, as a restoration of the traditional Ottoman military. Nevertheless, his proposal for a new European-style army in 1826 brought him into conflict with the Janissaries. When the Janissaries mutinied in protest, Mahmud had them massacred by troops loyal to the sultan. That incident cleared the way for a series of reforms that unfolded during the last thirteen years of Mahmud's reign.

The Reforms of Mahmud II

Mahmud's program remodeled Ottoman institutions along western European lines. Highest priority went to the creation of a more effective army. European drill masters dressed Ottoman soldiers in European-style uniforms and instructed them in European weapons and tactics. Before long, Ottoman recruits were studying at military and engineering schools that taught European curricula. Mahmud's reforms went beyond military affairs. His government created a system of secondary education for boys to facilitate the transition from mosque schools, which provided most primary education, to newly established scientific, technical, and military academies. Mahmud also tried to transfer power from traditional elites to the sultan and his cabinet by taxing rural landlords, abolishing the system of military land grants, and undermining the ulama, the Islamic leadership. To make his authority more effective, the sultan established European-style ministries, constructed new roads, built telegraph lines, and inaugurated a postal service. By the time of Mahmud's death in 1839, the Ottoman empire had shrunk in size, but it was also more manageable and powerful than it had been since the early seventeenth century.

Continuing defeats on the battlefield and the rise of separatist movements among subject peoples prompted the ruling classes to undertake more radical restructuring of the Ottoman state. The tempo of reform increased rapidly during the Tanzimat ("reorganization") era (1839–1876). Once again, the army was a principal target of reform efforts, but legal and educational reforms also had wide-ranging implications for Ottoman society. In designing their program, Tanzimat reformers drew considerable

Legal and Educational Reform

Sultan Abdül Hamid II ruled the Ottoman empire from 1876 to 1909, when the Young Turks deposed him and sent him into exile.

inspiration from Enlightenment thought and the constitutional foundations of western European states.

Tanzimat reformers attacked Ottoman law with the aim of making it acceptable to Europeans so they could have the capitulations lifted and recover Ottoman sovereignty. Using the French legal system as a guide, reformers promulgated a commercial code (1850), a penal code (1858), a maritime code (1863), and a new civil code (1870–1876). Tanzimat reformers also issued decrees designed to safeguard the rights of subjects. Key among them were measures that guaranteed public trials, rights of privacy, and equality before the law for all Ottoman subjects, whether Muslim or not. Matters pertaining to marriage and divorce still fell under religious law. But because state courts administered the new laws, legal reform undermined the ulama and enhanced the authority of the Ottoman state. Educational reforms also undermined the ulama, who controlled religious education for Muslims. A comprehensive plan for educational reform, introduced in 1846, provided for a complete system of primary and secondary schools leading to university-level instruction, all under the supervision of the state ministry of education. A still more ambitious plan, inaugurated in 1869, provided for free and compulsory primary education.

Opposition to the Tanzimat

Although reform and reorganization strengthened Ottoman society, the Tanzimat provoked spirited opposition from several distinct quarters. Harsh criticism came from religious conservatives, who argued that reformers posed a threat to the empire's Islamic foundation. Many devout Muslims viewed the extension of legal equality to Jews and Christians as an act contrary to the basic principles of Islamic law. Even some minority leaders opposed legal equality, fearing that it would diminish their own position as intermediaries between their communities and the Ottoman state. Criticism arose also from a group known collectively as the Young Ottomans. Although they did not share a common political or religious program—their views ranged from secular revolution to uncompromising Islam—Young Ottomans agitated for individual freedom, local autonomy, and political decentralization. Many Young Ottomans desired the establishment of a constitutional government along the lines of the British system. A fourth and perhaps the most dangerous critique of Tanzimat emerged from within the Ottoman bureaucracy itself. In part because of their exclusion from power, high-level bureaucrats were determined to impose checks on the sultan's power by forcing him to accept a constitution and, if necessary, even to depose the ruler.

The Young Turk Era

In 1876 a group of radical dissidents from the Ottoman bureaucracy seized power in a coup, formed a cabinet that included partisans of reform, and installed Abdül Hamid II as sultan (reigned 1876–1909). Convinced of the need to check the sultan's power, reformers persuaded Abdül Hamid to accept a constitution that limited his authority and established a representative government. Within a year, however, the sultan suspended the constitution, dissolved parliament, exiled many liberals, and executed others. For thirty years he ruled autocratically in an effort to rescue the empire from dismemberment by European powers. He continued to develop the army and administration according to Tanzimat principles, and he oversaw the formation of a police force, educational reforms, economic development, and the construction of railroads.

Reform and Repression

Abdül Hamid's despotic rule generated many liberal opposition groups. Though intended to strengthen the state, reform and reorganization actually undermined the position of the sultan. As Ottoman bureaucrats and army officers received an education in European curricula, they not only learned modern science and technology but also became acquainted with European political, social, and cultural traditions. Many of them fell out of favor with Abdül Hamid and spent years in exile, where they experienced European society firsthand. Educated subjects came to believe that the biggest problem of the Ottoman empire was the political structure that vested unchecked power in the sultan. For these dissidents, Ottoman society was in dire need of political reform and especially of a written constitution that defined and limited the sultan's power.

The most active dissident organization was the Ottoman Society for Union and Progress, better known as the Young Turk Party, although many of its members were neither young nor Turkish. Founded in 1889 by exiled Ottoman subjects living in Paris, the Young Turk Party vigorously promoted reform, and its members made effective use of recently established newspapers to spread their message. Young Turks called for universal suffrage, equality before the law, freedom of religion, free public education, secularization of the state, and the emancipation of women. In 1908 the Young Turks inspired an army coup that forced Abdül Hamid to restore parliament and the constitution of 1876. In 1909 they dethroned him and established Mehmed V Rashid (reigned 1909–1918) as a puppet sultan. Throughout the Young Turk era (1908–1918), Ottoman sultans reigned but no longer ruled.

The Young Turks

While pursuing reform within Ottoman society, the Young Turks sought to maintain Turkish hegemony in the larger empire. They worked to make Turkish the official language of the empire, even though many subjects spoke Arabic or a Slavic language as their native tongue. Thus Young Turk policies aggravated tensions between Turkish rulers and subject peoples outside the Anatolian heartland of the Ottoman empire. Syria and Iraq were especially active regions of Arab resistance to Ottoman rule. In spite of their efforts to shore up the ailing empire, reformers could not turn the tide of decline: Ottoman armies continued to lose wars, and subject peoples continued to seek autonomy or independence. By the early twentieth century, the Ottoman empire survived principally because European diplomats could not agree on how to dispose of the empire without upsetting the European balance of power.

Young Turks celebrate the success of their coup, which forced the sultan to establish a constitutional government in 1908.

Sources from the Past

Proclamation of the Young Turks

Beginning in the 1890s the Ottoman Society for Union and Progress, better known as the Young Turk Party, started agitating for the resignation of the Ottoman sultan Abdül Hamid and the restoration of the constitution of 1876. After years of underground activity, the Young Turks forced the sultan to reestablish a parliamentary government and reinstate the constitution in 1908. Shortly thereafter the Young Turks outlined their plans for a new Turkish state.

1. The basis for the Constitution will be respect for the predominance of the national will. One of the consequences of this principle will be to require without delay the responsibility of the minister before the Chamber, and, consequently, to consider the minister as having resigned, when he does not have a majority of the votes of the Chamber.

2. Provided that the number of senators does not exceed one third the number of deputies, the Senate will be named (which is not provided for in article 62 of the Constitution) as follows: one third by the Sultan and two thirds by the nation, and the term of senators will be of limited duration.

3. It will be demanded that all Ottoman subjects having completed their twentieth year, regardless of whether they possess property or fortune, shall have the right to vote. Those who have lost their civil rights will naturally be deprived of this right.

4. It will be demanded that the right freely to constitute political groups be inserted in a precise fashion in the constitutional charter, in order that article 1 of the Constitution of 1293 (1876) be respected. . . .

7. The Turkish tongue will remain the official state language. Official correspondence and discussion will take place in Turk. . . .

9. Every citizen will enjoy complete liberty and equality, regardless of nationality or religion, and be submitted to the same obligations. All Ottomans, being equal before the law as regards rights and duties relative to the State, are eligible for government posts, according to their individual capacity and their education. Non-Muslims will be equally liable to the military law.

10. The free exercise of the religious privileges which have been accorded to different nationalities will remain intact. . . .

14. Provided that the property rights of landholders are not infringed upon (for such rights must be respected and must remain intact, according to the law), it will be proposed that peasants be permitted to acquire land, and they will be accorded means to borrow money at a moderate rate. . . .

16. Education will be free. Every Ottoman citizen, within the limits of the prescriptions of the Constitution, may operate a private school in accordance with the special laws.

17. All schools will operate under the surveillance of the state. In order to obtain for Ottoman citizens an education of a homogeneous and uniform character, the official schools will be open, their instruction will be free, and all nationalities will be admitted. Instruction in Turk will be obligatory in public schools. In official schools, public instruction will be free.

Secondary and higher education will be given in the public and official schools indicated above; it will use the Turkish tongue as a basis. . . . Schools of commerce, agriculture and industry will be opened with the goal of developing the resources of the country.

FOR FURTHER REFLECTION

How do the plans of the Young Turks privilege their own age cohort within the Ottoman empire, particularly in regard to voting rights and education?

SOURCE: Rondo Cameron, ed. *Civilization since Waterloo: A Book of Source Readings.* Itasca, Ill.: F. E. Peacock, 1971, pp. 245–46.

The Russian Empire under Pressure

Like the Ottoman empire, the Russian empire experienced battlefield reverses that laid bare the economic and technological disparity between Russia and western European powers. Determined to preserve Russia's status as a great land power, the tsarist

Map 32.2 **The Russian empire, 1801–1914.** Note the sheer size of Russian territory in this period, and that the state included part of Europe, central Asia, and east Asia. How would straddling so much space and so many cultures have affected the process of industrialization and nationalism in Russia?

government embarked on a program of reform. The keystone of those efforts was the emancipation of the serfs. Social reform paved the way for government-sponsored industrialization, which began to transform Russian society during the last decades of the nineteenth century. Political liberalization did not accompany social and economic reform, because the tsars refused to yield their autocratic powers. The oppressive political environment sparked opposition movements that turned increasingly radical in the late nineteenth century. In the early twentieth century, domestic discontent reached crisis proportions and exploded in revolution.

Military Defeat and Social Reform

The nineteenth-century tsars ruled a multiethnic, multilingual, multicultural empire that stretched from Poland to the Pacific Ocean. Only about half the population spoke the Russian language or observed the Russian Orthodox faith. The Romanov tsars ruled their diverse and sprawling realm through an autocratic regime in which all initiative came from the central administration. The tsars enjoyed the support of the Russian Orthodox church and a powerful class of nobles who owned most of the land and were exempt from taxes and military duty. Peasants made up the vast majority of the population, and most of them were serfs bound to the lands that they cultivated.

The Crimean War

Serfdom was almost as cruel and exploitative as slavery, but most landowners, including the state, considered it a guarantee of social stability.

A respected and feared military power, Russia maintained its tradition of conquest and expansion. During the nineteenth century the Russian empire expanded in three directions: east into Manchuria, south into the Caucasus and central Asia, and southwest toward the Mediterranean. This last thrust led to interference in the Balkan provinces of the Ottoman empire. After defeating Turkish forces in a war from 1828 to 1829, Russia tried to establish a protectorate over the weakening Ottoman empire. This expansive effort threatened to upset the balance of power in Europe, which led to military conflict between Russia and a coalition including Britain, France, the Kingdom of Sardinia, and the Ottoman empire. The Crimean War (1853–1856) clearly revealed the weakness of the Russian empire, which could hold its own against Ottoman and Qing forces, but not against the industrial powers of western Europe. In September 1854, allied forces mounted a campaign against Sevastopol in the Crimean peninsula, headquarters of Russia's Black Sea Fleet. Unable to mobilize, equip, and transport troops to defeat European forces that operated under a mediocre command, Russian armies suffered devastating and humiliating defeats on their own territory. Russia's economy could not support the tsars' expansionist ambitions, and the Crimean War clearly demonstrated the weakness of an agrarian economy based on unfree labor. Military defeat compelled the tsarist autocracy to reevaluate the Russian social order and undertake an extensive restructuring program.

Emancipation of the Serfs

The key to social reform in Russia was emancipation of the serfs. Opposition to serfdom had grown steadily since the eighteenth century, not only among radicals, but also among high officials. Although some Russians objected to serfdom on moral grounds, many believed that it had become an obstacle to economic development and a viable state. Besides being economically inefficient, serfdom was a source of rural instability and peasant revolt: hundreds of insurrections broke out during the first four decades of the nineteenth century. As Tsar Alexander II (reigned 1855–1881) succinctly suggested to the nobility of Moscow, "It is better to abolish serfdom from above than to wait until the serfs begin to liberate themselves from below." Accordingly, in 1861 the tsar abolished the institution of serfdom, though it remained in practice for decades to come.

The government sought to balance the interests of lords and serfs, but on balance the terms of emancipation were unfavorable to most peasants. The government compensated landowners for the loss of their land and the serfs who had worked it. Serfs won their freedom, had their labor obligations gradually canceled, and gained opportunities to become landowners. But the peasants won few political rights, and they had to pay a redemption tax for most of the lands they received. Many disappointed peasants believed that their rulers forced them to pay for land that was theirs by right. A few peasants prospered and improved their position as the result of emancipation, but most found themselves in debt for the rest of their lives—a source of alienation and radicalization. Emancipation resulted in little if any increase in agricultural production.

Political and Legal Reform

Other important reforms came in the wake of the serfs' emancipation. To deal with local issues of health, education, and welfare, the government created elected district assemblies, or *zemstvos*, in 1864. Although all classes, including peasants, elected representatives to these assemblies, the *zemstvos* remained subordinate to the tsarist autocracy, which retained exclusive authority over national issues, and the landowning nobility, which possessed a disproportionately large share of both votes and seats. Legal reform was more fruitful than experimentation with representative government. The revision of the judiciary system in 1864 created a system of law courts based on western European models, replete with independent judges and a system of appellate courts. Legal reforms also instituted trial by jury for criminal offenses and elected justices of the peace who dealt with minor offenses. These reforms encouraged the emergence of attorneys and other legal experts, whose professional standards contributed to a decline in judicial corruption.

Industrialization

Social and political reform coincided with industrialization in nineteenth-century Russia. Tsar Alexander II emancipated the serfs partly with the intention of creating a mobile labor force for emerging industries, and the tsarist government encouraged industrialization as a way of strengthening the Russian empire. Thus, although Russian industrialization took place within a framework of capitalism, it differed from western European industrialization in that the motivation for development was political and military and the driving force was government policy rather than entrepreneurial initiative. Industrialization proceeded slowly at first, but it surged during the last two decades of the nineteenth century.

Tsar Alexander II of Russia. After signing the Treaty of Paris in 1856, ending the Crimean War, Alexander abolished serfdom in the Russian empire.

The prime mover behind Russian industrialization was Count Sergei Witte, minister of finance from 1892 to 1903. His first budget, submitted to the government in 1893, outlined his aims as "removing the unfavorable conditions which hamper the economic development of the country" and "kindling a healthy spirit of enterprise." Availing himself of the full power of the state, Witte implemented policies designed to stimulate economic development. The centerpiece of his industrial policy was an ambitious program of railway construction, which linked the far-flung regions of the Russian empire and also stimulated the development of other industries. Most important of the new lines was the trans-Siberian railway, which opened Siberia to large-scale settlement, exploitation, and industrialization. To raise domestic capital for industry, Witte remodeled the state bank and encouraged the establishment of savings banks. Witte supported infant industries with high protective tariffs while also securing large foreign loans from western Europe to finance industrialization. His plan worked. French and Belgian capital played a key role in developing the steel and coal industries, and British funds supported the booming petroleum industry in the Caucasus.

The Witte System

For a decade the Witte system played a crucial role in the industrialization of Russia, but peasant rebellions and strikes by industrial workers indicated that large segments of the population were unwilling to tolerate the low standard of living that Witte's policy entailed. Recently freed serfs often did not appreciate factory work, which forced them to follow new routines and adapt to the rhythms of industrial machinery. Industrial growth began to generate an urban working class, which endured conditions similar to those experienced by workers in other societies during the early stages of industrialization. Employers kept wages of overworked and poorly housed workers at the barest minimum. The industrial sections of St. Petersburg and Moscow became notorious for the miserable working and living conditions of factory laborers. In 1897 the government limited the maximum working day to 11.5 hours, but that measure did little to alleviate the plight of workers. The government prohibited the formation of trade unions and outlawed strikes, which continued to occur in spite of the restrictions. Economic exploitation and the lack of political freedom made workers

Industrial Discontent

Russian merchants in nineteenth-century Novgorod wear both western European and traditional Russian dress while taking tea.

increasingly receptive to revolutionary propaganda, and underground movements soon developed among them.

Not everyone was dissatisfied with the results of intensified industrialization. Besides foreign investors, a growing Russian business class benefited from government policy that protected domestic industries and its profits. Russian entrepreneurs reaped rich rewards for their roles in economic development, and they had little complaint with the political system. In contrast to western European capitalists, who had both material and ideological reasons to challenge the power of absolute monarchs and the nobility, Russian businesspeople generally did not challenge the tsarist autocracy.

Repression and Revolution

Protest

During the last three decades of the nineteenth century, antigovernment protest and revolutionary activity increased. Hopes aroused by government reforms gave impetus to reform movements, and social tensions arising from industrialization fueled protest by groups whose aims became increasingly radical. Peasants seethed with discontent because they had little or no land and, increasingly, mobile dissidents spread rebellious ideas between industrial cities. At the center of opposition were university students and a class of intellectuals collectively known as the intelligentsia. Their goals and methods varied, but they generally sought substantial political reform and thorough social change. Most dissidents drew inspiration from western European socialism, but they despised the individualism, materialism, and unbridled capitalism of western Europe and thus worked toward a socialist system more in keeping with Russian cultural traditions. Many revolutionaries were anarchists, who on principle opposed all forms of government and believed that individual freedom cannot be realized until all government is abolished. Some anarchists relied on terror tactics and assassination to achieve their goals. Insofar as they had a positive political program, the anarchists wanted to vest all authority in local governing councils elected by universal suffrage.

Repression

Some activists saw the main potential for revolutionary action in the countryside, and between 1873 and 1876 hundreds of anarchists and other radicals traveled to rural areas to enlighten and rouse the peasantry. The peasants did not understand their impassioned speeches, but the police did and soon arrested the idealists. Tsarist authorities sentenced some to prison and banished others to the remote provinces of Siberia. Frightened by manifestations of radicalism, tsarist authorities resorted to repression: they censored publications and sent secret police to infiltrate and break up dissident organizations. Repression, however, only radicalized revolutionaries further and encouraged them to engage in conspiratorial activities.

In the Baltic provinces, Poland, the Ukraine, Georgia, and central Asia, dissidents opposed the tsarist autocracy on ethnic as well as political and social grounds. In those lands, subject peoples speaking their own languages often used schools and political groups as foundations for separatist movements as they sought autonomy or independence from the Russian empire. Tsarist officials responded with a heavy-handed program of Russification to repress the use of languages other than Russian and to restrict educational opportunities to those loyal to the tsarist state. Throughout the Russian empire, Jews also were targets of suspicion, and tsarist authorities tolerated frequent pogroms (anti-Jewish riots) by subjects jealous of their Jewish neighbors' success in business affairs. To escape this violence, Jews migrated by the hundreds of thousands to western Europe and the United States in the late nineteenth century.

Japanese infantry charging during the Russo-Japanese war.

Terrorism

In 1876 a recently formed group called the Land and Freedom Party began to promote the assassination of prominent officials as a means to pressure the government into political reform. In 1879 a terrorist faction of the party, the People's Will, resolved to assassinate Alexander II, who had emancipated the serfs and had launched a program of political and social reform. After several unsuccessful attempts, an assassin exploded a bomb under Alexander's carriage in 1881. The first blast did little damage, but as Alexander inspected his carriage, a second and more powerful explosion killed the reforming tsar. The attack brought the era of reform to an end and prompted the tsarist autocracy to adopt an uncompromising policy of repression.

In 1894 Nicholas II (reigned 1894–1917) ascended the throne. A well-intentioned but weak ruler, Nicholas championed oppression and police control. To deflect attention from domestic issues and neutralize revolutionary movements, the tsar's government embarked on expansionist ventures in east Asia. Russian designs on Korea and Manchuria clashed with similar Japanese intentions, leading to a rivalry that ended in war. The Russo-Japanese war began with a Japanese surprise attack on the Russian naval squadron at Port Arthur in February 1904 and ended in May 1905 with the destruction of the Russian navy.

The Revolution of 1905

Russian military defeats brought to a head simmering political and social discontent and triggered widespread disturbances. In January 1905 a group of workers marched on the tsar's Winter Palace in St. Petersburg to petition Nicholas for a popularly elected assembly and other political concessions. Government troops met the petitioners with rifle fire, killing 130. The news of this Bloody Sunday massacre caused an angry uproar throughout the empire that culminated in labor unrest, peasant insurrections, student demonstrations, and mutinies in both the army and the navy. Organizing themselves at the village level, peasants discussed seizing the property of their landlords. Urban workers created new councils known as soviets to organize strikes and negotiate with employers and government authorities. Elected delegates from factories and workshops served as members of these soviets.

Revolutionary turmoil paralyzed Russian cities and forced the government to make concessions. Sergei Witte, whom Nicholas had appointed to conduct peace negotiations with Japan, urged the tsar to create an elected legislative assembly. The tsar reluctantly consented and permitted the establishment of the Duma, Russia's first parliamentary institution. Although the Duma lacked the power to create or bring down governments, from the Romanov perspective this act was a major concession. Still, the creation of the Duma did not end unrest. Between 1905 and 1907 disorder continued, and violence flared especially in the Baltic provinces, Poland, the Ukraine, Georgia, and central Asia, where ethnic tensions added to revolutionary sentiments. Through bloody reprisals the government eventually restored order, but the hour was late for the Romanov dynasty.

The Chinese Empire under Siege

The Chinese empire and the Qing dynasty experienced even more difficulties than did the Ottoman and Russian empires during the nineteenth century. European powers inflicted military defeats on Qing forces and compelled China's leaders to accept a series of humiliating treaties. The provisions of these treaties undermined Chinese sovereignty, carved China into spheres of influence that set the stage for economic exploitation, and handicapped the Qing dynasty's ability to deal with domestic disorder. As the government tried to cope with foreign challenges, it also faced dangerous internal upheavals, the most important of which was the Taiping rebellion. Caught between aggressive foreigners and insurgent rebels, China's ruling elites developed reform programs to maintain social order, strengthen the state, and preserve the Qing dynasty. The reforms had limited effect, however, and by the early twentieth century, China was in a seriously weakened condition.

The Opium War and the Unequal Treaties

In 1759 the Qianlong emperor restricted the European commercial presence in China to the waterfront at Guangzhou, where European merchants could establish warehouses. There Chinese authorities controlled not only European merchants but also the terms of trade. Foreign merchants could deal only with specially licensed Chinese firms known as *cohongs*, which bought and sold goods at set prices and operated under strict regulations established by the government. Besides the expense and inconvenience of the *cohong* system, European merchants had to cope with a market that had little demand for European products. As a result, European merchants paid for Chinese silk, porcelain, lacquerware, and tea largely with silver bullion.

The Opium Trade   Seeking increased profits in the late eighteenth century, officials of the British East India Company sought alternatives to bullion to exchange for Chinese goods. They gradually turned to trade in a product that was as profitable as it was criminal—opium. Using Turkish and Persian expertise, the East India Company grew opium in India and shipped it to China, where company officials exchanged it for Chinese silver coin. The silver then flowed back to British-controlled Calcutta and London, where company merchants used it to buy Chinese products in Guangzhou. The opium trade ex-

Chinese opium smokers. Chinese efforts to stop opium imports led to a humiliating defeat in the Opium War.

panded rapidly: annual imports of opium in the early nineteenth century amounted to about 4,500 chests, each weighing 60 kilograms (133 pounds), but by 1839 some 40,000 chests of opium entered China annually to satisfy the habits of drug addicts. With the help of this new commodity, the East India Company easily paid for luxury Chinese products.

Trade in opium was illegal, but it continued unabated for decades because Chinese authorities made little effort to enforce the law. Indeed, corrupt officials often benefited personally by allowing the illegal trade to go on. By the late 1830s, however, government officials had become aware that China had a trade problem and a drug problem as well. The opium trade not only drained large quantities of silver bullion from China but also created serious social problems in southern China. When government authorities took steps in 1838 to halt the illicit trade, British merchants started losing money. In 1839 the Chinese government stepped up its campaign by charging the incorruptible Lin Zexu with the task of destroying the opium trade. Commissioner Lin acted quickly, confiscating and destroying some 20,000 chests of opium. His uncompromising policy ignited a war that ended in a humiliating defeat for China.

Outraged by the Chinese action against opium, British commercial agents pressed their government into a military retaliation designed to reopen the opium trade. The ensuing conflict, known as the Opium War (1839–1842), made plain the military power differential between Europe and China. In the initial stages of the conflict, British naval vessels easily demonstrated their superiority on the seas. Meanwhile, equipped only with swords, knives, spears, and occasionally muskets, the defenders of Chinese coastal towns were no match for the controlled firepower of well-drilled British infantry armed with rifles. But neither the destruction of Chinese war fleets nor the capture of coastal forts and towns persuaded the Chinese to sue for peace.

The Opium War

Sources from the Past

Letter of Lin Zexu to Queen Victoria

In 1838 Qing emperor Daoguang sent Lin Zexu to Guangzhou to put an end to imports of opium into China. A leading Confucian scholar, Lin worked to persuade Chinese and foreigners alike that opium was a harmful and evil drug. In 1839 he composed a letter to Great Britain's Queen Victoria seeking her support in halting the flow of opium. Although never delivered, the letter illustrates Lin's efforts to stem the flow of opium by reason and negotiation before he resorted to sterner measures.

You have traded in China for almost 200 years, and as a result, your country has become wealthy and prosperous.

As this trade has lasted for a long time, there are bound to be unscrupulous as well as honest traders. Among the unscrupulous are those who bring opium to China to harm the Chinese; they succeed so well that this poison has spread far and wide in all the provinces. You, I hope, will certainly agree that people who pursue material gains to the great detriment of the welfare of others can be neither tolerated by Heaven nor endured by men. . . .

I have heard that the areas under your direct jurisdiction such as London, Scotland, and Ireland do not produce opium; it is produced instead in your Indian possessions such as Bengal, Madras, Bombay, Patna, and Malwa. In these possessions the English people not only plant opium poppies that stretch from one mountain to another but also open factories to manufacture this terrible drug. As months accumulate and years pass by, the poison they have produced increases in its wicked intensity, and its repugnant odor reaches as high as the sky. Heaven is furious with anger, and all the gods are moaning with pain! It is hereby suggested that you destroy and plow under all of these opium plants and grow food crops instead, while issuing an order to punish severely anyone who dares to plant opium poppies again. If you adopt this policy of love so as to produce good and exterminate evil, Heaven will protect you, and gods will bring you good fortune. Moreover, you will enjoy a long life and be rewarded with a multitude of children and grandchildren! . . .

The present law calls for the imposition of the death sentence on any Chinese who has peddled or smoked opium. Since a Chinese could not peddle or smoke opium if foreigners had not brought it to China, it is clear that the true culprits of a Chinese's death as a result of an opium conviction are the opium traders from foreign countries. Being the cause of other people's death, why should they themselves be spared from capital punishment? A murderer of one person is subject to the death sentence; just imagine how many people opium has killed! This is the rationale behind the new law which says that any foreigner who brings opium to China will be sentenced to death by hanging or beheading. Our purpose is to eliminate this poison once and for all and to the benefit of all mankind. . . .

Our Celestial Empire towers over all other countries in virtue and possesses a power great and awesome enough to carry out its wishes. But we will not prosecute a person without warning him in advance; that is why we have made our law explicit and clear. If the merchants of your honorable country wish to enjoy trade with us on a permanent basis, they must fearfully observe our law by cutting off, once and for all, the supply of opium. Under no circumstance should they test our intention to enforce the law by deliberately violating it.

FOR FURTHER REFLECTION

How does Lin Zexu convey his distaste for opium in the descriptive terms he attaches to the drug, and how do the punishments inflicted on opium peddlers suggest Lin Zexu's perception of opium's threat to China?

SOURCE: Dan J. Li. *China in Transition.* New York: Van Nostrand, 1969, pp. 64–67.

British forces broke the military stalemate when they decided to strike at China's jugular vein—the Grand Canal, which linked the Yangzi and Yellow River valleys—with the aid of steam-powered gunboats. Armed, shallow-draft steamers could travel speedily up and down rivers, projecting the military advantage that European ships enjoyed on the high seas deep into interior regions. In May 1842 a British armada of

Map 32.3 **East Asia in the nineteenth century.** Notice the division of China, which technically remained a sovereign nation, into spheres of influence by various European nations and Japan. What impact would such spheres of influence have had on the Chinese government in Beijing?

seventy ships—led by the gunboat *Nemesis*—advanced up the Yangzi River. The British fleet encountered little resistance, and by the time it reached the intersection of the river and the Grand Canal, the Chinese government had sued for peace. China experienced similar military setbacks throughout the second half of the nineteenth century in conflicts with Britain and France (1856–1858), France (1884–1885), and Japan (1894–1895).

Unequal Treaties

In the wake of those confrontations came a series of pacts collectively known in China as unequal treaties, which curtailed China's sovereignty. Beginning with the Treaty of Nanjing, which Britain forced China to accept at the conclusion of the Opium War in 1842, these agreements guided Chinese relations with foreign states until 1943. The Treaty of Nanjing (1842) ceded Hong Kong Island in perpetuity to Britain, opened five Chinese ports—including Guangzhou and Shanghai—to commerce and residence, compelled the Qing government to extend most-favored-nation status to Britain, and granted extraterritoriality to British subjects, which meant they were not subject to Chinese laws. The Treaty of Nanjing governed relations only between Britain and China, but France, Germany, Denmark, the Netherlands, Spain, Belgium, Austria-Hungary, the United States, and Japan later concluded similar unequal treaties with China. Collectively these treaties broadened the concessions given to foreign powers; they legalized the opium trade, permitted the establishment of Christian missions throughout China, and opened additional treaty ports. To ease sales of foreign goods, various treaties also prevented the Qing government from levying tariffs on imports to protect domestic industries. By 1900 ninety Chinese ports were under the effective control of foreign powers, foreign merchants controlled much of the Chinese economy, Christian missionaries sought converts throughout China, and foreign gunboats patrolled Chinese waters. Several treaties also released Korea, Vietnam, and Burma (now known as Myanmar) from Chinese authority and thereby dismantled the Chinese system of tributary states.

The Taiping Rebellion

The debilitation of the Chinese empire at the end of the nineteenth century was as much a result of internal turmoil as it was a consequence of foreign intrusion. Large-scale rebellions in the later nineteenth century reflected the increasing poverty and discontent of the Chinese peasantry. Between 1800 and 1900 China's population rose by almost 50 percent, from 330 million to 475 million. The amount of land under cultivation increased only slowly during the same period, so population growth strained Chinese resources. The concentration of land in the hands of wealthy elites aggravated peasant discontent, as did widespread corruption of government officials and increasing drug addiction. After 1850, rebellions erupted throughout China: the Nian rebellion (1851–1868) in the northeast, the Muslim rebellion (1855–1873) in the southwest, and the Tungan rebellion (1862–1878) in the northwest. Most dangerous of all was the Taiping rebellion (1850–1864), which raged throughout most of China and brought the Qing dynasty to the brink of collapse.

The Taiping Program

The village schoolteacher Hong Xiuquan provided both inspiration and leadership for the Taiping rebellion. His call for the destruction of the Qing dynasty and his program for the radical transformation of Chinese society appealed to millions of men and women. The Qing dynasty had ruled China since 1644, and Qing elites had adapted to Chinese ways, but many native Chinese subjects despised the Manchu ruling class as foreigners. The Taiping reform program contained many radical features that appealed to discontented subjects, including the abolition of private property, the creation of communal wealth to be shared according to needs, the prohibition of foot-

| The final assault on the Taipings at Nanjing by Qing forces in 1864, an operation that caught common people and their livestock in the crossfire.

binding and concubinage, free public education, simplification of the written language, and literacy for the masses. Some Taiping leaders also called for the establishment of democratic political institutions and the building of an industrial society. Although they divided their army into separate divisions of men and women soldiers, the Taipings decreed the equality of men and women. Taiping regulations prohibited sexual intercourse among their followers, including married couples, but Hong and other high leaders maintained large harems.

After sweeping through southeastern China, Hong and his followers in the Society of God Worshipers took Nanjing in 1853 and made it the capital of their Taiping ("Great Peace") kingdom. From Nanjing they campaigned throughout China, and as the rebels passed through the countryside whole towns and villages joined them— often voluntarily, but sometimes under coercion. By 1855 a million Taipings were poised to attack Beijing. Qing forces repelled them, but five years later, firmly entrenched in the Yangzi River valley, the Taipings threatened Shanghai.

The radical nature of the Taiping program ensured that the Chinese gentry would side with the Qing government to support a regime dedicated to the preservation of the established order. After imperial forces consisting of Manchu soldiers failed to defeat the Taipings, the Qing government created regional armies staffed by Chinese instead of Manchu soldiers and commanded by members of the scholar-gentry class. With the aid of European advisors and weapons, these regional armies gradually overcame the Taipings. By 1862 Hong Xiuquan had largely withdrawn from public affairs,

Taiping Defeat

Empress Dowager Cixi diverted government funds intended for the construction of modern warships to the building of a huge marble vessel to decorate a lake in the gardens of the Summer Palace near Beijing.

as he sought solace in religious reflection and diversion in his harem. After a lingering illness, he committed suicide in June 1864. In the following months Nanjing fell, and government forces slaughtered some one hundred thousand Taipings. By the end of the year, the rebellion was over. But the Taiping rebellion had taken a costly toll. It claimed twenty million to thirty million lives, and it caused such drastic declines in agricultural production that populations in war-torn regions frequently resorted to eating grass, leather, hemp, and even human flesh.

Reform Frustrated

The Taiping rebellion altered the course of Chinese history. Contending with aggressive foreign powers and lands ravaged by domestic rebellion, Qing rulers recognized that changes were necessary for the empire to survive. From 1860 to 1895, Qing authorities tried to fashion an efficient and benevolent Confucian government to solve social and economic problems while also adopting foreign technology to strengthen state power.

The Self-Strengthening Movement

Most imaginative of the reform programs was the Self-Strengthening Movement (1860–1895), which flourished especially in the 1860s and 1870s. Empowered with imperial grants of authority that permitted them to raise troops, levy taxes, and run bureaucracies, several local leaders promoted military and economic reform. Adopting the slogan "Chinese learning at the base, Western learning for use," leaders of the Self-Strengthening Movement sought to blend Chinese cultural traditions with European industrial technology. While holding to Confucian values and seeking to reestablish a stable agrarian society, movement leaders built modern shipyards, constructed railroads, established weapons industries, opened steel foundries with blast furnaces, and founded academies to develop scientific expertise.

Although it laid a foundation for industrialization, the Self-Strengthening Movement brought only superficial change to the Chinese economy and society. It did not introduce enough industry to bring real military and economic strength to China. It also encountered obstacles in the imperial government: the empress dowager Cixi (1835–1908)—a former imperial concubine who established herself as effective ruler of China during the last fifty years of the Qing dynasty—diverted funds intended for the navy to instead build a magnificent marble boat to grace a lake in the imperial gardens. Furthermore, the movement foundered on a contradiction: industrialization would bring fundamental social change to an agrarian land, and education in European curricula would undermine the commitment to Confucian values.

Spheres of Influence

In any case, the Self-Strengthening Movement also did not prevent continuing foreign intrusion into Chinese affairs. During the latter part of the nineteenth century, foreign powers began to dismantle the Chinese system of tributary states. In 1885 France incorporated Vietnam into its colonial empire, and in 1886 Great Britain detached Burma from Chinese control. In 1895 Japan forced China to recognize the independence of Korea and cede the island of Taiwan and the Liaodong Peninsula in southern Manchuria. By 1898 foreign powers had carved China into spheres of economic influence. Powerless to resist foreign demands, the Qing government granted exclusive rights for railway and mineral development to Germany in Shandong Province, to France in the southern border provinces, to Great Britain in the Yangzi

River valley, to Japan in the southeastern coastal provinces, and to Russia in Manchuria. Only distrust among the foreign powers prevented the total dismemberment of the Middle Kingdom.

Those setbacks sparked the ambitious but abortive Hundred Days reforms of 1898. The leading figures of the reform movement were the scholars Kang Youwei (1858–1927) and Liang Qichao (1873–1929), who published a series of treatises reinterpreting Confucian thought in a way that justified radical changes in the imperial system. Kang and Liang did not seek to preserve an agrarian society and its cultural traditions so much as to remake China and turn it into a powerful modern industrial society. Impressed by their ideas, the young and open-minded Emperor Guangxu launched a sweeping program to transform China into a constitutional monarchy, guarantee civil liberties, root out corruption, remodel the educational system, encourage foreign influence in China, modernize military forces, and stimulate economic development. The broad range of reform edicts produced a violent reaction from members of the imperial household, their allies in the gentry, and the young emperor's aunt, the ruthless and powerful Empress Dowager Cixi. After a period of 103 days, Cixi nullified the reform decrees, imprisoned the emperor in the Forbidden City, and executed six leading reformers. Kang and Liang, the spiritual guides of the reform movement, escaped to Japan.

The Hundred Days Reforms

Believing that foreign powers were pushing for her retirement, Cixi threw her support behind an antiforeign uprising known as the Boxer rebellion, a violent movement spearheaded by militia units calling themselves the Society of Righteous and Harmonious Fists. The foreign press referred to the rebels as Boxers. In 1899 the Boxers organized to rid China of "foreign devils" and their influences. With the empress dowager's encouragement, the Boxers went on a rampage in northern China, killing foreigners and Chinese Christians as well as Chinese who had ties to foreigners. Confident that foreign weapons could not harm them, some 140,000 Boxers besieged foreign embassies in Beijing in the summer of 1900. A heavily armed force of British, French, Russian, U.S., German, and Japanese troops quickly crushed the Boxer movement in bloody retaliation for the assault. The Chinese government had to pay a punitive indemnity and allow foreign powers to station troops in Beijing at their embassies and along the route to the sea.

The Boxer Rebellion

Because Cixi had instigated the Boxers' attacks on foreigners, many Chinese regarded the Qing dynasty as bankrupt. Revolutionary uprisings gained widespread public support throughout the country, even among conservative Chinese gentry. Cixi died in November 1908, one day after the sudden, unexpected, and mysterious death of the emperor. In her last act of state, the empress dowager appointed the two-year-old boy Puyi to the imperial throne. But Puyi never had a chance to rule: revolution broke out in the autumn of 1911, and by early 1912 the last emperor of the Qing dynasty had abdicated his throne.

The Transformation of Japan

In 1853 a fleet of U.S. warships steamed into Tokyo Bay and demanded permission to establish trade and diplomatic relations with Japan. Representatives of European lands soon joined U.S. agents in Japan. Heavily armed foreign powers intimidated the Tokugawa shogun and his government, the bakufu, into signing unequal treaties providing political and economic privileges similar to those obtained earlier from the Qing dynasty in China. Opposition forces in Japan used the humiliating intrusion of foreigners as an excuse to overthrow the discredited shogun and the Tokugawa bakufu. After

Crisis and Reform

ÉVÉNEMENTS DE CHINE
Quatorze têtes de Boxers aux murs de Tchio-Tchao

A French journal discussing events in China included an illustration of the Chinese rebels' severed heads being displayed on a wall in 1900.

restoring the emperor to power in 1868, Japan's new rulers worked for the transformation of Japanese society to achieve political and economic equality with foreign powers. The changes initiated during the Meiji period turned Japan into the political, military, and economic powerhouse of east Asia.

From Tokugawa to Meiji

By the early nineteenth century, Japanese society was in turmoil. Declining agricultural productivity, periodic crop failures and famines, and harsh taxation contributed to economic hardship and sometimes even led to starvation among the rural population. A few cultivators prospered during this period, but many had to sell their land and become tenant farmers. Economic conditions in towns and cities, where many peasants migrated in search of a better life, were hardly better than those in the countryside. As the price of rice and other commodities rose, the urban poor experienced destitution and hunger. Even samurai and daimyo faced hardship because they fell into debt to a growing merchant class. Under those conditions Japan experienced increasing peasant protest and rebellion during the late eighteenth and early nineteenth centuries.

The Tokugawa bakufu responded with conservative reforms. Between 1841 and 1843 the shogun's chief advisor, Mizuno Tadakuni, initiated measures to stem growing social and economic decline and to shore up the Tokugawa government. Mizuno canceled debts that samurai and daimyo owed to merchants, abolished several merchant guilds, and compelled peasants residing in cities to return to the land and cultivate rice. Most of his reforms were ineffective, and they provoked strong opposition that ultimately drove him from office.

Foreign Pressure

Another problem facing the Tokugawa bakufu was the insistence on the establishment of diplomatic and commercial relations by foreign lands. Beginning in 1844, British, French, and U.S. ships visited Japan seeking to establish relations. The United States in particular sought ports where its Pacific merchant and whaling fleets could stop for fuel and provisions. Tokugawa officials refused all those requests and stuck to the policy of excluding all European and American visitors to Japan except for a small number of Dutch merchants, who carried on a carefully controlled trade

A Japanese view of an audience of the first U.S. consul, Townsend Harris,
with the Tokugawa shogun and his officials in 1859.

in Nagasaki. In the later 1840s the bakufu began to make military preparations to resist potential attacks.

The arrival of a U.S. naval squadron in Tokyo Bay in 1853 abruptly changed the
situation. The American commander, Commodore Matthew C. Perry, trained his
guns on the bakufu capital of Edo (modern Tokyo) and demanded that the shogun
open Japan to diplomatic and commercial relations and sign a treaty of friendship.
The shogun had no good alternative and so quickly acquiesced to Perry's demands.
Representatives of Britain, the Netherlands, and Russia soon won similar rights. Like
Qing diplomats a few years earlier, Tokugawa officials agreed to a series of unequal
treaties that opened Japanese ports to foreign commerce, deprived the government
of control over tariffs, and granted foreigners extraterritorial rights.

The sudden intrusion of foreign powers precipitated a domestic crisis in Japan that
resulted in the collapse of the Tokugawa bakufu and the restoration of imperial rule.
When the shogun complied with the demands of U.S. and European representatives,
he aroused the opposition of conservative daimyo and the emperor, who resented the
humiliating terms of the unequal treaties and questioned the shogun's right to rule
Japan as "subduer of barbarians." Opposition to Tokugawa authority spread rapidly,
and the southern domains of Choshu and Satsuma became centers of discontented
samurai. By 1858 the imperial court in Kyoto—long excluded from playing an active
role in politics—had become the focal point for opposition. Dissidents there rallied
around the slogan "Revere the emperor, expel the barbarians."

*The End of
Tokugawa Rule*

Tokugawa officials did not yield power quietly. Instead, they vigorously responded to their opponents by forcibly retiring dissident daimyo and executing or
imprisoning samurai critics. In a brief civil war, however, bakufu armies suffered repeated defeats by dissident militia units trained by foreign experts and armed with
imported weapons. With the Tokugawa cause doomed, the shogun resigned his office. On 3 January 1868 the boy emperor Mutsuhito—subsequently known by his
regnal name, Meiji ("Enlightened Rule")—took the reins of power. Emperor Meiji
(1852–1912) reigned during a most eventful period in Japan's history.

The Meiji Restoration

Meiji Reforms

The Meiji restoration returned authority to the Japanese emperor and brought an end to the series of military governments that had dominated Japan since 1185. It also marked the birth of a new Japan. Determined to gain parity with foreign powers, a conservative coalition of daimyo, imperial princes, court nobles, and samurai formed a new government dedicated to the twin goals of prosperity and strength: "rich country, strong army." The Meiji government looked to the industrial lands of Europe and the United States to obtain the knowledge and expertise to strengthen Japan and win revisions of the unequal treaties. The Meiji government sent many students and officials abroad to study everything from technology to constitutions, and it also hired foreign experts to facilitate economic development and the creation of indigenous expertise.

Foreign Influences

Among the most prominent of the Meiji-era travelers were Fukuzawa Yukichi (1835–1901) and Ito Hirobumi (1841–1909). Fukuzawa began to study English soon after Perry's arrival in Japan, and in 1860 he was a member of the first Japanese mission to the United States. Later he traveled in Europe, and he reported his observations of foreign lands in a series of popular publications. He lauded the constitutional government and modern educational systems that he found in the United States and western Europe, and he argued strongly for equality before the law in Japan. Ito ventured abroad on four occasions. His most important journey came in 1882 and 1883, when he traveled to Europe to study foreign constitutions and administrative systems, as Meiji leaders prepared to fashion a new government. He was especially impressed with recently united Germany, and he drew inspiration from the German constitution in drafting a governing document for Japan.

Abolition of the Social Order

The first goal of the Meiji leaders was to centralize political power, a ticklish task that required destruction of the old social order. After persuading daimyo to yield their lands to the throne in exchange for patents of nobility, reformers replaced the old domains with prefectures and metropolitan districts controlled by the central government. Reformers then appointed new prefectural governors to prevent the revival of old domain loyalties. As a result, most daimyo found themselves effectively removed from power. The government also abolished the samurai class and the stipends that supported it. Gone as well were the rights of daimyo and samurai to carry swords and wear their hair in the distinctive topknot that signified their military status. When Meiji leaders raised a conscript army, they deprived the samurai of the military monopoly they had held for centuries. Many samurai felt betrayed by these actions, and Meiji officials sought to ease their discontent by awarding them government bonds. As the bonds diminished in value because of inflation, former warriors had to seek employment or else suffer impoverishment. Frustrated by these new circumstances, some samurai rose in rebellion, but the recently created national army crushed all opposition. By 1878 the national government no longer feared military challenges to its rule.

Revamping the Tax System

Japan's new leaders next put the regime on secure financial footing by revamping the tax system. Peasants traditionally paid taxes in grain, but because the value of grain fluctuated with the price of rice, so did government revenue. In 1873 the Meiji government converted the grain tax into a fixed-money tax, which provided the government with predictable revenues and left peasants to deal with market fluctuations in grain prices. The state also began to assess taxes on the potential productivity of arable land, no matter how much a cultivator actually produced. This measure virtually guaranteed that only those who maximized production could afford to hold on to their land. Others had to sell their land to more efficient producers.

The reconstruction of Japanese society continued in the 1880s under mounting domestic pressure for a constitution and representative government. Those demands coincided with the rulers' belief that constitutions gave foreign powers their strength and unity. Accordingly, in 1889 the emperor promulgated the Meiji constitution as "a voluntary gift" to his people. Drafted under the guidance of Ito Hirobumi, this document established a constitutional monarchy with a legislature, known as the Diet, composed of a house of nobles and an elected lower house. The constitution limited the authority of the Diet and reserved considerable power to the executive branch of government. The "sacred and inviolable" emperor commanded the armed forces, named the prime minister, and appointed the cabinet. Both the prime minister and the cabinet were responsible to the emperor rather than the lower house, as in European parliamentary systems. The emperor also had the right to dissolve the parliament, and whenever the Diet was not in session he had the prerogative of issuing ordinances. Effective power thus lay with the emperor, whom the parliament could advise but never control. The Meiji constitution recognized individual rights, but it provided that laws could limit those rights in the interests of the state, and it established property restrictions on the franchise, ensuring that delegates elected to the lower house represented the most prosperous social classes. In the elections of 1890 less than 5 percent of the adult male population was eligible to cast ballots. Despite its conservative features, the Meiji constitution provided greater opportunity for debate and dissent than ever before in Japanese society.

Constitutional Government

Economic initiatives matched efforts at political reconstruction. Convinced that a powerful economy was the foundation of national strength, the Meiji government created a modern transportation, communications, and educational infrastructure. The establishment of telegraph, railroad, and steamship lines tied local and regional markets into a national economic network. The government also removed barriers to commerce and trade by abolishing guild restrictions and internal tariffs. Aiming to improve literacy rates—40 percent for males and 15 percent for females in the nineteenth century—the government introduced a system of universal primary and secondary education. Universities provided advanced instruction for the best students, especially in scientific and technical fields. This infrastructure supported rapid industrialization and economic growth. Although most economic enterprises were privately owned, the government controlled military industries and established pilot programs to stimulate industrial development. During the 1880s the government sold most of its enterprises to private investors who had close ties to government officials. The result was a concentration of enormous economic power in the hands of a small group of people, collectively known as *zaibatsu*, or financial cliques. By the early twentieth century, Japan had joined the ranks of the major industrial powers.

Remodeling the Economy

Economic development came at a price, as the Japanese people bore the social and political costs of rapid industrialization. Japanese peasants, for example, supplied much of the domestic capital that supported the Meiji program of industrialization. The land tax of 1873, which cost peasants 40 to 50 percent of their crop yields, produced almost 90 percent of government revenue during the early years of Meiji development. Foreign exchange to purchase industrial equipment came chiefly from the export of textiles produced in a labor-intensive industry staffed by poorly paid workers.

Costs of Economic Development

The difficult lot of peasants came to the fore in 1883 and 1884 with a series of peasant uprisings aimed at moneylenders and government offices holding records of loans. The Meiji government deployed military police and army units to put down these uprisings, and authorities imprisoned or executed many leaders of the rebellions. Thereafter, the government did virtually nothing to alleviate the suffering of

This photograph of the emperor Mutsohito in European attire offers a visual image of transformations in Meiji Japan.

the rural population. Hundreds of thousands of families lived in destitution, haunted by malnutrition, starvation, and infanticide. Those who escaped rural society to take up work in the burgeoning industries learned that the state did not tolerate labor organizations that promoted the welfare of workers: Meiji law treated the formation of unions and the organization of strikes as criminal activities, and the government crushed a growing labor movement in 1901.

Nevertheless, in a single generation Meiji leaders transformed Japan into a powerful industrial society poised to play a major role in world affairs. Achieving political and economic equality with western European lands and the United States was the prime goal of Meiji leaders, who sought an end to humiliating treaty provisions. Serving as symbols of Japan's remarkable development were the ending of extraterritoriality in 1899, the conclusion of an alliance with Britain as an equal power in 1902, and convincing displays of military prowess in victories over the Chinese empire (1894–1895) and the Russian empire (1904–1905).

During the nineteenth century, Ottoman, Russian, Chinese, and Japanese societies faced severe challenges on both foreign and domestic fronts. Confrontations with western European and U.S. forces showed that the agrarian societies were militarily much weaker than industrializing lands. Ottoman, Russian, Chinese, and Japanese societies suffered also from domestic weaknesses brought on by growing populations, the slowing of agricultural productivity, official corruption, and declining imperial revenues. All those societies embarked on ambitious reform programs that drew inspiration from western European and U.S. models to solve the crises caused by domestic discontent and foreign intrusions on their sovereignty. But reform programs had very different results in different lands. In the Ottoman, Russian, and Chinese empires, conservative ruling elites were able to limit the scope of reform: although they generally supported industrialization and military reform, they stifled political and social reforms that might threaten their positions in society. In Japan, however, dissent led to the collapse of the Tokugawa bakufu, and reformers had the opportunity to undertake a much more thorough program of reform than did their counterparts in Ottoman, Russian, and Chinese societies. By the early twentieth century, on the basis of reforms implemented by Meiji leaders, Japan was becoming a political, military, and economic powerhouse.

CHRONOLOGY

1805–1848	Reign of Muhammad Ali in Egypt
1808–1839	Reign of Sultan Mahmud II
1814–1864	Life of Taiping leader Hong Xiuquan
1839–1842	Opium War
1839–1876	Tanzimat era
1850–1864	Taiping rebellion
1853	Arrival of Commodore Perry in Japan
1853–1856	Crimean War
1855–1881	Reign of Tsar Alexander II
1860–1895	Self-Strengthening Movement
1861	Emancipation of the Russian serfs
1868	Meiji restoration
1876	Promulgation of the Ottoman constitution
1889	Promulgation of the Meiji constitution
1894–1917	Reign of Tsar Nicholas II
1898	Hundred Days reforms
1900	Boxer rebellion
1904–1905	Russo-Japanese war
1905	Revolution of 1905 in Russia
1908–1918	Young Turk era

FOR FURTHER READING

Michael R. Auslin. *Negotiating with Imperialism: The Unequal Treaties and the Culture of Japanese Diplomacy.* Cambridge, Mass., 2004. Diplomatic history that examines Japan's interaction with Western imperialism and the country's emergence as a world power.

David Anthony Bello. *Opium and the Limits of Empire: Drug Prohibition in the Chinese Interior, 1729–1850.* Cambridge, Mass., 2005. Explores Qing China's efforts at controlling and prohibiting the domestic opium trade.

William L. Blackwell. *The Industrialization of Russia: An Historical Perspective.* New York, 1982. A useful overview.

Carter V. Findley. *Bureaucratic Reform in the Ottoman Empire: The Sublime Porte, 1789–1922.* Princeton, 1980. An important scholarly work on bureaucratic reform and the development of the Ottoman civil service.

Yukichi Fukuzawa. *The Autobiography of Yukichi Fukuzawa.* Trans. by E. Kiyooka. New York, 1966. Fascinating autobiography of the former samurai who introduced Japan to the larger world on the basis of his travels in Europe and the United States.

Marius B. Jansen and Gilbert Rozman, eds. *Japan in Transition: From Tokugawa to Meiji.* Princeton, 1986. Important collection of essays exploring economic and social change during the era of the Meiji restoration.

Rebecca E. Karl. *Staging the World: Chinese Nationalism at the Turn of the Twentieth Century.* Durham, 2002. Intellectual history arguing that Chinese nationalism resulted from global interactions.

Patrick Balfour Kinross. *The Ottoman Centuries: The Rise and Fall of the Turkish Empire.* New York, 1977. A general history of the Ottoman state.

Peter Kolchin. *Unfree Labor: American Slavery and Russian Serfdom.* Cambridge, Mass., 1987. A remarkable and stimulating comparative study of American slavery and Russian serfdom.

Tetsuo Najita and J. Victor Koschmann, eds. *Conflict in Modern Japanese History: The Neglected Tradition.* Princeton, 1982. Explores the role of conflict rather than consensus in Japanese society.

Sevket Pamuk. *The Ottoman Empire and European Capitalism, 1820–1913: Trade, Investment, and Production.* Cambridge, 1987. Closely examines complex economic entanglements.

James M. Polachek. *The Inner Opium War.* Cambridge, Mass., 1992. A scholarly treatment of the Opium War and its effects in China.

Hans Rogger. *Russia in the Age of Modernisation and Revolution, 1881–1917.* New York, 1983. An important study of Russian social and economic development.

Jonathan D. Spence. *God's Chinese Son: The Taiping Heavenly Kingdom of Hong Xiuquan.* New York, 1996. A readable work on the Taiping rebellion.

John W. Steinberg, ed. *The Russo-Japanese War in Global Perspective: World War Zero.* Boston, 2005. Collection of essays that examines the Russo-Japanese War as a harbinger of World War I.

Conrad D. Totman. *The Collapse of the Tokugawa Bakufu, 1862–1868.* Honolulu, 1980. A detailed political history of the bakufu's decline and fall.

Arthur Waley. *The Opium War through Chinese Eyes.* Stanford, 1968. Fascinating perspective on the Opium War drawing on eyewitness accounts by Chinese participants and observers.

Francis William Wcislo. *Reforming Rural Russia: State, Local Society, and National Politics, 1855–1914.* Princeton, 1990. Beginning with emancipation of the serfs, this work traces agrarian and political problems in Russian society.

Richard Wortman. *Scenarios of Power: Myth and Ceremony in the Russian Monarchy.* Princeton, 1995. An innovative study exploring the means by which Romanov rulers held on to their autocratic prerogatives despite fundamental changes in Russian society.

Avrahm Yarmolinsky. *Road to Revolution: A Century of Russian Radicalism.* New York, 1959. The most comprehensive introduction to Russian revolutionary movements in the nineteenth century.

Peter Zarrow. *China in War and Revolution, 1895–1949.* New York, 2005. Study of the impact of Qing China's loss of Korea on the formation of modern China.

33 The Building of Global Empires

Foundations of Empire
Motives of Imperialism
Tools of Empire

European Imperialism
The British Empire in India
Imperialism in Central Asia and Southeast Asia
The Scramble for Africa
European Imperialism in the Pacific

The Emergence of New Imperial Powers
U.S. Imperialism in Latin America and the Pacific
Imperial Japan

Legacies of Imperialism
Empire and Economy
Labor Migrations
Empire and Society
Nationalism and Anticolonial Movements

Few Europeans had traveled to south Africa by the mid-nineteenth century, but the discovery of diamonds and rich gold deposits brought both European settlers and dramatic change to the region. European prospectors flocked to south Africa to seek their fortune.

Among the arrivals was Cecil John Rhodes, an eighteen-year-old student at Oxford University, who in 1871 went to south Africa in search of a climate that would relieve his tuberculosis. Rhodes was persistent, systematic, and ambitious. He carefully supervised African laborers who worked his claims in the diamond fields, and he bought the rights to others' claims when they looked promising. By 1889, at age thirty-five, he had almost completely monopolized diamond mining in south Africa, and he controlled 90 percent of the world's diamond production. With ample financial backing, Rhodes built up a healthy stake in the gold-mining business, although he did not seek to monopolize gold the way he did diamonds. He also entered politics, serving as prime minister (1890–1896) of the British Cape Colony.

Yet Rhodes's ambitions went far beyond business and local politics. In his vision the Cape Colony would serve as a base of operations for the extension of British control to all of Africa, from Cape to Cairo. Rhodes led the movement to enlarge the colony by absorbing territories to the north settled by Dutch farmers. Under Rhodes's guidance, the colony annexed Bechuanaland (modern Botswana) in 1885, and in 1895 it added Rhodesia (modern Zambia and Zimbabwe) to its holdings. But Rhodes's plan did not stop with Africa: he urged the expansion of the British empire until it embraced all the world, and he even hoped to bring the United States of America back into the British fold. Rhodes considered British society the most noble, moral, and honorable in the world, and he regarded imperial expansion as a duty to humankind: "We are the finest race in the world," he said in 1877, "and the more of the world we inhabit, the better it is for the human race." In his sense of superiority to other peoples as well as his restless energy, his compulsion to expand, and his craving to extract mineral wealth from distant parts of the world, Rhodes represented well the views of European imperialists who carved the world into colonies during the nineteenth century.

Throughout history strong societies have often sought to dominate their weaker neighbors by subjecting them to imperial rule. They have built empires for various reasons: to gain control over natural resources, to subdue potential enemies, to seize wealth, to acquire territory for expansion, and to win glory. From the days of ancient Mesopotamia and Egypt to the present, imperialism has been a prominent theme of world history.

During the second half of the nineteenth century, as the Ottoman and Qing empires weakened, a handful of western European states wrote a new chapter in the history of imperialism.

OPPOSITE: **The battle of Omdurman on the Nile River, 2 September 1898.**

Strong nationalist sentiments enabled them to mobilize their populations for purposes of overseas expansion. Industrialization equipped them with the most effective tools and the most lethal weapons available anywhere in the world. Three centuries of experience with maritime trade in Asia, Africa, the Americas, and Oceania provided them with unparalleled knowledge of the world and its peoples. With those advantages, western European peoples conquered foreign armies, overpowered local rulers, and imposed their hegemony throughout the world. Toward the end of the century, the United States and Japan joined European states as new imperial powers.

The establishment of global empires had far-reaching effects. In many ways, imperialism tightened links between the world's societies. Imperial powers encouraged trade between dominant states and their overseas colonies, for example, and they organized mass migrations of laborers to work in agricultural and industrial ventures. Yet imperialism also fostered divisions between the world's peoples. Powerful tools, deadly weapons, and global hegemony tempted European peoples to consider themselves superior to their subjects throughout the world: modern racism is one of the legacies of imperialism. Another effect of imperialism was the development of nationalism in subject lands. Just as the incursion of Napoleonic armies stimulated the development of nationalism in Europe, so the imposition of foreign rule provoked nationalist responses in colonized lands. Although formal empires almost entirely dissolved in the twentieth century, the influence of global imperialism continues to shape the contemporary world.

Foundations of Empire

Even under the best of circumstances, campaigns to conquer foreign lands have always been dangerous and expensive ventures. They have arisen from a sense that foreign conquest is essential, and they have entailed the mobilization of political, military, and economic resources. In nineteenth-century Europe, proponents of empire advanced a variety of political, economic, and cultural arguments to justify the conquest and control of foreign lands. The imperialist ventures that they promoted enjoyed dramatic success partly because of the increasingly sophisticated technologies developed by European industry.

Motives of Imperialism

Modern Imperialism The building of empires is an old story in world history. By the nineteenth century, however, European observers recognized that empires of their day were different from those of earlier times. Accordingly, about midcentury they began to speak of *imperialism,* and by the 1880s the recently coined term had made its way into popular speech and writing throughout western Europe. In contemporary usage, imperialism refers to the domination of European powers—and later the United States and Japan as well—over subject lands in the larger world. Sometimes that domination came in the old-fashioned way, by force of arms, but often it arose from trade, investment, and business activities that enabled imperial powers to profit from subject societies and influence their affairs without going to the trouble of exercising direct political control.

Modern Colonialism Like the building of empires, the establishment of colonies in foreign lands is a practice dating from ancient times. In modern parlance, however, colonialism refers not just to the sending of colonists to settle new lands but also to the political, social, economic, and cultural structures that enabled imperial powers to dominate subject lands. In some lands, such as North America, Chile, Argentina, Australia, New Zealand,

and south Africa, European powers established settler colonies populated largely by migrants from the home societies. Yet contemporary scholars also speak of European colonies in India, southeast Asia, and sub-Saharan Africa, even though European migrants did not settle there in large numbers. European agents, officials, and businesspeople effectively turned those lands into colonies and profoundly influenced their historical development by controlling their domestic and foreign policies, integrating local economies into the network of global capitalism, introducing European business techniques, transforming educational systems according to European standards, and promoting European cultural preferences.

During the second half of the nineteenth century, many Europeans came to believe that imperial expansion and colonial domination were crucial for the survival of their states and societies—and sometimes for the health of their personal fortunes as well. European merchants and entrepreneurs sometimes became fabulously wealthy from business ventures in Asia or Africa, and they argued for their home states to pursue imperialist policies partly to secure and enhance their own enterprises. After making his fortune mining diamonds and gold, for example, Cecil Rhodes (1853–1902) worked tirelessly on behalf of British imperial expansion.

It is not difficult to understand why entrepreneurs such as Rhodes would promote overseas expansion, but their interests alone could not have driven the vast imperialist ventures of the late nineteenth century. In fact, a wide range of motives encouraged European peoples to launch campaigns of conquest and control. Some advocates argued that imperialism was in the economic interests of European societies as well as individuals. They pointed out that overseas colonies could serve as reliable sources of raw materials not available in Europe that came into demand because of industrialization: rubber, tin, and copper were vital products, for example, and by the late nineteenth century petroleum had also become a crucial resource for industrialized lands. Rubber trees were indigenous to the Amazon River basin, but imperialists established colonial rubber plantations in the Congo River basin and Malaya. Abundant supplies of tin were available from colonies in southeast Asia and copper in central Africa. The United States and Russia supplied most of the world's petroleum in the nineteenth century, but the oil fields of southwest Asia attracted the attention of European industrialists and imperialists alike.

Economic Motives of Imperialism

Proponents of imperialism also held that colonies would consume manufactured products and provide a haven for migrants in an age of rapidly increasing European population. In fact, manufactured goods did not flow to most colonies in large quantities, and European migrants went overwhelmingly to independent states in the Americas rather than to overseas colonies. Nevertheless, arguments arising from national economic interest generated considerable support for imperialism.

As European states extended their influence overseas, a geopolitical argument for imperialism gained prominence. Even if colonies were not economically beneficial, imperialists held, it was crucial for political and military reasons to maintain them. Some overseas colonies occupied strategic sites on the world's sea-lanes, and others offered harbors or supply stations for commercial and naval ships. Advocates of imperialism sought to gain those advantages for their own states and—equally important—to deny them to rivals.

Political Motives of Imperialism

Imperialism had its uses also for domestic politics. In an age when socialists and communists directly confronted industrialists, European politicians and national leaders sought to defuse social tension and inspire patriotism by focusing public attention on foreign imperialist ventures. Cecil Rhodes himself once observed that imperialism was an attractive alternative to civil war, and the German chancellor Otto von Bismarck worked to persuade both industrialists and workers that overseas expansion

Cecil Rhodes resting in the goldfields of south Africa, about 1897.

would benefit them all. By the end of the nineteenth century, European leaders frequently organized colonial exhibitions where subject peoples displayed their dress, music, and customs for tourists and the general public in imperial lands, all in an effort to win popular support for imperialist policies.

Cultural Justifications of Imperialism

Even spiritual motives fostered imperialism. Like the Jesuits in the early modern era, missionaries flocked to African and Asian lands in search of converts to Christianity. Missionaries often opposed imperialist ventures and defended the interests of their converts against European entrepreneurs and colonial officials. Nevertheless, their spiritual campaigns provided a powerful religious justification for imperialism. Furthermore, missionaries often facilitated communications between imperialists and subject peoples, and they sometimes provided European officials with information they needed to maintain control of overseas colonies. Missionary settlements also served as convenient meeting places for Europeans overseas and as distribution centers for European manufactured goods.

While missionaries sought to introduce Christianity to subject peoples, other Europeans worked to bring them "civilization" in the form of political order and social stability. French imperialists routinely invoked the *mission civilisatrice* ("civilizing mission") as justification for their expansion into Africa and Asia, and the English writer and poet Rudyard Kipling (1864–1936) defined the "white man's burden" as the duty of European and Euro-American peoples to bring order and enlightenment to distant lands.

Tools of Empire

Even the strongest motives would not have enabled imperialists to impose their rule throughout the world without the powerful technological advantages that industrialization conferred on them. Ever since the introduction of gunpowder in the thirteenth century, European states had competed vigorously to develop increasingly powerful military technologies. Industrialization enhanced those efforts by making it possible to produce huge quantities of advanced weapons and tools. During the nineteenth century,

Sources from the Past

Rudyard Kipling on the White Man's Burden

Rudyard Kipling lived in northern India for the first six years of his life. He grew up speaking Hindi, and he mixed easily with Indian subjects of the British empire. After attending a boarding school in England, he returned to India in 1882 and became a journalist and writer. Many of his works express his deep enchantment with India, but he also believed strongly in imperial rule. Indeed, he wrote his famous poem titled "The White Man's Burden" to encourage the United States to impose colonial rule in the Philippines. While recognizing the unpopularity of foreign rule, Kipling considered it a duty to bring order to colonial lands and to serve subject peoples.

Take up the White Man's burden—
   Send forth the best ye breed—
Go bind your sons to exile
   To serve your captives' need;
To wait in heavy harness,
   On fluttered folk and wild—
Your new-caught, sullen peoples,
   Half-devil and half-child.

Take up the White Man's burden—
   In patience to abide,
To veil the threat of terror
   And check the show of pride;
By open speech and simple,
   An hundred times made plain,
To seek another's profit,
   And work for another's gain.

Take up the White Man's burden—
   The savage wars of peace—
Fill full the mouth of Famine
   And bid the sickness cease;
And when your goal is nearest
   The end for others sought,
Watch Sloth and heathen Folly
   Bring all your hope to nought.

Take up the White Man's burden—
   No tawdry rule of kings,
But toil of serf and sweeper—
   The tale of common things.
The ports ye shall not enter,
   The roads ye shall not tread,
Go make them with your living,
   And mark them with your dead.

Take up the White Man's burden—
   And reap his old reward:
The blame of those ye better,
   The hate of those ye guard—
The cry of hosts ye humor
   (Ah, slowly!) toward the light;—
"Why brought ye us from bondage,
   "Our loved Egyptian night?"

Take up the White Man's burden—
   Ye dare not stoop to less—
Nor call too loud on Freedom
   To cloak your weariness;
By all ye cry or whisper,
   By all ye leave or do,
The silent, sullen peoples
   Shall weigh your Gods and you.

Take up the White Man's burden—
   Have done with childish days—
The lightly proffered laurel,
   The easy, ungrudged praise.
Comes now, to search your manhood
   Through all the thankless years,
Cold, edged with dear-bought wisdom,
   The judgment of your peers!

FOR FURTHER REFLECTION

Compare and contrast the sorts of adjectives Kipling uses to describe native peoples as opposed to Europeans; how does his very language usage convey his sense of white superiority?

SOURCE: Rudyard Kipling. "The White Man's Burden." *McClure's Magazine* 12, no. 4 (1899): 290–91.

industrialists devised effective technologies of transportation, communication, and war that enabled European imperialists to have their way in the larger world.

Transportation Technologies

The most important innovations in transportation involved steamships and railroads. Small steamboats plied the waters of the United States and western Europe from the early nineteenth century. During the 1830s British naval engineers adapted steam power to military uses and built large, ironclad ships equipped with powerful guns. These steamships traveled much faster than any sailing vessel, and as an additional advantage they could ignore the winds and travel in any direction. Because they could travel much farther upriver than sailboats, which depended on convenient winds, steamships enabled imperialists to project power deep into the interior regions of foreign lands. Thus in 1842 the British gunboat *Nemesis* led an expedition up the Yangzi River that brought the Opium War to a conclusion. Steam-powered gunboats later introduced European power to inland sites throughout Africa and Asia.

The construction of new canals enhanced the effectiveness of steamships. Both the Suez Canal (constructed 1859–1869) and the Panama Canal (constructed 1904–1914) facilitated the building and maintenance of empires by enabling naval vessels to travel rapidly between the world's seas and oceans. They also lowered the costs of trade between imperial powers and subject lands.

Once imperialists had gained control of overseas lands, railroads helped them to maintain their hegemony and organize local economies to their own advantage. Rail transportation enabled colonial officials and armies to travel quickly through the colonies. It also facilitated trade in raw materials and the distribution of European manufactured goods in the colonies.

Military Technologies

European industrialists also churned out enormous quantities of increasingly powerful weapons. The most advanced firearms of the early nineteenth century were smoothbore, muzzle-loading muskets. When large numbers of infantry fired their muskets at once, the resulting volley could cause havoc among opponents. Yet it took a skilled musketeer about one minute to reload a weapon, and because of its smoothbore, the musket was not a very accurate firearm. By midcentury European armies were using breech-loading firearms with rifled bores that were far more accurate and reliable than muskets. By the 1870s Europeans were experimenting with rifled machine guns, and in the 1880s they adopted the Maxim gun, a light and powerful weapon that fired eleven bullets per second.

Those firearms provided European armies with an arsenal vastly stronger than any other in the world. Accurate rifles and machine guns devastated opposing overseas forces, enabling European armies to impose colonial rule almost at will. In 1898, for example, a British army with twenty machine guns and six gunboats encountered a Sudanese force at Omdurman, near Khartoum on the Nile River. During five hours of fighting, the British force lost a few hundred men while machine guns and explosive charges fired from gunboats killed thousands of Sudanese. The battle of Omdurman opened the door for British colonial rule in Sudan.

Communications Technologies

Communications also benefited from industrialization. Oceangoing steamships reduced the time required to deliver messages from imperial capitals to colonial lands. In the 1830s it took as long as two years for a British correspondent to receive a reply to a letter sent to India by sailing ship. By the 1850s, however, after the introduction of steamships, correspondence could make the round-trip between London and Bombay in four months. After the opening of the Suez Canal in 1869, steamships traveled from Britain to India in less than two weeks.

The invention of the telegraph made it possible to exchange messages even faster. Telegraph wires carried communications over land from the 1830s, but only in the 1850s did engineers devise reliable submarine cables for the transmission of messages

Thousands of spectators gathered on the banks of the Suez Canal in 1869 to watch a parade of ships that opened the canal by proceeding from the Mediterranean to the Red Sea.

through the oceans. By 1870 submarine cables carried messages between Britain and India in about five hours. By 1902 cables linked all parts of the British empire throughout the world, and other European states maintained cables to support communications with their own colonies. Their monopoly on telegraphic communications provided imperial powers with distinct advantages over their subject lands. Imperial officials could rapidly mobilize forces to deal with troubles, and merchants could respond quickly to developments of economic and commercial significance. Rapid communication was an integral structural element of empire.

European Imperialism

Aided by powerful technologies, European states launched an unprecedented round of empire building in the second half of the nineteenth century. Imperial expansion began with the British conquest of India. Competition between imperial powers led to European intrusion into central Asia and the establishment of colonies in southeast Asia. Fearful that rivals might gain control over some region that remained free of imperial control, European states embarked on a campaign of frenzied expansion in the 1880s that brought almost all of Africa and Pacific Ocean territories into their empires.

The British Empire in India

The British empire in south Asia and southeast Asia grew out of the mercantile activities of the English East India Company, which enjoyed a monopoly on English trade with India. The East India Company obtained permission from the Mughal emperors of India to build fortified posts on the coastlines. There company agents traded for goods and stored commodities in warehouses until company ships arrived to transport them to Europe. In the seventeenth century, company merchants traded mostly for Indian pepper and cotton, Chinese silk and porcelain, and fine spices from southeast Asia. During the eighteenth century, tea and coffee became the most prominent trade items, and European consumers acquired a taste for both beverages that they have never lost.

Company Rule

After the death of the emperor Aurangzeb in 1707, the Mughal state entered a period of decline, and many local authorities asserted their independence of Mughal rule. The East India Company took advantage of Mughal weakness to strengthen and expand its trading posts. In the 1750s company merchants began campaigns of outright conquest in India, largely to protect their commercial interests from increasing disorder in the subcontinent. From their forts at Calcutta, Madras, and Bombay, the merchants extended their authority inland and won official rights to rule from the Mughal emperors and local authorities. They enforced their rule with a small British army and a large number of Indian troops known as sepoys.

A revolt by the sepoys led to the establishment of direct British imperial rule in India. In 1857 sepoy regiments received new Enfield rifles that fired bullets from cartridges. To protect them from moisture, the cartridges came in paper waxed with animal fat, and British officers instructed the sepoys to tear the paper off with their teeth. Hindu sepoys refused to comply out of concern that the protective fat came from cows, which they held sacred, and their Muslim counterparts refused on grounds that the fat might have come from pigs, which they considered foul. Even though British officials soon changed the procedures for packing and opening cartridges, in May 1857 Hindu sepoys staged a mutiny, killed their British officers, and proclaimed restoration of Mughal authority. Peasants and disgruntled elites joined the fray and transformed a minor mutiny into a large-scale rebellion that seriously threatened British rule in India. But the rebels had different interests and could not agree on a common program; in contrast, British forces benefited from powerful weapons and telegraphic communications, which enabled them to rush troops to trouble spots. The conflict produced some horrifying episodes of violence. At Cawnpore, near Lucknow, sepoys quickly overcame the British garrison and its population of 60 soldiers, 180 civilian men, and some 375 women and children. The rebels killed all the men—many of them as they surrendered—and two weeks later massacred the women and children. When a fresh British force arrived, it exacted revenge by subjecting rebels and suspects to summary execution by hanging. Elsewhere British forces punished mutineers by blowing them to bits with a cannon. By May 1858 the British had crushed the rebellion and restored their authority in India.

British Imperial Rule

To stabilize affairs and forestall future problems, the British government preempted the East India Company and imposed direct imperial rule in India. In 1858 Queen Victoria (reigned 1837–1901) assigned responsibility for Indian policy to the newly established office of secretary of state for India. A viceroy represented British royal authority in India and administered the colony through an elite Indian civil service staffed almost exclusively by the English. Indians served in low-level bureaucratic positions, but British officials formulated all domestic and foreign policy in India.

Under both the East India Company and direct colonial administration, British rule transformed India. As they extended their authority to all parts of India and Ceylon (modern Sri Lanka), British officials cleared forests, restructured landholdings, and encouraged the cultivation of crops, such as tea, coffee, and opium, that were especially valuable trade items. They built extensive railroad and telegraph networks that tightened links between India and the larger global economy. They also constructed new canals, harbors, and irrigation systems to support commerce and agriculture.

British colonial authorities made little effort to promote Christianity, but they established English-style schools for the children of Indian elites, whom they sought as supporters of their rule. They also suppressed Indian customs that conflicted with European law or values. Most prominent of those customs was sati, the practice of widows burning themselves on their husbands' funeral pyres. Although not universally observed, sati was not an uncommon practice among upper-class Hindus, who believed that women should serve their husbands loyally and follow them even in death. Under pressure from

A contemporary British print depicts the atrocities at Cawnpore. At left, sepoys kill British troops and men from the garrison, while women and children fall in the foreground. At the right, rebels stuff their victims' corpses in a well.

the East India Company, Indian law banned sati as early as 1829, but effective suppression of the practice came only after a long campaign by colonial authorities.

Imperialism in Central Asia and Southeast Asia

As the East India Company and British colonial agents tightened their grip on India, competition among European states kindled further empire-building efforts. Beginning in the early nineteenth century, French and Russian strategists sought ways to break British power and establish their own colonial presence in India. The French bid stalled after the fall of Napoleon, but Russian interest in India fueled a prolonged contest for power in central Asia.

Russian forces had probed central Asia as early as the sixteenth century, but only in the nineteenth century did they undertake a systematic effort to extend Russian authority south of the Caucasus. The weakening of the Ottoman and Qing empires turned central Asia into a political vacuum and invited Russian expansion into the region. By the 1860s cossacks had overcome Tashkent, Bokhara, and Samarkand, the great caravan cities of the silk roads, and approached the ill-defined northern frontier of British India. For the next half century, military officers and imperialist adventurers engaged in a risky pursuit of influence and intelligence that British agents referred to as the "Great Game."

Russian and British explorers ventured into parts of central Asia never before visited by Europeans. They mapped terrain, scouted mountain passes, and sought alliances

The Great Game

Map 33.1   **Imperialism in Asia, ca. 1914. Date is year of conquest.** Note the claims made by various industrial powers. Which territories remained unclaimed, and why? Which power claimed the most imperial territory in Asia?

with local rulers from Afghanistan to the Aral Sea—all in an effort to prepare for the anticipated war for India. In fact, the outbreak of global war in 1914 and the collapse of the tsarist state in 1917 ensured that the contest for India never took place. Nevertheless, imperial expansion brought much of central Asia into the Russian empire and subjected the region to a Russian hegemony that persisted until the disintegration of the Soviet Union in 1991.

Competition among European powers led also to further imperialism in southeast Asia. The Philippines had come under Spanish colonial rule in the sixteenth century, and many southeast Asian islands fell under Dutch rule in the seventeenth century. As imperial rivalries escalated in the nineteenth century, Dutch officials tightened their control and extended their authority throughout the Dutch East Indies, the archipelago that makes up the modern state of Indonesia. Along with cash crops of sugar, tea, coffee, and tobacco, exports of rubber and tin made the Dutch East Indies a valuable and productive colony.

British Colonies in Southeast Asia

In the interests of increasing trade between India, southeast Asia, and China, British imperialists moved in the nineteenth century to establish a presence in southeast Asia. As early as the 1820s, colonial officials in India came into conflict with the kings of Burma (modern Myanmar) while seeking to extend their influence to the Irrawaddy River delta. By the 1880s they had established colonial authority in Burma, which became a source of teak, ivory, rubies, and jade. In 1824 Thomas Stamford Raffles founded the port of Singapore, which soon became the busiest center of trade in the Strait of Melaka. Administered by the colonial regime in India, Singapore served as the base for the British conquest of Malaya (modern Malaysia) in the 1870s

Warships provide covering fire as British troops prepare to storm the Burmese port of Rangoon in 1824.

and 1880s. Besides offering outstanding ports that enabled the British navy to control sea-lanes linking the Indian Ocean with the South China Sea, Malaya provided abundant supplies of tin and rubber.

French Indochina

Although foiled in their efforts to establish themselves in India, French imperialists built the large southeast Asian colony of French Indochina, consisting of the modern states of Vietnam, Cambodia, and Laos, between 1859 and 1893. Like their British counterparts in India, French colonial officials introduced European-style schools and sought to establish close connections with native elites. Unlike their rivals, French officials also encouraged conversion to Christianity, and as a result the Roman Catholic church became prominent throughout French Indochina, especially in Vietnam. By century's end, all of southeast Asia had come under European imperial rule except for the kingdom of Siam (modern Thailand), which preserved its independence largely because colonial officials regarded it as a convenient buffer state between British-dominated Burma and French Indochina.

The Scramble for Africa

The most striking outburst of imperialism took place in Africa. As late as 1875 European peoples maintained a limited presence in Africa. They held several small coastal colonies and fortified trading posts, but their only sizable possessions were the Portuguese colonies of Angola and Mozambique, the French settler colony in northern Algeria, and a cluster of settler colonies populated by British and Dutch migrants in south Africa. After the end of the slave trade, a lively commerce developed around the exchange of African gold, ivory, and palm oil for European textiles, guns, and manufactured goods. This trade brought considerable prosperity and economic opportunity, especially to west African lands.

Between 1875 and 1900, however, the relationship between Africa and Europe dramatically changed. Within a quarter century European imperial powers partitioned and colonized almost the entire African continent. Prospects of exploiting African resources and nationalist rivalries between European powers help to explain this frenzied quest for empire, often referred to as the "scramble for Africa."

European Explorers in Africa

Henry Morton Stanley spent a great deal of time in the field, but here he appears, along with his gun bearer Kalulu, in front of a painted backdrop in a photographer's studio.

European imperialists built on the information compiled by a series of adventurers and explorers who charted interior regions of Africa that Europeans had never before visited. Some went to Africa as missionaries. Best known of them was Dr. David Livingstone, a Scottish minister, who traveled through much of central and southern Africa in the mid-nineteenth century in search of suitable locations for mission posts. Other travelers were adventurers such as the American journalist Henry Morton Stanley, who undertook a well-publicized expedition to find Livingstone and report on his activities. Meanwhile, two English explorers, Richard Burton and John Speke, ventured into east Africa seeking the source of the Nile River. The geographic information compiled by these travelers held great interest for merchants eager to exploit business opportunities in Africa.

Especially exciting was reliable information about the great African rivers—the Nile, Niger, Congo, and Zambesi—and the access they provided to inland regions. In the 1870s King Leopold II of Belgium (reigned 1865–1909) employed Henry Morton Stanley to help develop commercial ventures and establish a colony called the Congo Free State (modern-day Democratic Republic of the Congo) in the basin of the Congo River. To forestall competition from Belgium's much larger and more powerful European neighbors, Leopold announced that the Congo region would be a free-trade zone accessible to merchants and businesspeople from all European lands. In fact, however, he carved out a personal colony and filled it with lucrative rubber plantations run by forced labor. Working conditions in the Congo Free State were so brutal, taxes so high, and abuses so many that humanitarians protested Leopold's colonial regime. Predatory rule had culminated in the death of four to eight million Africans. In 1908 the Belgian government took control of the colony, known thereafter as Belgian Congo.

As Leopold colonized central Africa, Britain established an imperial presence in Egypt. As Muhammad Ali and other Egyptian rulers sought to build up their army, strengthen the economy, and distance themselves from Ottoman authority, they borrowed heavily from European lenders. In the 1870s crushing debt forced Egyptian officials to impose high taxes, which provoked popular unrest and a military rebellion. In 1882 a British army occupied Egypt to protect British financial interests and ensure the safety of the Suez Canal, which was crucial to British communications with India.

South Africa

Long before the nineteenth-century scramble, a European presence had grown at the southern tip of the African continent, where the Dutch East India Company had established Cape Town (1652) as a supply station for ships en route to Asia. Soon after, former company employees plus newly arrived settlers from Europe moved into lands beyond company control to take up farming and ranching. Many of these settlers, known first as Boers (the Dutch word for "farmer") and then as Afrikaners (the Dutch word for "African"), believed that God had predestined them to claim the people and resources of the Cape. The area under white settler control expanded during the eighteenth century as a steady stream of European migrants—chiefly Dutch, Germans, and French Huguenots fleeing religious persecution—continued to swell the colony's population. As European settlers spread beyond the reaches of the original colony, they began encroaching on lands occupied by Khoikhoi and Xhosa peoples. Competition for land soon led to hostility, and by the early eighteenth century, warfare, enslavement, and smallpox epidemics had led to the virtual extinction of the Khoikhoi. After a century of intermittent warfare, the Xhosa too had been decimated, losing lives, land, and resources to European settlers.

The British takeover of the Cape during the Napoleonic Wars (1799–1815) encouraged further Afrikaner expansion into the interior of south Africa. The establishment of British rule in 1806 deeply disrupted Afrikaner society, for in its wake came the im-

This 1912 photograph shows a stark portrait of the Belgian king's inhumane treatment of Africans in the Congo.

position of English law and language. The institution of slavery—a key defining feature of rural Afrikaner society—developed into the most contentious issue between British administrators and Afrikaner settlers. When the British abolished slavery in 1833, they not only eliminated the primary source of labor for white farmers but also dealt a crippling blow to Afrikaner financial viability and lifestyles. Chafing under British rule, Afrikaners started to leave their farms in Cape Colony and gradually migrated east in what they called the Great Trek. That colonial expansion sometimes led to violent conflict with indigenous peoples, but the superior firepower of Afrikaner *voortrekkers* (Afrikaans for "pioneers") overcame first Ndebele and then Zulu resistance. The colonizers interpreted their successful expansion as evidence that God approved of their dominance in south Africa. By the mid-nineteenth century, *voortrekkers* had created several independent republics: the Republic of Natal, annexed by the British in 1843; the Orange Free State in 1854; and the South African Republic (Transvaal territories) in 1860.

Britain's lenient attitude toward Afrikaner statehood took a drastic turn with the discovery of large mineral deposits in Afrikaner-populated territories—diamonds in 1867 and gold in 1886. The influx of thousands of British miners and prospectors led to tensions between British authorities and Afrikaners, culminating in the South African War (1899–1902; sometimes called the Boer War). Although the brutal conflict pitted whites against whites, it also took a large toll on black Africans, who served both sides as soldiers and laborers. The internment of 100,000 black Africans in British concentration camps, for example, left more than 10,000 dead. The Afrikaners conceded defeat in 1902, and by 1910 the British government had reconstituted the four former colonies as provinces in the Union of South Africa, a largely autonomous British dominion. British attempts at improving relations between English speakers and Afrikaners centered on shoring up the privileges of white colonial society and the domination of black Africans.

The Berlin Conference

Tensions between those European powers who were seeking African colonies led to the Berlin West Africa Conference (1884–1885), during which the delegates of twelve European states as well as the United States and the Ottoman empire—not a single African was present—devised the ground rules for the colonization of Africa. Half the nations represented, including the United States, had no colonial ambitions on the continent, but they had been invited to give the proceedings a veneer of unbiased international approval. The Berlin Conference produced agreement for future claims on African lands: each colonial power had to notify the others of its claims, and each claim had to be followed up by "effective occupation" of the claimed territory. Occupation was commonly accomplished either by getting a signed agreement from a local African ruler or by military conquest. Conference participants also spelled out noble-minded objectives for colonized lands: an end to the slave trade, the extension of civilization and Christianity, and commerce and trade. Although the conference did not parcel out African lands among the participant nations, it nevertheless served public notice that European powers were poised to carve the continent into colonies.

During the next twenty-five years, European imperialists sent armies to consolidate their claims and impose colonial rule. Armed with the latest weapons technology, including the newly developed machine gun and artillery with explosive shells, they rarely failed to defeat African forces. All too often, battles were one-sided. In 1898, at Omdurman, a city in central Sudan near the junction of the White and Blue Nile rivers, British forces killed close to 20,000 Sudanese in a matter of hours while suffering only minor losses themselves. The only indigenous African state to resist colonization successfully was Ethiopia. In 1895, Italian forces invaded Ethiopia, anticipating an easy victory. But any designs to establish a colony were abandoned when the well-equipped Ethiopian army annihilated the Italians at the battle of Adwa in 1896. Besides Ethiopia, the only African state to remain independent was Liberia, a small republic in west Africa populated by freed slaves that was effectively a dependency of the United States.

Systems of Colonial Rule

In the wake of rapid conquest came problems of colonial occupation. Imperial powers commonly assumed that, following an initial modest investment, colonial administration would become financially self-sufficient. For decades, Europeans struggled to identify the ideal system of rule, only to learn that colonial rule in Africa could be maintained only through exceedingly high expenditures.

The earliest approach to colonial rule involved "concessionary companies." European governments typically granted private companies large concessions of territory and empowered them to undertake economic activities such as mining, plantation agriculture, or railroad construction. Concessionary companies also had permission to implement systems of taxation and labor recruitment. Although that approach allowed European governments to colonize and exploit immense territories with only a modest investment in capital and personnel, company rule also brought liabilities. The brutal use of forced labor, which provoked a public outcry in Europe, and profits smaller than anticipated persuaded most European governments by the early twentieth century to curtail the powers of private companies and to establish their own rule, which took the form of either direct rule, typical of French colonies, or indirect rule, characteristic of British colonies.

Under direct rule, colonies featured administrative districts headed by European personnel who assumed responsibility for tax collection, labor and military recruitment, and the maintenance of law and order. Administrative boundaries intentionally cut across existing African political and ethnic boundaries to divide and weaken

1792-1841, thinker and litterdeur of Late Qing Dynasty
Academic studies should be pratical

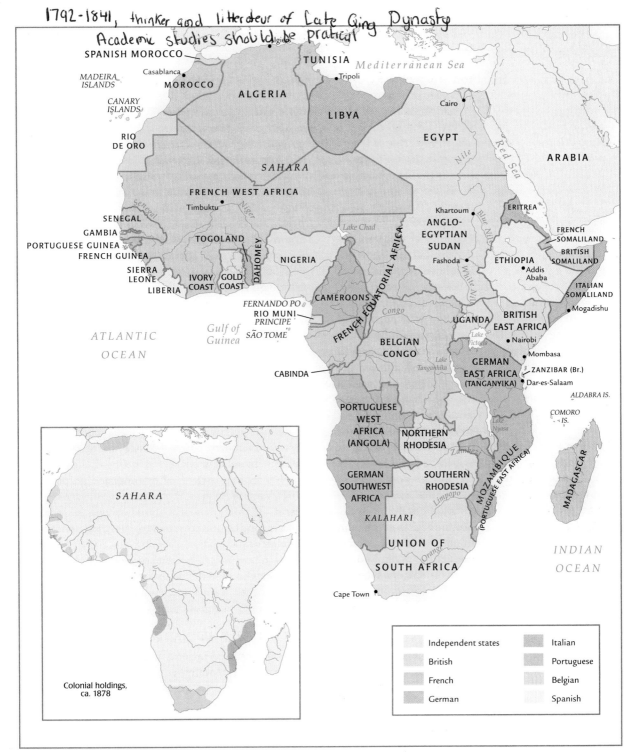

Map 33.2 **Imperialism in Africa, ca. 1914.** Note the dramatic difference between the map of 1878 and the later map.
How was it possible that Europeans were able to claim so much territory in such a short span of time?

Sources from the Past

Lord Lugard Justifies Imperialism and Indirect Rule in Africa

Frederick D. Lugard (1858–1945) played a major role in opening Africa to European colonialism. Born to missionary parents in Madras, India, he served as an army officer in Afghan, Sudan, and Burma. As an official of the British East Africa Company, he helped secure British rule in Uganda and persuaded his government to declare Uganda a protectorate in 1894. His name is especially associated with Nigeria, where as governor and governor-general (1912–1919) he welded the diverse territories of Nigeria into a single administrative unit and introduced a system of indirect rule. As the following passages show, Lugard was also an eloquent spokesperson for British imperialism in Africa.

The "Scramble for Africa" by the nations of Europe—an incident without parallel in the history of the world—was due to the growing commercial rivalry, which brought home to civilised nations the vital necessity of securing the only remaining fields for industrial enterprise and expansion. It is well, then, to realise that it is for our *advantage*—and not alone at the dictates of duty—that we have undertaken responsibilities in East Africa. It is in order to foster the growth of the trade of this country, and to find an outlet for our manufactures and our surplus energy, that our far-seeing statesmen and our commercial men advocate colonial expansion.

Money spent in such extension is circulated for the ultimate advantage of the masses. It is, then, beside the mark to argue that while there is want and misery at home money should not be spent in Africa. It has yet to be proved that the most effective way of relieving poverty permanently, and in accordance with sound political economy, is by distributing half-pence in the street. If our advent in Africa introduces civilisation, peace, and good government, abolishes the slave-trade, and effects other advantages for Africa, it must not be therefore supposed that this was our sole and only aim in going there. However greatly such objects may weigh with a large and powerful section of the nation, I do not believe that in these days our national policy is based on motives of philanthropy only. Though these may be our *duties*, it is quite possible that here (as frequently if not generally is the case) advantage may run parallel with duty. There are some who say we have no *right* in Africa at all, that "it belongs to the natives." I hold that our

right is the necessity that is upon us to provide for our ever-growing population—either by opening new fields for emigration, or by providing work and employment which the development of over-sea extension entails—and to stimulate trade by finding new markets, since we know what misery trade depression brings at home.

While thus serving our own interests as a nation, we may, by selecting men of the right stamp for the control of new territories, bring at the same time many advantages to Africa. Nor do we deprive the natives of their birthright of freedom, to place them under a foreign yoke. It has ever been the key-note of British colonial method to rule through and by the natives, and it is this method, in contrast to the arbitrary and uncompromising rule of Germany, France, Portugal, and Spain, which has been the secret of our success as a colonising nation, and has made us welcomed by tribes and peoples in Africa, who ever rose in revolt against the other nations named. In Africa, moreover, there is among the people a natural inclination to submit to a higher authority. That intense detestation of control which animates our Teutonic races does not exist among the tribes of Africa, and if there is any authority that we replace, it is the authority of the Slavers and Arabs, or the intolerable tyranny of the "dominant tribe."

FOR FURTHER REFLECTION

According to Lord Lugard, what aspects of European imperialism in Africa proved advantageous to Europeans at home?

SOURCE: Frederick D. Lugard. *The Rise of Our East African Empire*, 2 vols. Edinburgh and London: William Blackwood and Sons, 1893, 1:381–82.

potentially powerful indigenous groups. Direct rule aimed at removing strong kings and other leaders and replacing them with more malleable persons. Underlying the principle of direct rule was the desire to keep African populations in check and to permit European administrators to engage in a "civilizing mission." However, that approach to colonial rule presented its own difficulties. Key among them was the constant shortage of European personnel. For example, in French West Africa some thirty-six hundred Europeans tried to rule over an African population of more than nine million. The combination of long distances and slow transport limited effective communication between regional authorities and officials in remote areas. An inability to speak local languages and a limited understanding of local customs among European officials further undermined their effective administration.

The British colonial administrator Frederick D. Lugard (1858–1945) was the driving force behind the doctrine of indirect rule, which the British employed in many of their African colonies. In his book *The Dual Mandate in British Tropical Africa* (1922), he stressed the moral and financial advantages of exercising control over subject populations through indigenous institutions. He was particularly keen on using existing "tribal" authorities and "customary laws" as the foundation for colonial rule. Forms of indirect rule worked in regions where Africans had already established strong and highly organized states, but elsewhere erroneous assumptions concerning the "tribal" nature of African societies weakened the effectiveness of indirect rule. Bewildered by the complexities of African societies, colonial officials frequently imposed their own ideas of what constituted "tribal boundaries" or "tribal authorities." The invention of rigid tribal categories and the establishment of artificial tribal boundaries became one of the greatest obstacles to nation building and regional stability in much of Africa during the second half of the twentieth century.

European Imperialism in the Pacific

While scrambling for Africa, European imperial powers did not overlook opportunities to establish their presence in the Pacific Ocean basin. Imperialism in the Pacific took two main forms. In Australia and New Zealand, European powers established settler colonies and dominant political institutions. In most of the Pacific islands, however, they sought commercial opportunities and reliable bases for their operations but did not wish to go to the trouble or expense of outright colonization. Only in the late nineteenth century did they begin to impose direct colonial rule on the islands.

European mariners reconnoitered Australia and made occasional landfalls from the early sixteenth century, but only after the Pacific voyages of Captain James Cook did Europeans travel to the southern continent in large numbers. In 1770 Cook anchored his fleet for a week at Botany Bay, near modern Sydney, and reported that the region would be suitable for settlement. In 1788 a British fleet with about one thousand settlers, most of them convicted criminals, arrived at Sydney harbor and established the colony of New South Wales. The migrants supported themselves mostly by herding sheep. Lured by opportunity, voluntary migrants outnumbered convicts by the 1830s, and the discovery of gold in 1851 brought a surge in migration to Australia. European settlers established communities also in New Zealand. Europeans first visited New Zealand while hunting whales and seals, but the islands' fertile soils and abundant stands of timber soon attracted their attention and drew large numbers of migrants.

Settler Colonies in the Pacific

European migration rocked the societies of Australia and New Zealand. Diseases such as smallpox and measles devastated indigenous peoples at the same time that European migrants flooded into their lands. The aboriginal population of Australia fell from about 650,000 in 1800 to 90,000 in 1900, whereas the European population rose from a few thousand to 3.75 million during the same period. Similarly, the population of indigenous Maori in New Zealand fell from about 200,000 in 1800 to 45,000 a century later, while European numbers climbed to 750,000.

Increasing migration also fueled conflict between European settlers and native populations. Large settler societies pushed indigenous peoples from their lands, often

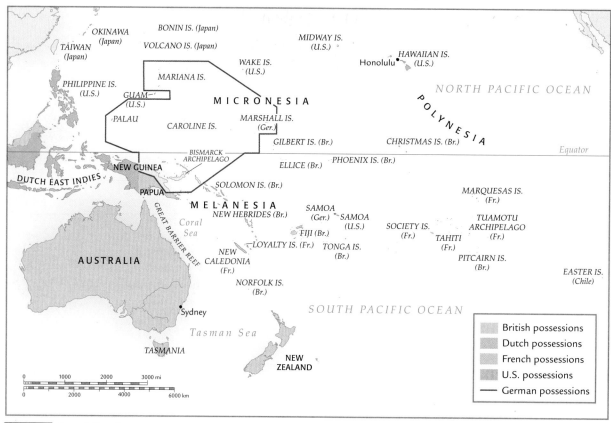

Map 33.3 **Imperialism in Oceania, ca. 1914.** Observe the many small, distant islands of the Pacific. Why would imperial powers have thought it so important to claim these islands in the late nineteenth and early twentieth centuries?

following violent confrontations. Because the nomadic foraging peoples of Australia did not occupy lands permanently, British settlers considered the continent *terra nullius*—"land belonging to no one"—that they could seize and put to their own uses. They undertook brutal military campaigns to evict aboriginal peoples from lands suitable for agriculture or herding. Despite native resistance, by 1900 the British had succeeded in displacing most indigenous Australians from their traditional lands and dispersing them throughout the continent.

A similarly disruptive process transpired in New Zealand. Representatives of the British government encouraged Maori leaders in 1840 to sign the Treaty of Waitangi, presumably designed to place New Zealand under British protection. Interpreted differently by the British and the Maori, the treaty actually signaled the coming of official British colonial control in New Zealand (1841) and thereafter inspired effective and long-lasting Maori opposition to British attempts to usurp their land and sovereignty. Conflicts over land confiscations and disputed land sales, for example, helped to spark the New Zealand Wars, a series of military confrontations between autonomous Maori groups and British troops and settlers that extended from the mid- to the late nineteenth century. Various Maori also cooperated in the Maori King Movement (or *Kingitanga*), beginning in 1856, as a means of forwarding Maori unity and sovereignty. While political and military battles continued, the British managed by the end of the century to force many Maori into poor rural communities separated from European settlements.

Imperialists in Paradise

Even though imported diseases ravaged indigenous populations, the Pacific islands mostly escaped the fate of Australia and New Zealand, where settlers overwhelmed and overpowered native populations. During the nineteenth century the principal European visitors to Pacific islands were whalers, merchants, and missionaries. Whalers frequented ports where they could relax, refit their ships, and drink rum. Merchants sought fragrant sandalwood and succulent sea slugs, both of which fetched high prices in China. Missionaries established both Roman Catholic and Protestant churches throughout the Pacific Ocean basin. Naval vessels sometimes made a show of force or intervened in disputes between islanders and Europeans—or between competing groups of Europeans.

An anonymous contemporary painting depicts the signing of the Treaty of Waitangi on 6 February 1840. British military and colonial officials look on as about fifty Maori chiefs put their names to the document.

Through most of the nineteenth century, however, imperialist powers had no desire to establish direct colonial rule over Pacific islands.

That situation changed in the late nineteenth century. Just as nationalist rivalries drove the scramble for Africa, so they encouraged imperialist powers to stake their claims in the Pacific. In an era of global imperialism, European states sought reliable coaling stations for their steamships and ports for their navies. France established a protectorate in Tahiti, the Society Islands, and the Marquesas as early as 1841 and imposed direct colonial rule in 1880. France also annexed New Caledonia in 1853. Britain made Fiji a crown colony in 1874, and Germany annexed several of the Marshall Islands in 1876 and 1878. At the Berlin Conference, European diplomats agreed on a partition of Oceania as well as Africa, and Britain, France, Germany, and the United States proceeded to claim almost all of the Pacific islands. By 1900 only the kingdom of Tonga remained independent, and even Tonga accepted British protection against the possibility of encroachments by other imperial powers.

Quite apart from their value as ports and coaling stations, the Pacific islands offered economic benefits to imperial powers. Hawai`i and Fiji were the sites of productive sugarcane plantations. Samoa, French Polynesia, and many Melanesian and Micronesian islands were sources of copra—dried coconut, which produced high-quality vegetable oil for the manufacture of soap, candles, and lubricants. New Caledonia had rich veins of nickel, and many small Pacific islands had abundant deposits of guano—bird droppings that made excellent fertilizer.

The Emergence of New Imperial Powers

Nineteenth-century imperialism was mostly a European affair. Toward the end of the century, however, two new imperial powers appeared on the world stage: the United States and Japan. Both lands experienced rapid industrialization in the late nineteenth century, and both built powerful armed forces. As European imperial powers planted their flags throughout the world, leaders of the United States and Japan decided that they too needed to establish a global imperial presence.

U.S. Imperialism in Latin America and the Pacific

The very existence of the United States was due to European imperialism. After the new republic had won its independence, U.S. leaders pursued their manifest destiny and brought almost all the temperate regions of North America under their authority. Like British migrants in Australia and New Zealand, Euro-American cultivators pushed indigenous peoples onto marginal lands and reservations. This domination of the North American continent represents a part of the larger story of European and Euro-American imperialism.

The Monroe Doctrine   The fledgling United States also tried to wield power outside North America. In 1823 President James Monroe (in office 1817–1825) issued a proclamation that warned European states against imperialist designs in the western hemisphere. In essence Monroe claimed the Americas as a U.S. protectorate, and his proclamation, known as the Monroe Doctrine, served as a justification for later U.S. intervention in hemispheric affairs. Until the late nineteenth century, the United States mostly exercised informal influence in the Americas and sought to guarantee free trade in the region. That policy benefited U.S. entrepreneurs and their European counterparts who worked to bring the natural resources and agricultural products of the Americas to the world market.

As the United States consolidated its continental holdings, U.S. leaders became interested in acquiring territories beyond the temperate regions of North America. In 1867 the United States purchased Alaska from Russia and in 1875 it claimed a protectorate over the islands of Hawai`i, where U.S. entrepreneurs had established highly productive sugarcane plantations. The Hawaiian kingdom survived until 1893, when a group of planters and businesspeople overthrew the last monarch, Queen Lili`uokalani (reigned 1891–1893), and invited the United States to annex the islands. U.S. president Grover Cleveland (in office 1885–1889 and 1893–1897) opposed annexation, but his successor, William McKinley (in office 1897–1901), was more open to American expansion and agreed to acquire the islands as U.S. possessions in 1898.

The Spanish-Cuban-   The United States emerged as a major imperial and colonial power after the brief
American War   Spanish-Cuban-American War (1898–1899). War broke out as anticolonial tensions mounted in Cuba and Puerto Rico—the last remnants of Spain's American empire—where U.S. business interests had made large investments. In 1898 the U.S. battleship *Maine* exploded and sank in Havana harbor. U.S. leaders claimed sabotage and declared war on Spain. The United States easily defeated Spain and took control and possession of Cuba and Puerto Rico. After the U.S. navy destroyed the Spanish fleet at Manila in a single day, the United States also took possession of Guam and the Philippines, Spain's last colonies in the Pacific, to prevent them from falling under German or Japanese control.

The United States quickly established colonial governments in most of its new possessions. Instability and disorder prompted the new imperial power to intervene also in the affairs of Caribbean and Central American lands, even those that were not U.S. possessions, to prevent rebellion and protect American business interests. U.S. military forces occupied Cuba, the Dominican Republic, Nicaragua, Honduras, and Haiti in the early twentieth century.

The consolidation of U.S. authority in the Philippines was an especially difficult affair. The Spanish-Cuban-American War coincided with a Filipino revolt against Spanish rule, and U.S. forces promised to support independence of the Philippines in exchange for an alliance against Spain. After the victory over Spain, however, President William McKinley decided to bring the Philippines under American control. The United States paid Spain twenty million dollars for rights to the colony, which was important to American businesspeople and military leaders because of its strategic position in the South China Sea. Led by Emilio Aguinaldo—known to his followers as the George Washington of his country—Filipino rebels turned their arms against the new intruders. The result was a bitter insurrection that raged until 1902 and flared sporadically until 1906. The conflict claimed the lives of 4,200 American soldiers, 15,000 rebel troops, and some 200,000 Filipino civilians.

To facilitate communication and transportation between the Atlantic and the Pacific oceans, the United States sought to build a canal across some narrow stretch

The Panama Canal

Queen Lili`uokalani, last monarch of Hawai`i, before her deposition in 1893. Wearing a European dress, the queen sits on a throne covered with a traditional royal cape made of bird feathers.

of land in Central America. Engineers identified the isthmus of Panama in northern Colombia as the best site for a canal, but Colombia was unwilling to cede land for the project. Under President Theodore Roosevelt (in office 1901–1909), an enthusiastic champion of imperial expansion, the United States supported a rebellion against Colombia in 1903 and helped rebels establish the breakaway state of Panama. In exchange for this support, the United States won the right to build a canal across Panama and to control the adjacent territory, known as the Panama Canal Zone. Given this expansion of U.S. interests in Latin America, Roosevelt added a corollary to the Monroe Doctrine in 1904. The "Roosevelt Corollary" exerted the U.S. right to intervene in the domestic affairs of nations within the hemisphere if they demonstrated an inability to maintain the security deemed necessary to protect U.S. investments. The Roosevelt Corollary, along with the Panama Canal when it opened in 1914, strengthened U.S. military and economic claims.

Imperial Japan

Strengthened by rapid industrialization during the Meiji era, Japan joined the ranks of imperial powers in the late nineteenth century. Japanese leaders deeply resented the unequal treaties that the United States and European powers forced them to accept in the 1860s. They resolved to eliminate the diplomatic handicaps imposed by the treaties and to raise Japan's profile in the world. While founding representative political institutions to demonstrate their trustworthiness to American and European diplomats, Japanese leaders also made a bid to stand alongside the world's great powers by launching a campaign of imperial expansion.

Early Japanese Expansion

The Japanese drive to empire began in the east Asian islands. During the 1870s Japanese leaders consolidated their hold on Hokkaido and the Kurile Islands to the north, and they encouraged Japanese migrants to populate the islands to forestall Russian expansion there. By 1879 they had also established their hegemony over Okinawa and the Ryukyu Islands to the south.

In 1876 Japan purchased modern warships from Britain, and the newly strengthened Japanese navy immediately began to flex its muscles in Korea. After a confrontation between the Korean navy and a Japanese surveying vessel, Meiji officials dispatched a gunboat expedition and forced Korean leaders to submit to the same kind of unequal treaty that the United States and European states had imposed on Japan. As European and U.S. imperialists divided up the world in the 1880s and 1890s, Meiji political and military leaders made plans to project Japanese power abroad. They developed contingency plans for a conflict with China, staged maneuvers in anticipation of a continental war, and built a navy with the capacity to fight on the high seas.

The Sino-Japanese War

Conflict erupted in 1894 over the status of Korea. Taking advantage of the unequal treaty of 1876, Japanese businesses had substantial interests in Korea. When an antiforeign rebellion broke out in Korea in 1893, Meiji leaders feared that the land might fall into anarchy and become an inviting target of European and U.S. imperialism. Qing rulers sent an army to restore order and reassert Chinese authority in Korea, but Meiji leaders were unwilling to recognize Chinese control over a land so important to Japanese business interests. Thus in August 1894 they declared war on China. The Japanese navy quickly gained control of the Yellow Sea and demolished the Chinese fleet in a battle lasting a mere five hours. The Japanese army then pushed Qing forces out of the Korean peninsula. Within a few months the conflict was over. When the combatants made peace in April 1895, Qing authorities recognized the independence of Korea, thus making it essentially a dependency of Japan. They also ceded Taiwan, the Pescadores Islands, and the Liaodong peninsula, which strengthened Japanese control over east Asian waters. Alongside territorial acquisitions, Japan gained unequal treaty rights in China like those enjoyed by European and American powers.

The unexpected Japanese victory startled European imperial powers, especially Russia. Tensions between Japan and Russia soon mounted, as both imperial powers had territorial ambitions in the Liaodong peninsula, Korea, and Manchuria. During the late 1890s Japanese military leaders vastly strengthened both their navy and their army with an eye toward a future conflict with Russia.

The Russo-Japanese War

War broke out in 1904, and Japanese forces overran Russian installations before reinforcements could arrive from Europe. The enhanced Japanese navy destroyed the Russian Baltic fleet, which had sailed halfway around the world to support the war effort. By 1905 the war was over, and Japan won international recognition of its colonial authority over Korea and the Liaodong peninsula. Furthermore, Russia ceded the southern half of Sakhalin island to Japan, along with a railroad and economic interests in southern Manchuria. Victory in the Russo-Japanese War transformed Japan into a major imperial power.

Legacies of Imperialism

Imperialism and colonialism profoundly influenced the development of world history. In some ways they tightened links between the world's peoples: trade and migration increased dramatically as imperial powers exploited the resources of subject lands and recruited labor forces to work in colonies throughout the world. Yet imperialism and colonialism also brought peoples into conflict and heightened senses of difference between peoples. (European, Euro-American, and Japanese imperialists all came to think of themselves as superior to the peoples they overcame.) Meanwhile, foreign intrusion stimulated the development of national identities in colonized lands, and over time these national identities served as a foundation for anticolonial independence movements.

Empire and Economy

One of the principal motives of imperialism was the desire to gain access to natural resources and agricultural products. As imperial powers consolidated their hold on foreign lands, colonial administrators reorganized subject societies so they would become efficient suppliers of timber, rubber, petroleum, gold, silver, diamonds, cotton, tea, coffee, cacao, and other products as well. As a result, global trade in those commodities surged during the nineteenth and early twentieth centuries. The advantages of that trade went mostly to the colonial powers, whose policies encouraged their subject lands to provide raw materials for processing in the industrialized societies of Europe, North America, and Japan.

Economic and Social Changes

Sometimes colonial rule transformed the production of crops and commodities that had long been prominent in subject societies. In India, for example, the cultivation of cotton began probably before 5000 B.C.E. For most of history, cultivators spun thread and wove their own cotton textiles or else supplied local artisans with raw materials. In the nineteenth century, however, colonial administrators reoriented the cultivation of cotton to serve the needs of the emerging British textile industry. They encouraged cultivators to produce cotton for export rather than for local consumption, and they built railroads deep into the subcontinent to transport raw cotton to the coast quickly, before rain and dust could spoil the product. They shipped raw cotton to England, where mechanized factories rapidly turned out large volumes of high-quality textiles. They also allowed the import of inexpensive British textiles, which undermined Indian cotton cloth production. The value of raw cotton exported from India went from 10 million rupees in 1849 to 60 million rupees in 1860 and 410 million rupees in 1913, whereas the value of finished cotton products imported into India rose from 50,000 rupees in 1814 to 5.2 million rupees in 1829 and 30 million rupees in 1890. Thus colonial policies transformed India from the world's principal center of cotton manufacture to a supplier of raw cotton and a consumer of textiles produced in the British isles.

In some cases, colonial rule led to the introduction of new crops that transformed both the landscape and the social order of subject lands. In the early nineteenth century, for example, British colonial officials introduced tea bushes from China to Ceylon and India. The effect on Ceylon was profound. British planters felled trees in much of the island, converted rain forests into tea plantations, and recruited Ceylonese women by the thousands to carry out the labor-intensive work of harvesting mature tea leaves. Consumption of tea in India and Ceylon was almost negligible, so increased supplies met the growing demand for tea in Europe, where the beverage became accessible to individuals of all social classes. The value of south Asian tea exports rose from about 309,000 pounds sterling in 1866 to 4.4 million pounds sterling in 1888 and 6.1 million pounds sterling in 1900. Malaya and Sumatra underwent a similar social transformation after British colonial agents planted rubber trees there in the 1870s and established plantations to meet the growing global demand for rubber products.

An engraving depicts the East India Railway about 1863. Though originally built to transport goods, railroads quickly became a popular means of passenger travel in India.

Labor Migrations

Efforts to exploit the natural resources and agricultural products of subject lands led imperial and colonial powers to encourage mass migrations of workers during the nineteenth and early twentieth centuries. Two patterns of labor migration were especially prominent during the imperial and colonial era. European migrants went mostly to temperate lands, where they worked as free cultivators or industrial laborers. In contrast, migrants from Asia, Africa, and the Pacific islands moved largely to tropical and subtropical lands, where they worked as indentured laborers on plantations or manual laborers for mining enterprises or large-scale construction projects. Between them, these two streams of labor migration profoundly influenced the development of societies, especially in the Americas and the Pacific basin.

European Migration   Between 1800 and 1914 some fifty million European migrants left their homes and sought opportunities overseas. Most of those migrants left the relatively poor agricultural societies of southern and eastern Europe, especially Italy, Russia, and Poland, although sizable numbers came also from Britain, Ireland, Germany, and Scandinavia. A majority of the migrants—about thirty-two million—went to the United States. Many of the early arrivals went west in search of cheap land to cultivate. Later migrants settled heavily in the northeast, where they provided the labor that drove U.S. industrialization after the 1860s. Settler colonies in Canada, Argentina, Australia, New Zealand, and south Africa also drew large numbers of European migrants, who mostly became free cultivators or herders but sometimes found employment as skilled laborers in mines or fledgling industries. Most European migrants traveled as free agents, but some went as indentured laborers. All of them were able to find opportunities in temperate regions of the world because of European and Euro-American imperialism in the Americas, south Africa, and Oceania.

Indentured Labor Migration   In contrast to their European counterparts, migrants from Asia, Africa, and the Pacific islands generally traveled as indentured laborers. As the institution of slavery went into decline, planters sought large numbers of laborers to replace slaves who left the plantations. The planters relied primarily on indentured laborers recruited from relatively poor and densely populated lands. Between 1820 and 1914 about 2.5 million indentured laborers left their homes to work in distant parts of the world. Labor recruiters generally offered workers free passage to their destinations and provided them with food, shelter, clothing, and modest compensation for their services in

to Fiji   to New Zealand   AUSTRALIA

JAPAN

KOREA   PHILIPPINES

HAWAII

CHINA

CANADA

MALAYA

UNITED STATES

INDIA

EUROPE

Equator

Tropic of Cancer

THE GUIANAS

AFRICA

PERU

SOUTH AMERICA

Equator

Tropic of Capricorn

MAURITIUS

RÉUNION

Tropic of Capricorn

SOUTH AFRICA

Legend:
→ European migrants
→ Japanese migrants
→ Chinese migrants
→ Indian migrants
→ African migrants
→ Filipino migrants
→ Korean migrants

Map 33.4 **Imperialism and migration during the nineteenth and early twentieth centuries.** An unprecedented intercontinental migration of people characterized the age of imperialism. What factors encouraged and facilitated migration on this extraordinary scale?

exchange for a commitment to work for five to seven years. Sometimes recruiters also offered free return passage to workers who completed a second term of service.

The majority of the indentured laborers came from India, but sizable numbers also came from China, Japan, Java, Africa, and the Pacific islands. Indentured laborers went mostly to tropical and subtropical lands in the Americas, the Caribbean, Africa, and Oceania. The indentured labor trade began in the 1820s when French and British colonial officials sent Indian migrants to work on sugar plantations in the Indian Ocean islands of Réunion and Mauritius. The arrangement worked well, and large numbers of Indian laborers later went to work on rubber plantations in Malaya and sugar plantations in south Africa, the Pacific island of Fiji, the Guianas, and the Caribbean islands of Trinidad, Tobago, and Jamaica. After the Opium War, recruiters began to seek workers in China. Large numbers of Chinese laborers went to sugar plantations in Cuba and Hawai`i, guano mines in Peru, tin mines in Malaya, gold mines in south Africa and Australia, and railroad construction sites in the United States, Canada, and Peru. After the Meiji restoration in Japan, a large contingent of Japanese laborers migrated to Hawai`i to work on sugar plantations, and a smaller group went to work in guano mines in Peru. Indentured laborers from Africa went mostly to sugar plantations in Réunion, the Guianas, and Caribbean islands. Those from Pacific islands went mostly to plantations in other Pacific islands and Australia.

Empire and Migration

All those large-scale migrations of the nineteenth century reflected the global influence of imperial powers. European migrations were possible only because European and Euro-American peoples had established settler societies in temperate regions around the world. Movements of indentured laborers were possible because colonial officials were able to recruit workers and dispatch them to distant lands where their compatriots had already established plantations or opened mines. In combination the nineteenth-century migrations profoundly influenced societies around the world by depositing large communities of people with distinctive ethnic identities in lands far from their original homes.

Empire and Society

Colonial Conflict

The policies adopted by imperial powers and colonial officials forced peoples of different societies to deal with one another on a regular and systematic basis. Their interactions often led to violent conflicts between colonizers and subject peoples. The sepoy rebellion was the most prominent effort to resist British colonial authority in India, but it was only one among thousands of insurrections organized by discontented Indian subjects between the mid-nineteenth and the mid-twentieth centuries. Colonized lands in southeast Asia and Africa also became hotbeds of resistance, as subject peoples revolted against foreign rule, tyrannical behavior of colonial officials, the introduction of European schools and curricula, high taxation, and requirements that subject peoples cultivate certain crops or provide compulsory labor for colonists' enterprises.

Many rebellions drew strength from traditional religious beliefs, and priests or prophets often led resistance to colonial rule. In Tanganyika, for example, a local prophet organized the large-scale Maji Maji rebellion (1905–1906) to expel German colonial authorities from east Africa. Rebels sprinkled themselves with *maji-maji* ("magic water"), which they believed would protect them from German weapons. The magic water was ineffective, and as many as seventy-five thousand insurgents died in the conflict. Nevertheless, rebellion was a constant threat to colonial rule. Even when subject peoples dared not revolt, since they could not match European weaponry, they resisted colonial rule by boycotting European goods, organizing political parties and pressure groups, publishing anticolonial newspapers and magazines, and pursuing anticolonial policies through churches and religious groups.

Colonial policies also led to conflicts among peoples brought together artificially into multicultural societies. When indentured laborers from different societies congregated on plantations, for example, tensions quickly developed between workers and their supervisors and among different groups of workers themselves. In Hawai`i, one of the most diverse multicultural societies created by the labor migrations of the nineteenth century, workers on sugar plantations came primarily from China, Japan, and Portugal, but there were also sizable contingents from the Philippines, Korea, and other Pacific islands. Workers and their families normally lived in villages dominated by their own ethnic groups, but there were plentiful opportunities for individuals and groups to mix with one another at work, at play, or in the larger society. Although the various ethnic communities readily adopted their neighbors' foods and sometimes took spouses from other groups, linguistic, religious, and cultural differences provided a foundation for strong ethnic identities throughout the plantation era and beyond.

Social and cultural differences were the foundation of an academic pursuit known as scientific racism, which became prominent especially after the 1840s. Theorists such as the French nobleman Count Joseph Arthur de Gobineau (1816–1882) took race as the most important index of human potential. In fact, there is no such thing as a biologically pure race, but nineteenth-century theorists assumed that the human species consisted of several distinct racial groups. In his dense, four-volume *Essay on the Inequality of the Human Races* (1853–1855), Gobineau divided humanity into four main racial groups, each of which had its own peculiar traits. Gobineau characterized Africans as unintelligent and lazy; Asians as smart but docile; the native peoples of the Americas as dull and arrogant; and Europeans as intelligent, noble, and morally superior to others. Throughout the later nineteenth and early twentieth centuries, racist thinkers sought to identify racial groups on the basis of skin color, bone structure, nose shape, cranial capacity, and other physical characteristics. Agreeing uniformly that Europeans were superior to other peoples, race theorists clearly reflected the dominance of European imperial powers in the larger world.

After the 1860s, scientific racists drew heavily from the writings of Charles Darwin (1809–1882), an English biologist whose book *The Origin of Species* (1859) argued that

Scientific Racism

Apollo Belvidere

Greek

Negro

Creole Negro

Young chimpanzee

Young chimpanzee

Scientific racists often argued that Europeans had reached a higher stage of evolution than other peoples. An illustration from a popular book by Josiah Clark Nott and G. R. Glidden, *Indigenous Races of the Earth*, deliberately distorted facial and skull features to suggest a close relationship between African peoples and chimpanzees.

all living species had evolved over thousands of years in a ferocious contest for survival. Species that adapted well to their environment survived, reproduced, and flourished, according to Darwin, whereas others declined and went into extinction. The slogan "survival of the fittest" soon became a byword for Darwin's theory of evolution. Theorists known as social Darwinists seized on those ideas, which Darwin had applied exclusively to biological matters, and adapted them to explain the development of human societies. The English philosopher Herbert Spencer (1820–1903) relied on theories of evolution to explain differences between the strong and the weak: successful individuals and races had competed better in the natural world and consequently evolved to higher states than did other, less fit peoples. On the basis of that reasoning, Spencer and others justified the domination of European imperialists over subject peoples as the inevitable result of natural scientific principles.

Popular Racism

On a more popular level, there was no need for elaborate scientific theories to justify racist prejudices. Representatives of imperial and colonial powers routinely adopted racist views on the basis of personal experience, which seemed to teach their superiority to subject peoples. In 1896, for example, the British military officer Colonel Francis Younghusband reflected on differences between peoples that he noticed during his travels throughout China, central Asia, and India. He granted that Asian peoples were physically and intellectually equal to Europeans, but he held that

> no European can mix with non-Christian races without feeling his moral superiority over them. He feels, from the first contact with them, that whatever may be their relative positions from an intellectual point of view, he is stronger morally than they are. And facts show that this feeling is a true one. It is not because we are any cleverer than the natives of India, because we have more brains or bigger heads than they have, that we rule India; but because we are stronger morally than they are. Our superiority over them is not due to mere sharpness of intellect, but to that higher moral nature to which we have attained in the development of the human race.

Racist views were by no means a monopoly of European imperialists: U.S. and Japanese empire builders also developed a sense of superiority over the peoples they conquered and ruled. U.S. forces in the Philippines disparaged the rebels they fought there as "gooks," and they did not hesitate to torture enemies in a conflict justified by President McKinley as an effort to "civilize and Christianize" the Filipinos. In the 1890s Japanese newspapers portrayed Chinese and Korean peoples as dirty, backward, stupid, and cowardly. Some scholars concocted speculative theories that the Japanese people were more akin to the "Aryans," who supposedly had conquered much of the Eurasian landmass in ancient times, than to the "Mongolians" who populated China and Korea. After their victory in the Russo-Japanese War, political and military leaders came to believe that Japan had an obligation to oversee the affairs of their backward neighbors and help civilize their little Asian brothers.

Nationalism and Anticolonial Movements

While imperialists convinced themselves of their racial superiority, colonial rule provoked subject peoples to develop a sense of their own identities. Just as Napoleon's invasions aroused national feelings and led to the emergence of nationalist movements in Europe, so imperial expansion and colonial domination prompted the formation of national identities and the organization of anticolonial movements in subject lands. The potential of imperialism and colonialism to push subject peoples toward nationalism was most evident in India.

Ram Mohan Roy

During the nineteenth century, educated Indian elites helped forge a sense of Indian identity. Among the most influential of them was Ram Mohan Roy (1772–1833), a prominent Bengali intellectual sometimes called the "father of modern India." Roy argued for the construction of a society based on both modern European science and the Indian tradition of devotional Hinduism. He supported some British colonial policies, such as the campaign to end the practice of sati, and he worked with Christian social reformers to improve the status of women by providing them with education and property rights. Yet Roy saw himself as a Hindu reformer who drew inspiration from the Vedas and Upanishads and who sought to bring Hindu spirituality to bear on the problems and conditions of his own time. During the last two decades of his life, Roy tirelessly published newspapers and founded societies to mobilize educated Hindus and advance the cause of social reform in colonial India.

Much of western India experienced severe famine in 1896–1897, and epidemics of bubonic plague broke out among weakened populations. British relief efforts were often heavy-handed and insensitive, and they did little to alleviate the problems.

Reform societies flourished in nineteenth-century India. Most of them appealed to upper-caste Hindus, but some were Muslim organizations, and a few represented the interests of peasants, landlords, or lower castes. After midcentury, reformers increasingly called for self-government or at least greater Indian participation in government. Their leaders often had received an advanced education at British universities, and they drew inspiration from European Enlightenment values such as equality, freedom, and popular sovereignty. But they invoked those values to criticize the British colonial regime in India and to call for political and social reform.

The most important of the reform groups was the Indian National Congress, founded in 1885, with British approval, as a forum for educated Indians to communicate their views on public affairs to colonial officials. Representatives from all parts of the subcontinent aired grievances about Indian poverty, the transfer of wealth from India to Britain, trade and tariff policies that harmed Indian businesses, the inability of colonial officials to provide effective relief for regions stricken by drought or famine, and British racism toward Indians. By the end of the nineteenth century, the congress openly sought Indian self-rule within a larger imperial framework. In 1916 the congress joined forces with the All-India Muslim League, the most prominent organization working to advance the political and social interests of Muslims, who made up about 25 percent of the Indian population.

The Indian National Congress

Faced with increasing demands for Indian participation in government, in 1909 colonial authorities granted a limited franchise that allowed wealthy Indians to elect representatives to local legislative councils. By that time, however, the drive for political reform had become a mass movement. Indian nationalists called for immediate independence, mounted demonstrations to build support for their cause, and organized boycotts of British goods. A few zealous nationalists turned to violence and sought to undermine British rule by bombing government buildings and assassinating colonial officials. Going into the twentieth century, Indian nationalism was a powerful movement that would bring independence from colonial rule in 1947.

Although local experiences varied considerably, Indian nationalism and independence movements served as models for anticolonial campaigns in other lands. In almost all cases the leaders of those movements were European-educated elites who absorbed Enlightenment values and then turned those values into an attack on European colonial rule in foreign lands.

———————

The construction of global empires in the nineteenth century noticeably increased the tempo of world integration. Armed with powerful transportation, communication, and military technologies, European peoples imposed their rule on much of Asia and almost all of Africa. They wielded enormous influence throughout the world, even where they did not establish imperial control, because of their wealth and economic power. Toward the end of the nineteenth century, the United States and Japan joined European states as global imperialists. All the imperial powers profoundly influenced the development of the societies they ruled. They shaped the economies and societies of their colonies by pushing them to supply natural resources and agricultural commodities in exchange for manufactured products. They created multicultural societies around the world by facilitating the movement of workers to lands where there was high demand for labor on plantations or in mines. They unintentionally encouraged the emergence of independence movements by provoking subject peoples to develop a sense of national identity. From the early twentieth century forward, much of global history has revolved around issues stemming from the world order of imperialism and colonialism.

CHRONOLOGY

1772–1833	Life of Ram Mohan Roy
1809–1882	Life of Charles Darwin
1816–1882	Life of Count Joseph Arthur de Gobineau
1824	Founding of Singapore by Thomas Stamford Raffles
1840	Treaty of Waitangi
1853–1902	Life of Cecil Rhodes
1857	Sepoy rebellion
1859–1869	Construction of the Suez Canal
1860–1864	Land wars in New Zealand
1865–1909	Reign of King Leopold II of Belgium
1884–1885	Berlin West Africa Conference
1885	Founding of the Indian National Congress
1894–1895	Sino-Japanese War
1897–1901	Term of office of U.S. president William McKinley
1898–1899	Spanish-Cuban-American War
1899–1902	South African War (Boer War)
1901–1909	Term of office of U.S. president Theodore Roosevelt
1904–1905	Russo-Japanese War
1904–1914	Construction of the Panama Canal
1905–1906	Maji Maji rebellion
1906	Founding of All-India Muslim League

FOR FURTHER READING

Michael Adas. *Machines as the Measure of Men: Science, Technology, and Ideologies of Western Dominance.* Ithaca, 1988. Argues that European imperialists judged other peoples on the basis of their technological expertise.

——. *Prophets of Rebellion: Millenarian Protest Movements against the European Colonial Order.* Cambridge, 1987. Fascinating study focusing on five rebellions against European colonial rule led by religious leaders.

Benedict Anderson. *Imagined Communities: Reflections on the Origin and Spread of Nationalism.* Rev. ed. London, 1991. Examines the emergence of nationalism in Europe and its spread to other parts of the world during the era of imperialism.

W. G. Beasley. *Japanese Imperialism, 1894–1945.* Oxford, 1987. The best study of the topic, emphasizing the relationship between Japanese industrialization and imperialism.

A. Adu Boahen. *African Perspectives on Colonialism.* Baltimore, 1987. A valuable synthetic work that examines African responses to imperial intrusions and colonial regimes.

Sugata Bose. *A Hundred Horizons: The Indian Ocean in the Age of Global Empires.* Cambridge, Mass., 2006. A bold interregional history that argues that the peoples of the Indian Ocean littoral shared a common historical destiny.

H. V. Bowen. *The Business of Empire: The East India Company and Imperial Britain, 1756–1833*. Cambridge, 2006. Detailed history of the company's rise to power in India.

John M. Carroll. *Edge of Empires: Chinese Elites and British Colonials in Hong Kong*. Cambridge, Mass., 2005. Study of the commercial and social interaction between Chinese and British in the formation of Hong Kong.

Nupur Chaudhuri and Margaret Strobel, eds. *Western Women and Imperialism: Complicity and Resistance*. Bloomington, 1992. A collection of essays examining the roles of women in the imperial era.

Bernard S. Cohn. *Colonialism and Its Forms of Knowledge: The British in India*. Princeton, 1996. Insightful essays on the cultural and intellectual manifestations of imperialism.

Philip D. Curtain. *The World and the West: The European Challenge and the Overseas Response in the Age of Empire*. Cambridge and New York, 2000. A work that focuses on cultural change as it examines how various peoples have responded to the establishment of European empires.

Saul David. *Victoria's War*. New York, 2006. High-quality military history, though ordinary people are essentially invisible.

D. K. Fieldhouse. *The Colonial Empires: A Comparative Survey from the Eighteenth Century*. London, 1966. Concentrates on the political history of European empires.

John Gallagher. *The Decline, Revival, and Fall of the British Empire*. Ed. by Anil Seal. Cambridge, 1982. A collection of essays that have deeply influenced scholarship on the British empire.

Ranajit Guha and Gayatri Chakravorty Spivak, eds. *Selected Subaltern Studies*. New York, 1988. A collection of essays dealing with the experiences of women, minorities, peasants, workers, rebels, and subordinate groups in colonial India.

Daniel R. Headrick. *The Tentacles of Progress: Technology Transfer in the Age of Imperialism, 1850–1940*. New York, 1988. Argues that imperial powers reserved the benefits of technological innovation for themselves by limiting the expertise that they shared with subject peoples.

———. *The Tools of Empire: Technology and European Imperialism in the Nineteenth Century*. New York, 1981. Surveys the role of transportation, communication, military, and medical technologies in the making of global empires.

Adam Hochschild. *King Leopold's Ghost: A Story of Greed, Terror, and Heroism in Colonial Africa*. Boston, 1998. A ghastly story of nearly forgotten greed and crime.

Peter H. Hoffenberg. *An Empire on Display: English, Indian, and Australian Exhibitions from the Crystal Palace to the Great War*. Berkeley, 2001. An imaginative work that shows how exhibitions shaped culture and society within and across borders of the British empire.

Peter Hopkirk. *The Great Game: The Struggle for Empire in Central Asia*. New York, 1992. Exciting account of the contest for power known as the Great Game.

Victor G. Kiernan. *The Lords of Human Kind: European Attitudes to the Outside World in the Imperial Age*. Rev. ed. Harmondsworth, 1972. Influential study of European paternalism and condescension toward colonial subjects.

Zine Magubane. *Bringing the Empire Home: Race, Class, and Gender in Britain and Colonial South Africa*. Chicago, 2004. Study of the ways that colonial England used racial stereotypes to justify its own social hierarchies as well as the colonial project.

David Northrup. *Indentured Labor in the Age of Imperialism, 1834–1922*. Cambridge, 1995. Careful study of indentured labor migrations and working conditions.

Thomas Pakenham. *The Scramble for Africa, 1876–1912*. New York, 1991. Detailed popular history of empire building in sub-Saharan Africa.

Robert I. Rotberg. *The Founder: Cecil Rhodes and the Pursuit of Power*. New York, 1988. An insightful psychohistorical biography of Cecil Rhodes.

H. L. Wesseling. *The European Colonial Empires: 1815–1919*. New York, 2004. Puts the process of colonization into a comparative and long-term perspective.

Kathleen Wilson, ed. *A New Imperial History: Culture, Identity, and Modernity in Britain and the Empire, 1660–1840*. New York, 2004. Study of the cultural impact of colonialism on Britain.

Louise Young. *Japan's Total Empire: Manchuria and the Culture of Wartime Imperialism*. Berkeley, 1988. An important work that analyzes the transforming power imperialism had on both the colonized and the colonizer.

VII CONTEMPORARY GLOBAL REALIGNMENTS, 1914 TO THE PRESENT

At the time the Great War erupted in 1914, Europeans and their descendants in North America dominated global affairs to an unprecedented extent, exercising political and economic control over peoples and their lands in most of Asia, nearly all of Africa, the Americas, and the Pacific islands. This global dominance was the outcome of three interconnected historical developments that took place between 1750 and 1914. Political revolutions in the Atlantic Ocean basin had encouraged the formation of national states, which could mobilize large-scale popular support. Extensive economic transformations paralleled the political reorganization of national communities, as peoples in western Europe and North America initiated processes of industrialization. Industrializing societies wielded enormous political and economic power. Their efficient transportation systems, fast communications networks, and powerful military technology supported imperial and colonial expansion. The ensuing cross-cultural encounters resulted in a high degree of interaction among the world's peoples.

States became belligerents, the Great War turned increasingly global in scope. By the time the war ended in 1918, the major European powers, including the victorious ones, had exhausted much of their economic wealth and global political primacy.

Global interdependence ensured that after the Great War most of the world needed to cope with postwar frustrations and economic instability, culminating in the Great Depression in 1929. Spawning political turmoil and social misery, postwar upheavals paved the way to fascist dictatorships in Italy and Germany and authoritarian regimes elsewhere. While the industrial world reeled under the impact of the Great Depression, the communist leadership of the Soviet Union, a state born out of revolution in 1917, embarked on a state-sponsored program of rapid industrialization. Amid great human suffering, a series of five-year plans transformed the Soviet Union into a major international power and the first socialist state. Meanwhile, the continued economic and political weakening of the European colonial powers encouraged political ferment in Asia, where nationalist movements tried to forge new identities free from imperial domination.

In 1914 a Europe torn by national rivalries, colonial disputes, and nationalist aspirations plunged into war. As the imperial powers of Europe drew on the human and material resources of their colonies and dependencies and as lands such as the Ottoman empire, Japan, and the United

Sparked as a result of the Great War and the Great Depression, World War II began in China in 1931 when Japanese forces established a colonial empire on Chinese territory. The conflict spread to Europe in the late 1930s when the Nazi regime embarked on a policy of territorial expansion. By 1941 all the world's major powers had been sucked into a maelstrom of violence and suffering that engulfed most European societies, almost all of Asia and the Pacific, and parts of Africa. World War II proved to be more destructive than any previous war and counted among its victims more civilians than soldiers. With the United States and the Soviet Union playing the lead roles, the Allied forces brought the conflict to a victorious end in 1945.

World War II completed the economic and political weakening of European societies and led to a second major realignment in the contemporary era. Two events—the immediate outbreak of the cold war and the dismantling of colonial empires—created and realigned the world of the late twentieth and twenty-first centuries. Because European powers no longer had the wherewithal to rule the world and their empires, two new superpowers filled a global void. The cold war, therefore, significantly contributed to global political transformations after World War II. It was a strategic struggle that developed between the United States and its allies on the one hand and the Soviet Union and its allied countries on the other. The conflict between the forces of capitalism and communism produced a new set of global relationships, shaping the foreign policies, economic systems, and political institutions of nations throughout the world. The cold war and its bipolar world ended suddenly in the late 1980s as the Soviet-dominated regimes of central and eastern Europe dissolved under the impact of mostly peaceful revolutions.

Although the cold war complicated the task of building nations from the wreckage of empires, in the three

decades after World War II an irresistible wave of independence movements swept away colonies and empires and led to the establishment of new nations in Africa and Asia. This end of empire was one of the most important outcomes of World War II and was perhaps the most spectacular phase of contemporary global realignments, but the initial euphoria that accompanied freedom from imperial control was tempered by neocolonial and postcolonial problems such as rapid population growth, lack of economic development, and regional and ethnic conflicts among the former colonial lands.

The cold war and decolonization reshaped the twentieth- and twenty-first-century world. Other transforming forces were also at work, among them globalization, a process that widened the extent and forms of cross-cultural interaction among the world's peoples. Technological advances dissolved old political, social, and economic barriers and promoted globalization. Improvements in information, communication, and transportation technologies, for instance, eased the movement of peoples, diseases, and cultural preferences across political and geographic borders. In this highly interdependent world, the task of dealing with problems of a global magnitude—such as human rights, epidemic diseases, gender equity, and environmental pollution—increasingly required international cooperation. Greater global integration encouraged similar economic and political preferences and fostered common cultural values, but forces promoting distinct cultural traditions and political identities also arose to challenge the universalizing effects of globalization.

34 The Great War:
The World in Upheaval

The Drift toward War
Nationalist Aspirations
National Rivalries
Understandings and Alliances

Global War
The Guns of August
Mutual Butchery
Total War: The Home Front

Conflict in East Asia and the Pacific
Battles in Africa and Southwest Asia

The End of the War
Revolution in Russia
U.S. Intervention and Collapse of the Central Powers
After the War
Challenges to European Preeminence

Archduke Francis Ferdinand (1863–1914) was aware that his first official visit to Sarajevo was fraught with danger. That ancient city was the capital of Bosnia-Herzegovina, twin provinces that had been under Ottoman rule since the fifteenth century and then occupied in 1878 and finally annexed by Austria-Hungary in 1908. These provinces became the hotbed of pan-Serbian nationalism. Ferdinand was on record as favoring greater autonomy for the provinces, but his words carried little weight with most Serbian nationalists, who hated the dynasty and the empire represented by the heir to the throne of Austria-Hungary.

It was a warm and radiant Sunday morning when Ferdinand's motorcade made its way through the narrow streets of Sarajevo. Waiting for him along the designated route were seven assassins armed with bombs and revolvers. The first would-be assassin did nothing, but the next man in line had more resolve and threw a bomb into the open car. Glancing off Ferdinand's arm, the bomb exploded near another vehicle and injured dozens of spectators. Trying to kill himself, the bomb thrower swallowed cyanide and jumped into a nearby river. The old poison only made him vomit, and the water was too shallow for drowning.

Undeterred, Ferdinand went on to a reception at city hall; after the reception he instructed his driver to take him to the hospital where those wounded in the earlier attack were being treated. While Ferdinand was on his way to the hospital, a young Bosnian Serb named Gavrilo Princip (1894–1918) lunged at the archduke's car and fired a revolver. The first bullet blew a gaping hole in the side of Ferdinand's neck. A second bullet intended for the governor of Bosnia went wild and entered the stomach of the expectant Duchess Sophie, the wife of the archduke. Turning to his wife, the archduke pleaded: "Sophie dear! Don't die! Stay alive for our children!" By the time medical aid arrived, however, the archduke and the duchess were dead.

In the meantime, Princip swallowed poison, which also only made him sick. When he tried to turn the gun on himself, a crowd intervened. After rescuing Princip from the mob, the police inflicted their own torture on the assassin: they kicked him, beat him, and scraped the skin from his neck with the edges of their swords. Three months later a court found Princip guilty of treason and murder, but because he committed his crime before his twentieth birthday, he could not be executed. Sentenced to twenty years in prison, Princip died in April 1918 from tuberculosis.

The assassination on 28 June 1914 brought to a head the tensions between the Austro-Hungarian empire and the neighboring kingdom of Serbia. As other European powers took sides, the stakes far outgrew Austro-Serbian conflicts. Nationalist aspirations, international rivalries, and an inflexible alliance system transformed that conflict into a general European war

---

OPPOSITE: **Nurse, wounded soldier, and child.**

and ultimately into a global struggle involving thirty-two nations. Twenty-eight of those nations, collectively known as the Allies and the Associated Powers, fought the coalition known as the Central Powers, which consisted of Germany, Austria-Hungary, the Ottoman empire, and Bulgaria. The shell-shocked generation that survived the carnage called this clash of arms the Great War. Sadly, though, a subsequent generation of survivors renamed the conflict World War I, because it was only the first of two wars that engulfed the world in the first half of the twentieth century.

The Great War lasted from August 1914 to November 1918 and ushered in history's most violent century. In geographic extent the conflict surpassed all previous wars, compelling men, women, and children on five continents to participate directly or indirectly in a struggle that many did not understand. The Great War also had the distinction of being the first total war in human history, as governments mobilized every available human and material resource for the conduct of war. This scope contrasted with those of past wars, which, though frequently waged with ruthlessness and savage efficiency, were less destructive because they rarely engaged the passions of entire nations. Moreover, total war depended on industrial nations' capacity to fight with virtually unlimited means and to conduct combat on a vast scale. The industrial nature of the conflict meant that it was the bloodiest in the annals of organized violence. It took the lives of millions of combatants and civilians, physically maimed untold multitudes, and emotionally scarred an entire generation. The military casualties passed a threshold beyond previous experience: approximately fifteen million soldiers died, and an additional twenty million combatants suffered injuries.

The war of 1914–1918 did more than destroy individual lives. It seriously damaged national economies. The most visible signs of that damage were huge public debts and soaring rates of inflation. The international economy witnessed a shift in power away from western Europe. By the end of the conflict, the United States loomed as an economic world power that, despite its self-imposed isolation during the 1920s and 1930s, played a key role in global affairs in the coming decades. Politically, the war led to the redrawing of European boundaries and caused the demise of four dynasties and their empires—the Ottoman empire, the Russian empire, the Austro-Hungarian empire, and the German empire. The Great War also gave birth to nine new nations: Yugoslavia, Austria, Hungary, Czechoslovakia, Poland, Lithuania, Latvia, Estonia, and Finland. The war helped unleash the Bolshevik Revolution of 1917, which set the stage for an ideological conflict between capitalism and communism that endured to the end of the twentieth century. Finally, the Great War was responsible for an international realignment of power. It undermined the preeminence and prestige of European society, signaling an end to Europe's global primacy.

The Drift toward War

The catalyst for war was the assassination of Archduke Francis Ferdinand, heir to the throne of the Austro-Hungarian empire, by a Serbian nationalist. Yet without deeper underlying developments, the assassin's bullets would have had limited effect. The underlying causes for the war of 1914–1918 were many, including intense nationalism, frustrated national ambitions and ethnic resentments, the pursuit of exclusive economic interests, abrasive colonial rivalries, and a general struggle over the balance of power in Europe and in the world at large. Between 1871 and 1914, European governments adopted foreign policies that increased steadily the danger of war. So as to not find themselves alone in a hostile world, national leaders sought alignments with other powers. The establishment and maintenance in Europe of two hostile alliances—the Allies and the Central Powers—helped spread the war from the Balkans.

Nationalist Aspirations

The French Revolution and subsequent Napoleonic conquests spread nationalism throughout most of Europe (see chapter 29). Inherent in nationalism was the idea that peoples with the same ethnic origins, language, and political ideals had the right to form sovereign states; this concept is termed *self-determination*. The dynastic and reactionary powers that dominated European affairs during the early nineteenth century either ignored or opposed the principle of self-determination, thereby denying national autonomy to Germans, Italians, and Belgians, among others. Before long, however, a combination of powerful nationalistic movements, revolutions, and wars allowed Belgians to gain independence from the Netherlands in 1830, promoted the unification of Italy in 1861, and secured the unification of Germany in 1871. Yet at the end of the nineteenth century, the issue of nationalism remained unresolved in other areas of Europe, most notably in eastern Europe and the Balkans. There the nationalist aspirations of subject minorities threatened to tear apart the multinational empires of the Ottoman, Habsburg, and Russian dynasties and with them the regional balance of power. In those instances, opposition to foreign rule played a large role in the construction of national identities and demands for self-determination.

The Ottoman empire had controlled the Balkan peninsula since the fifteenth century, but after 1829 the Turkish empire shriveled. European powers, especially Austria and Russia, were partly responsible for the shrinking of Ottoman territories in Europe, but the slicing away of Turkish territory resulted mostly from nationalist revolts by the sultan's subjects. Greece was the first to gain independence (in 1830), but within a few decades Serbia, Romania, and Bulgaria followed suit.

As the Ottoman territories succumbed to the forces of nationalism, Austria-Hungary confronted the nationalist aspirations of Slavic peoples—Poles, Czechs, Slovaks, Serbs, Croats, and Slovenes. Most menacing and militant were the Serbs, who pressed for unification with the independent kingdom of Serbia. Russia added fuel to this volatile situation by promoting Pan-Slavism, a nineteenth-century movement that stressed the ethnic and cultural kinship of the various Slav peoples of eastern and east central Europe and that sought to unite those peoples politically. Pan-Slavism, as advocated by Russian leaders, supported Slav nationalism in lands occupied by Austria-Hungary. The purpose behind that policy was to promote secession by Slav areas, thereby weakening Austrian rule and perhaps preparing territories for future Russian annexation. Russia's support of Serbia, which supported Slav nationalism, and Germany's backing of Austria-Hungary, which tried desperately to counter the threat of national independence, helped set the stage for international conflict.

National Rivalries

Aggressive nationalism was also manifest in economic competition and colonial conflicts, fueling dangerous rivalries among the major European powers. The industrialized nations of Europe competed for foreign markets and engaged in tariff wars, but the most unsettling economic rivalry involved Great Britain and Germany. By the twentieth century, Germany's rapid industrialization threatened British economic predominance. In 1870 Britain, the first industrial nation, produced almost 32 percent of the world's total industrial output, compared with Germany's share of 13 percent, but by 1914 Britain's share had dropped to 14 percent, roughly equivalent to that of Germany. British reluctance to accept the relative decline of British industry vis-à-vis German industry strained relations between the two economic powers.

The Naval Race   An expensive naval race further exacerbated tensions between the two nations. Germans and Britons convinced themselves that naval power was imperative to secure trade routes and protect merchant shipping. Moreover, military leaders and politicians saw powerful navies as a means of controlling the seas in times of war, a control they viewed as decisive in determining the outcome of any war. Thus, when Germany's political and military leaders announced their program to build a fleet with many large battleships, they seemed to undermine British naval supremacy. The British government moved to meet the German threat through the construction of super battleships known as *dreadnoughts*. Rather than discouraging the Germans from their naval buildup, the British determination to retain naval superiority stimulated the Germans to build their own flotilla of dreadnoughts. This expensive naval race contributed further to international tensions and hostilities between nations.

Colonial Disputes   Economic rivalries fomented colonial competition. During the late nineteenth and early twentieth centuries, European nations searched aggressively for new colonies or dependencies to bolster economic performance. In their haste to conquer and colonize, the imperial powers stumbled over each other, repeatedly clashing in one corner of the globe or another: Britain and Russia faced off in Persia (modern-day Iran) and Afghanistan; Britain and France in Siam (modern-day Thailand) and the Nile valley; Britain and Germany in east and southwest Africa; Germany and France in Morocco and west Africa.

Virtually all the major powers engaged in the scramble for empire, but the competition between Britain and Germany and that between France and Germany were the most intense and dangerous. Germany, a unified nation only since 1871, embarked on the colonial race belatedly but aggressively, insisting that it too must have its "place in the sun." German imperial efforts were frustrated, however, by the simple fact that British and French imperialists had already carved up most of the world. German-French antagonisms and German-British rivalries went far toward shaping the international alliances that contributed to the spread of war after 1914.

Between 1905 and 1914, a series of international crises and two local wars raised tensions and almost precipitated a general European war. The first crisis resulted from a French-German confrontation over Morocco in 1905. Trying to isolate the French diplomatically, the German government announced its support of Moroccan independence, which French encroachment endangered. The French responded to German intervention by threatening war. An international conference in Algeciras, Spain, in the following year prevented a clash of arms, but similar crises threatened the peace in subsequent years. Contributing to the growing tensions in European affairs were the Balkan wars. Between 1912 and 1913, the states of the Balkan peninsula—including Bulgaria, Greece, Montenegro, Serbia, and Romania—fought two consecutive wars for possession of European territories held by the Ottoman empire. The Balkan wars strained European diplomatic relations and helped shape the tense circumstances that led to the outbreak of the Great War.

Public Opinion   Public pressure also contributed to national rivalries. Characteristic of many European societies was a high degree of political participation and chauvinism on the part of citizens who identified strongly with the state. These citizens wanted their nation to outshine others, particularly in the international arena. New means of communication nourished the public's desire to see their country "come in first," whether in the competition for colonies or in the race to the South Pole. The content of cheap, mass-produced newspapers, pamphlets, and books fueled feelings of national arrogance and aggressive patriotism. However, public pressure calling for national greatness placed

Dissident cartoonist Walter Trier's satirical map of Europe in 1914.

policymakers and diplomats in an awkward situation. Compelled to achieve headline-grabbing foreign policy successes, these leaders ran the risk of paying for short-lived triumphs with long-lasting hostility from other countries.

Understandings and Alliances

In addition to a basic desire for security, escalating national rivalries and nationalist aspirations of subject minorities spawned a system of entangling alliances. While national interests guided the search for allies, each nation viewed its fulfillment of treaty obligations as crucial to self-preservation. Moreover, the complexity of those obligations could not hide the common characteristic underlying all the alliances: they outlined the circumstances under which countries would go to war to support one another. Intended to preserve the peace, rival alliance systems created a framework whereby even a small international crisis could set off a chain reaction leading to global war. Thus by 1914 Europe's major powers had transformed themselves into two hostile camps—the Triple Alliance and the Triple Entente.

The Triple Alliance, also known as the Central Powers, grew out of the close relationship that developed between the leaders of Germany and Austria-Hungary during the last three decades of the nineteenth century. In 1879 the governments of the two empires formed the Dual Alliance, a defensive pact that ensured reciprocal protection from a Russian attack and neutrality in case of an attack from any other power. Fear of a hostile France motivated Germans to enter into this pact, whereas Austrians viewed it as giving them a free hand in pursuing their Balkan politics without fear of Russian intervention. Italy, fearful of France, joined the Dual Alliance in 1882, thereby transforming

The Central Powers

it into the Triple Alliance. From the outset, however, the Italian policy of aggrandizement at the expense of the Ottoman empire and Italy's rivalry with Austria-Hungary in the Balkans threatened to wreck the alliance. Thus the Italian declaration of war on the Ottoman empire in 1911 and the subsequent drive to annex the Tripoli region of northern Africa strained the Triple Alliance because the German government tried to cultivate friendly relations with the Turks.

The Allies   The Central Powers sought to protect the political status quo in Europe, but the leaders of other nations viewed this new constellation of power with suspicion. This response was especially true of French leaders, who neither forgot nor forgave France's humiliating defeat during the Franco-Prussian War of 1870–1871. The French government was determined to curb the growing might of Germany.

The tsarist regime of Russia was equally disturbed by the new alignment of powers, especially by Germany's support of Austria, and British leaders were traditionally suspicious of any nation that seemed to threaten the balance of power on the Continent. The result was that the most unlikely bedfellows formed the Triple Entente, a combination of nations commonly referred to as the Allies. The Triple Entente originated in a series of agreements between Britain and France (1904) and between Britain and Russia (1907) that aimed to resolve colonial disputes. Between 1907 and 1914 cooperation between the leaders of Britain, France, and Russia led to the signing of a military pact in the summer of 1914. Reciprocal treaty obligations, which the governments felt compelled to honor lest they face the risk of being alone in a hostile world, made it difficult for diplomats to contain what otherwise might have been relatively small international crises.

War Plans   The preservation of peace was also difficult because the military staffs of each nation had devised inflexible military plans and timetables to be carried out in the event of war. For example, French military strategy revolved around Plan XVII, which amounted to a veritable celebration of offensive maneuvers. The French master plan could be summed up in one word, *attack*, to be undertaken always and everywhere. This strategy viewed the enemy's intentions as inconsequential and gave no thought to the huge number of casualties that would invariably result. German war plans in particular played a crucial role in the events leading to the Great War. Germany's fear of encirclement encouraged its military planners to devise a strategy that would avoid a war on two fronts. It was based on a strategy developed in 1905 by General Count Alfred von Schlieffen (1833–1913). The Schlieffen plan called for a swift knockout of France, followed by defensive action against Russia. German planners predicated their strategy on the knowledge that the Russians could not mobilize their soldiers and military supplies as quickly as the French, thus giving German forces a few precious weeks during which they could concentrate their full power on France. However brilliantly conceived, the Schlieffen plan raised serious logistical problems, not the least of which was moving 180,000 soldiers and their supplies into France and Belgium on five hundred trains, with fifty wagons each. More important, Germany's military strategy was a serious obstacle to those seeking to preserve the peace. In the event of Russian mobilization, Germany's leaders would feel compelled to stick to their war plans, thereby setting in motion a military conflict of major proportions.

Global War

War came to Europe during harvest time, and most ordinary people heard the news as they worked in the fields. They reacted not with enthusiasm but with shock and fear. Other people, especially intellectuals and young city dwellers, met the news with euphoria. Many of them had long expected war and saw it as a liberating release of pressure that would resolve the various political, social, and economic crises that had been building for years. The philosopher Bertrand Russell observed that the average Englishman positively wanted war, and the French writer Alain-Fournier noted that "this war is fine and just and great." In the capitals of Europe, people danced in the streets when their governments announced formal declarations of war. When the first contingents of soldiers left for the front, jubilant crowds threw flowers at the feet of departing men, who expected to return victorious after a short time.

Reality crushed any expectations of a short and triumphant war. On most fronts the conflict quickly bogged down and became a war of attrition in which the firepower of modern weapons slaughtered soldiers by the millions. For the first time in history, belligerent nations engaged in total war. Even in democratic societies, governments assumed dictatorial control to marshal the human and material resources required for continuous war. One result was increased participation of women in the labor force. Total war had repercussions that went beyond the borders of Europe. Imperial ties drew millions of Asians, Africans, and residents of the British dominions into the war to serve as soldiers and laborers. Struggles over far-flung colonies further underlined the global dimension of this war. Last, the war gained a global flavor through the entry of Japan, the United States, and the Ottoman empire, nations whose leaders professed little direct interest in European affairs.

British recruiting poster.

The Guns of August

The shots fired from Gavrilo Princip's revolver on that fateful day of 28 June 1914 were heard around the world, for they triggered the greatest war in human history up to that point. By July, Austrian investigators had linked the assassins to a terrorist group known as the Black Hand. Centered in neighboring Serbia, this organization was dedicated to the unification of all south Slavs, or Yugoslavs, to form a greater Serbia. As far as Serbian nationalists were concerned, the principal obstacle to Slavic unity was the Austro-Hungarian empire, which explains why the heir to the Habsburg throne was a symbolic victim. This viewpoint also explains Austria's unyielding and violent response to the murder.

The assassination set in motion a flurry of diplomatic activity that quickly escalated into war. Austrian leaders in Vienna were determined to teach the unruly Serbs a lesson, and on 23 July the Austrians issued a nearly unacceptable ultimatum to the government of Serbia. The Serbian government accepted all the terms of the ultimatum except one, which infringed on its sovereignty. The ultimatum demanded that Austrian officials take part in any Serbian investigation of persons found on Serbian territory connected to the assassination of Francis Ferdinand. On 28 July, after declaring the Serbian reply to be unsatisfactory, Austria-Hungary declared war on Serbia. The war had begun, and politicians and generals discovered that it could not be easily arrested. The subsequent sequence of events was largely determined by two factors:

Declarations of War

A German dispatch rider wearing a gas mask.

complex mobilization plans and the grinding logic of the alliance system. Mobilization called for the activation of military forces for imminent battle and the redirection of economic and social activities to support military efforts. Thus military planners were convinced that the timing of mobilization orders and adherence to precise timetables were crucial to the successful conduct of war.

On 29 July the Russian government mobilized its troops to defend its Serbian ally and itself from Austria. The tsar of Russia then ordered mobilization against Germany. Nicholas II (1868–1918) took that decisive step reluctantly and only after his military experts had convinced him that a partial mobilization against the Austrians would upset complex military plans and timetables. Delayed mobilization might invite defeat, they advised, should the Germans enter the war. That action precipitated a German ultimatum to Russia on 31 July, demanding that the Russian army cease its mobilization immediately. Another ultimatum addressed to France demanded to know what France's intentions were in case Germany and Russia went to war. The Russians replied with a blunt "impossible," and the French never answered. Thus on 1 August the German government declared war on Russia, and France started to mobilize.

After waiting two more days, the Germans declared war on France, on 3 August. On the same day, German troops invaded Belgium in accordance with the Schlieffen plan. Key to this plan was an attack on the weak left flank of the French army by a massive German force through Belgium. The Belgian government, which had refused to permit the passage of German troops, called on the signatories of the treaty of 1839, which guaranteed Belgium's neutrality. On 4 August the British government, one of the signatories, sent an ultimatum to Germany demanding that Belgian neutrality be respected. When Germany's wartime leaders refused, the British immediately declared war. A local conflict had become a general European war.

Mutual Butchery

Everyone expected the war to be brief. In the first weeks of August 1914, twenty million young men donned uniforms, took up rifles, and left for the front. Many of them looked forward to heroic charges, rapid promotions, and a quick homecoming. Some dreamed of glory and honor, and they believed that God was on their side. The inscription on the belt buckle of German recruits read *Gott mit uns* ("God is with us"), a sentiment echoed by Russian troops, who fought for "God and Tsar," and British soldiers, who went into battle "For God, King, and Country." Several years later Americans felt called on to "make the world safe for democracy." Similar attitudes prevailed among the political and military leaders of the belligerent nations. The war strategies devised by the finest military thinkers of the time paid little attention to matters of defense. Instead, they were preoccupied with visions of sweeping assaults, envelopments, and, above all, swift triumphs.

Map 34.1 **The Great War in Europe and southwest Asia, 1914–1918.** Note the locations of both the eastern and the western fronts in Europe during the war. Why didn't the same kind of trench warfare immobilize opposing armies on the eastern front the way it did on the western front?

The German thrust toward Paris in August 1914 came to a grinding halt along the river Marne, and both sides then undertook flanking maneuvers, a "race to the sea" that took them to the Atlantic coast. For the next three years, the battle lines remained virtually stationary, as both sides dug in and slugged it out in a war of attrition that lasted until the late autumn of 1918. Each belligerent tried to wear down the enemy by inflicting continuous damage and casualties, only to have their own forces suffer heavy losses in return. Trenches on the western front ran from the English Channel to

The Western Front

Stalemate and New Weapons

Air raid warden in helmet and gas mask, holding a wooden gas attack rattle in his gloved hand.

Switzerland. Farther south, Italy left the Triple Alliance in favor of neutrality but entered the war on the side of the Allies in 1915. By the terms of the Treaty of London the Allies promised, once victory was secured, to cede to Italy Austro-Hungarian-controlled territories, specifically south Tyrol and most of the Dalmatian coast. Allied hopes that the Italians would pierce Austrian defenses quickly faded. After the disastrous defeat at Caporetto in 1917, Italian forces maintained a defensive line only with the help of the French and the British.

The stalemate on the western and southern fronts reflected technological developments that favored defensive tactics. Barbed wire, which had confined cattle on America's Great Plains, proved highly effective in frustrating the advance of soldiers across "no-man's-land," the deadly territory between opposing trenches. The rapid and continuous fire of machine guns further contributed to the battlefield stalemate, turning infantry charges across no-man's-land into suicide missions. First deployed by Confederate troops during the U.S. Civil War, the machine gun had been a key weapon for overcoming resistance to colonial expansion before Europeans trained the weapon on one another during the Great War. The machine gun represented one of the most important advances in military technology and compelled military leaders on all sides to rethink their battlefield tactics.

The immobility of trench warfare and the desire to reintroduce movement to warfare prompted the development of weapons that supplied the power necessary to break the deadly stalemate. Industrial societies subsequently gave birth to many new and potent weapons. The most unconventional weapon was poisonous gas, first used by German troops in January 1915. Especially hated and much feared by troops in the trenches was mustard gas, a liquid agent that, when exposed to air, turned into a noxious yellow gas, hence its name. The effects of mustard gas did not appear for some twelve hours following exposure, but then it rotted the body from both within and without. After blistering the skin and damaging the eyes, the gas attacked the bronchial tubes, stripping off the mucous membrane. Death could occur in four to five weeks. In the meantime, victims endured excruciating pain and had to be strapped to their beds. Like the machine gun, gas proved a potent weapon, and both sides suffered heavy casualties totaling about 1.2 million soldiers. Such destructiveness convinced military leaders of the effectiveness of chemical agents, yet gas attacks failed to deliver the promised strategic breakthroughs, and the anticipated return to more fluid battle lines never materialized.

Other novel weapons developed during the war included tanks and airplanes. The British first introduced tanks in late 1915, and the Allies deployed them to break down defensive trenches and to restore fighting. Despite its proven short-term effectiveness during the final offenses of the war, the tank did not produce the longed-for strategic advantage. As a rule, German counterattacks quickly regained the ground won by tanks. Also of recent origin was the airplane, still in its infancy in 1914. Constantly refined and improved as the war progressed, the airplane by the end of the war showed dramatic improvements in speed, range, and altitude. However, because airplanes could not carry enough weapons to do serious damage to troops or installations on the ground, their real asset during the Great War was aerial reconnaissance. It was, in effect, an attempt to prevent the enemy from conducting aerial reconnaissance that led to the much publicized and glamorized aerial combat of the Great War featuring "ace fighters" and "dogfights." The plane and the tank figured more prominently as important strategic weapons during the Second World War. Other weapons systems, such as the submarine, had made earlier appearances in warfare but did not play a significant role until the Great War. It was not until the Great War, when the German navy deployed its diesel-powered submarine fleet against Allied commercial shipping, that the

A dogfight between German and British planes during the Great War.

submarine proved its military effectiveness. Although the German navy relied more heavily on submarines, the allied navies of Great Britain and the United States deployed their own fleets of diesel-powered submarines.

The most courageous infantry charges, even when preceded by pulverizing artillery barrages and clouds of poisonous gas, were no match for determined defenders. Shielded by the dirt of their trenches and by barbed wire and gas masks, they unleashed a torrent of lethal metal with their machine guns and repeating rifles. In every sector of the front, those who fought rarely found the glory they sought. Instead, they encountered death. No-man's-land was strewn with shell craters, cadavers, and body parts. The grim realities of trench warfare—the wet, cold, waist-deep mud, gluttonous lice, and corpse-fed rats—contrasted sharply with the ringing phrases of politicians and generals justifying the unrelenting slaughter. War had ceased to be a noble and sporting affair, if it ever was. *No-Man's-Land*

In eastern Europe and the Balkans, the battle lines were more fluid. After a staunch defense, a combination of Austrian and German forces overran Serbia, Albania, and Romania. Farther north, Russia took the offensive early by invading Prussia in 1914. The Central Powers recovered quickly, however, and by the summer of 1915 combined German-Austrian forces drove the Russian armies out of East Prussia and then out of Poland and established a defensive line extending from the Baltic to the Ukraine. Russian counterattacks in 1916 and 1917 collapsed in a sea of casualties. Those Russian defeats undermined the popularity of the tsar and his government and played a significant role in fostering revolutionary ferment within Russian society. *The Eastern Front*

Many battles took place, but some were so horrific, so devastating, and so futile that their names are synonymous with human slaughter. The casualty figures attested to this bloodletting. In 1916 the Germans tried to break the deadlock with a huge *Bloodletting*

Mutilated body on the western front.

assault on the fortress of Verdun. The French rallying cry was "They shall not pass," and they did not—but at a tremendous cost: while the victorious French counted 315,000 dead, the defeated Germans suffered a loss of 280,000. Survivors recovered fewer than 160,000 identifiable bodies. The rest were unrecognizable or had been blown to bits by high explosives and sucked into the mud. To relieve the pressure on Verdun, British forces counterattacked at the Somme, and by November they had gained a few thousand yards at the cost of 420,000 casualties. The Germans suffered similar losses, although in the end neither side gained any strategic advantage.

New Rules of Engagement

Dying and suffering were not limited solely to combatants: the Great War established rules of engagement that made civilians targets of warfare. Because they were crucial to the war effort, millions of people out of uniform became targets of enemy military operations. On 30 August 1914, Parisians looked up at the sky and saw a new weapon of war, a huge, silent German zeppelin (a hydrogen-filled dirigible) whose underbelly rained bombs, eventually killing one person. That event heralded a new kind of warfare—air war against civilians. A less novel but more effective means of targeting civilian populations was the naval blockade. Military leaders on both sides used blockades to deny food to whole populations, hoping that starving masses would force their governments to capitulate. The British blockade of Germany during the war contributed to the deaths of an estimated half million Germans.

Total War: The Home Front

Helmuth Karl von Moltke (1800–1891), former chief of the Prussian General Staff, showed an uncanny insight long before 1914 when he predicted that future wars would not end with a single battle, because the defeat of a nation would not be acknowledged until the whole strength of its people was broken. He was right. As the Great War ground on, it became a conflict of attrition in which the organization of material and human resources was of paramount importance. War became total, fought between entire societies, not just between armies; and total victory was the only acceptable outcome that might justify the terrible sacrifices made by all sides. The nature of total war created a military front and a home front. The term *home front* expressed the important reality that the outcome of the war hinged on how effectively each nation mobilized its economy and activated its noncombatant citizens to support the war effort.

The Home Front

As the war continued beyond Christmas 1914 and as war weariness and a decline in economic capability set in, the response of all belligerents was to limit individual freedoms and give control of society increasingly over to military leaders. Because patriotism and courage alone could not guarantee victory, the governments of belligerent nations assumed control of the home front. Initially, ministers and generals shrank from compulsive measures, even conscription of recruits, but they quickly

Sources from the Past

Dulce et Decorum Est

The Great War produced a wealth of poetry. The poetic response to war covered a range of moods, from early romanticism and patriotism to cynicism, resignation, and the angry depiction of horror. Perhaps the greatest of all war poets was Wilfred Owen (1893–1918), whose poems are among the most poignant of the war. Owen, who enlisted for service on the western front in 1915, was injured in March 1917 and sent home. Declared fit for duty in August 1918, he returned to the front. German machine-gun fire killed him on 7 November, four days before the armistice, when he tried to cross the Sambre Canal.

Bent double, like old beggars under sacks,
Knock-kneed, coughing like hags, we cursed through
   sludge,
Till on the haunting flares we turned our backs
And towards our distant rest began to trudge.
Men marched asleep. Many had lost their boots
But limped on, blood-shod. All went lame; all blind;
Drunk with fatigue; deaf even to the hoots
Of gas-shells dropping softly behind.

Gas! GAS! Quick, boys!—An ecstasy of fumbling,
Fitting the clumsy helmets just in time;
But someone still was yelling out and stumbling
And floundering like a man in fire or lime.—
Dim, through the misty panes and thick green light
As under a green sea, I saw him drowning.

In all my dreams, before my helpless sight,
He plunges at me, guttering, choking, drowning.

If in some smothering dreams you too could pace
Behind the wagon that we flung him in,
And watch the white eyes writhing in his face,
His hanging face, like a devil's sick of sin;
If you could hear, at every jolt, the blood
Come gargling from the froth-corrupted lungs,
Obscene as cancer, bitter as the cud
Of vile, incurable sores on innocent tongues,—
My friend, you would not tell with such high zest
To children ardent for some desperate glory,
The old Lie: Dulce et decorum est
Pro patria mori.*

*Author's note: "Sweet and fitting is it to die for one's country" comes from a line by the Roman poet Horace (65–8 B.C.E.)

FOR FURTHER REFLECTION

How does Owen poetically describe the effects of a gas attack? Is his literary depiction more or less effective than detached descriptions of war's effects?

SOURCE: Edmund Blunden, ed. *The Poems of Wilfred Owen.* London: Chattus & Windus, 1933, p. 66.

changed their minds. Each belligerent government eventually militarized civilian war production by subordinating private enterprises to governmental control and imposing severe discipline on the labor process.

Economic measures were foremost in the minds of government leaders because the war created unprecedented demands for raw materials and manufactured goods. Those material requirements compelled governments to abandon long-cherished ideals of a laissez-faire capitalist market economy and to institute tight controls over economic life. Planning boards reorganized entire industries, set production quotas and priorities, and determined what would be produced and consumed. Government authorities also established wage and price controls, extended work hours, and in some instances restricted the movement of workers. Because bloody battlefields caused an insatiable appetite for soldiers, nations responded by extending military service. In Germany, for example, men between the ages of sixteen and sixty were eligible to serve at the front. By constantly tapping into the available male population, the war created an increasing demand for workers at home. Unemployment—a persistent feature of all prewar

Women at War

■ **Women at work in an English munitions factory.**

economies—vanished virtually overnight.

As men marched off to war, women marched off to work. Conscription took men out of the labor force, and wartime leaders exhorted women to fill the gaps in the workforce. A combination of patriotism and high wages drew women into formerly "male" jobs. The lives of women changed as they bobbed their hair and left home or domestic service for the workplace. Some women took over the management of farms and businesses left by their husbands, who went off to fight. Others found jobs as postal workers and police officers. Behind the battle lines, women were most visible as nurses, physicians, and communications clerks.

Perhaps the most crucial work performed by women during the war was the making of shells. Several million women, and sometimes children, put in long, hard hours in munitions factories. This work exposed them to severe dangers. The first came from explosions, because keeping sparks away from highly volatile materials was impossible. Many women died in these incidents, although government censorship during the war made it difficult to know how many women perished in this fashion. The other, more insidious danger came from working with TNT explosives. Although the authorities claimed that this work was not dangerous, exposure to TNT caused severe poisoning, depending on the length of exposure. Before serious illnesses manifested themselves, TNT poisoning marked its victims by turning their skin yellow and their hair orange. The accepted though ineffectual remedy for TNT poisoning was rest, good food, and plenty of fresh milk.

Middle- and upper-class women often reported that the war was a liberating experience, freeing them from older attitudes that had limited their work and their personal lives. At the least, the employment of upper-class women spawned a degree of deliverance from parental control and gave women a sense of mission. They knew that they were important to the war effort. The impact of the Great War on the lives of working-class women, in contrast, was relatively minor. Working-class women in cities had long been accustomed to earning wages, and for them war work proved less than liberating. Most of the belligerent governments promised equal pay for equal work, but in most instances that promise remained unfulfilled. Although women's industrial wages rose during the war, measurable gaps always remained between the incomes of men and women. In the end, substantial female employment was a transitory phenomenon. With few exceptions, the Great War only briefly suspended traditional patterns of work outside the home. Nevertheless, the extension of voting rights to women shortly after the war, in Britain (1918, for women thirty years and older), Germany (1919), and Austria

(1919), was in part due to the role women assumed during the Great War. Later in the century, war and revolution continued to serve as at least temporary liberating forces for women, especially in Russia (1917) and China (1949), where new communist governments discouraged the patriarchal family system and supported sexual equality, including birth control.

To maintain the spirit of the home front and to counter threats to national unity, governments resorted to the restriction of civil liberties, censorship of bad news, and vilification of the enemy through propaganda campaigns. While some government officials busily censored war news, people who had the temerity to criticize their nation's war effort were prosecuted as traitors. In

Propaganda

"The Heroes of Belgium 1914." French propaganda poster expresses outrage at the German invasion of Belgium.

France, for example, former prime minister Joseph Caillaux spent two years in prison awaiting trial because he had publicly suggested that the best interest of France would be to reach a compromise peace with Germany.

The propaganda offices of the belligerent nations tried to convince the public that military defeat would mean the destruction of everything worth living for, and to that end they did their utmost to discredit and dehumanize the enemy. Posters, pamphlets, and "scientific" studies depicted the enemy as subhuman savages who engaged in vile atrocities. While German propaganda depicted Russians as semi-Asiatic barbarians, French authorities chronicled the atrocities committed by the German "Hun" in Belgium. In 1917 the *Times* of London published a story claiming that Germans converted human corpses into fertilizer and food. With much less fanfare a later news story admitted that this information resulted from a sloppy translation: the German word for *horse* had been mistakenly translated as "human." German propaganda stooped equally low. One widely distributed poster invoked images of bestial black Allied soldiers raping German women, including pregnant women, to suggest the horrors that would follow if the nation's war effort failed. Most atrocity stories originated in the fertile imagination of propaganda officers, and their falsehood eventually engendered public skepticism and cynicism. Ironically, public disbelief of wartime propaganda led to an inability to believe in the abominations perpetrated during subsequent wars.

Conflict in East Asia and the Pacific

To many Asian and African peoples, the Great War was a murderous European civil war that quickly turned into a global conflict. There were three reasons for the war's expansion. First, European governments carried their animosities into their colonies, embroiling them—especially African societies—in their war. Second, because Europe's human reserves were not enough to satisfy the appetite of war, the British and the French augmented their ranks by recruiting men from their colonies. Millions of Africans and Asians were drawn into the war. Behind their trenches the French employed laborers from Algeria, China, and French Indochina, and the British did not hesitate to draft Indian and African troops for combat. The British in particular relied on troops furnished by the dominion lands, including Australia, New Zealand, Canada, Newfoundland, and South Africa. Third, the Great War assumed global significance because the desires and objectives of some principal actors that entered the conflict—Japan, the United States, and the Ottoman empire—had little to do with the murder in Sarajevo or the other issues that drove the Europeans to battle.

Japan's Entry into the War

On 15 August 1914 the Japanese government, claiming that it desired "to secure firm and enduring peace in Eastern Asia," sent an ultimatum to Germany demanding the handover of the German-leased territory of Jiaozhou (northeastern China) to Japanese authorities without compensation. The same note also demanded that the German navy unconditionally withdraw its warships from Japanese and Chinese waters. When the Germans refused to comply, the Japanese entered the war on the side of the Allies on 23 August 1914. Japanese forces took the fortress of Qingdao, a German-held port in China's Shandong Province, in November 1914, and between August and November of that year took possession of the German-held Marshall Islands, the Mariana Islands, Palau, and the Carolines. Forces from New Zealand and Australia joined in the Japanese quest for German-held islands in the Pacific, capturing German-held portions of Samoa in August 1914 and German-occupied possessions in the Bismarck Archipelago and New Guinea.

The Twenty-one Demands

After seizing German bases on the Shandong peninsula and on Pacific islands, Japan shrewdly exploited Allied support and European preoccupation to advance its own imperial interests in China. On 18 January 1915 the Japanese presented the Chinese government with twenty-one secret demands. The terms of that ultimatum, if accepted, would have reduced China to a protectorate of Japan. The most important demands were that the Chinese confirm the Japanese seizure of Shandong from Germany, grant Japanese industrial monopolies in central China, place Japanese overseers in key government positions, give Japan joint control of Chinese police forces, restrict their arms purchases to Japanese manufacturers, and make those purchases only with the approval of the Tokyo government. China submitted to most of the demands but rejected others. Chinese diplomats leaked the note to the British authorities, who spoke up for China, thus preventing total capitulation. The Twenty-one Demands reflected Japan's determination to dominate east Asia and served as the basis for future Japanese pressure on China.

Battles in Africa and Southwest Asia

The geographic extent of the conflict also broadened beyond Europe when the Allies targeted German colonies in Africa. When the war of 1914–1918 erupted in Europe, all of sub-Saharan Africa (except Ethiopia and Liberia) consisted of European colonies, with the Germans controlling four: Togoland, the Cameroons, German Southwest Africa, and German East Africa.

■ **An Indian gun crew in the Somme area, 1916.**

Unlike the capture of German colonies in the Pacific, which Allied forces accomplished during the first three months of the war with relative ease, the conquest of German colonies in Africa was difficult. Togoland fell to an Anglo-French force after three weeks of fighting, but it took extended campaigns ranging over vast distances to subdue the remaining German footholds in Africa. The Allied force included British, French, and Belgian troops and large contingents of Indian, Arab, and African soldiers. Fighting took place on land and sea; on lakes and rivers; in deserts, jungles, and swamps; and in the air. Germs were frequently more deadly than Germans; tens of thousands of Allied soldiers and workers succumbed to deadly tropical diseases. The German flag did not disappear from Africa until after the armistice took effect on 11 November 1918.

Gallipoli

The most extensive military operations outside Europe took place in the southwest Asian territories of the Ottoman empire, which was aligned with the Central Powers at the end of 1914. Seeking a way to break the stalemate on the western front, Winston Churchill (1874–1965), first lord of the Admiralty (British navy), suggested that an Allied strike against the Ottomans—a weak ally of the Central Powers—would hurt the Germans. Early in 1915 the British navy conducted an expedition to seize the approach to the Dardanelles Strait in an attempt to open a warm-water supply line to Russia through the Ottoman-controlled strait. After bombing the forts that defended the strait, Allied ships took damage from floating mines and withdrew without accomplishing their mission. After withdrawing the battleships, the British high command decided to land a combined force of English, Canadian, Australian, and New Zealand soldiers on the beaches of the Gallipoli peninsula. The campaign was a disaster. Turkish defenders, ensconced in the cliffs above, quickly pinned down the Allied troops on the beaches. Trapped between the sea and the hills, Allied soldiers dug in and engaged in their own version of trench warfare. The resulting stalemate produced a total of 250,000 casualties on each side. Despite the losses, Allied leaders took nine months to admit that their campaign had failed.

Gallipoli was a debacle with long-term consequences. Although the British directed the ill-fated campaign, it was mostly Canadians, Australians, and New Zealanders who suffered terrible casualties. That recognition led to a weakening of imperial ties and paved the way for emerging national identities. In Australia the date of the fateful landing, 25 April 1915, became enshrined as Anzac Day (an acronym for Australian and New Zealand Army Corps) and remains the country's most significant day of public homage. On the other side, the battle for the strait helped launch the political career of the commander of the Turkish division that defended Gallipoli. Mustafa Kemal (1881–1938) went on to play a crucial role in the formation of the modern Turkish state.

Armenian Massacres

The war provided the pretext for a campaign of extermination against the Ottoman empire's two million Armenians, the last major non-Muslim ethnic group under Ottoman rule seeking autonomy and eventual independence. Friction between Christian Armenians and Ottoman authorities went back to the nineteenth century, when distinct nationalist feelings stirred many of the peoples who lived under Ottoman rule.

Initially, Armenians had relied on government reforms to prevent discrimination against non-Muslim subjects by corrupt officials and extortionist tax collectors. When abuses persisted, Armenians resorted to confrontation. Armenian demonstrations against Ottoman authorities in 1890 and 1895 led to reprisals by a government that had become increasingly convinced that the Armenians were seeking independence, as other Christian minorities of the Balkans had done in previous decades.

After 1913 the Ottoman state adopted a new policy of Turkish nationalism intended to shore up the crumbling imperial edifice. The new nationalism stressed Turkish culture and traditions, which only aggravated tensions between Turkish rulers and non-Turkish subjects of the empire. In particular, the state viewed Christian minorities as an obstacle

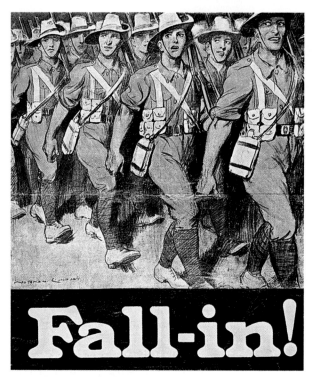

Australian recruiting poster.

to Turkism. During the Great War, the Ottoman government branded Armenians as a traitorous internal enemy, who threatened the security of the state, and then unleashed a murderous campaign against them. Forced mass evacuations, accompanied by starvation, dehydration, and exposure, led to the death of tens of thousands of Armenians. An equally deadly assault on the Armenians came by way of government-organized massacres that claimed victims through mass drowning, incineration, or assaults with blunt instruments.

Those wartime atrocities that took place principally between 1915 and 1917 have become known as Armenian genocide. Best estimates suggest that close to a million Armenians perished. Although it is generally agreed that the Armenian genocide did occur, the Turkish government in particular rejects the label of genocide and claims that Armenian deaths resulted not from a state-sponsored plan of mass extermination but from communal warfare perpetrated by Christians and Muslims, disease, and famine.

The Ottoman Empire

After successfully fending off Allied forces on the beaches of Gallipoli in 1915 and in Mesopotamia in 1916, Ottoman armies retreated slowly on all fronts. After yielding to the Russians in the Caucasus, Turkish troops were unable to defend the empire against invading British armies that drew heavily on recruits from Egypt, India, Australia, and New Zealand. As the armies smashed the Ottoman state—one entering Mesopotamia and the other advancing from the Suez Canal toward Palestine—they received significant support from an Arab revolt against the Turks. In 1916, abetted by the British, the nomadic bedouin of Arabia under the leadership of Ibn Ali Hussain, sherif of Mecca and king of the Hejaz (1856–1931), and others rose up against Turkish rule. The motivation for the Arab revolt centered on securing independence from the Ottoman empire and subsequently creating a unified Arab nation spanning lands from Syria to Yemen. The British government did not keep its promise of Arab independence after the war.

The End of the War

The war produced strains within all the belligerent nations, but most of them managed, often ruthlessly, to cope with food riots, strikes, and mutinies. In the Russian empire, the war amplified existing stresses to such an extent that the Romanov dynasty was forced to abdicate in favor of a provisional government in the spring of 1917. Eight months later, the provisional government yielded power to Bolshevik revolutionaries, who took Russia out of the war early in 1918. This blow to the Allies

Bolshevik (BOHL-sheh-vihk)

was more than offset by the entry of the United States into the conflict in 1917, which turned the tide of war in 1918. The resources of the United States finally compelled the exhausted Central Powers to sue for peace in November 1918.

In 1919 the victorious Allies gathered in Paris to hammer out a peace settlement that turned out to be a compromise that pleased few of the parties involved. The most significant consequence of the war was Europe's diminished role in the world. The war of 1914–1918 undermined Europe's power and simultaneously promoted nationalist aspirations among colonized peoples who clamored for self-determination and national independence. For the time being, however, the major imperialist powers kept their grip on their overseas holdings.

Revolution in Russia

The Great War had undermined the Russian state. In the spring of 1917, disintegrating armies, mutinies, and food shortages provoked a series of street demonstrations and strikes in Petrograd (St. Petersburg). The inability of police forces to suppress the uprisings, and the subsequent mutiny of troops garrisoned in the capital, persuaded Tsar Nicholas II (reigned 1894–1917) to abdicate the throne. Thus Russia ceased to be a monarchy, and the Romanov dynasty disappeared after more than three hundred years of uninterrupted rule. The March Revolution—the first of two revolutions in 1917—was an unplanned and incomplete affair.

The March Revolution

After its success in Petrograd, the revolution spread throughout the country, and political power in Russia shifted to two new agencies: the provisional government and the Petrograd soviet of Workers' and Soldiers' Deputies. Soviets, which were revolutionary councils organized by socialists, appeared for the first time during the Russian revolution of 1905 (see chapter 32). In 1917 soviets of Workers' and Soldiers' Deputies surfaced all over Russia, wielding considerable power through their control of factories and segments of the military. The period between March and November witnessed a political struggle between the provisional government and the powerful Petrograd soviet. At first the new government enjoyed considerable public support as it disbanded the tsarist police; repealed all limitations on freedom of speech, press, and association; and abolished laws that discriminated against ethnic or religious groups; but it failed to satisfy popular demands for an end to war and for land reform. It claimed that, being provisional, it could not make fundamental changes such as confiscating land and distributing it among peasants. Any such change had to be postponed for decision by a future constituent assembly. The government also pledged itself to "unswervingly carry out the agreements made with the Allies" and promised to continue the war to a victorious conclusion. The Petrograd soviet, in contrast, called for an immediate peace. Such radicals were the only ones in Russia determined to end the war and hence gained more support from the people of Russia.

The Struggle for Power

Into this tense political situation stepped Vladimir Ilyich Lenin (1870–1924), a revolutionary Marxist who had been living in exile in Switzerland. Born into a warm and loving family, Lenin grew up in the confines of a moderately prosperous family living in the provincial Russian town of Simbirsk. In 1887, shortly after his father's death, the police arrested and hanged his older brother for plotting to assassinate the tsar, an event that seared Lenin's youth. Following a brief career as a lawyer, Lenin spent many years abroad, devoting himself to studying Marxist thought and writing political pamphlets. In contrast to Marx, Lenin viewed the industrial working class as incapable of developing the proper revolutionary consciousness that would lead to effective political action. To Lenin the industrial proletariat required the leadership of a well-organized and highly disciplined party, a workers' vanguard that would serve as the catalyst for revolution and for the realization of a socialist society.

Lenin

Vladimir Lenin makes a speech in Red Square on the first anniversary (1918) of the Bolshevik Revolution.

In a moment of high drama, the German High Command transported Lenin and other revolutionaries in 1917 to Russia in a sealed train, hoping that this committed antiwar activist would stir up trouble and bring about Russia's withdrawal from the war. Lenin headed the Bolsheviks, the radical wing of the Russian Social Democratic Party. In April he began calling for the transfer of legal authority to the soviets and advocated uncompromising opposition to the war. Initially, his party opposed his radicalism, but he soon succeeded in converting his fellow Bolsheviks to his proposals.

The November Revolution

The Bolsheviks, who were a small minority among revolutionary working-class parties, eventually gained control of the Petrograd soviet. Crucial to that development was the provisional government's insistence on continuing the war, its inability to feed the population, and its refusal to undertake land reform. Those policies led to a growing conviction among workers and peasants that their problems could be solved only by the soviets. The Bolsheviks capitalized on that mood with effective slogans such as "All Power to the Soviets" and, most famous, "Peace, Land, and Bread." In September, Lenin persuaded the Central Committee of the Bolshevik Party to organize an armed insurrection and seize power in the name of the All-Russian National Congress of Soviets, which was then convening in Petrograd. During the night of 6 November and the following day, armed workers, soldiers, and sailors stormed the Winter Palace, the home of the provisional government. By the afternoon of 7 November, the virtually bloodless insurrection had run its course, and power passed from the provisional government into the hands of Lenin and the Bolshevik Party. The U.S. journalist John Reed (1887–1920), who witnessed the Bolshevik seizure of power, understood the significance of the events when he referred to them as "ten days that shook the world." Lenin and his followers were poised to destroy the traditional patterns and values of Russian society and challenge the institutions of liberal society everywhere.

Treaty of Brest-Litovsk

The Bolshevik rulers ended Russia's involvement in the Great War by signing the Treaty of Brest-Litovsk with Germany on 3 March 1918. The treaty gave the Germans possession or control of much of Russia's territory (the Baltic states, the Caucasus, Finland, Poland, and the Ukraine) and one-quarter of its population. The terms of the treaty were harsh and humiliating, but taking Russia out of the war gave the new government an opportunity to deal with internal problems. Russia's departure from the war meant that Germany could concentrate all its resources on the western front.

U.S. Intervention and Collapse of the Central Powers

The year 1917 was crucial for another reason: it marked the entry of the United States into the war on the side of the Allies. In 1914 the American public firmly opposed intervention in a European war. Woodrow Wilson (1856–1924) was reelected president in 1916 because he campaigned on a nonintervention platform. That sentiment soon changed. After the outbreak of the war, the United States pursued a

Sources from the Past

The State and Revolution

V. I. Lenin believed that the Great War would result in a revolutionary crisis that would lead to proletarian revolution. While hiding in Finland in the fall of 1917, Lenin composed the authoritative statement on Bolshevik political theory, published under the title The State and Revolution *(1918). Lenin argued that the capitalist state had to be destroyed by a dictatorship of the proletariat before communism could be realized.* The State and Revolution *was published after the Bolshevik seizure of power, prompting Lenin to write in a postscript: "It is more pleasant and useful to go through 'the experience of the revolution' than to write about it."*

In capitalist society, providing it develops under the most favorable conditions, we have a more or less complete democracy in the democratic republic. But this democracy is always hemmed in by the narrow limits set by capitalist exploitation, and consequently always remains, in reality, a democracy for the minority, only for the propertied classes, only for the rich. Freedom in capitalist society always remains about the same as it was in the ancient Greek republics: freedom for the slave-owners. Owing to the conditions of capitalist exploitation the modern wage slaves are so crushed by want and poverty that "they cannot be bothered with democracy," "they cannot be bothered with politics"; in the ordinary peaceful course of events the majority of the population is debarred from participation in public and political life.

But from this capitalist democracy—that is inevitably narrow, and stealthily pushes aside the poor, and is therefore hypocritical and false to the core—forward development does not proceed simply, directly and smoothly towards "greater and greater democracy," as the liberal professors and petty-bourgeois opportunists would have us believe. No, forward development, i.e., toward Communism, proceeds through the dictatorship

of the proletariat; and cannot do otherwise, for the *resistance* of the capitalist exploiters cannot be *broken* by anyone else or in any other way.

. . . the dictatorship of the proletariat imposes a series of restrictions on the freedom of the oppressors, the exploiters, the capitalists. We must suppress them in order to free humanity from wage slavery, their resistance must be crushed by force; . . .

Only in Communist society, when the resistance of the capitalists has been completely crushed, when the capitalists have disappeared, when there are no classes (i.e., when there is no difference between the members of society as regards their relation to the social means of production), *only* then "the state . . . ceases to exist," and it "*becomes possible to speak of freedom.*" Only then will there become possible and be realized a truly complete democracy, a democracy without any exceptions whatever.

FOR FURTHER REFLECTION

Why does Lenin argue that the political participation of "wage slaves" was in actuality very limited, even in democratic states?

SOURCE: V. I. Lenin. *The State and Revolution*. Peking: Foreign Languages Press, 1973, pp. 105–6.

---

neutrality that favored the Allies, and as the war progressed, the United States became increasingly committed economically to an Allied victory.

During the first two years of the war, the U.S. economy coped with a severe business recession that saw thousands of businesses fail and unemployment reach 15 percent. Economic recovery became dependent on sales of war materials, especially on British orders for munitions. Because U.S. companies sold huge amounts of supplies to the Allies, insistence on neutrality seemed hypocritical at best. With the war grinding on, the Allies took out large loans with American banks, which persuaded some Americans that an Allied victory made good financial sense. Moreover, by the spring of 1917, the Allies had depleted their means of paying for essential supplies from the United States and probably could not have maintained their war effort had the United States remained neutral. An Allied victory and, hence, the ability to pay off Allied war debts could be accomplished only by direct U.S. participation in the Great War.

Economic Considerations

In 1915 artist Willy Stower depicted a ship sinking as a result of a submarine attack.

Submarine Warfare

The official factor in the United States' decision to enter the war was Germany's resumption of unrestricted submarine warfare in February 1917. At the outset of the war, U.S. government officials asserted the traditional doctrine of neutral rights for American ships because they wanted to continue trading with belligerents, most notably the British and the French. With the German surface fleet bottled up in the Baltic, Germany's wartime leaders grew desperately dependent on their submarine fleet to strangle Britain economically and break the British blockade of the Central Powers. German military experts calculated that submarine attacks against the ships of Great Britain and all the ships headed to Great Britain would bring about the defeat of Great Britain in six months. German subs often sank neutral merchant ships without first giving a warning as required by international law. On 7 May 1915, a German submarine sank the British passenger liner *Lusitania* off the Irish coast with a loss of 1,198 lives, including 128 U.S. citizens. Technically, the ship was a legitimate target, because it carried 4,200 cases of ammunition and traveled through a declared war zone. Nevertheless, segments of the American public were outraged, and during the next two years the country's mood increasingly turned against Germany. Allied propaganda, especially British manipulation of information, also swayed public opinion.

America Declares War

Even though the British naval blockade directed at the Central Powers constantly interfered with American shipping, Woodrow Wilson nonetheless moved his nation to war against Germany. In January 1917, with his country still at peace, Wilson began to enumerate U.S. war aims, and on 2 April he urged the Congress of the United States to adopt a war resolution. In his ringing war message Wilson equated German "warfare against commerce" with "warfare against mankind," intoning that "the world must be made safe for democracy." Republican senator George W. Norris, arguing for U.S. neutrality, countered by saying "I feel that we are about to put the dollar sign upon the American flag." That protest was to no avail, and on 6 April 1917 the United States declared war against Germany. The U.S. entry proved decisive in breaking the stalemate.

The corrosive effects of years of bloodletting showed. For the first two years of the conflict, most people supported their governments' war efforts, but the continuing ravages of war took their toll everywhere. In April 1916 Irish nationalists mounted the Great Easter Rebellion, which attempted unsuccessfully to overthrow British rule in Ireland. The Central Powers suffered from food shortages as a result of the British blockade, and increasing numbers of people took to the streets to demonstrate against declining food rations. Food riots

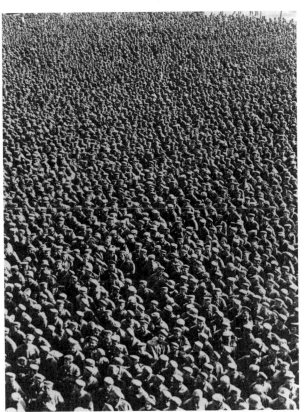

Collapsing Fronts

German prisoners taken in France in the autumn of 1918.

were complemented by strikes as prewar social conflicts reemerged. Governments reacted harshly to those challenges, pouncing on strikers, suppressing demonstrators, and jailing dissidents. Equally dangerous was the breakdown of military discipline. At the German naval base in Kiel, sailors revolted in the summer of 1917 and again, much more seriously, in the fall of 1918. In the wake of another failed offensive during the spring of 1917, which resulted in ghastly casualties, French soldiers lost confidence in their leadership. When ordered to attack once again, they refused. The extent of the mutiny was enormous: 50,000 soldiers were involved, resulting in 23,385 courts-martial and 432 death sentences. So tight was French censorship that the Germans, who could have taken advantage of this situation, did not learn about the mutiny until the war was over.

Against the background of civilian disillusionment and deteriorating economic conditions, Germany took the risk of throwing its remaining might at the western front in the spring of 1918. The gamble failed, and as the offensive petered out, the Allies broke through the front and started pushing the Germans back. By that time Germany had effectively exhausted its human and material means to wage war. Meanwhile, Bulgaria capitulated to the invading Allies on 30 September, the Ottomans concluded an armistice on 30 October, and Austria-Hungary surrendered on 4 November. Finally, the Germans accepted an armistice, which took effect on 11 November 1918. At last the guns went silent.

After the War

The immediate effects of the Great War were all too obvious. Aside from the physical destruction, which was most visible in northern France and Belgium, the war had killed, disabled, orphaned, or rendered homeless millions of people. Conservative estimates suggest that the war killed fifteen million people and wounded twenty million others. In the immediate postwar years, millions more succumbed to the effects of starvation, malnutrition, and epidemic diseases.

The Influenza Pandemic of 1918

The end of the Great War coincided with the arrival of one of the worst pandemics ever recorded in human history. No one knows its origins or why it vanished in mid-1919, but by the time this virulent influenza disappeared, it had left more than twenty million dead. The disease killed more people than did the Great War, and it hit young adults—a group usually not severely affected by influenza—with particular ferocity. Contemporaries called it the Spanish flu because the first major documented outbreak of the disease occurred in Spain in late 1918.

The Great War did not cause the flu pandemic of 1918–1919, but wartime traffic on land and sea probably contributed to the spread of the infection. It killed swiftly wherever it went. From the remotest villages in Arctic climates and crowded cities in India and the United States to the battlefields of Europe, men and women were struck down by high fever. Within a few days they were dead. One estimate puts deaths in India alone at seven million. In Calcutta, the postal service and the legal system ground to a halt. In the United States, the flu killed more Americans than all the wars fought in the twentieth century put together. In cutting a swath across west Africa, it left in its deadly path more than one million victims. The Pacific islands suffered worst of all as the flu wiped out up to twenty-five percent of their entire population.

The influenza plague never discriminated. It struck the rich as fiercely as the poor. It decimated men and women equally. It did not distinguish between the hungry and the well nourished, and it took the sick as well as the healthy. The presence or absence of doctors and nurses never made any difference. There was no cure for the flu of 1918.

The Paris Settlement

Before the costs of the war were assessed fully, world attention shifted to Paris. There, in 1919, the victorious powers convened to arrange a postwar settlement and set terms for the defeated nations. At the outset, people on both sides of the war had high hopes for the settlement, but in the end it left a bitter legacy. Because the twenty-seven nations represented at Paris had different and often conflicting aims, many sessions of the conference deteriorated into pandemonium. Ultimately, Georges Clemenceau (1841–1929), Lloyd George (1863–1945), and Woodrow Wilson—the representative leaders of France, Great Britain, and the United States—dominated the deliberations. The Allies did not permit representatives of the Central Powers to participate. In addition, the Allies threatened to renew the war if the terms they laid down were not accepted. Significantly, the Soviet Union was not invited to the conference. Throughout this time the British blockade of Germany remained in effect, adding a sense of urgency to the proceedings. That situation later gave rise to the charge of a dictated peace, especially because no foreign troops set foot on German soil.

Wilson's Fourteen Points

One year before the opening of the Paris Peace Conference in January 1918, U.S. president Woodrow Wilson forwarded a proposal for a just and enduring postwar peace settlement. Wilson's postwar vision had subsequently prompted the defeated Central Powers to announce their acceptance of his so-called Fourteen Points as the basis for the armistice. They also expected the Allies to use them as the foundation for later peace treaties. Key among Wilson's Fourteen Points were the following recommendations: open covenants (agreements) of peace, openly arrived at; absolute freedom of navigation on the seas in peace and war; the removal of all economic barriers and the establishment of an equality of trade conditions among all nations; adequate guarantees for a reduction in national armaments; adjustments of colonial disputes to give equal weight to the interests of the controlling government and the colonial population; and a call for "a general association of nations." The idealism expressed in the Fourteen Points gave Wilson a position of moral leadership among the Allies. Those same allies also opposed various points of Wilson's peace formula, because those points compromised the secret wartime agreements by which they had agreed to distribute among themselves territories and possessions of the defeated nations. The defeated powers, in turn, later felt betrayed when they faced the harsh peace treaties that so clearly violated the spirit of the Fourteen Points.

The final form of the treaties represented a series of compromises among the victors. The hardest terms originated with the French, who desired the destruction or the permanent weakening of German power. Thus, in addition to requiring Ger-

The Peace Treaties

Political leaders signing the Treaty of Versailles.

many to accept sole responsibility and guilt for causing the war, the victors demanded a reduction in the military potential of the former Central Powers. For example, the Treaty of Versailles (1919) denied the Germans a navy and an air force and limited the size of the German army to 100,000 troops. In addition, the Allies prohibited Germany and Austria from entering into any sort of political union. The French and the British agreed that the defeated Central Powers must pay for the cost of the war and required the payment of reparations either in money or in kind. Although the German government and the public decried the Treaty of Versailles as being excessively harsh, it was no more severe in its terms that the Treaty of Brest-Litovsk that the Germans imposed on Russia in 1918.

The Paris peace conference resulted in several additional treaties. Bulgaria accepted the Treaty of Neuilly (1919), ceding only small portions of territory, because the Allies feared that major territorial changes in the Balkans would destabilize the region. That view did not apply to the dual monarchy of Austria-Hungary, whose imperial unity disintegrated under the impact of the war. The peacemakers recognized the territorial breakup of the former empire in two separate treaties: the Treaty of St. Germain (1919), between the Allies and the Republic of Austria, and the Treaty of Trianon (1920), between the Allies and the Kingdom of Hungary. Both Austria and Hungary suffered severe territorial losses, which the Allies claimed were necessary in order to find territorial boundaries that accorded closely with the principle of self-determination. For example, the peace settlement reduced Hungarian territory to one-third of its prewar size and decreased the nation's population from 28 to 8 million people.

Arrangements between the defeated Ottoman empire and the Allies proved to be a more complicated and protracted affair. The Treaty of Sèvres (1920) effectively dissolved the empire, calling for the surrender of Ottoman Balkan and Arab provinces and the occupation of eastern and southern Anatolia by foreign powers. The treaty was acceptable to the government of sultan Mohammed VI, but not to Turkish nationalists who rallied around their wartime hero Mustafa Kemal. As head of the Turkish nationalist movement, Mustafa Kemal set out to defy the Allied terms. He organized a national army that drove out Greek, British, French, and Italian occupation forces and abolished the sultanate and replaced it with the Republic of Turkey, with Ankara as its capital. In a great diplomatic victory for Turkish nationalists, the Allied powers officially recognized the Republic of Turkey in a final peace agreement, the Treaty of Lausanne (1923).

Atatürk

As president of the republic, Mustafa Kemal, now known as Atatürk ("Father of the Turks"), instituted an ambitious program of modernization that emphasized economic development and secularism. Government support of critical industries and businesses, and other forms of state intervention in the economy designed to ensure rapid economic development, resulted in substantial long-term economic progress. The government's policy of secularism dictated the complete separation between the existing Muslim religious establishment and the state. The policy resulted in the replacement of religious with secular institutions of education and justice, the emancipation of women, including their right to vote, the adoption of European-derived law, Hindu-Arabic numerals, the Roman alphabet, and western clothing. Theoretically heading a constitutional democracy, Atatürk ruled Turkey as a virtual dictator until his death in 1938.

Turkey's postwar transformations and its success in refashioning the terms of peace proved to be something of an exception. In the final analysis, the peace settlement was strategically weak because too few participants had a stake in maintaining it and too many had an interest in revising it. German expansionist aims in Europe, which probably played a role in the nation's decision to enter the Great War, remained unresolved, as did Italian territorial designs in the Balkans and Japanese influence in China. Those issues virtually ensured that the two decades following the peace settlement became merely a twenty-year truce, characterized by power rivalries and intermittent violence that led to yet another global war.

The League of Nations

In an effort to avoid future destructive conflicts, the diplomats in Paris created the League of Nations. The League was the first permanent international security organization whose principal mission was to maintain world peace. At the urging of U.S. president Woodrow Wilson, the Covenant of the League of Nations was made an integral part of the peace treaties, and every signatory to a peace treaty had to accept this new world organization. Initially, the League seemed to be the sign of a new era: twenty-six of its forty-two original members were countries outside Europe, suggesting that it transcended European interests.

The League had two major flaws that rendered it ineffective. First, though designed to solve international disputes through arbitration, it had no power to enforce its decisions. Second, it relied on *collective security* as a tool for the preservation of global peace. The basic premise underlying collective security arrangements was the concept that aggression against any one state was considered aggression against all the other states, which had pledged to aid one another. Shared deterrence could assume different forms, such as diplomatic pressure, economic sanctions, and, ultimately, force. However, the basic precondition for collective security—participation by all the great powers—never materialized, because at any given time one or more of the major powers did not belong to the League. The United States never joined the organization because the U.S. Senate rejected the idea. Germany, which viewed the League as a club of Allied victors, and Japan, which saw it as an instrument of imperialism, left the League of Nations in 1933, as did some smaller powers. Italy, chastised by the League for imperial adventures in Ethiopia, withdrew from it in 1937. The Soviet Union, which regarded the League as a tool of global capitalism, joined the organization in 1934, only to face expulsion in 1940. Although its failure to stop aggression in the 1930s led to its demise in 1940, the League established the pattern for a permanent international organization and served as a model for its successor, the United Nations.

Self-Determination

One of the principal themes of the peacemaking process was the concept of self-determination, which was promoted most intensely by Woodrow Wilson. Wilson believed that self-determination was the key to international peace and cooperation. With respect to Europe, that principle sometimes translated into reality. For example, Poland, Czechoslovakia, and Yugoslavia (Kingdom of Serbs, Croats, and Slovenes until 1929) already existed as sovereign states by 1918, and by the end of the confer-

Map 34.2 **Territorial changes in Europe after the Great War.** Observe the territories ceded by the Central Powers and the Soviet Union. Which power lost the most territory, and why?

ence, the principle of self-determination had triumphed in many areas that were previously under the control of the Austro-Hungarian and Russian empires. Yet in other instances peacemakers pushed the principle aside for strategic and security reasons, such as in Austria and Germany, whose peoples were denied the right to form one nation. At other times, diplomats violated the notion of self-determination because they found it impossible to redraw national boundaries in accordance with nationalist aspirations without creating large minorities on one side or the other of a boundary line. Poland was one case in point; one-third of the population did not speak Polish. A more complicated situation existed in Czechoslovakia. The peoples who gave the republic its name—the Czechs and the Slovaks—totaled only 67 percent of the population, with the remaining population consisting of Germans (22 percent), Ruthenes (6 percent), and Hungarians (5 percent). On the surface, the creation of Yugoslavia ("Land of the South Slavs") represented a triumph of self-determination, because it politically united related peoples who for centuries had chafed under foreign rule. Beneath that unity, however, there lingered the separate national identities embraced by Serbs, Croats, and Slovenes.

The Mandate System

However imperfect the results, the peacemakers at Paris tried to apply the principle of self-determination and nationality throughout Europe. Elsewhere, however, they did not do so. The unwillingness to apply the principle of self-determination became most obvious when the victors confronted the issue of what to do with Germany's former colonies and the Arab territories of the Ottoman empire. Because the United States rejected the establishment of old-fashioned colonies, the European powers came up with the enterprising idea of trusteeship. Article 22 of the Covenant of the League of Nations referred to the colonies and territories of the former Central Powers as areas "inhabited by peoples not yet able to stand by themselves under the strenuous conditions of the modern world." As a result, "The tutelage of such peoples should be entrusted to the advanced nations who . . . can best undertake this responsibility." The League divided the mandates into three classes based on the presumed development of their populations in the direction of fitness for self-government. The administration of the mandates fell to the victorious powers of the Great War.

The Germans interpreted the mandate system as a division of colonial booty by the victors, who had conveniently forgotten to apply the tutelage provision to their own colonies. German cynicism was more than matched by Arab outrage. The establishment of mandates in the former territories of the Ottoman empire violated promises (made to Arabs) by French and British leaders during the war. They had promised Arab nationalists independence from the Ottoman empire and had promised Jewish nationalists in Europe a homeland in Palestine. Where the Arabs hoped to form independent states, the French (in Lebanon and Syria) and the British (in Iraq and Palestine) established mandates. The Allies viewed the mandate system as a reasonable compromise between the reality of imperialism and the ideal of self-determination. To the peoples who were directly affected, the mandate system smacked of continued imperial rule draped in a cloak of respectability.

Challenges to European Preeminence

The Great War changed Europe forever, but to most Europeans the larger world and the Continent's role in it remained essentially unchanged. With the imperial powers still ruling over their old colonies and new protectorates, it appeared that European global hegemony was more secure. Yet that picture did not correspond to reality. The Great War did irreparable damage to European power and prestige and set the stage for a process of decolonization that gathered momentum during and after the Second World War. The war of 1914–1918 accelerated the growth of nationalism in the European-controlled parts of the world, fueling desires for independence and self-determination.

Weakened Europe

The decline in European power was closely related to diminished economic stature, a result of the commitment to total war. In time, Europe overcame many war-induced economic problems, such as high rates of inflation and huge public debts, but other economic dislocations were permanent and damaging. Most significant was the loss of overseas investments and foreign markets, which had brought huge financial returns. Nothing is more indicative of Europe's reduced economic might than the reversal of the economic relationship between Europe and the United States. Whereas the United States was a debtor nation before 1914, owing billions of dollars to European investors, by 1919 it was a major creditor.

A loss of prestige overseas and a weakening grip on colonies also reflected the undermining of Europe's global hegemony. Colonial subjects in Africa, Asia, and the Pacific often viewed the Great War as a civil war among the European nations, a bloody spectacle in which the haughty bearers of an alleged superior society vilified

Map 34.3 **Territorial changes in southwest Asia after the Great War.** The Great War completed the process of disintegration of the Ottoman empire and left much of the region in limbo. What was the reaction in the region when European statesmen assigned former Ottoman territories to French or British control under the League of Nations mandates?

and slaughtered one another. Because Europe seemed weak, divided, and vulnerable, the white overlords no longer appeared destined to rule over colonized subjects. The colonials who returned home from the war in Europe and southwest Asia reinforced those general impressions with their own firsthand observations. In particular, they were less inclined to be obedient imperial subjects.

Revolutionary Ideas

The war also helped spread revolutionary ideas to the colonies. The U.S. war aims spelled out in the Fourteen Points raised the hopes of peoples under imperial rule and promoted nationalist aspirations. The peacemakers repeatedly invoked the concept of self-determination, and Wilson publicly proposed that in all colonial questions "the interests of the native populations be given equal weight with the desires of European governments." Wilson seemed to call for nothing less than national independence and self-rule. Nationalists struggling to organize anti-imperialist resistance also sought inspiration from the Soviet Union, whose leaders denounced all forms of imperialism and pledged their support to independence movements. Taken together, these messages were subversive to imperial control and had a great appeal for colonial peoples. The postwar disappointments and temporary setbacks experienced by nationalist movements did not diminish their desire for self-rule and self-determination.

———

The assassination of the Austrian archduke Francis Ferdinand had a galvanizing effect on a Europe torn by national rivalries, colonial disputes, and demands for self-determination. In the summer of 1914, inflexible war plans and a tangled alliance system transformed a local war between Austria-Hungary and Serbia into a European-wide clash of arms. With the entry of the Ottoman empire, Japan, and the United States, the war of 1914–1918 became a global conflict. Although many belligerents organized their societies for total war and drew on the resources of their overseas empires, the war remained at a bloody stalemate until the United States entered the conflict in 1917. The tide turned, and the combatants signed an armistice in November 1918. The Great War, a brutal encounter between societies and peoples, inflicted ghastly human casualties, severely damaged national economies, and discredited established political and cultural traditions. The war also altered the political landscape of many lands as it destroyed four dynasties and their empires and fostered the creation of several new European nations. In Russia the war served as a backdrop for the world's first successful socialist revolution. In the end the Great War sapped the strength of European colonial powers while promoting nationalist aspirations among colonized peoples.

CHRONOLOGY

1914	Assassination of Archduke Francis Ferdinand
1915	German submarine sinks the *Lusitania*
1915	Japan makes Twenty-one Demands on China
1915	Gallipoli campaign
1916	Battles at Verdun and the Somme
1917	German resumption of unrestricted submarine warfare
1917	United States declaration of war on Germany
1917	Bolshevik Revolution
1918	Treaty of Brest-Litovsk
1918	Armistice suspends hostilities
1919	Paris Peace Conference
1920	First Meeting of the League of Nations
1923	Atatürk proclaims Republic of Turkey

FOR FURTHER READING

Joanna Bourke. *Dismembering the Male: Men's Bodies, Britain, and the Great War.* Chicago, 1996. A study that examines the most intimate site of the war—the bodies of the men who fought it.

Robert B. Bruce. *A Fraternity of Arms: America and France in the Great War.* Lawrence, Kans., 2003. Military history arguing that America's cooperation with France constituted the crucial alliance in World War I.

Jonathan W. Daly. *The Watchful State: Security Police and Opposition in Russia, 1906–1917.* DeKalb, Ill., 2004. Study of the Russian secret police and their policies toward early revolutionary activities.

Belinda Davis. *Home Fires Burning: Food, Politics, and Everyday Life in World War I Berlin.* Chapel Hill, 2000. Effectively covers daily life in wartime and also offers insights into how government policies during the war affected the reconstruction of society following it.

Modris Eckstein. *Rites of Spring: The Great War and the Birth of the Modern Age.* Boston, 1989. An imaginative cultural study that ranges widely.

Gerald D. Feldman. *Army, Industry, and Labor in Germany, 1914–1918.* Princeton, 1966. A pioneering work on the impact of total war on the home front.

Niall Ferguson. *The Pity of War: Explaining World War I.* New York, 2000. A stimulating example of revisionist history that shifts the blame for the war away from Germany and onto England.

Paul Fussell. *Great War and Modern Memory.* Oxford, 1975. An original and deeply moving piece of cultural history.

Peter Gatrell. *Russia's First World War: A Social and Economic History.* London, 2005. Traces the impact of World War I on Russian society before the revolution.

Felix Gilbert. *The End of the European Era, 1890 to the Present.* New York, 1979. An information-laden study that argues that the Great War destroyed Europe's centrality in the world.

Paul G. Halpern. *A Naval History of World War I.* Annapolis, 1994. Unlike most other treatments, this work covers all participants in all major theaters.

Gerd Hardach. *The First World War, 1914–1918.* Berkeley, 1977. A brief and excellent introduction to the economic aspects of the conflict.

Maureen Healy. *Vienna and the Fall of the Habsburg Empire: Total War and Everyday Life in World War I.* New York, 2004. Argues that hardships and domestic conflicts among civilians led to the fall of Vienna, which preceded the collapse of the empire.

Margaret Randolph Higonnet et al. *Behind the Lines.* New Haven, 1990. Women's work and the war industry take center stage.

Hubertus F. Jahn. *Patriotic Culture in Russia during World War I.* Ithaca, 1995. Charts the rise and fall of Russian patriotism through popular culture.

James Joll. *The Origins of the First World War.* 2nd ed. London, 1991. The most lucid and balanced introduction to a complex and controversial subject.

John Keegan. *The First World War.* New York, 1999. A comprehensive and a stunningly vivid account of the Great War.

John Maynard Keynes. *The Economic Consequences of the Peace.* New York, 1920. A classic and devastating critique of the Versailles treaty.

John H. Morrow. *The Great War. An Imperial History.* New York, 2003. A global history of the Great War that places the conflict squarely in the context of imperialism.

Michael S. Neiberg. *Fighting the Great War.* Cambridge, Mass., 2005. A good blend of narrative and analysis, this work highlights the global reach of the conflict.

Richard Pipes. *The Russian Revolution 1899–1919.* 2nd ed. London, 1992. An up-to-date and well-argued interpretation.

Erich Remarque. *All Quiet on the Western Front.* New York, 1958. A fictional account of trench warfare.

Hew Strachan. *The First World War.* Vol. 1: *To Arms.* New York, 2001. The first of three anticipated volumes, this is a masterly work that treats the war in global rather than European terms.

Barbara Tuchman. *The Guns of August.* New York, 1962. Spellbinding narrative of the coming of the war.

Robert Wohl. *The Generation of 1914.* Cambridge, 1979. Elegantly captures the ideas and attitudes of the generations that experienced the Great War.

An Age of Anxiety

Probing Cultural Frontiers
Postwar Pessimism
Revolutions in Physics and Psychology
Experimentation in Art and Architecture

Global Depression
The Great Depression
Despair and Government Action
Economic Experimentation

Challenges to the Liberal Order
Communism in Russia
The Fascist Alternative
Italian Fascism
German National Socialism

Born on a lovely spring day in 1889, in a quaint Austrian village, he was the apple of his mother's eye. He basked in Klara's warmth and indulgence as a youth, enjoying the fine life of a middle-class child. As he grew older, he sensed a tension that long stayed with him, a vague anxiety that stemmed from the competing expectations of his parents. Contented with the dreamy indolence allowed by Klara, he bristled at the demands of his father, Alois. Alois expected him to follow in his footsteps, to study hard and enter the Austrian civil service. He had no desire to become a bureaucrat. In fact, he envisioned a completely different life for himself. He wanted to be an artist. His school grades slipped, and that seemed an appropriate way to express his discontent and sabotage his father's pedestrian plans for his future.

Alois's unexpected death in 1903 freed him from that awful future. He now had the time and the familial sympathy to daydream and indulge his imagination. He left school in 1905, not at all dissatisfied with having achieved only a ninth-grade education, because now he could pursue his heart's desire: an education as an artist. He followed his ambitions to Vienna, only to find bitter disappointment when the Vienna Academy of Fine Arts rejected him as an art student in 1907. His beloved Klara died the following year, and he meandered the city streets of Vienna, living off a pension and the money he inherited from his mother. He immersed himself in Vienna, admiring the architecture of the city and attending the opera when his funds permitted. He especially enjoyed the music of Richard Wagner, whose embrace of heroic German myth matched his own imaginative predilections.

Having finally run through all of his money, he hit bottom and began staying at a homeless shelter. It was interesting, though, to hear the different political points of view spouted by the shelter's other inhabitants. They discussed compelling issues of the day, such as race, and he listened intently to those who hailed the supremacy of the Aryan race and the inferiority of the Jews. He immersed himself in reading, particularly the newspapers and pamphlets that gave him more information about those disturbing political issues. He came to hate Jews and Marxists, whom he thought had formed an evil union with the goal of destroying the world. He also despised liberalism and democracy, and in cheap cafés he began directing political harangues at anyone who would listen.

Still, he had his art, and he found he could just barely survive on the earnings he made from selling his pretty postcards covered with painted replicas of famous works or his original sketches of Viennese buildings. He believed, too, that his political and social life had become much more exciting, as he was now publicly debating issues and learning to speak up about the concerns of

OPPOSITE: In his disturbing painting of the *Seven Deadly Sins* (1933), Otto Dix features Hitler, clearly identified by a black moustache, in the guise of envy. Fearing retribution while the Führer remained in power, Dix added the moustache after Hitler's death.

This is one of the few known photographs of a young Adolf Hitler, taken in 1923.

the day—and what anxious, perilous, but interesting times these were. He felt compelled to leave Vienna in 1913, however, if only to avoid the Austrian military draft. He was not willing to serve or die for what he believed was a decaying Austria-Hungary empire.

He found refuge in Munich, Germany, and there volunteered for service in the German army, which had just embarked on its crusade in the greatest war ever fought. He discovered in himself a real talent for military service, and he remained in the army for the duration of the war, 1914–1918. Twice wounded and decorated for bravery, he nonetheless found himself in despair at war's end. He languished in a military hospital, temporarily blinded by the mustard gas that had enveloped him during his last days of fighting. An impotent rage coursed through him when he learned of Germany's defeat. He knew with all his being that the Jews were responsible for this humiliation, and he also knew what he had to do: he had to enter the political arena in his chosen fatherland and save the nation. Adolf Hitler had finally found his mission in life.

Affected by and in turn affecting the anxiety and malaise of the early decades of the twentieth century, Hitler (1889–1945) stood as just one personification of Europe's age of anxiety. Torn between divergent visions of his future and embittered by a sense of dislocation and fear stemming from the drastic changes engulfing the society around him, Hitler dedicated himself to discovering a way out of the anxiety for the nation he had adopted. His solutions ultimately brought about more rather than less anxiety, but the novelty and cruelty of his political and military agendas reflected brilliantly the traumatic consequences of the Great War and the Great Depression.

Just as Adolf Hitler changed as a result of his life experiences in the early twentieth century, so too did European society as a whole. Badly shaken by the effects of years of war, Europeans experienced a shock to their system of values, beliefs, and traditions. Profound scientific and cultural transformations that came to the fore in the postwar decades also contributed to a sense of loss and anxiety. As peoples in Europe and around the world struggled to come to terms with the aftermath of war, an unprecedented economic contraction gripped the international community.

Against the background of the Great Depression, dictators in Russia, Italy, and Germany tried to translate blueprints for utopias into reality. While Joseph Stalin and his fellow communists recast the former tsarist empire into a dictatorship of the proletariat, Benito Mussolini and his fascists along with Adolf Hitler and his Nazi party forged new national communities. These political innovations unsettled many Europeans and much of the world, contributing significantly to the anxiety of the age. Such shifts in political thought matched in their radical-ness, however strangely, the vast alterations taking place in the intellectual and cultural realms of European society after the Great War.

Probing Cultural Frontiers

The Great War discredited established social and political institutions and long-held beliefs about the superiority of European society. Writers, poets, theologians, and other intellectuals lamented the decline and imminent death of their society. While some wrote obituaries, however, others embarked on bold new cultural paths that established the main tendencies of contemporary thought and taste. Most of these cultural innovators began their work before the war, but it was in the two decades following the war that a revolution in science, psychology, art, and architecture at-tained its fullest development and potency.

The discoveries of physicists undermined the Newtonian universe, in which a set of inexorable natural laws governed events, with a new and disturbing cosmos. Un-certainty governed this strange universe, which lacked objective reality. Equally dis-comforting were the insights of psychoanalysis, which suggested that human behavior was fundamentally irrational. Disquieting trends in the arts and architecture paral-leled the developments in science and psychology. Especially in painting, an aversion to realism and a pronounced preference for abstraction heralded the arrival of new aesthetic standards.

Postwar Pessimism

"You are all a lost generation," noted Gertrude Stein (1874–1946) to her fellow American writer Ernest Hemingway (1899–1961). Stein had given a label to the group of American intellectuals and literati who congregated in Paris in the postwar years. This "lost generation" expressed in poetry and fiction the malaise and disillu-sion that characterized U.S. and European thought after the Great War. The vast ma-jority of European intellectuals rallied enthusiastically to the war in 1914, viewing it as a splendid adventure. The brutal realities of industrialized warfare left no room for heroes, however, and most of these young artists and intellectuals quickly became dis-illusioned. During the 1920s they spat out their revulsion in a host of war novels such as Ernest Hemingway's *A Farewell to Arms* (1929) and Erich Maria Remarque's *All Quiet on the Western Front* (1929), works overflowing with images of meaningless death and suffering.

Postwar writers lamented the decline of Western society. A retired German school-teacher named Oswald Spengler (1880–1936) made headlines when he published *The Decline of the West* (1918–1922). In this work, which might have been seen as an obit-uary of civilization, Spengler proposed that all societies pass through a life cycle of growth and decay comparable to the biological cycle of living organisms. His analysis of the history of western Europe led him to conclude that European society had en-tered the final stage of its existence. All that remained was irreversible decline, marked by imperialism and warfare. Spengler's gloomy predictions provided a kind of comfort to those who sought to rationalize their postwar despair, as did his conviction that all the nations of the world were equally doomed. In England the shock of war caused the historian Arnold J. Toynbee (1889–1975) to begin his twelve-volume classic, *A Study of History* (1934–1961), that sought to discover how societies develop through time. In this monumental comparative study, Toynbee analyzes the genesis, growth, and disintegration of twenty-six societies.

Religious Uncertainty

Theologians joined the chorus of despair. In 1919 Karl Barth (1886–1968), widely recognized as one of the most notable Christian theologians, published a religious bombshell entitled *Epistle to the Romans*. In his work Barth sharply attacked the liberal Christian theology that embraced the idea of progress, that is, the tendency of European thinkers to believe in limitless improvement as the realization of God's purpose. Other Christians joined the fray, reminding a generation of optimists that Christ's kingdom is not of this world. The Augustinian, Lutheran, and Calvinist message of original sin—the depravity of human nature—fell on receptive ears as many Christians refused to accept the idea that contemporary human society was in any way a realization of God's purpose. The Russian orthodox thinker Niokolai Berdiaev (1874–1948) summed up these sentiments: "Man's historical experience has been one of steady failure, and there are no grounds for supposing it will be ever anything else."

Attacks on Progress

The Great War destroyed long-cherished beliefs such as belief in the universality of human progress. Many idols of nineteenth-century progress came under attack, especially science and technology. The scientists' dream of leading humanity to a beneficial conquest of nature seemed to have gone awry, because scientists had spent the war making poisonous gas and high explosives. Democracy was another fallen idol. The idea that people should have a voice in selecting the leaders of their government enjoyed widespread support in European societies. By the early twentieth century, the removal of property and educational restrictions on the right to vote resulted in universal male suffrage in most societies. In the years following the Great War, most European governments extended the franchise to women. Those developments led to an unprecedented degree of political participation as millions of people voted in elections and referendums, but many intellectuals abhorred what they viewed as a weak political system that championed the tyranny of the average person. Because they viewed democracy as a product of decay and as lacking in positive values, many people idealized elite rule. In Germany a whole school of conservatives lamented the "rule of inferiors." Common people, too, often viewed democracy as a decaying political system because they associated it with corrupt and ineffective party politics. However, antidemocratic strains were not confined to Germany. The widely read essay "Revolt of the Masses" (1930) by the Spanish philosopher José Ortega y Gasset (1883–1955) warned readers about the masses who were destined to destroy the highest achievements of Western society.

One of the best-known faces of the twentieth century, Albert Einstein was the symbol of the revolution in physics.

Revolutions in Physics and Psychology

The postwar decade witnessed a revolution in physics that transformed the character of science. Albert Einstein (1879–1955) struck the first blow with his theory of special relativity (1905), showing that there is no single spatial and chronological framework in the universe. According to the theory, it no longer made sense to speak of space and time as absolutes, because the measurement of those two categories always varies with the motion of the observer. That is, space and time are relative to the person measuring them. To the layperson such notions—usually expressed in incomprehensible mathematical formulas—suggested that science had reached the limits of what could be known with certainty. A common-sense universe had vanished, to be replaced by a radically new one in which reality or truth was merely a set of mental constructs.

More disquieting even than Einstein's discoveries was the theory formulated by Werner Heisenberg (1901–1976), who in 1927 published a paper, "About the Quantum-Theoretical Reinterpretation of Kinetic and Mechanical Relationships," which established the "uncertainty principle." Accord-

A striking painted portrait of Sigmund Freud.

The Uncertainty Principle

ing to Heisenberg, it is impossible to specify simultaneously the position and the velocity of a subatomic particle. The more accurately one determines the position of an electron the less precisely one can determine its velocity, and vice versa. In essence, scientists cannot observe the behavior of electrons objectively, because the act of observation interferes with them. The indeterminacy of the atomic universe demanded that the exact calculations of classical physics be replaced by probability calculations.

It quickly became evident that the uncertainty principle had important implications beyond physics. It also carried broader philosophical ramifications. Heisenberg's theory called into question established notions of truth and violated the fundamental law of cause and effect. Likewise, objectivity as it was understood was no longer a valid concept, because the observer was always part of the process under observation. Accordingly, any observer—an anthropologist studying another society, for instance—had to be alert to the fact that his or her very presence became an integral part of the study.

Equally unsettling as the advances in physics were developments in psychology that challenged established concepts of morality and values. In an indeterminate universe governed by relativity, the one remaining fixed point was the human psyche, but the insights of Sigmund Freud (1856–1939) proved disturbing as well. Beginning in 1896, the medical doctor from Vienna embarked on research that focused on psychological rather than physiological explanations of mental disorders. Through his clinical observations of patients, Freud identified a conflict between conscious and unconscious

Freud's Psychoanalytic Theory

Paul Gauguin, *Nafea Fan Ipoipo* ("When are you to be married?"; 1892). Gauguin sought the spiritual meaning for his art in the islands of the South Pacific. This painting of two Tahitian women revealed his debt to impressionism, but also showed his innovations: strong outlines, flat colors, and flattened forms.

mental processes that lay at the root of neurotic behavior. That conflict, moreover, suggested to him the existence of a repressive mechanism that keeps painful memories or threatening events away from the conscious mind. Freud believed that dreams held the key to the deepest recesses of the human psyche. Using the free associations of patients to guide him in the interpretation of dreams, he identified sexual drives and fantasies as the most important source of repression. For example, Freud claimed to have discovered a so-called Oedipus complex in which male children develop an erotic attachment to their mother and hostility toward their father.

From dreams Freud analyzed literature, religion, politics, and virtually every other type of human endeavor, seeking always to identify the manifestations of the repressed conscious. He was convinced that his theory, known as *psychoanalysis,* provided the keys to understanding all human behavior. In the end, Freudian doctrines shaped the psychiatric profession and established a powerful presence in literature and the arts. During the 1920s, novelists, poets, and painters acknowledged Freud's influence as they focused on the inner world—the hidden depths of memory and emotion—of their characters. The creators of imaginative literature used Freud's bold emphasis on sexuality as a tool for the interpretation and understanding of human behavior.

Experimentation in Art and Architecture

The roots of contemporary painting go back to nineteenth-century French avant-garde artists who became preoccupied with how a subject should be painted. The common denominator among the various schools was disdain for realism and concern for freedom of expression. The aversion to visual realism was heightened by the spread of photography. When everyone could create naturalistic landscapes or portraits with a camera, it made little sense for artists to do so laboriously with paint and brush. Thus painters began to think of canvas not as a reproduction of reality but as an end in itself. The purpose of a painting was not to mirror reality but to create it.

By the beginning of the twentieth century, the possibilities inherent in this new aesthetic led to the emergence of a bewildering variety of pictorial schools, all of which promised an entirely new art. Regardless of whether they called themselves *les fauves* ("wild beasts"), expressionists, cubists, abstractionists, dadaists, or surrealists, artists generally agreed on a program "to abolish the sovereignty of appearance." Paintings no longer depicted recognizable objects from the everyday world, and beauty was expressed in pure color or shape. Some painters sought to express feelings and emotions through violent distortion of forms and the use of explosive colors; others, influenced by Freudian psychology, tried to tap the subconscious mind to communicate an inner vision or a dream.

Pablo Picasso's *Les Demoiselles d' Avignon* (1907) was the first of what would be called cubist works. This image had a profound influence on subsequent art.

Artistic Influences

The artistic heritages of Asian, Pacific, and African societies fertilized various strains of contemporary painting. Nineteenth-century Japanese prints, for example, influenced French impressionists such as Edgar Degas (1834–1917), whose study of them led him to experiment with visual angles and asymmetrical compositions. The deliberate violation of perspective by Japanese painters and their stress on the flat, two-dimensional surface of the picture, their habit of placing figures off center, and their use of primary colors, encouraged European artists to take similar liberties with realism. In a revolt against rational society, the postimpressionist painter Paul Gauguin (1848–1903) fled to central America and Tahiti. He was inspired by the "primitive" art he found there, claiming that it held a sense of wonder that "civilized" people no longer possessed. In Germany a group of young artists known as the "Bridge" made a point of regularly visiting the local ethnographic museum to be inspired by the boldness and power of indigenous art. The early works of Pablo Picasso (1881–1973), the leading proponent of cubism, displayed the influence of African art forms.

Designed by Walter Gropius in 1925, this building introduced the functional international style of architecture that dominated for the next half century.

By the third decade of the twentieth century, it was nearly impossible to generalize about the history of contemporary painting. All artists were acknowledged to have a right to their own reality, and generally accepted standards that distinguished between "good" and "bad" art disappeared.

Bauhaus

During the first decades of the twentieth century, architecture underwent a revolutionary transformation as designers deliberately set out to create a completely different building style that broke with old forms and traditions. The modernistic trends in architecture coalesced with the opening of the *Bauhaus,* an institution that brought together architects, designers, and painters from several countries. Located first in Weimar and then Dessau, Germany, the Bauhaus was a community of innovators bent on creating a building style and interior designs that were uniquely suited to the urban and industrial landscape of the twentieth century.

The first director of the Bauhaus was Walter Gropius (1883–1969) whose theory of design became the guiding principle first of the Bauhaus and subsequently of contemporary architecture in general. To Gropius, design was functional, based on a marriage between engineering and art. The buildings Gropius designed featured simplicity of shape and extensive use of glass and always embodied the new doctrine that form must follow function. The second director of the Bauhaus, Ludwig Mies von der Rohe (1886–1969), exerted an equally profound influence on modern architecture. He experimented with steel frames around which he stretched non-load-bearing walls of glass. His designs became the basis for the ubiquitous glass-box skyscrapers that first adorned cities such as Chicago and New York and later dominated the skylines of most major cities.

The style initiated by the Bauhaus architects, the international style, gradually prevailed after 1930 because its functionalism was well suited to the construction of large apartment and office complexes. The work of the world-famous Swiss-French architect Le Corbusier (Charles Édouard Jeanneret, 1887–1965) proved the broad appeal of the new architecture. At the request of Jawaharlal Nehru (1889–1964), India's first prime minister, Le Corbusier laid out the new capital city of the Punjab, Chandigarh, and designed for it three concrete government buildings. Governments and businesses eagerly embraced the new style, but the public never quite warmed to the glass box, a cold and impersonal structure that seemed to overwhelm the individual.

Global Depression

After the horrors and debilitating upheavals of the Great War, much of the world yearned for a return to normality and prosperity. By the early 1920s the efforts of governments and businesses to rebuild damaged economies seemed to bear fruit. Prosperity, however, was short-lived. In 1929 the world plunged into an economic depression that was so long-lasting, so severe, and so global that it has become known as the Great Depression. The old capitalist system of trade and finance collapsed, and until a new system took its place after 1945, a return to worldwide prosperity could not occur.

The Great Depression

By the middle of the 1920s, some semblance of economic normality had returned, and most countries seemed on the way to economic recovery. Industrial productivity had returned to prewar levels as businesses repaired the damages the war had inflicted on industrial plants, equipment, and transportation facilities. But that prosperity was fragile, perhaps false, and many serious problems and dislocations remained in the international economy.

The economic recovery and well-being of Europe, for example, were tied to a tangled financial system that involved war debts among the Allies, reparations paid by Germany and Austria, and the flow of U.S. funds to Europe. In essence, the governments of Austria and Germany relied on U.S. loans and investment capital to finance reparation payments to France and England. The French and British governments, in turn, depended on those reparation payments to pay off loans taken out in the United States during the Great War. By the summer of 1928, U.S. lenders and investors started to withdraw capital from Europe, placing an intolerable strain on the financial system.

Economic Problems

There were other problems as well. Improvements in industrial processes reduced worldwide demand for certain raw materials, causing an increase in supplies and a drop in prices. Technological advances in the production of automobile tires, for instance, permitted the use of reclaimed rubber. The resulting glut of natural rubber had devastating consequences for the economies of the Dutch East Indies, Ceylon, and Malaysia, which relied on the export of rubber. Similarly, the increased use of oil undermined the coal industry, the emergence of synthetics hurt the cotton industry, and the growing adoption of artificial nitrogen virtually ruined the nitrate industry of Chile.

One of the nagging weaknesses of the global economy in the 1920s was the depressed state of agriculture, the result of overproduction and falling prices. During the Great War, when Europe's agricultural output declined significantly, farmers in the United States, Canada, Argentina, and Australia expanded their production. At the end of the war, European farmers resumed their agricultural activity, thereby contributing to worldwide surpluses. Above-average global harvests between 1925 and 1929 aggravated the situation. As production increased, demand declined, and prices collapsed throughout the world. By 1929 the price of a bushel of wheat was at its lowest level in 400 years, and farmers everywhere became impoverished. The reduced income of farm families contributed to high inventories of manufactured goods, which in turn caused businesses to cut back production and to dismiss workers.

The Crash of 1929

The United States enjoyed a boom after the Great War: industrial wages were high, and production and consumption increased. Many people in the United States invested their earnings and savings in speculative ventures, particularly the buying of stock on margin—putting up as little as 3 percent of a stock's price in cash and borrowing the remainder from brokers and banks or by mortgaging their homes. By October 1929, hints of a worldwide economic slowdown and warnings from experts that stock prices were overvalued prompted investors to pull out of the market. On Black Thursday (24 October), a wave of panic selling on the New York Stock Exchange caused stock prices to plummet. Investors who had overextended themselves in a frenzy of speculative stock purchases watched in agony. Thousands of people, from poor widows to industrial tycoons, lost their life savings, and by the end of the day eleven financiers had committed suicide. The crisis deepened when lenders called in loans, thereby forcing more investors to sell their securities at any price.

Economic Contraction Spreads

In the wake of this financial chaos came a drastic decrease in business activity, wages, and employment. Consumer demand no longer sufficed to purchase all the goods that businesses produced, and when businesses realized that they could not sell their inventories, they responded with cutbacks in production and additional layoffs. With so many people unemployed or underemployed, demand plummeted further, causing more business failures and soaring unemployment. In 1930 the slump deepened, and by 1932 industrial production had fallen to half of its 1929 level. National income had dropped by approximately half. Forty-four percent of U.S. banks were out of business, and the deposits of millions of people had disappeared. Because much of the world's prosperity depended on the export of U.S. capital and the strength of U.S. import markets, the contraction of the U.S. economy created a ripple effect that circled the globe.

Most societies experienced economic difficulties throughout the 1930s. Although the severity of the economic contraction varied in intensity, virtually every industrialized society saw its economy shrivel. Nations that relied on exports of manufactured goods to pay for imported fuel and food—Germany and Japan in particular—suffered the most. The depression also spread unevenly to primary producing economies in Latin America, Africa, and Asia. Hardest hit were countries that depended on the export of a few primary products—agricultural goods, such as coffee, sugar, and cotton, and raw materials, such as minerals, ores, and rubber.

Industrial Economies

U.S. investors, shaken by the collapse of stock prices, tried to raise money by calling in loans and liquidating investments, and Wall Street banks refused to extend short-term loans as they became due. Banking houses in Austria and Germany became vulnerable to collapse, because they had been major recipients of U.S. loans. Devastated by the loss of U.S. capital, the German economy experienced a precipitous economic slide that by 1932 resulted in 35 percent unemployment and a 50 percent decrease in industrial production. As the German economy ground to a virtual halt, the rest of Europe—which was closely integrated with the German economy—sputtered and stalled. Although Germany lost the Great War, it remained a leading economic power throughout the postwar years. Because no military engagements took place on German soil, the national economy—its natural resources, infrastructure, and productive capacity—were spared the physical destruction that seriously disrupted the economies of other lands such as France or Russia. Germany did not escape the ravages of the depression. The situation in Europe deteriorated further when businesses, desperate to raise capital by exporting goods to the United States, found that U.S. markets had virtually disappeared behind tariff walls. Foreign trade fell sharply between

1929 and 1932, causing further losses in manufacturing, employment, and per capita income. Because of its great dependence on the U.S. market, the Japanese economy felt the depression's effects almost immediately. Unemployment in export-oriented sectors of the economy skyrocketed as companies cut back on production.

The Great Depression destroyed the international financial and commercial network of the capitalist economies. As international cooperation broke down, governments turned to their own resources and practiced economic nationalism. By imposing tariff barriers, import quotas, and import prohibitions, politicians hoped to achieve a high degree of economic self-sufficiency. In an age of global interdependence, such goals remained unobtainable, and economic nationalism invariably backfired. Each new measure designed to restrict imports provoked retaliation by other nations whose interests were affected. After the U.S. Congress passed the Smoot-Hawley Tariff in 1930, which raised duties on most manufactured products to prohibitive levels, the governments of dozens of other nations immediately retaliated by raising tariffs on imports of U.S. products. The result was a sharp drop in international trade. Instead of higher levels of production and income, economic nationalism yielded the opposite. Between 1929 and 1932, world production declined by 38 percent and trade dropped by more than 66 percent.

Economic Nationalism

Despair and Government Action

By 1933 unemployment in industrial societies reached thirty million, more than five times higher than in 1929. Men lost their jobs because of economic contraction, and a combination of economic trends and deliberate government policy caused women to lose theirs also. Unemployment initially affected women less directly than men because employers preferred women workers, who were paid two-thirds to three-quarters the wages of men doing the same work. But before long, governments enacted policies to reduce female employment, especially for married women. The notion that a woman's place was in the home was widespread. In 1931 a British royal commission on unemployment insurance declared that "in the case of married women as a class, industrial employment cannot be regarded as the normal condition." More candid was the French Nobel Prize–winning physician Charles Richet (1850–1935), who insisted that removing women from the workforce would solve the problem of male unemployment and increase the nation's dangerously low birthrate.

In January 1932, ten thousand hunger strikers marched on Washington, D.C., seeking government relief for their misery.

Personal Suffering

Dorothea Lange, *Migrant Mother, Nipomo California* **(1936). A famous photograph of the Great Depression.**

The Great Depression caused enormous personal suffering. The stark, gloomy statistics documenting the failure of economies do not convey the anguish and despair of those who lost their jobs, savings, and homes, and often their dignity and hope. For millions of people the struggle for food, clothing, and shelter grew desperate. Shantytowns appeared overnight in urban areas, and breadlines stretched for blocks. Marriage, childbearing, and divorce rates declined, while suicide rates rose. The acute physical and social problems of those at the bottom of the economic ladder often magnified social divisions and class hatreds. Workers and farmers especially came to despise the wealthy, who, despite their reduced incomes, were shielded from the worst impact of the economic downturn and continued to enjoy a comfortable lifestyle. Adolescents completing their schooling faced an almost nonexistent job market.

That the Great Depression deflated economies and hope was especially noticeable in the literature of the period. Writers castigated the social and political order, calling repeatedly for a more just society. The U.S. writer John Steinbeck (1902–1968) chillingly captured the official heartlessness and the rising political anger inspired by the depression. In *The Grapes of Wrath* (1939), the Joad family, prototypical "Okies," migrated from Oklahoma to California to escape the dust bowl. In describing their journey Steinbeck commented on the U.S. government's policy of "planned scarcity," in which surplus crops were destroyed to raise prices while citizens starved. In one of the novel's most famous passages, Steinbeck portrayed the nation's rising political anguish:

> The people come with nets to fish for potatoes in the river and the guards hold them back; they come in rattling cars to get the dumped oranges, but the kerosene is sprayed. And they stand still and watch potatoes float by, listen to the screaming pigs being killed in a ditch and covered with quicklime, watch the mountains of oranges slop down to a putrefying ooze; and in the eyes of the people there is the failure; and in the eyes of the hungry there is a growing wrath. In the souls of the people the grapes of wrath are filling and growing heavy, growing heavy for the vintage.

Economic Experimentation

Classical economic thought (see chapter 29) held that capitalism was a self-correcting system that operated best when left to its own devices. Governments responded to the economic crisis in one of two ways. Initially, most governments did nothing, hoping against all odds that the crisis would resolve itself. When the misery spawned by the depression sparked calls for action, some governments assumed more active roles, pursuing deflationary measures by balancing national budgets and curtailing public spending. In either case, rather than lifting national economies out of the doldrums, the classical prescriptions for economic ills worsened the depression's impact and intensified the plight of millions of people. Far from self-correcting, capitalism

Human faces of the Great Depression: children bathing in the Ozark Mountains, Missouri, 1940.

seemed to be dying. Many people called for a fundamental revision of economic thought.

John Maynard Keynes (1883–1946), the most influential economist of the twentieth century, offered a novel solution. His seminal work, *The General Theory of Employment, Interest, and Money* (1936), was his answer to the central problem of the depression—that millions of people who were willing to work could not find employment. To Keynes the fundamental cause of the depression was not excessive supply, but inadequate demand. Accordingly, he urged governments to play an active role and stimulate the economy by increasing the money supply, thereby lowering interest rates and encouraging investment. He also advised governments to undertake public works projects to provide jobs and redistribute incomes through tax policy, an intervention which would result in reduced unemployment and increased consumer demand, which would lead to economic revival. Such measures were necessary even if they caused governments to run deficits and maintain unbalanced budgets.

Keynes

Although Keynes's theories did not become influential with policymakers until after World War II, the administration of U.S. president Franklin Delano Roosevelt (1882–1945) applied similar ideas. Roosevelt took aggressive steps to reinflate the economy and ease the worst of the suffering caused by the depression. His proposals for dealing with the national calamity included legislation designed to prevent the collapse of the banking system, to provide jobs and farm subsidies, to give workers the right to organize and bargain collectively, to guarantee minimum wages, and to provide social security in old age. This program of sweeping economic and social reforms was called the "New Deal." Its fundamental premise, that the federal government was justified in intervening to protect the social and economic welfare of the people, represented a major shift in U.S. government policy and started a trend toward social reform legislation that continued long after the depression years. Ultimately, the enormous military spending during World War II did more to end the Great Depression in the United States and elsewhere than did the specific programs of the New Deal or similar approaches.

The New Deal

Sources from the Past

Franklin Delano Roosevelt: Nothing to Fear

Franklin Delano Roosevelt (1882–1945) assumed the presidency of the United States on 4 March 1933, during the very depths of the Great Depression. In his inaugural address to the nation, he conveyed both the anxiousness of the times and the seemingly unquenchable optimism that carried him—and his nation—through hard times. A vastly wealthy man serving as president during a time of devastating penury, Roosevelt nonetheless gained the admiration and respect of his people because of his warm eloquence and compassion. Although he hid his condition quite successfully during his time in public, FDR had contracted polio in the 1920s and had lost the use of his legs. This "crippled" president became a metaphor for the United States' economic collapse, but also for its ability to overcome fear itself.

I am certain that my fellow Americans expect that on my induction into the Presidency I will address them with a candor and a decision which the present situation of our Nation impels. This is preeminently the time to speak the truth, the whole truth, frankly and boldly. Nor need we shrink from honestly facing conditions in our country today. This great Nation will endure as it has endured, will revive and will prosper. So, first of all, let me assert my firm belief that the only thing we have to fear is fear itself—nameless, unreasoning, unjustified terror which paralyzes needed efforts to convert retreat into advance. In every dark hour of our national life a leadership of frankness and vigor has met with that understanding and support of the people themselves which is essential to victory. I am convinced that you will again give that support to leadership in these critical days.

In such a spirit on my part and on yours we face our common difficulties. They concern, thank God, only material things. Values have shrunken to fantastic levels; taxes have risen; our ability to pay has fallen; government of all kinds is faced by serious curtailment of income; the

means of exchange are frozen in the currents of trade; the withered leaves of industrial enterprise lie on every side; farmers find no markets for their produce; the savings of many years in thousands of families are gone.

More important, a host of unemployed citizens face the grim problem of existence, and an equally great number toil with little return. Only a foolish optimist can deny the dark realities of the moment. . . .

Happiness lies not in the mere possession of money; it lies in the joy of achievement, in the thrill of creative effort. The joy and moral stimulation of work no longer must be forgotten in the mad chase of evanescent profits. These dark days will be worth all they cost us if they teach us that our true destiny is not to be ministered unto but to minister to ourselves and to our fellow men.

FOR FURTHER REFLECTION

How does Roosevelt believe U.S. citizens can profit from the dark days of the Great Depression, and why is it that all they have to fear is fear itself?

SOURCE: Franklin D. Roosevelt, First Inaugural Address, 4 March 1933, available at The Avalon Project at http://www.yale.edu/lawweb/avalon/president/inaug/froos1.htm.

Challenges to the Liberal Order

Amid the gloom and despair of the Great Depression, some voices proclaimed the promise of a better tomorrow. Marxists believed that capitalist society was on its deathbed, and they had faith that a new and better system based on rule by the proletariat was being born out of the ashes of the Russian empire. The new rulers of Russia, Vladimir Ilyich Lenin and then Joseph Stalin, transformed the former tsarist empire into the world's first socialist society, the Union of Soviet Socialist Republics (1922).

Other people, uncomfortable with the abolition of private property and the "dictatorship of the proletariat," found solace in activist political movements that claimed to have an alternative formula for the reconstruction of society. Fascist movements across Europe promoted their alternatives to socialism and offered revolutionary answers to the economic, social, and political problems that seemed to defy solution by traditional liberal democratic means. Among those fascist movements, the Italian and German ones figured most prominently.

Communism in Russia

In 1917 Lenin and his fellow Bolsheviks had taken power in the name of the Russian working class, but socialist victory did not bring peace and stability to the lands of the former Russian empire. After seizing power, Lenin and his supporters had to defend the world's first dictatorship of the proletariat against numerous enemies, including dissident socialists, anti-Bolshevik officers and troops, peasant bands, and foreign military forces.

Opposition to the Bolshevik Party—by now calling itself the Russian Communist Party—erupted into a civil war that lasted from 1918 to 1920. Operating out of its new capital in Moscow, Lenin's government began a policy of crushing all opposition. The communists began the Red Terror campaign in which suspected anticommunists known as Whites were arrested, tried, and executed. The secret police killed some 200,000 opponents of the regime. In July 1918 the Bolsheviks executed Tsar Nicholas II, Empress Alexandra, their five children, and their remaining servants because they feared that the Romanov family would fall into the hands of the Whites, thereby strengthening counterrevolutionary forces. White terror was often equally as brutal as Red terror. The peasantry, although hostile to the communists, largely supported the Bolsheviks, fearing that a victory by the Whites would result in the return of the monarchy. However, foreign military intervention supported White resistance to the communist takeover. Russia's withdrawal from the Great War and anticommunist sentiment inflamed Russia's former allies (notably Britain, France, Japan, and the United States), who sent troops and supplies to aid White forces. Although their numbers were negligible, the foreigners' presence sometimes had the effect of bonding otherwise hostile groups to the Reds. Poorly organized and without widespread support, the Whites were defeated by the Red Army in 1920. Estimates place the number of lives lost in the civil war at ten million, with many more people dying from disease and starvation than from the fighting. The political system that emerged from the civil war bore the imprint of political oppression, which played a significant role in the later development of the Soviet state.

Civil War

The new rulers of Russia had no plans to transform the economy, but in the course of the civil war they embarked on a hasty and unplanned course of nationalization, a policy known as *war communism*. After officially annulling private property, the Bolshevik government assumed control or ownership of banks, industry, and other privately held commercial properties. Landed estates and the holdings of monasteries and churches became national property, although the Bolsheviks explicitly exempted the holdings of poor peasants from confiscation. The abolition of private trade was unpopular, and when the party seized crops from peasants to feed people in the cities, the peasants drastically reduced their production. By 1920 industrial production had fallen to about one-tenth of its prewar level and agricultural output to about one-half its prewar level.

War Communism

In 1921, as the Reds consolidated their military victories, Lenin faced the daunting prospect of rebuilding a society that had been at war since 1914. The workers, in whose name he had taken power, were on strike. Other problems included depopulated cities, destroyed factories, and an army that demobilized soldiers faster than the workforce could absorb them. Lenin and the party tried to take strict control of the country by

The New Economic Policy

■ **Joseph Stalin at a Soviet congress in 1936.**

crushing workers' strikes, peasant rebellions, and a sailors' revolt. Yet Lenin recognized the need to make peace with those whose skills would rekindle industrial production. Faced with economic paralysis, in the spring of 1921 he decided on a radical reversal of war communism.

Demonstrating his pragmatism and willingness to compromise, Lenin implemented the New Economic Policy (NEP), which temporarily restored the market economy and some private enterprise in Russia. Large industries, banks, and transportation and communications facilities remained under state control, but the government returned small-scale industries (those with fewer than twenty workers) to private ownership. The government also allowed peasants to sell their surpluses at free market prices. Other features of the NEP included a vigorous program of electrification and the establishment of technical schools to train technicians and engineers. Lenin did not live to see the success of the NEP. After suffering three paralytic strokes, he died in 1924. His death was followed by a bitter struggle for power among the Bolshevik leaders.

Joseph Stalin

Many old Bolsheviks continued to argue for a permanent or continuous revolution, asserting that socialism in Russia would fail if socialism did not move from a national to an international stage. Others in the Politburo, the central governing body of the Communist Party, favored establishing socialism in one country alone, thus repudiating the role of the Union of Soviet Socialist Republics as torchbearer of worldwide socialist revolution. Joseph Stalin (1879–1953), who served in the unglamorous bureaucratic position of general secretary, promoted the idea of socialism in one country. A Georgian by birth, an Orthodox seminarian by training, and a Russian nationalist by conviction, Stalin indicated his unified resolve to gain power in his adopted surname, which meant "man of steel." Speaking Russian with a heavy accent, he was an intellectual misfit among the Bolshevik elite. However, by 1928, Stalin lived up to his name and completely triumphed over his rivals in the party, clearing the way for an unchallenged dictatorship of the Soviet Union.

First Five-Year Plan

Stalin decided to replace Lenin's NEP with an ambitious plan for rapid economic development known as the First Five-Year Plan. The basic aims of this and subsequent five-year plans, first implemented in 1929, were to transform the Soviet Union from a predominantly agricultural country to a leading industrial power. The First Five-Year Plan set targets for increased productivity in all spheres of the economy but emphasized heavy industry—especially steel and machinery—at the expense of consumer

Men and women drive tractors out of one of the Soviet Union's Machine Tractor Stations to work fields where mechanization had been a rare sight.

goods. Through Gosplan, the central state planning agency, Stalin and the party attempted to coordinate resources and the labor force on an unprecedented scale. As the rest of the world teetered on the edge of economic collapse, this blueprint for maximum centralization of the entire national economy offered a bold alternative to market capitalism. Stalin repeatedly stressed the urgency of this monumental endeavor, telling his people, "We are 50 to 100 years behind the advanced countries. Either we do it, or we shall go under."

Integral to the drive for industrialization was the collectivization of agriculture. The Soviet state expropriated privately owned land to create collective or cooperative farm units whose profits were shared by all farmers. The logic of communist ideology demanded the abolition of private property and market choices, but more practical considerations also played a role. Stalin and his regime viewed collectivization as a means of increasing the efficiency of agricultural production and ensuring that industrial workers would be fed. Collectivization was enforced most ruthlessly against *kulaks*—relatively wealthy peasants who had risen to prosperity during the NEP but accounted for only 3 to 5 percent of the peasantry.

Collectivization of Agriculture

In some places, outraged peasants reacted to the government's program by slaughtering their livestock and burning their crops. Millions of farmers left the land and migrated to cities in search of work, thereby further taxing the limited supplies of housing, food, and utilities. Unable to meet production quotas, peasants often starved to death on the land they once owned. When Stalin called a halt to collectivization in 1931, proclaiming the policymakers "dizzy with success," half the farms in the Soviet Union had been collectivized. Estimates of the number of peasant lives lost have fluctuated wildly, but even the most cautious place it at three million.

The First Five-Year Plan set unrealistically high production targets. Even so, the Soviet leadership proclaimed success after only four years. The Soviet Union industrialized under Stalin even though the emphasis on building heavy industry first and consumer industries later meant that citizens postponed the gratifications of industrialization. Before refrigerators, radios, or automobiles became available, the government constructed steelworks and hydroelectric plants. The scarcity or nonexistence of consumer goods was to some degree balanced by full employment, low-cost utilities, and—when available—cheap housing and food. Set against the collapse of the U.S. stock market and the depression-ridden capitalist world, the ability of a centrally planned economy to create more jobs than workers could fill made it appear an attractive alternative.

The Great Purge

Nevertheless, the results of Stalin's First Five-Year Plan generated controversy as the Communist Party prepared for its seventeenth congress in 1934, the self-proclaimed "Congress of Victors." The disaster of collectivization and the ruthlessness with which it was carried out had raised doubts about Stalin's administration. Although themes of unity and reconciliation prevailed, Stalin learned of a plan to bring more pluralism back into leadership. The Congress of Victors became the "Congress of Victims" as Stalin incited a civil war within the party that was climaxed by highly publicized trials of former Bolshevik elites for treason and by a purge of two-thirds of the delegates. Between 1935 and 1938 Stalin removed from posts of authority all persons suspected of opposition, including two-thirds of the members of the 1934 Central Committee and more than one-half of the army's high-ranking officers. The victims faced execution or long-term suffering in labor camps. In 1939 eight million Soviet citizens were in labor camps, and three million were dead as a result of the "cleansing," as Stalin's supporters termed this process.

The outside world watched the events unfolding within the Soviet Union with a mixture of contempt, fear, and admiration. Most observers recognized that the political and social upheavals that transformed the former Russian empire were of worldwide importance. The establishment of the world's first dictatorship of the proletariat challenged the values and institutions of liberal society everywhere and seemed to demonstrate the viability of communism as a social and political system.

The Fascist Alternative

While socialism was transforming the former Russian empire, another political force swept across Europe after the Great War. Fascism, a political movement and ideology that sought to create a new type of society, developed as a reaction against liberal democracy and the spread of socialism and communism. The term *fascism* derives from the *fasces,* an ancient Roman symbol of punitive authority consisting of a bundle of wooden rods strapped together around an axe. In 1919 Benito Mussolini adopted this symbol for the Italian Fascist movement that governed Italy from 1922 to 1943. Movements comparable to Italian fascism subsequently developed and sometimes dominated political life in many European societies, most notably in Germany in the guise of National Socialism (Nazism). Although fascism enjoyed widespread popularity in many European countries, it rarely threatened the political order and, with the exception of Italy and Germany, never overthrew a parliamentary system. Political and economic frustrations made fertile ground for fascist appeals outside Europe, and potential fascist movements sprang up during the 1930s in Japan, China, and South Africa; in Latin American societies such as Brazil and Argentina; and in several Arab lands. Nevertheless, that potential for fascism never reproduced the major characteristics of European fascism, and fascism remained basically a European phenomenon of the era between the two world wars.

Defining Fascism

During the 1920s and 1930s, fascism attracted millions of followers and proved especially attractive to middle classes and rural populations. These groups became radicalized by economic and social crises and were especially fearful of class conflict and the perceived threat from the political left. Fascism also proved attractive to nationalists of all classes, who denounced their governments for failing to realize the glorious objectives for which they had fought during the Great War. Asserting that society faced a profound crisis, fascists sought to create a new national community, which they defined either as a nation-state or as a unique ethnic or racial group. As part of their quest, fascist movements commonly dedicated themselves to the revival of allegedly lost national traditions and, hence, differed widely. Nevertheless, most fascist movements shared certain common features, such as the veneration of the state, a devotion to a strong leader, and an emphasis on ultranationalism, ethnocentrism, and militarism.

Fascist ideology consistently invoked the primacy of the state, which stood at the center of the nation's life and history and which demanded the subordination of the individual to the service of the state. Strong and often charismatic leaders, such as Benito Mussolini in Italy or Adolf Hitler in Germany, embodied the state and claimed indisputable authority. Consequently, fascists were hostile to liberal democracy, its devotion to individualism, and its institutions, which they viewed as weak and decadent. Fascism was also extremely hostile to class-based visions of the future promoted by socialism and communism. Fascist movements emphasized chauvinism (a belligerent form of nationalism) and xenophobia (a fear of foreign people), which they frequently linked to an exaggerated ethnocentrism. Some fascist leaders, accordingly, viewed national boundaries as artificial restraints limiting their union with ethnic or racial comrades living in other states. The typical fascist state embraced *militarism,* a belief in the rigors and virtues of military life as an individual and national ideal. In practice, militarism meant that fascist regimes maintained large and expensive military establishments, tried to organize much of public life along military lines, and generally showed a fondness for uniforms, parades, and monumental architecture.

Italian Fascism

The first fascist movement grew up in Italy after the Great War. Conditions conducive to the rise of fascism included a widespread disillusionment with uninspired political leadership and ineffective government, extensive economic turmoil and social discontent, and a growing fear of socialism. In addition, there was vast disappointment over Italy's skimpy territorial spoils from the peace settlement after the Great War.

The guiding force behind Italian fascism was Benito Mussolini, a former socialist and, from 1912 to 1914, editor of Italy's leading socialist daily *Avanti!* ("Forward!"). In 1914 he founded his own newspaper, *Il Popolo d'Italia* ("The People of Italy"), which encouraged Italian entry into the Great War. Mussolini was convinced that the war represented a turning point for the nation. The soldiers returning from the front, he argued, would spearhead the thorough transformation of Italian society and create a new type of state. After the Great War, the one-time socialist advanced a political program that emphasized virulent nationalism, demanded repression of socialists, and called for a strong political leader. In 1919 he established the *Fasci Italiani di Combattimento* (Italian Combat Veteran League).

Benito Mussolini

Mussolini's movement gained widespread support after 1920, and by 1921 his league managed to elect thirty-five fascists to the Italian parliament. Much of the newly found public support resulted from the effective use of violence against socialists by fascist armed squads known as Blackshirts. The Italian socialist party had organized militant strikes throughout Italy's northern industrial cities, causing considerable chaos. By early 1921 Italy was in a state of incipient civil war. In 1922, Mussolini and his followers decided the time was ripe for a fascist seizure of power, and on 28 October, they staged a march on Rome. While Mussolini stayed safely in Milan awaiting the outcome of events, thousands of his black-shirted troops converged on Rome. Rather

The Fascist State

Italian dictator Benito Mussolini strikes a dramatic pose on horseback in 1940.

than calling on the military to oppose the fascist threat, King Victor Emmanuel III hastily asked Mussolini on 29 October to become prime minister and form a new government. Mussolini inaugurated a fascist regime in 1922.

Between 1925 and 1931, Italy's fascists consolidated their power through a series of laws that provided the legal basis for the nation's transformation into a one-party dictatorship. In 1926 Mussolini seized total power as dictator and subsequently ruled Italy as *Il Duce* ("the leader"). The regime moved quickly to eliminate all other political parties, curb freedom of the press, and outlaw free speech and association. A Special Tribunal for the Defense of the State, supervised by military officers, silenced political dissent. Marked as antifascist subversives, thousands of Italians found themselves imprisoned or exiled on remote islands, and some faced capital punishment. Allying himself and his movement with business and landlord interests, *Il Duce* also crushed labor unions and prohibited strikes. In an effort to harmonize the interests of workers, employers, and the state, the regime tried to establish a corporatist order. This order was based on the vague fascist concept of corporatism, which viewed society as an organic entity through which the different interests in society came under the control of the state. Thus, in theory, a National Council of Corporations settled labor disputes and supervised wage settlements; but, in reality, this scheme was little more than a propaganda effort. In 1932, on the tenth anniversary of the fascist seizure of power, Mussolini felt confident enough to announce "that the twentieth century will be a century of fascism, the century of Italian power."

Racism and anti-Semitism were never prominent components of Italian fascism, but in 1938 the government suddenly issued anti-Semitic laws that labeled Jews unpatriotic, excluded them from government employment, and prohibited all marriages between Jews and so-called Aryans. This development may have been occasioned by Mussolini's newfound friendship with fellow dictator, Adolf Hitler. In 1936 Mussolini told his followers that from now on, world history would revolve around a Rome-Berlin Axis. In May 1939 the leaders of fascist Italy and Nazi Germany formalized their political, military, and ideological alliance by signing a ten-year Pact of Steel. This Pact of Steel illustrated the strong links between the Italian and German variants of fascism.

A 1924 painting of Hitler as a knight in shining armor, as the standard bearer for National Socialism, became the state sanctioned Hitler portrait for 1938; reproductions in poster and postcard form proved very popular.

German National Socialism

After Adolf Hitler's postwar political awakening, he came into contact with an obscure political party sympathetic to his ideas. In 1921 he became chairman of the party now known as the National Socialist German Workers' Party. National Socialism (the Nazi movement) made its first major appearance in 1923 when party members and Hitler attempted to overthrow the democratic Weimar Republic that had replaced the German empire in 1919. The revolt quickly fizzled under the gunfire of police units; Hitler was jailed, and the Nazi movement and its leader descended into obscurity. When Hitler emerged from prison in 1924, he resolved to use new tactics. Recognizing the futility of armed insurrection, he reorganized his movement and launched it on a "path of legality." Hitler and his followers were determined to gain power legally through the ballot box and, once successful, to discard the very instrument of their success.

Hitler and the Nazi Party

National Socialism made rapid gains after 1929 because it had broad appeal. Hitler attracted disillusioned people who felt alienated from society and frightened by the specter of socialist revolution. A growing number of people blamed the young German

The Struggle for Power

Sources from the Past

Mein Kampf

Mein Kampf (My Struggle) *is the title of a book written by Adolf Hitler in which he presented his political views. Crudely written and turgid in style, it became the bible of the Nazi movement and the blueprint for the Third Reich. Hitler's basic theme was racial. He believed that a titanic struggle between a superior Aryan race and inferior non-Aryan races—including, most notably, Jews—determined the course of history. Originally, the term* Aryan *designated a language group, not a mythological breed of people.*

So humans invariably wander about the garden of nature, convinced that they know and understand everything, yet with few exceptions are blind to one of the fundamental principles Nature uses in her work: the intrinsic segregation of the species of every living thing on the earth.

Any cross-breeding between two not completely equal beings will result in a product that is in between the level of the two parents. That means that the offspring will be superior to the parent who is at a biologically lower level of being but inferior to the parent at a higher level. This means the offspring will be overcome in the struggle for existence against those at the higher level. Such matings go against the will of Nature for the higher breeding of life.

As little as nature approves the mating of higher and lower individuals, she approves even less the blending of higher races with lower ones; for indeed otherwise her previous work toward higher development perhaps over hundreds of thousands of years might be rendered useless with one blow. If this were not the case, progressive development would stop and even deterioration might set in. . . . All the great civilizations of the past died out because contamination of their blood caused them to become decadent.

. . . What we see before us today as human culture, all the yields of art, science, and technology, are almost exclusively the creative product of the Aryans. Indeed this fact alone leads to the not unfounded conclusion that the Aryan alone is the founder of the higher type of humanity, and further that he represents the prototype of what we understand by the word: MAN.

The Jew provides the greatest contrast to the Aryan.

Since the Jew—for reasons I will deal with shortly—never had a civilization of his own, others have always provided the foundations of his intellectual labors. His intellect has always developed by the use of those cultural achievements he has found ready at hand around him. Never has it happened the other way around.

He stops at nothing, and his vileness becomes so monstrous that no one should be surprised if among our people the hateful figure of the Jew is taken as the personification of the devil and the symbol of evil. . . .

FOR FURTHER REFLECTION

Although he twisted their meaning, the precepts of science were adapted by Hitler to support his racial theories. Why would he take such an approach? Was it particularly effective?

SOURCE: Adolf Hitler. *Mein Kampf.* Boston: Houghton Mifflin, 1939, pp. 390–414.

democracy for Germany's misfortunes: a humiliating peace treaty—the Treaty of Versailles—that identified Germany as responsible for the Great War and assigned reparation payments to the Allies; the hyperinflation of the early 1920s that wiped out the savings of the middle class; the suffering brought on by the Great Depression; and the seemingly unending and bitter infighting among the nation's major political parties. Adolf Hitler promised an end to all those misfortunes by creating a new order that would lead to greatness for Germany. By stressing racial doctrines, particularly anti-Semitism, the Nazis added a unique and frightening twist to their ideology. Although the Nazis avoided class divisions by recruiting followers from all strata of society, National Socialism in the main appealed to the members of the lower-middle classes:

ruined shopkeepers and artisans, impoverished farmers, discharged white-collar workers, and disenchanted students.

The impact of the Great Depression and political infighting led to bloody street battles, shaking the foundations of Germany's fragile young democracy. The leaders of the nation's democratic and liberal parties groped for solutions to mounting unemployment but were hindered by lack of consensus and the public's loss of faith in the democratic system. The electorate became radicalized. Fewer and fewer Germans were willing to defend a parliamentary system they considered ineffective and corrupt. Between 1930 and 1932 the Nazi Party became the largest party in parliament, and the reactionary and feeble president, Paul von Hindenburg (1847–1934), decided to offer Hitler the chancellorship. Promising to gain a majority in the next elections, Hitler lost little time in transforming the dying republic into a single-party dictatorship. He promised a German *Reich,* or empire, that would endure for a thousand years.

Under the guise of a state of national emergency, the Nazis used all available means to impose their rule. They began by eliminating all working-class and liberal opposition. The Nazis suppressed the German communist and socialist parties and abrogated virtually all constitutional and civil rights. Subsequently, Hitler and his government outlawed all other political parties, made it a crime to create a new party, and made the National Socialist Party the only legal party. Between 1933 and 1935 the regime replaced Germany's federal structure with a highly centralized state that eliminated the autonomy previously exercised by state and municipal governments. The National Socialist state then guided the destruction of trade unions and the elimination of collective bargaining, subsequently prohibiting strikes and lockouts. The Nazis also purged the judiciary and the civil service, took control of all police forces, and removed enemies of the regime—both real and imagined—through incarceration or murder.

Consolidation of Power

Once securely in power, the Nazi regime translated racist ideology, especially the notions of racial superiority and racial purity, into practice. The leaders of the Third Reich pursued the creation of a race-based national community by introducing eugenic measures designed to improve both the quantity and the quality of the German "race." Implicit in this racial remodeling was the conviction that there was no room for the "racially inferior" or for "biological outsiders."

The Racial State

Alarmed by declining birthrates, the Nazis launched a campaign to increase births of "racially valuable" children. This battle against the empty cradle meshed agreeably with Nazi ideology, which relegated women primarily to the role of wife and mother. Through tax credits, special child allowances, and marriage loans, the authorities tried to encourage marriage and, they hoped, procreation among young people. Legal experts rewrote divorce laws so that a husband could get a divorce decree solely on the ground that he considered his wife sterile. At the same time, the regime outlawed abortions, closed birth control centers, restricted birth control devices, and made it difficult to obtain information about family planning. The Nazis also became enamored with a relatively inexpensive form of propaganda: pronatalist (to increase births) propaganda. They set in motion a veritable cult of motherhood. Annually on 12 August—the birth date of Hitler's mother—women who bore many children received the Honor Cross of the German Mother in three classes: bronze for those with more than four children, silver for those with more than six, and gold for those with more than eight. By August 1939 three million women carried this prestigious award, which many Germans cynically called the "rabbit decoration." In the long term, however, any efforts by the Nazis to increase the fecundity of German women failed, and the birthrate remained below replacement level. German families were unwilling to change their reproductive preferences for fewer children.

Women and Race

Nazi Eugenics

"Mother and Child" was the slogan on this poster, idealizing and encouraging motherhood. The background conveys the Nazi predilection for the wholesome country life, a dream that clashed with the urban reality of German society.

The quantity of offspring was not the only concern of the new rulers, who were obsessed with quality. Starting in 1933, the regime initiated a compulsory sterilization program for men and women whom the regime had identified as having "hereditarily determined" sicknesses, including schizophrenia, feeble-mindedness, manic depression, hereditary blindness, hereditary deafness, chronic alcoholism, and serious physical deformities. Between 1934 and 1939 more than thirty thousand men and women underwent compulsory sterilization. Beginning in 1935 the government also sanctioned abortions—otherwise illegal in Germany—of the "hereditary ill" and "racial aliens." The mania for racial health culminated in a state-sponsored euthanasia program that was responsible for the murder of approximately two hundred thousand women, men, and children. Between 1939 and 1945 the Nazis systematically killed—by gassing, lethal injections, or starvation—those people judged useless to society, especially the physically and mentally handicapped. Nazi eugenics measures served as a precursor to the wholesale extermination of peoples classified as racial inferiors, such as gypsies and Jews.

Anti-Semitism

Anti-Semitism, or prejudice against Jews, was a key element in the designs to achieve a new racial order and became the hallmark of National Socialist rule. Immediately after coming to power in 1933 the Nazis initiated systematic measures to suppress Germany's Jewish population. Although Nazi anti-Semitism was based on biological racial theories dating to the nineteenth century, government authorities used religious descent to determine who was a Jew. A flood of discriminatory laws and directives designed to humiliate, impoverish, and segregate Jews from the rest of society followed. In 1935 the notorious Nuremberg Laws deprived German Jews of their citizenship and prohibited marriage and sexual intercourse between Jews and other Germans. The Nazi party, in cooperation with government agencies, banks, and businesses, took steps to eliminate Jews from economic life and expropriate their wealth. Jewish civil servants lost their jobs, and Jewish lawyers and doctors lost their gentile, or non-Jewish, clients. Party authorities also supervised the liquidation of

Jewish-owned businesses or argued for their purchase—at much less than their true value—by companies owned or operated by gentiles.

The official goal of the Nazi regime was Jewish emigration. Throughout the 1930s thousands of Jews left Germany, depriving the nation of many of its leading intellectuals, scientists, and artists. The exodus gained urgency after what came to be known as *Kristallnacht* ("the night of broken glass"). During the night of 9–10 November 1938, the Nazis arranged for the destruction of thousands of Jewish stores, the burning of most synagogues, and the murder of more than one hundred Jews throughout Germany and Austria. This *pogrom* (Yiddish for "devastation") was a signal that the position of Jews in Hitler's Reich was about to deteriorate dramatically. Although they had difficulty finding refuge, approximately 250,000 Jews left Germany by 1938. Those staying behind, especially the poor and the elderly, contemplated an uncertain destiny.

A Nazi "racial expert" uses a caliper to measure the racial purity of a German.

I n the decades after the Great War, European intellectuals questioned and challenged established traditions. While scientists and social thinkers conceived new theories that reshaped human knowledge and perceptions, artists forged a contemporary aesthetic. In an age of global interdependence, the U.S. stock market crash of 1929 ushered in a period of prolonged economic contraction and social misery that engulfed much of the world. As most of the industrialized world reeled under the impact of the Depression, the leadership of the Soviet Union embarked on a state-sponsored program of rapid industrialization. Though causing widespread human suffering, a series of five-year plans transformed the Soviet Union into a major industrial and military power.

Italians under the leadership of Mussolini rebuilt their state through fascist policies and imperial expansion. In Germany the effects of the Great Depression paved the way for the establishment of the Nazi state, which was based on the principle of racial inequality. Although many peoples suffered under the racist regime, Jews were the principal victims. Adolf Hitler's mission in life, envisioned in the wake of the Great War, was coming to a spectacular conclusion that culminated in another world war. That war brought both the fulfillment and the destruction of the goals and dreams he had crafted in an age of anxiety.

CHRONOLOGY

1905	Einstein publishes special theory of relativity
1907	Picasso paints *Les Demoiselles d'Avignon*
1918–1920	Civil war in Russia
1919	Mussolini launches fascist movement in Italy
1919	Walter Gropius founds the Bauhaus
1921–1928	Lenin's New Economic Policy
1927	Heisenberg establishes the uncertainty principle
1928–1932	First Soviet Five-Year Plan
1929	U.S. stock market crash
1929	Beginning of Great Depression
1929	Hemingway and Remarque publish antiwar novels
1933–1945	Hitler is ruler in Germany
1935–1938	Stalin's Great Purge in the Soviet Union
1939	Steinbeck publishes *The Grapes of Wrath*

FOR FURTHER READING

Geoffrey Barraclough. *Introduction to Contemporary History.* New York, 1964. An older but still useful introduction to global affairs since 1900.

Jeremy Bernstein. *Einstein.* New York, 1973. This brief and lucid treatment of Einstein's key concepts and ideas is comprehensible to the layperson.

Malcolm Bradbury and James McFarlane, eds. *Modernism, 1890–1930.* Atlantic Highlands, N.J., 1978. A comprehensive survey of the new trends in literature.

Martin Broszat. *The Hitler State: The Foundation and Development of the Internal Structure of the Third Reich.* New York, 1981. An account that does justice to the complexity of the Nazi movement and its rule.

Michael Burleigh. *The Third Reich: A New History.* New York, 2000. A new treatment of the Nazi dictatorship that stresses the tacit consent of the German people.

Robert Conquest. *Stalin: Breaker of Nations.* New York, 1991. A compelling and absorbing biography.

Peter Conrad. *Modern Times, Modern Places.* New York, 1999. Evocative appraisal of twentieth-century art and thought.

Sarah Davies and James Harris, eds. *Stalin: A New History.* New York, 2005. Reassessment of the Soviet leader based on newly available sources.

Richard Evans. *The Coming of the Third Reich.* New York, 2004. The first of a projected three-volume series, this work chronicles the Nazi movement's rise to power.

———. *The Third Reich in Power, 1933–1939.* New York, 2005. The second work in a planned three-volume series, this book starts with the Nazis' assumption of power, and ends at the beginning of World War II in Europe.

Sheila Fitzpatrick. *The Russian Revolution, 1917–1932.* 2nd ed. New York, 1984. This work stands out for the author's ability to make complex processes accessible to the general reader and still instruct the specialist.

George Gamow. *Thirty Years That Shook Physics.* Garden City, N.Y., 1966. A leading physicist engagingly tells the story of modern physics.

Peter Gay. *Freud: A Life for Our Time.* New York, 1988. A balanced biography of one of the most influential social thinkers of the twentieth century.

George Heard Hamilton. *Painting and Sculpture in Europe, 1880–1940.* 6th ed. New Haven, 1993. A classic that presents a discerning overview of the subject.

Ian Kershaw. *Hitler: 1889–1936: Hubris.* New York, 1999.

———. *Hitler: 1936–1945: Nemesis.* New York, 2000. One of the foremost historians of the Nazi era pens the definitive biography of Adolf Hitler.

———. *The Nazi Dictatorship: Problems and Perspectives of Interpretation.* 2nd ed. London, 1989. A superb assessment that also provides the best introduction to the enormous literature on the Third Reich.

Charles Kindleberger. *The World in Depression, 1929–1939.* London, 1973. A sophisticated analysis that focuses on developments in the United States and Europe.

A. J. H. Latham. *The Depression and the Developing World, 1914–1939.* London, 1981. One of the few works that looks beyond the industrialized world to give a global perspective on the subject.

Michael Mann. *Fascists.* New York, 2004. Comparative analysis of fascist movements in interwar Europe.

Colleen McDannell. *Picturing Faith: Photography and the Great Depression.* New Haven, 2004. Examination of depression-era photographs as evidence of the importance of religion in American life.

Robert Paxton. *The Anatomy of Fascism.* New York, 2004. A groundbreaking and fascinating history of fascism.

Nikolaus Pevsner. *Pioneers of Modern Design: From William Morris to Walter Gropius.* Rev. ed. New York, 1964. This work chronicles the rise of the international style in architecture.

Richard Pipes. *The Russian Revolution.* New York, 1990. When the Communist Party collapsed in 1991, this sweeping study was quickly translated into Russian and became a national bestseller.

Eli Zaretsky. *Secrets of the Soul: A Social and Cultural History of Psychoanalysis.* New York, 2004. Flawed but useful history of the broad social impacts of Freud's theories.

36 Nationalism and Political Identities in Asia, Africa, and Latin America

Asian Paths to Autonomy
India's Quest for Home Rule
China's Search for Order
Imperial and Imperialist Japan

Africa under Colonial Domination
Africa and the Great War
The Colonial Economy
African Nationalism

Latin American Struggles with Neocolonialism
The Impact of the Great War and the Great Depression
The Evolution of Economic Imperialism
Conflicts with a "Good Neighbor"

Shanfei lived in politically exciting times. The daughter of a wealthy landowning man of the Chinese gentry, she grew up with luxuries and opportunities unknown to most girls. Her father allowed her to attend school, and her mother clothed her in beautiful silk dresses. Shanfei, however, matured into a woman who rejected the rich trappings of her youth. Her formative years were marked by political ferment and the unsettling cultural changes that engulfed the globe in the wake of the Great War. The rise of nationalism and communism in China after the revolution of 1911 and the Russian revolution in 1917 guided the transformation of Shanfei—from a girl ruled by tradition and privilege, she became an active revolutionary dedicated to the cause of women and communism.

With the exception of Shanfei's father, the members of her family in Hunan province took in the new spirit of the first decades of the twentieth century. Her brothers returned from school with strange and compelling ideas, including some that challenged the subordinate position of women in China. Shanfei's mother, to all appearances a woman who accepted her subservience to her husband, proved instrumental to Shanfei's departure from the common destiny of Chinese girls. She listened quietly to her sons as they discussed new views, and then she applied them to her daughter. She used every means at her disposal to persuade her husband to educate their daughter. She wept, begged, and cajoled. He relented but still insisted that Shanfei receive an old-fashioned education and submit to foot binding and childhood betrothal.

When Shanfei was eleven years old, her father suddenly died, and his death emboldened her mother. She ripped the bandages off Shanfei's feet and sent her to a modern school far from home. In the lively atmosphere of her school, Shanfei bloomed into an activist. At sixteen she incited a student strike against the administration of her school, transferred to a more modern school, and became famous as a leader in the student movement. She went to school with men and broke tradition in her personal and political life. In 1926 Shanfei abandoned her studies to join the Communist Youth, and she gave up her fiancé for a free marriage to the man she loved: a peasant leader in the communist movement.

The twists of fate that altered the destiny of Shanfei had parallels throughout the colonial world after 1914. Two major events, the Great War and the Great Depression, defined much of the turmoil of those years. Disillusion and radical upheaval marked areas as distinct as Asia, Africa, and Latin America. As peoples around the world struggled to come to terms with the aftermath of war, an unprecedented economic contraction gripped the international economy. The Great Depression complicated peoples' struggles for national sovereignty and financial

OPPOSITE: In this cigarette advertisement from 1935, Chinese women are shown challenging traditions. They are "new women," affected by the radical changes in identity and behavior taking place after the Great War and during the Great Depression.

solvency, especially in Asia, where Japan's militarist leaders sought to build national strength through imperial expansion. Latin American states worked to alter the economic domination of its "good neighbor" to the north while African peoples suffered a contraction in living standards along with the economically weakened imperial industrialists.

European empires still appeared to dominate global relations, but the Great War had opened fissures within the European and U.S. spheres of influence. Beneath colonial surfaces, nationalist and communist ferment brewed. Nationalist and anti-imperial movements gathered strength, and in the postwar years resistance to foreign rule and a desire for national unity were stronger than ever. This situation was especially true in India and China, where various visions of national identity competed, but it also pertained to those in Africa and Latin America who struggled against the domination of imperial powers. While peoples in Africa worked to become independent of outright imperial control, those in Latin America had to fight off the more indirect economic effects of postindependence colonialism, usually termed *neocolonialism*. The roots of all of these developments lay in the global storm of a world war that shook the foundations of established traditions, which crumbled in Shanfei's home in Hunan as much as in the Kikuyu highlands and Mexico City.

Asian Paths to Autonomy

The Paris peace settlement had barely altered the prewar colonial holdings of Europeans, yet indirectly the Great War affected relations between Asian peoples and the imperial powers. In the decades following the Great War, nationalism developed into a powerful political force in Asia, especially in India and China, where growing numbers of people were influenced by the self-determination concept that was one of the legacies of the Paris Peace Conference. Achieving the twin ideals of independence from foreign powers and national unity became a dream of intellectuals and a goal of new political leaders. Even as foreign control was being rejected, Asian leaders availed themselves of European ideologies such as nationalism and socialism, but in their search for new identities untainted by the dependent past, Asians either transformed or adapted those ideologies to fit indigenous traditions. In that sense, peoples in India and China followed in the footsteps of Japan, which had already adapted European and U.S. economic strategies to its advantage. Still dissatisfied with its status, Japan used militarism and imperial expansion in the interwar years to enhance its national identity.

Indian, Chinese, and Japanese societies underwent a prolonged period of disorder and struggle until a new order emerged. In India the quest for national identity focused on gaining independence from British rule, a pursuit that was complicated by sectarian differences between Hindus and Muslims. The Chinese path to national identity was fraught with foreign and civil war as two principal groups—the Nationalist and Communist Parties—contended for power. Deeply divided by ideologies, both parties opposed foreign domination, rejected the old Confucian order, and sought a unified Chinese state. Japanese militarists made China's quest for national unity more difficult, because Japan struggled to overcome its domestic problems through conquests that focused on China.

India's Quest for Home Rule

By the beginning of the twentieth century, Indian nationalism threatened the British empire's hold on India. The construction of a vast railway network across India to facilitate the export of raw materials contributed to the idea of national unity by bringing the people of the subcontinent within easy reach of one another. Moreover, because it was impossible for a small group of foreigners to control and administer such a vast country, the British had created an elite of educated Indian administrators to help in this task. A European system of education familiarized the local middle-class intelligentsia with the political and social values of European society. Those values, however—democracy, individual freedom, and equality—were the antithesis of empire, and they promoted nationalist movements.

Of all the associations dedicated to the struggle against British rule, the greatest and most influential was the Indian National Congress, founded in 1885. This organization, which enlisted the support of many prominent Hindus and Muslims, at first stressed collaboration with the British to bring self-rule to India, but after the Great War the congress pursued that goal in opposition to the British. The formation of the Muslim League, established in 1906 with the encouragement of the British government, added a new current into the movement for national liberation. Both organizations were dedicated to achieving independence for India, but members of the Muslim League increasingly worried that Hindu oppression and continued subjugation of India's substantial Muslim minority might replace British rule.

Indian National Congress

During the Great War, large numbers of Indians—Hindus and Muslims—rallied to the British cause, and nationalist movements remained inactive. But as the war led to scarcities of goods and food, social discontent increasingly focused on the British colonizer. Indian nationalists also drew encouragement from ideas emanating from Washington, D.C., and St. Petersburg. They read Woodrow Wilson's Fourteen Points, which called for national self-determination, and Lenin's appeal for a united struggle by proletarians and colonized peoples. The British government responded to the upsurge of nationalist activity that came in the wake of the peace settlement with a series of repressive measures that precipitated a wave of violence and disorder throughout the Indian subcontinent.

Into this turmoil stepped Mohandas Karamchand Gandhi (1869–1948), one of the most remarkable and charismatic leaders of the twentieth century. Gandhi grew up in a prosperous and pious Hindu household, married at thirteen, and left his hometown in 1888 to study law in London. In 1893 he went to South Africa to accept a position with an Indian firm, and there he quickly became involved in organizing the local Indian community against a system of racial segregation that made Indians second-class citizens. During the twenty-five years he spent in South Africa, Gandhi embraced a moral philosophy of *ahimsa* (tolerance and nonviolence) and developed the technique of passive resistance that he called *satyagraha* ("truth and firmness"). His belief in the virtue of simple living led him to renounce material possessions, dress in the garb of a simple Indian peasant, and become a vegetarian. He renounced sex—testing his willpower by chastely sleeping with various comely young women—and extolled the virtues of a daily saltwater enema. He also spent an hour each morning in careful study of the Bhagavad Gita (Sanskrit for "The Lord's Song"), one of the most sacred writings of Hinduism, which he regarded as a spiritual dictionary.

Mohandas K. Gandhi

Returning to India in 1915, Gandhi became active in Indian politics. He succeeded in transforming the Indian National Congress from an elitist body of anglicized gentlemen into a mass organization that became an effective instrument of Indian nationalism. Although the reform program of the congress appeared remote from the needs of common people, Gandhi spoke in a language that they could understand. His unique mixture of spiritual intensity and political activism appealed to a broad section of the Indian population, and in the eyes of many he quickly achieved the stature of a political and spiritual leader, their Mahatma, or "great soul." Although he was a member of the merchant caste, Gandhi was determined to eradicate the injustices of the caste system. He fought especially hard to improve the status of the lowest classes of society, the casteless Untouchables, whom he called *harijans* ("children of God").

Under Gandhi's leadership the congress launched two mass movements: the Non-Cooperation Movement of 1920–1922 and the Civil Disobedience Movement of 1930. Convinced that economic self-sufficiency was a prerequisite for self-government, Gandhi called on the Indian people to boycott British goods and return to wearing rough homespun cotton clothing. He disagreed with those who wanted India to industrialize, advocating instead manual labor and the revival of rural cottage industries. Gandhi furthermore admonished his people to boycott institutions operated by the British in India, such as schools, offices, and courts. Despite Gandhi's cautions against the use of force, violence often accompanied the protest movement. The British retaliated with arrests. That the British authorities could react brutally was shown in 1919 in the city of Amritsar in Punjab, where colonial troops freely used their rifles to disperse an unarmed crowd, killing 379 demonstrators.

The India Act

When repressive measures failed to quell the movement for self-rule, the British offered a political compromise. After years of hesitation and deliberation, the British parliament enacted the Government of India Act, which gave India the institutions of a self-governing state. The legislation allowed for the establishment of autonomous legislative bodies in the provinces of British India, the creation of a bicameral (two-chambered) national legislature, and the formation of an executive arm under the control of the British government. On the urging of Gandhi, the majority of Indians approved the measure, which went into effect in 1937.

The India Act proved unworkable, however, because India's six hundred nominally sovereign princes refused to cooperate and because Muslims feared that Hindus would dominate the national legislature. Muslims had reason for concern because they already faced economic control by Hindus, a fact underlined during the Great Depression, which had a severe impact on India. On top of Indians suffering the typical devastations associated with agricultural economies during depression, they had to cope with added hurdles erected by an imperial government that did not respond with energetic efforts to mitigate the effects of the economic crisis. Moreover, the Great Depression exacerbated conflict between Muslims and Hindus, as Muslims constituted the majority of indebted tenant farmers, who found themselves increasingly unable to pay rents and debts. Their landlords were mainly Hindus. Muslims felt keenly what they perceived as economic exploitation by Hindus, and their recognition of this economic discrimination bolstered calls for a separate Muslim state. Muhammad Ali Jinnah (1876–1948), an eloquent and brilliant lawyer who headed the Muslim League, warned that a unified India represented nothing less than a threat to the Muslim faith and its Indian community. In place of one India, he proposed two states, one of which would be the "land of the pure," or Pakistan. Jinnah's proposal reflected an uncomfortable reality that society in India was split by hostility between Hindus and Muslims, making national unification an illusory goal.

China's Search for Order

As Shanfei's life story suggested, during the first half of the twentieth century China was in a state of almost continual revolutionary upheaval. The conflict's origins dated from the nineteenth century, when the Chinese empire came under relentless pressure from imperialist powers that rushed in to fill the vacuum created by China's internal political disintegration (see chapter 32). As revolutionary and nationalist uprisings gained widespread support, a revolution in 1911 forced the Xuantong emperor, still a

Sources from the Past

"Self-Rule Is My Birthright"

Bal Gangadhar Tilak (1856–1920) was a fiery Indian nationalist who galvanized public support for India's independence movement. Although he was a great Sanskrit scholar and a very successful journalist, people best remember Tilak as a political activist who sought a Hindu revival and independence from Great Britain. His slogan, "Swaraj (Self-Rule) is my birthright," inspired millions of Indians. Whereas the British labeled him the "Father of Indian Unrest," Mohandas K. Gandhi more generously called him the "Maker of Modern India." What follows is an excerpt from Tilak's address to the Indian National Congress in 1907, calling for a boycott of British goods and resistance to British rule.

One fact is that this alien government has ruined the country. In the beginning, all of us were taken by surprise. We were almost dazed. We thought that everything that the rulers did was for our good and that this English Government has descended from the clouds to save us from the invasions of Tamerlane and Chingis Khan, and, as they say, not only from foreign invasions but from internecine warfare. We felt happy for a time, but it soon came to light that the peace which was established in this country did this . . . —that we were prevented from going at each other's throats, so that a foreigner might go at the throat of us all. Pax Britannica has been established in this country in order that a foreign Government may exploit the country. That this is the effect of this Pax Britannica is being gradually realized in these days. It was an unhappy circumstance that it was not realized sooner. . . . English education, growing poverty, and better familiarity with our rulers, opened our eyes. . . . Your industries are ruined utterly, ruined by foreign rule; your wealth is going out of the country and you are reduced to the lowest level which no human being can occupy. In this state of things, is there any other remedy by

which you can help yourself? The remedy is not petitioning but boycott. We say prepare your forces, organize your power, and then go to work so that they cannot refuse you what you demand. . . . Every Englishman knows that they are a mere handful in this country and it is the business of every one of them to befool you in believing that you are weak and they are strong. This is politics. We have been deceived by such policy so long. What the new party wants you to do is realize the fact that your future rests entirely in your own hands. . . . We shall not give them assistance to collect revenue and keep peace. We shall not assist them in fighting beyond the frontiers or outside India with Indian blood and money. We shall not assist them in carrying on the administration of justice. We shall have our own courts, and when time comes we shall not pay taxes. Can you do that by your united efforts? If you can, you are free from to-morrow. . . .

FOR FURTHER REFLECTION

What does Tilak suggest the British duped Indians into believing, and how would an Indian boycott let the British know that Indians would no longer be fooled?

SOURCE: Bal Gangadhar Tilak. *Bal Gangadhar Tilak: His Writings and Speeches.* Madras: Ganesh and Co., 1923, pp. 56–65.

child (also known as Puyi), to abdicate. The Qing empire fell with relative ease. Dr. Sun Yatsen (1866–1925), a leading opponent of the old regime, proclaimed a Chinese republic in 1912 and briefly assumed the office of president. The dynasty was dead, but there remained the problems of how to bury it and what to put in its place.

The revolution of 1911 did not establish a stable government. Indeed, the republic soon plunged into a state of political anarchy and economic disintegration marked by the rule of warlords, who were disaffected generals from the old imperial Chinese army, and their troops. While the central government in Beijing ran the post office and a few other services, the warlords established themselves as provincial or regional rulers. Because the warlords were responsible for the neglect of irrigation projects crucial to the survival of farmers, for the revival of the opium trade, which they protected, and for the decline of crucial economic investments, they contributed to the deterioration of Chinese society. They never founded a new dynasty, nor did they create the semblance

The Republic

of a stable central state. Yet warlords were just one symbol of the disintegration of the political order. The fragmented relationship between native authority and foreign powers was another. Since the nineteenth century, a collection of treaties, known in China as the unequal treaties, had guided Chinese relations with foreign countries. Those treaties had established a network of foreign control over the Chinese economy that effectively prevented economic development. The continued sway of unequal treaties and other concessions permitted foreigners to intervene in Chinese society. Foreigners did not control the state, but through their privileges they impaired its sovereignty.

Chinese Nationalism   After the Great War, nationalist sentiment developed rapidly in China. Youths and intellectuals, who in the previous decade had looked to Europe and the United States for models and ideals for the reform of China, eagerly anticipated the results of the 1919 Peace Conference in Paris. They expected the U.S. government to support the termination of the treaty system and the restoration of full Chinese sovereignty. Those hopes were shattered, however, when the peacemakers approved increasing Japanese interference in China. That decision gave rise to the May Fourth Movement. Spearheaded by students and intellectuals in China's urban areas, the movement galvanized the country, and all classes of Chinese protested against foreign, especially Japanese, interference. In speeches, newspapers, and novels, the movement's leaders pledged themselves to rid China of imperialism and reestablish national unity. Student leaders such as Shanfei rallied their comrades to the cause.

Disillusioned by the cynical self-interest of the United States and the European powers, some Chinese became interested in Marxist thought as modified by Lenin (see chapter 34) and the social and economic experiments under way in the Soviet Union. The anti-imperialist rhetoric of the Soviet leadership struck a responsive chord, and in 1921 the Chinese Communist Party (CCP) was organized in Shanghai. Among its early members was Mao Zedong (1893–1976), a former teacher and librarian who viewed a Marxist-inspired social revolution as the cure for China's problems. Mao's political radicalism extended to the issue of women's equality, which he and other communists championed. As Shanfei's personal experience suggested, Chinese communists believed in divorce, opposed arranged marriages, and campaigned against the practice of foot binding.

Sun Yatsen   The most prominent nationalist leader at the time, Sun Yatsen, did not share the communists' enthusiasm for a dictatorship of the proletariat and the triumph of communism. Sun's basic ideology, summarized in his *Three Principles of the People,* called for elimination of special privileges for foreigners, national reunification, economic development, and a democratic republican government based on universal suffrage. To realize those goals, he was determined to bring the entire country under the control of his Nationalist People's Party, or *Guomindang.* In 1923 members of the small CCP began to augment the ranks of the Guomindang and by 1926 made up one-third of the Guomindang's membership. Both organizations availed themselves of the assistance offered by the Soviet Union. Under the doctrine of Lenin's democratic centralism—stressing centralized party control by a highly disciplined group of professional revolutionaries—Soviet advisors helped reorganize the Guomindang and the CCP into effective political organizations. In the process, the Soviets bestowed on China the basis of a new political system.

Civil War   After the death of Sun Yatsen in 1925, the leadership of the Guomindang fell to Jiang Jieshi (Chiang Kai-shek, 1887–1975), a young general who had been trained in Japan and the Soviet Union. In contrast to the communists, he did not hold a vision for social revolution that involved the masses of China. Before long, Jiang Jieshi launched a political and military offensive, known as the Northern Expedition, that aimed to unify the nation and bring China under Guomindang rule. Toward the end

The struggle for control in China, 1927–1936. Compare the continental territories controlled by Japan and the Guomindang in 1934. How would the size of Japan's territories in Manchuria and Korea influence Chinese abilities to challenge Japanese expansion?

of his successful campaign, in 1927, Jiang Jieshi brutally and unexpectedly turned against his former communist allies, bringing the alliance of convenience between the Guomindang and the CCP to a bloody end. In the following year, nationalist forces occupied Beijing, set up a central government in Nanjing, and declared the Guomindang the official government of a unified and sovereign Chinese state. Meanwhile, the badly mauled communists retreated to a remote area of southeastern China, where they tried to reconstitute and reorganize their forces.

The nationalist government had to deal with many concerns, but Chinese leaders evaded one major global crisis—the Great Depression. China's large agrarian economy and small industrial sector were connected only marginally to the world economy. Foreign trade in such items as tea and silk, which did decline, made up only a small part of China's economy, which was otherwise dominated by its large domestic markets. Although the new government in China generally avoided having to contend with global economic devastation, it did have to confront three major problems during the 1930s.

Adversaries in the struggle for power in China: at left, Jiang Jieshi (Chiang Kai-shek); at right, Mao Zedong.

First, the nationalists actually controlled only part of China, leaving the remainder of the country in the hands of warlords. Second, by the early 1930s communist revolution was still a major threat. Third, the Guomindang faced increasing Japanese aggression. In dealing with those problems, Jiang Jieshi gave priority to eliminating the CCP and its Red Army. No longer able to ward off the relentless attacks of nationalist forces, the communists took flight in October 1934 to avoid annihilation. Bursting through a military blockade around their bases in Jiangxi province in southeastern China, some eighty-five thousand troops and auxiliary personnel of the Red Army began the legendary Long March, an epic journey of 10,000 kilometers (6,215 miles). After traveling across difficult terrain and fighting for survival against hunger, disease, and Guomindang forces, the marchers arrived in a remote area of Shaanxi province in northwestern China in October 1935 and established headquarters at Yan'an. Although thousands had died in this forced retreat, the Long March inspired many Chinese to join the Communist Party. During the Long March, Mao Zedong emerged as the leader and the principal theoretician of the Chinese communist movement. He came up with a Chinese form of Marxist-Leninism, or Maoism, an ideology grounded in the conviction that peasants rather than urban proletarians were the foundation for a successful revolution. Village power, Mao believed, was critical in a country where most people were peasants.

Imperial and Imperialist Japan

After the Great War, Japan achieved great power status and appeared to accept the international status quo that the major powers fashioned in the aftermath of war. After joining the League of Nations as one of the "big five" powers, the Japanese government entered into a series of international agreements that sought to improve relations among countries with conflicting interests in Asia and the Pacific. As a signatory to several Washington Conference treaties in 1922, Japan agreed to limit naval development, pledged to evacuate Shandong province of China, and guaranteed China's territorial integrity. In 1928 the Japanese government signed the Kellogg-Briand Pact, which renounced war as an instrument of national policy. Concerns about earlier Japanese territorial ambitions, highlighted by the Twenty-One Demands on China in 1915, receded from the minds of the international community.

Japan's limited involvement in the Great War gave a dual boost to its economy. Japanese businesses profited from selling munitions and other goods to the Allies throughout the war, and they gained a bigger foothold in Asia as the war led Europe's trading nations to neglect Asian markets. Economic prosperity was short-lived, however, as the postwar economy of Japan faced serious challenges. Rapid inflation and labor unrest appeared by 1918, followed by a series of recessions that culminated in a giant economic slump caused by the Great Depression. Like the economies of other industrial nations tied into the global economy, Japan's economy experienced plummeting industrial production, huge job layoffs, declining trade, and financial chaos. Economic contraction set the stage for social unrest and radical politics.

Public demands for sweeping political and social reforms, including a broadening of the franchise, protection for labor unions, and welfare legislation, figured prominently in Japanese domestic politics throughout the 1920s. Yet conservatives blocked any major advances beyond the suffrage law of 1925, which established universal male suffrage. By the early 1930s an increasingly frustrated public blamed its government for the nation's continuing economic problems and became more disenchanted with leading politicians tainted by bribery scandals and corrupt connections to business conglomerates. Right-wing political groups called for an end to party rule, and xenophobic nationalists dedicated themselves to the preservation of a unique Japanese culture and the eradication of western influences. A campaign of assassinations, targeting political and business leaders, culminated in the murder of prime minister Inukai Tsuyoshi (1855–1932).

Politicians who supported Japan's role in the international industrial-capitalist system faced increasing opposition from those who were inclined toward a militarist vision of a self-sufficient Japan that would dominate east Asia. The hardships of the depression undermined support for the internationalist position, and the militarists were able to benefit from Japanese martial traditions and their own unwillingness to be constrained by international cooperation. China's unification, aided by international attempts to reinstate its sovereignty, threatened Japan's economic interests in Manchuria. Moreover, political instability, the result of nationalists and communists vying for power, made China an inviting target. Manchuria had historically been Chinese territory, but by the twentieth century it was a sphere of influence where Japan maintained the Manchurian Railroad (built in 1906), retained transit rights, and stationed troops. In 1931 Japan's military forces in Manchuria acted to assert control over the region.

On the night of 18 September 1931, Japanese troops used explosives to blow up a few feet of rail on the Japanese-built South Manchuria Railway north of Mukden. They accused the Chinese of attacking their railroad. This "Mukden incident" became the pretext for war between Japanese and Chinese troops. Although the civilian government in Japan tried to halt this military incursion, by 1932 Japanese troops controlled all of Manchuria, thereby ensuring Japan preeminence and protecting its long-term economic and industrial development of the region. The Japanese established a puppet state called Manchukuo, but in reality Japan had absorbed Manchuria into its empire, challenged the international peace system, and begun a war. In response to the Manchurian invasion, the Guomindang (Nationalist Party) leader Jiang Jieshi appealed to the League of Nations to halt Japanese aggression. After a lengthy investigation, the league called for the withdrawal of Japanese forces and for the restoration of Chinese sovereignty. The Japanese responded by leaving the league,

The Mukden Incident

and, although China gained the moral high ground in international eyes, nothing was done to stop the aggression. This reaction set the pattern for future responses to the actions of expansionist nations such as Japan. Embarking on conquests in east Asia, Japanese militarists found a sure means to promoting a new militant Japanese national identity. They also helped provoke a new global conflagration.

The Great War and the Great Depression made signal contributions to the ongoing nationalist and political upheavals taking place throughout Asia. New ideologies and old conflicts intersected to complicate the processes of independence and national unification in India and China. The global economic crisis led to some lessening of European imperial influence, while it prompted an industrialized Japan to exert its imperial will on the Asian sphere. Only the aftermath of another world war brought any resolution to the turmoil within and among Asian nations.

Africa under Colonial Domination

The Great War and the Great Depression similarly complicated quests for national independence and unity in Africa. The colonial ties that bound African colonies to European powers ensured that Africans became participants in the Great War, willing or not. European states transmitted their respective animosities and their military conflicts to African soil and drew on their colonies for the recruitment of soldiers and carriers. The forced recruitment of military personnel led some Africans to raise arms against their colonial overlords, but Europeans generally prevailed in putting down those uprisings. African contributions to the Great War and the wartime rhetoric of self-determination espoused by U.S. President Woodrow Wilson led some Africans to anticipate a different postwar world. The peacemakers in Paris, however, ignored African pleas for social and political reform.

Rather than retreating, colonialism consolidated its hold on the African continent. In the decades following the peace settlement of 1919, the European powers focused on the economic exploitation of their colonies. The imposition of a rapacious form of capitalism destroyed the self-sufficiency of many African economies and turned the resulting colonial economies into extensions of those of the colonizing powers. As a result, African economic life became enmeshed in the global economy. The persistence of colonialism led to the development of African nationalism and the birth of embryonic nationalist movements. During the decades following the Great War, African intellectuals searched for new national identities and looked forward to the construction of nations devoid of European domination and exploitation.

Africa and the Great War

The Great War had a profound impact on Africa. The conflict of 1914–1918 affected Africans because many belligerents were colonial powers who ruled over the greater part of Africa. Except for Spanish-controlled territories, which remained neutral, every African colony took sides in the war. In practice this meant that the German colonial administration faced the combined colonial forces of Great Britain, France, Belgium, Italy, and Portugal. Even the last remaining independent states on the continent—Liberia and Ethiopia—did not avoid involvement. Whereas Lij Iyasu (reigned 1913–1916), the uncrowned, pro-Muslim boy emperor of Ethiopia, aligned his nation with Turkey until he was overthrown by pro-Christian nobles in 1916, Liberia joined the Allies in 1917 when the United States entered the war.

A Senegalese regiment of the French Colonial Infantry on parade in Africa during the Great War.

War in Africa

Although Germany had been a latecomer in the race for overseas colonies, German imperialists had managed to carve out a rudimentary colonial empire in Africa that included Togo, Cameroon, German South-West Africa, and German East Africa. Thus, one immediate consequence of war for Africans in 1914 was that the Allies invaded those German colonies. Specific strategic interests among the Allies varied. British officers and soldiers, trying to maintain naval supremacy, attempted to put German port facilities and communications systems out of action. The British also anticipated that victory in the German colonies would bring victors' spoils after the war. France's objective was to recover territory in Cameroon that it had ceded to Germany in 1911. The Germans, in contrast, simply tried to hold on to what they had. Outnumbered ten to one, the Germans could not hope to win the war in Africa. Yet, by resorting to guerrilla tactics, some fifteen thousand German troops tied sixty thousand Allied forces down and postponed defeat until the last days of the war.

More than one million African soldiers participated directly in military campaigns, in which they witnessed firsthand the spectacle of white people fighting one another. Colonial "masters" sent them to fight on African soil, in the lands of southwest Asia, and on the western front in Europe. The colonial powers also encouraged their African subjects in uniforms to kill the enemy "white man," whose life until now had been sacrosanct because of his skin color. Even more men, as well as women and children, served as carriers to support armies in areas where supplies could not be hauled by conventional methods such as road, rail, or pack animal. The colonial powers raised recruits for fighting and carrier services in three ways: on a purely voluntary basis; in levies supplied by African chiefs that consisted of volunteer and impressed personnel; and through formal conscription. In French colonies, military service became compulsory for all males between the ages of twenty and twenty-eight, and by the end of the war over 480,000 colonial troops had served in the French army. The British also raised recruits in their African colonies. In 1915 a compulsory service order made all men ages eighteen to twenty-five liable for military service. In the Congo, the Belgians impressed more than half a million porters. Ultimately more than 150,000 African soldiers and carriers lost their lives, and many more suffered injury or became disabled.

Challenges to European Authority

While the world's attention was focused on the slaughter taking place in European lands between 1914 and 1918, Africans mounted bold challenges to European colonial authority. As the war dragged on, European commercial and administrative personnel began to leave the colonies in large numbers, whether for combat in Europe or for enlistment in locally based units for campaigns in Africa. That spread an already thin European presence even thinner, a fact not missed by colonial subjects. Africans took the opportunity to stage armed uprisings and other forms of protest. When they could least afford trouble, colonial regimes had no choice but to divert scarce military resources to meet those challenges.

The cause of widespread revolts varied. In some cases, as in Libya, revolts simply represented continued resistance to European rule. In other cases, the departure of European personnel, which seemed to signal a weakening of power, encouraged those who had previously only contemplated revolt. In yet other instances, pan-Islamic opposition to the war manifested itself in uprisings. The British had nervous moments, for example, when the Sufi brotherhood, based in Libya and still busy battling Italian occupation there, responded to a Turkish call for holy war and invaded western Egypt. The Mumbo cult in Kenya targeted Europeans and their Christian religion, declaring that "all Europeans are our enemies, but the time is shortly coming when they will disappear from our country." The major inspiration for most revolts, however, stemmed from the resentment and hatred engendered by the compulsory conscription of soldiers and carriers. No matter the cause, colonial authorities responded ruthlessly and succeeded in putting down all the revolts.

The Colonial Economy

The decades following the Great War witnessed a thorough transformation of African economic life. Colonial powers pursued two key economic objectives in Africa: they wanted to make sure that the colonized paid for the institutions—bureaucracies, judiciary, police, and military forces—that kept them in subjugation; and they developed export-oriented economies characterized by the exchange of unprocessed raw materials or minimally processed cash crops for manufactured goods from abroad. In pursuit of those goals, colonial authorities imposed economic structures that altered, subordinated, or destroyed previously self-sufficient African economies. In their place came colonial economies, tightly integrated into and dependent on a European-dominated global economy. The Great Depression of the 1930s exposed the vulnerability of dependent colonial economies. As international markets for primary products shrank under the impact of the depression, European companies that controlled the export of African products suffered accordingly. Trade volume often fell by half, and commodity prices dropped even more sharply.

Infrastructure

Africa's economic integration required investment in infrastructures. Thus, during the early twentieth century, the new colonial economy first became visible in the form of port facilities, roads, railways, and telegraph wires. Efficient transportation and communication networks not only facilitated conquest and rule but also linked the agricultural or mineral wealth of a colony to the outside world. Although Europeans later claimed that they had given Africa its first modern infrastructure, Europeans and their businesses were usually its main beneficiaries. It was Africans who paid for the

EAST-AFRICAN TRANSPORT-NEW STYLE

This poster, produced by the Empire Marketing Board, presented an idealized image of the dominant European role in forwarding African economic progress.

infrastructure with their labor and taxes, yet Europeans never considered the needs of local African economies.

Farming and Mining

Colonial taxation was an important tool designed to drive Africans into the labor market. To earn the money to pay the taxes levied on land, houses, livestock, and people themselves, African farmers had to become cash crop farmers or seek wage labor on plantations and in mines. Cash crop farming embraced the largest proportion of Africans. In most colonies, farmers who kept their land specialized in one or two crops, generally destined for export to the country governing them. African farmers grew a variety of cash crops for the international marketplace, among them peanuts from Senegal and northern Nigeria, cotton from Uganda, cocoa from the Gold Coast, rubber from the Congo, and palm oil from the Ivory Coast and the Niger delta. In areas with extensive white settlement, such as in Kenya, Rhodesia, and South Africa, settler agriculture was most prominent. Production of agricultural commodities intended for overseas markets remained in the hands of white settlers, whose governments saw to it that they received large and productive areas of land. In British-controlled Kenya, for example, four thousand white farmers seized the Kikuyu highlands, which comprised seven million acres of the colony's richest land. In South Africa, the government reserved 88 percent of all land for whites, who made up just 20 percent of the total population.

Colonial mining enterprises relying on African labor loomed large in parts of central and southern Africa. Engaged in the extraction of mineral wealth such as copper, gold, and diamonds, these enterprises recruited men from rural areas and paid them minimal wages. The recruitment practices set in motion a vast pattern of labor migration that persisted throughout the twentieth century. The absence of male labor and the payment of minimal wages had the effect of impoverishing the rural areas. In many cases, the wives left behind could not grow enough food to feed their children and elderly relatives.

Labor Practices

Where taxation failed to create a malleable native labor force, colonial officials resorted to outright forced labor. Indeed, forms of forced labor and barely disguised variants of slavery were prominent features of the colonial economy. A white settler in Kenya candidly expressed the view held by many colonial administrators: "We have stolen his land. Now we must steal his limbs. Compulsory labor is the corollary to our occupation of the country." Much of the labor abuse originated with concessionary companies, which were authorized by their governments to exploit a region's resources with the help of their own system of taxation and labor recruitment. Frequently, the conduct of such companies with respect to labor practices was downright brutal. For example, the construction of railways and roads often depended on forced labor regimes. When the French undertook the construction of the Congo-Ocean railway from Brazzaville to the port at Point-Noir, they rounded up some ten thousand workers annually. Within a few years, between fifteen and twenty thousand African laborers had perished from starvation, disease, and maltreatment.

African Nationalism

In the decades following the Great War, European powers consolidated their political control over the partitioned continent and imposed economies designed to exploit Africa's natural and labor resources. Many Africans were disappointed that their contributions to the war went unrewarded. In place of anticipated social reforms or some degree of greater political participation came an extension and consolidation of the colonial system. Nevertheless, ideas concerning self-determination, articulated by U.S. President Woodrow Wilson during the war, and the notion of the accountability of colonial powers that had been sown during the war gained adherents among a group of African nationalists. Those ideas influenced the growth of African nationalism and the development of incipient nationalist movements. An emerging class of native urban intellectuals, frequently educated in Europe, became especially involved in the formation of ideologies that promised freedom from colonialism and promoted new national identities.

Africa's New Elite

Colonialism prompted the emergence of a novel African social class, sometimes called the "new elite." This elite derived its status and place in society from employment and education. The upper echelons of Africa's elite class contained high-ranking civil servants, physicians, lawyers, and writers, most of whom had studied abroad either in western Europe or sometimes in the United States. A case in point was Jomo Kenyatta (1895–1978), who spent almost fifteen years in Europe, during which time he attended various schools and universities, including the London School of Economics. An immensely articulate nationalist, Kenyatta later led Kenya to independence from the British. Even those who had not gone abroad had familiarized themselves with the writings of European authors. Below them in status stood teachers, clerks, and interpreters who had obtained a European-derived primary or secondary education. Although some individuals were self-employed, such as lawyers and doctors, most of them held jobs with colonial governments, with foreign companies, or with Christian missions. In short, these were the Africans who spoke and understood the language of the colonizer, moved with ease in the world of the colonizer, and outwardly adopted the cultural norms of the colonizer such as wearing European-style clothes or adopting European names. It was within the ranks of this new elite that ideas concerning African identity and nationhood germinated.

Because colonialism had introduced Africans to European ideas and ideologies, African nationalists frequently embraced the European concept of the nation as a means of forging unity among disparate African groups. As they saw it, the nation as

Sources from the Past

Africa for Africans

Marcus Garvey (1887–1940) is best remembered as a pivotal figure in black nationalism, one who inspired nationalist movements as well as many African leaders. A powerful orator, Garvey preached the greatness of the African heritage and called on European colonial powers to leave Africa. Convinced that blacks in the diaspora could never secure their rights as minorities, this "Black Moses" rejected the idea of integration and instead championed a "Back to Africa" movement. According to Garvey, a Jamaican who garnered notoriety during his time in the United States, only in ancestral Africa would it be possible to establish an autonomous black state that featured its own unique culture.

George Washington was not God Almighty. He was a man like any Negro in this building, and if he and his associates were able to make a free America, we too can make a free Africa. Hampden, Gladstone, Pitt and Disraeli were not the representatives of God in the person of Jesus Christ. They were but men, but in their time they worked for the expansion of the British Empire, and today they boast of a British Empire upon which "the sun never sets." As Pitt and Gladstone were able to work for the expansion of the British Empire, so you and I can work for the expansion of a great African Empire. Voltaire and Mirabeau were not Jesus Christs, they were but men like ourselves. They worked and overturned the French Monarchy. They worked for the Democracy which France now enjoys, and if they were able to do that, we are able to work for a democracy in Africa. Lenin and Trotsky were not Jesus Christs, but they were able to overthrow the despotism of Russia, and today they have given to the world a Social Republic, the first of its kind. If Lenin and Trotsky were able to do that for Russia, you and I can do that for Africa. Therefore, let no man, let no power on earth, turn you from this sacred cause of liberty. I prefer to die at this moment rather than not to work for the freedom of Africa. If liberty is good for certain sets of humanity it is good for all. Black men, Colored men, Negroes have as much right to be free as any other race that God Almighty ever created, and we

desire freedom that is unfettered, freedom that is unlimited, freedom that will give us a chance and opportunity to rise to the fullest of our ambition and that we cannot get in countries where other men rule and dominate.

We have reached the time when every minute, every second must count for something done, something achieved in the cause of Africa. . . . It falls to our lot to tear off the shackles that bind Mother Africa. Can you do it? You did it in the Revolutionary War. You did it in the Civil War; You did it at the Battles of the Marne and Verdun; You did it in Mesopotamia. You can do it marching up the battle heights of Africa. Let the world know that 400,000,000 Negroes are prepared to die or live as free men. Despise us as much as you care. Ignore us as much as you care. We are coming 400,000,000 strong. We are coming with our woes behind us, with the memory of suffering behind us—woes and suffering of three hundred years—they shall be our inspiration. My bulwark of strength in the conflict of freedom in Africa, will be the three hundred years of persecution and hardship left behind in this Western Hemisphere.

FOR FURTHER REFLECTION

In his speech, how does Marcus Garvey convey the significance of Africa for both Africans and those involved in the black diaspora?

SOURCE: Amy Jacques Garvey, compiler. *Philosophy and Opinions of Marcus Garvey or Africa for Africans.* London: Frank Cass and Co., 1967, pp. 73–74.

articulated by European thinkers and statesmen provided the best model for mobilizing their resources and organizing their societies, and it offered the best chance to mount effective resistance to colonialism. Although the concept of the nation proved a useful general framework for African nationalists, there remained differences as to what constituted a nation or a people's national identity.

Some nationalists in search of a national identity looked to the precolonial past for inspiration. There they found identities based on ethnicity, religion, and languages, and

Forms of Nationalism

| A European colonialist takes advantage of African labor and is "Traveling in Hammock," as this 1912 photograph's title suggests.

they believed that any future nation must reconstitute institutions crucial to those identities, such as distinctively African forms of spiritual and political authority. Race had provided colonial powers with one rationale for conquest and exploitation; hence it was not surprising that some nationalists used the concept of an African race as a foundation for identity, solidarity, and nation building. Race figured as an important concept in another important strain of African nationalism, which originated in the western hemisphere among the descendants of slaves. Typically it was U.S. blacks and Afro-Caribbean intellectuals who thought of themselves as members of a single race and who promoted the unification of all people of African descent into a single African state. Representatives of this Pan-Africanism were the black U.S. activist and intellectual W. E. B. DuBois (1868–1963) and the Jamaican nationalist leader Marcus Garvey (1887–1940), who preached black pride and called on blacks living in the African diaspora to go "Back to Africa." Still other nationalists discarded the concept of a unique racial identity altogether and looked rather for an African identity rooted in geography. This approach commonly translated into a desire to build the nation on the basis of borders that defined existing colonial states. Collectively these ideas influenced the development of nationalist movements during the 1930s and 1940s, but it took another world war before these ideas translated into demands for independence from colonialism.

Latin American Struggles with Neocolonialism

The postcolonial history of Latin American states in the early twentieth century offered clues about what the future might hold for those areas in Asia and Africa still chafing under colonial dominion but seeking independence. Having gained their independence in the nineteenth century, most sovereign nations in Latin America thereafter struggled to achieve political and economic stability in the midst of interference from foreign powers. The era of the Great War and the Great Depression proved crucial to solidifying and exposing to view the neocolonial structures that guided affairs in Latin America. Generally seen as an indirect and more subtle form of imperial control, neocolonialism usually took shape as foreign economic domination but did not exclude more typically imperial actions such as military intervention and political interference. In Central and South America, as well as in Mexico and the Caribbean, this new imperial influence came not from former colonial rulers in Spain and Portugal but, rather, from wealthy, industrial-capitalist powerhouses such as Great Britain and especially the United States. Neocolonialism impinged on the independent political and economic development of Latin American states, but it did not prevent nationalist leaders from devising strategies to combat the newfound imperialism.

The Impact of the Great War and the Great Depression

The Great War and the Russian revolution, along with the ongoing Mexican revolution, spread radical ideas and the promise of new political possibilities throughout Latin America. The disparate ideals emerging from this time of political ferment found receptive audiences in Latin America before but especially during the global economic crisis of the Great Depression. Marxism, Vladimir Lenin's theories on capitalism and imperialism, and a growing concern for the impoverished Indian masses as well as exploited peasants and workers in Latin American societies informed the outlooks of many disgruntled intellectuals and artists. Although those revolutionary doctrines did not achieve full-scale adoption by Latin American states during the interwar era, their increasing popularity and perceived viability as political options suggested the alternatives open to nations in the future. The Enlightenment-derived liberalism that had shaped independence movements and the political systems of many postindependence nations no longer served as the only form of political legitimacy.

Reorientation of Political and Nationalist Ideals

The Great War had propelled the United States into a position of world economic leadership. The peoples of Latin America came to experience most intensely this new U.S. economic power, and it was probably no coincidence that the capitalism embraced by the United States came under attack. One of the first institutions in Latin America to witness this rebelliousness was the university. Taking their inspiration from two revolutions inimical to ideals of the United States, university students hailed the Mexican and Russian revolutions and in the 1920s began to demand reforms. Students wanted more representation within the educational system, and their political activism resulted in the long-term politicization of the student bodies at Latin American universities. Universities thereafter became training grounds for future political leaders, including Fidel Castro (1926–), and the ideas explored within an academic setting—from Marxism to anti-imperialism—exerted great influence on those budding politicians.

University Protests and Communist Parties

The currency of radicalism also expressed itself in the formation of political parties that either openly espoused communism or otherwise adopted rebellious agendas for change. Peruvians, for example, created a number of radical new political parties, many of which had connections to a self-educated young Marxist intellectual, José Carlos Mariátegui (1895–1930). Mariátegui felt particular concern for the poor and for the Indians, who constituted approximately 50 percent of Peru's population. He castigated Peru's leaders in journals and newspapers for not helping the downtrodden, and he suffered exile to Europe as a result. He came back from Europe a dedicated Marxist and in 1928 established the Socialist Party of Peru. Mariátegui continued to write and

Diego Rivera's *Imperialism* was one in a series of paintings on the United States and offered a visual critique of U.S. neocolonialism in Latin America.

rally in support of laborers, and he was in the midst of helping to create the Peruvian Communist Party when he died from cancer in 1930.

The same agitation that filled José Carlos Mariátegui affected others in Peru and led in the 1920s and 1930s to violence and strikes. The *Alianza Popular Revolucionaria Americana* (Popular American Revolutionary Alliance, or APRA) gave another voice to those critical of Peru's ruling system. This party's followers, known as *Apristas,* advocated indigenous rights and anti-imperialism among other causes. *Aprismo* offered a radical but noncommunist alternative to Peruvians, and it stemmed from the ideas of Victor Raúl Haya de la Torre (1895–1979). Haya de la Torre began his political activism as a student protester and as a supporter of a workers' movement. Exiled like Mariátegui, Haya de la Torre nonetheless imparted his eclectic views to APRA, including both staunch anti-imperialism and a plan for capitalist development that had peasants and workers cooperating with the middle class. The more traditional power of the military and landed elites in Peru managed to contain these rebellious movements, but the cultural and political popularity of radicalism and its intellectual proponents persisted.

Diego Rivera and Radical Artistic Visions

The ideological transformations apparent in Latin America became stunningly and publicly visible in the murals painted by famed Mexican artist Diego Rivera (1886–1957). Artistically trained in Mexico in his youth, Rivera went to study in Europe in 1907 and did not return to Mexico until 1921. Influenced by the art of both Renaissance artists and cubists, Rivera also experienced the turmoil and shifting political sensibilities taking place during the Great War and its aftermath. He blended his artistic and political visions in vast murals that he intended for viewing and appreciation by the masses. He believed that art should be on display for working people. Along with other Mexican muralists, such as David Alfaro Siqueiros (1896–1974) and José Clemente Orozco (1883–1949), Rivera shaped the politicized art of Mexico for decades.

Diego Rivera celebrated indigenous Mexican art and pre-Columbian folk traditions, and he incorporated radical political ideas in his style and approach to mural painting. The government commissioned him in the late 1920s and 1930s to create large frescoes for public buildings, and Rivera artistically transcribed the history of Mexico, replete with its social ills, on the walls of such structures as the National Palace and the Ministry of Education in Mexico City. An activist in the Mexican Communist Party, he taught briefly in Moscow in the late 1920s. In the early 1930s the Detroit Institute of Arts commissioned him to paint murals for a U.S. audience, and this migration of his art to the United States soon caused a controversy.

In 1933 Rivera received a request to paint murals for the RCA building in Rockefeller Center in New York City. He included in one panel a portrait of Vladimir Lenin, which outraged those who had commissioned the work. His mural was destroyed. Rivera in turn undertook a series of twenty-one paintings on United States history titled *Portrait of America*. He labeled one of the most pointed and critical paintings *Imperialism*, which visualized and advertised the economic interference and political repressiveness engendered by U.S. neocolonialism in Latin America. Rivera depicted massive guns and tanks extending over the New York Stock Exchange. In the foreground and at the edges of the Stock Exchange are a variety of Latin American victims of this monied-military oppression, including Central Americans laboring for the United Fruit Company and others toiling for the Standard Oil Company. Overlooking all of this in the upper-right corner is Augusto César Sandino (1893–1934), the martyred nationalist hero who opposed U.S. intervention in Nicaragua. Rivera made visible the impact of U.S. imperialism on Latin American societies, and by doing so he helped spread political activism in the Americas.

The Evolution of Economic Imperialism

Latin American states were no strangers to foreign economic domination in the nineteenth and early twentieth centuries. Their export-oriented economies had long been tied to global finances and had long been subject to controls imposed by foreign investors, largely those from Great Britain and the United States. The major evolution in economic neocolonialism during this period concerned the growing predominance of the United States in the economic affairs of Latin American nations. The Great War sealed this transition to U.S. supremacy, and U.S. investments in Latin America soared in the 1920s. Between 1924 and 1929, U.S. banks and businesses more than doubled their financial interests in Latin America as investments grew from $1.5 billion to $3.5 billion. Much of that money went toward the takeover of businesses extracting vital minerals, such as copper-mining firms in Chile and oil-drilling concerns in Venezuela.

United States Economic Domination

That U.S. neocolonialism was meant to be largely economic became evident in the policies of President William Howard Taft (1857–1931). In his final address to Congress in 1912, Taft argued that the United States should substitute "dollars for bullets" in its foreign policy. He wanted businesses to develop foreign markets through peaceful commerce and believed that expensive military intervention should be avoided as much as possible. Likewise, by replacing European investments with U.S. investments, the United States would face fewer tests of the Monroe Doctrine or its 1904 Roosevelt corollary, which justified direct intervention in Latin American nations deemed unstable by the United States. This new vision of U.S. expansion abroad, dubbed "dollar diplomacy" by critics, encapsulated the gist of what those in Latin America perceived as "Yankee imperialism."

Dollar Diplomacy

The economic crisis of the Great Depression demonstrated the extent to which Latin America had become integrated in the world economy. With some exceptions, exports had continued in the interwar period to help nations achieve basic solvency and even enough economic expansion to institute social reforms. The Great Depression, however, halted fifty years of economic growth in Latin America and illustrated the region's susceptibility to global economic crises. The increasing U.S. capital investments for nascent industries and other financial concerns during the 1920s could not

Economic Depression and Experimentation

Map 36.2 The United States in Latin America, 1895–1941. Note the number of states where U.S. troops intervened in local politics. On what basis did U.S. policymakers justify those interventions?

be maintained during this catastrophic economic downturn. Most Latin American states, because they exported agricultural products or raw materials, were further vulnerable to the effects of the depression. The prices of sugar from the Caribbean, coffee from Brazil and Colombia, wheat and beef from Argentina, tin from Bolivia, nitrates from Chile, and many other products fell sharply after 1929. Attempts by producers to raise prices by holding supplies off the market—Brazilians, for example, set fire to coffee beans or used them in the construction of highways—failed, and throughout Latin America unemployment rates increased rapidly. The drastic decline in the price of the region's exports and the drying-up of foreign capital prompted Latin American governments to raise tariffs on foreign products and impose various other restrictions on foreign trade. Those same conditions also encouraged domestic manufacturing, which made important gains in many Latin American nations.

Although the weaknesses of export-oriented economies and industrial development financed by foreigners became evident during the Great Depression, the international crisis also allowed Latin American nations to take alternative paths to economic development. Economic policy stressing internal economic development was most visible in Brazil, where dictator-president (1930–1945, 1950–1954) Getúlio Dornelles Vargas (1883–1954) turned his nation into an *estado novo* (new state). Ruling with the backing of the military but without the support of the landowning elite, Vargas and his government during the 1930s and 1940s embarked on a program of industrialization that created new enterprises. Key among them was the iron and steel industry. The Vargas regime also implemented protectionist policies that shielded domestic production from foreign competition, which pleased both industrialists and urban workers. Social welfare initiatives accompanied industrial development, protecting workers with health and safety regulations, minimum wages, limits on working hours, unemployment compensation, and retirement benefits. The Great Depression contributed in many ways to the evolution of both economic neocolonialism and economic experimentation within Latin American states.

Conflicts with a "Good Neighbor"

The pressures of the Great Depression and the instability of global politics led to a reassessment of U.S. foreign policy in Latin America during the late 1920s and 1930s. U.S. leaders realized the costliness and the ineffectiveness of their previous direct interventions in Latin America, especially when committing U.S. Marines as peacekeeping forces. To extricate U.S. military forces and rely more fully on dollar diplomacy, policymakers instituted certain innovations that nonetheless called into question any true change of heart among U.S. neocolonialists. They approved "sweetheart treaties" that guaranteed U.S. financial control in the Caribbean economies of Haiti and the Dominican Republic, for example, and the U.S. Marines provided training for indigenous police forces to keep the peace and maintain law and order. These national guards tended to be less expensive than maintaining forces of U.S. Marines, and the guards' leaders usually worked to keep cordial relations with the United States. This revamped U.S. approach to relations with Latin America became known as the "Good Neighbor Policy," and it was most closely associated with the administration of Franklin D. Roosevelt (1882–1945). Although Roosevelt appeared more well-intentioned in his exercise of the policy, events in Nicaragua before and during the beginning of his administration highlighted the limits of U.S. neighborliness.

The "Good Neighbor Policy"

U.S. financial interests had long influenced the economy of Nicaragua, and those substantial investments—whether in the transportation industry or in bananas—served to justify U.S. intervention when revolts or civil wars broke out. The mid- and late 1920s again witnessed the outbreak of civil war in Nicaragua and the repeated insertion of the Marines to restore order. Leading the opposition to Nicaraguan conservatives and the occupation of Nicaragua by U.S. Marines was Augusto César Sandino, a nationalist and liberal general who refused to accept any peace settlement that left Marines on Nicaraguan soil.

Nicaragua and the Guarda Nacional

As part of a plan to remove U.S. forces, the United States established and trained the *Guarda Nacional,* or National Guard, in Nicaragua. The U.S.-supervised elections of 1932 brought Juan Batista Sacasa (president, 1932–1936) into power, and U.S. troops departed, having positioned the brutal but trusted Anastacio Somoza Garcia (1896–1956) as commander of the Guard. Even though conflicts between Sandino's forces and Somoza's Guard persisted, Sandino explored options with Sacasa and Somoza for ending the rebellion given the departure of the Marines. Officers from the National Guard murdered Sandino in 1934, and Somoza soon after fulfilled his ambitions and became president of his country. Somoza endeavored successfully to maintain the loyalty of the National Guard and to prove himself a good neighbor to the United States. He visited Washington, D.C., in 1939 and renamed the Nicaraguan capital city's main thoroughfare after Roosevelt. He also began to collect what became the largest fortune in Nicaragua's history and to establish a political dynasty that ruled

Cárdenas' Mexico

A 1920s photograph of Nicaraguan patriot leader Augusto César Sandino.

the nation for decades to come. In the meantime, Sandino gained heroic status as a martyr who died in part because he fought the good neighbor to the north.

However flawed, the Good Neighbor Policy evolved under Roosevelt into a more conciliatory U.S. approach to Latin American relations. The interventionist corollary to the Monroe Doctrine enunciated previously by President Theodore Roosevelt (1859–1919) was formally renounced in December 1933, when Secretary of State Cordell Hull attended the Seventh International Conference of American States in Montevideo, Uruguay. Hull signed the "Convention on the Rights and Duties of States," which held that "no state has the right to intervene in the internal or external affairs of another." That proposition faced a severe challenge in March 1938 when Mexican president Lázaro Cárdenas (1895–1970) nationalized the oil industry, much of which was controlled by foreign investors from the United States and Great Britain.

Given the history of tempestuous relations between the United States and Mexico, including multiple U.S. military incursions into Mexico during the revolution, there was little chance for a peaceful resolution to this provocative move on the part of Cárdenas. The reluctance of U.S. and British oil companies to adhere to an arbitration decree granting concessions to Mexican oil workers prompted him to this drastic act. His radical persuasions also drove Cárdenas to this extreme, as did his intent to implement some of the progressive provisions of the Constitution of 1917. Despite calls for a strong U.S. and British response, Roosevelt and his administration officials resisted the demands of big businesses and instead called for a cool, calm response and negotiations to end the conflict. This plan prevailed, and the foreign oil companies ultimately had to accept only $24 million in compensation rather than the $260 million that they initially demanded. Cárdenas cleverly based the compensation price on the tax value claimed by the oil companies, and his nationalization of the oil industry proved popular with the Mexican people.

Neighborly Cultural Exchanges

Although the nationalization crisis in Mexico ended in a fashion that suggested the strength of the Good Neighbor Policy, a good deal of the impetus for that policy came from economic and political concerns associated with the Great Depression and the deterioration of international relations in the 1930s. The United States wanted to cultivate Latin American markets for its exports, and it wanted to distance itself from the militarist behavior of Asian and European imperial powers. The U.S. government knew it needed to improve relations with Latin America, if only to secure those nations' support in the increasingly likely event of another global war. Widespread Mexican migration to the United States during and after the Great War suggested the attractiveness of the United States for at least some Latin Americans. Filling the migration void left by Europeans prevented from coming to the United States by the war and by the U.S. immigration restriction laws of the 1920s, Mexican men, women, and children entered the United States in the hundreds of thousands to engage in agricultural and industrial work. The migrants suffered the animosity of some U.S. citizens, who considered them "cheap Mexican labor," but the political power of agribusinesses prevented the government from instituting legal restrictions on Mexican migration. Federal and local officials managed, however, to deport thousands of Mexicans during the Great Depression.

Trying to contribute to the repairing of relations and the promoting of more positive images of Latin American and U.S. relations, Hollywood adopted a Latin American singing and dancing sensation, Carmen Miranda (1909–1955). Born in Portugal but raised from childhood in Brazil, Miranda found fame on a Rio de Janeiro radio station and recorded hundreds of hit songs. A Broadway producer lured her to the United States, but she gained her greatest visibility in such films as *Down Argentine Way* (1940) and many others produced during World War II. Carmen Miranda appeared as an exotic Latin American woman,

This Hollywood publicity photo of Carmen Miranda features the type of lively costuming that made her a colorful favorite in both the United States and Latin America.

usually clothed in sexy, colorful costumes that featured amazing headdresses adorned with the fruits grown in Latin America—such as bananas. She softened representations of Latin Americans for audiences in the United States, providing a less threatening counterpoint to laboring migrants or women guerrilla fighters in Mexico's revolution. She also became a source of pride for Brazilians, who reveled in her Hollywood success. Hollywood's espousal of Roosevelt's Good Neighbor Policy proved a success.

Equally successful as a marketing device, although one that illustrated the continued limitations of the Good Neighbor Policy, was the United Fruit Company's appropriation of Carmen Miranda's image for the selling of the bananas that symbolized U.S. economic control of regions throughout Central America and the Caribbean. The United Fruit Company owned 160,000 acres of land in the Caribbean by 1913, and already by 1918 U.S. consumers bought fully 90 percent of Nicaragua's bananas. Not content with such market control, the United Fruit Company's advertising executives in 1944 crafted "Chiquita Banana," a female banana look-alike of Carmen Miranda. In singing radio commercials, Chiquita Banana taught U.S.

Chiquita Banana, an advertising icon used to promote a good image of the United Fruit Company, was a replica in fruit of the singing and acting sensation Carmen Miranda.

consumers about the storage and various uses of bananas ("I'm Chiquita Banana / And I've come to say / Bananas have to ripen / In a certain way"). This singing banana promoted the sales of United Fruit Company bananas, and for consumers in the United States, it gave the prototypical neocolonial company in Latin America a softer, less threatening image—one that challenged, for example, the more ideologically raw representation in Diego Rivera's *Imperialism*.

I n the decades after the Great War, and in the midst of the Great Depression, intellectuals and political activists in Asia, Africa, and Latin America challenged the ideological and economic underpinnings of empire and neocolonialism. Often embracing the ideas and theories that disseminated around the globe as a result of the war, including self-determination, socialism, communism, and anti-imperialism, radicals and nationalists revised understandings of political identity in the colonial and neocolonial worlds.

Japanese and U.S. imperial practices incited military and civil discord within their respective spheres, while European colonial rulers continued to limit, often brutally, the freedom of peoples in India and Africa. Like Shanfei, young intellectuals and older political leaders alike emerged transformed in these years. Their efforts to inspire nationalism and to achieve economic and political autonomy came to fruition later—after another world war had come and gone.

CHRONOLOGY

1912	Taft establishes dollar diplomacy as U.S. foreign policy
1914–1918	2.5 million African troops and carriers serve in the Great War
1919	May Fourth Movement in China
1920	Non-Cooperation Movement in India
1921	Rivera returns to Mexico to paint
1928	Socialist Party of Peru is founded
1929	Beginning of Great Depression
1930	Civil Disobedience Movement in India
1930s–1940s	Vargas's *Estado Novo* in Brazil
1931	Japanese invasion of Manchuria
1933	Roosevelt begins practice of the Good Neighbor Policy
1934	Long March by Chinese Communists
1934	Sandino is murdered in Nicaragua
1935	Government of India Act
1938	Cárdenas nationalizes oil industry in Mexico

FOR FURTHER READING

A. Adu Boahen, ed. *Africa under Colonial Domination, 1880–1935.* Berkeley, 1985. Part of the ambitious UNESCO General History of Africa (vol. 7), this work reflects how different Africans view their history.

Judith Brown. *Modern India: The Origins of Asian Democracy.* 2nd ed. Oxford, 1994. This survey is a good introduction to the past two hundred years of Indian history.

Victor Bulmer-Thomas, John H. Coatsworth, and Robert Cortés Conde, eds. *The Cambridge Economic History of Latin America.* Vol. 2: *The Long Twentieth Century.* Cambridge, 2006. Scholarly collection of essays that outlines the region's main economic trends and developments.

Ian Buruma. *Inventing Japan, 1853–1964.* New York, 2003. A respected journalist compresses a century of complex history into a short and elegant book.

Prasenjit Duara. *Sovereignty and Authenticity: Manchukuo and the East Asian Modern.* Lanham, Md., 2003. Using the Japanese puppet state of Manchukuo as a focal point, this is a technical and highly demanding but impressive study of imperialism, nationalism, and modernity.

Cynthia Enloe. *Bananas, Beaches & Bases: Making Feminist Sense of International Politics.* Berkeley, 1989. A gendered analysis of U.S. and other foreign policies through such categories as tourism and diplomats' spouses.

William Gould. *Hindu Nationalism and the Language of Politics in Late Colonial India.* New York, 2004. Political history of India on the eve of independence.

Robert E. Hannigan. *The New World Power: American Foreign Policy, 1898–1917.* Philadelphia, 2002. A detailed account of U.S. foreign relations that links class, race, and gender influences to policymakers.

John Iliffe. *Africans: The History of a Continent.* New York, 1995. A well-written introductory text that is organized thematically rather than chronologically.

Lawrence James. *Raj: The Making and Unmaking of British India.* New York, 1998. A sweeping, narrative account of the Raj and British influence in the Indian subcontinent.

Robert W. July. *A History of the African People.* 5th ed. Long Grove, Ill., 1997. A critically acclaimed survey that explores themes that cut across time and place.

Patrick Marnham. *Dreaming with His Eyes Wide Open: A Life of Diego Rivera.* Berkeley, 2000. An engaging and well-received biography, which includes an appendix with reprints of Rivera's major mural paintings.

Jim Masselos. *Indian Nationalism: A History.* 3rd ed. Columbia, 1998. A keen work that remains the standard, most readable introduction to Indian leaders and movements.

Michael C. Meyer, William L. Sherman, and Susan M. Deeds. *The Course of Mexican History.* 6th ed. Oxford, 1999. An updated survey of Mexican history from pre-Columbian to modern times.

Roland Oliver and Anthony Atmore. *Africa since 1800.* 4th ed. Cambridge, 1994. An updated version of a well-regarded survey.

Michael E. Parish. *Anxious Decades: America in Prosperity and Depression, 1920–1941.* New York, 1992. A detailed portrait of the United States between the world wars, featuring treatments of foreign relations with Latin America.

Anthony Read and David Fisher. *The Proudest Day: India's Long Road to Independence.* New York, 1998. Written for the general reader, this is a compelling and colorful account of India's road to freedom.

Mahir Saul and Patrick Royer. *West African Challenge to Empire: Culture and History in the Volta-Bani Anti-Colonial War.* Athens, Ohio, 2002. Anthropological study of the largest anticolonial movement the French faced in West Africa in 1915–1916.

Elizabeth Schmidt. *Mobilizing the Masses: Gender, Ethnicity, and Class in the Nationalist Movement in Guinea, 1939–1958.* Portsmouth, N.H., 2005. Details the emergence of lesser-known but powerful subaltern anticolonial networks that preceded formal nationalist organizations in French West Africa.

Vera Schwarcz. *The Chinese Enlightenment: Intellectuals and the Legacy of May Fourth Movement of 1919.* Berkeley, 1986. A gracefully written, thoughtful work.

Jonathan D. Spence. *Mao Zedong.* New York, 1999. Blending history with cultural analysis, this intimate portrait of Mao is informative despite its brevity.

Steve Striffler and Mark Moberg, eds. *Banana Wars: Power, Production, and History in the Americas.* Durham, 2003. Interdisciplinary analysis of the transformative impact of the banana industry on global trade and the consequences for Latin American societies and economies.

Odd Arne Westad. *Decisive Encounters: The Chinese Civil War, 1946–1950.* Stanford, 2003. An engagingly written work that introduces the reader to the salient political and military events that led to the eventual defeat of the Guomindang.

Louise Young. *Japan's Total Empire: Manchuria and the Culture of Wartime Imperialism.* Berkeley, 1999. An important and penetrating work on the nature of Japanese imperialism.

37 New Conflagrations: World War II

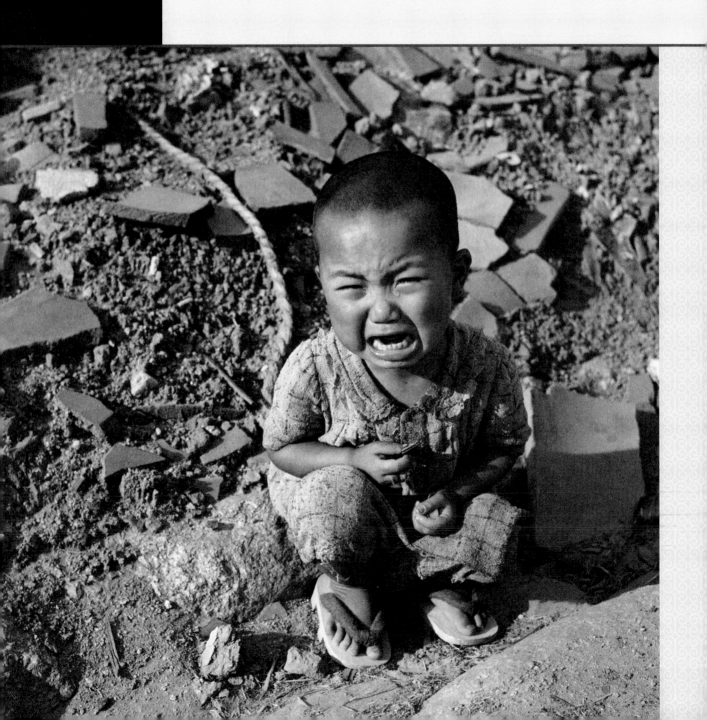

Origins of World War II
Japan's War in China
Italian and German Aggression

Total War: The World under Fire
Blitzkrieg: Germany Conquers Europe
The German Invasion of the Soviet Union
Battles in Asia and the Pacific
Defeat of the Axis Powers

Life during Wartime
Occupation, Collaboration, and Resistance
The Holocaust
Women and the War

Neither Peace nor War
Postwar Settlements and Cold War
Global Reconstruction and the United Nations

On 6 August 1945, as he listened to the armed services radio on Saipan (a U.S.-controlled island in the north Pacific), U.S. marine Victor Tolley heard the news: the president of the United States announced that a "terrible new weapon" had been deployed against the city of Hiroshima, Japan. Tolley and the other marines rejoiced, realizing that the terrible new weapon—the atomic bomb—might end the war and relieve them of the burden of invading Japan. A few days later Tolley heard that the city of Nagasaki had also been hit with an atomic bomb. He remembered the ominous remarks that accompanied the news of this atomic destruction: radio announcers suggested it might be decades before the cities would be inhabitable.

Imagine Tolley's astonishment when a few weeks later, after the Japanese surrender, he and his buddies were assigned to the U.S. occupation forces in Nagasaki. Assured by a superior officer that Nagasaki was "very safe," Tolley lived there for three months, during which he became very familiar with the devastation wrought by the atomic bomb. On his first day in Nagasaki, Tolley investigated the city. As he noted, "It was just like walking into a tomb. There was total silence. You could smell this death all around ya. There was a terrible odor."

Tolley also became acquainted with some of the Japanese survivors in Nagasaki, which proved to be an eye-opening experience. After seeing "young children with sores and burns all over," Tolley, having become separated from his unit, encountered another young child. He and the boy communicated despite the language barrier between them. Tolley showed the child pictures of his wife and two daughters. The Japanese boy excitedly took Tolley home to meet his surviving family, his father and his pregnant sister. Tolley recalled,

> This little kid ran upstairs and brought his father down. A very nice Japanese gentleman. He could speak English. He bowed and said, "We would be honored if you would come upstairs and have some tea with us." I went upstairs in this strange Japanese house. I noticed on the mantel a picture of a young Japanese soldier. I asked him, "Is this your son?" He said, "That is my daughter's husband. We don't know if he's alive. We haven't heard." The minute he said that, it dawned on me that they suffered the same as we did. They lost sons and daughters and relatives, and they hurt too.

Before his chance meeting with this Japanese family, Tolley had felt nothing except contempt for the Japanese. He pointed out, "We were trained to kill them. They're our enemy. Look what they did in Pearl Harbor. They asked for it and now we're gonna give it to 'em. That's how I felt until I met this young boy and his family." But after coming face-to-face with his enemies, Tolley saw only their common humanity, their suffering, and their hurt. The lesson he learned was that "these people didn't want to fight us."

OPPOSITE: A Japanese child crouches and cries in the rubble of Hiroshima in the aftermath of the atomic bombing, expressing the profound sadness of war and its devastating weapons.

The civility that reemerged at the end of the war was little evident during the war years. The war began and ended with Japan. In 1931 Japan invaded Manchuria, thereby ending the post–Great War peace, and the United States concluded hostilities by dropping atomic bombs on Hiroshima and Nagasaki. Between 1931 and 1945 the conflict expanded well beyond east Asia. By 1941 World War II was a truly global war. Hostilities spread from east Asia and the Pacific to Europe, north Africa, and the Atlantic, and large and small nations from North America, Asia, Europe, Africa, and Australia came into close contact for the duration of the war. Beyond its immense geographic scope, World War II exceeded even the Great War (1914–1918) in demonstrating the willingness of societies to make enormous sacrifices in lives and other resources to achieve complete victory. In this total war, contacts with enemies, occupiers, and liberators affected populations around the world. World War II redefined gender roles and relations between colonial peoples and their masters, as women contributed to their nations' war efforts and as colonial peoples exploited the war's weakening of imperial nations. The cold war and the atomic age that began almost as soon as World War II ended complicated the task of recovering economic health and psychological security, but they also brought forth institutions, programs, and policies that promoted global reconstruction. New sets of allies and newly independent nations emerged after the war, signaling that a new global order had arisen. The United States and the Soviet Union in particular gained geopolitical strength during the early years of the cold war as they competed for global influence, and previously colonial peoples constructed sovereign states as European empires crumbled under the pressures of another global conflagration.

Origins of World War II

In 1941 two major alliances squared off against each other. Japan, Germany, and Italy, along with their conquered territories, formed the Axis powers, the name of the alignment between Nazi Germany and Fascist Italy that had been formed in October 1936. The term was used later to include Germany's other allies in World War II, especially Japan. The Allied powers included France and its empire; Great Britain and its empire and Commonwealth allies (such as Canada, Australia, and New Zealand); the Soviet Union; China; and the United States and its allies in Latin America. The construction of these global alliances took place over the course of the 1930s and early 1940s.

Driven in part by a desire to revise the peace settlements that followed the Great War and affected by the economic distress of the worldwide depression, Japan, Italy, and Germany engaged in a campaign of territorial expansion that ultimately broke apart the structure of international cooperation that had kept the world from violence in the 1920s. These *revisionist powers,* so called because they revised, or overthrew, the terms of the post–Great War peace, confronted nations that were committed to the international system and to the avoidance of another world war. To expand their global influence, the revisionist nations remilitarized and conquered territories they deemed central to their needs and to the spread of their imperial control. The Allies acquiesced to the revisionist powers' early aggressive actions, but by the late 1930s and early 1940s the Allies decided to engage the Axis powers in a total war.

Japan's War in China

The global conflict opened with Japan's attacks on China in the 1930s: the conquest of Manchuria between 1931 and 1932 was the first step in the revisionist process of expansionism and aggression. Within Japan a battle continued between supporters

Japanese soldiers execute Chinese prisoners.

and opponents of the aggressive policies adopted in Manchuria, but during the course of the 1930s the militarist position dominated, and for the most part civilians lost control of the government and the military. In 1933, after the League of Nations condemned its actions in Manchuria, Japan withdrew from the league and followed an ultranationalist and promilitary policy.

Seeing territorial control as essential to its survival, Japan launched a full-scale invasion of China in 1937. A battle between Chinese and Japanese troops at the Marco Polo Bridge in Beijing in July 1937 was the opening move in Japan's undeclared war against China. Japanese troops took Beijing and then moved south toward Shanghai and Nanjing, the capital of China. Japanese naval and air forces bombed Shanghai, killing thousands of civilians, and secured it as a landing area for armies bound for Nanjing. By December 1937 Shanghai and Nanjing had fallen, and during the following six months Japanese forces won repeated victories.

The Rape of Nanjing   China became the first nation to experience the horrors of World War II: brutal warfare against civilians and repressive occupation. During the invasion of China, Japanese forces used methods of warfare that led to mass death and suffering on a new, almost unimaginable, level. Chinese civilians were among the first to feel the effects of aerial bombing of urban centers; the people of Shanghai died by the tens of thousands when Japanese bombers attacked the city to soften Chinese resistance. What became known as the Rape of Nanjing demonstrated the horror of the war as the residents of Nanjing became victims of Japanese troops inflamed by war passion and a sense of racial superiority. Over the course of two months, Japanese soldiers raped seven thousand women, murdered hundreds of thousands of unarmed soldiers and civilians, and burned one-third of the homes in Nanjing. Four hundred thousand Chinese lost their lives as Japanese soldiers used them for bayonet practice and machine-gunned them into open pits.

Chinese Resistance   Despite Japanese military successes and the subsequent Japanese occupation of Chinese lands, Chinese resistance persisted throughout the war. Japanese aggression aroused feelings of nationalism among the Chinese that continued to grow as the war wore on. By September 1937 nationalists and communists had agreed on a "united front" policy against the Japanese, uniting themselves into standing armies of some 1.7 million soldiers. Although Chinese forces failed to defeat the Japanese, who retained naval and air superiority, they tied down half the Japanese army, 750,000 soldiers, by 1941.

Throughout the war, the coalition of nationalists and communists threatened to fall apart. Although neither side was willing to risk open civil war, the two groups engaged in numerous military clashes as their forces competed for both control of enemy territory and political control within China. Those clashes rendered Chinese resistance less effective, and while both sides continued the war against Japan, each fought ultimately for its own advantage. The nationalists suffered major casualties in their battles with Japanese forces, but they kept the Guomindang government alive by moving inland to Chongqing. Meanwhile, the communists carried on guerrilla operations against the Japanese invaders. Lacking air force and artillery, communist guerrillas staged hit-and-run operations from their mountain bases, sabotaged bridges and railroads, and harassed Japanese troops. The guerrillas did not defeat the Japanese, but they captured the loyalty of many Chinese peasants through their resistance to the Japanese and their moderate policies of land reform. At the end of the war, the communists were poised to lead China.

The Japanese invasion of China met with intense international opposition, but by that time Japan had chosen an-

Japanese soldiers in 1938 engaged in strenuous physical education and kept fit in order to fight the Chinese.

other path—and it was an auspicious time to further its attack on the international system. Other world powers, distracted by depression and military aggression in Europe, could offer little in the way of an effective response to Japanese actions. The government of Japan aligned itself with the other revisionist nations, Germany and Italy, by signing the Tripartite Pact, a ten-year military and economic pact, in September 1940. Japan also cleared the way for further empire building in Asia and the Pacific basin by concluding a neutrality pact with the Soviet Union in April 1941, thereby precluding hostilities on any other front, especially in Manchuria. Japan did not face determined opposition to its expansion until December 1941, when conflict with the United States created a much broader field of action for Japan and its growing empire.

Italian and German Aggression

Italy's expansionism helped destabilize the post–Great War peace and spread World War II to the European continent. Italians suffered tremendously in World War I. Six hundred thousand Italian soldiers died, and the national economy never recovered sufficiently for Italy to function as an equal to other European military and economic powers. Many Italians expected far greater recompense and respect than they received at the conclusion of the Great War. Rather than being treated as a real partner in victory by Britain and France, Italy found itself shut out of the divisions of the territorial spoils of war.

Benito Mussolini promised to bring glory to Italy through the acquisition of territories that it had been denied after the Great War. Italy's conquest of Ethiopia in 1935 and 1936, when added to the previously annexed Libya, created an overseas empire. Italy also intervened in the Spanish Civil War (1936–1939) on the side of General Francisco Franco (1892–1975), whose militarists overthrew the republican government, and annexed Albania in 1939. (Mussolini viewed Albania as a bridgehead for expansion into the Balkans.) The invasion and conquest of Ethiopia in particular infuriated other nations; but, as with Japan's invasion of Manchuria, the League of Nations offered little effective opposition.

Italy

What angered nonrevisionists about Italy's conquest of Ethiopia was not just the broken peace. The excessive use of force against the Ethiopians also rankled. Mussolini sent an army of 250,000 soldiers armed with tanks, poison gas, artillery, and aircraft to conquer the Ethiopians, who were entirely unprepared for the assault. The mechanized troops mowed them down. Italy lost 2,000 soldiers while 275,000 Ethiopians lost their lives. Despite its victories in Ethiopia, Italy's prospects for world glory never appeared quite as bright as Japan's, especially since few Italians wanted to go to war. Throughout the interwar years, Italy played a diplomatic game that kept European nations guessing as to its future intentions, but by 1938 it was firmly on the side of the Axis.

Japan and Italy were the first nations to challenge the post–World War I settlements through territorial conquest, but it was Germany that systematically undid the Treaty of Versailles and the fragile peace of the interwar years. Most Germans and their political leaders deeply resented the harsh terms imposed on their nation in 1919, but even the governments of other European nations eventually recognized the extreme nature of the Versailles Treaty's terms and turned a blind eye to the revisionist actions of Adolf Hitler (1889–1945) and his government. Hitler came to power in 1933, riding a wave of public discontent with Germany's postwar position of powerlessness and the suffering caused by the Great Depression. Hitler referred to the signing of the 1918 armistice as the "November crime" and blamed it on those he viewed as Germany's internal enemies: Jews, communists, and liberals of all sorts. Neighboring European states—Poland,

Germany

■ **Ethiopian soldiers train with outmoded equipment that proves no match for Italian forces.**

France, Czechoslovakia, Yugoslavia, Hungary, and Austria—also shared in the blame. Hitler's scheme for ridding Germany of its enemies and reasserting its power was remilitarization—which was legally denied to Germany under the Versailles Treaty. Germany's dictator abandoned the peaceful efforts of his predecessors to ease the provisions of the treaty and proceeded unilaterally to destroy it step-by-step. Hitler's aggressive foreign policy helped relieve the German public's feeling of war shame and depression trauma. After withdrawing Germany from the League of Nations in 1933, his government carried out an ambitious plan to strengthen the German armed forces. Hitler reinstated universal military service in 1935, and in the following year his troops entered the previously demilitarized Rhineland that bordered France. Germany joined with Italy in the Spanish Civil War, where Hitler's troops, especially the air force, honed their skills. In 1938 Hitler began the campaign of expansion that ultimately led to the outbreak of World War II in Europe.

Germany's forced *Anschluss* ("union") with Austria took place in March 1938. Hitler justified this annexation as an attempt to reintegrate all Germans into a single homeland. Europe's major powers, France and Britain, did nothing in response, thereby enhancing Hitler's reputation in the German military and deepening his already deep contempt for the democracies. Soon thereafter, using the same rationale, the Nazis attempted to gain control of the Sudetenland, the western portion of Czechoslovakia. This region was inhabited largely by ethnic Germans, whom Hitler conveniently regarded as persecuted minorities. Although the Czech government was willing to make concessions to the Sudeten Germans, Hitler in September 1938 demanded the immediate cession of the Sudetenland to the German Reich. Against the desires of the Czechoslovak government, the leaders of France and Britain accommodated Hitler and allowed Germany to annex the Sudetenland. Neither the French nor the British were willing to risk a military confrontation with Germany to defend Czechoslovakian territory.

Peace for Our Time   At the Munich Conference held in September 1938, European politicians formulated the policy that came to be known as *appeasement*. Attended by representatives of Italy, France, Great Britain, and Germany, the meeting revealed how most nations outside the revisionist sphere had decided to deal with territorial expansion by aggressive nations, especially Germany. In conceding demands to Hitler, or "appeasing" him, the

British and French governments extracted a promise that Hitler would cease further efforts to expand German territorial claims. Their goal was to keep peace in Europe, even if it meant making major concessions. Because of public opposition to war, the governments of France and Britain approved the Munich accord. Britain's prime minister Neville Chamberlain (1869–1940) arrived home from Munich to announce that the meeting had achieved "peace for our time." Unprepared for war and distressed by the depression, nations sympathetic to Britain and France also embraced peace as an admirable goal in the face of aggression by the revisionist nations.

Hitler, however, refused to be bound by the Munich agreement, and in the next year German troops occupied most of Czechoslovakia. As Hitler next threatened Poland, it became clear that the policy of appeasement was a practical and moral failure, which caused Britain and France to abandon it by guaranteeing the security of Poland. By that time Joseph Stalin (1879–1953) was convinced that British and French leaders were conspiring to deflect German aggression toward the Soviet Union. Despite deep ideological differences that divided communists from Nazis, Stalin accordingly sought an accommodation with the Nazi regime. In August 1939 the foreign ministers of the Soviet Union and Germany signed the Russian-German Treaty of Nonaggression, an agreement that shocked and outraged the world. By the terms of the pact, the two nations agreed not to attack each other, and they promised neutrality in the event that either of them went to war with a third party. Additionally, a secret protocol divided eastern Europe into German and Soviet spheres of influence. The protocol provided for German control over western Poland while granting the Soviet Union a free hand in eastern Poland, eastern Romania, Finland, Estonia, Latvia, and Lithuania. Hitler was ready to conquer Europe.

Total War: The World under Fire

Two months after the United States became embroiled in World War II, President Franklin Roosevelt (1882–1945) delivered one of his famous radio broadcasts, known as fireside chats. In it he explained the nature of the war: "This war is a new kind of war," he said. "It is warfare in terms of every continent, every island, every sea, every air lane." There was little exaggeration in FDR's analysis. Before World War II was over, almost every nation had participated in it. Battles raged across the vast Pacific and Atlantic oceans, across Europe and northern Africa, and throughout much of Asia. Virtually every weapon known to humanity was thrown into the war. More than the Great War, this was a conflict where entire societies engaged in warfare and mobilized every available material and human resource.

The war between Japan and China had already stretched over eight years when European nations stormed into battle. Between 1939 and 1941, nations inside and outside Europe were drawn into the conflict. They included the French and British colonies in Africa, India, and the British Dominion allies: Canada, Australia, and New Zealand. Germany's stunning military successes in 1939 and 1940 focused attention on Europe, but after the Soviet Union and the United States entered the war in 1941, the conflict took on global proportions. Almost every nation in the world had gone to war by 1945.

Blitzkrieg: Germany Conquers Europe

During World War II it became common for aggressor nations to avoid overt declarations of war. Instead, the new armed forces relied on surprise, stealth, and swiftness for their conquests. Germany demonstrated the advantages of that strategy in Poland.

German dive-bombers like this one dominated the early air war in World War II and played a significant role in Blitzkrieg.

German forces, banking on their air force's ability to soften resistance and on their *Panzer* ("armored") columns' unmatched mobility and speed, moved into Poland unannounced on 1 September 1939. Within a month they subdued its western expanses while the Soviets took the eastern sections in accordance with the Nazi-Soviet pact. The Germans stunned the world, especially Britain and France, with their *Blitzkrieg* ("lightning war") and sudden victory.

While the forces of Britain and France coalesced to defend Europe without facing much direct action with Nazi forces, the battle of the Atlantic already raged. This sea confrontation between German *Unterseeboote* ("U-boats," or submarines) and British ship convoys carrying food and war matériel proved decisive in the European theater of war. The battle of the Atlantic could easily have gone either way—to the German U-boats attempting to cut off Britain's vital imports or to the convoys devised by the British navy to protect its ships from submarine attacks. Although British intelligence cracked Germany's secret code to the great advantage of the Allies, advance knowledge of the location of submarines was still not always available. Moreover, the U-boats began traveling in wolf packs to negate the effectiveness of convoys protected by aircraft and destroyers.

The Fall of France

As the sea battle continued, Germany prepared to break through European defenses. In April 1940 the Germans occupied Denmark and Norway, then launched a full-scale attack on western Europe. Their offensive against Belgium, France, and the Netherlands began in May, and again the Allies were jolted by Blitzkrieg tactics. Belgium and the Netherlands fell first, and the French signed an armistice in June. The fall of France convinced Italy's Benito Mussolini that the Germans were winning the war, and it was time to enter the conflict and reap any potential benefits his partnership with the Germans might offer.

Before the battle of France, Hitler had boasted to his staff, "Gentlemen, you are about to witness the most famous victory in history!" Given France's rapid fall, Hitler was not far wrong. Field Marshal Erwin Rommel put it more colorfully: "The war has become practically a lightning Tour de France!" In a moment of exquisite triumph, Hitler had the French sign their armistice in the very railroad car in which the Germans had signed the armistice in 1918. Trying to rescue some Allied troops before the fall of France, the British engineered a retreat at Dunkirk, but it could not hide the bleak failure of the Allied troops. Britain now stood alone against the German forces.

The Battle of Britain

The Germans therefore launched the Battle of Britain, led by its air force, the *Luftwaffe.* They hoped to defeat Britain almost solely through air attacks. "The Blitz," as the British called this air war, rained bombs on heavily populated metropolitan areas, especially London, and killed more than forty thousand British civilians. The Royal Air Force staved off defeat, however, forcing Hitler to abandon plans to invade Britain. By the summer of 1941, Hitler's conquests included the Balkans, and the battlefront extended to north Africa, where the British fought both the Italians and the Germans. The swastika-bedecked Nazi flag now waved from the streets of Paris to the Acropolis in Athens, and Hitler had succeeded beyond his dreams in his quest to reverse the outcome of World War I.

The German Invasion of the Soviet Union

Flush with victory in the spring of 1941, Hitler turned his sights on the Soviet Union. This land was the ul-

Adolf Hitler proudly walks through conquered Paris in 1940, with the Eiffel Tower as a backdrop.

timate German target, from which Jews, Slavs, and Bolsheviks could be expelled or exterminated to create more *Lebensraum* ("living space") for resettled Germans. Believing firmly in the bankruptcy of the Soviet system, Hitler said of Operation Barbarossa, the code name for the June invasion of the Soviet Union, "You only have to kick in the door, and the whole rotten structure will come crashing down."

On 22 June 1941, Adolf Hitler ordered his armed forces to invade the Soviet Union. For the campaign against the Soviet Union, the German military assembled the largest and most powerful invasion force in history, attacking with 3.6 million soldiers, thirty-seven hundred tanks, and twenty-five hundred planes. The governments of Hungary, Finland, and Romania declared war on the Soviet Union and augmented the German invasion force with their own military contingents totaling about thirty divisions. The invasion, along a front of 3,000 kilometers (1,900 miles), took Stalin by surprise and caught the Red Army off guard. By December 1941 the Germans had captured the Russian heartland, Leningrad had come under siege, and German troops had reached the gates of Moscow. Germany seemed assured of victory.

Operation Barbarossa

However, German Blitzkrieg tactics that had earlier proved so effective in Poland and western Europe failed the Germans in the vast expanses of Russia. Hitler and his military leaders underestimated Soviet personnel reserves and industrial capacity. Within a matter of weeks the 150 German divisions faced 360 divisions of the Red Army. Also, in the early stages of the war Stalin ordered Soviet industry to relocate to areas away from the front. About 80 percent of firms manufacturing war matériel moved to the Ural Mountains between August and October 1941. As a result, the

The devastation caused by German bombardments is visible in the wreckage of a London neighborhood in 1944.

capacity of Soviet industry outstripped that of German industry. The Soviets also received crucial equipment from their allies, notably trucks from the United States. By the time the German forces reached the outskirts of Moscow, fierce Soviet resistance had produced eight hundred thousand German casualties.

The arrival of winter—the most severe in decades—helped Soviet military efforts and prevented the Germans from capturing Moscow. So sure of an early victory were the Germans that they did not bother to supply their troops with winter clothing and boots. One hundred thousand soldiers suffered frostbite, and two thousand of them underwent amputation. The Red Army, in contrast, prepared for winter and found further comfort as the United States manufactured thirteen million pairs of felt-lined winter boots. By early December, Soviet counterattacks along the entire front stopped German advances.

German forces regrouped and inflicted heavy losses on the Red Army during the spring. The Germans briefly regained the military initiative, and by June 1942 German armies raced toward the oil fields of the Caucasus and the city of Stalingrad. As the Germans came on Stalingrad in September, Soviet fortunes of war reached their nadir. At this point the Russians dug in. "Not a step back," Stalin ordered, and he called on his troops to fight a "patriotic" war for Russia. Behind those exhortations lay a desperate attempt to stall the Germans with a bloody street-by-street defense of Stalingrad until the Red Army could regroup for a counterattack.

Battles in Asia and the Pacific

Before 1941 the United States was inching toward greater involvement in the war. After Japan invaded China in 1937, Roosevelt called for a quarantine on aggressors, but his plea fell mostly on deaf ears. However, as war broke out in Europe and tensions with Japan increased, the United States took action. In 1939 it instituted a cash-and-carry policy of supplying the British, in which the British paid cash and carried the materials on their ships. More significant was the lend-lease program initiated in 1941, in which the United States "lent" destroyers and other war goods to the British in return for the lease of naval bases. The program later extended such aid to the Soviets, the Chinese, and many others.

German victories over the Dutch and French in 1940 and Great Britain's precarious military position in Europe and in Asia encouraged the Japanese to project their influence into southeast Asia. Particularly attractive were the Dutch East Indies (now Indonesia) and British-controlled Malaya, regions rich in raw materials such as tin,

Outside Moscow, Soviet women dig antitank trenches against the Nazi onslaught.

Pearl Harbor

rubber, and petroleum. In September of 1940, moving with the blessings of the German-backed Vichy government of France, Japanese forces began to occupy French Indochina (now Vietnam, Laos, and Cambodia). The government of the United States responded to that situation by freezing Japanese assets in the United States and by imposing a complete embargo on oil. Great Britain, the Commonwealth of Nations, and the independent colonial government of the Dutch East Indies supported the U.S. oil embargo. Economic pressure, however, did not persuade the Japanese to accede to U.S. demands, which included the renunciation of the Tripartite Pact and the withdrawal of Japanese forces from China and southeast Asia. To Japanese militarists, given the equally unappetizing alternatives of succumbing to U.S. demands or engaging the United States in war, war seemed the lesser of two evils. In October 1941, defense minister general Tojo Hideki (1884–1948) assumed the office of prime minister, and he and his cabinet set in motion plans for war against Great Britain and the United States.

The Japanese hoped to destroy American naval capacity in the Pacific with an attack at Pearl Harbor and to clear the way for the conquest of southeast Asia and the creation of a defensive Japanese perimeter that would thwart the Allies' ability to strike at Japan's homeland. On 7 December 1941, "a date which will live in infamy," as Franklin Roosevelt concluded, Japanese pilots took off from six aircraft carriers to attack Hawai`i. More than 350 Japanese bombers, fighters, and torpedo planes struck in two waves, sinking or disabling eighteen ships and destroying more than two hundred. Except for the U.S. aircraft carriers, which were out of the harbor at the time, American naval power in the Pacific was devastated.

Flames consumed U.S. battleships in Pearl Harbor after the Japanese attack on 7 December 1941.

On 11 December 1941, though not compelled to do so by treaty, Hitler and Mussolini declared war on the United States. That move provided the United States with the only reason it needed to declare war on Germany and Italy. The United States, Great Britain, and the Soviet Union came together in a coalition that linked two vast and interconnected theaters of war, the European and Asian-Pacific theaters, and ensured the defeat of Germany and Japan. Adolf Hitler's gleeful reaction to the outbreak of war between Japan and the United States proved mistaken: "Now it is impossible for us to lose the war: We now have an ally who has never been vanquished in three thousand years." More accurate was Winston Churchill (1874–1965), prime minister of Britain, who expressed a vast sense of relief and a more accurate assessment of the situation when he said, "So we had won after all!"

Japanese Victories   After Pearl Harbor the Japanese swept on to one victory after another. The Japanese coordinated their strike against Pearl Harbor with simultaneous attacks against the Philippines, Guam, Wake Island, Midway Island, Hong Kong, Thailand, and British Malaya. For the next year the Japanese military maintained the initiative in southeast Asia and the Pacific, capturing Borneo, Burma, the Dutch Indies, and several Aleutian Islands off Alaska. Australia and New Zealand were now in striking distance. The Japanese navy emerged almost unscathed from these campaigns. The humiliating surrender of British-held Singapore in February 1942 dealt a blow to British prestige and shattered any myths of European military invincibility.

Singapore was a symbol of European power in Asia. The slogan under which Japan pursued expansion in Asia was "Asia for Asians," implying that the Japanese would lead Asian peoples to independence from the despised European imperialists and the international order they dominated. In this struggle for Asian independence, Japan re-

Map 37.1 **High tide of Axis expansion in Europe and north Africa, 1942–1943.** Observe the number of nations occupied by or allied with the Axis powers. Given Axis dominance in Europe, what factors finally allowed the Allies to turn the tide of war in their favor?

Legend:
- Neutral nations
- Axis nations
- Axis-occupied areas
- Allied areas
- Allied with Germany

quired the region's resources and therefore sought to build a "Greater East Asia Co-Prosperity Sphere." The appeal to Asian independence at first struck a responsive chord, but conquest and brutal occupation made it soon obvious to most Asians that the real agenda was "Asia for the Japanese." Proponents of the Greater East Asia Co-Prosperity Sphere advocated Japan's expansion in Asia and the Pacific while cloaking their territorial and economic designs with the idealism of Asian nationalism.

Defeat of the Axis Powers

The entry of the Soviet Union and the United States into the war in 1941 was decisive, because personnel reserves and industrial capacity were the keys to the Allied victories in the European and Asia-Pacific theaters. Despite the brutal exploitation of conquered territories, neither German nor Japanese war production matched that of the Allies, who outproduced their enemies at every turn. The U.S. automotive industry alone, for instance, produced more than four million armored, combat, and supply vehicles of all kinds during the war. Not until the United States joined the struggle in 1942 did the tide in the battle in the Atlantic turn in favor of the Allies. Although German submarines sank a total of 2,452 Allied merchant ships and 175 Allied warships in the course of six years, U.S. naval shipyards simply built more "Liberty Ships" than the Germans could sink. By the end of 1943, sonar, aircraft patrols, and escort aircraft from carriers finished the U-boat as a strategic threat.

Allied Victory in Europe

By 1943, German forces in Russia lost the momentum and faced bleak prospects as the Soviets retook territory. Moscow never fell, and the battle for Stalingrad, which ended in February 1943, marked the first large-scale victory for Soviet forces. Desperate German counteroffensives failed repeatedly, and the Red Army, drawing on enormous personnel and material reserves, pushed the German invaders out of Russian territory. By 1944 the Soviets had advanced into Romania, Hungary, and Poland, reaching the suburbs of Berlin in April 1945. At that point, the Soviets had inflicted more than six million casualties on the German enemy—twice the number of the original German invasion force. The Red Army had broken the back of the German war machine.

With the Eastern front disintegrating under the Soviet onslaught, British and U.S. forces attacked the Germans from north Africa and then through Italy. In August 1944 the Allies forced Italy to withdraw from the Axis and to join them. In the meantime, the Germans also prepared for an Allied offensive in the west, where the British and U.S. forces opened a front in France. On D-Day, 6 June 1944, British and U.S. troops landed on the French coast of Normandy. Although the fighting was deadly for all sides, the Germans were overwhelmed. With the two fronts collapsing around them and round-the-clock strategic bombing by the United States and Britain leveling German cities, German resistance faded. Since early 1943 Britain's Royal Air Force had committed itself to area bombing in which centers of cities became the targets of nighttime raids. U.S. planes attacked industrial targets in daytime. The British firebombing raid on Dresden in February 1945 literally cooked German men, women, and children in their bomb shelters: 135,000 people died in the firestorm. A brutal street-by-street battle in Berlin between Germans and Russians, along with a British and U.S. sweep through western Germany, forced Germany's unconditional surrender on 8 May 1945. A week earlier, on 30 April, as fighting flared right outside his Berlin bunker, Hitler committed suicide, as did many of his Nazi compatriots. He therefore did not live to see the Soviet red flag flying over the Berlin *Reichstag*, Germany's parliament building.

Turning the Tide in the Pacific

The turning point in the Pacific war came in a naval engagement near the Midway Islands on 4 June 1942. The United States prevailed there partly because U.S. aircraft carriers had survived the attack on Pearl Harbor. Although the United States had few carriers, it did have a secret weapon: a code-breaking operation known as *Magic*, which enabled a cryptographer monitoring Japanese radio frequencies to discover the plan to attack Midway. On the morning of 4 June, thirty-six carrier-launched dive-bombers attacked the Japanese fleet, sinking three Japanese carriers in one five-minute strike and a fourth one later in the day. This victory changed the character of the war in the Pacific. Although there was no immediate shift in Japanese fortunes, the Allies took the offensive. They adopted an island-hopping strategy, capturing islands from which they could make direct air assaults on Japan. Deadly, tenacious fighting characterized these battles in which the United States and its allies gradually retook islands in the Marianas and Philippines and then, early in 1945, moved toward areas more threatening to Japan: Iwo Jima and Okinawa.

Iwo Jima and Okinawa

The fighting on Iwo Jima and Okinawa was savage. Innovative U.S. amphibious tactics were matched by the vigor and sacrifice of Japanese soldiers and pilots. On Okinawa the Japanese introduced the *kamikaze*—pilots who volunteered to fly planes with just enough fuel to reach an Allied ship and dive-bomb into it. In the two-month battle, the Japanese flew nineteen hundred kamikaze missions, sinking dozens of ships and killing more than five thousand U.S. soldiers. The kamikaze, and the

kamikaze (KAH-mih-kah-zee)

Sources from the Past

A Hiroshima Maiden's Tale

Yamaoka Michiko, at fifteen years of age, worked as an operator at a telephone exchange in Hiroshima and attended girls' high school. Many young women had been mobilized for work during World War II, and they viewed even civilian work on telephone exchanges as a means of helping to protect Japan during wartime. On the morning of 6 August 1945, when the first U.S. atomic bomb used in battle devastated Hiroshima, Yamaoka Michiko had just started off for work.

That morning I left the house at about seven forty-five. I heard that the B-29s [U.S. bomber planes] had already gone home. Mom told me, "Watch out, the B-29s might come again." My house was one point three kilometers from the hypocenter [the exact point of the atomic bomb's impact in Hiroshima]. My place of work was five hundred meters from the hypocenter. I walked toward the hypocenter. . . . I heard the faint sound of planes. . . . The planes were tricky. Sometimes they only pretended to leave. I could still hear the very faint sound of planes. . . . I thought, how strange, so I put my right hand above my eyes and looked up to see if I could spot them. The sun was dazzling. That was the moment.

There was no sound. I felt something strong. It was terribly intense. I felt colors. It wasn't heat. You can't really say it was yellow, and it wasn't blue. At that moment I thought I would be the only one who would die. I said to myself, "Goodbye, Mom."

They say temperatures of seven thousand degrees centigrade hit me. You can't really say it washed over me. It's hard to describe. I simply fainted. I remember my body floating in the air. That was probably the blast, but I don't know how far I was blown. When I came to my senses, my surroundings were silent. There was no wind. I saw a threadlike light, so I felt I must be alive. I was under stones. I couldn't move my body. I heard voices crying, "Help! Water!" It was then I realized I wasn't the only one. . . .

"Fire! Run away! Help! Hurry up!" They weren't voices but moans of agony and despair. "I have to get help and shout," I thought. The person who rescued me was Mom, although she herself had been buried under our collapsed house. Mom knew the route I'd been taking. She came, calling out to me. I heard her voice and cried for help. Our surroundings were already starting to burn. Fires burst out from just the light itself. It didn't really drop. It just flashed. . . .

My clothes were burnt and so was my skin. I was in rags. I had braided my hair, but now it was like a lion's mane. There were people, barely breathing, trying to push their intestines back in. People with their legs wrenched off. Without heads. Or with faces burned and swollen out of shape. The scene I saw was a living hell.

Mom didn't say anything when she saw my face and I didn't feel any pain. She just squeezed my hand and told me to run. She was going to rescue my aunt. Large numbers of people were moving away from the flames. My eyes were still able to see, so I made my way toward the mountain, where there was no fire, toward Hijiyama. On this flight I saw a friend of mine from the phone exchange. She'd been inside her house and wasn't burned. I called her name, but she didn't respond. My face was so swollen she couldn't tell who I was. Finally, she recognized my voice. She said, "Miss Yamaoka, you look like a monster!" That's the first time I heard that word. I looked at my hands and saw my own skin was hanging down and the red flesh exposed. I didn't realize my face was swollen up because I was unable to see it. . . .

I spent the next year bedridden. All my hair fell out. When we went to relatives' houses later they wouldn't even let me in because they feared they'd catch the disease. There was neither treatment nor assistance for me. . . . It was just my Mom and me. Keloids [thick scar tissue] covered my face, my neck. I couldn't even move my neck. One eye was hanging down. I was unable to control my drooling because my lip had been burned off. . . .

The Japanese government just told us we weren't the only victims of the war. There was no support or treatment. It was probably harder for my Mom. Once she told me she tried to choke me to death. If a girl had terrible scars, a face you couldn't be born with, I understand that even a mother could want to kill her child. People threw stones at me and called me Monster. That was before I had my many operations.

FOR FURTHER REFLECTION

What did Yamaoka Michiko's psychological and physical reaction to the atomic bombing of Hiroshima suggest about the nature of these new weapons? Why did friends and relatives treat her as if she were a "monster"?

SOURCE: Yamaoka Michiko. "Eight Hundred Meters from the Hypocenter." In Haruko Taya Cook and Theodore F. Cook, *Japan at War: An Oral History.* New York: The New Press, 1992, pp. 384–87.

Map 37.2 **World War II in Asia and the Pacific.** Compare the geographical conditions of the Asian-Pacific theater with those of the European theater. What kinds of resources were necessary to win in the Asian-Pacific theater as opposed to the European theater?

Japanese Surrender

defense mounted by Japanese forces and the 110,000 Okinawan civilians who died refusing to surrender, convinced many people in the United States that the Japanese would never capitulate.

The fall of Saipan in July 1944 and the subsequent conquest of Iwo Jima and Okinawa brought the Japanese homeland within easy reach of U.S. strategic bombers. Because high-altitude strikes in daylight failed to do much damage to industrial sites, military planners changed tactics. The release of napalm firebombs during low-altitude sorties at night met with devastating success. The firebombing of Tokyo in March 1945 destroyed 25 percent of the city's buildings, annihilated approximately one hundred thousand people, and made more than a million homeless. The final blows came on 6 and 9 August 1945, when the United States used its revolutionary new weapon,

A photograph titled "Planes over Tokyo Bay," taken from the U.S.S. *Missouri,* visually captured a sense of U.S. power and victory on V-J Day, 1945.

the atomic bomb, against the cities of Hiroshima and Nagasaki. The atomic bombs either instantaneously vaporized or slowly killed by radiation poisoning upward of two hundred thousand people.

The Soviet Union declared war on Japan on 8 August 1945, and this new threat, combined with the devastation caused by the bombs, persuaded Emperor Hirohito (1901–1989) to surrender unconditionally. The Japanese surrendered on 15 August, and the war was officially over on 2 September 1945. When Victor Tolley sipped his conciliatory cup of tea with a Nagasaki family, the images of ashen Hiroshima and firebombed Tokyo lingered as reminders of how World War II brought the war directly home to millions of civilians.

Life during Wartime

The widespread bombing of civilian populations during World War II, from its beginning in China to its end in Hiroshima and Nagasaki, meant that there was no safe home front during the war. So too did the arrival of often brutal occupation forces in the wake of Japanese and German conquests in Asia and Europe. Strategic bombing slaughtered men, women, and children around the world, and occupation troops forced civilians to labor and die in work and extermination camps. In this total war, civilian death tolls far exceeded military casualties. Beside the record of the war's brutality can be placed testimony to the endurance of the human spirit personified in the contributions of resistance groups battling occupying forces, in the mobilized women, and in the survivors of bombings or concentration camps.

Occupation, Collaboration, and Resistance

Axis bombardments and invasion were followed by occupation, but the administration imposed on conquered territories by Japanese and German forces varied in character. In territories such as Manchukuo, Japanese-controlled China, Burma, and the Philippines, Japanese authorities installed puppet governments that served as agents of Japanese rule. Thailand remained an independent state after it aligned itself with Japan, for which it was rewarded with grants of territory from bordering Laos and Burma. Other conquered territories either were considered too unstable or unreliable for self-rule or were deemed strategically too important to be left alone. Thus territories such as Indochina (Laos, Cambodia, and Vietnam), Malaya, the Dutch East Indies, Hong Kong, Singapore, Borneo, and New Guinea came under direct military control.

In Europe, Hitler's racist ideology played a large role in determining how occupied territories were administered. As a rule, Hitler intended that most areas of western and northern Europe—populated by racially valuable people, according to him—would become part of a Greater Germanic Empire. Accordingly, Denmark retained its elected government and monarchy under German supervision. In Norway and Holland, whose governments had gone into exile, the Germans left the civilian administration intact. Though northern France and the Atlantic coast came under military rule, the Vichy government remained the civilian authority in the unoccupied southeastern part of the country. Named for its locale in central France, the Vichy government provided a prominent place for those French willing to collaborate with German rule. The Germans had varying levels of involvement in eastern European and Balkan countries, but most conquered territories came under direct military rule as a prelude for harsh occupation, economic exploitation, and German settlement.

Exploitation   Japanese and German authorities administered their respective empires for economic gain and proceeded to exploit the resources of the lands under their control for their own benefit regardless of the consequences for the conquered peoples. The occupiers pillaged all forms of economic wealth that could fuel the German and Japanese war machines. The most notorious form of economic exploitation involved the use of slave labor. As the demands of total war stimulated an insatiable appetite for workers, Japanese and German occupation authorities availed themselves of prisoners of war and local populations to help meet labor shortages. In Poland, the Soviet Union, France, Italy, and the Balkan nations, German occupiers forced millions of people to labor in work camps and war industries, and the Japanese did likewise in China and Korea. These slave laborers worked under horrific conditions and received little in the way of sustenance. Reaction to Japanese and German occupation varied from willing collaboration and acquiescence to open resistance.

Collaboration   The majority of people resented occupation forces but usually went on with life as much as possible. That response was especially true in many parts of Japanese-occupied lands in Asia, where local populations found little to resent in the change from one colonial administration to another. In Asia and Europe, moreover, local notables often joined the governments sponsored by the conquerors because collaboration offered them the means to gain power. In many instances, bureaucrats and police forces collaborated because they thought it was better that natives rule than Germans or Japanese. Businesspeople and companies often collaborated because they prospered financially from foreign rule. Still other people became collaborators and assisted occupation authorities by turning in friends and neighbors to get revenge for past grievances. In western Europe, anticommunism motivated Belgians, French, Danish, Dutch, and Norwegians to join units of Hitler's elite military formations, the Waffen SS, creating in the process a multinational army tens of thousands strong. In China several Guomindang generals went over to the Japanese, and local landowners and merchants in some regions of China set up substantial trade networks between the occupiers and the occupied.

Resistance

Occupation and exploitation created an environment for resistance that took various forms. The most dramatic forms of resistance were campaigns of sabotage, armed assaults on occupation forces, and assassinations. Resistance fighters as diverse as Filipino guerrillas and Soviet partisans harassed and disrupted the military and economic activities of the occupiers by blowing up ammunition dumps, destroying communication and transportation facilities, and sabotaging industrial plants. More quietly, other resisters gathered intelligence, hid and protected refugees, or passed on clandestine newspapers. Resistance also comprised simple acts of defiance such as scribbling anti-German graffiti or walking out of bars and restaurants when Japanese soldiers entered. In the Netherlands, people associated the royal House of Orange with national independence and defiantly saluted traffic lights when they turned orange.

German and Japanese citizens faced different decisions about resistance than conquered peoples did. They had no antiforeign axe to grind, and any form of noncompliance constituted an act of treason that might assist the enemy and lead to defeat. Moreover, many institutions that might have formed the core of resistance in Japan and Germany, such as political parties, labor unions, or churches, were weak or had been destroyed. As a result, there was little or no opposition to the state and its policies in Japan, and in Germany resistance remained generally sparse and ineffective. The most spectacular act of resistance against the Nazi regime came from a group of officers and civilians who tried to kill Adolf Hitler on 20 July 1944. The plot failed when their bomb explosion killed several bystanders but inflicted only minor injuries on Hitler.

Atrocities

Occupation forces did not hesitate to retaliate when resistance to occupation arose. When in May 1942 members of the Czech resistance assassinated Reinhard Heydrich, the deputy leader of the SS (a Nazi security agency that carried out the most criminal tasks of the regime, including mass murder), the Nazis eliminated the entire village of Lidice as punishment. Six days after Heydrich succumbed to his wounds, SS personnel shot the village's 179 men on the spot, transported 50 women to a concentration camp where they died, and then burned and dynamited the village to the ground. SS security forces, after examining the surviving 90 children, deemed them racially "pure" and dispersed them throughout Germany to be raised as Germans. Likewise, in the aftermath of the failed attempt on Adolf Hitler's life in 1944, many of the conspirators ended up dying while suspended from meat hooks, a process recorded on film for Hitler. Equally brutal reprisals took place under Japanese rule. After eight hundred forced Chinese laborers escaped from their camp in the small Japanese town of Hanaoka, the townspeople, the local militia, and the police hunted them down. At least fifty of the slave laborers were tortured to death, some beaten as they hung by their thumbs from the ceiling of the town hall.

Attempts to eradicate resistance movements in many instances merely fanned the flames of rebellion because of the indiscriminate reprisals against civilians. Despite the

Titled "Abyss of Human Horror," this photograph shows a survivor of the concentration camp at Nordhausen, Germany, on its liberation by Allies in 1945.

deadly retaliation meted out to people who resisted occupation, widespread resistance movements grew throughout the war. Life in resistance movements was tenuous at best and entailed great hardship—changing identities, hiding out, and risking capture and death. Nevertheless, the resisters kept alive their nations' hopes for liberation.

The Holocaust

By the end of World War II, the Nazi regime and its accomplices had physically annihilated millions of Jews, Slavs, Gypsies, homosexuals, Jehovah's Witnesses, communists, and others targeted as undesirables. Jews were the primary target of Hitler's racially motivated genocidal policies, and the resulting Holocaust epitomized the tragedy of conquest and occupation in World War II. The Holocaust, the near destruction of European Jews by Germany, was a human disaster on a scale previously unknown.

The murder of European Jews was preceded by a long history of vilification and persecution of Jews. For centuries Jewish communities had been singled out by Christian society as a "problem," and by the time the Nazi regime assumed power in 1933, anti-Semitism had contributed significantly to the widespread tolerance for anti-Jewish measures. Marked as outsiders, Jews found few defenders in their societies. Nazi determination to destroy the Jewish population and Europeans' passive acceptance of anti-Semitism laid the groundwork for genocide. In most war-torn European countries, the social and political forces that might have been expected to rally to the defense of Jews did not materialize.

Initially, the regime encouraged Jewish emigration. Although tens of thousands of Jews availed themselves of the opportunity to escape from Germany and Austria, many more were unable to do so. Most nations outside the Nazi orbit limited the migration of Jewish refugees, especially if the refugees were impoverished, as most of them were because Nazi authorities had previously appropriated their wealth. This situation worsened as German armies overran Europe, bringing an ever-larger number of Jews under Nazi control. At that point Nazi "racial experts" toyed with the idea of deporting Jews to Nisko, a proposed reservation in eastern Poland, or to the island of Madagascar, near Africa. Those ideas proved to be impractical and threatening. The concentration of Jews in one area led to the dangerous possibility of the creation of a separate Jewish state, hardly a solution to the so-called Jewish problem in the Nazi view.

The Final Solution   The German occupation of Poland in 1939 and invasion of the Soviet Union in the summer of 1941 gave Hitler an opportunity to solve what he considered the problem of Jews in Germany and throughout Europe. When German armies invaded the Soviet Union in June 1941, the Nazis also dispatched three thousand troops in mobile detachments known as SS *Einsatzgruppen* ("action squads") to kill entire populations of Jews and Roma (or Gypsies) and many non-Jewish Slavs in the newly occupied territories. The action squads undertook mass shootings in ditches and

Sources from the Past

"We Will Never Speak about It in Public"

On 4 October 1943, Heinrich Himmler, leader of the SS and chief of the German police, gave a three-hour speech to an assembly of SS generals in the city of Posen (Poznan), in what is now Poland. In the following excerpt, Himmler justified Nazi anti-Jewish policies that culminated in mass murder. The speech, recorded on tape and in handwritten notes, was entered into evidence at the Nuremberg war crimes trials in 1945.

I also want to speak to you here, in complete frankness, of a really grave chapter. Amongst ourselves, for once, it shall be said quite openly, but all the same we will never speak about it in public. . . .

I am referring here to the evacuation of the Jews, the extermination of the Jewish people. This is one of the things that is easily said: "The Jewish people are going to be exterminated," that's what every Party member says, "sure, it's in our program, elimination of the Jews, extermination—it'll be done." And then they all come along, the 80 million worthy Germans, and each one has his one decent Jew. Of course, the others are swine, but this one, he is a first-rate Jew. Of all those who talk like that, not one has seen it happen, not one has had to go through with it. Most of you men know what it is like to see 100 corpses side by side, or 500 or 1,000. To have stood fast through this and except for cases of human weakness to have stayed decent, that has made us hard. This is an unwritten and never-to-be-written page of glory in our history. . . .

The wealth they possessed we took from them. I gave a strict order, which has been carried out by SS *Obergruppenfuehrer* Pohl, that this wealth will of course be turned over to the Reich in its entirety. We have taken

none of it for ourselves. Individuals who have erred will be punished in accordance with the order given by me at the start, threatening that anyone who takes as much as a single Mark of this money is a dead man. A number of SS men, they are not very many, committed this offense, and they shall die. There will be no mercy. We had the moral right, we had the duty towards our people, to destroy this people that wanted to destroy us. But we do not have the right to enrich ourselves by so much as a fur, as a watch, by one Mark or a cigarette or anything else. We do not want, in the end, because we destroyed a bacillus, to be infected by this bacillus and to die. I will never stand by and watch while even a small rotten spot develops or takes hold. Wherever it may form we will together burn it away. All in all, however, we can say that we have carried out this most difficult of tasks in a spirit of love for our people. And we have suffered no harm to our inner being, our soul, our character. . . .

FOR FURTHER REFLECTION

Himmler argued that SS officers and soldiers "stayed decent" while overseeing the extermination of the Jews; why then does he focus so much attention on punishing those who took money from the dead Jews?

SOURCE: International Military Tribunal. *Trial of the Major War Criminal*, Nuremberg, Germany, 1948; volume 29, Document 1919-PS. Translation Copyright 2002 Yad Vashem.

ravines that became mass graves. By the spring of 1943, the special units had killed over one million Jews, and tens of thousands of Soviet citizens and Roma.

Sometime during 1941 the Nazi leadership committed to the "final solution" of the Jewish question, a solution that entailed the attempted murder of every Jew living in Europe. At the Wannsee Conference on 20 January 1942, fifteen leading Nazi bureaucrats gathered to discuss and coordinate the implementation of the final solution. They agreed to evacuate all Jews from Europe to camps in eastern Poland, where they would be worked to death or exterminated. Soon German forces—aided by collaborating authorities in foreign countries—rounded up Jews and deported them to specially constructed concentration camps in occupied Poland. The victims from nearby Polish ghettos and distant assembly points all across Europe traveled to their destinations by train. On the way the sick and the elderly often perished in overcrowded

Map 37.3 **The Holocaust in Europe, 1933–1945.**
Observe the geographical locations of the concentration and extermination camps. Why were there more concentration camps in Germany and more extermination camps in Poland?

freight cars. The Jewish victims packed into these suffocating railway cars never knew their destinations, but rumors of mass deportations and mass deaths nonetheless spread among Jews remaining at large and among the Allied government leaders, who were apparently apathetic to the fate of Jews.

In camps such as Kulmhof (Chelmno), Belzec, Majdanek, Sobibòr, Treblinka, and Auschwitz, the final solution took on an organized and technologically sophisticated character. Here, the killers introduced gassing as the most efficient means for mass extermination, though other means of destruction were always retained, such as electrocution, phenol injections, flamethrowers, hand grenades, and machine guns. The largest of the camps was Auschwitz, where at least one million Jews perished. Nazi camp personnel subjected victims from all corners of Europe to industrial work, starvation, medical experiments, and outright extermination. The German commandant of Auschwitz explained proudly how his camp became the most efficient at killing Jews: by using the fast-acting crystallized prussic acid Zyklon B as the gassing agent, by enlarging the size of the gas chambers, and by lulling victims into thinking they were going through a delousing process. At Auschwitz and elsewhere, the Germans also constructed large crematories to incinerate the bodies of gassed Jews and hide the evidence of their crimes. This systematic murder of Jews constituted what war crime tribunals later termed a "crime against humanity."

Jewish Resistance   The murder of European Jewry was carried out with the help of the latest technology and with the utmost efficiency. For most of the victims, the will to resist was sapped by prolonged starvation, disease, and mistreatment. Nevertheless, there was fierce Jewish resistance throughout the war. Thousands of Jews joined anti-Nazi partisan groups and resistance movements while others led rebellions in concentration camps or participated in ghetto uprisings from Minsk to Krakow. The best-known uprising took place in the Warsaw ghetto in the spring of 1943. Lacking adequate weapons, sixty thousand Jews who remained in the ghetto that had once held four hundred thousand rose against their tormentors. It took German security forces using tanks and flamethrowers three weeks to crush the uprising. Approximately 5.7 million Jews perished in the Holocaust.

Women and the War

Observing the extent to which British women mobilized for war, the U.S. ambassador to London noted, "This war, more than any other war in history, is a woman's war." A poster encouraging U.S. women to join the WAVES (Women Appointed for Volunteer Emergency Service in the navy) mirrored the thought: "It's A Woman's War Too!" While hundreds of thousands of women in Great Britain and the United States joined the armed forces or entered war industries, women around the world were affected by the war in a variety of ways. Some nations, including Great Britain and the United States, barred women from engaging in combat or carrying weapons, but Soviet and Chinese women took up arms, as did women in resistance groups. In fact, women often excelled at resistance work because they were women: they were less suspect in the eyes of occupying security forces and less subject to searches. Nazi forces did not discriminate, though, when rounding up Jews for transport and extermination: Jewish women and girls died alongside Jewish men and boys.

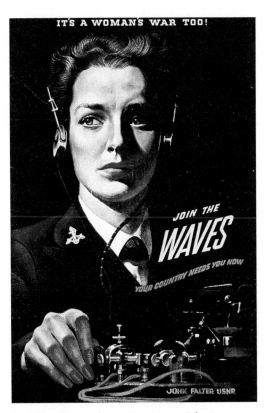

A WAVES recruitment poster proclaims "It's A Woman's War Too!"

Women's Roles

Women who joined military services or took jobs on factory assembly lines gained an independence and confidence previously denied them, but so too did women who were forced to act as heads of household in the absence of husbands killed or away at war, captured as prisoners of war, or languishing in labor camps. Women's roles changed during the war, often in dramatic ways, but those new roles were temporary. After the war, women warriors and workers were expected to return home and assume their traditional roles as wives and mothers. In the meantime, though, women made the most of their opportunities. In Britain, women served as noncombatant pilots, wrestled with the huge balloons and their tethering lines designed to snag Nazi aircraft from the skies, drove ambulances and transport vehicles, and labored in the fields to produce foodstuffs. More than 500,000 women joined British military services, and approximately 350,000 women did the same in the United States.

Comfort Women

Women's experiences in war were not always ennobling or empowering. The Japanese army forcibly recruited, conscripted, and dragooned as many as two hundred thousand women age fourteen to twenty to serve in military brothels, called "comfort houses" or "consolation centers." The army presented the women to the troops as a gift from the emperor, and the women came from Japanese colonies such as Korea, Taiwan, and Manchuria and from occupied territories in the Philippines and elsewhere in southeast Asia. The majority of the women came from Korea and China.

Once forced into this imperial prostitution service, the "comfort women" catered to between twenty and thirty men each day. Stationed in war zones, the women often

■ **British women handle a balloon used for defense in the Battle of Britain.**

confronted the same risks as soldiers, and many became casualties of war. Others were killed by Japanese soldiers, especially if they tried to escape or contracted venereal diseases. At the end of the war, soldiers massacred large numbers of comfort women to cover up the operation. The impetus behind the establishment of comfort houses for Japanese soldiers came from the horrors of Nanjing, where the mass rape of Chinese women had taken place. In trying to avoid such atrocities, the Japanese army created another horror of war. Comfort women who survived the war experienced deep shame and hid their past or faced shunning by their families. They found little comfort or peace after the war.

Neither Peace nor War

The end of World War II produced moving images of peace: Soviet and U.S. soldiers clasping hands in camaraderie at the Elbe River, celebrating their victory over the Germans; Victor Tolley sharing a quiet bowl of tea with a Japanese boy and his family; Allied bombers being transformed into ships of mercy, delivering food and medicine to conquered peoples in Germany and Japan. A sense of common humanity refused to die in this deadliest of wars, although further tests of that humanity awaited in the postwar world.

The two strongest powers after World War II, the Soviet Union and the United States, played a central role in shaping, influencing, and rebuilding the postwar world. Each sought to create a world sympathetic to Soviet communist or U.S. capitalist hegemony. The struggle to align postwar nations on one side or the other centered on areas that were liberated by the Soviet Union and the United States, although ultimately it was not limited to those territories.

Postwar Settlements and Cold War

Although the peoples of victorious nations danced in the streets on Victory in Europe (V-E) Day and Victory in Japan (V-J) Day, they also gazed at a world transformed by war—a world seriously in need of reconstruction and healing. At least sixty million people perished in World War II. The Soviets lost more than twenty million, one-third of whom were soldiers; fifteen million Chinese, mostly civilians, died; Germany and Japan suffered the deaths of four million and two million people, respectively; six million Poles were also dead; in Great Britain four hundred thousand people died; and the United States lost three hundred thousand. The Holocaust claimed the lives of almost six million European Jews. In Europe and Asia tens of millions of displaced persons further contributed to the difficulty of rebuilding areas destroyed by war.

At the end of the war in Europe, eight million Germans fled across the Elbe River to surrender or to seek refuge in the territories soon to be occupied by Great Britain and the United States. They wanted to avoid capture and presumed torture by the Red Army and Soviet occupiers. The behavior of Soviet troops, who pillaged and raped with abandon in Germany, did little to alleviate the fears of those facing Soviet occupation. Joining the refugees were twelve million German and Soviet prisoners of war making their way home, along with the survivors of work and death camps and three million refugees from the Balkan lands. This massive population shift put a human face on the political transformations taking place in Europe and around the world.

The Origins of the Cold War

At the same time, the cold war between the Soviet Union and the United States began. This long-drawn-out conflict (1947–1991) divided global populations, categorizing humans and nations as sympathetic either to the Soviet Union or to the United States. The cold war came to define the postwar era as one of political, ideological, and economic hostility between the two superpowers. Cold war hostilities affected nations around the globe, although the rivals usually refrained from armed conflict in Europe but not in Asia.

Throughout most of World War II, Hitler had rested some of his hopes for victory on his doubts about the unlikely alliance fighting against him. He believed that the alliance of the communist Soviet Union, the imperialist Great Britain, and the unwarlike U.S. democracy would break up over ideological differences. Even when the staunch anticommunist Harry S. Truman (1884–1972) assumed the presidency after Roosevelt's death, however, the Grand Alliance held—at least on the surface. Hitler underestimated the extent to which opposition to his regime could unite such unusual allies. Winston Churchill had made the point in vivid terms when Britain aligned itself with the Soviet Union after the German invasion: "If Hitler invaded Hell, I would at least make favorable reference to the Devil in the House of Commons."

Yalta and Potsdam

The necessity of defeating the Axis nations glued the Allies together, although there were tensions among them. The Soviets bristled at the delay of Britain and the United States in opening the second front, and differences of opinion over postwar settlements arose during the wartime conferences held at Yalta (February 1945) and Potsdam. Yalta, a resort on the Black Sea coast of the Crimea, served as the setting for the second wartime conference (4–11 February 1945) of the three principal Allied leaders: Premier Joseph Stalin of the Soviet Union, Prime Minister Winston Churchill of Great Britain, and President Franklin D. Roosevelt of the United States.

Roosevelt succeeded in gaining Stalin's agreement to enter the war against Japan "within two or three months after Germany's surrender" and to collaborate in the establishment of the United Nations. The Allies also agreed that the major war criminals would be tried before an international court. The main issue discussed at the conference, however, centered on how to deal with the liberated countries of eastern Europe. In the end, all sides agreed to "the earliest possible establishment through free elections of governments responsive to the will of the people." The Potsdam Conference (16 July–2 August 1945) took place in a Berlin suburb and was the last wartime summit conference of the Allies. The focal points of discussion were the immediate Allied control of Germany, the occupation of Austria, and the demarcation of the boundaries of Poland.

By the time of the Yalta Conference, the Soviets were 64 kilometers (40 miles) from Berlin, and they controlled so much territory that Churchill and Roosevelt could do little to alter Stalin's plans for eastern Europe. They attempted to persuade Stalin to allow democracy in Poland, even having supported a democratic Polish government in exile, but Stalin's plans for Soviet-occupied nations prevailed. The Soviets suppressed noncommunist political parties and prevented free elections in Poland, Hungary, Romania, and Bulgaria. They installed a communist government in Poland and took similar steps elsewhere in eastern Europe, adhering to the Allied principle of occupying and controlling those territories liberated by one's armed forces.

At Yalta Stalin ensured that the Red Army's presence would dictate the future of states liberated by the Soviets, and at Potsdam Truman initiated the harder-line stance of the United States, confident now that little Soviet aid would be needed to defeat Japan. The successful test of the atomic bomb while Truman was at Potsdam stiffened the president's resolve, and tensions over postwar settlements intensified. Having just fought a brutal war to guarantee the survival of their ways of life, neither the United States nor the Soviet Union would easily forgo the chance to remake occupied territories as either capitalist or communist allies.

Postwar Territorial Divisions

In Europe and Asia, postwar occupation and territorial divisions reflected both hard postwar realities and the new schism between the Soviet Union and the United States. All that the Allies agreed on was the dismemberment of the Axis states and their possessions. The Soviets took over the eastern sections of Germany, and the United States, Britain, and France occupied the western portions. The capital city of Berlin, deep within the Soviet area, remained under the control of all four powers. Because of the rising hostility between the Soviets and their allies, no peace treaty was signed with Germany, and by the late 1940s these haphazard postwar territorial arrangements had solidified into a divided Germany. As Churchill proclaimed in 1946, an "iron curtain" had come down on Europe. Behind that curtain were the nations controlled by the Soviet Union, including East Germany and Poland, while on the other side were the capitalist nations of western Europe. A somewhat similar division occurred in Asia. Whereas the United States alone occupied Japan, Korea remained occupied half by the Soviets and half by the Americans.

The Truman Doctrine

The enunciation of the Truman Doctrine on 12 March 1947 crystallized the new U.S. perception of a world divided between free and enslaved peoples. Articulated partly in response to crises in Greece and Turkey, where communist movements seemed to threaten democracy and U.S. strategic interests, the Truman doctrine starkly drew the battle lines of the cold war. As Truman explained to the U.S. Congress,

At the present moment in world history nearly every nation must choose between alternative ways of life. The choice is too often not a free one. One way of life is based upon the will of the majority, and is distinguished by free institutions, representative government, free elections, guarantees of individual liberty, freedom of speech and religion, and freedom from political oppression. The second way of life is based upon the will of a minority forcibly imposed upon the majority. It relies upon terror and repression, a controlled press and radio, fixed elections, and the suppression of personal freedoms. I believe that it must be the policy of the United States to support free peoples who are resisting attempted subjugation by armed minorities or by outside pressures.

The United States then committed itself to an interventionist foreign policy, dedicated to the "containment" of communism, which meant preventing any further expansion of Soviet influence. The United States sent vast sums of money to Greece and Turkey, and the world was polarized into two armed camps, each led by a superpower that provided economic and military aid to nations within its sphere of influence.

Global Reconstruction and the United Nations

As an economic adjunct to the Truman Doctrine, the U.S. government developed a plan to help shore up the destroyed infrastructures of western Europe. The European Recovery Program, commonly called the Marshall Plan after U.S. secretary of state George C. Marshall (1880–1959), proposed to rebuild European economies through cooperation and capitalism, forestalling communist or Soviet influence in the devastated nations of Europe. Proposed in 1947 and funded in 1948, the Marshall Plan provided more than $13 billion to reconstruct western Europe.

The Marshall Plan

Although initially included in the nations invited to participate in the Marshall Plan, the Soviet Union resisted what it saw as capitalist imperialism and countered with a plan for its own satellite nations. The Soviet Union established the Council for Mutual Economic Assistance (COMECON) in 1949, offering increased trade within the Soviet Union and eastern Europe as an alternative to the Marshall Plan. The Soviet and U.S. recovery plans for Europe benefited the superpowers by providing lucrative markets or resources. Yet even those economic programs were cut back as more spending shifted to building up military defenses.

The creation of the U.S.-sponsored North Atlantic Treaty Organization (NATO) and the Soviet-controlled Warsaw Pact signaled the militarization of the cold war. In 1949 the United States established NATO as a regional military alliance against Soviet aggression. The original members included Belgium, Canada, Denmark, France, Great Britain, Iceland, Italy, Luxembourg, the Netherlands, Norway, Portugal, and the United States. The intent of the alliance was to maintain peace in postwar Europe through collective defense. When NATO admitted West Germany and allowed it to rearm in 1955, the Soviets formed the Warsaw Pact as a countermeasure. A military alliance of seven communist European nations, the Warsaw Pact matched the collective defense policies of NATO. Europe's contrasting economic and military alliances were part of postwar global reconstruction, and they gave definition to the early cold war.

NATO and the Warsaw Pact

The United States and the Soviet Union became global superpowers as a result of World War II—either through territorial aggrandizement and a massive army, in the case of the Soviet Union, or through tremendous economic prosperity and industrial capacity, in the case of the United States. The dislocation of European and Asian peoples aided the superpowers' quests for world hegemony, but so too did their idealism—however much that idealism cloaked self-interest. Each superpower wanted to guard its preciously won victory by creating alliances and alignments that would support its way of life. The territorial rearrangements of the postwar world, either a direct result of the war or a consequence of the decolonization that followed, gave both superpowers a vast field in which to compete.

Despite their many differences, the superpowers were among the nations that agreed to the creation of the United Nations (UN), a supranational organization

The United Nations

dedicated to keeping world peace. The commitment to establish a new international organization derived from Allied cooperation during the war, and in 1944 representatives from China, Great Britain, the Soviet Union, and the United States finalized most of the proposals for the organization at Dumbarton Oaks in Washington, D.C. The final version of the United Nations charter was hammered out by delegates from fifty nations at the United Nations Conference in San Francisco in 1945. The United Nations was dedicated to maintaining international peace and security and promoting friendly relations among the world's nations. It offered an alternative for global reconstruction that was independent of the cold war.

It rapidly became clear, however, that international peace and security eluded both the United Nations and the superpowers. The cold war dominated postwar reconstruction efforts. It remained cold for the most part, characterized by ideological and propaganda campaigns, although certain events came perilously close to warming up the conflict—as when the Chinese communists gained victory over the nationalists in 1949, thereby joining the Soviets as a major communist power. The cold war also became hot in places such as Korea between 1950 and 1953, and it had the potential to escalate into a war more destructive than World War II. The Soviet Union broke the U.S. monopoly on the atomic bomb in September 1949, and from that point on the world held its collective breath, because a nuclear war was too horrible to contemplate.

———————

At the end of World War II, it was possible for a U.S. marine to enjoy the hospitality of a Japanese family in Nagasaki, but not for Soviet and U.S. troops to continue embracing in camaraderie. World War II was a total global war that forced violent encounters between peoples and radically altered the political shape of the world. Beginning with Japan and China in 1931, this global conflagration spread to Europe and its empires and to the Pacific Ocean and the rest of Asia. Men, women, and children throughout the world became intimate with war as victims of civilian bombing campaigns, as soldiers and war workers, and as slave laborers and comfort women. When the Allies defeated the Axis powers in 1945, destroying the German and Japanese empires, the world had to rebuild as another war began. The end of the war saw the breakup of the alliance that had defeated Germany and Japan, and within a short time the United States and the Soviet Union and their respective allies squared off against each other in a cold war, a rivalry waged primarily on political, economic, and propaganda fronts. The cold war helped determine the new shape of the world as nations reconstructed under the auspices of either the United States or the Soviet Union, the two superpowers of the postwar era.

CHRONOLOGY

1937	Invasion of China by Japan
1937	The Rape of Nanjing
1938	German *Anschluss* with Austria
1939	Nazi-Soviet Pact
1939	Invasion of Poland by Germany
1940	Fall of France, Battle of Britain
1941	German invasion of the Soviet Union
1941	Attack on Pearl Harbor by Japan
1942	U.S. victory at Midway
1943	Soviet victory at Stalingrad
1944	D-Day, Allied invasion at Normandy
1945	Capture of Berlin by Soviet forces
1945	Atomic bombing of Hiroshima and Nagasaki
1945	Establishment of United Nations
1947	Truman Doctrine
1948	Marshall Plan
1949	Establishment of NATO
1955	Establishment of Warsaw Pact

FOR FURTHER READING

Gar Alperovitz. *Atomic Diplomacy: Hiroshima and Potsdam.* Rev. ed. New York, 1985. The classic account of the atomic origins of the cold war.

Christopher Bayly and Tim Harper. *Forgotten Armies: The Fall of British Asia, 1941–1945.* Cambridge, 2005. Broad study of the impact of World War II on Britain's Asian empire.

Herbert P. Bix. *Hirohito and the Making of Modern Japan.* New York, 2001. A groundbreaking, unvarnished biography that details the strong and decisive role the emperor played in wartime operations during World War II.

Christopher R. Browning with contributions by Jürgen Matthäuss. *The Origins of the Final Solution: The Evolution of Nazi Jewish Policy, September 1939–March 1942.* Lincoln, Neb., and Jerusalem, 2004. Standard work on the evolution of Nazi anti-Jewish policies from persecution to mass murder.

Ian Buruma. *The Wages of Guilt: Memories of War in Germany and Japan.* New York, 1995. A moving account of how societies deal with the war crimes of World War II.

Winston Churchill. *The Second World War.* 6 vols. New York, 1948–60. An in-depth account of the war from one of the major players.

Haruko Taya Cook and Theodore F. Cook. *Japan at War: An Oral History.* New York, 1992. Views of World War II in the words of the Japanese who witnessed it.

John Dower. *War without Mercy: Race and Power in the Pacific War.* New York, 1986. An insightful and important work on how race influenced the Japanese and U.S. war in the Pacific.

Dwight Eisenhower. *Crusade in Europe.* New York, 1948. An account of the European war from the military point of view of the supreme Allied commander.

Paul Fussell. *Understanding and Behavior in the Second World War.* Oxford, 1989. A dissection of the culture of war; see the author's similar treatment of World War I.

Tsuyoshi Hasegawa. *Racing the Enemy: Stalin, Truman, and the Surrender of Japan.* Cambridge, Mass., 2005. Impressive international history of the end of World War II in the Pacific that argues the Soviet threat was the decisive factor in Japan's surrender, not Truman's use of nuclear weapons.

Brian Masaru Hayashi. *Democratizing the Enemy: The Japanese American Internment.* Princeton, 2004. Important account of the experience of Japanese Americans in World War II.

Margaret Higgonet, Jane Jenson, Sonya Michel, and Margaret Weitz, eds. *Behind the Lines: Gender and the Two World Wars.* New Haven, 1987. A penetrating series of articles on women in both world wars, focusing generally on U.S. and European experiences.

Raul Hilberg. *The Destruction of the European Jews.* New York, 1967. One of the most important works on the Holocaust.

Akira Iriye. *The Origins of the Second World War in Asia and the Pacific.* New York, 1987. An examination of the Asian and Pacific origins of the war by one of the field's leading scholars.

———. *Power and Culture: The Japanese-American War, 1941–1945.* Cambridge, Mass., 1981. An incisive account of the Pacific war.

John Keegan. *The Second World War.* New York, 1989. An exhaustive military history.

Charles S. Maier, ed. *The Origins of the Cold War and Contemporary Europe.* New York, 1978. An anthology of essays that concentrates on the relationship of the U.S.-Soviet tension and the social and political development of European nations.

Williamson Murray and Alan R. Millet. *A War to Be Won: Fighting in the Second World War, 1937–1945.* Cambridge, Mass., 2000. A fine single-volume history focusing on military operations.

Richard Rhodes. *The Making of the Atomic Bomb.* New York, 1986. An in-depth account of how the atomic bomb was created, with special emphasis on the scientists' role.

Martin Sherwin. *A World Destroyed: The Atomic Bomb and the Grand Alliance.* New York, 1975. A classic study of how the bomb influenced the end of the war.

You-Li Sun. *China and the Origins of the Pacific War, 1931–1941.* New York, 1993. An account of the origins of the war in which China takes center stage.

Studs Terkel. *"The Good War": An Oral History of World War II.* New York, 1984. A valuable collection of oral histories on the war from a U.S. perspective.

Gerhard L. Weinberg. *Visions of Victory: The Hopes of Eight World War II Leaders.* Cambridge, 2005. A close examination of eight political leaders and their visions for the postwar world.

———. *A World at Arms: A Global History of World War II.* Cambridge, 1994. An exhaustive look at the war from a global perspective.

38 The Bipolar World

The Formation of a Bipolar World
The Cold War in Europe
Confrontations in Korea and Cuba
Cold War Societies

Challenges to Superpower Hegemony
Defiance, Dissent, and Intervention in Europe
The People's Republic of China
Détente and the Decline of Superpower Influence

The End of the Cold War
Revolutions in Eastern and Central Europe
The Collapse of the Soviet Union
Toward an Uncertain Future

In the summer of 1959, the world was treated to a verbal slugfest—subsequently known as the kitchen debate—between representatives of the world's two most powerful nations. In July of that year the vice president of the United States, Richard M. Nixon (1913–1994), arrived in Moscow to open the American National Exhibition, a rare display of U.S. goods on Russian soil. Nixon's host, Soviet premier Nikita S. Khrushchev (1894–1971), was in no mood, however, to embrace his guest from the capitalist United States. The U.S. Congress had just passed the "captive nations" resolution, which openly criticized the Soviet Union for mistreating its satellite nations, and Khrushchev was convinced that Nixon's visit to Moscow was timed to humiliate the Soviet leader publicly.

Before visiting the exhibit, Khrushchev and Nixon met privately and exchanged heated words about captive nations. According to Nixon's memoirs, the colorful and candid Soviet premier initiated the conversation by remarking, "It stinks like fresh horse shit, and nothing smells worse than that." The equally frank Nixon—aware that Khrushchev had tended pigs in his youth—quickly replied, "There is something that smells worse than horse shit and that is pig shit." Having thus set the mood, Nixon and Khrushchev descended on the exhibit, where they continued their barbed exchange.

The high point of their vocal showdown took place in the kitchen of a U.S. model house built expressly for the exhibit. Without hesitation, Khrushchev mocked the many modern appliances in the kitchen, including a lemon juicer and a built-in dishwasher. In his opinion they epitomized "the capitalist attitude toward women." Besides, Khrushchev argued, the working class could never afford such useless gadgets in the first place. Stung by the criticism, Nixon poked a finger at the chest of the Soviet premier and boisterously declared that any U.S. steelworker could purchase this $14,000 home. What followed was an unrehearsed polemical discourse on communism and capitalism, climaxing with a dispute concerning the relative merits of everything from dishwashers to missiles.

The kitchen debate between Nixon and Khrushchev took place at the height of the cold war and illustrated how deep the rift between the United States of America and the Union of Soviet Socialist Republics (USSR) had grown since 1945. The cold war was a strategic struggle that developed after World War II between the United States and its allies on the one hand and the USSR and its allied communist countries on the other. Yet the confrontation was more than an instance of great-power rivalry; it was also a tense encounter between rival social and economic systems and competing political ideologies. It was this clash between the

---

OPPOSITE: The visceral beauty of nuclear explosions, such as this one in the Marshall Islands in 1954, masked the terror and the tensions that beset the Soviet Union, the United States, and the rest of the world during the cold war.

forces of capitalism and communism that gave rise to a new set of global relationships, shaping the foreign policies, economic systems, and political institutions of nations throughout the world. The cold war signaled a major realignment in international relations and the global balance of power.

The geopolitical and ideological rivalry between the Soviet Union and the United States lasted almost five decades and affected every corner of the world. The cold war was responsible for the formation of military and political alliances, the creation of client states, and an arms race of unprecedented scope. It engendered diplomatic crises, spawned military conflicts, and at times brought the world to the brink of nuclear annihilation. It was a contest in which neither side gave way, yet in the end the United States and the Soviet Union always avoided a direct clash of arms, hence the term *cold war*. However devoid of direct military conflict, the cold war nonetheless spurred ideological clashes and led to changing societal and economic practices in the Soviet Union and United States. Societies in this atmosphere could not avoid scrutiny and comparison. Discontented women and African-Americans in U.S. society protested the failings of democratic capitalism, while Soviet and east European societies had difficulty matching the increasing wealth and consumerism of western European and U.S. societies.

The Formation of a Bipolar World

The cold war began at the end of World War II, and its initial arena was war-torn Europe. By the time Germany surrendered in the spring of 1945, the wartime alliance between the Soviet Union and the United States was disintegrating. With the advent of peace, the one-time partners increasingly sacrificed cooperation for their own national interests. The competing ideologies of capitalism and communism shaped the postwar aims of the two superpowers. (The term *superpower* came into use during this period to distinguish their supreme global power from the more limited resources of other, merely great, powers.) The hostility between these new adversaries resulted in a divided world. First Europe, and Germany in particular, was split into separate blocs and states. Then the cold war became global in scale as the superpowers came into conflict in nations as far afield as Korea and Cuba.

The Cold War in Europe

Among the first manifestations of the cold war was the division of the European continent into competing political, military, and economic blocs—one dependent on the United States and the other subservient to the USSR—separated by what Winston Churchill called an "iron curtain." In essence, both blocs adopted the political institutions, economic systems, and foreign policies of the two superpowers. Thus western European nations that were tied to the United States embraced parliamentary political systems and capitalist economic structures and adjusted their foreign policies to the U.S. vision of the postwar world. On the other hand, under the watchful eyes of Soviet occupation armies, the governments of eastern European states adopted Soviet political and economic institutions and supported Moscow's foreign policy goals. Outside Europe, members of the socialist and capitalist blocs often diverged significantly from the political and economic norms of their patrons. Nevertheless, when it suited their needs, both sides in the cold war welcomed regimes that practiced neither democracy nor socialism.

A Divided Germany   The fault lines of cold war Europe were most visible in Germany. There in 1948–1949 an international crisis arose when the Soviet Union pressured the western powers to relinquish their jurisdiction over Berlin. After the collapse of Hitler's

Soviet Premier Nikita Khrushchev and U.S. Vice President Richard Nixon sharing a rare "lighter" moment during the kitchen debate.

Third Reich, the forces of the United States, the Soviet Union, Britain, and France occupied Germany and its capital, Berlin, both of which they divided for administrative purposes into four zones. In accordance with agreements made at Yalta, specific travel corridors running through the Soviet occupation zone of Germany gave the French, British, and Americans access from their sectors in Berlin to their respective zones of occupation in western Germany. Tensions mounted between Soviet authorities and their western counterparts in 1947–1948 after the western powers decided to merge their occupation zones in Germany into a single economic unit and to introduce a new currency, the German mark, throughout their occupation zones and in their sectors of Berlin.

The Soviets retaliated by blockading all road, rail, and water links between Berlin and western Germany. The Soviet Union maintained that western economic measures violated wartime agreements and, on 24 June 1948, announced that the four-power administration of Berlin was no longer in effect and that the Allies no longer had any jurisdiction there. Two days later, in the first serious test of the cold war, the Americans and British responded with an airlift designed to keep the city's inhabitants alive, fed, and warm. For eleven months, in a daunting display of airpower, American and British aircrews flew around-the-clock missions to supply West Berlin with the necessities of life. Tensions remained high during the airlift, but the cold war did not turn hot. Stymied by British and U.S. resolve and stung by an embargo on exports from communist countries, the Soviet leadership called off the blockade in May 1949, though the airlift continued until September. The blockade failed to force the British, French, and Americans to vacate their advance outpost deep in communist-controlled eastern Europe. In the aftermath of the blockade, the U.S., British, and French zone of occupation coalesced to form the Federal Republic of Germany (West Germany) in May 1949. In October the German Democratic Republic (East Germany) emerged out of the Soviet zone of occupation. A similar process repeated itself in Berlin, which was deep within the Soviet zone. The Soviet sector formed East Berlin and became the capital of the new East Germany. The remaining three sectors united to form West Berlin, and the West German capital moved to the small town of Bonn.

Blockade and Airlift

Map 38.1 **Occupied Germany, 1945–1949.** Locate the city of Berlin in Soviet-controlled territory. How was it possible for the British, American, and French to maintain their zones of control in Berlin, given such geographical distance from western Germany?

Berlin Wall

By 1961 the communist East German state was hemorrhaging from a steady drain of refugees who preferred life in capitalist West Germany. Between 1949 and 1961 nearly 3.5 million East Germans—many of them young and highly skilled—left their homeland, much to the embarrassment of East Germany's communist leaders. In August 1961 the communists reinforced their fortification along the border between East and West Germany, following the construction of a fortified wall dividing the city of Berlin. The wall, which began as a layer of barbed wire, quickly turned into a barrier several layers deep, replete with watchtowers, searchlights, antipersonnel mines, and border guards ordered to shoot to kill. Although the erection of the Berlin Wall was an obvious violation of four-power control in Germany, the United States and its British and French partners avoided a direct confrontation with the Soviet Union for fear that the crisis would escalate into a full shooting war. In subsequent years several thousand East Germans escaped to West Germany, often by ingenious means, but several hundred others paid with their lives for attempting to do so. Meanwhile, the Berlin Wall accomplished its purpose of stemming the flow of refugees, though at the cost of shaming a regime that obviously lacked legitimacy among its own people.

The Nuclear Arms Race

A central feature of the cold war world was a costly arms race and the terrifying proliferation of nuclear weapons. The struggle between the United States and the

Soviet Union led to the creation of two military blocs: the North Atlantic Treaty Organization, or NATO (1949), intended to serve as a military counterweight to the Soviet forces in Europe, and the Warsaw Treaty Organization, or Warsaw Pact (1955), established as a response to the rearming of West Germany. Because the United States was determined to retain military superiority and because the Soviet Union was equally determined to reach parity with the United States, both sides amassed enormous arsenals of thermonuclear weapons and developed a multitude of systems for deploying those weapons. Not until the 1960s did the Soviet Union approach parity, and by the end of that decade both sides had achieved what Richard Nixon later called "essential equivalence" in their strategic forces. Thus by 1970 both superpowers had acquired the capacity for mutually assured destruction, or MAD. Yet the balance of terror restrained the contestants and stabilized their relationship, with two important exceptions.

Barbed wire and a concrete wall in front of the Brandenburg Gate in Berlin symbolized the cold war division of Europe.

Confrontations in Korea and Cuba

With the unforeseen outbreak of hostilities on the Korean peninsula in the summer of 1950, the focus of the cold war shifted from Europe to east Asia. At the end of World War II, the leaders of the Soviet Union and the United States had partitioned Korea along the thirty-eighth parallel of latitude into a northern Soviet zone and a southern U.S. zone. Because the superpowers were unable to agree on a framework for the reunification of the country, in 1948 they consented to the establishment of two separate Korean states: in the south, the Republic of Korea, with Seoul as its capital and the conservative anticommunist Syngman Rhee (1875–1965) as its president; in the north, the People's Democratic Republic of Korea, with Pyongyang as its capital and the revolutionary communist Kim Il Sung (1912–1995) as its leader. After arming their respective clients, each of which claimed sovereignty over the entire country, U.S. and Soviet troops withdrew.

On the early morning of 25 June 1950, the unstable political situation in Korea came to a head. Determined to unify Korea by force, the Pyongyang regime ordered more than one hundred thousand troops across the thirty-eighth parallel in a surprise attack, quickly pushing back South Korean defenders and capturing Seoul on 27 June. Convinced that the USSR had sanctioned the invasion, the U.S. government lost no time persuading the United Nations to adopt a resolution requesting all member states "to provide the Republic of Korea with all necessary aid to repel the aggressors." Armed with a UN mandate and supported by token ground forces from twenty countries, the U.S. military went into action. U.S. forces were unable to dislodge the North Koreans, who inflicted a series of humiliating defeats on the Americans during the summer of 1950. In September, however, following an extremely risky but successful amphibious operation at Incheon (near Seoul) far behind North Korean lines, U.S. forces went on the offensive. Americans and their allies eventually pushed North Korean forces back to the thirty-eighth parallel, thereby fulfilling the UN mandate. Sensing an opportunity to unify all of Korea under a friendly government, U.S. leaders sent American forces into North Korea, where they soon occupied Pyongyang. Subsequent U.S. advances toward the Yalu River on the Chinese border caused the government of the

The Korean War

In August 1950, U.S. troops marched toward North Korea while South Koreans moved in the opposite direction to escape the fighting.

People's Republic of China to issue a warning: the U.S. incursion across the thirty-eighth parallel threatened Chinese national interests and could result in Chinese intervention in the Korean conflict.

When U.S. leaders gave no indication of heeding China's warning, some three hundred thousand Chinese soldiers surged across the Yalu River into North Korea. A combined force of Chinese and North Koreans pushed U.S. forces and their allies back into the south, and the war settled into a protracted stalemate near the original border at the thirty-eighth parallel. After two more years of desultory fighting that raised the number of deaths to three million people—mostly Korean civilians—both sides finally agreed to a cease-fire in July 1953. The failure to conclude a peace treaty ensured that the Korean peninsula would remain in a state of suspended strife that constantly threatened to engulf the region in a new round of hostilities. The war had also intensified the bitterness between north and south, making the prospect for a unified Korea even more remote.

The Globalization of Containment

Beyond the human casualties and physical damage it wrought, the Korean conflict also encouraged the globalization of containment. Viewing the North Korean offensive as part of a larger communist conspiracy to conquer the world, the U.S. government extended military protection and economic aid to the noncommunist governments of Asia. It also entered into security agreements that culminated in the creation of the Southeast Asian Treaty Organization (SEATO), an Asian counterpart of NATO. By 1954 U.S. president Dwight D. Eisenhower (1890–1969), who had contemplated using nuclear weapons in Korea, accepted the famous "domino theory." This strategic theory rationalized worldwide U.S. intervention on the assumption that if one country became communist, neighboring ones would collapse to communism the way a row of dominoes falls sequentially until none remains standing. Subsequent U.S. administrations extended the policy of containment to areas beyond the nation's vital interests and applied it to local or imagined communist threats in Central and South America, Africa, and Asia.

Cuba: Nuclear Flashpoint

The Cuban missile crisis of 1962, which brought the superpowers to the brink of a nuclear exchange, dramatically underscored the risks inherent in extending the cold war throughout the world. The one region the United States had declared off-limits to all foreign intrusion, including Soviet influence, was the western hemisphere; the

▨ **Prime Minister Fidel Castro of Cuba addresses a rally.**

United States believed its dominance here was undisputed. Ironically, the cold war confrontation that came closest to unleashing nuclear war took place not at the expected flashpoints in Europe or Asia but on the island of Cuba.

In 1959 a revolutionary movement headed by Fidel Castro Ruz (1926–) overthrew the autocratic Fulgencio Batista y Zaldivar (1901–1973), whose regime had gone to great lengths to maintain the country's traditionally subservient relationship with the United States and especially with the U.S. sugar companies that controlled Cuba's economy. Denouncing Yankee imperialism, Castro worked to limit its operations, purging the Batista supporters remaining in Cuba and seizing foreign properties and businesses, most of which were U.S. owned. He also accepted assistance from the Soviet Union, which fueled U.S. fears about his communist leanings. The U.S. government promptly retaliated by cutting off Cuban sugar imports to the U.S. market and imposing a severe export embargo of U.S. goods on Cuba. Officials in the Eisenhower administration also cut diplomatic relations with Cuba and secretly began planning an invasion of the island.

The severing of ties between Cuba and the United States gave the Soviet Union an unprecedented opportunity to contest the dominant position of the United States in its own hemisphere. Soviet support also provided Castro with a buffer against U.S. hostility, and Castro's regime accepted a generous Soviet offer of military and economic aid, including an agreement to purchase half of Cuba's sugar production. Before long thousands of Soviet technicians, advisors, and diplomatic personnel arrived in Cuba. In return for the Soviet largesse, Castro declared his support for the USSR's foreign policy. This he did loudly and dramatically on 26 September 1960. Clad in battle fatigues, he delivered a four-and-a-half-hour lecture to the UN General Assembly.

Cuba's alignment with the Soviet Union spurred the U.S. government to action.   *The Bay of Pigs*
Newly elected President John F. Kennedy (1917–1963) gave the go-ahead to the invasion of Cuba planned by the previous administration and intended to overthrow

Castro and his supporters. In April 1961 a force of 1,500 anti-Castro Cubans trained, armed, and transported by the Central Intelligence Agency (CIA) landed on Cuba at a place called the Bay of Pigs. The arrival of the invasion force failed to incite any internal uprising, and when the promised American air support failed to appear, the invasion quickly fizzled. Within three days, Castro's military had either captured or killed the entire invasion force. The Bay of Pigs fiasco diminished U.S. prestige, especially in Latin America. It also, contrary to U.S. purposes, actually strengthened Castro's position in Cuba and his commitment to communism. In December 1961 Castro publicly announced, "I have been a Marxist-Leninist all along, and will remain one until I die." The failure of the Bay of Pigs led members of the U.S. government and CIA to institute "Operation Mongoose," a clandestine campaign aimed at destabilizing Cuba and assassinating Castro. The invasion attempt likely encouraged Castro to accept and the Soviets to deploy nuclear missiles in Cuba as a deterrent to any future invasion.

The Cuban Missile Crisis

On 22 October 1962 President Kennedy went on national television to inform the public about the U.S. discovery of offensive nuclear missiles and launch sites in Cuba and to frame the nation's response to this crisis. The Soviet government apparently took this bold step to protect the Castro government, give the USSR greater diplomatic leverage vis-à-vis the United States, undermine U.S. credibility in the region, and gain more influence in Latin America. Whatever the precise motives, the deployment of nuclear missiles that could reach targets in the United States within minutes represented an unacceptable threat to U.S. national security. Under pressure from Congress to deal with the Soviet menace, President Kennedy delivered his public ultimatum, calling on the Soviet leadership to withdraw all missiles from Cuba and stop the arrival of additional nuclear armaments. To back up his demand, Kennedy imposed an air and naval quarantine on the island nation that went into effect two days later. The superpowers seemed poised for nuclear confrontation, and for a week the world's peoples held their collective breath.

Negotiations between the U.S. and the U.S.S.R. continued during these emotional days, and Nikita Khrushchev best understood the seriousness of the risk of a superpower nuclear showdown over Cuba. He agreed to Kennedy's demand that he withdraw the missiles on the condition that the United States pledge to not invade Cuba. He also received a promise from Kennedy, though one not to be made public, that U.S. missiles in Turkey would be removed. Khrushchev informed the public of the end of the crisis in a worldwide radio broadcast on 28 October, and global tension began to ebb. Nonetheless, the Cuban missile crisis revealed the dangers of the bipolar world, because the world trembled during this crisis, awaiting the apocalypse that potentially lurked behind any superpower encounter.

Cold War Societies

The global political arena after World War II resounded with clashes stemming from the cold war and decolonization. The conflicts emanating from those dual forces naturally had repercussions in societies around the world. Postwar social transformations demonstrated how domestic policies and international affairs often become linked, particularly as peoples living in disparate parts of the world discovered commonalities and differences, mutual sympathies and antipathies. Cold war competition for allies prodded the United States and the Soviet Union to commit their financial resources, military and diplomatic personnel, and goods and services to diverse countries that experienced firsthand encounters with superpower representatives. Officials

Map 38.2 **The cold war, 1949–1962.** Note the size of the territories and the number of states allied to both sides. Were these alliances a source of global stability or global instability?

NATO

BELGIUM
BRITAIN
CANADA
DENMARK
W. GERMANY
GREECE
ICELAND
ITALY

LUXEMBOURG
NETHERLANDS
NORWAY
PORTUGAL
SPAIN
TURKEY
UNITED STATES

WARSAW PACT

BULGARIA
CZECHOSLOVAKIA
EAST GERMANY
HUNGARY
POLAND
ROMANIA
SOVIET UNION

NATO Nations

NATO dependencies 1960

Other nations allied to the U.S. by treaty

U.S.S.R.

WARSAW Pact 1955

Communist satellite states

China

of the superpowers also came face-to-face with one another for the first time in the late 1950s, and those meetings suggested the extent to which Soviet and U.S. societies had also transformed as a result of the cold war and decolonization.

Domestic Containment and Female Liberation

When Nikita Khrushchev and Richard Nixon squared off in the kitchen debate in Moscow, their argument underscored the importance of women and domesticity as a means of understanding the differences between their respective societies—and by extension, between all capitalist and communist societies. Citizens of the United States, like Nixon, celebrated the wondrous home appliances that made the lives of housewives and mothers so comfortable and that distinguished these U.S. women from their toiling Soviet counterparts. Clinging to the notion that U.S. women best served their families and their nation by staying home and rearing patriotic children, social and political leaders in the United States believed that families provided the best defense against communist infiltration in their nation. Women did not need to work, as they did in the Soviet Union, because their husbands earned enough to support the family in suburban splendor and because a mother's most important job was keeping the family happy and loyal.

Cold war concerns about the spread of communism reached into the domestic sphere, particularly in the United States. Politicians, FBI agents, educators, and social commentators warned of communist spies trying to undermine the institutions of U.S. life, and Senator Joseph McCarthy (1909–1957) became infamous in the early 1950s for his unsuccessful quest to expose communists in the U.S. government. Supporting any radical or liberal cause, or behaving in any odd way, subjected citizens of the United States to suspicions about their loyalty. Thousands of citizens—especially those who were or once had been members of the Communist Party—lost their jobs and reputations after being deemed risks to their nation's security. Conformity to a socially sanctioned way of life became the norm during the early, most frightening, years of the cold war. Staying safely protected in family life meant avoiding suspicion and ignoring some of the more anxious elements of the cold war as waged by the United States—the atomic peril in particular. Some scholars have dubbed this U.S. retreat to the home and family "domestic containment," indicating its similarity to the U.S. foreign policy of the containment of international communism.

Although the burden of domestic containment fell on all members of the family, women were most affected by its restraints. Married women in the United States worked in larger numbers during the cold war than during World War II, and many resented having to feel shame or guilt at not living up to the domestic ideals being showcased on the new and widely viewed television shows that sustained the U.S. public during the cold war. Not all women aspired to be June Cleaver on *Leave It to Beaver* (1957–1963 TV show), and female discontent with postwar domesticity in the United States helped to fuel the modern feminist movement. Aligning themselves to some extent with women in societies such as the Soviet Union and taking inspiration from women in Asia and Africa who fought for their independence from the colonial powers—and often won legal equality as a result—U.S. women rejected cold war norms and agitated for equal rights.

Building on the dissatisfaction that surfaced after World War II with their often forcible return to the home from war work, women in European and North American societies expressed a newfound understanding of their oppression at the hands of men. French writer Simone de Beauvoir (1908–1986) wrote *The Second Sex* in 1949, denouncing the second-class status of women. In 1963 U.S. author Betty Friedan (1921–) published *The Feminine Mystique*, laying bare the severe unhappiness of women who presumably enjoyed the best life the United States could offer. Feminists provided one signal that not all was well within the capitalist orbit, as African-Americans and university students around the world also contested elements of cold war life. When student radicals objected to U.S. policies in Vietnam, for example, by rioting and demonstrating from the mid-1960s to the early 1970s, it became clear that a consensus about cold war policies had broken down. Women activists adopted the language and terms of Marxism and anticolonialism in their quest for equality and independence. They referred to women as an "oppressed class" and argued against male "colonization" of female bodies and for "women's liberation." Support for domestic containment, and containment itself, wavered.

A cross-fertilization between domestic and foreign policies and between European, American, and decolonizing societies took place throughout the early cold war years. This condition was particularly noticeable in regard to black nationalism, in the Caribbean, the United States, and the newly emerging states in Africa. The reggae music of Jamaican Bob Marley (1945–1981) spread throughout the world, rallying blacks to the cause. Marley's song "Get Up Stand Up," although written as a form of resistance to persistent racism and poverty in Jamaica, nonetheless spoke to millions of blacks struggling for their freedom. In his song, Marley urged people to stand up for their rights and to continue fighting for them.

Black Nationalism

Africans and African-Americans were influenced by the radical ideas of another black nationalist from Jamaica, Marcus Garvey (1887–1940), who advocated that U.S. blacks seek repatriation in Africa. Kwame Nkrumah (1909–1972), who later led Ghana to independence from colonial rule, familiarized himself with the works of Garvey while studying in the United States. Moderate civil rights leaders in the United States who distanced themselves from more radical forms of black nationalism, however, also adopted the ideas and strategies of other nationalist leaders fighting for independence from colonial rule. Dr. Martin Luther King Jr. (1929–1968), the most prominent of these leaders, relied openly on the Indian leader Mohandas K. Gandhi's examples of passive nonresistance and boycotting in the struggle to win African-Americans their equality and independence in the United States.

The coinciding of the cold war with the modern civil rights movement in the United States showed the links between domestic and foreign policies. The Soviet Union could and did use the appalling conditions of African-Americans to expose the weaknesses of the capitalist system in the United States. In virtually every sphere of life, southern U.S. states institutionalized segregation, a system of laws and customs designed to separate blacks and whites. African-Americans contended with segregation and the loss of voting rights, widespread discrimination, and extralegal violence. Discrimination was less pronounced in northern states, where African-Americans could usually vote, but informal segregation practices also influenced northern society. U.S. politicians and lawmakers recognized the adverse propaganda value of this institutionalized racism during the cold war. The U.S. Supreme Court in 1954 ruled segregation in the schools illegal in *Brown v. Board of Education*, but it was direct action on the part of African-Americans—through the civil rights movement—that brought down segregation and impediments to voting.

The Civil Rights Movement

The civil rights movement was first and foremost a challenge to segregation. In 1955, when Rosa Parks, an African-American woman living in Montgomery, Alabama, refused to give up her seat on a bus to a white man—as required by law—she accelerated a civil rights revolution that resulted in major advances for blacks in the United States. African-Americans in Montgomery refused to ride city buses until they were desegregated, and the Montgomery bus boycott—led by Martin Luther King—proved the effectiveness of Gandhi's methods. King went on to lead numerous marches and demonstrations and, despite the violence visited on him and his followers, to win major civil rights battles. Until his assassination in 1968, King clung to his

Sources from the Past

Nikita Khrushchev on the Capitalist Iron Curtain

In early 1946 Winston Churchill (1874–1965) delivered his "Iron Curtain" speech, stirring audiences with its image of a Europe firmly and frighteningly divided between communist and capitalist nations and marking, for some, the beginning of the cold war. Fifteen years after Churchill delivered his speech, Nikita Khrushchev (1894–1971) acknowledged the power of Churchill's imagery by using it in his own speech to the Communist Party Congress. In his 1961 "Report to the Communist Party Congress," Soviet premier Khrushchev blasted capitalism with the same force Churchill had employed in his earlier condemnation of communism.

Comrades! The competition of the two world social systems, the socialist and the capitalist, has been the chief content of the period since the 20th Party Congress [February 1956]. It has become the pivot, the foundation of world development at the present historical stage. Two lines, two historical trends, have manifested themselves more and more clearly in social development. One is the line of social progress, peace and constructive activity. The other is the line of reaction, oppression and war.

In the course of the peaceful competition of the two systems, capitalism has suffered a profound moral defeat in the eyes of all peoples. The common people are daily convinced that capitalism is incapable of solving a single one of the urgent problems confronting mankind. It becomes more and more obvious that only on the paths to socialism can a solution to these problems be found. Faith in the capitalist system and the capitalist path of development is dwindling. Monopoly capital, losing its influence, resorts more and more to intimidating and suppressing the masses of the people, to methods of open dictatorship in carrying out its domestic policy and to aggressive acts against other countries. But the masses of the people offer increasing resistance to reaction's acts.

The ruling circles of some imperialist powers have elevated subversive activities against the socialist countries to the level of state policy. With cynical frankness, the United States of America is spending hundreds of millions of dollars on espionage and subversion against socialist countries and organizing so-called "guerrilla units," assembling in them criminal elements and cut-throats prepared to undertake the vilest crimes for money. For

several successive years the United States has been holding provocational "captive nations weeks." The hired agents of the monopolies call "captive" all those peoples who have liberated themselves from imperialist bondage and taken the path of free development. Truly, imperialist demagogy and hypocrisy know no bounds!

Our society is open to those people who come to us from abroad with open hearts. It is open to honest trade, to scientific, technical and cultural exchanges, to the exchange of truthful information. If it's an iron curtain we're talking about, where it really exists is in the world of capitalism, which, though dubbing itself the "free world," every now and then fearfully slams its gates shut to Soviet people, one moment to our cooks, the next to our chess players. There was a case where one state, which calls itself the "most open," was afraid to let in Soviet dancers. Can they really have feared that Russian folk dancing might shake the foundations of the capitalist world?!

We have long proposed to the capitalist world that we compete not in an arms race but in improving the working people's lives. We are confident that capitalism cannot stand up under that kind of competition! We are confident that in the end all peoples will make the correct choice, will give their preference to the truly free world of communism and turn their backs on the so-called "free world" of capitalism.

FOR FURTHER REFLECTION

Why did Khrushchev contend that faith in capitalism had dwindled and that the true "iron curtain" closed capitalist nations to outside contacts?

SOURCE: Nikita Khrushchev. "Report to the Communist Party." In *Current Soviet Policies IV*, ed. Charlotte Saikowski and Leo Gruliow, from the translations of *The Current Digest of the Soviet Press*, 1962.

dream of black equality in the United States, a nation pressured by the cold war and African liberation movements to accede rights to its black population.

The United States fell short in cold war ideological battles in its treatment of African-Americans, but the Soviet Union had difficulty matching the United States and its allies in the provision of material wealth, leisure, and consumer goods. Like women and domesticity, consumerism became one means of distinguishing communist and capitalist societies. This issue too gave bite to the kitchen debate between Nixon and Khrushchev. As the two squabbled over the significance of appliances, it was apparent that the Soviet Union and its satellites had achieved success with military and scientific endeavors, but had not provided their people with the stuff of dreams—automobiles, Hollywood movies, record albums, supermarkets, or month-long paid vacations. European and North American peoples suffered atomic anxiety and the insecurity of living in the cold war world, but the postwar economic prosperity that stemmed in part from waging the cold war relieved some of that pain.

Cold War Consumerism

The contrasting economic and social conditions of western and eastern Europe after World War II demonstrated the different lifestyles that emerged in Europe during the cold war. Western European nations experienced what many people termed an economic miracle, recovering swiftly from the war's devastation. Starting with an infusion of $13 billion from the U.S. Marshall Plan between 1948 and 1952, west European government leaders rebuilt their nations by encouraging economic growth and by providing social services that outpaced those in the United States—including, over time, the guarantee of a thirty-day paid vacation. The increased standard of living and consumerism in western Europe was visible in the rapidly growing numbers of Europeans driving the automobiles they could afford. In 1955 only five million people owned cars in western Europe. By 1963 that figure had jumped to forty-four million.

Although Soviet and eastern European societies could not compete with the abundance of consumer goods available in the United States and western Europe, they could take pride and some comfort from the technological triumphs enjoyed by the Soviet Union in the late 1950s and early 1960s. Soviet experts demonstrated to the world their apparent superiority in science and technology when in the late 1950s news spread that a workable intercontinental ballistic missile (ICBM) had been tested. That success was overshadowed on 4 October 1957 by the more spectacular Soviet launching into space of the first satellite, *Sputnik*. Between the ICBM and *Sputnik*, the Soviets grabbed the initiative in the newly dubbed space race, an extraterrestrial form of the cold war. The Soviet head start in this race provoked panic among U.S. citizens and politicians. A deep questioning of U.S. social and educational systems followed, and it intensified in April 1961 when the Soviets rocketed cosmonaut Yuri Gagarin (1934–1968) into space, where he became the first man to orbit the earth.

The Space Race

The United States soon copied those Soviet successes in space with its own—launching the satellite *Explorer I* in 1958 and sending astronaut John Glenn (1921–) into orbit in 1962. When John F. Kennedy became president, having worried for years about the missile and space gaps between the United States and the Soviet Union, he dedicated himself and the National Aeronautics and Space Administration (NASA) to the task of landing a man on the moon. That came to fruition on 20 July 1969 when *Apollo XI* gently set down on the moon's Sea of Tranquility and thereby ensured that Americans were the first to make this "great leap for mankind." The moon landing reassured U.S. citizens of their world status, but the earlier years of the cold war had left them insecure about missile gaps and diminished scientific ingenuity in a society relentlessly devoted to consumerism.

However buoyed by their scientific prowess, the peoples of the Soviet Union and eastern European nations experienced less economic growth and enjoyed far fewer

Peaceful Coexistence

consumer items and far less leisure than did their counterparts in western Europe and North America. After the war, Stalin imposed Soviet economic planning on governments in east Europe and expected the peoples of the Soviet Union and eastern Europe to conform to anticapitalist ideological requirements in their cultural productions. Rebellious artists and novelists found themselves silenced or denounced in an exaggerated and reversed form of McCarthyism (anticommunist repression) that affected government workers, writers, and filmmakers in the United States in the same years. A relaxation of economic and cultural dictates took place after Stalin's death in 1953 and during most of the years of Khrushchev's leadership in the Soviet Union. With respect to foreign policy, Khrushchev emphasized the possibility of "peaceful coexistence" between different social systems and the achievement of communism by peaceful means. This change in Soviet doctrine reflected the recognition that a nuclear war was more likely to lead to mutual annihilation than to victory. The peaceful coexistence that Khrushchev fostered with the United States appeared to apply to domestic Soviet and eastern European societies also. There were limits to this Soviet liberalization, though: Soviet troops cracked down on Hungarian rebels in 1956, and Soviet novelist Boris Pasternak (1890–1960), author of *Dr. Zhivago*, was not allowed to receive his Nobel Prize for literature in 1958.

Societies in the Soviet Union and the United States may have resembled each other in some ways—in their domestic censorship policies, in their space racing, in their pursuit of nuclear superiority, and in their quest for cold war supremacy—but they also resembled each other in their basic humanity: a fact that may have prevented the ultimate tipping of the balance of terror. A few weeks after the famous kitchen debate, Khrushchev visited the United States and became the first Soviet leader to set foot on U.S. soil. Despite some tense moments, Khrushchev's tour of the United States contributed to a thaw in the cold war, however brief. In his September 1959 travels, which included stops in New York, California, and Iowa, he showed himself to be a formidable leader and a warm and witty man. Television coverage of his trip allowed millions in the United States to see the previously perceived demonic Soviet premier as a human being—understanding his disappointment at not getting to see Disneyland because of security concerns, watching him talk with U.S. farmers, and listening as he thanked his U.S. hosts on his departure for their hospitality. This encounter between a Soviet leader and a U.S. audience suggested the ever-shifting possibilities for peace in the perilous cold war world. The search for peace and security in a bipolar world was revamping societies in the Euro-American world and beyond. When peace remained elusive, however, the superpowers confronted challenges on many fronts, some coming from their own allies and others from small nations seeking freedom from any superpower interference.

Challenges to Superpower Hegemony

The global preeminence of the two new superpowers evoked challenges from several quarters. In western Europe, French politicians sought to free their nation from superpower dominance by transforming Europe into an independent strategic bloc. That gambit ultimately failed, although it set the stage for a cautious, more independent political course on the part of other western European nations. Eastern European states also tried to gain independence, or at least to gain a measure of autonomy from the Soviet Union. Except for Yugoslavia, which resisted Soviet pressure and became a nonaligned, or neutral, state, the nations of the Soviet bloc did not fare well in their autonomy endeavors. On several occasions, Soviet tanks ruthlessly crushed rebels' efforts to leave the Soviet orbit. The leadership of the People's Republic of China mounted the most serious challenge to Soviet hegemony within the communist world. What began as a quarrel over national interests and disagreements concerning ideology grew into a schism. Finally, in Vietnam and Afghanistan, respectively, the United States and the Soviet Union suffered serious political and military setbacks that signaled the decline of superpower hegemony.

Defiance, Dissent, and Intervention in Europe

The first direct assault on the bipolar world emanated from France under the leadership of President Charles de Gaulle (1890–1970), who dreamed of a Europe that could act as a third force in world affairs. De Gaulle's pursuit of independence stemmed from dissatisfaction with the international order dictated by leaders in Washington and Moscow. In particular, he regarded subservience to U.S. authority and unqualified support for U.S. global objectives as intolerable conditions.

De Gaulle and many of his compatriots believed that France could never regain great power status—a standing it once held as a great continental and imperial power—if it depended for security on U.S. military protection. Moreover, military dependence carried with it the risk that a nuclear confrontation between the superpowers over issues unrelated to European interests could engulf Europe by virtue of its alliance with the United States. De Gaulle and others also questioned the credibility of the American promise to defend Europe against a Soviet attack by threatening nuclear retaliation against the Soviet Union.

France under de Gaulle

De Gaulle pursued independent policies wherever he could. Thus in 1963, despite U.S. disapproval, the French government rejected a partial nuclear test ban treaty that had been signed by the Soviet Union, Great Britain, and the United States and recognized by the communist People's Republic of China. The focus of French policy, however, was disengagement from the U.S.-dominated NATO and the development of an independent nuclear strike force. The latter became a realistic proposition in 1964 when the French detonated their first atomic bomb in the Sahara desert. Four years later the French military put together a nuclear delivery system consisting of long-range bombers and land- and submarine-based missiles. French military doctrine and capability—the *force de frappe* or nuclear strike force—failed to convince Europeans to leave the protective fold of the United States, however, and by the time de Gaulle left office in 1969 his grand design for France and Europe had nearly disappeared. Nevertheless, the vision of a Europe free from superpower domination persisted in a different guise.

There were many challenges to the hegemonic position of the Soviet Union during the cold war decades. The first opposition from within the communist world emanated from Yugoslavia, where a postwar communist regime came to power without the assistance of the Soviet Union. That fact, along with strong support at home, enabled Josip Broz, known as Marshal Tito (1892–1980), to rule the federation of Yugoslavia with an iron hand from 1945 until his death and to assert his nation's independence. Tito's resistance to Soviet control led to a major split with Stalin, and in 1948 Stalin expelled Yugoslavia from the Soviet bloc. In foreign affairs, Tito pursued an independent course that consisted of maintaining good relations with eastern European communist states and establishing strong ties with nonaligned nations, states that refused to take one side or the other in the cold war.

Tito's Yugoslavia

Developments within the Soviet Union caused more serious changes in eastern Europe. Within three years after Stalin's death in 1953, several communist leaders startled the world when they openly attacked Stalin and questioned his methods of rule. The most vigorous denunciations came from Stalin's successor, Nikita Khrushchev, during

De-Stalinization

Czech citizens confront Warsaw Pact troops in Prague during the Soviet invasion in the spring of 1968.

a secret speech at the Twentieth Party Congress in February 1956. Khrushchev subsequently embarked on a policy of de-Stalinization, that is, the end of the rule of terror and the partial liberalization of Soviet society. Government officials removed portraits of Stalin from public places, renamed institutions and localities bearing his name, and commissioned historians to rewrite textbooks to deflate Stalin's reputation. The de-Stalinization period, which lasted from 1956 to 1964, also brought a thaw in government control and resulted in the release of millions of political prisoners. One of these was Alexandr Solzhenitsyn (1919–) who, thanks to Khrushchev's support, was able to publish his novel *One Day in the Life of Ivan Denisovich* (1962), a short and moving description of life in a Siberian forced labor camp. The new political climate in the Soviet Union tempted communist leaders elsewhere to experiment with domestic reforms and seek a degree of independence from Soviet domination.

The Hungarian Challenge

The most serious challenge to Soviet control in eastern Europe came in 1956 from nationalist-minded communists in Hungary. When the communist regime in Hungary embraced the process of de-Stalinization, large numbers of Hungarian citizens demanded democracy and the breaking of ties to Moscow and the Warsaw Pact. In the wake of massive street demonstrations joined by the Hungarian armed forces, communist Imre Nagy (1896–1958) gained power and visibility as a nationalist leader who announced Hungary's neutrality and withdrawal from the Warsaw Pact. Soviet leaders viewed those moves as a serious threat to their security system. In the late autumn of 1956, Soviet tanks entered Budapest and crushed the Hungarian uprising. Soviet authorities installed János Kádár (1912–1989) as a dependable communist leader who adhered strictly to a pro-Soviet line of foreign policy and secretly executed Nagy, along with many others who had mistakenly trusted a Soviet promise of safe conduct.

The Prague Spring

Twelve years after the Hungarian tragedy, Soviets again intervened in eastern Europe, this time in Czechoslovakia. In 1968 the Communist Party leader, Alexander Dubček (1921–1992), launched a "democratic socialist revolution." He supported a liberal movement known as the "Prague Spring" and promised his fellow citizens "socialism with a human face." The Czechs' move toward liberal communism aroused fear in the Soviet Union because such ideas could lead to the unraveling of

Soviet control in eastern Europe. Intervention by the Soviet army, aided by East German, Bulgarian, and Polish units, brought an end to the Prague Spring. Khrushchev's successor, Leonid Ilyich Brezhnev (1906–1982), justified the invasion of Czechoslovakia by the Doctrine of Limited Sovereignty. This policy, more commonly called the "Brezhnev doctrine," reserved the right to invade any socialist country that was deemed to be threatened by internal or external elements "hostile to socialism." The destruction of the dramatic reform movement in Czechoslovakia served to reassert Soviet control over its satellite nations in eastern Europe and led to tightened controls within the Soviet Union.

The People's Republic of China

The birth of a communist China further transformed the cold war. With the defeat of Japan in 1945, the civil war in China resumed. Between August 1945 and the end of 1946, the nationalists and the communists conducted negotiations for a peaceful settlement, but at the same time, each side fought limited military engagements with the other and raced to take over territories once held by the Japanese. By mid-1948 the strategic balance favored the communists, who inflicted heavy military defeats on the nationalists throughout 1948 and 1949. With the People's Liberation army controlling most of mainland China, the national government under Jiang Jieshi (Chiang Kai-shek) sought refuge on the island of Taiwan, taking along most of the nation's gold reserves. From Taiwan, Jiang Jieshi continued to proclaim that the government in Taiwan was the legitimate government of all China. That rhetoric, however, did not prevent Mao Zedong, the chairman of the Chinese Communist Party, from proclaiming the establishment of the People's Republic of China on 1 October 1949. That declaration brought to an end the long period of imperialist intrusion in China and spawned a close relationship between the world's largest and most powerful socialist states. Idolizing the achievements of the Soviet Union, Chinese leaders under Mao Zedong set out to imitate Soviet socialism.

The reorganization of all aspects of Chinese society amounted to a frontal attack on Chinese traditions. First came the formation of new political institutions that were anchored in a constitution that took effect in 1954. Although the constitution stipulated a national assembly chosen by popular election, it was the Communist Party that monopolized political power through a central committee and a politburo, chaired by Mao. To protect its authority, the government orchestrated campaigns to mobilize revolutionary enthusiasm and remove from power all of those likely to be a threat to the new leaders. In a 1951 campaign that singled out individuals previously affiliated with the nationalist government or its armed forces, tens of thousands were executed while many more disappeared in labor reform camps.

Next came the economic and social transformation of Chinese society, which centered on rapid industrialization and the collectivization of agriculture (making landownership collective, not individual). Emulating the Soviet experiment of 1929, the Chinese introduced their first Five-Year Plan in 1955. Designed to speed up economic development, the Five-Year Plan emphasized improvements in infrastructure and the expansion of heavy industry at the expense of consumer goods. A series of agrarian laws promoted the unprecedented transfer of wealth among the population, virtually eliminating economic inequality on the village level. After confiscating the landholdings of rich peasants and landlords—effectively removing their source of income and influence—the government redistributed the land so that virtually every peasant had at least a small plot of land. After the government took over the grain market and prohibited farmers from marketing their crops, however, collective farms

Economic and Social Transformations

replaced private farming. Health care and primary education anchored to collectives permitted the extension of social services to a larger part of the population. In the wake of economic reforms came social reforms, many of which challenged and often eliminated Chinese family traditions. Supporting equal rights for women, Chinese authorities introduced marriage laws that eliminated such practices as child or forced marriages, gave women equal access to divorce, and legalized abortion. Foot binding, a symbol of women's subjugation, also became a practice of the past.

Fraternal Cooperation

Moscow and Beijing drew closer during the early years of the cold war. That relationship was hardly astonishing because the leaders of both communist states felt threatened by a common enemy, the United States, which sought to establish anticommunist bastions throughout Asia. Most disconcerting to Soviet and Chinese leaders was the American-sponsored rehabilitation of their former enemy, Japan, and client states South Korea and Taiwan. The Chinese-Soviet partnership matured during the early 1950s and took on a distinct form when Beijing recognized Moscow's undisputed authority in world communism in exchange for Russian military equipment and economic aid. In return, Soviet diplomats instigated a campaign in the United Nations to transfer the Chinese seat in the Security Council from Taiwan to the communist government on the mainland. The Soviet tendency to lecture the Chinese on how to construct a socialist society nonetheless undermined the growing partnership between the two nations.

Cracks in the Alliance

As the Chinese embarked on a crash program of industrialization, the Soviet Union rendered valuable assistance in the form of economic aid and technical advisors. By the mid-1950s the Soviet Union was China's principal trading partner, annually purchasing roughly half of all Chinese exports. Before long, however, cracks appeared in the Soviet-Chinese alliance. From the Chinese perspective, Soviet aid programs were far too modest and had too many strings attached. For example, Soviet military aid to China during the Korean War had to be repaid in full at a time when China was in desperate need of capital. Likewise, in 1955 the Soviet Union supplied more economic aid to noncommunist countries such as Egypt and India than to China. Another source of friction was the conflict between China and India over Tibet. After forcibly restoring Chinese sovereignty over Tibet in 1950, the Chinese ruthlessly quelled an armed resurrection in favor of Tibetan independence eleven years later. Beijing accused the government of India of fomenting the revolt, and both sides subsequently became involved in border clashes high in the Himalayas. Most infuriating to the Chinese, however, was Moscow's announcement of neutrality in the conflict, which the Soviets belied by giving a loan to India that exceeded any similar loan ever granted to China. Border clashes between Chinese and Soviet forces in central Asia and Siberia further fueled the smoldering conflict between the two communist states.

By the end of 1964, the rift between the Soviet Union and the People's Republic of China became embarrassingly public, with both sides engaging in name-calling. Because Nikita Khrushchev, fearing nuclear attack, was pursuing a policy of peaceful coexistence with the United States and western Europe at the time, the Chinese government accused the Soviets of being "revisionists," a highly insulting term in the communist vocabulary. The Soviets, for their part, accused the Chinese of being dangerous "left-wing adventurists" because Mao Zedong asserted the inevitability of war with capitalist nations. In addition to name-calling, both nations openly competed for influence in Africa and Asia, especially in the nations that had recently gained independence. The fact that the People's Republic had conducted successful nuclear tests in 1964 enhanced its prestige. An unanticipated outcome of the Chinese-Soviet split was that many countries gained an opportunity to pursue a more independent course by playing capitalists against communists and by playing Soviet communists against Chinese communists.

Détente and the Decline of Superpower Influence

Amid the complications of the cold war and the challenges issuing from allies and enemies alike, Soviet and U.S. leaders began adjusting to the reality of an unmanageable world—a reality they could no longer ignore. By the late 1960s the leaders of the Soviet Union and the United States agreed on a policy of *détente,* or a reduction in hostility, trying to cool the costly arms race and slow their competition in developing countries. Although détente did not resolve the deep-seated antagonism between the superpowers, it did signal the relaxation of cold war tensions and prompted a new spirit of cooperation.

Between 1972 and 1974, U.S. and Soviet leaders exchanged visits and signed agreements calling for cooperation in areas such as health research, environmental protection, science and technology, space ventures, and expanded cultural exchange programs. However, the spirit of détente was most visible in negotiations designed to reduce the threat posed by strategic nuclear weapons. In 1972 U.S. and Soviet negotiators concluded their Strategic Arms Limitations Talks (SALT) with two agreements and reached another accord in 1979. The two cold war antagonists cooperated despite the tensions caused by the U.S. incursion into Vietnam, Soviet involvement in Angola and other African states, and continued Soviet repression of dissidents in eastern Europe.

An Era of Cooperation

By the early 1980s, however, relations between the superpowers had deteriorated notably. The establishment of full diplomatic relations between the United States and the People's Republic of China in January 1979 and the announcement in 1981 that the United States would sell weapons to the Chinese military undermined U.S.-Soviet cooperation. The situation was aggravated in December 1979 by Soviet armed intervention to save a Marxist regime in Afghanistan. That action doomed ratification of the most recent SALT agreement by the U.S. Congress and led the U.S. government to impose economic sanctions. The era of détente nonetheless reflected a significant transformation of superpower relations. It coincided with a marked decline in superpower influence, which also changed relations between the superpowers and threatened their standing in the world. First the United States in Vietnam and then the Soviet Union in Afghanistan experienced serious military and political setbacks that undermined their global status.

The Demise of Détente

Throughout its long history, Vietnam resisted Chinese and French imperialism and, most recently, U.S. military intrusion and political influence. (See chapter 39 for Vietnam's colonial struggles against France.) In the early part of the cold war's globalization, U.S. leaders extended aid to noncommunist Vietnamese in the south after the French were defeated. Nationalist communists had installed themselves in the north. U.S. involvement in South Vietnam steadily escalated and militarized under Presidents Eisenhower, Kennedy, and Lyndon B. Johnson (1908–1973), until by 1968 more than half a million U.S. troops served in-country in defense of South Vietnamese democracy. Heavy bombing campaigns were also unleashed on North Vietnam. Even with the major U.S. presence, U.S. and South Vietnamese military leaders and troops achieved only a stalemate in their struggles with the North Vietnamese and with South Vietnamese communists organized as the National Liberation Front (NLF), derisively termed the Viet Cong or VC by U.S. soldiers. War weariness and outright, militant protests against the U.S. role in Vietnam spread in the United States, signaling a public distancing from U.S. cold war policy—especially as more and more young men died on the other side of the world.

The U.S. Defeat in Vietnam

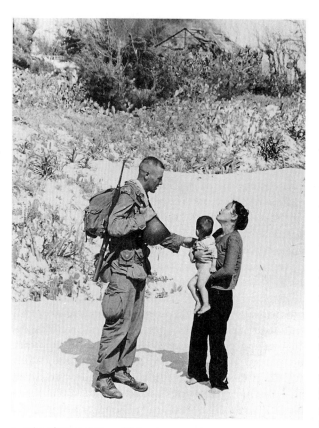

The Vietnam War: with her home going up in flames behind her, a Vietnamese woman pleads with a U.S. soldier.

Recognizing his country's distaste for the U.S. role in the Vietnam War, presidential candidate Richard Nixon pledged in 1968 to end the war. After his election, he implemented his strategy of turning over the war to the South Vietnamese (termed *Vietnamization*) by escalating the conflict. Nixon extended the war into Cambodia through bombing and invasion in 1969 and 1970, and he resumed heavy bombing of North Vietnam. At the same time, however, he opened diplomatic channels to the Soviet Union and China, hoping to get them to pressure North Vietnam into a negotiated end to the war. Under those circumstances the continuation of the battle in Vietnam seemed futile. U.S. troops gradually withdrew from the conflict, and in January 1973 the U.S. phase of the Vietnam War ended with the Paris Peace Accords, a complex set of agreements signed by Britain, France, the Soviet Union, the United States, North Vietnam, the National Liberation Front, and South Vietnam. Although the U.S. presence in Vietnam came to an end, the war did not. Within two years the agreements were torn up as forces from North Vietnam and the NLF continued their struggle to conquer South Vietnam and unite their nation. They achieved their goals with the military defeat of South Vietnam in 1975 and unification in 1976.

Soviet Setbacks in Afghanistan

Muslim Afghanistan had quietly remained aloof from the cold war as a nonaligned nation until 1978, when a pro-Soviet coup drew the republic into the cold war, precipitated foreign intervention, and fomented civil war. Once in power, the leftist People's Democratic Party of Afghanistan (PDPA) wasted little time in introducing radical reforms in education and land and family law. This movement caused a backlash. Especially in rural areas, Islamic religious and ethnic leaders objected to rapid social change and to the PDPA's brutal methods and called for armed resistance. By the summer of 1979, antigovernment rebels controlled much of the Afghan countryside. At that point the Soviet Union intervened, installing the Marxist Babrak Karmal as president. With the help of Soviet air and land forces and civilian advisors, Karmal tried to establish control over the country. He promised to combine social and economic reform with respect for Islam and Afghan traditions. Nevertheless, the Soviet-backed government remained unpopular, and a national resistance movement spread throughout the country.

For nine years, well-equipped Soviet forces fought a brutal, unsuccessful campaign against Afghan mujahideen, or Islamic warriors, who gradually gained control of most of the countryside. Weapons and money from the United States, Saudi Arabia, Iran, Pakistan, and China sustained the mujahideen in their struggle. The Central Intelligence Agency of the United States supplied the decisive weapons in the war: ground-to-air Stinger missiles, which could be used to shoot down heavily armored Soviet helicopters, and thousands of mules to haul supplies from Pakistan.

In 1986 the Soviet leadership replaced the unpopular Karmal with the equally unpopular Muhammad Najibullah, a Soviet favorite who had been in charge of the Afghan secret police. In the same year, the Kremlin also decided to pull its troops out of the costly, unpopular, and unwinnable war. A cease-fire negotiated by the United Nations in 1988 led to a full Soviet withdrawal in 1989. However, the fighting continued and by 1992 civil war broke out among factions within the mujahideen. The shared Islamic identity that mobilized and unified the mujahideen in their struggle against Soviet forces gave way to ancient tribal, ethnic, and religious rivalries. By 1994 the Taliban, an organization claiming to be an army of religious students, began a campaign to unify the Afghan lands. In 1996 they captured the capital of Kabul after an eleven-month siege, executed Najibullah, and proclaimed the Islamic State of Afghanistan.

The experiences of the superpowers in Vietnam and Afghanistan demonstrated that they had overextended their influence by involving their military forces in conflicts that did little to further their cold war policies. Those forays taxed their nations financially but, more important, caused dissatisfaction with cold war politics within the superpower nations. Internationally, the wars in Vietnam and Afghanistan undermined the prestige of the superpowers and exposed the hollowness of their claims to military superiority.

Cold War Countercultural Protests

While de Gaulle, Brezhnev, and Nixon worked from within their political systems to modify international relations, their citizens and others throughout the world agitated for the abolition of the cold war systems. By 1964 cultural criticism of the cold war and its leaders had clearly influenced the films coming out of Hollywood. The political oppression that tried to stifle dissent in the United States in the late 1940s and 1950s lifted by the early 1960s. The 1964 release of Stanley Kubrick's film *Dr. Strangelove or: How I Learned to Stop Worrying and Love the Bomb* was proof positive. The film comedically represented the leaders of the United States and the USSR as insane morons whose irrational policies guaranteed the destruction of all life on earth through nuclear war.

Dr. Strangelove belonged to an era of European and North American cultural ferment that had its roots in the global changes caused by the cold war. Anxiety about nuclear weapons and doubts about cold war policies flourished in the 1960s and 1970s, and the world's youth formed the vanguard in a countercultural revolution that challenged the basic political and cultural precepts of post–World War II societies. Disturbed by their nations' apparent commitment to war and social conformity, European and American students in particular took to the streets or disrupted their universities through mass demonstrations designed to promote peace, end the nuclear arms race and the war in Vietnam, and abolish unfair university rules and restrictions. In the United States, students at the University of California at Berkeley formed the Free Speech Movement in 1964 to encourage free political expression on campus; four years later, students in France erected barricades in Paris reminiscent of nineteenth-century French revolts.

Rock and Roll

Student activism suggested the extent to which global youth experienced empowerment in these years, whether in France, the United States, or China, where Red

Guard youths controlled much of the Cultural Revolution. This youthful influence also accounted for the worldwide popularity of rock and roll, a new form of musical expression born in the postwar era. Whereas U.S. singer Elvis Presley (1935–1977) shocked parents and attracted the young with his wild rock and roll music and dancing, British groups such as the Beatles and the Rolling Stones invaded the United States and the world in the 1960s (this phenomenon was called the "British invasion"). Rock and roll in the 1960s and 1970s also underscored the political radicalism of youths disaffected from their states' leaders and policies. The Beatles sang of "Revolution," and the Rolling Stones wrote rock musical odes to a "Street Fighting Man."

Watergate

Although himself a fan of Elvis Presley, Richard Nixon became a victim of the societal discontentment aroused by the cold war and exploited by the young. In an atmosphere of increased scrutiny of leaders, Nixon's operations in the Vietnam War (bombing and invading Cambodia) and in the Watergate scandal (1972–1974) were exposed by journalists and members of the U.S. Congress. Upset at news leaks to the *New York Times* about his unauthorized bombings in Cambodia, Nixon ordered wiretaps placed on the phone lines of reporters and members of his staff. This action started the trend toward criminal activities in the Nixon White House that culminated in the scandal surrounding a break-in at the Democratic National Headquarters (at the Watergate building) during the 1972 presidential elections.

The burglars were caught, Nixon and his staff attempted to cover up the crimes committed for the president's benefit, and journalistic and congressional investigations ultimately unraveled the criminal links that led to Nixon's resignation in August 1974. Richard Nixon was a prominent leader associated with the cold war throughout his entire political career. He left office in disgrace and reinforced the negative images of politicians featured in films such as *Dr. Strangelove* and in the youth movement. His fate suggested the vulnerability of cold war leaders whose hegemony was contested abroad and at home.

The End of the Cold War

Whereas superpower leaders intimately associated with the cold war such as Richard Nixon lost face and power, new superpower leaders such as Mikhail S. Gorbachev (1931–) arose and helped bring an end to the cold war. Some older U.S. cold warriors also made final pushes against the Soviet Union, most notably Ronald Reagan (1911–2004), president during most of the 1980s (1981–1989). Reagan reinvigorated cold war animosities, zeroing in on communism and the USSR, which he called "the evil empire." Beyond adopting this rhetorical fervor, Reagan advocated steep increases in military spending, including a controversial proposal called the Strategic Defense Initiative in 1983. Popularly termed "Star Wars" after the contemporary science fiction film, the Strategic Defense Initiative presumably would have provided the United States with full high-tech protection from nuclear attack, thereby limiting or ending one of the Soviet Union's main threats to U.S. security.

Reagan's cold war rhetoric and budgets challenged détente and the Soviet ability to match U.S. spending, but internal changes in the Soviet Union and eastern Europe worked most effectively to end communism and the cold war. Whether forced by internal dissent or by the horrendous military and economic costs of the cold war, the superpowers soon backed down from their traditional polarizing division of the world. The result was the collapse of the bipolar world, whose disintegration began in eastern Europe and the Soviet Union. Between 1989 and 1990, through a series of mostly nonviolent revolutions, the peoples of eastern and central Europe regained their independence, instituted democratic forms of government, and adopted market-based economies.

The downfall of communist regimes in Europe was the direct consequence of interrelated economic and political developments. The economic weakness of the communist regimes in eastern and central Europe and the Soviet Union became so apparent as to require reforms. The policies espoused by Soviet leader Mikhail Gorbachev, who came to power in 1985, represented an effort to address this economic deterioration, but they also unleashed a tidal wave of revolution that brought down governments from Czechoslovakia to the Soviet Union. As communism unraveled throughout eastern and central Europe, Gorbachev desperately tried to save the Soviet Union from disintegration by restructuring the economy and liberalizing society. Caught between the rising tide of radical reforms and the opposition of entrenched interests, however, there was little he could do except watch as events unfolded beyond his control. By the time the Soviet Union collapsed in 1991, the Soviet vision of socialism had ceased to inspire either fear or emulation. The cold war system of states and alliances became irrelevant to international relations.

Revolutions in Eastern and Central Europe

The inability to connect communism with nationalism left communist regimes vulnerable throughout eastern and central Europe. Those regimes were born in Moscow, transplanted by the Soviet army, and

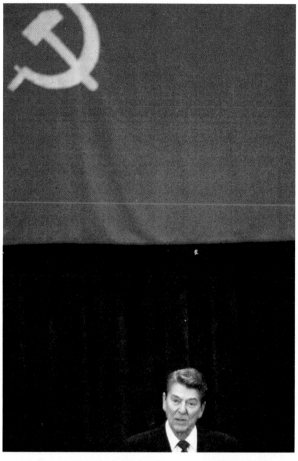

At a U.S./U.S.S.R. summit in 1985, a Soviet flag served as a dramatic backdrop and counterpoint to U.S. President Ronald Reagan's speech.

shored up by tanks and bayonets. To most eastern and central Europeans, the Soviet-imposed governments lacked legitimacy from the beginning, and despite the efforts of local communist leaders, the regimes never became firmly established.

For a while it seemed possible that Stalin's "friendly governments" might succeed in establishing rapport with indigenous populations. By the end of World War II, conservative political parties had lost credibility because they had not supported democracy in the interwar period and had subsequently aided the Nazis during the war. Conversely, left-wing parties had acquired a solid record of opposition to authoritarian regimes in general and German rule in particular. As for the Soviet Union, its prestige was high after the war because it played a major role in defeating fascism and liberating eastern and central Europe from German rule.

Moscow's Legacies

Emanating from the Soviet Union was the hope that reform might push the regimes of eastern and central Europe toward less harsh and more enlightened communist rule. Nikita Khrushchev's denunciation of the Stalin era and his vision of a more prosperous and humane communism inspired a generation of reformers in the Soviet Union and Europe. The brutal Soviet interventions in 1956 (Hungary) and 1968 (Czechoslovakia), however, dashed the aspirations and dreams of reformers. By the early 1970s, intellectuals and dissidents abandoned all hope for a humane socialism. The Polish intellectual Leszek Kolakowski echoed the sentiments of many reformers when he bitterly

Gorbachev's Impact

Polish demonstrators raise a placard with Mikhail Gorbachev's photograph, illustrating the impact of his reforms on the collapse of communism in Europe.

complained in 1971 that "the dead and by now also grotesque creature called Marxist-Leninism still hangs at the necks of the rulers like a hopeless tumor."

Despite economic stagnation, an accelerated arms race with the Reagan administration that further strained the Soviet economy, and obvious signs of discontent, the rulers of eastern and central Europe were too reluctant to confront the challenge and restructure their ailing systems. It remained for a new Soviet leader, Mikhail S. Gorbachev, to unleash the forces that resulted in the disappearance of the Soviet empire in Europe. By the time Gorbachev visited East Berlin in 1989 on the fortieth anniversary of the German Democratic Republic, he had committed himself to a restructuring of the Soviet Union and to unilateral withdrawal from the cold war. In public interviews he surprised his grim-faced hosts with the announcement that the Brezhnev Doctrine was no longer in force and that from then on each country would be responsible for its own destiny. As one observer put it, the "Sinatra doctrine" ("I did it my way") replaced the Brezhnev Doctrine. The new Soviet orientation led in rapid succession to the collapse or overthrow of regimes in Poland, Bulgaria, Hungary, Czechoslovakia, Romania, and East Germany.

Revolutions in Eastern Europe

The end of communism came first in Poland, where Solidarity—a combined trade union and nationalist movement—put pressure on the crumbling rule of the Communist Party. The Polish government legalized the previously banned Solidarity movement and agreed to multiparty elections in 1989 and 1990. The voters favored Solidarity candidates, and Lech Walesa (1943–), the movement's leader, became president of Poland. In Bulgaria popular unrest forced Todor Zhivkov (1911–1998), eastern Europe's longest surviving communist dictator, to resign in November 1989. Two months later a national assembly began dismantling the communist state. Hungarians tore down the Soviet-style political system during 1988 and 1989. In 1990 they held free elections and launched their nation on the rocky path toward democracy and a market economy.

The disintegration of communism continued elsewhere in eastern Europe. In Czechoslovakia a "velvet revolution" swept communists out of office and restored democracy by 1990. The term *velvet revolution* derived from the fact that aside from the initial suppression of mass demonstrations, little violence was associated with the transfer of power in societies formerly ruled by an iron fist. The communist leadership stood by and watched events take their course. In 1993 disagreements over the time frame for shifting to a market economy led to a "velvet divorce," breaking Czechoslovakia into two new nations, the Czech Republic and Slovakia. In Romania, in contrast, the regime of dictator Nicolae Ceauşescu (1918–1989) refused to acknowledge the necessity of reform. In 1989 *Securitate,* a brutal secret police force, savagely repressed demonstrations, setting off a national uprising that ended within four days and left Ceauşescu and his wife dead.

East Germany had long been a staunchly communist Soviet satellite. Its aging leader, Erich Honecker (1912–1994), openly objected to Gorbachev's ideas and clung to Stalinist policies. When he showed genuine bewilderment at the fact that East German citizens fled the country by the thousands through openings in the iron curtain in Hungary and Czechoslovakia, his party removed him from power. It was too late for anything other than radical changes, and when the East German regime decided to open the Berlin Wall to intra-German traffic on 9 November 1989, the end of the German Democratic Republic was in sight. The end to a divided Berlin was also in sight, literally, as thousands of east and west Berliners tore down the Berlin wall in the last weeks of 1989. In 1990 the two Germanies, originally divided by the cold war, formed a united nation.

Berliners climb the wall after it fell on 9 November 1989.

The Collapse of the Soviet Union

The desire to concentrate attention and resources on urgent matters at home motivated Gorbachev's decision to disengage his nation from the cold war and its military and diplomatic extensions. When he came to power in 1985, Gorbachev was keenly aware of the need for economic reform and the liberalization of Soviet society, although he never intended to abolish the existing political and economic system. Yet it proved impossible to fix parts of the system without undermining the whole. The desire of the Communist Party to control every aspect of the system precluded partial reforms.

Gorbachev's reform efforts focused on the ailing economy. Antiquated industrial plants, obsolete technologies, and inefficient government control of production resulted in shoddy and outmoded products. The diversion of crucial resources to the military made it impossible to produce enough consumer goods—regardless of their quality. The failure of state and collective farms to feed the population compelled the Soviet government to import grains from the United States, Canada, and elsewhere. By 1990 the government imposed rationing to cope with the scarcity of essential consumer goods and food. Economic stagnation in turn contributed to the decline of the Soviet standard of living. Ominous statistics documented the disintegration of the state-sponsored health care system: infant mortality increased while life expectancy decreased. Funding of the educational system dropped precipitously, and pollution threatened to engulf the entire country. Demoralization affected ever-larger numbers

Gorbachev's Reforms

of Soviet citizens as divorce rates climbed, corruption intensified, and alcoholism became more widespread.

Under the slogan of *uskorenie,* or "acceleration," Gorbachev tried to shock the economy out of its coma. Yet the old methods of boosting production and productivity through bureaucratic exhortation and harassment paid few dividends; in fact, they called attention to the drawbacks of centralized economic control. Gorbachev then contemplated different kinds of reform, using the term *perestroika,* or "restructuring," to describe his efforts to decentralize the economy. To make perestroika work, the Soviet leader linked it to *glasnost,* a term that referred to the opening of Soviet society to public criticism and admission of past mistakes.

Perestroika and Glasnost

Perestroika proved more difficult to implement than Gorbachev imagined, and glasnost unleashed a torrent of criticism that shook the Soviet state to its foundations. When Gorbachev pushed economic decentralization, the profit motive and the cost-accounting methods he instituted engendered the hostility of those whose privileged positions depended on the old system. Many of Gorbachev's comrades and certain factions of the military objected to perestroika and worked to undermine or destroy it. Glasnost also turned out to be a two-edged sword as it opened the door to public criticism of party leaders and Soviet institutions in a way unimaginable a short time earlier. While discontent with Soviet life burst into the open, long-repressed ethnic and nationalist sentiments bubbled to the surface, posing a threat to the multiethnic Soviet state. Only half of the 285 million Soviet citizens were Russian. The other half included numerous ethnic minorities, most of which never fully reconciled themselves to Soviet dominance.

By the summer of 1990, Gorbachev's reforms had spent themselves. As industrial and agricultural production continued their downward slide against a backdrop of skyrocketing inflation, the Soviet economy disintegrated. Inspired by the end of the Soviet empire in eastern and central Europe, many minorities now contemplated secession from the Soviet Union. The Baltic peoples—Estonians, Latvians, and Lithuanians—were first into the fray, declaring their independence in August 1991. In the following months the remaining twelve republics of the Soviet Union followed suit. The largest and most prominent of the Soviet republics, the Russian Soviet Federated Socialist Republic, and its recently elected president Boris N. Yeltsin (1931–2007), led the drive for independence. Soviet leaders vacillated between threats of repression and promises of better treatment, but neither option could stop the movement for independence.

Collapse

Although the pace of reform was neither quick nor thorough enough for some, others convinced themselves that they had gone too far. While Gorbachev was vacationing in the Crimea in August 1991, a group of conspirators—including discontented party functionaries, disillusioned KGB (secret police) officials, and dissatisfied military officers—decided to seize power. Gorbachev's former friend and ally, the flamboyant Boris Yeltsin, crushed the coup with the help of loyal Red Army units. Gorbachev emerged unscathed from house arrest, but his political career had ended. He watched from the sidelines as Yeltsin dismantled the Communist Party and pushed the country toward market-oriented economic reforms. As the Soviet system disintegrated, several of its constituent regions moved toward independence. On 25 December 1991 the Soviet flag fluttered for the last time atop the Kremlin, and by the last day of that year the Union of Soviet Socialist Republics ceased to exist.

Toward an Uncertain Future

In many ways the cold war provided comfort to the world—however cold that comfort seemed at the time. World War II left most of the major imperialist, fascist, and

Map 38.3 **The collapse of the Soviet Union and European communist regimes, 1991.** Note the number of states suddenly created by the breakup of the Soviet Union. How would this affect the ability of each to survive, both economically and politically?

militarist nations in shambles, and the United States and the Soviet Union stepped into what could have been an uncomfortable vacuum in global leadership. Perilous and controlling it may have been, but the cold war that resulted from the ideological contest between the superpowers had ordered and defined the world for almost fifty years. The cold war also shaped how the nations and peoples of the world perceived themselves—as good capitalists fighting evil communists, as progressive socialists battling regressive capitalists, or as nonaligned peoples striving to follow their own paths. Although those perceptions placed constraints on the choices open to them, particularly given the control exerted by the United States and the USSR at the peak of their power, the choices nonetheless were familiar. At the end of the cold war, those easy choices disappeared. The stunning impact of the end of the cold war reverberated in policy-making circles and on the streets.

The most immediate and obvious loss that accompanied the end of the cold war involved the alliance systems built by the two former superpowers. At one time, critics of the cold war routinely denounced military alliances such as NATO or the Warsaw Pact for promoting an expensive arms race and for constantly threatening to transform local conflicts into nuclear confrontations between the superpowers. After the end of the cold war, it became fashionable to praise the same alliances for their ability to manage rather than to escalate such conflicts. Moreover, many observers praised the cold war system for providing peace and security around the world despite the nuclear balance of terror. The loss of deterrence against global disorder and violence was matched by a corresponding lack of certainty regarding the future and by a declining sense of purpose in an era no longer characterized by ideological struggle.

A Future without Divisions

The disappearance of communist regimes in eastern Europe, the dissolution of the Soviet Union, and the increasing market orientation of the People's Republic of China virtually guaranteed the diminishing popularity of the communist model. To be sure, a few states, such as Cuba and North Korea, clung to communism, but their economies teetered on the edge of collapse, and, without the support once furnished by the Soviet Union, their long-term viability as communist regimes was doubtful. The end of the cold war suggested the possibility of a radical shift in power relations, a global realignment that marked a new era of world history devoid of the categories embraced during the cold war.

———————————

The cold war defined much of the global political landscape after World War II. The United States and the Soviet Union stepped into the void created by the disappearance of European empires after 1945, and global encounters between the proponents of democracy and communism stretched from a divided Europe to Korea, Cuba, Vietnam, and Afghanistan. Adding elements of tension to these conflicts were the increasingly sophisticated nuclear weapons and delivery systems that threatened radioactive disaster and human annihilation. Like the nuclear weapons systems, neither cold war societies nor the cold war remained static. The cold war evolved from mutual hostility to peaceful coexistence and détente, finally reaching extinction at the close of the twentieth century. Facing opposition at home and military humiliation abroad, the superpowers relinquished their hegemonic dreams of world control. From its beginning to its end, the cold war suggested the powerful new global forces at work in the wake of World War II. The process of decolonization—itself complicated by the cold war—also symbolized this same phenomenon of radical postwar alterations in the global balance of power.

CHRONOLOGY

1948–1949	Berlin blockade and airlift
1949	Division of Berlin and Germany
1949	Establishment of People's Republic of China
1950–1953	Korean War
1956	Uprising in Hungary
1959	Castro comes to power in Cuba
1961	Bay of Pigs invasion
1961	Construction of Berlin Wall
1962	Cuban missile crisis
1964	Sino-Soviet rift
1965–1973	U.S. troops to Vietnam
1968	Prague Spring
1973	U.S. Defeat in Vietnam
1989	Soviet withdrawal from Afghanistan
1989	Fall of Berlin Wall
1990	Reunification of Germany
1991	Collapse of the Soviet Union
1991	End of the cold war

FOR FURTHER READING

Pertti Ahonen. *After the Expulsion: West Germany and Eastern Europe, 1945–1990.* New York, 2003. Study of the diplomatic problems faced by postwar West Germany.

David Calleo. *Beyond American Hegemony: The Future of the Western Alliance.* New York, 1987. A broad treatment of Europe during and after the cold war.

Samuel Farber. *Origins of the Cuban Revolution Reconsidered.* Chapel Hill, 2006. Argues that the Cuban Revolution of 1959–1961 was born of endemic ideologies and political visions rather than being simply a reaction to American policy.

John Lewis Gaddis. *The Cold War: A New History.* New York, 2005. A fresh and concise history of the cold war by the dean of cold war historians.

———. *Strategies of Containment: A Critical Appraisal of Postwar American National Security Policy.* New York, 1982. Insightful work that traces the U.S. policy of containment from its inception to the late 1970s.

Greg Grandin. *The Last Colonial Massacre: Latin America in the Cold War.* Chicago, 2004. Using Guatemala as a case study, this impassioned work argues that the cold war in the region was a contest not between U.S. liberalism and Soviet communism but between different versions of democracy.

Margot A. Henriksen. *Dr. Strangelove's America: Society and Culture in the Atomic Age.* Berkeley, 1997. Analyzes the crucial role the bomb played in shaping postwar U.S. society.

Akira Iriye. *The Cold War in Asia: A Historical Introduction.* Englewood Cliffs, N.J., 1974. A leading diplomatic historian provides an excellent introduction to the subject.

Madeline Kalb. *The Congo Cables: The Cold War in Africa—From Eisenhower to Kennedy.* New York, 1982. Proper attention for an often neglected aspect of the cold war.

Bruce Kuniholm. *The Origins of the Cold War in the Near East.* Princeton, 1980. A dissection of great power diplomacy and conflicts that focuses on Greece, Turkey, and Iran.

Walter Lafeber. *America, Russia, and the Cold War, 1945–1992.* 7th ed. New York, 1993. A standard work that emphasizes the corrosive effects the cold war had on democratic values in the United States.

Elaine Tyler May. *Homeward Bound: American Families in the Cold War Era.* New York, 1988. An insightful analysis of how the cold war and atomic age affected family and gender roles in U.S. society.

Roy A. Medvedev and Zhores A. Medvedev. *Khrushchev: The Years in Power.* New York, 1976. One of the more insightful accounts of Khrushchev and de-Stalinization.

Louis A. Perez. *Cuba: Between Reform and Revolution.* 3rd ed. New York, 2005. A sweeping history vividly written.

Christopher A. Preble. *John F. Kennedy and the Missile Gap.* DeKalb, Ill., 2004. Explores the ways that President Kennedy used the myth of a missile gap to further American economic interests.

William Stueck. *Rethinking the Korean War: A New Diplomatic and Strategic History.* Princeton, 2002. Reappraisal of the Korean War in a cold war context.

William Taubman. *Stalin's America Policy: From Entente to Détente to Cold War.* New York, 1982. An important work that focuses on the Soviet perspective of the cold war.

Odd Arne Westad. *The Global War: Third World Interventions and the Making of Our Times.* New York, 2005. Integrates the Third World into the history of the cold war by tracing U.S. and Soviet interventions.

Stephen Whitfield. *The Culture of the Cold War.* Baltimore, 1991. An in-depth analysis of how the cold war and domestic anti-communism shaped U.S. culture from the 1940s to the early 1960s.

Daniel Yergin. *Shattered Peace: The Origins of the Cold War and the National Security State.* Boston, 1977. An interpretative history that looks at the origins of the cold war and its impact on U.S. political life.

39

The End of Empire

Independence in Asia
India's Partitioned Independence
Nationalist Struggles in Vietnam
Arab National States and the Problem of Palestine

Decolonization in Africa
Forcing the French out of North Africa
Black African Nationalism and Independence
Freedom and Conflict in Sub-Saharan Africa

After Independence: Long-Term Struggles in the Postcolonial Era
Communism and Democracy in Asia
Islamic Resurgence in Southwest Asia and North Africa
Politics and Economics in Latin America
War and Peace in Sub-Saharan Africa

"Hé Ram" were the last words that escaped his lips after three bullets savagely ripped through his frail body. Roughly translated, he uttered, "O! God," and then died. It had begun as a day much like any other in the life of Mohandas K. Gandhi (1869–1948), or "Bapuji" as he was fondly called—a dear father of the country of India. On 30 January 1948, a few months after India gained its independence from Great Britain, he awakened at Birla House in Delhi at an early hour, 3:00 A.M., to continue his work hammering out solutions to the problems that plagued his land. That morning, he labored on a draft of a new constitution for the Indian National Congress, stressing as usual his major concerns for his newly independent and strife-ridden nation: that villages be empowered, that discrimination based on the caste system be abolished, that religious intolerance and violence between Hindus and Muslims cease. Still distraught over the partitioning of his land into a Hindu India and Muslim Pakistan, he had weakened himself after independence through fasts and hunger strikes staged as *satyagraha,* or "truth and firmness," protests against the killings of Hindus and Muslims and the mistreatment of Pakistan. He weighed a mere 107 pounds that day.

Alternating between working, talking with visitors, and napping, Gandhi finally took a meal at 4:30 P.M. He nibbled on raw and cooked vegetables and oranges, and drank goat's milk and a special brew made with aloe juice, lemons, ginger, and strained butter. A little over half an hour later, he made his way to the evening prayer meeting he was to lead. A bit late, the skies already darkening, he took a shortcut across the emerald green, finely trimmed lawns of Birla House to reach the dais where he would speak. As he approached the dais, he stopped to press his palms together, offering the traditional Hindu greeting to the crowd waiting at the meeting. At that moment, out of the crowd stepped a large and impatient man who suddenly pulled a Beretta pistol from his pants pocket and fired the three shots that ended the life of the man many credited with Indian independence, the man seen as the very soul and conscience of India. The force of the shots crumpled Gandhi's thin body, his chest and abdomen riddled by bullets. As he slumped to the ground, his glasses fell from his face, his sandals slipped from his feet, and large crimson blood stains spread starkly over his white homespun shawl. After he whispered "Hé Ram," his breathing stilled.

Two days before he was assassinated by the Hindu extremist Nathuram Godse, Gandhi prophetically said, "If I am to die by the bullet of a mad man, I must do so smiling. There must be no anger within me. God must be in my heart and on my lips." Gandhi died as he had wanted, and as he lived, without anger and with God on his lips. His assassination, however, stood in bleak contrast to the nonviolence embraced by Gandhi throughout his life. Gandhi

OPPOSITE: **This saintly image of Mohandas K. Gandhi captures his spiritual significance to the independence movement in India both before and after his death.**

could have been forgiven some anger given the apparent failure of his nonviolence doctrine in the days after independence—a failure made publicly evident in communal killings after partition and personally evident in his violent death. Not all Hindus agreed with Gandhi's rejection of violence and avowal of religious tolerance for Muslims. Before he was executed by hanging in 1949, his assassin Godse declared Gandhi a "curse for India, a force for evil."

Gandhi's murder suggested the troubles and traumas faced by nations and peoples adjusting to independence from colonial rule, but his martyrdom also enshrined his principles of nonviolence and religious tolerance in Indian life after independence. Gandhi's death discredited Hindu extremism and halted communal violence, for a time. He became a more mythic hero in India, a new national symbol to be invoked in times of trouble and violence. His life and death spoke to the promise and perils of independence and its aftermath. Despite the hazards of life in a world without empires, peoples in the colonial world fought tenaciously for independence and then for national unity after World War II.

Like the cold war, decolonization contributed significantly to the global political transformation after World War II. Decolonization, in essence the relinquishing of all colonial possessions by imperial powers or the end to empires, brought the world to its current international standing. Imperial agents lost their control, new independent states gained autonomy and self-determination, and—given the concurrent developments in the cold war—the globe was no longer demarcated by clearly identifiable spheres of influence. These two developments, the cold war and the end of empire, intertwined to reshape the world in the late twentieth century. The end of empire was one of the most important outcomes of World War II, as dozens of new, independent nations emerged from the British, French, Dutch, Spanish, and Portuguese empires established in previous centuries. With the emergence of two superpowers dedicated to the overthrow of empire, the stage was set for a drastic overturning of colonial rule. As cold war animosities deepened, however, the leaders of the Soviet Union and the United States tended to view new nations and struggling nationalist movements through a cold war prism. Emerging nations were often confronted by the demand that they take sides and choose between capitalism and communism. At times that demand compromised their independence, particularly in new nations deemed strategically important by the superpowers. Because the pressure exerted by the superpowers included the threat of nuclear weapons, the leaders of newly independent nations worried about upsetting the global balance of nuclear terror.

The demands of the cold war, however, could not dim the joy that colonized peoples felt on gaining independence. The imperial encounters engineered by European societies in the previous centuries ceased swiftly after World War II, leaving previously colonial peoples in charge of their own destinies. No brief treatment of such a broad and variegated process as decolonization can do justice to each individual nation, particularly because more than ninety nations gained independence between the end of World War II and 1980. Nations achieved independence at different times: India and Pakistan became independent nations as early as 1947, Zimbabwe (Southern Rhodesia) as late as 1980. Algerians in North Africa fought a long, hard war against the French for freedom, whereas some peoples in sub-Saharan Africa followed less torturous routes to independence. Vietnam became deeply embroiled in the cold war even as it successfully fought French imperial domination, whereas other countries managed to avoid through neutrality or nonalignment becoming too perilously enmeshed in that ideological contest. Regardless of freedom's timetable, new and developing nations around the world discovered, as Gandhi had, that independence was just the first step on a much longer, and often much more difficult, road to national unity and social and economic stability.

Peoples in the former colonial world labored to build national identities, balancing their traditions against demands for development. Such difficulties were true for nations in areas of the world where independence came long ago and in areas where peoples achieved independence from colonial or imperial rule recently. Latin American nations still struggled to achieve political stability free from European and U.S. interference, and South Africans put an end to white rule only after decades of political fighting and negotiation. Asian and African lands faced daunting challenges in their pursuit of domestic or regional goals in a rapidly changing world, and they worked to transform their societies in the midst of religious, sectarian, or ethnic crises or neoimperial or superpower pressures. Despite all the complications of decolonization and its aftermath, colonial peoples in Asia and Africa fought for freedom and then for security. The desire of nations to seek peace and stability after independence seemed reasonable, especially because independence often led to numerous problems. Freedom did not remain elusive for the nations of Asia, Africa, and Latin America, but peace often did—a fact Gandhi acknowledged in the days after Indian independence and on the day of his death.

Independence in Asia

In the wake of World War II, the power of Asian nationalism was irrepressible. New nations emerged throughout Asia, from India and Pakistan in south Asia to diverse Arab nations in southwest Asia and to Vietnam, Cambodia, and Laos in southeast Asia. These lands encountered different conditions in their quests for independence and freedom from imperial control, but everywhere Asian nationalists rallied their people against colonialism and imperialism. Whether fighting against colonial powers, which established formal political and territorial control, or against imperial powers, which often exercised a more informal and indirect control, Asians were successful. The result of their efforts, measured in years or decades, was independence and the end of empire in Asia.

India's Partitioned Independence

In the 1930s Great Britain had granted numerous reforms in response to the tireless campaign of Mohandas K. Gandhi and the Congress Party, as well as Muhammad Ali Jinnah and the Muslim League. The gradual trend toward Indian self-rule, as in the India Act of 1935, faced challenges in the form of increasing calls for independent yet separate Hindu and Muslim states. World War II, however, interrupted the drive for any sort of self-rule.

Under the leadership of Winston Churchill, who despised Gandhi and vowed never "to preside over the liquidation of the British empire," measures for home rule were suspended, and India was ordered to support the war effort. British recalcitrance about Indian independence evaporated after the war, however. The British people voted Churchill out of office. His conservative government was replaced with a Labour government more inclined to dismantle the empire. The economic devastation of the war made it unrealistic for Britain to continue bearing the financial burden of empire in India.

The Coming of Self-Rule

The issue of Muslim separatism grew in importance as the probability of Indian independence became more pronounced, and Muslims increasingly feared their minority status in a free India dominated by Hindus. Muhammad Ali Jinnah (1876–1948), leader of the Muslim League, felt no qualms about frankly expressing Muslim concerns and desires for a separate Muslim state, even as Congress Party leaders such as Jawaharlal Nehru (1889–1964) and Gandhi urged all Indians to act and feel as one nation, undivided by what came to be known as communalism—emphasizing religious over national identity. In August 1946, in the midst of negotiations with the British to reach

Jawaharlal Nehru (left) and Mohandas K. Gandhi, Hindu leaders of India's independence movement.

Partition and Violence

terms regarding independence, the Muslim League called for a Day of Direct Action, even though the league's leaders recognized that Muslim demonstrations might lead to rioting and fighting between Muslims and Hindus. Some six thousand people died in the Great Calcutta Killing that resulted, further fueling communal feeling and adding weight to Jinnah's claim: "The only solution to India's problem is Pakistan."

The idea of partition, the division of India into separate Hindu and Muslim states, violated the stated ideals of men such as Gandhi and Nehru, who sickened at the prospect and only reluctantly came to accept the notion of a divided and independent India—perhaps in part because they belonged to the vast Hindu majority in South Asia. Gandhi nonetheless condemned the division of his homeland as "vivisection," using a term that refers to the cutting up of a living body. He avoided the celebrations on 15 August 1947 that accompanied independence for India and Pakistan, glumly prophesying that "rivers of blood" would flow in the wake of partition. His vision came true as the terms of partition were announced and hundreds of thousands of Muslim and Hindu refugees migrated to either Muslim Pakistan (divided between parts of Bengal in the east and Punjab in the west) or Hindu India. By mid-1948 an estimated ten million refugees made the tortuous journey to one or the other state, and between half a million and one million people had died in the violence that accompanied those massive human migrations. Gandhi undertook measures, including hunger strikes, in the hope of quelling the violence between Muslims and Hindus; he continually urged all Indians and Pakistanis to adhere to the practice of nonviolence. When Gandhi was shot he became a martyr to his cause, killed by the violence he so abhorred.

Sources from the Past

Muhammad Ali Jinnah on the Need for a Muslim Pakistan

Muhammad Ali Jinnah (1876–1948) served as the most visible and articulate leader of India's Muslims during the first half of the twentieth century. Like Mohandas K. Gandhi, he initially promoted cooperation and unity among Muslims and Hindus in order to achieve freedom from British rule. He came to feel strongly, however, that Muslims in an independent but Hindu-controlled India would only suffer from the discrimination they already faced from the Hindu majority. In the following speech to the Muslim League in 1940, Jinnah formulated some of the reasons why Muslims indeed deserved and already constituted their own nation.

It is extremely difficult to appreciate why our Hindu friends fail to understand the real nature of Islam and Hinduism. They are not religions in the strict sense of the word, but are, in fact, different and distinct social orders, and it is a dream that the Hindus and Muslims can ever evolve a common nationality, and this misconception of one Indian nation has gone far beyond the limits and is the cause of most of your troubles and will lead India to destruction if we fail to revise our notions in time. The Hindus and Muslims belong to two different religious philosophies, social customs, literatures. They neither intermarry nor interdine together and, indeed, they belong to two different civilizations which are based mainly on conflicting ideas and conceptions. Their aspects on life and of life are different. It is quite clear that Hindus and Mussalmans [Muslims] derive their inspiration from different sources of history. They have different epics, different heroes, and different episodes. Very often the hero of one is the foe of the other and, likewise, their victories and defeats overlap. To yoke together two such nations under a single state, one as a numerical minority and the other as a majority, must lead to growing discontent. . . .

[W]e know that the history of the last twelve hundred years has failed to achieve unity and has witnessed, during the ages, India always divided into Hindu India and Muslim India. The present artificial unity of India dates back only to the British conquest and is maintained by the British bayonet, but termination of the British regime, which is implicit in the recent declaration of His Majesty's government, will be the herald of the entire break-up with worse disaster than has ever taken place during the last one thousand years under Muslims. Surely that is not the legacy which Britain would bequeath to India after one hundred fifty years of her rule, nor would Hindu and Muslim India risk such a sure catastrophe. Muslim India cannot accept any constitution which must necessarily result in a Hindu majority government. Hindus and Muslims brought together under a democratic system forced upon the minorities can only mean Hindu raj [rule]. . . .

Mussalmans are a nation according to any definition of a nation, and they must have their homelands, their territory, and their state. We wish to live in peace and harmony with our neighbors as a free and independent people. We wish our people to develop to the fullest our spiritual, cultural, economic, social, and political life in a way that we think best and in consonance with our own ideals and according to the genius of our people. Honesty demands and the vital interests of millions of our people impose a sacred duty upon us to find an honorable and peaceful solution, which would be just and fair to all.

FOR FURTHER REFLECTION

How does Jinnah employ the idea of "difference" to justify his calls for a separate Muslim state in an independent India?

SOURCE: Muhammad Ali Jinnah, "Hindus and Muslims: Two Separate Nations," from *Sources of Indian Tradition,* 2nd ed., vol. 2, edited by Stephen Hay. New York, 1988, pp. 228–31.

After Gandhi's death Nehru announced, "The light has gone out of our lives and there is darkness everywhere." That sentiment expressed the void left by Gandhi's assassination, but efforts to build up the separate and independent nations of India and Pakistan continued. The hostility between migrating Hindus and Muslims spilled over into the enmity between the two states, complicating efforts to build their independent

Conflict between India and Pakistan

Map 39.1 **Decolonization in Asia. Date is year of independence.** Note the dates of independence for the colonies of Great Britain, the Netherlands, the United States, and France. Why did independence occur in such a short time span for most of these colonies?

nations. War broke out in 1947 over the province of Kashmir, which was claimed by both states, and their continuing hostility made India and Pakistan vulnerable to the pressures of the cold war. When Pakistan lost the battle over Kashmir, it sought an alliance with the United States to strengthen its position. As India's prime minister, Nehru favored a policy of nonalignment, but India accepted military aid from the Soviet Union. Partition gave the superpowers a tenuous foothold in South Asia, given Nehru's successful neutrality and his ability to garner economic and military aid from both superpowers.

Though mired in violence, Indian independence became a reality with momentous consequences for the process of decolonization. India was the jewel in the crown of the British empire, and its breakaway marked a significant turning point. Just as Gandhi's nonviolent resistance to British rule inspired nationalists around the globe before and after World War II, independence in India and Pakistan further encouraged anti-imperial movements throughout Asia and Africa. Moreover, once India left the British empire, there could be little doubt about the fate of Britain's remaining imperial possessions.

Unlike the Dutch and the French, who at times tenaciously battled to maintain imperial control in Asia, the British recognized that Europeans could not rule in Asia without the cooperation of colonial peoples. Also unlike the Dutch and the French, the British could rely on their own models of decolonization, previously tested in Canada. Like Canada, India and Pakistan gained independence yet retained ties to

Britain, becoming Dominion members in the British Commonwealth and adopting English as their first official language.

Another way in which Indian independence inspired other nations and set a pattern for grappling with decolonization in the midst of a cold war was through Nehru's promotion of a nonalignment strategy. Nehru proved instrumental in fashioning a compelling position for newly independent nations caught in the cold war and in the superpower tug-of-war contests for the loyalties of new nations. He became one of the impassioned defenders of nonalignment, especially at the Bandung Conference where he was one of the most visible participants. In a speech made at the conference, he articulated the policy clearly:

> The preservation of peace forms the central aim of India's policy. It is in the pursuit of this policy that we have chosen the path of nonalinement [nonalignment] in any military or like pact of alliance. Nonalinement does not mean passivity of mind or action, lack of faith or conviction. It does not mean submission to what we consider evil. It is a positive and dynamic approach to such problems that confront us. We believe that each country has not only the right to freedom but also to decide its own policy and way of life. Only thus can true freedom flourish and a people grow according to their own genius.

Leaders of new African and Asian countries first discussed nonalignment at the Bandung Conference. In April 1955 leaders from twenty-three Asian and six African nations met in Bandung, Indonesia, partly to find a "third path," an alternative to choosing either the United States or the Soviet Union. Besides neutrality in the cold war, the Bandung Conference stressed the struggle against colonialism and racism, and Indonesian president Achmad Sukarno (1901–1970) proudly proclaimed Bandung "the first international conference of coloured peoples in the history of mankind." Bandung was the precursor of the broader Nonaligned Movement, which held occasional meetings so that its members could discuss matters of common interest, particularly their relations with the United States and the Soviet Union. The movement's primary goal was to maintain formal neutrality. However, the Nonaligned Movement suffered from a chronic lack of unity among its members and ultimately failed to present a genuinely united front. Although theoretically nonaligned with either cold war superpower, many member states had close ties to one or the other, and this situation caused dissension within the movement. For example, the Philippines and Cuba clearly supported the U.S. and Soviet camps, respectively. Nevertheless, other individual states avoided becoming pawns in the cold war, and the new nations succeeded in declaring independence from the cold war by announcing the policy of nonalignment.

Nationalist Struggles in Vietnam

In contrast to India, Vietnam over time had more difficulty in keeping its nationalist struggle for independence separate from the complications of the cold war. In its fight for independence, Vietnam became deeply enmeshed in the cold war contest between capitalism and communism, but immediately after World War II the Vietnamese first engaged in a battle to free themselves from French colonial control. Vietnam's nationalist communist leader, Ho Chi Minh (1890–1969), had exploited wartime conditions to advance the cause of Vietnamese independence.

After the Japanese conquest of Vietnam, which effectively ended French rule, Ho helped oust the Japanese from Vietnam in the waning days of World War II. He then issued the Vietnamese Declaration of Independence, which was modeled on the U.S. declaration. However, the French, humiliated by their country's easy defeat and occupation by the Germans, sought to reclaim their world-power status through their

Nonalignment

Suez Canal - artifical sea level waterway in Egypt connecting Med/Red Sea 1869

route between Europe & Asia without going around Africa

Fighting the French

Ho Chi Minh, leader of North Vietnam from 1945 to 1969 and one of southeast Asia's most influential communist leaders.

imperial possessions. Armed with British and U.S. weapons, the French recaptured Saigon and much of southern Vietnam in 1945. Faced with the hostility of the northern nationalist communists, organized as the Viet Minh, the French retook the north brutally, bombing Hanoi and Haiphong and killing at least ten thousand civilians. By 1947 the French appeared to have secured their power, especially in the cities, but that security proved to be temporary. Much like the Chinese communists in their battles against the Japanese and then against the nationalists in the postwar years, the Vietnamese resistance forces, led by Ho Chi Minh and General Vo Nguyen Giap (1912–), took to the countryside and mounted a campaign of guerrilla warfare. The Vietnamese communists grew increasingly influential in the anti-imperial war, especially after 1949 when communist China sent aid and arms to the Viet Minh. Thus strengthened, they defeated the French at their fortress in Dienbienphu in 1954. The French had to sue for peace at the conference table.

The Geneva Conference and Partial Independence

The peace conference, held in Geneva in 1954, determined that Vietnam should be temporarily divided at the seventeenth parallel; North Vietnam would be controlled by Ho Chi Minh and the communist forces, whereas South Vietnam would remain in the hands of noncommunists. The communist affiliation of Ho and his comrades, along with the globalization of the cold war that accompanied the Korean War, persuaded the United States to lend its support first to the French war effort and then to the government of South Vietnam. U.S. president Dwight Eisenhower applied the domino theory to Vietnam. Violating the terms of the Geneva Agreements, which required elections that would likely have brought Ho to power, South Vietnam's leaders, with U.S. support, avoided elections and sought to build a government that would prevent the spread of communism in South Vietnam and elsewhere in Asia. Ngo Dinh Diem (1901–1963), the first president of the Republic of (South) Vietnam, and other South Vietnamese leaders did not garner popular support with the people, however, and growing discontent sparked the spread of guerrilla war in the south.

In 1960 Vietnamese nationalists formed the National Liberation Front to fight for freedom from South Vietnamese rule. Although Vietnamese from the south made up the majority in this organization, it received direction, aid, weapons, and ultimately troops from the north also. In turn, the government in the north received economic and military assistance from the Soviet Union and China, and a cold war stalemate ensued.

Cold War Stalemate

Given the lack of popular support for Diem and U.S.-style democratic reforms, the nationalist communist attacks against the South Vietnamese government met with continued success. In 1965 President Lyndon Johnson (1908–1973) embarked on a course of action that exponentially increased U.S. involvement in Vietnam. He ordered a bombing campaign against North Vietnam and sent U.S. ground troops to augment the South Vietnamese army. Yet, even with the overwhelming firepower and military personnel, the best the United States and South Vietnam could achieve against the Viet Cong was a draw. North Vietnam found a stalemate quite acceptable. Vietnamese forces fought for freedom from outside interference of any sort and could show patience while making progress toward independence. They were trapping U.S. troops in a quagmire and a war of attrition typical of successful guerrilla operations against powerful foes. Still, the nationalists' aspirations were thwarted and a long struggle remained. The stalemate in Vietnam dragged on, demonstrating the perils of cold war politics in the age of decolonization for democrats and communists, for small nations and superpowers (see chapter 38 for the U.S. defeat in Vietnam).

Arab National States and the Problem of Palestine

With the exception of Palestine, the Arab states of southwest Asia had little difficulty freeing themselves from the colonial powers of France and Britain by the end of World War II. Before the war, Arab states agitated for concessions under the mandate system, which limited Arab nationalist aspirations after the Great War. In fact, Egypt had almost complete autonomy from British rule, an autonomy limited by British military control of the strategic Suez Canal and the oil-rich Persian Gulf.

After the war, although Syria, Iraq, Lebanon, and Jordan gained complete independence, significant vestiges of imperial rule impeded Arab sovereignty. The battle to rid southwest Asia of those remnants of imperialism took some twists and turns as the superpowers interfered in the region, drawn by its vast reserves of oil, the lifeblood of the cold war's military-industrial complexes. Throughout, one ambiguous legacy of imperialism—Palestine—absorbed much of the region's energies and emotions.

Arab Independence

Great Britain served as the mandate power in Palestine after the Great War, and before and during its mandate made conflicting promises to the Palestinian Arabs and to the Jews migrating to Palestine to establish a secure homeland where they could avoid persecution. With the Balfour Declaration of 1917, the British government committed itself to the support of a homeland for Jews in Palestine, a commitment engendered in part by the vibrant Zionist movement that had been growing in Europe since the 1890s. Zionists were dedicated to combating the violent anti-Semitism prevailing in central and eastern Europe by establishing a national Jewish state. The Zionist dream of returning to Palestine, considered the site of the original Jewish homeland, received a boost from the Balfour Declaration and from the Allies' support for it at the Paris Peace Conference in 1919. Thus the British were compelled to allow Jewish migration to Palestine under their mandate, but they also had to allay the fears of those in possession of the land—the Palestinian Arabs. The British therefore limited the migration and settlement of Jews and promised to protect the Arabs' political and economic rights.

Palestine

This British attempt to balance the causes of two conflicting groups was unsuccessful, and large-scale violence was prevented only through the use of imperial military forces. To this day the dilemma of how to reconcile the claims of two peoples who became staunch foes remains unresolved. Arab Palestinians rejected British rule and Jewish settlement, seeing both as links in an imperial chain of control. The Jews migrating to Palestine were mostly of European descent, and threatened Arab interests when they purchased land and established kibbutzim, or communal farms. The Palestinian Muslims perceived the Jews as alien interlopers in their land. In the 1920s and 1930s, Arab resentment against the British and the Jews exploded in anti-Jewish riots and demonstrations. At the same time, European Jews were dangerously under attack. Under the pressure of Nazi persecution, Jews migrated to Palestine in increasing numbers in the 1930s, and Zionists in Palestine armed themselves to protect Jewish settlers against Arab reprisals. Those conditions exacerbated the tense situation in Palestine.

At the end of World War II, a battle brewed. As Arab states around Palestine gained their freedom from imperial rule, they developed a pan-Arab nationalism sparked by support for their fellow Arabs in Palestine and opposition to the possibility of a Jewish state there. The Holocaust, along with the British policy of limiting Jewish migration to Palestine after the war, intensified the Jewish commitment to build a state capable of defending the world's remaining Jews—and the tens of thousands of Palestinian Jews who had fought in the British army during the war were seen as potential defenders of the new state.

The Creation of Israel

The British could not adjudicate the competing claims of the Arabs and the Jews in Palestine. While the Arabs insisted on complete independence under Arab rule, in 1945 the Jews embarked on a course of violent resistance to the British to compel recognition of Jewish demands for self-rule and open immigration. The British gave up in 1947, stating that they intended to withdraw from Palestine and turn over the region to the newly created United Nations. Delegates to the UN General Assembly debated the idea of dividing Palestine into two states, one Arab and the other Jewish. The United States and the Soviet Union lent their support to that notion, and in November 1947 the General Assembly announced a proposal for the division of Palestine into two distinct states. Arabs inside and outside Palestine found this solution unacceptable, and in late 1947 civil war broke out. Arab and Jewish troops battled each other as the British completed their withdrawal from Palestine, and in May 1948 the Jews in Palestine proclaimed the creation of the independent state of Israel. This act precipitated what turned out to be the first of many Arab-Israeli wars as Egypt, Jordan, Syria, Lebanon, and Iraq led the war on Israel in support of the Palestinian Arabs.

The Arab states, expecting a swift and triumphant victory over the outnumbered Jewish forces, underestimated the staying power and military skills of the new Israeli military. Arab attacks and campaigns, although boldly fought, were uncoordinated, and the Israelis managed to achieve a stunning victory, gaining territories far larger than those that would have been granted to the Jewish state under the United Nations partition plan. A truce went into effect in early 1949 under UN auspices, and the partition of Palestine resulted. Jerusalem and the Jordan River valley were divided between the new Israeli state and the Kingdom of Jordan, while Israel controlled the coastal areas of Palestine and the Negev Desert to the Red Sea. During and after the fighting, hundreds of thousands of Palestinian Arabs fled, first from the war and then from the prospect of life under Jewish political control, and for the surrounding Arab states these refugees served as a symbol of the Arabs' defeat in Palestine and as a spur to the Arab nations' determination to rid their region of the hated presence of Israel.

Egypt and Arab Nationalism

Egyptian military leaders, particularly officers under the leadership of Gamal Abdel Nasser (1918–1970), committed themselves to opposing Israel and taking command of the Arab world. Forsaking constitutional government and democratic principles, they began a political revolution and campaign of state reform through militarism, suppressing the ideological and religious opposition organized by communists and the Muslim Brotherhood. In July 1952 Nasser and other officers staged a bloodless coup that ended the monarchy of Egypt's King Farouk. After a series of complicated intrigues, Nasser named himself prime minister in 1954 and took control of the government. He then labored assiduously to develop Egypt economically and militarily and make it the fountainhead of pan-Arab nationalism.

In his efforts to strengthen Egypt, Nasser adopted an internationalist position akin to Nehru's nonalignment policy in India. Nasser's neutralism, like Nehru's, was based on the belief that cold war power politics were a new form of imperialism. Nasser condemned states that joined with foreign powers in military alliances, such as the Bagh-

Map 39.2 **The Arab-Israeli conflict, 1949–1982.** Compare the boundaries proposed by the UN partition of Palestine with those claimed by Israel after 1948–49. What were the strategic advantages of the extra territories claimed by Israel in 1948–49?

dad Pact, a British- and U.S.-inspired alliance that included Turkey, Iraq, and Iran. Nevertheless, he saw in the new bipolar world opportunities that could be exploited for the advancement of Egypt, and he used his political savvy to extract pledges of economic and military assistance from the United States and the Soviet Union. Nasser demonstrated how newly independent nations could evade becoming trapped in either ideological camp and could force the superpowers to compete for influence.

Nasser also dedicated himself to ridding Egypt and the Arab world of imperial interference, which included destroying the state of Israel. He gave aid to the Algerians in their war against the French. Nasser did not neglect the remaining imperial presence in Egypt: he abolished British military rights to the Suez Canal in 1954. Through such actions and through his country's antipathy toward Israel, he laid claim to pan-Arab leadership throughout southwest Asia and north Africa.

Nasser sealed his reputation during the Suez crisis, which left him in a dominant position in the Arab world. The crisis erupted in 1956, when Nasser decided to nationalize the Suez Canal and use the money collected from the canal to finance construction of a massive dam of the Nile River at Aswan. When he did not bow to international pressure to provide multinational control of the vital Suez Canal, British, French, and Israeli forces combined to wrest control of the canal away from him. Their military campaign was successful, but they failed miserably on the diplomatic level and tore at the fabric of the bipolar world system. They had not consulted

The Suez Crisis

Gamal Abdel Nasser was president of Egypt from 1954 until his death in 1970.

with the United States, which strongly condemned the attack and forced them to withdraw. The Soviet Union also objected forcefully, thereby gaining a reputation for being a staunch supporter of Arab nationalism. Nasser gained tremendous prestige, and Egypt solidified its position as leader of the charge against imperial holdovers in southwest Asia and north Africa.

Despite Nasser's successes, he did not manage to rid the region of Israel, which was growing stronger with each passing year. More wars were fought in the decades to come, and peace between the Arab states and Israel seemed not only elusive but at times impossible. Although the partition that took place in Palestine appeared to lend itself to manipulation by the superpowers, the region of southwest Asia confused, complicated, and undermined elements of bipolarism. The strategic importance of oil dictated that both superpowers vie for favor in the Arab states, and while the United States became a firm ally of Israel, the Soviet Union also supported Israel's right to exist. The Suez crisis further tangled cold war power politics because it divided the United States and its allies in western Europe. Southwest Asia proved successful at ousting almost all imperial control and at challenging the bipolar worldview.

Decolonization in Africa

In the 1950s the superpowers' influence intensified. For African lands, that situation often meant delays in decolonization. Also complicating the decolonization process were internal divisions in African societies, which undermined attempts to forge national or pan-African identities. Tribal, ethnic, religious, and linguistic divides within and between state boundaries, all of which colonial rulers had exploited, posed a challenge to African leaders, particularly once independence came and the imperial enemy departed. Given the variety of barriers to African independence, from imperial resistance and the cold war to internal tribal conflicts, it is not astonishing that independence came more slowly in Africa than in other regions of the world.

Forcing the French out of North Africa

In Africa as in southeast Asia, the French resisted decolonization. In Algeria the French fought a bloody war that began in 1954, the year France suffered its defeat at Dienbienphu. Somewhat ironically, while it focused its efforts on Algeria in the 1950s and 1960s, France allowed all its other territories in Africa to gain independence. In 1956 France granted independence to its colonies in Morocco and Tunisia, and thirteen French colonies in west and equatorial Africa won their independence in 1960, a year that came to be known as "the year of Africa."

France in Africa

France's concessions to its other African colonies illustrated its determination to control Algeria at all costs. The French people expressed differing opinions on the Algerian conflict, being less determined than their government leaders. French settlers demanded that the government in Paris defend their cause in north Africa. Two

French paratroopers search for terrorists near Algiers, January 1957.

million French settled or were born there by the mid-1940s. The end of World War II, however, marked the beginning of a revitalized nationalist movement in Algeria, fueled by desire for independence from France and freedom from domination by white settlers. The event that touched off the Algerian revolt came in May 1945. French colonial police in the town of Sétif fired shots into an otherwise peaceful demonstration in support of Algerian and Arab nationalism. Algerian rioting and French repression of the disturbances took place in the wake of the incident. In the resulting melee more than eight thousand Algerian Muslims died, along with approximately one hundred French.

The Algerian war of liberation began in 1954 under the command of the Front de Libération Nationale (FLN, or National Liberation Front). The FLN adopted tactics similar to those of nationalist liberation groups in Asia, relying on bases in outlying mountainous areas and resorting to guerrilla warfare. The French did not realize the seriousness of the challenge they faced until 1955, when the FLN moved into more urbanized areas. In an attack on the town of Constantine, the FLN killed dozens of French settlers. France sent thousands of troops to Algeria to put down the revolution, and by 1958 it had committed half a million soldiers to the war. The war became ugly: Algerians serving with the French had to kill fellow Algerians or be killed by them; Algerian civilians became trapped in the crossfire of war, often accused of and killed for aiding FLN guerrillas; thousands of French soldiers died. By the war's end in 1962, when the Algerians gained independence from France, hundreds of thousands of Algerians had died.

War in Algeria

One ideological legacy for Africa stemmed from Algeria's war of independence. Frantz Fanon (1925–1961) gained fame as an Algerian revolutionary and as an influential proponent of national liberation for colonial peoples through violent revolution. Born in Martinique in the West Indies, Fanon studied psychiatry and medicine in France, went to Algeria to head a hospital's psychiatric department, and then participated in Algeria's battle to free itself from French rule. Fanon furthered his fame and provided ideological support for African nationalism and revolution in his writings. In works such as *The Wretched of the Earth* (1961), he urged the use of violence against colonial oppressors as a means of overcoming the racist degradation experienced by

Frantz Fanon

peoples in developing or colonial nations outside the Soviet-U.S. sphere. Fanon died shortly before Algerians achieved independence, but his ideas influenced the independence struggles ongoing in Africa.

Black African Nationalism and Independence

Before and during World War II, nationalism flourished in sub-Saharan Africa. African nationalists celebrated their blackness and Africanness in contrast to their European colonial rulers. Drawing from the pan-African movements that emerged in the United States and the Caribbean, African intellectuals, especially in French-controlled west Africa, established a movement to promote *Négritude* ("Blackness"). Reviving Africa's great traditions and cultures, poets and writers expressed a widely shared pride in Africa.

Growth of African Nationalism

This celebration of African culture was accompanied by grassroots protests against European imperialism. A new urban African elite slowly created the sorts of associations needed to hold demonstrations and fight for independence. Especially widespread, if sporadic, were workers' strikes against oppressive labor practices and the low wages paid by colonial overlords in areas such as the Gold Coast and Northern Rhodesia. Some independent Christian churches also provided avenues for anticolonial agitation, as prophets such as Simon Kimbangu in the Belgian Congo promised his churchgoers that God would deliver them from imperial control.

In the years after World War II, African poets associated with the *Négritude* movement continued to express their attachment to Africanness and encourage Africans to turn away from European culture and colonial rule. Bernard Dadié's poem "Dry Your Tears, Africa!" illustrates those sentiments:

Dry your tears, Africa!
Your children come back to you
Out of the storms and squalls of fruitless journeys. . . .
Over the gold of the east
and the purple of the setting sun,
the peaks of proud mountains
and the grasslands drenched with light
They return to you. . . .
And our senses are now opened
to the splendour of your beauty
to the smell of your forests
to the charms of your waters
to the clearness of your skies
to the caress of your sun. . . .

African Independence

The dreams and hopes of African nationalists frequently had to be placed on hold in the early years after World War II. Often assuming that black Africans were incapable of self-government, imperial powers planned for a slow transition to independence. The presence of white settlers in certain African colonies also complicated the process of decolonization. The politics of the cold war allowed imperial powers to justify oppressive actions in the name of rooting out a subversive communist presence. Despite the delays, however, sub-Saharan states slowly but surely won their independence as each newly independent nation inspired and often aided other lands to win their freedom.

Agitation for independence in sub-Saharan Africa took on many forms, peaceful and violent, and decolonization occurred at a different pace in different nations. Ghana became independent in 1957, but independence came much later to Angola

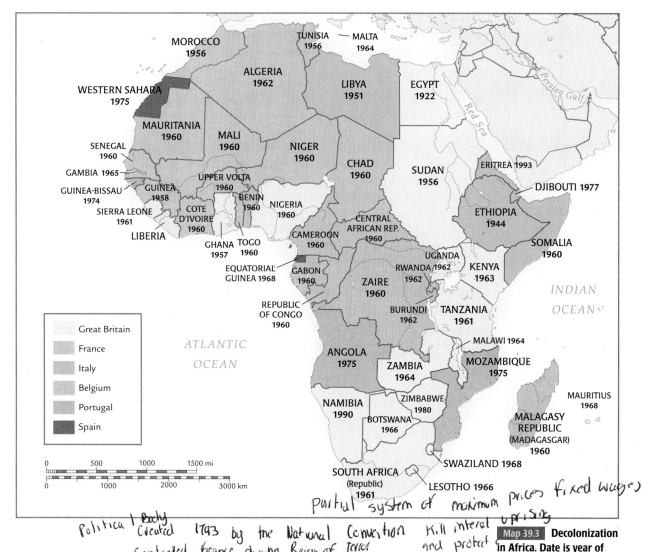

Handwritten annotations below map:

Partial system of maximum prices fixed wages

Political Body Created 1793 by the National Convention Kill internal uprising
Controlled France during Reign of Terror and protect

Map 39.3 **Decolonization in Africa. Date is year of independence.** Compare this map with Map 33.2. How do the borders of the newly independent African states compare with those drawn by European powers in the late nineteenth century?

(1975) and Zimbabwe, formerly Southern Rhodesia (1980). Freedom's aftermath often showcased the sorts of divisions and problems that tempered the joy of decolonization. The outbreak of civil war (as in Rwanda, Burundi, and Angola), economic instability, and political and ethnic divisiveness hampered postindependence nation building, but sub-Saharan African states nonetheless made the break from empire. African nations in many instances symbolized and sealed their severance from imperial control by adopting new names that shunned the memory of European rule and drew from the glory of Africa's past empires. Ghana set the pattern, and the map of Africa soon featured similar references to precolonial African places: Zambia, Malawi, Zimbabwe. As Dadié predicted, Africans had opened their political senses to the splendor of Africa past and present.

Freedom and Conflict in Sub-Saharan Africa

Ghana's success in achieving its freedom from British rule in 1957 served as a hallmark in Africa's end of empire. Under the leadership of Kwame Nkrumah (1909–1972), political parties and strategies for mass action took shape. Although the British subjected

Roadside portraits of Queen Elizabeth II and Kwame Nkrumah in Accra. The British monarch made a postindependence visit to Ghana in November 1961.

Ghana

Nkrumah and other nationalists to jail terms and repressive control, gradually they allowed reforms and negotiated the transfer of power in their Gold Coast colony.

After it became independent in 1957, Ghana emboldened and inspired other African nationalist movements. Nkrumah, as a leader of the first sub-Saharan African nation to gain independence from colonial rule, became a persuasive spokesperson for pan-African unity. His ideas and his stature as an African leader symbolized the changing times in Africa. In preparation for the 1961 visit of Britain's Queen Elizabeth II (1926–), the people of Ghana erected huge side-by-side posters of the queen and their leader, Nkrumah. Those roadside portraits offered a stunning vision of newfound equality and distinctiveness. Ex-colonial rulers, dressed in royal regalia, faced off against new African leaders, clothed in traditional African fabrics, the once-dominating white faces matched by the proud black faces.

Anticolonial Rebellion in Kenya

The process of attaining independence did not always prove as nonviolent as in Ghana. The battle that took place in the British colony of Kenya in east Africa demonstrated the complexity and difficulty of African decolonization. The situation in Kenya turned tense and violent in a clash between powerful white settlers and nationalists, especially the Kikuyu, one of Kenya's largest ethnic groups. Beginning in 1947, Kikuyu rebels embarked on an intermittently violent campaign against Europeans and alleged traitorous Africans. The settlers who controlled the colonial government in Nairobi refused to see the uprisings as a legitimate expression of discontent with colonial rule. Rather, they branded the Kikuyu tribes as radicals bent on a racial struggle for primacy. As one settler put it, "Why the hell can't we fight these apes and worry about the survivors later?" Members of the militant nationalist movements were labeled by the British government as Mau Mau subversives or communists.

In reality, Kikuyu radicalism and violence had much more to do with nationalist opposition to British colonial rule, especially land policies in Kenya. Kikuyu resent-

Sources from the Past

Kwame Nkrumah on African Unity

As the leader of the first African nation to gain independence, Kwame Nkrumah (1909–1972) became a respected spokesperson for African unity as a strategy for dealing with decolonization during the cold war. In his book I Speak of Freedom: A Statement of African Ideology *(1961), Nkrumah made an eloquent case for an African solution for the problems of African independence during a global cold war.*

It is clear that we must find an African solution to our problems, and that this can only be found in African unity. Divided we are weak; united, Africa could become one of the greatest forces for good in the world.

Never before have a people had within their grasp so great an opportunity for developing a continent endowed with so much wealth. Individually, the independent states of Africa, some of them potentially rich, others poor, can do little for their people. Together, by mutual help, they can achieve much. But the economic development of the continent must be planned and pursued as a whole. A loose confederation designed only for economic cooperation would not provide the necessary unity of purpose. Only a strong political union can bring about full and effective development of our natural resources for the benefit of our people.

The political situation in Africa today is heartening and at the same time disturbing. It is heartening to see so many new flags hoisted in place of the old; it is disturbing to see so many countries of varying sizes and at different levels of development, weak and, in some cases, almost helpless. If this terrible state of fragmentation is allowed to continue it may well be disastrous for us all.

Critics of African unity often refer to the wide differences in culture, language and ideas in various parts of Africa. This is true, but the essential fact remains that we are all Africans, and have a common interest in the independence of Africa. The difficulties presented by questions of language, culture and different political systems are not insuperable. If the need for political union is agreed by us all, then the will to create it is born; and where there's a will there's a way.

The greatest contribution that Africa can make to the peace of the world is to avoid all the dangers inherent in disunity, by creating a political union which will also by its success, stand as an example to a divided world. A union of African states will project more effectively the African personality. It will command respect from a world that has regard only for size and influence.

We have to prove that greatness is not to be measured in stockpiles of atom bombs. I believe strongly and sincerely that with the deep-rooted wisdom and dignity, the innate respect for human lives, the intense humanity that is our heritage, the African race, united under one federal government, will emerge not as just another world bloc to flaunt its wealth and strength, but as a Great Power whose greatness is indestructible because it is not built on fear, envy and suspicion, nor won at the expense of others, but founded on hope, trust, friendship and directed to the good of all mankind.

FOR FURTHER REFLECTION

How does Nkrumah's call for African unity rather than fragmentation reflect the tensions between decolonization and the ongoing cold war?

SOURCE: Kwame Nkrumah. *I Speak of Freedom: A Statement of African Ideology.* New York: Frederick A. Praeger, 1961, x–xii.

ment of the British stemmed from their treatment in the 1930s and 1940s, when white settlers pushed them off the most fertile highland farm areas and reduced them to the status of wage slaves or relegated them to overcrowded "tribal reserves." Resistance began in the early 1940s with labor strikes and violent direct action campaigns designed to force or frighten the white settlers off their lands. In the 1950s, attacks on white settlers and black collaborators escalated, and in 1952 the British established a state of emergency to crush the anticolonial guerrilla movement through detention and counterinsurgency programs. Unable or unwilling to distinguish violent activism

Rebel suspects in a British internment camp, Nairobi, Kenya.

from nonviolent agitation, the British moved to suppress all nationalist groups and jailed Kenya nationalist leaders, including Jomo Kenyatta (1895–1978) in 1953. Amid growing resistance to colonial rule, the British mounted major military offenses against rebel forces, supporting their army troops with artillery, bombers, and jet fighters. By 1956 the British had effectively crushed all military resistance in a conflict that claimed the lives of twelve thousand Africans and one hundred Europeans.

Despite military defeat, Kikuyu fighters broke British resolve in Kenya and gained increasing international recognition of African grievances. The British resisted the radical white supremacism and political domineering of the settlers in Kenya and instead responded to calls for Kenya independence. In 1959 the British lifted the state of emergency, and as political parties formed, nationalist leaders like Kenyatta reemerged to lead those parties. By December 1963 Kenya had negotiated its independence.

After Independence: Long-Term Struggles in the Postcolonial Era

Political and economic stability proved elusive after independence, particularly in those developing nations struggling to build political and economic systems free from the domination of more powerful nations. The legacies of imperialism, either direct or indirect, hindered the creation of democratic institutions in many parts of the world—in recently decolonized nations, such as those of Africa, and in some of the earliest lands to gain independence, such as those of Latin America. Continued interference by the former colonial powers, by the superpowers, or by more developed nations impeded progress, as did local elites with ties to the colonial powers. The result was an unstable succession of governments based on an authoritarian one-party system or on harsh military rule. South Africa and India, however, transformed themselves into functioning democracies despite deep racial and religious divides. In Asia and the Islamic world, some governments kept order by relying on tightly centralized rule, as in China, or on religion, as in Iran after the 1979 revolution. Few developing or newly industrialized countries, however, escaped the disruption of war or revolution that also characterized the postcolonial era.

Communism and Democracy in Asia

Except for Japan and India, the developing nations in south, southeast, and east Asia adopted some form of authoritarian or militarist political system, and many of them followed a communist or socialist path of political development. Under Mao Zedong (1893–1976), China served as a guide and inspiration for those countries seeking a means of political development distinct from the ways of their previous colonial masters.

Mao's China　　Mao reunified China for the first time since the collapse of the Qing dynasty, transforming European communist ideology into a distinctly Chinese communism. After 1949 he embarked on programs designed to accelerate development in China and to distinguish Chinese communism from Soviet communism. The Great Leap Forward (1958–1961) and the Great Proletarian Cultural Revolution (1966–1976) were far-reaching policies that hampered the political and economic development that Mao so urgently sought.

Mao envisioned his Great Leap Forward as a way to overtake the industrial production of more developed nations, and to that end he worked to collectivize all land and to manage all business and industrial enterprises collectively. Private ownership was abolished, and farming and industry became largely rural and communal. The Great Leap Forward—or "Giant Step Backward" as some have dubbed it—failed. Most disastrous was its impact on agricultural production in China: the peasants, recalcitrant and exhausted, did

A 1966 poster shows Mao Zedong inspiring the people to launch the Great Proletarian Cultural Revolution.

not meet quotas, and a series of bad harvests also contributed to one of the deadliest famines in history. Rather than face reality, Mao blamed the sparrows for the bad harvests, accusing these counterrevolutionaries of eating too much grain. He ordered tens of millions of peasants to kill the feathered menaces, leaving insects free to consume what was left of the crops. Between 1959 and 1962 as many as twenty million Chinese may have died of starvation and malnutrition in this crisis.

In 1966 Mao tried again to mobilize the Chinese and reignite the revolutionary spirit with the inauguration of the Great Proletarian Cultural Revolution. Designed to root out the revisionism Mao perceived in Chinese life, especially among Communist Party leaders and others in positions of authority, the Cultural Revolution subjected millions of people to humiliation, persecution, and death. The elite—intellectuals, teachers, professionals, managers, and anyone associated with foreign or bourgeois values—constituted the major targets of the Red Guards, youthful zealots empowered to cleanse Chinese society of opponents to Mao's rule. Victims were beaten and killed, jailed, or sent to corrective labor camps or to toil in the countryside. The Cultural Revolution, which cost China years of stable development and gutted its educational system, did not die down until after Mao's death in 1976. It fell to one of Mao's heirs, Deng Xiaoping, to heal the nation.

The Cultural Revolution

Although he was a colleague of Mao, Deng Xiaoping (1904–1997) suffered the same fate as millions of other Chinese during the Cultural Revolution: he had to recant criticisms of Mao, identify himself as a petit-bourgeois intellectual, and labor in a tractor-repair factory. When a radical faction failed to maintain the Cultural Revolution after Mao's death, China began its recovery from the turmoil. Deng came to power in

Deng's Revolution

Tiananmen Square

The student democracy movement in Tiananmen Square, Beijing, June 1989.

1981, and the 1980s are often referred to as the years of "Deng's Revolution." Deng moderated Mao's commitment to Chinese self-sufficiency and isolation and engineered China's entry into the international financial and trading system, a move that was facilitated by the normalization of relations between China and the United States in the 1970s.

To push the economic development of China, Deng opened the nation to the influences that were so suspect under Mao—foreign, capitalist values. His actions included sending tens of thousands of Chinese students to foreign universities to rebuild the professional, intellectual, and managerial elite needed for modern development. Those students were exposed to the democratic societies of western Europe and the United States. When they staged pro-democracy demonstrations in Beijing's Tiananmen Square in 1989, Deng, whose experiences in the Cultural Revolution made him wary of zealous revolutionary movements, approved a bloody crackdown. Not surprisingly, Deng faced hostile world opinion after crushing the student movement. The issue facing China as it entered the global economy was how (or whether) to reap economic benefits without compromising its identity and its authoritarian political system. This issue gained added weight as Hong Kong, under British administration since the 1840s and in the throes of its own democracy movement, reverted to Chinese control in 1997. Chinese leaders in the twenty-first century have managed to maintain both centralized political control over China and impressive economic growth and development. The evidence of China's increasing global power and prominence should become especially visible during the 2008 summer Olympics in Beijing.

Indian Democracy

The flourishing of democracy in India stands in stark contrast to the political trends in developing nations in Asia and throughout the world. While other nations turned to dictators, military rule, or authoritarian systems, India maintained its political stability and its democratic system after gaining independence in 1947. Even when faced with the crises that shook other developing nations—ethnic and religious conflict, wars, poverty, and overpopulation—India remained committed to free elections and a critical press. Its first postindependence prime minister, Jawaharlal Nehru, guided his nation to democratic rule.

In 1966 Indira Gandhi (1917–1984), Nehru's daughter (and no relation to Mohandas K. Gandhi), became leader of the Congress Party. She served as prime minister of India from 1966 to 1977 and from 1980 to 1984, and under her leadership India embarked on the "green revolution" that increased agricultural yields for India's eight hundred million people. Although the new agricultural policies aided wealthier farmers, the masses of peasant farmers fell deeper into poverty. Beyond the poverty that drove Indians to demonstrations of dissatisfaction with Gandhi's government, India was beset by other troubles—overpopulation and continuing sectarian conflicts.

Those problems prompted Indira Gandhi to take stringent action to maintain control. To quell growing opposition to her government, she declared a national emergency (1975–1977) that suspended democratic processes. She used her powers under the emergency to forward one of India's most needed social reforms, birth control. But rather than persuading or tempting Indians to control the size of their families (offering gifts of money for those who got vasectomies, for example), the government engaged in repressive birth control policies, including involuntary sterilization. A record eight million sterilization operations were performed in 1976 and 1977. The riots that ensued, and the fear of castration among men who might be forced to undergo vasectomies, added to Gandhi's woes.

When Indira Gandhi allowed elections to be held in 1977, Indians voted against her because of her abrogation of democratic principles and her harsh birth control policies. She returned to power in 1980, however, and again faced great difficulty keeping the state of India together in the face of religious, ethnic, and secessionist movements. One such movement was an uprising by Sikhs who wanted greater autonomy in the Punjab region. The Sikhs, representing perhaps 2 percent of India's population, practiced a religion that was an offshoot of Hinduism, and they had a separate identity—symbolized by their distinctive long hair and headdresses—and a history of militarism and self-rule. Unable or unwilling to compromise in view of the large number of groups agitating for a similar degree of autonomy, Indira Gandhi ordered the army to attack the sacred Golden Temple in Amristar, which harbored armed Sikh extremists. In retaliation, two of her Sikh bodyguards—hired for their martial skills—assassinated her a few months later in 1984.

Indira Gandhi's son Rajiv Gandhi (1944–1991) took over the leadership of India in 1985 and offered reconciliation to the Sikhs. He was assassinated by a terrorist in 1991 while attempting to win back the office he lost in 1989. Despite those setbacks, however, Nehru's heirs maintained democracy in India and continued to work on the problems plaguing Indian development—overpopulation, poverty, and sectarian division. The legacy of Mohandas K. Gandhi lived on in the form of brutal assassinations and continued quests for peace and religious tolerance.

Indira Gandhi delivers a speech in 1972.

chinese fleet admiral from 1405~1433 led 7 naval expeditions to establish chinese control over trade imperial impress foreign people in the India Ocean Basin

Islamic Resurgence in Southwest Asia and North Africa

The geographic convergence of the Arab and Muslim worlds in southwest Asia and north Africa encouraged the development of Arab nationalism in states of those regions that gained independence in the year after World War II. Whether in Libya, Algeria, or Egypt in north Africa or in Syria, Saudi Arabia, or Iraq in southwest Asia, visions of Arab nationalism, linked to the religious force of Islam, dazzled nations that wished to fend off European and U.S. influence. In north Africa, Egypt's Gamal

*Muslim Revival
and Arab Disunity*

Abdel Nasser provided the leadership for this Arab nationalism, and Arab-Muslim opposition to the state of Israel held the dream together.

The hopes attached to pan-Arab unity did not materialize. Although Arab lands shared a common language and religion, divisions were frequent and alliances shifted over time. The cold war split the Arab-Muslim world; some states allied themselves with the United States, and others allied with the Soviet Union. Some countries also shifted between the two, as Egypt did when it left the Soviet orbit for the U.S. sphere in 1976. Governments in these nations included military dictatorships, monarchies, and Islamist revolutionary regimes. Religious divisions also complicated the attainment of Arab unity, because Sunni and Shia Muslims followed divergent theologies and foreign policies.

In southwest Asia, peace seemed a distant prospect for decades, given the political turmoil caused by the presence of Israel in the midst of Arab-Islamic states, many of which allied themselves with the Soviet Union as Israel became a staunch ally of the United States. Israel soundly defeated Egypt and Syria in the 1967 Arab-Islamic War and in the 1973 Arab-Israeli, or Yom Kippur, War, so named by Israel because the Arab attack took place on the major Jewish holy day of Yom Kippur. Those conflicts greatly intensified the tensions in the region, but the wars also ultimately led to a long series of peace negotiations. Anwar Sadat (1918–1981), who replaced Nasser as Egypt's president, masterminded the Yom Kippur surprise attack on Israel, but he also facilitated the peace process. The United States helped negotiate the peace. In 1976 Sadat renounced his nations' friendship treaty with the Soviet Union, and in 1977 he traveled to Israel in an attempt to break a deadlock in the negotiations. Between 1978 and 1980 the leaders of Egypt and Israel signed peace treaties.

Sadat was assassinated in 1981 by opponents of his policies toward Israel, and the Arab states along with the Palestinian Liberation Organization (PLO) worked to isolate Egypt. The PLO, the political organization that served as a government in exile for Palestinians displaced from Israel, had been created in 1964 under the leadership of Yasser Arafat (1929–2004) to promote Palestinian rights. Despite more violence by Israelis and Palestinians in the 1990s, these implacable foes moved to end hostilities. In 1993 and 1995 Arafat and Israeli prime minister Yitzhak Rabin (1922–1995) signed peace treaties that advanced the notion of limited Palestinian self-rule in Israeli-occupied territories. The assassination of Rabin in 1995 by a Jewish extremist who opposed the peace agreements, as well as other hurdles, blocked the peace process. Although hope for a peaceful resolution of the long-running conflict between Israel and the Palestinians has persisted, deadly clashes such as the 2006 Israel-Lebanon conflict illuminate the complexity of this region's politics as well as the fragility of peace. The forces of Hezbollah, a Lebanese Shia resistance group benefiting from support from Iran and fighting against any Israeli occupation of Lebanese territory, instigated a conflict that saw Hezbollah rockets launched against Israel, Israeli air strikes and artillery barrages devastating parts of Lebanon, and many dead Lebanese and displaced Lebanese and Israelis. A UN-mandated cease-fire went into effect in August 2006, but hostility itself has not disappeared. Cease-fires and tentative moves toward peace have not, however, negated Muslim desires for solidarity and strength. A revival of Muslim traditions found expression in Islamism.

Islamism

At the heart of Islamism was the desire for the reassertion of Islamic values in Muslim politics. In this view, the Muslim world had been slipping into a state of decline, brought about by the abandonment of Islamic traditions. Many Muslims had become skeptical about European and American models of economic development and political and cultural norms, which they blamed for economic and political failure as well as for secularization and its attendant breakdown of traditional social and religious values. Disillusionment and even anger with European and American societies, and especially with the United States, became widespread. The solution to the problems faced by Muslim societies lay, according to Islamists, in the revival of Islamic identity, values, and power. The vast majority of Islamic activists have sought to bring about change through peaceful means, but an extremist minority has claimed a mandate from God that calls for violent transformations. Convinced that the Muslim world is under siege, extremists used the concept of *jihad*—the right and duty to defend Islam and the Islamic community from unjust attack—to rationalize and legitimize terrorism and revolution.

The Arab-Muslim world was divided on a number of issues, but the revolution that took place in Iran in 1979 demonstrated the power of Islam as a means of staving off secular foreign influences. Islamist influences penetrated Iran during the lengthy regime of Shah Mohammed Reza Pahlavi (1919–1980), whom the CIA helped bring to power in 1953. The vast sums of money that poured in from Iran's oil industry helped finance industrialization, and the United States provided the military equipment that enabled Iran to become a bastion of anticommunism in the region. In the late 1970s, however, opposition to the shah's government coalesced. Shia Muslims despised the shah's secular regime, Iranian small businesses detested the influence of U.S. corporations on the economy, and leftist politicians rejected the shah's repressive policies. The shah fled the country in early 1979 as the revolution gained force, and power was captured by the Islamist movement under the direction of Ayatollah Ruhollah Khomeini (1900–1989).

The Iranian Revolution

The revolution took on a strongly anti-U.S. cast, partly because the shah was allowed to travel to the United States for medical treatment. In retaliation, Shia militants captured sixty-nine hostages at the U.S. embassy in Tehran, fifty-five of whom remained captives until 1981. In the meantime, Iranian leaders shut U.S. military bases and confiscated U.S.-owned economic ventures. This Islamic power play against a developed nation such as the United States inspired other Muslims to undertake terrorist actions. The resurgent Islam of Iran did not lead to a new era of solidarity, however. Iranian Islam was the minority sect of Shia Islam, and one of Iran's neighbors, Iraq, attempted to take advantage of the revolution to invade Iran.

By the late 1970s Iraq had built a formidable military machine, largely owing to oil revenues and the efforts of Saddam Hussein (1937–2006), who became president of Iraq in 1979. Hussein launched his attack on Iran in 1980, believing that victory would be swift and perhaps hoping to become the new leader of a revived pan-Arab nationalism. (Iran is Muslim in religion, but not ethnically Arab, as are Iraq, Kuwait, and Saudi Arabia.) Although they were initially successful, Iraqi troops faced a determined counterattack by Iranian forces, and the conflict became a war of attrition that did not end until 1988.

The Iran-Iraq War killed as many as one million soldiers. In Iran the human devastation is still visible, if not openly acknowledged, in a nation that permits little dissent from Islamist orthodoxy. Young people are showing signs of a growing discontent caused by the war and by the rigors of a revolution that also killed thousands. Signs of recovery and a relaxation of Islamist strictness appeared in Iran in the late 1990s, but the destruction from war also remained visible. Islamism has reemerged in twenty-first-century Iran and has aroused some international concern, particularly for the United States. A conservative supreme leader, the Ayatollah Khamenei (1939–), and a conservative president, Mahmoud Ahmadinejad (1956–), represented this trend. Ahmadinejad took office in 2005 and touted Iran's nuclear program and his antipathy to the state of Israel, which had the effect of increasing his status in the Islamic world while intensifying tensions with the United States.

The Iran-Iraq War

Iranians show their devotion to the Ayatollah Khomeini at his funeral in 1989.

Iraqis continued on a militant course. Two years after the end of the Iran-Iraq War, Hussein's troops invaded Kuwait (1990) and incited the Gulf War (1991). The result was a decisive military defeat for Iraq, at the hands of an international coalition led by the United States, and further hardships for the Iraqi people. Hussein's troubles deepened in the wake of the 11 September 2001 terrorist attacks against the United States as President George W. Bush (1946–) vastly expanded his nation's war on terror (see chapter 40). A coalition of forces aligned with the United States launched a preemptive invasion of Iraq in 2003 to destroy Hussein's "weapons of mass destruction" and Iraq's capacity to harbor global terrorists. Iraqi military units suffered defeat and coalition forces captured Saddam Hussein in December 2003. Tried and found guilty of crimes against the Iraqi people, Hussein faced execution by hanging on 30 December 2006. Deadly conflicts have persisted, however, as both Iraqis and U.S. occupation forces have become targets for those Iraqis disgruntled with new Iraqi leaders and with the continued presence of foreign troops in Iraq.

Politics and Economics in Latin America

The uneasy aftermath of independence visible throughout Asia also affected states on the other side of the world—states that gained their freedom from colonial rule more than a century before postwar decolonization. Nations in Central and South America along with Mexico grappled with the conservative legacies of Spanish and Portuguese colonialism, particularly the political and economic power of the landowning elite of European descent. Latin America moreover had to deal with neocolonialism, because the United States not only intervened militarily when its interests were threatened but also influenced economies through investment and full or part ownership of enterprises such as the oil industry. In the nineteenth century Latin American states may have looked to the United States as a model of liberal democracy, but by the twentieth century U.S. interference provoked negative reactions. That condition was true after World War I, and it remained true during and after World War II.

Mexico   Only President Lázaro Cárdenas (in office 1934–1940) had substantially invoked and applied the reforms guaranteed to Mexicans by the Constitution of 1917. The constitution's provisions regarding the state's right to redistribute land after confiscation and compensation, as well as its claim to government ownership of the subsoil and its products, found a champion in Cárdenas. He brought land reform and redistribution to a peak in Mexico, returning forty-five million acres to peasants, and he wrested away control of the oil industry from foreign investors. Cárdenas's nationalization of Mexico's oil industry allowed for the creation of the *Petróleos Mexicanos* (PEMEX), a national oil company in control of Mexico's petroleum products. The revenues generated by PEMEX contributed to what has been called "El Milagro Mexicano," or the Mexican economic miracle, a period of prosperity that lasted for decades. Conservative governments thereafter, controlled by the one-party rule of the Institutional Revolutionary Party (PRI), often acted harshly and experimented with various economic strategies that decreased or increased Mexico's reliance on foreign markets and capital. The PRI came under attack in the 1990s as Mexican peasants in the Chiapas district protested their political oppression. Cuauhtemoc Cárdenas, the son of Lázaro Cárdenas, took on the leadership of an opposition party, the Democratic Revolutionary Party (PRD), and this shift to democratic political competition and multiparty elections has continued into the twenty-first century. Vincente Fox Quesada (1942–) won the 2000 presidential election as a candidate for the National Action Party (PAN), breaking the PRI's long-term monopoly on the office. Another PAN candidate, Felipe de Jesús Calderón Hinojosa (1962–) replaced him as president in 2006, but only after a hotly contested race and an extremely narrow victory over the PRD's Andres Manuel Lopez Obrador (1953–).

Argentina

Mexico served as one model for political development in Latin America, and Argentina seemed to be another candidate for leadership in South America. It had a reasonably expansive economy based on cattle raising and agriculture, a booming urban life, the beginnings of an industrial base, and a growing middle class in a population composed mostly of migrants from Europe. Given its geographic position far to the south, Argentina remained relatively independent of U.S. control and became a leader in the Latin American struggle against U.S. and European economic and political intervention in the region. A gradual shift to free elections and a sharing of political power beyond that exercised by the landowning elite also emerged. Given the military's central role in its politics, however, Argentina became a model of a less positive form of political organization: the often brutal and deadly sway of military rulers.

Juan Perón

During World War II, nationalistic military leaders gained power in Argentina and established a government controlled by the army. In 1946 Juan Perón (1895–1974), a former colonel in the army, was elected president. Although he was a nationalistic militarist, his regime garnered immense popularity among large segments of the Argentine population, partly because he appealed to the more downtrodden Argentines. He promoted a nationalistic populism, calling for industrialization, support of the working class, and protection of the economy from foreign control.

Evita

However opportunistic Perón may have been, his popularity with the masses was real. His wife, Eva Perón (1919–1952), helped to foster that popularity, as Argentinians warmly embraced their "Evita" (little Eva). She rose from the ranks of the desperately poor. An illegitimate child who migrated to Buenos Aires at the age of fifteen, she found work as a radio soap-opera actress. She met Perón in 1944, and they were married shortly thereafter. Reigning in the Casa Rosada (the Pink House) as Argentina's first lady from 1946 to 1952, Eva Perón transformed herself into a stunningly beautiful political leader, radiant with dyed gold-blonde hair and clothed in classic designer fashions. While pushing for her husband's political reforms, she also tirelessly ministered to the needs of the poor, often the same *descamisados,* or "shirtless ones," who formed the core of her husband's supporters. Endless lines of people came to see her

■ **Eva Perón waves to adoring *descamisados* in Buenos Aires in 1950.**

in her offices at the labor ministry—asking for dentures, wedding clothes, medical care, and the like. Eva Perón accommodated those demands and more: she bathed lice-ridden children in her own home, kissed lepers, and created the Eva Perón Foundation to institutionalize and extend such charitable endeavors. When she died of uterine cancer at the age of thirty-three, the nation mourned the tragic passing of a woman who came to be elevated to the status of "Santa Evita."

Some saw Eva Perón not as a saint but as a grasping social climber and a fascist sympathizer (she had, for example, made an official visit to General Franco's Spain) and saw her husband as a political opportunist, but after Juan Perón's ouster from office in 1955, support for the Perónist party remained strong. However, with the exception of a brief return to power by Perón in the mid-1970s, brutal military dictators held sway for the next three decades. Military rule took a sinister turn in the late 1970s and early 1980s when dictators approved the creation of death squads that fought a "dirty war" against suspected subversives. Between six thousand and twenty-three thousand people disappeared between 1976 and 1983. Calls for a return to democratic politics increased in the aftermath of the dirty war, demands that were intensified by economic disasters and the growth of the poor classes.

Guatemala and Nicaragua

The political models and options open to states in Latin America were rather diverse, even though cold war issues complicated some political choices made after World War II. The establishment of communist and socialist regimes in Central and South America—or the instigation of programs and policies that hinted of progressive liberalism or anti-Americanism—regularly provoked a response from the United States. The United States did not need the impetus of a communist threat to justify its intervention in Latin America, because the northern neighbor had upheld the right to make southern incursions since the enunciation of the Monroe Doctrine in 1823. Moreover, one hundred years later, Latin America had become the site of fully 40 percent of U.S. foreign investments. Nonetheless, cold war imperatives shaped many U.S. actions in Latin America in the postwar years, especially in Cuba (see chapter 38) and the Central American nations of Guatemala and Nicaragua.

Democratically elected president of Guatemala in 1951, Jacobo Arbenz Guzmán (1913–1971) publicly announced in 1953 a government seizure of hundreds of thousands of acres of uncultivated land owned by the United Fruit Company, a private enterprise controlled mainly by U.S. investors. Foreign companies such as the United Fruit Company dominated Guatemala's economy and its major export crop of bananas. President Arbenz was attempting to reassert Guatemala's control over its economy and its lands—for redistribution to the peasants. He offered monetary compensation to the company, based on the land's declared value for tax payments, but both the company and the United States government found that amount insufficient. U.S. officials also believed Arbenz's policies to be communist inspired, and they feared a spread of such radical doctrines throughout Central America.

President Dwight Eisenhower therefore empowered the CIA to engineer the overthrow of Arbenz's government. The United States sent arms to Guatemala's neighbors, Nicaragua and Honduras, to shore up their defenses against communism, and the CIA trained noncommunist Guatemalans under Colonel Carlos Castillo Armas (1914–1957) to attack and weaken the Arbenz government. With a continued supply of U.S. weapons and air support, Castillo Armas and his troops forced the fall of Arbenz in 1954. Castillo Armas established a military government, returned land to the United Fruit Company, and ruthlessly suppressed opponents with methods that included torture and murder. After his assassination in 1957, Guatemalans plunged into a civil war that did not end until the 1990s.

Anastacio Somoza Garcia (1896–1956) served as president of Nicaragua during the CIA-backed coup that removed Arbenz from Guatemalan government, and he demonstrated himself to be a staunch anticommunist U.S. ally. He had funneled weapons to Guatemalan rebels opposing Arbenz, and he outlawed the communist party in Nicaragua during the cold war. Somoza first grasped power in the 1930s, propelled into a position of leadership when members of his Nicaraguan National Guard killed nationalist Augusto César Sandino (1893–1934). Sandino had led a guerrilla movement aimed at ending U.S. interference in Nicaragua, including the stationing of U.S. Marines. Somoza and his sons, Luis Somoza Debayle (d. 1967) and Anastacio Somoza Debayle (1928–1980), controlled Nicaraguan politics for more than forty years.

The brutality, corruption, and pro-U.S. policies of the Somoza family—which extended to allowing the United States to use Nicaragua as a staging place during the Bay of Pigs attack on Cuba in 1961—alienated other Latin American nations as well as Nicaraguans. In the early 1960s, a few Nicaraguans honored the memory and mission of Augusto Sandino and created a movement opposing the Somozas by founding the Frenté Sandinista de Liberacíon Nacional (FSLN), or the Sandinista Front for National Liberation. The Sandinistas, as they became known, garnered support over the decades for their guerrilla operations aimed at overthrowing the Somozas, but they did not take power until 1979. The assumption of power by the Sandinistas, many of whom were avowed Marxists dedicated to a socialist agenda, was in some respects surprisingly supported by the actions of the United States.

Under President Jimmy Carter (1924–), U.S. cold war policies in Latin America moderated. In some cases, the United States refused to interfere in Latin American nations pursuing more autonomy or progressive and even socialist goals. Carter helped make Anastacio Somoza Debayle's position untenable in 1978 by withdrawing U.S. military and economic aid, and when the dictator fled Nicaragua in 1979, the United States offered recognition and aid to the new Sandinista government. Carter's commitment to human rights contributed to this shift in U.S. cold war policy—which also led to withdrawal of U.S. support for Latin American dictators and to the negotiations of the 1979 Panama Canal Treaty that gave Panama sovereignty over all its territory, including the Canal Zone (restored by treaty to Panama on 31 December 1999).

This thaw in U.S.–Latin American cold war relations did not last long. President Ronald Reagan (1911–2004) abandoned Carter's policies and renewed attacks on communism. Nicaraguan Sandinistas felt the full force of Reagan's anticommunism after his assumption of the presidency in 1981, especially because he believed that the Sandinistas were abetting communist rebels elsewhere in Central America, as in El Salvador. He halted aid to Nicaragua and instituted an economic boycott of the country. In 1983 Reagan offered increasing support—monetary and military—to the Contras, a CIA-trained counterrevolutionary group dedicated to overthrowing the Sandinistas and engaging over time in such activities as the bombing of oil facilities and the mining of harbors. Members of the U.S. Congress and public expressed wariness about Reagan's ventures in Nicaragua, and in 1984 Congress imposed a two-year ban on all military aid to the Contras. Representatives of the Reagan administration went outside the law to provide funds for the Contras in 1986, illegally using the profits that accrued from secretly selling weapons to Iran—a scandal that became public and highly visible in late 1986 and early 1987.

In the face of U.S. efforts to destabilize Sandinista rule in Nicaragua, Central American leaders decided to take action themselves on their region's troubles. President Oscar Arias Sánchez (1940–) of Costa Rica became especially influential in promoting a negotiated end to the Contra war in Nicaragua. A 1989 agreement provided for the presence of a UN peacekeeping force, for monitored elections, and for the disarming of the Contras. Elections in the following decade brought new political parties to the forefront, and the Sandinistas worked to form coalition governments with opposition parties. Sandinista power was weakened but not eliminated despite the overwhelming interference of the United States, and democratic politics and a normalization of relations with the United States emerged in Nicaragua in the late twentieth century.

Nicaragua's experiences after World War II suggested clearly the political complications associated with the cold war and with continued U.S. interference in Latin America. The economic and political conditions in South and Central America nonetheless made experiments with revolutionary doctrines and Marxist programs attractive to many of the region's peoples. These interested people included members of normally conservative institutions such as the Catholic Church; numerous priests in Latin America embraced what was called "liberation theology," a mixture of Catholicism and Marxism meant to combat the misery and repression of the masses through revolutionary salvation. Brutal regimes ordered the assassinations of hundreds of priests preaching this message of liberation, including Archbishop Oscar Romero in El Salvador in 1980.

Liberation for Nations and Women   Revolutionary ideologies and political activism also provided opportunities for Latin American women to agitate for both national and women's liberation. Nicaraguan women established the Association of Women Concerned about National Crisis in 1977 and fought as part of the FSLN to rid their nation of Somoza's rule. In 1979 they renamed the organization the Luisa Amanda Espinoza Association of Nicaraguan Women (AMNLAE) to honor the first woman who died in the battle against Somoza. The group's slogan—"No revolution without women's emancipation: no emancipation without revolution"—suggested the dual goals of Nicaraguan women. By the mid-1980s, AMNLAE had over 80,000 members. Despite facing problems typical to women's movements trying to navigate between national and personal needs, AMNLAE has been credited with forwarding women's participation in the public and political spheres, an impressive accomplishment in a region where women's suffrage had often been delayed. Although women in Ecuador attained voting rights in 1929, women in Nicaragua could not vote until 1955; Paraguay's women waited for suffrage rights until 1961, when that nation became the last in Latin America to incorporate women into the political process.

The late twentieth century witnessed a revival of democratic politics in Latin America, but economic problems continued to limit the possibility of widespread change or the achievement of economic and social equity. In many Latin American nations, the landowning elites who gained power during the colonial era were able to maintain their dominant position, which resulted in societies that remained divided between the few rich, usually backed by the United States, and the masses of the poor. It was difficult to structure such societies without either keeping the elite in power or promoting revolution on behalf of the poor, and the task of fashioning workable state and economic systems was made even more troublesome given the frequency of foreign interference, both military and economic. Despite the difficulties, the mid-twentieth century offered economic promise. During World War II, many Latin American nations took advantage of world market needs and pursued greater industrial development. Profits flowed into these countries during and after the war, and nations in the region experienced sustained economic growth through expanded export trade and diversification of foreign markets. Exports included manufactured goods and traditional export commodities such as minerals and foodstuffs such as sugar, fruits, and coffee.

The Search for Economic Equity

Latin American nations realized the need to reorient their economies away from exports and toward internal development, but the attempts to do so fell short. One influential Argentine economist, Raul Prebisch (1901–1985), who worked for the United Nations Commission for Latin America, explained Latin America's economic problems in global terms. Prebisch crafted the "dependency" theory of economic development, pointing out that developed industrial nations—such as those in North America and Europe—dominated the international economy and profited at the expense of less developed and industrialized nations burdened with the export-oriented, unbalanced economies that were a legacy of colonialism. To break the unequal relationship between what Prebisch termed the "center" and "periphery," developing nations on the periphery of international trade needed to protect and diversify domestic trade and to use strategies of import-substituting industrialization to promote further industrial and economic growth.

Prebisch's theories about the economic ills of the developing world, though influential at the time, have since declined in currency. Many Latin American nations remained committed to export trade and foreign investment, and economic expansion resulted from an infusion of funds from developed nations. The global recession of the 1970s and 1980s halted that expansion. Latin American states incurred huge foreign debts, and declining commodity prices reduced export profits so much that it became almost impossible for them to pay the interest on those debts. The recession and debt crisis hit Latin America hard, and renegotiating debt payments to developed nations opened the region to outside pressures on domestic economic policies—reducing commitments to social welfare and income redistribution, for example. Latin American economies have shown resilience in the late twentieth and early twenty-first centuries, however, and Latin American nations have maintained links to global markets and money. Their economies appeared strong enough to limit the effects of their export-oriented systems and their use of foreign investment monies, and further economic growth should aid in the search for a social and economic equity that have been elusive in Latin America from colonial times.

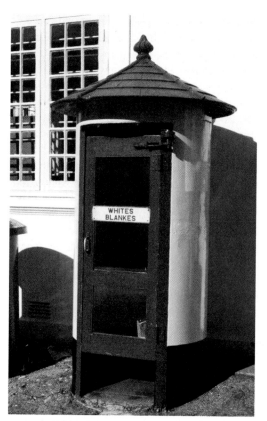

Whites telephone kiosk. The South African system of apartheid institutionalized racial segregation.

War and Peace in Sub-Saharan Africa

The optimism that arose in Africa after World War II faded over time. There seemed little prospect for widespread political stability in sub-Saharan Africa. Civilians running newly independent states were replaced by military leaders in a large number of unsettling coups. In Africa, as in Latin America, this condition largely reflected the impact of colonialism: European powers carved Africa into territories whose boundaries were artificial conveniences that did not correspond to economic or ethnic divisions. As a result, achieving national unity was difficult, especially because there were numerous conflicts between ethnic groups within states. Political institutions foundered, and the grinding poverty in which most African peoples lived increased tensions and made the absence of adequate administration and welfare programs more glaring. Poverty also prevented nations from accumulating the capital that could have contributed to a sound political and economic infrastructure.

The Aftermath of Decolonization

The Organization of African Unity (OAU), created in 1963 by thirty-two member states, recognized some of those problems and attempted to prevent conflicts that could lead to intervention by former colonial powers. The artificial boundaries of African states, though acknowledged as problematic, were nonetheless held inviolable by the OAU to prevent disputes over boundaries. Pan-African unity was also promoted, at least by the faction headed by Kwame Nkrumah, as another way for African states to resist interference and domination by foreign powers. But, although national borders have generally held, unity has not; African nations have been unable to avoid internal conflicts. Nkrumah, the former president of Ghana, is a case in point: he was overthrown in 1966, and Ghanaians tore down the statues and photographs that celebrated his leadership. Thus in Ghana, as in many other sub-Saharan states, politics evolved into dictatorial one-party rule, with party leaders forgoing multiparty elections in the name of ending political divisiveness. Several African nations fell prey to military rule. South Africa managed in part to solve its political crisis and discord, providing a model for multiethnic African transformation even as ethnic violence flared.

South Africa

As elsewhere in Africa, the presence of large numbers of white settlers in South Africa long delayed the arrival of black freedom. South Africa's black population, though a majority, remained dispossessed and disfranchised. Anticolonial agitation thus was significantly different in South Africa than in the rest of sub-Saharan Africa: it was a struggle against internal colonialism, against an oppressive white regime that denied basic human and civil rights to tens of millions of South Africans.

The ability of whites to resist majority rule had its roots in the South African economy, the strongest on the continent. That strength had two sources: extraction of minerals and industrial development, which received a huge boost during World War II. The growth of the industrial sector opened many jobs to blacks, creating the possibility of a change in their status. Along with black activism and calls for serious political reform after World War II, these changes struck fear into the hearts of white South Africans. In 1948 the Afrikaner National Party, which was dedicated to quashing any move toward black independence, came to power. Under the National Party the government instituted a harsh new set of laws designed to control the restive black population; these new laws constituted the system known as apartheid, or "separateness."

Apartheid

The system of apartheid asserted white supremacy and institutionalized the racial segregation established in the years before 1948. The government designated approximately 87 percent of South Africa's territory for white residents. Remaining areas were designated as homelands for black and colored citizens. Nonwhites were classified according to a variety of ethnic identifications—colored or mixed-race peoples, Indians, and "Bantu," which in turn was subdivided into numerous distinct tribal affiliations (for example, Zulu, Xhosa, Sotho). As other imperial powers had done in Africa, white South Africans divided the black and colored population in the hope of preventing the rise of unified liberation movements. The apartheid system, complex and varied in its composition, evolved into a system designed to keep blacks in a position of political, social, and economic subordination.

However divided the nonwhite population might be, the dispossessed peoples all found in apartheid an impetus for resistance to white rule. The African National Congress (ANC), formed in 1912, gained new young leaders such as Nelson Mandela (1918–), who inspired direct action campaigns to protest apartheid. In 1955 the ANC published its Freedom Charter, which proclaimed the ideal of multiracial democratic rule for South Africa. Because its goals directly challenged white rule, the ANC and all black activists in South Africa faced severe repression. The government declared all its opponents communists and escalated its actions against black activists. Protests increased in 1960, the so-called year of Africa, and on 21 March 1960 white police gunned down black demonstrators in Sharpeville, near Johannesburg. Sixty-nine blacks died and almost two hundred were wounded. Sharpeville instituted a new era of radical activism.

When the white regime banned black organizations such as the ANC and jailed their adherents, international opposition to white South African rule grew. Newly freed nations in Asia and Africa called for UN sanctions against South Africa, and in 1961 South Africa declared itself a republic, withdrawing from the British Commonwealth. Some leaders of the ANC saw the necessity of armed resistance, but in 1963 government forces captured the leaders of ANC's military unit, including Nelson Mandela. The court sentenced them to life in prison, and Mandela and others became symbols of oppressive white rule. Protests against the system persisted in the 1970s and 1980s, spurred especially by student activism and a new black-consciousness movement. The combined effects of widespread black agitation and a powerful international anti-apartheid boycott eventually led to reform and a growing recognition that, if it was to survive, South Africa had to change.

When F. W. de Klerk (1936–) became president of South Africa in 1989, he and the National Party began to dismantle the apartheid system. De Klerk released Mandela from jail in 1990, legalized the ANC, and worked with Mandela and the ANC to negotiate the end of white minority rule. Collaborating and cooperating, the National Party, the ANC, and other African political groups created a new constitution and in April 1994 held elections that were open to people of all races. The ANC won

The End of Apartheid

overwhelmingly, and Mandela became the first black president of South Africa. In 1963, at the trial that ended in his jail sentence, Mandela proclaimed, "I have cherished the ideal of a democratic and free society in which all persons live together in harmony and with equal opportunities. It is an ideal which I hope to live for and to achieve. But if needs be, it is an ideal for which I am prepared to die." Mandela lived to see his ideal fulfilled. In 1994, as president, he proclaimed his nation "free at last." Mandela left office in 1999, replaced by Thabo Mbeki (1942–) as both president of the ANC and president of South Africa. An ANC activist in exile for decades before the end of apartheid, Mbeki was reelected in 2004. Although his fiscally conservative policies have alienated some in South Africa, his nation has remained the most stable, prosperous, and industrialized country in Africa.

The Democratic Republic of the Congo

Outside South Africa political stability remained difficult to achieve. The fleeting character of African political identity and stability can be seen in the history of the land once known as the Belgian Congo, which was reconfigured as Zaire in 1971 and renamed the Democratic Republic of the Congo in 1997. Mobutu Sese Seko (1930–1997) took power in 1960 by having Zaire's first prime minister, Patrice Lumumba (1925–1961), killed in a military coup in 1961. Lumumba was a Maoist Marxist, and the United States supported Mobutu's coup. Mobutu thereafter received support from the United States and other European democracies hoping to quell subversive uprisings. With international backing and financial support, Mobutu ruled Zaire in dictatorial fashion, using his power to amass personal fortunes for himself, his family, and his allies but devastating Zaire's economy. One observer termed Mobutu and his cronies "a vampire elite" as they plundered one of the richest African nations.

Mobutu's full adopted name, Mobutu Sese Seko Kuku Ngbendu Wa Za Banga, means "the all-powerful warrior who, by his endurance and will to win, goes from conquest to conquest, leaving fire in his wake." Mobutu endured until 1997, when he was ousted by Laurent Kabila. Having earlier called Zaire "a fabrication of the dictator," Kabila changed the nation's name to the Democratic Republic of the Congo. Kabila's first concern was stability, which translated into vast personal power for himself as president, head of the military, and head of state. Kabila promised that this stage was a transition phase, preparatory to a democratic and stable Republic of Congo. However, a year after his revolution, Kabila came under attack by rebels in Congo who were aided by the governments of neighboring Uganda and Rwanda. In January 2001 during a failed coup attempt, a bodyguard shot and killed Kabila. His surviving son, Joseph, took over the reins of power. Joseph Kabila (1971–) worked to promote democratic elections and a new constitution, which an interim parliament approved in 2005, even though he faced disruptions from persistent outbreaks of violence within Congo and between Congo and bordering states. In elections held in 2006, Kabila was democratically elected to his position as president.

Developing Economies

Most African nations are less developed countries—countries that have the world's lowest per capita incomes and little industrial development. Africa contains 10 percent of the world's population but accounts for only 1 percent of its industrial output. By the mid-1980s only seven African nations had per capita incomes of $1,000 or more, and the continent had the world's highest number of low-income states. Africa is rich in mineral resources, raw materials, and agricultural products, but it lacks the capital, technology, foreign markets, and managerial class necessary to exploit its natural wealth. An ever-growing population compounds Africa's economic woes. Sub-Saharan Africa has one of the highest rates of population growth in the world—between 2.5 and 3 percent per year. While the populations of African states continue to grow, so do hopes for a new generation of economic solutions that can promote the health and welfare of those populations.

Africa's economic prospects after decolonization were not always so bleak, and they may improve in coming decades. The postwar period saw growing demand for Africa's commodity exports, and many African nations initiated or continued financial links with ex-colonial powers to finance economic development. After the 1970s, however, nations in Africa and Latin America faced the same crises: huge foreign debts, falling commodity prices, and rising import costs. Africa's burdens were complicated by droughts, famines, and agricultural production that could not keep pace with population growth. Leaders of African nations were among the strongest supporters of the New International Economic Order that was called for by a coalition of developing nations. These states sought a just allocation of global wealth, especially by guaranteeing prices and markets for commodities. African states have continued to attempt wider integration into the global economy, as well as to nurture closer economic and political cooperation among themselves. The African Union (AU), which superseded the Organization of African Unity and encompassed the African Economic Community (AEC, 1991), has fifty-three member nations and has been committed to working toward economic unity and integration in Africa. These nations seek to strengthen themselves by combating the conflicts so disruptive of African life and by establishing a common market designed in planned stages to unify Africa.

In the years immediately before and after World War II, a few nations controlled the political and economic destiny of much of the world. The imperial and colonial encounters between European elites and indigenous peoples defined much of the recent history of the world before the mid-twentieth century. The decades following 1945 witnessed the stunning reversal of that state of affairs, as European empires fell and dozens of newly independent nations emerged. Decolonization changed the world's political, economic, and social landscape in often radical ways, and the peoples of these newly free countries thereafter labored to reshape their national identities and to build workable political and economic systems. The effervescence of liberty and independence at times gave way to a more sober reality in the days, years, and decades after liberation. Religious and ethnic conflict, political instability, economic challenges, and neoimperialism dampened spirits and interfered with the ability of nations to achieve peace and stability. Nothing, however, could ever truly diminish the historic significance of what transpired in the colonial world after World War II. The global balance of power had been irrevocably altered by this attainment of worldwide independence. The fall of those age-old empires, along with the disappearance of the superpowers' bipolar cold war world, pointed to the emergence of a new kind of world order: one without borders.

From the end of 15 century Europeans began to dominate the planet. Even though China had a superior fleet, they chose to defend instead of explore. Europeans tended to be private operators with no central control. This promoted internal competition. Europeans sought value in tropical products where chines thought foreigners had nothing to offer.

CHRONOLOGY

1946	Perón elected president of Argentina
1947	Partition of India
1948	Creation of Israel
1948–1989	Apartheid in South Africa
1954	Overthrow of Arbenz in Guatemala
1954	French defeat at Dienbienphu
1954–1962	Algerian war of liberation
1955	Bandung Conference
1956	Suez crisis
1957	Ghana gains independence
1958–1961	Great Leap Forward in China
1963	Founding of Organization of African Unity
1964	Creation of Palestinian Liberation Organization (PLO)
1973	Arab-Israeli War
1979	Revolution in Iran
1979	Sandinistas in power in Nicaragua
1980–1988	Iran-Iraq War
1990–1991	Gulf War
1997	Transfer of British Hong Kong to People's Republic of China
1999	Canal Zone returned to Panama
2003	U.S.-led invasion of Iraq
2006	Execution of Saddam Hussein

FOR FURTHER READING

David Anderson. *Histories of the Hanged: The Dirty War in Kenya and the End of Empire.* New York, 2005. History of Kenya's Kikuyu insurrection as a consequence of British colonial violence and land appropriation.

Franz Ansprenger. *The Dissolution of the Colonial Empires.* New York, 1989. A discerning and thorough treatment of the dismantling of European empires and colonies.

Mark Borthwick, ed. *Pacific Century: The Emergence of Modern Pacific Asia.* Boulder, 1992. An excellent source for an overview of southeast and east Asia.

Greg Campbell. *Blood Diamonds: Tracing the Deadly Path of the World's Most Precious Stones.* New York, 2002. A look at the dark side of the Sierra Leone–centered diamond trade.

M. E. Chamberlain. *Decolonization: The Fall of European Empires.* Oxford, 1985. A brief but competent summary of the demise of empires.

Gloria Chuku. *Igbo Women and Economic Transformation in Southeastern Nigeria, 1900–1960.* New York, 2004. Study of the impact of colonial policies on gender relations in postcolonial Nigeria from economic and political perspectives.

Nancy L. Clark and William H. Worger. *South Africa: The Rise and Fall of Apartheid.* New York, 2004. A survey of the history of the apartheid regime from 1948 to its collapse in the 1990s.

Michael J. Cohen. *Palestine and the Great Powers 1945–48.* 2nd ed. Princeton, 1992. An evenhanded assessment of the role played by the great powers in the partition of Palestine and the creation of Israel.

Basil Davidson. *The Black Man's Burden: Africa and the Curse of the Nation State.* New York, 1992. A critical postindependence account that emphasizes the shortcomings of nationalism and the national state.

Prasenjit Duara, ed. *Decolonization (Rewriting Histories).* New York, 2004. The perspective of the colonized is privileged through a selection of writings by leaders of the colonizing countries.

Carlene J. Edie. *Politics in Africa: A New Beginning?* New York, 2002. Examines the domestic and external pressures that have transformed postcolonial African states and societies.

Caroline Elkins. *Imperial Reckoning: The Untold Story of Britain's Gulag in Kenya.* New York, 2004. Powerful study of British atrocities in late colonial Kenya.

R. N. Gwynne. *New Horizons? Third World Industrialization in an International Framework.* New York, 1990. Examines diverse forms of industrialization in the developing world.

Robert Hardgrave Jr. and Stanley A. Hardgrave. *India: Government and Politics in a Developing Nation.* 4th ed. San Diego, 1986. A work that centers on Indian postindependence politics.

Seth Jacobs. *America's Miracle Man in Vietnam: Ngo Dinh Diem, Religion, Race, and U.S. Intervention in Southeast Asia, 1950–1957.* Durham, 2004. Suggests that the decision to support the Catholic South Vietnamese president was a product of heightened religiosity in 1950s America.

Sunil Khilani. *The Idea of India.* New York, 1988. A lively and incisive analysis of the many meanings of India.

Phyllis M. Martin and Patrick O'Meara, eds. *Africa.* 3rd ed. Bloomington, 1995. An insightful collection of articles addressing the cultural, social, economic, and political development of Africa.

Mark Mathabane. *Kaffir Boys: The True Story of a Black Youth's Coming of Age in Apartheid South Africa.* New York, 1986. A gripping real-life story.

Robert A. Mortimer. *The Third World Coalition in International Politics.* New York, 1980. Surveys the political evolution of the nonaligned world.

Timothy H. Parsons. *The 1964 Army Mutinies and the Making of Modern East Africa.* Westport, Conn., 2003. Detailed analysis of soldiers' anticolonial protests in Tanganyika, Uganda, and Kenya.

Thomas E. Skidmore and Peter H. Smith. *Modern Latin America.* New York, 1992. Excellent overview covering the region from the 1880s to the 1980s and supported by an extensive bibliography.

Charles Smith. *Palestine and the Arab-Israeli Conflict.* New York, 1988. A lucid and readable history of the wars between Israel and its Arab adversaries.

Thomas W. Walker. *Nicaragua. Living in the Shadow of the Eagle.* 4th ed. Boulder, 2003. Best and most comprehensive treatment of the nation in the past two decades.

Jeffrey N. Wasserstrom and Elizabeth J. Perry, eds. *Popular Protest and Political Culture in Modern China.* 2nd ed. Boulder, 1994. A collection of essays in which scholars from various disciplines take a critical look at contemporary China.

40 A World without Borders

The Global Economy
Economic Globalization
Economic Growth in Asia
Trading Blocs

**Cross-Cultural Exchanges
and Global Communications**
Global Barbie
Consumption and Cultural Interaction
The Age of Access

Global Problems
Population Pressures and Environmental Degradation
Economic Inequities and Labor Servitude
Global Diseases
Global Terrorism
Coping with Global Problems: International Organizations

Crossing Boundaries
Women's Traditions and Feminist Challenges
Migration
Cross-Cultural Travelers

On 9 November 1989, Kristina Matschat felt excitement and tension in the night air of Berlin. She had joined thousands of other East Germans at Checkpoint Charlie, one of the most famous crossing points in the Berlin Wall. Anticipating that some momentous event was soon to occur at the wall, that the wall might come down that night, she also shivered in fear at the proximity of the *Volkspolizei* ("people's police")—the same officers who since 1961 gunned down East Germans attempting to scale the wall and escape to freedom in West Berlin. She wore running shoes in case she needed to sprint away if shooting broke out or tanks rumbled through East Berlin to prevent the destruction of the wall.

She remembered that "everybody was full of fear—but also full of hope." Bitter memories flooded her consciousness as she recalled not being allowed to study what she wanted in school, not being able to speak freely of her discontent in case her friends were government spies, and not being able to locate disgruntled colleagues whom the government had condemned as "unwanted elements." Her hope overcame her fears, though, as she chanted with her fellow compatriots, "Tear the wall down! Open the gates!" She could see that on the other side of the wall massive crowds of West Berliners had gathered to join their demonstration. Thrilled by this open protest against the most salient symbol of the cold war, she was nonetheless psychologically unprepared for victory when it came. Just before midnight East German soldiers suddenly began not only opening gates in the Wall but also gently helping East Germans cross to the West, often for the first time in their lives. Her near disbelief at the swift downfall of Berlin's decades-old barricade registered in the word she heard shouted over and over again by those passing through the wall: *Wahnsinn* ("craziness").

Kristina Matschat remained at the wall until 3:00 or 4:00 A.M., celebrating with the hundreds of thousands of other Berliners who now mingled, drinking champagne and dancing on top of the wall. While celebrating the fall of the barbed wire and mortar structure, she became aware of the significance of a world without borders: "Suddenly we were seeing the West for the first time, the forbidden Berlin we had only seen on TV or heard about from friends. When we came home at dawn, I felt free for the first time in my life. I had never been happier." The fall of the Berlin Wall brought down one of the world's most notorious borders and symbolized the breaching of all sorts of boundaries in the contemporary world.

Along with decolonization, the fall of the Berlin Wall, and the end of the cold war, many other forces were at work to create a new, more open, world. One pronounced feature of this

OPPOSITE: **This stunning digitally crafted photograph, called "Omnipotent Technology" (1999), blurs the boundaries between art and reality. Its composition of an ethnically fluid face from computer chips and hardware suggests how global identity has morphed and how computers have breached borders between humans and machines.**

1131

world was an increased level of economic interaction between countries and a tighter economic integration of the world. The forces driving the world economy in this direction, often referred to as *globalization,* included advances in communication technology, an enormous expansion of international trade, and the emergence of new global enterprises as well as governments and international organizations that favored market-oriented economics. Global economic interaction and integration were not all new, of course. Ancient Rome and China, for example, controlled and economically integrated vast regions of the ancient world. In more recent centuries, the nations of western Europe—through their global outreach and encounters with far-flung societies—created worldwide empires in which goods and people moved freely. The more recent phenomenon of globalization, however, has been different and unprecedented in both scope and speed, and it has the potential to transform the social and political as well as the economic contours of the world.

Although certain formal national borders changed only after decolonization and the end of the cold war, cultural and technological developments since World War II had steadily broken down the distances between countries and peoples. Cultural integration resulted from the never-ending stream of ideas, information, and values spreading from one society to another. Consumer goods, popular culture, television, computers, and the Internet all spread outward from advanced capitalist and industrialized nations, particularly Europe and the United States, and other societies had to come to terms with this breakdown of cultural and technological barriers. Cultural traditions from Europe and the United States were challenged as often as they were accepted, as most of the world's peoples attempted to blend foreign traditions with their own.

The world's peoples themselves underwent changes in a world with fewer barriers. Women struggled to close the divide between the sexes, at times fighting for equal economic, social, and political rights and at other times abiding by gender expectations while waiting for new opportunities to improve their condition. As populations grew at often alarming rates, women spent much of their time at the traditional female task of child rearing, but both women and men embarked on migrations when their societies could no longer adequately support their growing populations. They moved to the cities or to other nations either to escape suffering or to seek new fortunes.

The populations moving around the globe revealed the diminishing significance of national boundary lines, but they also posed problems that could not be solved by any one state acting alone. International organizations such as the United Nations acknowledged that global problems needed global solutions, underscoring anew the tenuousness of borders in the contemporary world. The global troubles posed by epidemic diseases, labor servitude, terrorism, and human rights also crossed national boundaries and prompted international cooperation. Not everyone experienced the ecstasy Kristina Matschat felt at the Berlin Wall when that most restrictive border disappeared, but global interconnectedness made it more difficult to maintain boundaries among the peoples and countries of the world.

The Global Economy

The global economy came into public view after the spectacular collapse of communism in 1990. Economists pointed to a new economic order characterized by the expansion of trade between countries, the growth of foreign investments, the unfettered movement of capital, the privatization of former state enterprises, a wave of deregulation that undermined the control that national governments once exercised over economic activity, and the emergence of a new breed of corporations. Supporting the new global economy were technological developments in communications; semiconductors, fiber-optic cables, and satellites have virtually eliminated geographic distances, causing an ever-faster integration of the market economy. The forces driving the world economy toward increased economic integration have been responsible for a process termed *globalization*.

Economic Globalization

The early origins of economic globalization derived from the establishment of international organizations such as the International Monetary Fund (IMF). Founded at the Bretton Woods Conference in New Hampshire in 1944, the IMF began the promotion of market economies, free trade, and high growth rates.

Free Trade

International trade proved to be a key driving force behind economic globalization. Trade across long distances especially has figured prominently in the shaping of human history, and for at least the past five hundred years it has served as an integrating force. Of more recent origin is the phrase *free trade,* meaning freedom from state-imposed limits and constraints on trade across borders. The issue of free trade engendered a debate about the extent to which free trade enhances the prosperity of a society. In the aftermath of World War II, leaders from industrialized nations, especially from the United States, took a decisive stand on the issue.

GATT and WTO

U.S. politicians and business leaders wanted to establish an international trading system that suited their interests, and they pushed for the elimination of restrictive trading practices that stood in the way of free trade. The main vehicle for the promotion of unrestricted global trade was the General Agreement on Tariffs and Trade (GATT), which was signed by the representatives of 23 noncommunist nations in 1947. GATT members held a series of negotiations with the intent of removing or loosening barriers to free trade. After the round of negotiations that ended in 1994, the member nations of GATT (now totaling 123) signed an agreement to establish the World Trade Organization (WTO), which took over the activities of GATT in 1995. The WTO has developed into a forum for settling international trade disputes, with the power to enforce its decisions. Numbers tell the story of the fortunes of free trade. World trade (exports and imports) between 1948 and 1966 grew by 6.6 percent annually and by 9.2 percent annually between 1966 and 1977. Although trade slowed in the 1980s, by 1990 world trade exceeded six trillion U.S. dollars, roughly double the figure for 1980.

Global Corporations

The emergence of a new breed of corporation played another key role in the development of the new economic order. Global corporations have increasingly replaced the more traditional international or multinational forms of corporate enterprises. International companies were born out of the desire to extend business activities across borders in pursuit of specific activities such as importation, exportation, and the extraction of raw materials. International companies evolved into multinationals, which conducted their business in several countries but had to operate within the confines of specific laws and customs of a given society. During the past twenty-five years, the transformation of the corporate landscape has resulted in the birth of some fifty thousand global corporations. In contrast to the multinational, the typical global corporation relies on a small headquarters staff while dispersing all other corporate functions across the globe in search of the lowest possible operating costs. Global corporations treat the world as a single market and act as if the nation-state no longer exists. Many multinational corporations, such as General Motors, Siemens AG, and Nestlé, have transformed themselves into global enterprises, both benefiting from and contributing to the ongoing process of globalization.

Global corporations have become the symbols of the new economy. They also have begun to transform the political and social landscape of many societies. During the past

This image of a "Balanced World Economy" (1996) artistically expresses the precariousness of economic globalization.

fifty-five years, major corporations throughout the developed world have been operating under the constraints of a social compact with their employees and communities. Through a combination of collective bargaining agreements, tax laws, and environmental regulations, these companies had to contribute to the welfare of their respective home communities. Highly mobile global corporations that are no longer bound to any particular location have managed, however, to escape those obligations and break the social compact. Competing with companies around the world, the global corporation has moved jobs from high-wage facilities to foreign locations where wages are low and environmental laws are weak or nonexistent. The implications of this development are serious. For example, U.S. federal tax receipts show that corporations that once paid 30 percent of all federal taxes now pay only 12 percent. This trend is not confined to the United States but is visible throughout the industrialized world. In all instances, declining corporate taxes mean less money for social services and welfare programs.

The efforts of governments to entice businesses into keeping their operations at home by reducing the corporate tax burden have been only partially successful. Equally ineffective may be the ongoing efforts by governments and citizens' groups to compel corporations to resume their former social and economic obligations.

Economic Growth in Asia

Globalization and the speeding up of worldwide economic integration also benefited from economic developments in east and southeast Asia, where the economies of Japan, China, and the so-called Asian tigers underwent dramatic economic growth. This Asian "economic miracle" was largely a result of economic globalization.

Japan

U.S. policies jump-started Japan's economic revival after its defeat in 1945, and by 1949 the Japanese economy had already attained its prewar level of productivity. Just as western European countries had benefited from the Marshall Plan, so Japan benefited from direct U.S. financial aid ($2 billion), investment, and the timely abandonment of war reparations. In addition, there were no restrictions on the entry of Japanese products into the U.S. market. The United States, in its role as Japan's military protector, contributed to long-term economic growth as well. Because a 1952 mutual defense treaty stipulated that Japan could never spend more than 1 percent of its gross national product on defense, Japan's postwar leaders channeled the nation's savings into economic development.

At first sight Japan's economy was ill equipped for intensive economic growth. Japan had lost its overseas empire and was hampered by a large population and a lack of natural resources. Japan's economic planners sidestepped many of those disadvantages by promoting an economic policy that emphasized export-oriented growth supported by low wages. The large and mostly compliant workforce, willing to endure working conditions and wages considered intolerable by organized labor in western Europe and the United States, gave Japanese employers a competitive edge over international rivals. Although Japanese industries had to pay for the import of most raw materials, the low cost of Japanese labor ensured the production of goods that were cheap enough to compete on the basis of price.

Initially, the Japanese economy churned out labor-intensive manufactured goods such as textiles, iron, and steel slated for export to markets with high labor costs, particularly the United States. During the 1960s Japanese companies used their profits to switch to more capital-intensive manufacturing and produced radios, television sets, motorcycles, and automobiles. In the 1970s, Japanese corporations took advantage of a highly trained and educated workforce and shifted their economic resources toward technology-intensive products such as random access memory chips, liquid crystal displays, and CD-ROM drives. By that time the label "Made in Japan," once associated with cheap manufactured goods, signified state-of-the-art products of the highest quality. Japan's economic achievements gave its banks, corporations, and government an increasingly prominent voice in global affairs. By the 1980s Japan seemed poised to overtake the United States as the world's largest economy. In the 1990s, however, it became clear that postwar growth rates were not sustainable, and the Japanese economy sputtered into a recession that has continued into the twenty-first century. Nevertheless, the Japanese success story served as an inspiration for other Asian countries.

The Little Tigers

The earliest and most successful imitators of the Japanese model for economic development were Hong Kong, Singapore, South Korea, and Taiwan. Their remarkable and rapid growth rates earned them the sobriquet of the "four little tigers," and by the 1980s these newly industrializing countries had become major economic powers.

Like Japan, all four countries suffered from a shortage of capital, lacked natural resources, and had to cope with overpopulation. But like Japan a generation earlier, they transformed apparent disadvantages into advantages through a program of export-driven industrialization. By the 1990s the four little tigers were no longer simply imitators of Japan but had become serious competitors. As soon as new Japanese products had carved out market niches, corporations based in the four little tigers moved in and undercut the original item with cheaper versions. Before long, Indonesia, Thailand, and Malaysia joined the original tigers in their quest for economic development and prosperity.

The Rise of China

China provides yet-another economic success story. Within four years of the establishment of the People's Republic (1949), the government of Mao Zedong started to place the economy under state control and began a series of five-year plans. Because of the disastrous policies associated with the Great Leap Forward (1958–1961) and the Proletarian Cultural Revolution (1966–1976), China's leaders launched economic reforms in the late 1970s that reversed some earlier policies and opened Chinese markets to the outside world, encouraged foreign investment, and imported foreign technology. With the economy growing dramatically, the government in 1992 signaled the creation of a socialist market economy. In effect, the planned economic system of the past gave way to a market economy, where demand for goods and services determined production and pricing, and where the role of the government was limited to providing a stable but competitive environment. Besides acting as a major exporter, China benefited from its large pool of cheap labor and its enormous domestic markets have made the Chinese economy the destination of choice for foreign investment capital. In December 2001 China became a member of the World Trade Organization and moved closer to gaining global economic superpower status.

Perils of the New Economy

For the supporters of the new global economy, the spectacular economic development of so many Asian societies was proof that globalization could deliver on the promise of unprecedented prosperity. By the late 1990s, however, critics could point to the perils of the new global economy as many of the Asian tigers went from boom to bust economies.

At the center of this bust was a financial crisis that came to a head in 1997. In the preceding twenty years, the developing Asian economies had started to embrace the market, opening their borders to imports and courting foreign investments. Almost overnight these previously poor countries became the darlings of international investors, who willingly poured billions of dollars into the now-attractive national economies. Much of the investment went into creating rapid economic growth, while other investments funded highly speculative business projects. After years of generous lending and growing national debts, the international investment community suddenly lost confidence in the booming economies and withdrew support. The crisis began in Thailand in mid-1997, when investments that once easily poured into the country now left it equally quickly, causing the value of the baht (Thai national currency) to plummet. In quick succession, the Thai stock market lost 75 percent of its value, and the country found itself in the grip of a depression. For no obvious reason, the financial panic—and with it economic contraction—then moved to Malaysia, Indonesia, the Philippines, and South Korea. In each instance, the rise and fall of the individual economies resulted from their integration in the new global economy, which rewarded and punished its new participants with equal ease.

Emerging Economies in Asia and Beyond

Contrary to all expectations, the nations hit so hard by the financial crisis recovered quickly. Their recovery was matched by other emerging economies that included Brazil, China, India, Mexico, and Russia, eastern European nations, and several countries in Africa. In 2005 these emerging economies accounted for over half of global economic output, measured in purchasing-power parity (which takes into consideration lower prices in poorer countries). During the first five years of the twenty-first century, the annual growth rate of emerging economies averaged almost 7 percent—the fastest pace on record. Experts predict that by 2040 the world's ten largest economies will include Brazil, China, India, Mexico, and Russia. Among the emerging economies, China already figures as an economic titan. The IMF predicts that China will surpass the United States as the world's largest economy within the next three decades.

Emerging nations scour the earth for raw materials, are responsible for a steep rise in world energy demand and consumption, and cause an alarming increase in emissions of greenhouse gases and air pollution. The once-poor world is not only getting richer but also increasingly making its weight felt in international organizations on everything from trade issues to membership in the United Nations Security Council. What all this means is that the rich developed countries no longer dominate the global economy the way they did during the nineteenth and twentieth centuries. This shift is not as astonishing as it first seems, as some of today's emerging economies are simply regaining their former preeminence. Until the late nineteenth century, for example, China and India were the world's biggest economies.

Trading Blocs

Accepting free trade and open markets meant acknowledging global economic interdependence; no single economic power could fully control global trade and commerce. In the rapidly changing global economy, groups of nations have therefore entered into economic alliances designed to achieve advantages and greater strength for their partners in the competitive global economy.

The most famous and most strongly integrated regional bloc is the European Union, which is characterized by a common market and free trade. In March 1957, representatives of six nations—France, West Germany, Italy, the Netherlands, Belgium, and Luxembourg—took a significant step in this direction by signing the Treaty of Rome. This treaty established the European Economic Community—renamed the European Community in 1967. At the heart of this new community of nations lay the dismantling of tariffs and other barriers to free trade among member nations. Subsequent treaties creating political institutions such as the Council of Ministers and the European Parliament facilitated the long-range goal of European political integration. The development of a supranational organization dedicated to increasing European economic and political integration culminated in the Maastricht Treaty of 1993, which established the European Union. Twenty-seven European nations have submerged much of their national sovereignty in the European Union, and since 1999 thirteen members have adopted a common currency. In the future, this tight economic integration is expected to lead to a European Political Union.

European Union

One of the earliest and most successful economic alliances was the Organization of Petroleum Exporting Countries (OPEC), a producer cartel established in 1960 by the oil-producing states of Iran, Iraq, Kuwait, Saudi Arabia, and Venezuela, and later joined by Qatar, Libya, Indonesia, Abu Dhabi, Algeria, Nigeria, Ecuador, and Gabon. The mostly Arab and Muslim member states of OPEC sought to raise the price of oil through cooperation, but OPEC demonstrated during the Arab-Israeli War of 1973 that cooperation had political as well as economic potential. The cartel ordered an embargo on oil shipments to the United States, Israel's ally, and quadrupled the price of oil between 1973 and 1975. The huge increase in the cost of petroleum triggered a global economic downturn, as did a curtailment of oil exports in the later 1970s. OPEC's policies therefore contributed to the global recession and debt crisis that hurt

OPEC

Map 40.1   **European Union membership, 2004.** In 2007 the European Union celebrated the fiftieth anniversary of its founding as a supranational and intergovernmental organization that encompasses twenty-seven member states. What major challenge faced the European Union in the twenty-first century?

many developing nations, but its members—also developing nations—demonstrated how the alliance could exert control over the developed world and its financial system. OPEC's influence diminished in the 1980s and 1990s as a result of overproduction and dissension among its members over the Iran-Iraq War and the Gulf War.

ASEAN

Another well-established economic partnership is the Association of Southeast Asian Nations, or ASEAN. Established in 1967 by the foreign ministers of Thailand, Malaysia, Singapore, Indonesia, and the Philippines, its principal objectives were to accelerate economic development and promote political stability in southeast Asia. Originally conceived as a bulwark against the spread of communism in the region, the economic focus of ASEAN became sharper after it signed cooperative agreements with Japan in 1977 and the European Community in 1980. In 1992 member states agreed to establish a free-trade zone and to cut tariffs on industrial goods over a fifteen-year period.

NAFTA

The United States, although still home to the largest national economy in the world, also saw the need to become involved in regional trade groupings. The United States entered its own regional alliance, approving the North American Free Trade Agreement (NAFTA) with Canada and Mexico in 1993. NAFTA, which went into effect in 1994, constitutes the world's second-largest free-trade zone, but it is a much looser bloc, lacking the economic coordination so typical of the European Union. There are plans to expand NAFTA to all noncommunist nations in the Americas, underscoring the increasing commitment to the elimination of tariffs and other barriers to regional and global free trade.

Globalization and Its Critics

The global economy is still very much a work in progress, and it not clear what the long-term effects will be on the economies and societies it touches. To its supporters, the global economy delivers markets that operate with maximum efficiency, speedily directing goods and services wherever there is demand for them and always expecting the highest returns possible. Proponents of globalization also argue that the new economy is the only way to bring prosperity—the kind previously enjoyed only by industrialized nations—to the developing world. To its critics—nongovernmental organizations ranging from labor unions to tribal-rights activists—the global economy is an untamed juggernaut that is neither inevitable nor desirable, a force that rewards the few and impoverishes the many. The specific charges leveled by antiglobalization groups and coalitions are many. They assert that globalization diminishes the sovereignty of local and national governments and transfers the power to shape economic and political destinies to transnational corporations and global institutions such as the IMF and the WTO. Detractors of globalization also claim that the hallmark of globalization—rapid economic development—is responsible for the destruction of the environment, the widening gap between rich and poor societies, and the worldwide homogenization of local, diverse, and indigenous cultures. It is certain that globalization has been accompanied by serious social and economic problems. It is less certain, however, if anyone can succeed in taming its power.

Cross-Cultural Exchanges and Global Communications

[handwritten annotation: Spanish trading ships once or twice a year / Pacific ocean between Manila in the Philippines and Acapuco in New Mexico. 1565 / Served primary income for Spanish colonist in Manila / Spice trades]

The demise of European colonial empires, the fall of the Berlin Wall, and the end of the cold war brought down the most obvious political barriers of the post–World War II world. Long before then, however, cultural and technological developments had started a similar process of breaching boundaries. By showcasing the consumer goods of capitalist societies and spreading news of each new chapter in the fall of communism, television in fact had helped spur the revolutions that ended the cold war. As Kristina Matschat testified, before the Berlin Wall fell she had seen West Berlin only on television. One of the first products of the global consumer culture imbibed by East Germans was Coca-Cola, served to them by store owners in West Berlin.

Like trade and business organizations, cultural practices have also become globalized, thriving on a continuous flow of information, ideas, tastes, and values. At the turn of the twentieth century, local traditions—commonly derived from gender, social class, or religious affiliation—still determined the cultural identity of the vast majority of people. At the end of the twentieth century, thanks in part to advances in technology and communications, information and cultural practices were becoming truly global. Their impact was summarized in a jingle popularized by the Walt Disney corporation during the 1964–1965 World's Fair in New York City: "It's a small world after all."

Global Barbie

In October 1996 the Associated Press flashed a news story over its wires (and onto the Internet, through CNN Interactive) with the headline "Iran's Answer to Barbie." The story described the creation of the Sara doll, who would fight American cultural influences as embodied in the Barbie dolls on store shelves in Tehran. Sara's creator clearly meant the doll to compete with Barbie while promoting the chaste dress and pure values expected of Islamic girls and women. Sara is clothed in long flowing robes and head coverings. She and her brother doll, Dara (an Islamic cleric), pose a stark contrast to the plastic couple from the United States, Barbie and Ken, who show no shame in exposing their bodies and premarital relationship to the world. The cultural gulf between Sara and Dara and Barbie and Ken was intentional; according to Majid Ghaderi, the designer of the dolls and the director of Iran's Institute for the Intellectual Development of Children and Young Adults, "Barbie is an American woman who never wants to get pregnant and have babies. She never wants to look old, and this contradicts our culture."

Sara versus Barbie in Iran

Ghaderi viewed Barbie as a metaphor for unwanted cultural dominance: "Barbie is like a Trojan Horse. Inside it, it carries Western cultural influences, such as makeup and indecent clothes. Once it enters our society, it dumps these influences on our children." Whether Sara will effectively counter Barbie in Iran is still an open question, but the influence of Islamic clerics on Iranian notions of feminism is apparent. Shopkeepers in Tehran do not expect the doll to do well against Barbie but generally support the idea behind Sara. As one merchant said, "I myself believe that Barbie dolls are not good for our children, although they are beautiful." Feminists might chafe at the idea of Barbie representing a type of emancipated woman that is not welcome in the Islamic world. Iranian Muslims equate women's liberation with not getting pregnant, staying young, and wearing makeup and little else. They associate it with a plastic figurine whose impossibly ideal dimensions have given women fits. However, Barbie does serve as one symbol of the U.S. cultural products that are swamping global markets. And Iran's Sara demonstrates how countries have attempted to maintain their cultural traditions.

Barbie in Japan

That Iranian officials perceived Barbie as a Trojan horse bringing in foreign, feminist values—and created the traditional Sara doll to oppose Barbie's influence—suggests how strongly some societies strive to counteract foreign cultural influences. At the same time, however, the U.S. cultural system adapted to the demands and sensibilities of the world, modifying its products to conform to indigenous expectations. When Mattel Corporation wanted to market Barbie in Japan, it had to adjust to Japanese cultural sensibilities. Japanese girls preferred Licca, a doe-eyed, brunette, younger doll. They found Barbie's eyes scary, her smile too aggressively toothy, and her attitude too much of a professional woman on the go. Because Barbie challenged Japanese notions of a less-emancipated femininity, Mattel reformed Barbie: she was marketed in family settings, with stroller and children, and she had a rounder face, bigger eyes, a closed mouth, and less shockingly blonde hair. Barbie sales increased. As the manager at a major Japanese toy company concluded, "I don't think their doll is considered American like before. Now there are kids who play with Licca and Barbie together. It's a borderless era."

Consumption and Cultural Interaction

New communications media have tied the world together and have promoted a global cultural integration whose hallmark is consumption. Beginning in the eighteenth century, industrialization and the subsequent rise in per capita income gave birth to a type of society in which the consumption of goods and services satisfied wants and desires rather than needs or necessities. Although the desire to consume is hardly novel, the modern consumer culture means more than simple consumption. It implies that consumers want more than they need and that the items they consume take on symbolic value. Consumption, in other words, has become a means of self-expression as well as a source for personal identity and social differentiation. The peculiar shape of this consumer culture resulted from two seemingly contradictory trends: a tendency toward homogenization of cultural products and heightened awareness of local tastes and values. Critics sometimes refer to the homogenizing aspect of global culture as the "Americanization" or "McDonaldization" of the world.

Those terms suggest that the consumer culture that developed in the United States during the mid-twentieth century has been exported throughout the world, principally through advertising. Thus it is no accident that young people clad in blue jeans and T-shirts sing the same Usher or Eminem lyrics in San Francisco, Sarajevo, and Beijing. Still, nothing symbolizes the global marketing of U.S. mass culture more than the spread of its food and beverage products. While Pepsi and Coca-Cola fight battles over the few places on earth that their beverages have not yet dominated, fast-food restaurants such as Burger King, McDonalds, and Pizza Hut sell their standardized foods throughout the world. The closing of many bistros and cafés in France, for instance, is the result of more French people opting for fashionable fast food instead of taking the time for more traditional and lengthy lunches. So successful has the global spread of U.S. mass culture been that it seems to threaten local or indigenous cultures everywhere.

The export of U.S. products and services is not the sole determinant of global cultural practices, however, as the Barbie examples illustrate. Because the contemporary consumer culture stresses minute differences between products and encourages consumers to make purchase decisions based on brand names designed to evoke particular tastes, fashion, or lifestyle, it also fosters differentiation. Indeed, global marketing often emphasizes the local or indigenous value of a product. Genuinely Australian products, such as Drizabone wet-weather gear and Foster's Lager, have become international commodities precisely because they are Australian in origin. Likewise, young upwardly mobile consumers continue to prefer Rolex watches from Switzerland, Armani clothes from Italy, miniature electronics from Japan, and Perrier mineral water from France.

Pan-American Culture

The experiences in the Americas demonstrate that U.S. patterns of cultural consumption have not simply dominated the globe without competition or critical evaluation. For example, as she was dying, the Argentine political and cultural icon Eva Perón is reputed to have said, "I will return and I will be millions." Her prophecy has come true in the images of her that continually appear around the world, especially in the Americas. In Buenos Aires, city housing projects are named after her, a new Argentine film about her life played in 1996, and her face appears on souvenir T-shirts sold in the streets. In an Argentine supper club, the show's cast members sing "Don't Cry for Me, Argentina" as their grand finale, and audiences rise to their feet applauding. The song is from the musical *Evita* by Sir Andrew Lloyd Webber and Tim Rice, which was first performed in London and subsequently became a hit on Broadway (1979). While Argentine performers sing a Euro-American song, their

Evita has become an icon in the United States and Europe, not only in the musical, but also in the 1996 film *Evita* starring Madonna.

Although Latin American critics often decry the spell cast by North American popular culture on Latin American audiences, Evita-mania has indicated that the sharing or imposing of cultural practices is a two-way phenomenon. A trend in Latin America is Music Television (MTV) Latino, perceived by many critics as another case of foreign cultural intrusion, where Latin video deejays speak "Spanglish" or "Chequenos" ("check us out"), mixing Spanish and English. Yet, whereas Latin Americans once had called for protection against such alien influence, by the 1990s many had relaxed their guard. They see evidence of increased cultural sharing among Latin societies, noting that MTV and cable television have come to serve as a means of communication and unity by making the nations of Latin America more aware of one another. While the sheer dominance and size of the U.S. entertainment-technology industry keeps cultural sharing lopsided, cultural dominance is also limited by those societies' ability to blend and absorb a variety of foreign and indigenous practices.

The Age of Access

Throughout history technological advances such as in shipbuilding provided the means to dissolve boundaries between localities and peoples and thus allowed cultural transmission to take place. Today virtually instantaneous electronic communications have dissolved time and space. Contemporary observers have labeled our era "the age of access." Communication by radio, telephone, television, fax machine, and networked computers has spawned a global village that has swept away the social, economic, and political isolation of the past. However, because it takes capital to purchase the necessary equipment, maintain and upgrade it, and train people to use it, many societies find it difficult to plug into the global village. The existing gulf between the connected and the unconnected has the potential therefore to become one border in a world without borders.

Preeminence of the English Language

This new world of global interconnectedness is not without its detractors. Critics have charged, for instance, that mass media are a vehicle for cultural imperialism because most electronic media and the messages they carry emanate from advanced capitalist societies. A specific consequence is that English is becoming the primary language of global communications systems, effectively restricting vernacular languages to a niche status.

The Internet reinforces the contemporary fact that English has become the universal tongue of the twenty-first century. As a result of British colonialism, subjugated peoples the world over had been compelled to learn English and become at least bilingual, speaking their own languages along with those of the colonizer. In more recent times, many peoples have voluntarily adopted the language of a politically and economically preeminent English-speaking society, especially the United States. In this fashion, English has almost become a universal language, enjoying acceptance in scientific, diplomatic, and commercial circles. However understandable, English-language dominance on the Internet rankles some users. Xia Hong, a manager for an Internet access provider in Shanghai, articulates this concern:

> There's no question about it: the Internet is an information colony. From the moment you go online, you're confronted with English hegemony. It's not merely a matter of making the Net convenient for users in non-English-speaking countries. People have to face the fact that English speakers are not the whole world. What's the big deal about them, anyway? Our ideal is to create an exclusively Chinese-language network. It will be a Net that has Chinese characteristics, one that is an information superhighway for the masses.

Such sentiments apparently reflect the thinking of Chinese political leaders, for authorities are going to great lengths to ensure that China and its communications system do not become a spiritual colony of capitalist powers such as the United States. Accordingly, officials of China's Public Security Bureau—an agency that concerns itself with crimes ranging from murder to cultural espionage—are trying to contain the influence of the Internet by erecting around China a so-called "firewall" or *fanghuo*

A citizen of Kuwait lugs a television through streets filled with European and U.S. consumer products. From tennis shoes to automobiles to English-language signs, cultural interpenetration is occurring around the globe.

qiang (a direct translation from the English). The more prevailing and popular phrase for it is *wangguan* (literally, "net wall"), a name that invokes many centuries of Chinese efforts to repulse foreign invaders. However, because the original Great Wall had limited success, the fate of its digital successor remains an open question.

Some societies have managed to adapt European and U.S. technology to meet their needs while opposing cultural interference. Television, for example, has been used to promote state building around the world, since most television industries are state controlled. In Zaire, for example, the first television picture residents saw each day was of Mobutu Sese Seko. He especially liked to materialize in segments that pictured him walking on clouds—a miraculous vision of his unearthly power. The revolution in electronic communications has been rigidly controlled in other societies—including Vietnam and Iraq—where authorities limit access to foreign servers on the Internet. They thus harness the power of technology for their own purposes while avoiding cultural interference.

Adaptations of Technology

Global Problems

By the end of the twentieth century, many traditional areas of state responsibility—whether pertaining to population policies, health concerns, or environmental issues—needed to be coordinated on an intergovernmental level. Global problems demanded global solutions, and together they compelled the governments of individual states to surrender some of their sovereignty to larger international organizations such as the United Nations. Issues concerning labor servitude, poverty, epidemic diseases, terrorism, and human rights demanded attention and action on a scale greater than the nation-state.

Population Pressures and Environmental Degradation

The past hundred years or so have been accompanied by vast population increases. As the result of advances in agriculture, industry, science, medicine, and social organization, the world experienced a fivefold population increase over a period of three hundred years: from 500 million people in 1650 to 2.5 billion in 1950. After World War II

Table 40.1 Population (in Millions) for Major Areas of the World, 1900–2050

Major Area	1900	1950	1975	2005	2050
Africa	133	224	416	906	1937
Asia	947	1396	2395	3905	5217
Europe	408	547	676	728	653
Latin America	74	167	322	561	783
North America	82	172	243	331	438
Oceania	6	13	21	33	48
World (total)	1650	2519	4074	6465	9076

SOURCE: *World Population Prospects: The 2004 Revision. Highlights.* New York: United Nations, 2005.

the widespread and successful use of vaccines, antibiotics, and insecticides, along with improvements in water supplies and increased agricultural yields, caused a dramatic decline in worldwide death rates. The rapid decline in mortality among people who also maintained high levels of fertility led to explosive population growth in many areas of Asia and Africa. In some developing nations, population growth now exceeds 3.1 percent, a rate that ensures the doubling of the population within twenty-three years. In 2005 roughly 6.5 billion people shared the planet, and the population division of the United Nations has estimated that the earth's population will stabilize around 9 billion in 2050. In the meantime, 75 million people are joining the world's total population each year, and unless fertility declines to replacement levels—that is, two children per woman—the world's population will grow forever.

More optimistic voices, however, have pointed out that the odds of a population explosion and its dreaded consequences are exaggerated and are in fact receding. In part this decline is the result of the AIDS crisis, which is taking a heavy demographic toll in societies where fertility rates are high. More important, fertility rates have been falling fast in the past two decades, both in rich and in poor societies. The same optimists also argue that despite rapid population growth, wages have risen and the cost of everything extracted or grown from the earth has declined. Equally significant is the fact that food production has more than kept pace with the growing population.

The Planet's Carrying Capacity

A large population changes the earth and its environment, raising an important question: How many people can the earth support? The exact carrying capacity of the planet is, of course, a matter of debate, but by many measures the earth seems to strain already to support the current population. Scientists and concerned citizens have become increasingly convinced that human society cannot infinitely expand beyond the physical limits of the earth and its resources. Beginning in 1967 a group of international economists and scientists—dubbed the Club of Rome—attempted to specify the limits of both economic and population growth in relation to the capacity of the planet to support humanity. Praised by some observers as the conscience of the world and decried by others as being excessively negative, the club issued a report in 1972 with the subtitle, "The Limits to Growth." Because the world's physical resources are in finite supply, the Club of Rome concluded, any transgression of those limits would be calamitous. Two decades later, fifteen hundred scientists, including ninety-nine Nobel laureates and representatives from a dozen of the world's most prestigious academies, signed a document titled, "Warning to Humanity" (1992). The report sounded a clear alarm, stating that "human beings and the natural world are on a collision course . . . [that] may so alter the living world that it will be unable to sustain life in the manner that we know."

Smokestacks in Siberia releasing carbon dioxide emissions into the atmosphere.

The prophets of doom are not without their detractors, who have eagerly pointed out that the predictions of the Club of Rome and similar ones by other organizations and by concerned governments have not been borne out by the facts. For example, the Club of Rome predicted that the global reserves of oil, natural gas, silver, tin, uranium, aluminum, copper, lead, and zinc were approaching exhaustion and that prices would rise steeply. In every case but tin, reserves have actually grown since 1972. Eight years later the price for virtually all minerals—excepting only zinc and manganese—had dropped and continue to do so. The Club of Rome's inaccurate predictions have not diminished its dystopian confidence. In a more recent and widely acclaimed work, *Beyond the Limits* (1999), the Club of Rome, while acknowledging that its earlier predictions had been too pessimistic, persisted in being equally pessimistic about the future.

Environmental Impact

The problem is not simply one of depleting nonrenewable resources or expanding populations. The prodigious growth of the human population is at the root of many environmental problems. As people are born, pollution levels increase, more habitats and animal and plant species disappear, and more natural resources are consumed. In recent decades, two environmental issues have taken center stage: biodiversity and global warming.

Biodiversity relates to the maintenance of multiple species of plants and animals. The most serious threat to biodiversity emerged from the destruction of natural habitats in the wake of urbanization, extension of agricultural activity, and exploitation of mineral and timber resources. Extinction currently threatens some 4,500 animal

Silent Spring

One of the earliest and most effective warnings about modern environmental damage appeared in 1962. Silent Spring, *written by scientist Rachel Carson (1907–1964), offers a critical and dramatic investigation into the environmental disaster caused by chemical pesticides. Carson's book created a sensation, and* Silent Spring *is often credited with inspiring the environmental movement. Carson began her exposé of chemical pollution with "A Fable for Tomorrow," where she metaphorically details the results of chemical pollution on a symbolic American town and suggests the true meaning of a "silent spring."*

There was once a town in the heart of America where all life seemed to live in harmony with its surroundings. The town lay in the midst of a checkerboard of prosperous farms, with fields of grain and hillsides of orchards where, in spring, white clouds of bloom drifted above the green fields. In autumn, oak and maple and birch set up a blaze of color that flamed and flickered across a backdrop of pines. Then foxes barked in the hills and deer silently crossed the fields, half hidden in the mists of the fall mornings.

Along the roads, laurel, viburnum and alder, great ferns and wildflowers delighted the traveler's eye through much of the year. Even in winter the roadsides were places of beauty, where countless birds came to feed on the berries and on the seed heads of the dried weeds rising above the snow. The countryside was, in fact, famous for the abundance and variety of its bird life, and when the flood of migrants was pouring through in the spring and fall people traveled from great distances to observe them. Others came to fish the streams, which flowed clear and cold out of the hills and contained shady pools where trout lay. So it had been from the days many years ago when the first settlers raised their houses, sank their wells, and built their barns.

Then a strange blight crept over the area and everything began to change. Some evil spell had settled on the community: mysterious maladies swept the flocks of chickens; the cattle and sheep sickened and died. Everywhere was a shadow of death. The farmers spoke of much illness among their families. In the town the doctors had become more and more puzzled by the new kinds of sickness appearing among their patients. There had been several sudden and unexplained deaths, not only among adults but even among children, who would be stricken suddenly while at play and die within a few hours.

There was a strange stillness. The birds, for example—where had they gone? Many people spoke of them, puzzled and disturbed. The feeding stations in the backyards were deserted. The few birds seen anywhere were moribund; they trembled violently and could not fly. It was spring without voices. On the mornings that had once throbbed with the dawn chorus of robins, catbirds, doves, jays, wrens, and scores of other bird voices there was now no sound; only silence lay over the fields and woods and marsh.

On the farms the hens brooded, but no chicks hatched. The farmers complained that they were unable to raise any pigs—the litters were small and the young survived only a few days. The apple trees were coming into bloom but no bees droned among the blossoms, so there was no pollination and there would be no fruit.

The roadsides, once so attractive, were now lined with browned and withered vegetation as though swept by fire. These, too, were silent, deserted by all living things. Even the streams were now lifeless. Anglers no longer visited them, for all the fish had died.

In the gutters under the eaves and between the shingles of the roofs, a white granular powder still showed a few patches; some weeks before it had fallen like snow upon the roofs and the lawns, the fields and streams.

No witchcraft, no enemy action had silenced the rebirth of life in this stricken world. The people had done it themselves.

This town does not actually exist, but it might easily have a thousand counterparts in America or elsewhere in the world. I know of no community that has experienced all the misfortunes I describe. Yet every one of these disasters has actually happened somewhere, and many real communities have already suffered a substantial number of them. A grim specter has crept upon us almost unnoticed, and this imagined tragedy may easily become a stark reality we all shall know.

FOR FURTHER REFLECTION

What were the multiform effects of the "strange blight" creeping over the American environment, and who proved responsible for these disasters?

SOURCE: Rachel Carson. *Silent Spring.* Boston: Houghton Mifflin, 1962, 1994, pp. 1–3.

A poster advertising China's one-child family rule.

species. Global warming refers to a rise in global temperature, which carries potentially dire consequences for humanity. Atmospheric pollution causes global warming because the emission of greenhouse gases prevents solar heat from escaping from the earth's atmosphere.

Like the glass panes in a greenhouse, hydrocarbon emissions from automobiles, carbon dioxide emissions from burning fossil fuel, and methane emitted from the stool of farm animals trap heat within the atmosphere, leading to a rise in global temperatures. Even a seemingly modest rise of one to three degrees Celsius in the temperature of the atmosphere might have serious consequences, such as a rise in sea levels that would completely inundate low-lying islands and coastal areas on all continents. In the ancient Japanese capital of Kyoto, at a conference dedicated to pressing environmental problems, the delegates of 159 countries agreed in 1997 to cut greenhouse gas emissions blamed for global warming. Although the conference delegates agreed that developed nations should cut the emissions of carbon dioxide and other dangerous gases, the conference did not require developing countries—some of them major polluters, such as India and China—to reduce their emissions.

Population Control

For decades the issue of population control was highly politicized. Political leaders in developing countries, for example, charged representatives of industrialized countries with racism when they raised concerns regarding overpopulation. Industrialized nations were also accused of trying to safeguard their outrageous consumption patterns of the world's nonrenewable resources. Some leaders, such as Mexico's Luis Echeverria, went so far as to promote pronatalist measures (to increase births), urging his fellow citizens to have numerous children. The problems caused by rapid population growth eventually persuaded many governments to take action to control fertility. By that time, the old pervasive notion that a large population is a source of national power had given way to the idea that the best way to promote the health and well-being of a population is to control its growth.

As death rates declined persistently throughout the world during the latter part of the twentieth century, reducing birthrates became a central concern of many governments, and to date some eighty countries have adopted birth control programs.

The United Nations and two of its specialized agencies, the World Health Organization and the UN Fund for Population Activities, have aided many countries in organizing and promoting family-planning programs. However, the availability and promotion of contraceptives does not guarantee effective control of fertility. Whereas China has, however stringently, significantly reduced its population growth rate and some Latin American societies also have a decline in their birthrates, people in other societies have resisted efforts to reduce birthrates. In some instances, resistance stems from both religious and political motives. In India, for example, the Hindu emphasis on fertility has impeded birth control efforts. Thus global attempts to prevent excessive population growth have had mixed results.

Economic Inequities and Labor Servitude

The unequal distribution of resources and income, and the resulting poverty, have materialized as key concerns of the contemporary world. Several hundred million people, especially in the developing areas of eastern Europe, Africa, Latin America, and Asia, struggle daily for sufficient food, clean water, adequate shelter, and other basic necessities. Poverty is a lack of basic human necessities, and its effects are as wide-ranging as they are devastating. Malnutrition among the poor has led to starvation and death. As one of the most persistent effects of poverty, malnutrition is also responsible for stunted growth, poor mental development, and high rates of infection. Typically, vitamin and mineral deficiencies accompany malnutrition, causing mental disorders, organ damage, and vision failure among poor children and adults. Because of inadequate shelter, lack of safe running water, and the absence of sewage facilities, the poor have been exposed disproportionally to bacteria and viruses carried by other people, insects, and rodents. Poverty has correlated strongly with higher-than-average infant mortality rates and lower-than-average life expectancies.

The Causes of Poverty   The division between rich and poor has been a defining characteristic of all complex societies. Although relative poverty levels within a given society remain a major concern, it is the continuing division between rich and poor societies that has attracted the attention of the international community. A worldwide shortage of natural resources as well as the uneven distribution of resources have figured as major causes of poverty and have divided nations into the haves and have-nots. Excessively high population densities and environmental degradation have caused the depletion of available resources, leading to shortages of food, water, and shelter and ultimately to poverty. The other major cause of poverty, the unequal distribution of resources in the world economy, resulted from five hundred years of colonialism, defined by the appropriation of labor and natural resources. Pervasive poverty characterizes many former colonies and dependencies. All of these developing societies have tried to raise income levels and eliminate poverty through diversified economic development, but only a few, such as South Korea, Singapore, Malaysia, and Indonesia, have accomplished their aims. In the meantime, economic globalization has generated unprecedented wealth for developed nations, creating an even deeper divide between rich and poor countries.

Labor Servitude   Poor economic conditions have been closely associated with forms of servitude similar to slavery. Although legal slavery ceased to exist when Saudi Arabia and Angola abolished slavery officially in the 1960s, forced and bonded labor practices continue to affect millions of poor people in the developing world. Of particular concern is child-labor servitude. According to the International Labor Organization, a specialized agency of the United Nations, more than 250 million children between ages five and fourteen work around the world, many in conditions that are inherently harmful to their physical health and emotional well-being. Child-labor servitude is most pronounced in south and southeast Asia, affecting an estimated 50 million children in India alone. Most child labor occurs in agriculture, domestic service, family businesses, and the sex trade, making it difficult to enforce existing prohibitions and laws against those practices. Many children are born into a life of bonded labor because their parents have worked in debt bondage, a condition whereby impoverished persons work for very low wages, borrow money from their employer, and pledge their labor as security.

A growing and related global problem that touches societies on every continent is the trafficking of persons. In this insidious form of modern slavery, one to two million human beings annually are bought and sold across international and within national boundaries. Trafficking has appeared in many forms. In Russia and the Ukraine, for example, traffickers lure victims with the promise of well-paying jobs abroad. Once the victims arrive in the countries of their destination, they become captives of ruthless traffickers who force them into bonded labor, domestic servitude, or the commercial sex industry through threats and physical brutality—including rape, torture and starvation, incarceration, and death. Most of the victims of trafficking are girls and women, which is a reflection of the low social and economic status of women in many countries. In south Asia, for instance, it is common for poverty-stricken parents or other relatives to sell young women to traffickers for the sex trade or forced labor. The trafficking industry is one of the fastest growing and most lucrative criminal enterprises in the world, generating billions of dollars annually in profits.

Trafficking

Global Diseases

Since the dawn of history, disease has played a significant role in the development of human communities. Its impact has been as dramatic as it has been destructive. For example, the most devastating impact of the Columbian exchange (see chapter 23) came in the wake of diseases that Europeans introduced into the Americas following the voyages of Christopher Columbus and others. The introduction of diseases to populations that lacked any form of immunity killed perhaps as many as 90 percent of native Americans in the span of 150 years. More recently, an influenza pandemic that swept the globe in 1918 and 1919 killed between twenty and forty million people, far more than died as the result of the Great War that had just ended. Since then, medical experts, public health officials, and scientists scored major victories in their fight against diseases, eradicating smallpox and diphtheria, for example. Buoyed by those successes, the United Nations in 1978 called for the elimination of all infectious diseases by the year 2000. That goal was unrealistic, and in the meantime ancient diseases once thought under control, such as malaria and tuberculosis, are on the rise again. Equally ominous, public health officials have identified new lethal diseases such as Ebola fever and HIV/AIDS.

The most serious epidemic threat comes from acquired immunodeficiency syndrome (AIDS). This fatal disorder of the immune system is caused by the human immunodeficiency virus (HIV), which slowly attacks and destroys the immune system, leaving the infected individual vulnerable to diseases that eventually cause death. AIDS is the last stage of HIV infection, during which time these diseases arise. The HIV infection is spread through sexual contact with an infected person, contact with contaminated blood, and transmission from mother to child during pregnancy and, after birth, through breast feeding. Factors contributing to the spread of AIDS include poverty, ignorance, the prohibitive cost of drugs, and, some say, sexual promiscuity.

HIV/AIDS

Medical experts identified AIDS for the first time in 1981 among homosexual men and intravenous drug users in New York and San Francisco. Subsequently, evidence for an epidemic appeared among heterosexual men, women, and children in sub-Saharan

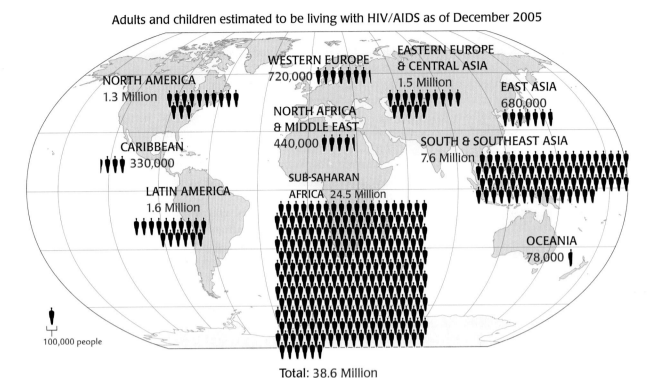

Adults and children estimated to be living with HIV/AIDS as of December 2005

Total: 38.6 Million

Map 40.2 **Global estimates of HIV/AIDS.** HIV infection in humans is one of the most destructive pandemics in recorded history, having claimed the lives of twenty-five million people since scientists first identified it in 1981. What regions of the world have been most affected?

AIDS in Africa

Africa, and rather quickly AIDS developed into a worldwide epidemic that affected virtually every nation. At the end of 2005, the number of people living with HIV/AIDS was 38.6 million, and over 20 million AIDS deaths had occurred since the beginning of the epidemic.

The AIDS epidemic is a serious public health threat throughout the world, but the disease has struck the developing world hardest, especially sub-Saharan Africa. Statistics paint a grim picture. Of the 38.6 million people identified with HIV/AIDS worldwide, 24.5 million of them currently live in sub-Saharan Africa. If current trends persist, AIDS deaths and the loss of future population from the demise of women in childbearing ages will lead to a 70-million drop in population by 2010. Between 2005 and 2010, the life expectancy in the region is expected to decline from fifty-nine years to forty-five. Africa is also home to 80 percent of the children who are living with HIV/AIDS worldwide. AIDS has touched children in two ways: as a disease infecting children and as a disease that leaves them orphans. Thus far the epidemic has orphaned 10 million children, and unless this pattern is reversed Africa will have 40 million AIDS orphans, most of whom will grow up with little or no social nurturing.

The AIDS epidemic threatens to overwhelm the social and economic fabric of African societies, rolling back decades of progress toward a healthier and more prosperous future. The health infrastructure of most African nations cannot cope with the impact of the AIDS epidemic. Although sophisticated palliative treatments—not cures—are available, only the wealthy can afford them. Most Africans are desperately poor. As the AIDS epidemic deepens, it leaves an economically devastated continent in its wake. Families who must care for a member who is ill with AIDS often deplete financial resources that would otherwise be used to cover necessities or to invest in children's futures. When AIDS claims the lives of people in their most productive years, grieving orphans and elders must contend with the sudden loss of financial support, communities must bear the burden of caring for those left behind, and countries must draw on a diminishing number of trained and talented workers.

There are signs that HIV incidence may stabilize in sub-Saharan Africa. So many people in the sexually active population have been affected that only a small pool of people is still able to acquire the infection. In addition, successful prevention programs in a small number of countries, notably in Uganda, have reduced infection rates and contributed to a regional downturn of the epidemic.

The good news from Africa is tainted by bad news from Asia. Although infection rates in Asia remain low, health officials fear that the disease will spread faster as it traverses India, the world's second most populous nation. There is fear that the infection rate will escalate during the next decade, causing the epidemic in India to dwarf the problems seen in Africa. Although no vaccine has yet emerged to prevent or cure HIV infection, some advances have been made. When scientists first identified AIDS, there was no treatment for the disease. Existing anti-viral drugs at best delayed the inevitable and at worst failed completely. By 1995, though, researchers succeeded in developing a new class of drugs known as protase inhibitors and, in combination with some of the older drugs, they produced what is now known as highly active anti-retroviral therapy or HAART. In most cases, HAART can prolong life indefinitely. The high cost of these sophisticated drugs initially prevented poor people from sharing in their benefits, but this too is changing. By 2007 over one million people in sub-Saharan Africa routinely received anti-AIDS drugs, and optimistic estimates suggest that by 2010 effective AIDS drugs will be available to all who might benefit from them. New prevention techniques parallel improved drug treatments. Although an effective vaccine remains elusive, scientists have come up with new prevention techniques that, unlike condom use, do not require male involvement. Holding out great promise are vaginal microbicides designed to prevent the virus from entering the body and prophylactic drug regimens that create a hostile environment for any virus that does make it into the bloodstream.

Global Terrorism

Terrorism has become a persistent feature of the globalized world. Although not a recent phenomenon, since it has been practiced throughout history, terrorism attained its greatest impact in a world distinguished by rapid technological advances in transportation, communications, and weapons development. Heightened media awareness, especially the ubiquity of worldwide television coverage, has exposed the grievances and demands of terrorists to millions of viewers, but it has also transformed the practice of terrorism. Acts of terror therefore punctuated the era following World War II, as individuals and groups the world over attempted to destabilize or overthrow political systems within or outside the borders of their countries. Terrorism figured prominently in anticolonial conflicts in Algeria and Vietnam; in struggles over a homeland between national groups such as Israelis and Palestinians; in clashes between religious denominations such as Protestants and Catholics in Northern Ireland; and between revolutionary forces and established regimes in lands such as Indonesia, Iran, and Nicaragua.

No universally agreed-on definition of terrorism exists, a fact underlined by the often-cited glib observation that "one person's terrorist is another person's freedom fighter." Most experts agree, nevertheless, that a key feature of terrorism is the deliberate and systematic use of violence against civilians, with the aim of advancing political,

Defining Terrorism

religious, or ideological causes. Terrorists use violent means—from hijackings and hostage-taking to assassinations and mass murder—to magnify their influence and power. In contrast to the populations and institutions they fight, terrorists and their organizations are limited in size and resources. Despite their ability to destabilize societies, terrorist organizations have rarely if ever realized their stated goals. In fact, terrorist tactics have more commonly discredited otherwise potentially worthy and commendable causes. During the last decades of the twentieth century and the first decade of the twenty-first century, terrorism increasingly assumed a global character because sustained terror campaigns require sophisticated financial support networks, a reliable and sustained supply of weapons technology, and places of sanctuary. Aside from regional initiatives such as those emanating from the European Union, however, the international community did not respond to the threat of global terrorism in a coherent or unified manner. The thorny issues of what constitutes terrorism and how to respond to it gained renewed attention, however, as a result of the terror attacks against the United States in September 2001.

11 September

On the morning of the second Tuesday in September, New York City and Washington, D.C., became the targets of a coordinated terrorist attack that was unprecedented in scope, sophistication, and destructiveness. Hijackers seized four passenger jetliners and used them as guided missiles. Two of the planes crashed into the World Trade Center towers, causing the collapse of the two towers, the ancillary destruction of adjacent skyscrapers, and thousands of deaths. Before the morning was over, another plane crashed into the Pentagon, the nerve center of the U.S. military in Washington, D.C., and the fourth jet crashed into a field outside Pittsburgh, Pennsylvania. Intended for another Washington, D.C., landmark, the fourth jet was thwarted in its mission when passengers stormed the hijackers. As millions around the world watched events unfold on television, the U.S. government launched an intensive investigation and identified the Islamic militant Osama bin Laden (1957–) as the mastermind behind the attacks. Officials also accused bin Laden of directing previous attacks on U.S. interests in Africa and southwest Asia. Before the dust of the collapsed World Trade towers had settled, U.S. President George W. Bush (1946–) declared war on Osama bin Laden and global terrorism itself.

Osama bin Laden headed *al-Qaeda* ("the base"), the core of a global terrorist network. The estranged son of a Saudi construction magnate and the seventeenth of fifty-two children, Osama bin Laden became a popular figure in the U.S.-backed effort to aid *mujahideen* (Islamic warriors) who fought Soviet forces in Afghanistan. By the end of the Persian Gulf War (1990–1991), however, he began to regard the United States and its allies with unqualified hatred. The stationing of U.S. troops on the holy soil of Saudi Arabia, the bombing of Iraq, and supporting Israeli oppression of Palestinians, bin Laden claimed, were tantamount to a declaration of war against God. Convinced that he was carrying out God's will, bin Laden in 1998 publicly called on every Muslim to kill Americans and their allies "wherever he finds them and whenever he can." Viewed by many as the personification of evil, yet admired by some for his convictions and aims, Osama bin Laden has moved to the forefront of Islamist violence.

War in Afghanistan and Iraq

Another related radical manifestation of Islam's resurgence was the creation of the Islamic State of Afghanistan in 1996 by the Taliban movement. The Taliban emerged out of the disorder and devastation of the Afghan-Soviet war (1979–1988) and the later civil war (see chapter 38). Promoting itself as a new force for unity and determined to create an Islamic state according to its own austere interpretation of Islam, the Taliban proclaimed its followers the liberators who brought peace to Afghanistan. In that pursuit of the purest Muslim state on earth, Taliban intolerance figured prominently, and Islamist strictures quickly alienated people both inside and outside

Afghanistan. Dominated by Pashtuns—the majority ethnic group of Afghanistan—the Taliban under its leading *mullah* (male religious leader) Mohammed Omar fought a series of holy wars against other ethnic and Muslim groups, such as Afghanistan's Shia minority. At the same time, the Taliban provided sanctuary and training grounds for Islamist fighters in southwest and central Asia, most notably for Osama bin Laden and al-Qaeda.

The Taliban espoused a strict brand of Islam that barred women from education and the workplace. As all forms of European and American dress became taboo, women had to be completely veiled in *burkas*, and men had to eschew neckties and grow full, untrimmed beards. The stringent form of Taliban-promoted Islam also called for a ban on television, movie theaters, photographs, and most styles of music. Some of those rules had little to do with pure Islam, but a religious police, the Ministry of the Promotion of Virtue and Prevention of Vice, enforced them with an extremely harsh code of justice. The United Nations and most governments in the world withheld recognition of the Taliban as Afghanistan's legitimate government. De jure recognition came instead to a Taliban opposition force, the Northern Alliance, composed of the country's smaller religious and ethnic groups, mainly Tajiks, Uzbeks, and Hazaras. The Northern Alliance became a crucial ally of the United States in its mission to find and punish those responsible for the 11 September attacks.

When the United States government announced its war against global terrorism it also pointedly targeted "those harboring terrorists," that is, governments and states that supported and provided sanctuary for terrorists. The refusal of the Taliban government to surrender Osama bin Laden prompted the United States and its allies on 7 October 2001 to begin military operations against Taliban military positions and terrorist training camps. The U.S. military and its international allies generally limited their operations to intelligence missions and massive air strikes, fighting the war on the ground through Afghan proxies, most notably the forces of the Northern Alliance. By November, U.S.-led bombardments permitted Northern Alliance troops to capture Kabul and other key Afghan cities. In a decisive military campaign, the United States' coalition smashed both the Taliban and al-Qaeda. The war against terrorism beyond Afghanistan, however, promised to be a long-term struggle necessitating a great deal of international cooperation.

Another international action against terrorism came in March 2003, when President Bush coordinated what he termed "Operation Iraqi Freedom." A multinational coalition force some three hundred thousand strong, largely made up of U.S. and British troops but also including those from approximately two dozen other nations, carried out an invasion of Iraq designed to wage further war on terrorism by ousting the regime of Saddam Hussein and creating a democratic state. One special target was Hussein's suspected stockpile of chemical and biological weapons, otherwise termed "weapons of mass destruction," devastating implements of war that could presumably be employed by global terrorists to wreak destruction on a scale even greater than that of 11 September 2001. Hussein himself made another special target, although he eluded capture for months. Coalition forces managed to establish their military supremacy in Iraq, but they did not uncover any such cache of weapons nor did they immediately control Hussein. President Bush declared an end to major battle operations on 1 May 2003, and coalition forces since that time struggled in their efforts to occupy and stabilize Iraq. Hussein was finally caught in December 2003 and executed in 2006, but deadly resistance in Iraq persisted.

The costs of the Iraq war climbed in terms of both casualties and expenditures. Tens of thousands of Iraqi military personnel and civilians have died, as have almost four thousand coalition soldiers by mid 2007. The United States has spent approximately

Contracts between the Ottoman Empire and European powers particulary

France to inhibit and regulate trade, to accelerate the dominance of

A photographer captured the ruin of Saddam Hussein in this image of a tiled mural pitted and pocked by the destruction in Baghdad as a result of Operation Iraqi Freedom.

$4 billion per month to maintain troops in Iraq. While President Bush sustained the United States' willingness to pay such a price, some critics in the United States and around the globe balked at the president's aggressive approach to the war on terrorism. Dubbed by some the "Bush Doctrine of Deterrence," his preemptive strike against Iraq—which had not overtly committed a terrorist act or been proven to harbor terrorists—set a troubling precedent in U.S. foreign policy. Moreover, the increased presence of foreign military personnel in Iraq may only serve to intensify the sort of Islamist fervor already fanned by Osama bin Laden.

Coping with Global Problems: International Organizations

Although the world's nations and peoples are becoming increasingly interdependent, governments still operate on the basis of the territorially delimited state. Because global economic and cultural interdependence demands that political activity focus on cross-societal concerns and solutions, nations are under pressure to surrender portions of their sovereignty. Moreover, as national borders become less important in the face of new economic and cultural connections, the effectiveness of national governments has declined. The widespread recognition that the national state is ill equipped to handle problems of a global magnitude has led to an increase in the number of organizations dedicated to solving global problems through international coordination and action. Often categorized as nongovernmental international organizations and governmental international organizations, these institutions are important because they have the potential to tackle problems that do not respect territorial boundaries and are beyond the reach of national governments.

Contemporary efforts at global cooperation have antecedents in the past. A proto- *Nongovernmental* typical nongovernmental organization (NGO) is the Red Cross, an international hu- *Organizations* manitarian agency. Founded on the initiative of the Swiss philanthropist Jean Henri Dunant (1828–1910), this agency was originally dedicated to alleviating the suffer- ings of wounded soldiers, prisoners of war, and civilians in time of war. In 1864 the representatives of twelve nations signed the first Geneva Convention, which laid down the rules for the treatment of the wounded and the protection of medical personnel and hospitals. The convention adopted the red cross as a symbol of neutral aid. (Most Muslim countries use a red crescent.) Later protocols—signed by most nations—re- vised and amended the original principles enunciated in the first Geneva Convention to include protection for noncombatants as well. The Red Cross ultimately extended its mission to peacetime, rendering medical aid and other help for victims of natural disasters such as floods, earthquakes, and famines.

An especially prominent contemporary NGO is Greenpeace, founded in 1970, an environmental organization dedicated to the preservation of the earth's natural re- sources and its diverse animal and plant life. In their pursuit of a green and peaceful world, Greenpeace activists have gained international notoriety and fame for their dar- ing exploits, which are calculated to attract media attention to environmental con- cerns. With the world watching, Greenpeace members in small rubber rafts have disrupted whaling expeditions by placing themselves between the whales and the hunters' harpoons. On other occasions, Greenpeace has convinced major news net- works to broadcast disturbing pictures of the slaughter of baby harp seals. After getting the attention of the media, Greenpeace activists worked to prevent further slaughter by spraying red paint on the seals, making their fur worthless for commercial purposes.

The premier international governmental organization is the United Nations, which *The United Nations* superseded the League of Nations (1920–1946). This association of sovereign nations attempts to find solutions to global problems and to deal with virtually any matter of concern to humanity. Unlike a national parliament, the UN does not legislate. Yet, in its meeting rooms and corridors, representatives of the vast majority of the world's countries have a voice and a vote in shaping the international community of nations.

Under its charter a principal purpose of the UN is "to maintain international peace and security." Cynics are quick to point to the UN's apparent inability to achieve that goal, citing as evidence the eight-year war between Iraq and Iran, the civil war in Somalia, and the many years of bloodshed in Afghanistan. However flawed its role as an international peacemaker and a forum for conflict resolution, the UN has com- piled an enviable record with respect to another role defined in its charter, namely, "to achieve international cooperation in solving international problems of an eco- nomic, social, cultural, or humanitarian character." Quietly and without attracting attention from the news media, the specialized agencies of the UN have achieved nu- merous successes. For example, in 1980 the World Health Organization proclaimed the worldwide eradication of smallpox as a result of its thirteen-year global program. On other fronts, UN efforts resulted in more than a 50 percent decrease in both in- fant and child mortality rates in developing countries between 1960 and 2002. The organization's efforts also promoted an increase in female literacy, especially in Africa, where for the first time in history the majority of women—50.8 percent in 2000— were deemed to be literate. The UN as well worked to provide access to safe water for over one billion people living in rural areas.

Governmental and nongovernmental organizations have focused much of their *Human Rights* attention on the protection of human rights, the notion that all persons are entitled to some basic rights, especially rights that protect an individual against state conduct prohibited by international law or custom. The concept of human rights originated with Greco-Roman natural law doctrines and subsequently evolved into specific efforts to protect the rights of humanity such as the abolition of slavery and the implementation of universal suffrage. Universal recognition and acceptance of the concept of human rights came in the aftermath of World War II, especially with the exposure of crimes that the Nazi regime unleashed on its own citizens and all those that had come under Nazi control during the war. The Nuremberg war crimes trials, designed to bring Nazi leaders to justice, challenged the notion of unlimited national sovereignty and created the concept of "crimes against humanity," which warranted international judgment and punishment. In the charter establishing the United Nations in 1945, fifty member nations pledged to achieve "universal respect for, and observance of, human rights, and fundamental freedoms." In 1948, the National Assembly of the UN adopted the Universal Declaration of Human Rights, which contributed to the codification of international human rights laws. The declaration singled out specific human rights violations such as extrajudicial or summary executions, arbitrary arrest and torture, and slavery or involuntary servitude as well as discrimination on racial, sexual, or religious grounds. The concern for human rights is shared by nongovernmental organizations such as Amnesty International and the Human Rights Watch, which bring the pressure of world public opinion to bear on offending governments. By the late 1980s, human rights had emerged as one of the principal themes of global politics.

Given the present level of global interaction, international coordination to solve global problems is a necessity. However, collaboration within and between international organizations has often been inadequate. Meetings, talks, and consultations have frequently deteriorated into arguments. At the height of the cold war, this situation hampered progress in finding solutions to crucial problems. Contentious issues have sometimes paralyzed the UN and its affiliated organizations, because societies at different stages of economic development have pursued sometimes conflicting social and political goals. Cultural diversity continues to make it difficult for people to speak a common language. Despite the shortcomings of international organizations, however, for the present they represent the closest thing humanity has to a global system of governance that can help the world's peoples meet the challenges of international problems.

Crossing Boundaries

Human populations also underwent radical transformations. Peoples throughout the world challenged gender definitions and embarked on large-scale migrations. Women in Europe, the United States, China, and the Soviet Union gained greater equality with men, partly by advocating women's liberation and a nonbiological or culturally defined understanding of gender. Elsewhere, women continued to follow their societies' dictates for acceptable female behavior, although extraordinary circumstances propelled some women to prominence even in countries that resisted the feminist revolution. Both women and men also experienced either forced or voluntary migrations and in the process helped to create an increasingly borderless world.

Women's Traditions and Feminist Challenges

The status of women began changing after World War II. Women gained more economic, political, social, and sexual rights in highly industrialized states than in devel-

Women belonging to the U.S. feminist group the National Organization for Women march for equal rights in Washington, D.C., in 1992.

oping nations, but nowhere have they achieved full equality with men. Although women have increasingly challenged cultural norms requiring their subordination to men and confinement in the family, attainment of basic rights for women has been slow. Agitation for gender equality is often linked to women's access to employment, and the industrialized nations have the largest percentage of working women. Women constitute 40 to 50 percent of the workforce in industrial societies, compared with only 20 percent in developing countries. In Islamic societies, 10 percent or less of the workforce is composed of women. In all countries, women work primarily in low-paying jobs designated as female—that is, teaching, service, and clerical jobs. Forty percent of all farmers are women, many at the subsistence level. Rural African women, for example, do most of the continent's subsistence farming and produce more than 70 percent of Africa's food. Whether they are industrial, service, or agricultural workers, women earn less than men earn for the same work and are generally kept out of the highest paid professional careers.

Feminism and Equal Rights

The discrimination that women faced in the workplace was a major stimulus for the feminist movement in industrialized nations. Women in most of those nations had gained the right to vote after the Great War, but they found that political rights did not guarantee economic or sexual equality. After World War II, when more and more women went to work, women started to protest job discrimination, pay differentials between women and men, and their lack of legal equality. In the 1960s those complaints expanded into a feminist movement that criticized all aspects of gender inequality. In the United States, for example, the civil rights movement that demanded equality for African-Americans influenced the women's movement and provided a training ground for many women activists.

Women started to expose the ways in which a biologically determined understanding of gender led to their oppression. In addition to demanding equality in the

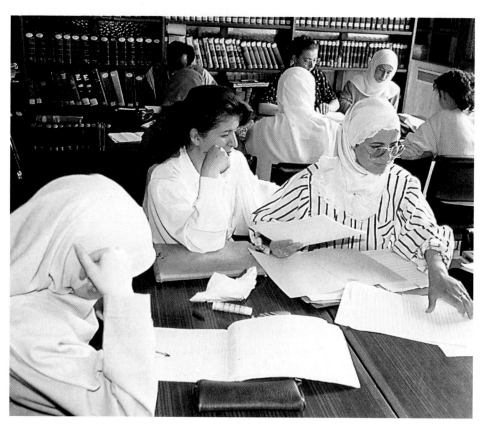

■ **Education offers hope for the future of Muslim and Arab women.**

workplace, women demanded full control over their bodies and their reproductive systems. Access to birth control and abortion became as essential to women's liberation as economic equality and independence. Only with birth control measures would women be able to determine whether or when to have children and thus avoid the notion that "biology is destiny." The U.S. Civil Rights Act of 1964 prohibited discrimination on the basis of both race and sex, and the introduction of the birth control pill in the 1960s and legal protection of abortion in the 1970s provided a measure of sexual freedom. The gender equality that an Equal Rights Amendment would have secured never materialized, however, because the amendment failed to achieve ratification before the 1982 deadline.

Gender Equality in China

Some socialist or communist societies transformed their legal systems to ensure basic equality. Legally, the position of women most closely matched that of men in communist or formerly communist countries such as the Soviet Union, Cuba, and China. "Women hold up half the sky," Mao Zedong had declared, and that eloquent acknowledgment of women's role translated into a commitment to fairness. The communist dedication to women's rights led to improvement in the legal status of Chinese women once the communists gained power in China. In 1950 communist leaders passed a marriage law that declared a "new democratic marriage system, which is based on free choice of partners, on monogamy, on equal rights for both sexes, and on protection of the lawful interests of women and children." The law abolished patriarchal practices such as child betrothal and upheld equal rights for men and women in the areas of work, property ownership, and inheritance.

Critics argue that despite such laws China's women have never gained true equality. Certainly few women have gained high status in the Communist Party's leadership. And although most women in China have full-time jobs outside the home, they do not receive wages equal to those of men. They do most of the work at home as well. Nevertheless, they are able to enter most professions, although most Chinese women engage in menial work. Long-standing Confucian values continue to degrade the status of women, especially in rural areas. Parents almost universally prefer boys over girls. One unintended consequence of China's population policies, which limits couples to one child, is the mysterious statistical disappearance of a large number of baby girls. Demographers estimate that annually more than one-half million female births go unrecorded in government statistics. Although no one can with certainty account for the "missing" girls, some population experts speculate that a continued strong preference for male children causes parents to send baby girls away for adoption or to be raised secretly, or in some cases to single them out for infanticide.

Domesticity and Abuse

Although girls and women in industrial and communist nations are guaranteed basic if not fully equal legal rights and are educated in roughly the same numbers as boys and men, women in other areas of the world have long been denied access to education. Expected to stay at home, girls and women have high illiteracy rates in these societies. In Arab and Muslim lands, women are twice as likely as men to be illiterate, and in some places nine of ten women are illiterate. This situation is beginning to change. Fifty years ago most women in these societies were illiterate, but in the past twenty-five years girls have begun to catch up with boys in education.

The same cannot be said for girls and women in India, despite some real advances made during the late twentieth century. By 2001 female literacy had reached 54 percent, and yet women remained largely confined to the home. Labor force participation remained low. Fewer than one-quarter of women of all ages were engaged in work, while the birthrate remained high even with the greater availability of birth control measures. This condition has ensured a life of domesticity for many Indian women. The issue that has most dramatically illustrated the perilous status of women in south Asia, though, is the prevalence of dowry deaths. What makes the birth of girl children in India so burdensome is the custom of paying dowries (gifts of money or goods) to the husband and his family upon a woman's marriage, a requirement that is difficult for many Indian families to meet. If the husband and his family perceive the dowry as inadequate, if the husband wants a new wife without returning his first wife's dowry, or even if the wife has simply annoyed the husband or her in-laws, the wife is doused with kerosene and set on fire—so that her death can be explained as a cooking accident. In 1995 the government of India reported six thousand dowry deaths, though unofficial estimates put the number closer to twenty-five thousand.

This form of domestic abuse has not been restricted to India and Hindu women, but has spread through south Asia. In Pakistan more than five hundred husbands set fire to their wives between 1994 and 1997. The motives for burnings go beyond dowry, because husbands have set fire to wives who overcooked or oversalted the men's food. The victims themselves, some of whom survive, voice perhaps the saddest aspect of this treatment: resignation to their fate. One Pakistani survivor noted, "It's my fate. From childhood, I have seen nothing but suffering." These attitudes may be changing, though, as Indian and Pakistani women activists challenge these practices and establish shelters for women threatened with burning.

Women Leaders

Around the world most women have the right to vote. They do not, however, exert political power commensurate with their numbers. Some women have nonetheless attained high political offices or impressive leadership positions. The same south Asia that revealed so many continued barriers to women's rights on a day-to-day basis

Opposition leader and Nobel Prize winner Aung San Suu Kyi at a gateside meeting in Rangoon, Myanmar.

also elevated numerous women to positions of power, breaking down other political barriers. Indira Gandhi (1917–1984) and Benazir Bhuto (1953–) led India and Pakistan as effective politicians, having been raised by fathers who themselves were prominent in politics. In 1994 Chandrika Bandaranaike Kumaratunga (1945–) became the first female president of Sri Lanka. Both her parents had previously served as prime ministers; her mother, Sirimavo Bandaranaike (1916–), became the first elected woman prime minister in 1960. As president, Kumaratunga appointed her mother to serve a third term as prime minister.

In Myanmar (formerly Burma), Daw Aung San Suu Kyi (1945–) has emerged as a leader, also deriving her political authority from her father Aung San, assassinated in 1947. Assuming the leadership of the democracy movement after her return from exile in 1988, Suu Kyi called for a nonviolent revolution against Myanmar's "fascist government." The government placed her under house arrest from 1989 to 1995, during which time she created a new political institution, the "gateside meeting," speaking to her followers from behind the gates of her home. In the 1990 elections Suu Kyi and her party won a landslide victory, but they were not allowed to come to power. Awarded the Nobel Peace Prize for her efforts in 1991, she could not accept the award personally because she was still under house arrest.

Women demonstrated their leadership abilities in a variety of ways. They became highly visible political figures, as in south Asia, or they more anonymously joined organizations or participated in activities designed to further the cause of women's rights. The United Nations launched a Decade for Women program in 1975, and since then global conferences on the status of women have been held regularly, attracting large crowds. Even in Iran, where the Islamic revolution severely limited opportunities for women, internal forces could radically transform the image and role of women. Today revolutionary patrols walk the streets of Tehran making sure that women conform to the society's rule of dress and behavior, but during the war with Iraq, Iranian women became revolutionaries, picking up guns and receiving weapons training. They protected their national borders while defying gender boundaries.

Rank	Urban Area	Country	Population (thousands)
1	Tokyo	Japan	27,242
2	Mexico City	Mexico	16,908
3	São Paulo	Brazil	16,792
4	New York	United States	16,390
5	Bombay	India	15,725
6	Shanghai	China	13,659
7	Los Angeles	United States	12,576
8	Calcutta	India	12,118
9	Buenos Aires	Argentina	11,931
10	Seoul	Republic of Korea	11,768
11	Beijing	China	11,414
12	Lagos	Nigeria	10,878
13	Osaka	Japan	10,618
14	Delhi	India	10,298
15	Rio de Janeiro	Brazil	10,264
16	Karachi	Pakistan	10,119

Table 40.2 World's Urban Areas of 10 Million or More Inhabitants in 1996

SOURCE: United Nations, *World Population Prospects: The 1998 Revisions.*

Migration

Migration, the movement of people from one place to another, is as old as humanity and has shaped the formation and identity of societies throughout the world. The massive influx of outsiders has transformed the ethnic, linguistic, and cultural composition of indigenous populations. With the advent of industrialization during the eighteenth century, population experts distinguished between two types of migration: internal migration and external or international migration. Internal migration describes the flow of people from rural to urban areas within one society, whereas external migration describes the movement of people across long distances and international borders. Both types of migration result from push factors, pull factors, or a combination of both. Lack of resources such as land or adequate food supplies, population pressure, religious or political persecution, or discriminatory practices aimed at ethnic minorities push people to move. Conversely, opportunities for better employment, the availability of arable land, or better services such as health care and education pull people to move. In the most general sense, migration is caused by differences, and because differences among societies are widening, the potential for migration has increased.

The largest human migrations today are rural-urban flows. During the last half of the twentieth century, these internal migrations led to rapid urbanization in much of the world. Today the most highly urbanized societies are those of western and northern Europe, Australia, New Zealand, and temperate South America and North America. In these societies the proportion of people living in urban areas exceeds 75 percent; in some countries, such as Germany, it exceeds 85 percent. (A more recent phenomenon visible in developed countries is a reverse migration, from the city to the country.) The societies of tropical Latin America are in an intermediate stage of urbanization, with 50 to 65 percent of the population living in cities. In many countries in Africa and Asia, the process of urbanization has just begun. Although most people still reside in rural areas, the rate of urbanization is very high.

Internal Migration

■ **A Rio de Janeiro slum.**

Urbanization   Urbanization has proved to be a difficult and challenging transformation for rural folk who have chosen or been forced to adjust to a new way of life. In Latin America, Africa, and south Asia, large numbers of people have migrated to metropolitan areas in search of relief from rural poverty. Once in the cities, though, they often find themselves equally destitute. Life is bleak in the slums outside Bombay; in the shantytowns around Kinshasa or Nairobi; and in the *barriadas, barrios,* and *villas miserias* of Lima, Mexico City, and Buenos Aires. More than ten million people cram the environs of cities such as Calcutta, Cairo, and Mexico City, straining those cities' resources. The few services originally available to the slum dwellers—potable water, electricity, and medical care—have diminished with the continuous influx of new people. Among the unemployed or underemployed, disease runs rampant, and many suffer from malnutrition.

External Migration   A combination of voluntary and forced international migrations has transformed the human landscape, especially during the past five hundred years. Between the sixteenth and twentieth centuries, more than sixty million European migrants, for example, colonized the Americas, Australia, Oceania, and the northern half of Asia. Between 1820 and 1980, in the course of the Atlantic migration, thirty-seven million migrants of European descent made their home in the United States. Slave migrations supplemented those voluntary movements of people. Between the sixteenth and nineteenth centuries, slave traders consigned about twelve million Africans to the Americas, though many died in the appalling conditions of the Atlantic voyages.

During World War II the Nazi regime initiated the largest mass expulsions of the twentieth century, deporting eight million people to forced-labor sites and extermi-

Afghan refugees fled to Iran in 1986, joining the ranks of the hundreds of thousands of forced displaced persons in the contemporary world.

nation camps. Following the war, the Soviet regime expelled ten million ethnic Germans from eastern and central Europe and transported them back to Germany. The largest migrations in the second half of the twentieth century have consisted of refugees fleeing war. For example, the 1947 partition of the Indian subcontinent into two independent states resulted in the exchange of six million Hindus from Pakistan and seven million Muslims from India. More recently, three million to four million refugees fled war-torn Afghanistan during the 1980s. According to UN estimates, at the end of 2003 there were some ten million refugees who lived outside their countries of origin and who could not return because of fear of persecution.

Many of these migrants left their home countries because they wanted to escape the ravages of war, but economic inequities between societies have caused most international migration. That is, people leave their country of birth in search of better jobs and more readily available health care, educational opportunities, and other services provided by the new society. Thus most contemporary mass migrations involve movement from developing countries to developed ones. Since 1960 some thirteen million "guest workers" from southern Europe, Turkey, and northern Africa have taken up permanent residence in western Europe, and more than ten million permanent migrants—mostly from Mexico—have entered the United States. Foreigners currently make up more than half the working population in the oil-producing countries of southwest Asia. Approximately 130 million people currently live outside their country of citizenship, collectively constituting a "nation of migrants" equivalent in size to Japan, the world's eighth most populous nation.

International mass migrations have accelerated and broadened the scope of cross-cultural interaction. After their arrival on foreign shores, migrants established cultural and ethnic communities that maintained their social customs and native languages. The sounds of foreign languages as well as the presence of ethnic foods, arts, and music have transformed especially large cities into multicultural environments. Although the arrival of migrants has enriched societies in many ways, it has also sparked resentment and conflict. People in host countries often believe that foreigners and their ways of life

Migrant Communities

undermine national identity, especially if defined by language and other cultural characteristics. Beyond that, many citizens of host societies view migrants, who are often willing to work for low wages and not join labor unions, as competitors for jobs. When unemployment rates climb, there is a tendency to look for scapegoats, and all too frequently the blame falls on migrants. In many countries, governments have come under pressure to restrict immigration or even expel foreign residents. Moreover, xenophobia, or an unreasonable fear of foreigners, has sometimes produced violence and racial tension, as when skinheads (shaved-head youths) in England assaulted members of ethnic minority groups or when neo-Nazis in Germany bombed the community centers of Turkish workers. Thus, while migrants are reshaping the world outside their home countries, international mass migration poses challenges both to the migrants themselves and to the host society.

Cross-Cultural Travelers

A more recent and transient form of migration is tourism. Although travelers have established cultural links between societies since the beginning of recorded history, travel for a long time took place mainly in connection with military conquest, religious pilgrimage, trade, or diplomacy. If more people did not take to travel, it was because most had little incentive to leave their homes, especially when transport was slow, expensive, and inconvenient. So risky was travel that most people regarded travelers as either very courageous or very foolish.

Mass Tourism

Industrial society gave birth to mass tourism by providing both safer and faster transport and by institutionalizing two modern features of social life—leisure and travel. By the mid-nineteenth century, tourism—travel for recreation or study—had become a growing industry in western Europe and the United States. In England, Thomas Cook (1808–1892) established the first travel agency, bearing his name and offering guided tours first of Europe in the 1850s and subsequently of the United States. For the more independent-minded travelers, his agency arranged travel and hotel accommodations. In Germany, Karl Baedeker (1801–1859) and his son exploited the economic potential of tourism. They established a publishing firm that specialized in travel guides that were popular not only in their original German editions but also in French and English translations.

In the early and mid-1800s, it became fashionable in Europe for the affluent to vacation, often for extended periods, and then later in the century working people began to copy the fashions of the wealthy. Working-class families took to the road during holidays to escape the grimy drudgery of the industrial city and, in the process, created working-class pleasure zones such as seaside resorts in Britain, Coney Island in the United States, or Varna at the Black Sea. People journeyed for pleasure and engaged in activities they normally did not do, such as breathing fresh air, wearing oddly colorful clothes, or taking long walks for no reason at all. By the twentieth century, leisure travel took on added symbolic value when travelers could show off the special clothes required for their journeys, such as ski apparel or bikinis. Others established that they had traveled through changes in their physical appearance, which could include varying degrees of sunburn or a leg encased in plaster. After World War II, companies created the packaged tour, which enabled millions of tourists to swarm across the world. Today middle-class tourists, new age travelers, and ecotourists—often weighted down by duty-free goods—busily crisscross the entire planet in their search for rarely visited sites.

Effects of Mass Tourism

Travel and tourism have become the largest industry on the planet. The industry is sustained by growing personal wealth, which continues to produce more tourists, and by cheaper and more efficient transport, especially the jet plane. According to World Travel and Tourism Council estimates, the total economic value of goods and services attributable to tourism in 1996 were $3.6 trillion, or 10.6 percent of the gross global product. The tourism business also provided work for approximately 255 million people. The attraction of an industry that generates wealth and jobs relatively quickly—and often with minimal investment compared with establishing a manufacturing industry, for example—has served as a powerful incentive for both governments and businesses in the developed and the developing worlds to further promote tourism. On the downside, tourism most often creates low-paying jobs, and most of the profits flow to the developed world, where the majority of tourism businesses are located. The travel boom has also sparked concerns connected to the cultural impact of mass tourism. Tourism has acted as a globalizing influence, sometimes initiating dramatic and irreversible changes within the cultural traditions of host communities. Large numbers of visitors have the tendency to transform local cultural traditions into commodities, which are then consumed like any other commodity. Religious rituals, ethnic rites, and festivals are reduced and sanitized to conform to tourist expectations, resulting in a "reconstructed ethnicity."

The decades following World War II were largely dominated by cold war politics and by nations seeking their independence from colonial rule. Borders created by the bipolar world and European empires dissolved and reshaped the world's landscape. Another barrier-crushing development that became visible at the end of the century was economic globalization, a process responsible for the unprecedented integration of the global economy. A growing share of the world's societies embraced market-oriented economies and thus hitched their fortunes to the vagaries of the global marketplace.

Globalization pointed to the new relevance of international organizations and to the increasing irrelevance of national boundaries; it signified the arrival of a world without borders. Technological and cultural developments likewise combined to break down barriers and create a global village that connected diverse peoples. Although many societies resisted cultural influences from Europe and the United States, the prevalence of communications technology and cultural diffusion made interactions and encounters inevitable. Women's efforts to achieve greater equality with men also collided with cultural traditions; and, although many barriers to women's liberation remain, others have fallen. The global movement of human populations crisscrossed boundaries, both internal and external, and contributed to global problems that could be solved only through international cooperation. In the borderless world of contemporary times, nothing less is acceptable.

CHRONOLOGY

1947	Establishment of GATT
1948	UN adopts Universal Declaration of Human Rights
1950	World population at 2.5 billion
1960	Introduction of birth control pill
1960	Creation of OPEC
1967	Establishment of ASEAN
1967	Birth of European Community
1970	Founding of Greenpeace
1981	Identification of AIDS
1982	Defeat of Equal Rights amendment in U.S.
1992	Beginning of socialist market economy in China
1993	Establishment of NAFTA
1995	WTO supersedes GATT
2000	World population at 6 billion
2001	China joins WTO
2001	Terrorist attacks against the United States
2003	Operation Iraqi Freedom

FOR FURTHER READING

Peter Baldwin. *Disease and Democracy: The Industrialized World Faces AIDS.* Berkeley, 2005. Probing comparative history of the public health policies implemented by Western democracies to contain domestic AIDS epidemics in the 1980s and 1990s.

Jagdish Bhagwati. *In Defense of Globalization.* New York, 2004. A convincing rebuttal to popular fallacies about global economic integration.

André Burguière et al. *A History of the Family.* Vol. 2: *The Impact of Modernity.* Cambridge, Mass., 1996. A collection of in-depth articles on modern families in different parts of the world.

Joel E. Cohen. *How Many People Can the Earth Support?* New York, 1997. An author who treads where few demographers dare to go.

Tim Flannery. *The Weather Makers: How Man Is Changing the Climate and What It Means for Life on Earth.* New York, 2006. A passionate and clear account that looks at the connection between human-made climate change and global warming.

John Bellamy Foster. *The Vulnerable Planet: A Short Economic History of the Environment.* New York, 1994. Sympathetic account of technological and environmental change.

Thomas L. Friedman. *The Lexus and Olive Tree.* New York, 1999. A readable overview that does justice to the complexities of globalization.

Kevin J. Gaston and John I. Spicer. *Biodiversity: An Introduction.* 2nd ed. Oxford, 2004. A simple and concise overview of biodiversity—what it is and why it is important.

Karl Gerth. *China Made: Consumer Culture and the Creation of the Nation.* Cambridge, Mass., 2003. Links notions of nationalism and consumerism in twentieth-century China.

Francis Harris, ed. *Global Environmental Issues.* New York, 2004. A clear, nontechnical introduction to a broad range of environmental issues.

Margaret Jean Hay and Sharon Stichter. *African Women South of the Sahara.* Boston, 1984. An analysis of social and economic change and how it affected African women in the twentieth century.

Nikki R. Keddie and Beth Baron, eds. *Women in Middle Eastern History: Shifting Boundaries in Sex and Gender.* New Haven, 1992. A sensitive selection of articles by the leading scholars in the field.

Naomi Klein. *No Space, No Choice, No Jobs, No Logo: Taking Aim at the Brand Bullies.* New York, 2000. Part cultural analysis and part political manifesto, this work makes an angry case against multinational corporations.

Joanna Liddle and Rama Doshi. *Daughters of Independence: Gender, Caste, and Class in India.* New Delhi, 1986. A work on the contemporary women's movement that covers the Indian caste system, British colonial rule, and class structure.

Michael Mandelbaum. *The Dawn of Peace in Europe.* New York, 1997. An elegant work focusing on the central question of continental security.

J. R. McNeill. *Something New under the Sun: An Environmental History of the Twentieth-Century World.* New York, 2000. A brilliant but dark tale of the past century's interaction between humans and the environment.

Julian L. Simon. *Population Matters: People, Resources, Environment, and Immigration.* New Brunswick, N.J. 1990. Broad and general treatment of demographic, environmental, and economic problems.

Joseph Stiglitz. *Globalization and Its Discontents* New York, 2002. A former chief economist at the World Bank and the 2002 Nobel Prize winner takes aim at the institutions that govern globalization, especially the IMF.

Wang Gungwu, ed. *Global History and Migrations.* Boulder, 1997. A fine collection of essays on topics that range from the Atlantic slave trade to diasporas and their relationship to the nation-state.

Malcom Waters. *Globalization.* New York, 1995. A crisp, to-the-point guide that covers globalization and its consequences and is framed by sociological theory.

Martin Wolf. *Why Globalization Works.* 2nd ed. New Haven, 2005. A sophisticated defense of the global market economy and free trade.

Margery Wolfe. *Revolution Postponed: Women in Contemporary China.* New Haven, 1985. Explores one of the more problematic legacies of the Chinese Revolution.

Glossary and Pronunciation Key

AH *a* sound, as in *car, father*
IH short *i* sound, as in *fit, his, mirror*
OO long *o* sound, as in *ooze, tool, crew*
UH short *u* sound, as in *up, cut, color*
A short *a* sound, as in *asp, fat, parrot*
EE long *e* sound, as in *even, meet, money*
OH long *o* sound, as in *open, go, tone*
EH short *e* sound, as in *ten, elf, berry*
AY long *a* sound, as in *ape, date, play*
EYE long *i* sound, as in *ice, high, bite*
OW dipthong *o* sound, as in *cow, how, bow*
AW dipthong *a* sound, as in *awful, paw, law*

Note on emphasis: Syllables in capital letters receive the accent. If there is no syllable in capitals, then all syllables get equal accent.

Abbasid (ah-BAH-sihd) Cosmopolitan Arabic dynasty (750–1258) that replaced the Umayyads; founded by Abu al-Abbas and reached its peak under Harun al-Rashid.

Abolitionism Antislavery movement.

Absolutism Political philosophy that stressed the divine right theory of kingship: the French king Louis XIV was the classic example.

Abu Bakr (ah-BOO BAHK-uhr) First caliph after the death of Muhammad.

Achaemenid empire (ah-KEE-muh-nid) First great Persian empire (558–330 B.C.E.), which began under Cyrus and reached its peak under Darius.

Aeschylus (ES-kuh-luhs) Greek tragedian, author of the *Oresteia*.

Age grades Bantu institution in which individuals of roughly the same age carried out communal tasks appropriate for that age.

Ahimsa (uh-HIM-suh) Jain term for the principle of nonviolence to other living things or their souls.

Ahura Mazda (uh-HOORE-uh MAHZ-duh) Main god of Zoroastrianism who represented truth and goodness and was perceived to be in an eternal struggle with the malign spirit Angra Mainyu.

Al-Andalus (al-ANN-duh-luhs) Islamic Spain.

Ali'i nui Hawaiian class of high chiefs.

Allah (AH-lah) God of the monotheistic religion of Islam.

Amon-Re (AH-muhn RAY) Egyptian god, combination of the sun god Re and the air god Amon.

Angkor (AHN-kohr) Southeast Asian Khmer kingdom (889–1432) that was centered on the temple cities of Angkor Thom and Angkor Wat.

Anti-Semitism Term coined in the late nineteenth century that was associated with a prejudice against Jews and the political, social, and economic actions taken against them.

Antonianism African syncretic religion, founded by Dona Beatriz, that taught that Jesus Christ was a black African man and that heaven was for Africans.

Apartheid (ah-PAHR-teyed) South African system of "separateness" that was implemented in 1948 and that maintained the black majority in a position of political, social, and economic subordination.

Appeasement British and French policy in the 1930s that tried to maintain peace in Europe in the face of German aggression by making concessions.

Arianism Early Christian heresy that centered on teaching of Arius (250–336 C.E.) and contained the belief that Jesus was a mortal human being and not coeternal with God; Arianism was the focus of Council of Nicaea.

Artha Hindu concept for the pursuit of economic well-being and honest prosperity.

Arthashastra (AR-thah-sha-strah) Ancient Indian political treatise from the time of Chandragupta Maurya; its authorship was traditionally ascribed to Kautalya, and it stressed that war was inevitable.

Aryans (AIR-ee-anns) Indo-European migrants who settled in India after 1500 B.C.E.; their union with indigenous Dravidians formed the basis of Hinduism.

Association of Southeast Asian Nations (ASEAN.) Regional organization established in 1967 by Thailand, Malaysia, Singapore, Indonesia, and the Philippines; the organization was designed to promote economic progress and political stability; it later became a free-trade zone.

Assyrians (uh-SEAR-ee-uhns) Southwest Asian people who built an empire that reached its height during the eighth and seventh centuries B.C.E.; it was known for a powerful army and a well-structured state.

Astrolabe Navigational instrument for determining latitude.

Aten Monotheistic god of Egyptian pharaoh Akhenaten (r. 1353–1335 B.C.E.) and a very early example of monotheism.

Audiencias Spanish courts in Latin America.

Australopithecus (ah-strah-loh-PITH-uh-kuhs) "Southern ape," oldest known ancestor of humans; it lived from around four million down to around one million years ago, and it could walk on hind legs, freeing up hands for use of simple tools.

Austronesians People who as early as 2000 B.C.E. began to explore and settle islands of the Pacific Ocean basin.

Avesta Book that contains the holy writings of Zoroastrianism.

Axum African kingdom centered in Ethiopia that became an early and lasting center of Coptic Christianity.

Aztec empire Central American empire constructed by the Mexica and expanded greatly during the fifteenth century during the reigns of Itzcoatl and Motecuzoma I.

Balfour Declaration British declaration from 1917 that supported the creation of a Jewish homeland in Palestine.

Bantu (BAN-too) African peoples who originally lived in the area of present-day Nigeria; around 2000 B.C.E. they began a centuries-long migration that took them to most of sub-Saharan Africa; the Bantu were very influential, especially linguistically.

Bedouins (BEHD-oh-ihnz) Nomadic Arabic tribespeople.

Benefice Grant from a lord to a vassal, usually consisting of land, which supported the vassal and signified the relationship between the two.

Berlin Conference Meeting organized by German chancellor Otto von Bismarck in 1884–1885 that provided the justification for European colonization of Africa.

Bhagavad Gita (BUH-guh-vahd GEE-tuh) "Song of the Lord," an Indian short poetic work drawn from the lengthy *Mahabharata* that was finished around 400 C.E. and that expressed basic Hindu concepts such as karma and dharma.

Bhakti (BAHK-tee) Indian movement that attempted to transcend the differences between Hinduism and Islam.

Black Hand Pre–World War I secret Serbian society; one of its members, Gavrilo Princip, assassinated Austrian archduke Francis Ferdinand and provided the spark for the outbreak of the Great War.

Blitzkrieg German style of rapid attack through the use of armor and air power that was used in Poland, Norway, Denmark, Belgium, the Netherlands, and France in 1939–1940.

Boddhisatvas (BOH-dih-SAT-vuhs) Buddhist concept regarding individuals who had reached enlightenment but who stayed in this world to help people.

Bolshevik (BOHL-shih-vehk) Russian communist party headed by Lenin.

Bourgeoisie Middle class in modern industrial society.

Brahmins (BRAH-minz) Hindu caste of priests.

Brezhnev Doctrine Policy developed by Leonid Brezhnev (1906–1982) that claimed for the Soviet Union the right to invade any socialist country faced with internal or external enemies; the doctrine was best expressed in Soviet invasion of Czechoslovakia.

Buddha (BOO-duh) The "enlightened one," the term applied to Siddhartha Gautama after his discoveries that would form the foundation of Buddhism.

Buddhism (BOO-diz'm) Religion, based on Four Noble Truths, associated with Siddhartha Gautama (563–483 B.C.E.), or the Buddha; its adherents desired to eliminate all distracting passion and reach nirvana.

Bunraku (boon-RAH-koo) Japanese puppet theater.

Byzantine Empire (BIHZ-ann-teen) Long-lasting empire centered at Constantinople; it grew out of the end of the Roman empire, carried the legacy of Roman greatness, and was the only classical society to survive into the early modern age; it reached its early peak during the reign of Justinian (483–565).

Caesaropapism Concept relating to the mixing of political and religious authority, as with the Roman emperors, that was central to the church-versus-state controversy in medieval Europe.

Cahokia (kuh-HOH-kee-uh) Large structure in modern Illinois that was constructed by the mound-building peoples; it was the third largest structure in the Americas before the arrival of the Europeans.

Caliph (KAL-ihf) "Deputy," Islamic leader after the death of Muhammad.

Capetian (cah-PEE-shuhn) Early French dynasty that started with Hugh Capet.

Capitalism An economic system with origins in early modern Europe in which private parties make their goods and services available on a free market.

Capitulation Highly unfavorable trading agreements that the Ottoman Turks signed with the Europeans in the nineteenth century that symbolized the decline of the Ottomans.

Carolingians Germanic dynasty that was named after its most famous member, Charlemagne.

Carthage Northern African kingdom, main rival to early Roman expansion, that was defeated by Rome in the Punic Wars.

Çatal Hüyük Important Neolithic settlement in Anatolia (7250–6150 B.C.E.).

Cathars Medieval heretics, also known as the Albigensians, who considered the material world evil; their followers renounced wealth and marriage and promoted an ascetic existence.

Catholic Reformation Sixteenth-century Catholic attempt to cure internal ills and confront Protestantism; it was inspired by the reforms of the Council of Trent and the actions of the Jesuits.

Caudillos (KAW-dee-ohs) Latin American term for nineteenth-century local military leaders.

Central Powers World War I term for the alliance of Germany, Austria-Hungary, and the Ottoman empire.

Chaghatai One of Chinggis Khan's sons, whose descendants ruled central Asia through the Chaghatai khanate.

Chan Buddhism (CHAHN BOO-diz'm) Influential branch of Buddhism in China, with an emphasis on intuition and sudden flashes of insight instead of textual study.

Chanchan (chahn-chahn) Capital of the pre-Incan, South American Chimu society that supported a large population of fifty thousand.

Chavín cult Mysterious but very popular South American religion (1000–300 B.C.E.).

Chimu Pre-Incan South American society that fell to Incas in the fifteenth century.

Chinampas Agricultural gardens used by Mexica (Aztecs) in which fertile muck from lake bottoms was dredged and built up into small plots.

Chivalry European medieval code of conduct for knights based on loyalty and honor.

Chola Southern Indian Hindu kingdom (850–1267), a tightly centralized state that dominated sea trade.

Chucuito Pre-Incan South American society that rose in the twelfth century and fell to the Incas in the fifteenth century.

City-state Urban areas that controlled surrounding agricultural regions and that were often loosely connected in a broader political structure with other city-states.

Cohong Specially licensed Chinese firms that were under strict government regulation.

Collectivization Process beginning in the late 1920s by which Stalin forced the Russian peasants off their own land and onto huge collective farms run by the state; millions died in the process.

COMECON The Council for Mutual Economic Assistance, which offered increased trade within the Soviet Union and eastern Europe; it was the Soviet alternative to the United States's Marshall Plan.

Communalism A term, usually associated with India, that placed an emphasis on religious rather than national identity.

Communism Philosophy and movement that began in middle of the nineteenth century with the work of Karl Marx; it has the same general goals as socialism, but it includes the belief that violent revolution is necessary to destroy the bourgeois world and institute a new world run by and for the proletariat.

Confucianism (kuhn-FYOO-shuhn-iz'm) Philosophy, based on the teachings of the Chinese philosopher Kong Fuzi (551–479 B.C.E.), or Confucius, that emphasizes order, the role of the gentleman, obligation to society, and reciprocity.

Congress of Vienna Gathering of European diplomats in Vienna, Austria, from October 1814 to June 1815. The representatives of the "great powers" that defeated Napoleon—Britain, Austria, Prussia, and Russia—dominated the proceedings, which aimed to restore the prerevolutionary political and social order.

Conquistadores (kohn-KEE-stah-dohr-ayz) Spanish adventurers such as Cortés and Pizarro who conquered Central and South America in the sixteenth century.

Constitutionalism Movement in England in the seventeenth century that placed power in Parliament's hands as part of a constitutional monarchy and that increasingly limited the power of the monarch; the movement was highlighted by the English Civil War and the Glorious Revolution.

Containment Concept associated with the United States and specifically with the Truman Doctrine during the cold war that revolved around the notion that the United States would contain the spread of communism.

Corporation A concept that reached mature form in 1860s in England and France; it involved private business owned by thousands of individual and institutional investors who financed the business through the purchase of stocks.

Corpus iuris civilis (KOR-puhs yoor-uhs sih-VEE-lihs) *Body of the Civil Law,* the Byzantine emperor Justinian's attempt to codify all Roman law.

Criollos (kree-OH-lohs) Creoles, people born in the Americas of Spanish or Portuguese ancestry.

Cross staff Device that sailors used to determine latitude by measuring the angle of the sun or the pole star above the horizon.

Cuneiform Written language of the Sumerians, probably the first written script in the world.

Daimyo (DEYEM-yoh) Powerful territorial lords in early modern Japan.

Dao Key element in Chinese philosophy that means the "way of nature" or the "way of the cosmos."

Daodejing (DOW-DAY-JIHNG) Book that is the fundamental work of Daoism.

Daoism (DOW-i'zm) Chinese philosophy with origins in the Zhou dynasty; it is associated with legendary philosopher Laozi, and it called for a policy of noncompetition.

Dar al-Islam The "house of Islam," a term for the Islamic world.

Declaration of Independence Drafted by Thomas Jefferson in 1776; the document expressed the ideas of John Locke and the Enlightenment, represented the idealism of the American rebels, and influenced other revolutions.

Declaration of the Rights of Man and the Citizen Document from the French Revolution (1789) that was influenced by the American Declaration of Independence and in turn influenced other revolutionary movements.

Decolonization Process by which former colonies achieved their independence, as with the newly emerging African nations in the 1950s and 1960s.

Deism (DEE-iz'm) An Enlightenment view that accepted the existence of a god but denied the supernatural aspects of Christianity; in deism, the universe was an orderly realm maintained by rational and natural laws.

Descamisados "Shirtless ones," Argentine poor who supported Juan and Eva Peron.

Détente A reduction in cold war tension between the United States and the Soviet Union from 1969 to 1975.

Devshirme Ottoman requirement that the Christians in the Balkans provide young boys to be slaves of the sultan.

Dharma (DAHR-muh) Hindu concept of obedience to religious and moral laws and order; also, the basic doctrine of Buddhism.

Dhimmi (dihm-mee) Islamic concept of a protected people that was symbolic of Islamic toleration during the Mughal and Ottoman empires.

Dhow Indian, Persian, and Arab ships, one hundred to four hundred tons, that sailed and traded throughout the Indian Ocean basin.

Diaspora People who have settled far from their original homeland but who

still share some measure of ethnic identity.

Dionysus Greek god of wine, also known as Bacchus; Greek plays were performed in his honor.

Dravidians Peoples who produced the brilliant Harappan society in India, 3000–1500 B.C.E.

Dreadnoughts A class of British battleships whose heavy armaments made all other battleships obsolete overnight.

Duma Russian parliament, established after the Revolution of 1905.

Dutch learning European knowledge that reached Tokugawa Japan.

East India Company British joint-stock company that grew to be a state within a state in India; it possessed its own armed forces.

Eight-legged essay Eight-part essays that an aspiring Chinese civil servant had to compose, mainly based on a knowledge of Confucius and the Zhou classics.

Encomienda (ehn-KOH-mee-ehn-dah) System that gave the Spanish settlers (*encomenderos*) the right to compel the indigenous peoples of the Americas to work in the mines or fields.

Engenho Brazilian sugar mill; the term also came to symbolize the entire complex world relating to the production of sugar.

Enlightenment Eighteenth-century philosophical movement that began in France; its emphasis was on the preeminence of reason rather than faith or tradition; it spread concepts from the Scientific Revolution.

Epicureans (ehp-ih-kyoo-REE-uhns) Hellenistic philosophers who taught that pleasure—as in quiet satisfaction—was the greatest good.

Equal-field system Chinese system during the Tang dynasty in which the goal was to ensure an equitable distribution of land.

Essenes Jewish sect that looked for the arrival of a savior; they were similar in some of their core beliefs to the early Christians.

Etruscans (ih-TRUHS-kuhns) Northern Italian society that initially dominated the Romans; the Etruscans helped convey Greek concepts to the expanding Romans.

Eunuchs (YOO-nihks) Castrated males, originally in charge of the harem, who grew to play major roles in government; eunuchs were common in China and other societies.

European Community (EC) Organization of European states established in 1957; it was originally called the European Economic Community and was renamed the EC in 1967; it promoted economic growth and integration as the basis for a politically united Europe.

European Union Established by the Maastricht Treaty in 1993, a supranational organization for even greater European economic and political integration.

Fascism Political ideology and mass movement that was prominent in many parts of Europe between 1919 and 1945; it sought to regenerate the social, political, and cultural life of societies, especially in contrast to liberal democracy and socialism; fascism began with Mussolini in Italy, and it reached its peak with Hitler in Germany.

Five Pillars The foundation of Islam: (1) profession of faith, (2) prayer, (3) fasting during Ramadan, (4) alms giving, and (5) pilgrimage, or hajj.

Five-year plans First implemented by Stalin in the Soviet Union in 1928; five-year plans were a staple of communist regimes in which every aspect of production was determined in advance for a five-year period; five-year plans were opposite of the free market concept.

Four Noble Truths The foundation of Buddhist thought: (1) life is pain, (2) pain is caused by desire, (3) elimination of desire will bring an end to pain, (4) living a life based on the Noble Eightfold Path will eliminate desire.

Front de Libération Nationale (FLN) The Algerian organization that fought a bloody guerilla war for freedom against France.

Fulani (foo-LAH-nee) Sub-Saharan African people who, beginning in the seventeenth century, waged a series of wars designed to impose their own strict interpretation of Islam.

Gathas (GATH-uhs) Zoroastrian hymns believed to be compositions by Zarathustra.

Gauchos (GOW-chohz) Argentine cowboys, highly romanticized figures.

General Agreement on Tariffs and Trade (GATT) Free trade agreement first signed in 1947; by 1994 it had grown to 123 members and formed the World Trade Organization (WTO).

Ghana (GAH-nuh) Kingdom in west Africa during the fifth through the thirteenth century whose rulers eventually converted to Islam; its power and wealth was based on dominating trans-Saharan trade.

Ghazi (GAH-zee) Islamic religious warrior.

Ghaznavids Turkish tribe under Mahmud of Ghazni who moved into northern India in the eleventh century and began a period of greater Islamic influence in India.

Gilgamesh Legendary king of the Mesopotamian city-state of Uruk (ca. 3000 B.C.E.), subject of the *Epic of Gilgamesh,* world's oldest complete epic literary masterpiece.

Glasnost (GLAHS-nohst) Russian term meaning "openness" introduced by Mikhail Gorbachev in 1985 to describe the process of opening Soviet society to dissidents and public criticism.

Globalization The breaking down of traditional boundaries in the face of increasingly global financial and cultural trends.

Global warming The emission of greenhouse gases, which prevents solar heat from escaping the earth's atmosphere and leads to the gradual heating of the earth's environment.

Golden Horde Mongol tribe that controlled Russia from the thirteenth to the fifteenth century.

Greater East Asia Co-Prosperity Sphere Japanese plan for consolidating east and southeast Asia under their control during World War II.

Great Game Nineteenth-century competition between Great Britain and Russia for the control of central Asia.

Great Zimbabwe Large sub-Saharan African kingdom in the fifteenth century.

Greenpeace An environmental organization founded in 1970 and dedicated to the preservation of earth's natural resources.

Guomindang (GWOH-mihn-dahng) Chinese nationalist party founded by Sun Yatsen (1866–1925) and later led by Jiang Jieshi; it has been centered in Taiwan since the end of the Chinese civil war.

Gupta (GOOP-tah) Indian dynasty (320–550 C.E.) that briefly reunited India after the collapse of the earlier Mauryan dynasty.

Hacienda (HAH-see-ehn-dah) Large Latin American estates.

Hagia Sophia (HAH-yah SOH-fee-uh) Massive Christian church constructed by the Byzantine emperor Justinian and later converted into a mosque.

Hajj (HAHJ) Pilgrimage to Mecca.

Hammurabi's Code (hahm-uh-RAH-beez) Sophisticated law code associated with the Babylonian king Hammurabi (r. 1792–1750 B.C.E.).

Harappan (hah-RAP-puhn) Early brilliant Indian society centered in Harappa and Mohenjo-daro.

Harijans "Children of God," Gandhi's term for the Untouchables.

Hebrews Semitic-speaking nomadic tribe influential for monotheistic belief in Yahweh.

Heian (HAY-ahn) Japanese period (794–1185), a brilliant cultural era notable for the world's first novel, Murasaki Shikibu's *The Tale of Genji.*

Hellenistic Era Phase in Greek history (328–146 B.C.E.), from the conquest of Greece by Philip of Macedon until Greece's fall to the Romans; this era was a more cosmopolitan age facilitated by the conquests of Alexander the Great.

Hieroglyphics (heye-ruh-GLIPH-iks) Ancient Egyptian written language.

Hijra Muhammad's migration from Mecca to Medina in 622, which is the beginning point of the Islamic calendar and is considered to mark the beginning of the Islamic faith.

Hinayana (HEE-nah-yah-nuh) Branch of Buddhism known as the "lesser vehicle," also known as Theravada Buddhism; its beliefs include strict, individual path to enlightenment, and it is popular in south and southeast Asia.

Hinduism Main religion of India, a combination of Dravidian and Aryan concepts; Hinduism's goal is to reach spiritual purity and union with the great world spirit; its important concepts include dharma, karma, and samsara.

Holocaust German attempt in World War II to exterminate the Jews of Europe.

Home front Term made popular in World War I and World War II for the civilian "front" that was symbolic of the greater demands of total war.

Hominid (HAWM-ih-nihd) A creature belonging to the family Hominidae, which includes human and humanlike species.

Homo erectus (HOH-MOH ee-REHK-ruhs) "Upright-walking human," which existed from two million to two hundred thousand years ago; *Homo erectus* used cleavers and hand axes and learned how to control fire.

Homo sapiens (HOH-MOH SAY-pee-uhns) "Consciously thinking human," which first appeared around two hundred fifty thousand years ago and used sophisticated tools.

Huitzilopochtli (wee-tsee-loh-pockt-lee) Sun god and patron deity of the Aztecs.

Hundred Days of Reform Chinese reforms of 1898 led by Kang Youwei and Liang Qichao in their desire to turn China into a modern industrial power.

Hyksos (HICK-sohs) Invaders who seized the Nile delta and helped bring an end to the Egyptian Middle Kingdom.

Iconoclasts (eye-KAHN-oh-klasts) Supporters of the movement, begun by the Byzantine Emperor Leo III (r. 717–741), to destroy religious icons because their veneration was considered sinful.

Ilkhanate (EEL-kahn-ate) Mongol state that ruled Persia after abolition of the Abbasid empire in the thirteenth century.

Imperialism Term associated with the expansion of European powers and their conquest and colonization of African and Asian societies, mainly from the sixteenth through the nineteenth century.

Inca empire Powerful South American empire that would reach its peak in the fifteenth century during the reigns of Pachacuti Inca and Topa Inca.

Indentured labor Labor source for plantations; wealthy planters would pay the laboring poor to sell a portion of their working lives, usually seven years, in exchange for passage.

Indo-Europeans Tribal groups from southern Russia who, over a period of millennia, embarked on a series of migrations from India through western Europe; their greatest legacy was the broad distribution of Indo-European languages throughout Eurasia.

Indra Early Indian god associated with the Aryans; Indra was the king of the gods and was associated with warfare and thunderbolts.

Investiture (ihn-VEHST-tih-tyoor) One aspect of the medieval European church-versus-state controversy, the granting of church offices by a lay leader.

Iroquois (EAR-uh-kwoi) Eastern American Indian confederation made up of the Mohawk, Oneida, Onondaga, Cayuga, and Seneca tribes.

Islam Monotheistic religion announced by the prophet Muhammad (570–632); influenced by Judaism and Christianity, Muhammad was considered the final prophet because the earlier religions

had not seen the entire picture; the Quran is the holy book of Islam.

Jainism (JEYEN-iz'm) Indian religion associated with the teacher Vardhamana Mahavira (ca. 540–468 B.C.E.) in which every physical object possessed a soul; Jains believe in complete nonviolence to all living beings.

Jati Indian word for a Hindu subcaste.

Jizya (JIHZ-yuh) Tax in Islamic empires that was imposed on non-Muslims.

Joint-stock companies Early forerunner of the modern corporation; individuals who invested in a trading or exploring venture could make huge profits while limiting their risk.

Ka'ba (KAH-buh) Main shrine in Mecca, goal of Muslims embarking on the hajj.

Kabuki (kah-BOO-kee) Japanese theater in which actors were free to improvise and embellish the words.

Kama Hindu concept of the enjoyment of physical and sexual pleasure.

Kamikaze (KAH-mih-kah-zee) A Japanese term meaning "divine wind" that is related to the storms that destroyed Mongol invasion fleets; the term is symbolic of Japanese isolation and was later taken by suicide pilots in World War II.

Kanun (KAH-noon) Laws issued by the Ottoman Süleyman the Magnificent, also known as Süleyman Kanuni, "the Lawgiver."

Kapu Hawaiian concept of something being taboo.

Karma (KAHR-mah) Hindu concept that the sum of good and bad in a person's life will determine his or her status in the next life.

Khoikhoi South African people referred to pejoratively as the Hottentots by Europeans.

Kongo Central African state that began trading with the Portuguese around 1500; although their kings, such as King Affonso I (r. 1506–1543), converted to Christianity, they nevertheless suffered from the slave trade.

Koumbi-Saleh Important trading city along the trans-Saharan trade route from the eleventh to the thirteenth century.

Kshatriyas (KSHAHT-ree-uhs) Hindu caste of warriors and aristocrats.

Kulaks Land-owning Russian peasants who benefited under Lenin's New Economic Policy and suffered under Stalin's forced collectivization.

Kush Nubian African kingdom that conquered and controlled Egypt from 750 to 664 B.C.E.

Lamaist Buddhism (LAH-muh-ihst BOO-diz'm) Branch of Buddhism that was similar to shamanism in its acceptance of magic and supernatural powers.

La Reforma Political reform movement of Mexican president Benito Juárez (1806–1872) that called for limiting the power of the military and the Catholic church in Mexican society.

Latifundia (LAT-ih-FOON-dee-uh) Huge state-run and slave-worked farms in ancient Rome.

League of Nations Forerunner of the United Nations, the dream of American president Woodrow Wilson, although its potential was severely limited by the refusal of the United States to join.

Lebensraum (LAY-behnz-rowm) German term meaning "living space"; the term is associated with Hitler and his goal of carving out territory in the east for an expanding Germany.

Legalism Chinese philosophy from the Zhou dynasty that called for harsh suppression of the common people.

Levée en Masse (leh-VAY on MASS) A term signifying universal conscription during the radical phase of the French revolution.

Lex talionis (lehks tah-lee-oh-nihs) "Law of retaliation," laws in which offenders suffered punishments similar to their crimes; the most famous example is Hammurabi's Laws.

Li (LEE) Confucian concept, a sense of propriety.

Linear A Minoan written script.

Linear B Early Mycenaean written script, adapted from the Minoan Linear A.

Luddites Early-nineteenth-century artisans who were opposed to new machinery and industrialization.

Machismo (mah-CHEEZ-moh) Latin American social ethic that honored male strength, courage, aggressiveness, assertiveness, and cunning.

Madrasas (MAH-drahs-uhs) Islamic institutions of higher education that originated in the tenth century.

Magyars (MAH-jahrs) Hungarian invaders who raided towns in Germany, Italy, and France in the ninth and tenth centuries.

Mahabharata (mah-hah-BAH-rah-tah) Massive ancient Indian epic that was developed orally for centuries; it tells of an epic civil war between two family branches.

Mahayana (mah-huh-YAH-nah) The "greater vehicle," a more metaphysical and more popular northern branch of Buddhism.

Majapahit Southeast Asian kingdom (1293–1520) centered on the island of Java.

Mali (MAH-lee) West African kingdom founded in the thirteenth century by Sundiata; it reached its peak during the reign of Mansa Musa.

Manchus Manchurians who conquered China, putting an end to the Ming dynasty and founding the Qing dynasty (1644–1911).

Mandate of Heaven Chinese belief that the emperors ruled through the mandate, or approval, of heaven contingent on their ability to look after the welfare of the population.

Mandate system System that developed in the wake of World War I when the former colonies ended up mandates under European control, a thinly veiled attempt at continuing imperialism.

Manichaeism (man-ih-KEE-iz'm) Religion founded by the prophet Mani in the third century C.E., a syncretic version of Zoroastrian, Christian, and Buddhist elements.

Manor Large estates of the nobles during the European middle ages, home for the majority of the peasants.

Maori (mow-ree) Indigenous people of New Zealand.

Marae Polynesian temple structure.

Marathon Battlefield scene of the Athenian victory over the Persians in 490 B.C.E.

Maroons Runaway African slaves.

Marshall Plan U.S. plan, officially called the European Recovery Program, that offered financial and other economic aid to all European states that had suffered from World War II, including Soviet bloc states.

Mauryan empire Indian dynasty (321–185 B.C.E.) founded by Chandragupta Maurya and reaching its peak under Ashoka.

Maya (Mye-uh) Brilliant Central American society (300–1100) known for math, astronomy, and a sophisticated written language.

May Fourth Movement Chinese movement that began 4 May 1919 with a desire to eliminate imperialist influences and promote national unity.

Medes (meeds) Indo-European branch that settled in northern Persia and eventually fell to another branch, the Persians, in the sixth century B.C.E.

Meiji Restoration (MAY-jee) Restoration of imperial rule under Emperor Meiji in 1868 by a coalition led by Fukuzawa Yukichi and Ito Hirobumi; the restoration enacted western reforms to strengthen Japan.

Melaka (may-LAH-kah) Southeast Asian kingdom that was predominantly Islamic.

Mesopotamia Term meaning "between the rivers," in this case the Tigris and Euphrates; Sumer and Akkad are two of the earliest societies.

Mestizo (mehs-TEE-zoh) Latin American term for children of Spanish and native parentage.

Métis (may-TEE) Canadian term for individuals of mixed European and indigenous ancestry.

Millet An autonomous, self-governing community in the Ottoman empire.

Ming Chinese dynasty (1368–1644) founded by Hongwu and known for its cultural brilliance.

Minoan (mih-NOH-uhn) Society located on the island of Crete (ca. 2000–1100 B.C.E.) that influenced the early Mycenaeans.

Missi dominici (mihs-see doh-mee-nee-chee) "Envoys of the lord ruler," the noble and church emissaries sent out by Charlemagne.

Mithraism (MITH-rah-iz'm) Mystery religion based on worship of the sun god Mithras; it became popular among the Romans because of its promise of salvation.

Mochica (moh-CHEE-kuh) Pre-Incan South American society (300–700) known for their brilliant ceramics.

Moksha Hindu concept of the salvation of the soul.

Monotheism (MAW-noh-thee-iz'm) Belief in only one god, a rare concept in the ancient world.

Monroe Doctrine American doctrine issued in 1823 during the presidency of James Monroe that warned Europeans to keep their hands off Latin America and that expressed growing American imperialistic views regarding Latin America.

Mughals (MOO-guhls) Islamic dynasty that ruled India from the sixteenth through the eighteenth century; the construction of the Taj Mahal is representative of their splendor; with the exception of the enlightened reign of Akbar, the increasing conflict between Hindus and Muslims was another of their legacies.

Muhammad (muh-HAH-mehd) Prophet of Islam (570–632).

Muslim A follower of Islam.

Mycenaean (meye-seh-NEE-uhn) Early Greek society on the Peloponese (1600–1100 B.C.E.) that was influenced by the Minoans; the Mycenaeans' conflict with Troy is immortalized in Homer's *Odyssey*.

Nara era Japanese period (710–794), centered on the city of Nara, that was the highest point of Chinese influence.

National Policy Nineteenth-century Canadian policy designed to attract migrants, protect industries through tariffs, and build national transportation systems.

NATO The North Atlantic Treaty Organization, which was established by the United States in 1949 as a regional military alliance against Soviet expansionism.

Ndongo (n'DAWN-goh) Angolan kingdom that reached its peak during the reign of Queen Nzinga (r. 1623–1663).

Neandertal (nee-ANN-duhr-tawl) Early humans (100,000 to 35,000 years ago) who were prevalent during the Paleolithic period.

Negritude (NEH-grih-tood) "Blackness," a term coined by early African nationalists as a means of celebrating the heritage of black peoples around the world.

Neo-Confucianism (nee-oh-kuhn-FYOO-shuhn-iz'm) Philosophy that attempted to merge certain basic elements of Confucian and Buddhist thought; most important of the early Neo-Confucianists was the Chinese thinker Zhu Xi (1130–1200).

Neolithic New Stone Age (10,000–4000 B.C.E.), which was marked by the discovery and mastery of agriculture.

Nestorian (neh-STOHR-ee-uhn) Early branch of Christianity, named after the fifth-century Greek theologian Nestorius, that emphasized the human nature of Jesus Christ.

New Economic Policy (NEP) Plan implemented by Lenin that called for minor free market reforms.

Nirvana (nuhr-VAH-nuh) Buddhist concept of a state of spiritual perfection and enlightenment in which distracting passions are eliminated.

Noble Eightfold Path Final truth of the Buddhist Four Noble Truths that called for leading a life of balance and constant contemplation.

North American Free Trade Agreement (NAFTA) Regional accord established in 1993 between the United States,

Canada, and Mexico; it formed world's second largest free-trade zone.

Nubia (NOO-bee-uh) Area south of Egypt; the kingdom of Kush in Nubia invaded and dominated Egypt from 750 to 664 B.C.E.

Oceania Term referring to the Pacific Ocean basin and its lands.

Olmecs Early Mesoamerican society (1200–100 B.C.E.) that centered on sites at San Lorenzo, La Venta, and Tres Zapotes and that influenced later Maya.

Oracle bones Chinese Shang dynasty (1766–1122 B.C.E.) means of foretelling the future.

Organization of African Unity (OAU) An organization started in 1963 by thirty-two newly independent African states and designed to prevent conflict that would lead to intervention by former colonial powers.

Organization of Petroleum Exporting Countries (OPEC) An organization begun in 1960 by oil-producing states originally for purely economic reasons but that later had more political influence.

Osiris Ancient Egyptian god that represented the forces of nature.

Ottoman empire Powerful Turkish empire that lasted from the conquest of Constantinople (Istanbul) in 1453 until 1918 and reached its peak during the reign of Süleyman the Magnificent (r. 1520–1566).

Paleolithic Old Stone Age, a long period of human development before the development of agriculture.

Palestinian Liberation Organization (PLO) Organization created in 1964 under the leadership of Yasser Arafat to champion Palestinian rights.

Paris Peace Accords Agreement reached in 1973 that marked the end of the United States's role in the Vietnam War.

Parsis (pahr-SEES) Indian Zoroastrians.

Parthians Persian dynasty (247 B.C.E.–224 C.E.) that reached its peak under Mithradates I.

Pater familias (PAH-tur fuh-MEE-lee-ahs) Roman term for the "father of the family," a theoretical implication that gave the male head of the family almost unlimited authority.

Patriarch (PAY-tree-ahrk) Leader of the Greek Orthodox church, which in 1054 officially split with the Pope and the Roman Catholic church.

Patricians Roman aristocrats and wealthy classes.

Pax Romana (Pahks roh-MAH-nah) "Roman Peace," a term that relates to the period of political stability, cultural brilliance, and economic prosperity beginning with unification under Augustus and lasting through the first two centuries C.E.

Peninsulares (pehn-IHN-soo-LAH-rayz) Latin American officials from Spain or Portugal.

Perestroika (PAYR-eh-stroy-kuh) "Restructuring," a Russian term associated with Gorbachev's effort to reorganize the Soviet state.

Pharaohs (FARE-ohs) Egyptian kings considered to be gods on earth.

Plebians (plih-BEE-uhns) Roman common people.

Polis (POH-lihs) Greek term for the city-state.

Popol Vuh (paw-pawl vuh) Mayan creation epic.

Prehistory The period before the invention of writing.

Proletariat Urban working class in a modern industrial society.

Protestant Reformation Sixteenth-century European movement during which Luther, Calvin, Zwingli, and others broke away from the Catholic church.

Ptolemaic (TAWL-oh-may-ihk) Term used to signify both the Egyptian kingdom founded by Alexander the Great's general Ptolemy and the thought of the philosopher Ptolemy of Alexandria (second century C.E.), who used mathematical formulas in an attempt to prove Aristotle's geocentric theory of the universe.

Putting-out system Method of getting around guild control by delivering unfinished materials to rural households for completion.

Qadi Islamic judge.

Qanat (kah-NAHT) Persian underground canal.

Qi (chee) Chinese concept of the basic material that makes up the body and the universe.

Qin (chihn) Chinese dynasty (221–207 B.C.E.) that was founded by Qin Shihuangdi and was marked by the first unification of China and the early construction of defensive walls.

Qing (chihng) Chinese dynasty (1644–1911) that reached its peak during the reigns of Kangxi and Qianlong.

Qizilbash (gih-ZIHL-bahsh) Term meaning "red heads," Turkish tribes that were important allies of Shah

Ismail in the formation of the Safavid empire.

Quetzalcoatl (keht-zahl-koh-AHT'l) Aztec god, the "feathered serpent," who was borrowed originally from the Toltecs; Quetzalcoatl was believed to have been defeated by another god and exiled, and he promised to return.

Quinto (KEEN-toh) The one-fifth of Mexican and Peruvian silver production that was reserved for the Spanish monarchy.

Quipu (KEE-poo) Incan mnemonic aid comprised of different-colored strings and knots that served to record events in the absence of a written text.

Quran (koo-RAHN) Islamic holy book that is believed to contain the divine revelations of Allah as presented to Muhammad.

Ramayana (rah-mah-yah-nah) Ancient Indian masterpiece about the hero Rama that symbolized the victory of *dharma* (order) over *adharma* (chaos).

Rape of Nanjing Japanese conquest and destruction of the Chinese city of Nanjing in the 1930s.

Realpolitik (ray-AHL-poh-lih-teek) The Prussian Otto von Bismarck's "politics of reality," the belief that only the willingness to use force would actually bring about change.

Reconquista (ray-kohn-KEE-stah) Crusade, ending in 1492, to drive the Islamic forces out of Spain.

Reconstruction System implemented in the American South (1867–1877) that was designed to bring the Confederate states back into the union and also extend civil rights to freed slaves.

Romanov (ROH-mah-nahv) Russian dynasty (1610–1917) founded by Mikhail Romanov and ending with Nicholas II.

Rubaiyat (ROO-bee-aht) "Quatrains," famous poetry of Omar Khayyam that was later translated by Edward Fitzgerald.

Safavid (SAH-fah-vihd) Later Persian empire (1501–1722) that was founded by Shah Ismail and that became a center for Shiism; the empire reached its peak under Shah Abbas the Great and was centered on the capital of Isfahan.

Sakk Letters of credit that were common in the medieval Islamic banking world.

Saljuqs (sahl-JYOOKS) Turkish tribe that gained control over the Abbasid empire and fought with the Byzantine empire.

Samsara (sahm-SAH-ruh) Hindu term for the concept of transmigration, that is, the soul passing into a new incarnation.

Samurai (SAM-uhr-eye) A Japanese warrior.

Sasanids (suh-SAH-nids) Later powerful Persian dynasty (224–651) that would reach its peak under Shapur I and later fall to Arabic expansion.

Sati (SUH-TEE) Also known as *suttee*, Indian practice of a widow throwing herself on the funeral pyre of her husband.

Satraps (SAY-traps) Persian administrators, usually members of the royal family, who governed a satrapy.

Satyagraha (SAH-tyah-GRAH-hah) "Truth and firmness," a term associated with Gandhi's policy of passive resistance.

Scholasticism Medieval attempt of thinkers such as St. Thomas Aquinas to merge the beliefs of Christianity with the logical rigor of Greek philosophy.

Scientific racism Nineteenth-century attempt to justify racism by scientific means; an example would be Gobineau's *Essay on the Inequality of the Human Races*.

Seleucids (sih-LOO-sihds) Persian empire (323–83 B.C.E.) founded by Seleucus after the death of Alexander the Great.

Self-determination Belief popular in World War I and after that every people should have the right to determine their own political destiny; the belief was often cited but ignored by the Great Powers.

Self-Strengthening Movement Chinese attempt (1860–1895) to blend Chinese cultural traditions with European industrial technology.

Semitic (suh-miht-ihk) A term that relates to the Semites, ancient nomadic herders who spoke Semitic languages; examples of Semites were the Akkadians, Hebrews, Aramaics, and Phoenicians, who often interacted with the more settled societies of Mesopotamia and Egypt.

Sepoys Indian troops who served the British.

Serfs Peasants who, though not chattel slaves, were tied to the land and who owed obligation to the lords on whose land they worked.

Shamanism (SHAH-mah-niz'm) Belief in shamans or religious specialists who possessed supernatural powers and who communicated with the gods and the spirits of nature.

Shari'a (shah-REE-ah) The Islamic holy law, drawn up by theologians from the Quran and accounts of Muhammad's life.

Shia (SHEE-ah) Islamic minority in opposition to the Sunni majority; their belief is that leadership should reside in the line descended from Ali.

Shintoism (SHIHN-toh-iz'm) Indigenous Japanese religion that emphasizes purity, clan loyalty, and the divinity of the emperor.

Shiva (SHEE-vuh) Hindu god associated with both fertility and destruction.

Shogun (SHOH-gun) Japanese military leader who ruled in place of the emperor.

Shudras (SHOO-druhs) Hindu caste of landless peasants and serfs.

Siddhartha Gautama (sih-DHAR-tuh GOW-tau-mah) Indian *kshatriya* who achieved enlightenment and became known as the Buddha, the founder of Buddhism.

Sikhs (SIHKS) Adherents of an Indian syncretic faith that contains elements of Hinduism and Islam.

Silk roads Ancient trade routes that extended from the Mediterranean in the west to China in the east.

Social Darwinism Nineteenth-century philosophy, championed by thinkers such as Herbert Spencer, that attempted to apply Darwinian "survival of the fittest" to the social and political realm; adherents saw the the elimination of weaker nations as part of a natural process and used the philosophy to justify war.

Socialism Political and economic theory of social organization based on the collective ownership of the means of production; its origins were in the early nineteenth century, and it differs from communism by a desire for slow or moderate change compared with the communist call for revolution.

Solidarity Polish trade union and nationalist movement in the 1980s that was headed by Lech Walesa.

Song (SOHNG) Chinese dynasty (960–1279) that was marked by an increasingly urbanized and cosmopolitan society.

Soviets Russian elected councils that originated as strike committees during the 1905 St. Petersburg disorders; they represented a form of local self-government that went on to become the primary unit of government in the Union of Soviet Socialist Republics. The term was also used during the cold war to designate the Soviet Union.

Spanish Inquisition Institution organized in 1478 by Fernando and Isabel of Spain to detect heresy and the secret practice of Judaism or Islam.

Srivijaya (sree-VIH-juh-yuh) Southeast Asian kingdom (670–1025), based on the island of Sumatra, that used a powerful navy to dominate trade.

Stateless societies Term relating to societies such as those of sub-Saharan Africa after the Bantu migrations that featured decentralized rule through family and kinship groups instead of strongly centralized hierarchies.

Stoics (STOH-ihks) Hellenistic philosophers who encouraged their followers to lead active, virtuous lives and to aid others.

Strabo (STRAH-boh) Greek geographer (first century C.E.).

Strategic Arms Limitations Talk (SALT) Agreement in 1972 between the United States and the Soviet Union.

Stupas (STOO-pahs) Buddhist shrines.

Sufis (SOO-fees) Islamic mystics who placed more emphasis on emotion and devotion than on strict adherence to rules.

Sui (SWAY) Chinese dynasty (589–618) that constructed the Grand Canal, reunified China, and allowed for the splendor of the Tang dynasty that followed.

Süleyman (SOO-lee-mahn) Ottoman Turkish ruler Süleyman the Magnificent (r. 1520–1566), who was the most powerful and wealthy ruler of the sixteenth century.

Sumerians (soo-MEHR-ee-uhns) Earliest Mesopotamian society.

Sundiata (soon-JAH-tuh) Founder of the Mali empire (r. 1230–1255), also the inspiration for the *Sundiata*, an African literary and mythological work.

Sunni (SOON-nee) "Traditionalists," the most popular branch of Islam; Sunnis believe in the legitimacy of the early caliphs, compared with the Shiite belief that only a descendent of Ali can lead.

Suu Kyi, Aung San (SOO KEY, AWNG SAHN) Opposition leader (1945–) in Myanmar; she was elected leader in 1990 but she was not allowed to come to power; she was a Nobel Peace Prize recipient in 1991.

Swahili (swah-HEE-lee) East African city-state society that dominated the coast from Mogadishu to Kilwa and was active in trade.

Taino (TEYE-noh) A Caribbean tribe who were the first indigenous peoples from the Americas to come into contact with Christopher Columbus.

Taiping rebellion (TEYE-pihng) Rebellion (1850–1864) in Qing China led by Hong Xiuquan, during which twenty to thirty million were killed; the rebellion was symbolic of the decline of China during the nineteenth century.

Taliban Strict Islamic organization that ruled Afghanistan from 1996 to 2002.

Tang Taizong (TAHNG TEYE-zohng) Chinese emperor (r. 627–649) of the Tang dynasty (618–907).

Tanzimat "Reorganization" era (1839–1876), an attempt to reorganize the Ottoman empire on Enlightenment and constitutional forms.

Temüjin (TEM-oo-chin) Mongol conqueror (ca. 1167–1227) who later took the name Chinggis Khan, "universal ruler."

Tenochtitlan (the-NOCH-tee-tlahn) Capital of the Aztec empire, later Mexico City.

Teotihuacan (tay-uh-tee-wah-KAHN) Central American society (200 B.C.E.–750 C.E.); its Pyramid of the Sun was the largest structure in Mesoamerica.

Teutonic Knights Crusading European order that was active in the Baltic region.

Third Rome Concept that a new power would rise up to carry the legacy of Roman greatness after the decline of the Second Rome, Constantinople; Moscow was referred to as the Third Rome during the fifteenth century.

Three Principles of the People Philosophy of Chinese Guomindang leader Sun Yatsen (1866–1925) that emphasized nationalism, democracy, and people's livelihood.

Tian (TEE-ehn) Chinese term for heaven.

Tikal (tee-KAHL) Maya political center from the fourth through the ninth century.

Timur-i lang (tee-MOOR-yee LAHNG) "Timur the Lame," known in English as Tamerlane (ca. 1336–1405), who conquered an empire ranging from the Black Sea to Samarkand.

Tokugawa (TOH-koo-GAH-wah) Last shogunate in Japanese history (1600–1867); it was founded by Tokugawa Ieyasu who was notable for unifying Japan.

Toltecs Central American society (950–1150) that was centered on the city of Tula.

Trail of Tears Forced relocation of the Cherokee from the eastern woodlands to Oklahoma (1837–1838); it was symbolic of U.S. expansion and destruction of indigenous Indian societies.

Triangular trade Trade between Europe, Africa, and the Americas that featured finished products from Europe, slaves from Africa, and American products bound for Europe.

Triple Alliance Pre–World War I alliance of Germany, Austria-Hungary, and Italy.

Triple Entente (ahn-TAHNT) Pre–World War I alliance of England, France, and Russia.

Truman Doctrine U.S. policy instituted in 1947 by President Harry Truman in which the United States would follow an interventionist foreign policy to contain communism.

Tsar (ZAHR) Old Russian term for king that is derived from the term *caesar*.

Twelver Shiism (SHEE'i'zm) Branch of Islam that stressed that there were twelve perfect religious leaders after Muhammad and that the twelfth went into hiding and would return someday; Shah Ismail spread this variety through the Safavid empire.

Uighurs (WEE-goors) Turkish tribe.

Ukiyo Japanese word for the "floating worlds," a Buddhist term for the insignificance of the world that came to represent the urban centers in Tokugawa Japan.

Ulaanbaatar (OO-lahn-bah-tahr) Mongolian city.

Ulama Islamic officials, scholars who shaped public policy in accordance with the Quran and the *sharia*.

Umayyad (oo-MEYE-ahd) Arabic dynasty (661–750), with its capital at Damascus, that was marked by a tremendous period of expansion to Spain in the west and India in the east.

Umma (UM-mah) Islamic term for the "community of the faithful."

United Nations (UN) Successor to the League of Nations, an association of sovereign nations that attempts to find solutions to global problems.

Upanishads (oo-PAHN-ee-shahds) Indian reflections and dialogues (800–400 B.C.E.) that reflected basic Hindu concepts.

Urdu (OOR-doo) A language that is predominant in Pakistan.

Uruk (OO-rook) Ancient Mesopotamian city from the fourth millennium B.C.E. that was allegedly the home of the fabled Gilgamesh.

Vaishyas (VEYES-yuhs) Hindu caste of cultivators, artisans, and merchants.

Vaqueros (vah-KEHR-ohs) Latin American cowboys, similar to the Argentine gaucho.

Varna (VAHR-nuh) Hindu word for caste.

Varuna (vuh-ROO-nuh) Early Aryan god who watched over the behavior of mortals and preserved the cosmic order.

Vedas (VAY-duhs) "Wisdom," early collections of prayers and hymns that provide information about the Indo-European Aryans who migrated into India around 1500 B.C.E.; *Rig Veda* is the most important collection.

Velvet revolution A term that describes the nonviolent transfer of power in Czechoslovakia during the collapse of Soviet rule.

Venta, La (VEHN-tuh, lah) Early Olmec center (800–400 B.C.E.).

Venus figurines Small Paleolithic statues of women with exaggerated sexual features.

Vernacular (ver-NA-kyoo-lar) The language of the people; Martin Luther translated the Bible from the Latin of the Catholic church into the vernacular German.

Versailles (vehr-SEYE) Palace of French King Louis XIV.

Viet Minh North Vietnamese nationalist communists under Ho Chi Minh.

Vijayanagar (vee-juh-yah-NAH-gahr) Southern Indian kingdom (1336–1565) that later fell to the Mughals.

Vishnu (VIHSH-noo) Hindu god, preserver of the world, who was often incarnated as Krishna.

Vodou (voh-DOW) Syncretic religion practiced by African slaves in Haiti.

Volksgeist (FOHLKS-geyest) "People's spirit," a term that was coined by the German philosopher Herder; a nation's volksgeist would not come to maturity unless people studied their own unique culture and traditions.

Volta do mar (VOHL-tah doh MAHR) "Return through the sea," a fifteenth-century Portuguese sea route that took advantage of the prevailing winds and currents.

Voltaire (vohl-TAIR) Pen name of French philosophe Francois-Marie Arouet (1694–1778), author of *Candide*.

Waldensians Twelfth-century religious reformers who criticized the Roman

Catholic church and who proposed that the laity had the right to preach and administer sacraments; they were declared heretics.

Walesa, Lech (WAH-lehn-sah, LEHK) Leader of the Polish Solidarity movement.

Wanli (wahn-LEE) Chinese Ming emperor (r. 1572–1620) whose refusal to meet with officials hurried the decline of the Ming dynasty.

War Communism The Bolshevik policy of nationalizing industry and seizing private land during the civil war.

Warsaw Pact Warsaw Treaty Organization, a military alliance formed by Soviet bloc nations in 1955 in response to rearmament of West Germany and its inclusion in NATO.

Wind wheels Prevailing wind patterns in the Atlantic and Pacific Oceans north and south of the equator; their discovery made sailing much safer and quicker.

Witte, Sergei (VIHT-tee, SAYR-gay) Late-nineteenth-century Russian minister of finance who pushed for industrialization.

World Health Organization (WHO) United Nation organization designed to deal with global health issues.

World Trade Organization (WTO) An organization that was established in 1995 with more than 120 nations and whose goal is to loosen barriers to free trade.

Wuwei (woo-WAY) Daoist concept of a disengagement from the affairs of the world.

Xia (shyah) Early Chinese dynasty (2200–1766 B.C.E.).

Xianyang (SHYAHN-YAHNG) Capital city of the Qin empire.

Xiao (SHAYOH) Confucian concept of respect for one's parents and ancestors.

Xinjiang (shin-jyahng) Western Chinese province.

Xuanzang (SHWEN-ZAHNG) Seventh-century Chinese monk who made a famous trip to India to collect Buddhist texts.

Yahweh (YAH-way) God of the monotheistic religion of Judaism that influenced later Christianity and Islam.

Yangshao (YAHNG-show) Early Chinese society (2500–2200 B.C.E.).

Yangzi (YAHNG-zuh) River in central China.

Yongle (YAWNG-leh) Chinese Ming emperor (r. 1403–1424) who pushed for foreign exploration and promoted cultural achievements such as the *Yongle Encyclopedia*.

Young Turks Nineteenth-century Turkish reformers who pushed for changes within the Ottoman empire, such as universal suffrage and freedom of religion.

Yu (yoo) Legendary founder of the Xia dynasty (ca. 2200 B.C.E.).

Yuan (yoo-AHN) Chinese dynasty (1279–1368) that was founded by the Mongol ruler Khubilai Khan.

Yucatan (yoo-kuh-TAN) Peninsula in Central America, home of the Maya.

Yurts (yuhrts) Tents used by nomadic Turkish and Mongol tribes.

Zaibatsu (zeye-BAHT-soo) Japanese term for "wealthy cliques," which are similar to American trusts and cartels but usually organized around one family.

Zambos (ZAHM-bohs) Latin American term for individuals born of indigenous and African parents.

Zamudio, Adela (ZAH-moo-dee-oh, ah-DEH-lah) Nineteenth-century Bolivian poet, author of "To Be Born a Man."

Zarathustra (zar-uh-THOO-struh) Persian prophet (ca. sixth century B.C.E.) who founded Zoroastrianism.

Zemstvos (ZEHMST-voh) District assemblies elected by Russians in the nineteenth century.

Zen Buddhism Japanese version of Chinese Chan Buddhism, with an emphasis on intuition and sudden flashes of insight instead of textual study.

Zhou (JOH) Chinese dynasty (1122–256 B.C.E.) that was the foundation of Chinese thought formed during this period: Confucianism, Daoism, Zhou Classics.

Zhu Xi (ZHOO-SHEE) Neo-Confucian Chinese philosopher (1130–1200).

Ziggurats (ZIG-uh-rahts) Mesopotamian temples.

Zimbabwe (zihm-BAHB-way) Former colony of Southern Rhodesia that gained independence in 1980.

Zoroastrianism (zohr-oh-ASS-tree-ahn-iz'm) Persian religion based on the teaching of the sixth-century-B.C.E. prophet Zarathustra; its emphasis on the duality of good and evil and on the role of individuals in determining their own fate would influence later religions.

Credits

CHAPTER 29

Text Credits p. 804, From *Women in Revolutionary Paris, 1789–1795: Selected Documents Translated With Notes And Commentary.* Translated with notes and commentary by Darline Gay Levy, Harriet Branson Applewhite, and Mary Durham Johnson. Copyright 1979 by the Board of Trustees of the University of Illinois. Used with permission of the editors and the University of Illinois Press. **Photo Credits p. 780,** © Bridgeman-Giraudon/Art Resource, NY; **p. 785,** © HIP/Art Resource, NY; **p. 786,** Yale University Art Gallery/Art Resource, NY; **p. 788,** © Bulloz/Agence Réunion des Musées Nationaux/Art Resource, NY; **p. 791,** © Bibliotheque Nationale de France, Paris (RCC 17519); **p. 792,** © Archivo Iconografico, S.A./Corbis; **p. 796,** © Snark/Art Resource, NY; **p. 797,** © The Granger Collection, New York; **p. 799,** © Van Butcher/Photo Researchers, Inc.; **p. 803,** © Réunion des Musées Nationaux/Art Resource, NY; **p. 806,** © The Granger Collection, New York; **p. 807,** © Erich Lessing/Art Resource, NY; **p. 808,** © akg-images; **p. 810,** Schloss Friedrichsruhe/© The Bridgeman Art Library.

CHAPTER 30

Photo Credits pp. 814, 819, © Corbis; **p. 820,** Science Museum, London/© The Bridgeman Art Library; **p. 822,** © Ann Ronan Picture Library/HIP/The Image Works; **p. 826,** Guildhall Library, Corporation of London/© The Bridgeman Art Library; **p. 828,** © HIP/Art Resource, NY; **p. 834,** © Culver Pictures; **p. 835,** © Museum of the City of New York; **p. 838,** Deutsches Historisches Museum, Berlin; **p. 840,** © The Art Archive/Private Collection/Laurie Platt Winfrey; **p. 841,** The Metropolitan Museum of Art, Rogers Fund, 1942 (42.95.7). Image copyright © The Metropolitan Museum of Art/Art Resource, NY.

CHAPTER 31

Text Credits p. 859, From *Latin American Civilization* by Benjamin Keen. New York: Westview Press, 1996. Copyright © 1996 Westview Press. Used by permission of Westview Press, a member of Perseus Books Group; **p. 871,** From *Been in the Storm So Long* by Leon F. Litwack, copyright © 1979 by Leon F. Litwack. Used by permission of Alfred A. Knopf, a division of Random House, Inc.; **p. 886,** Rondo Cameron, ed., *Civilization Since Waterloo: A Book of Source Readings.* Itasca, Ill.: F.E. Peacock, 1971, pp. 245–46. Reprinted by permission. **Photo Credits p. 846,** © Bettmann/Corbis; **p. 851,** Library of Congress; **p. 852,** © PoodlesRock/Corbis; **p. 853,** Library of Congress; **p. 858,** © Erich Lessing/Art Resource, NY; **p. 860,** © Lake County Museum, Corbis; **p. 861,** © Micael Maslan Historic Photographs/Corbis; **p. 864,** © Museum of the City of New York/Corbis; **p. 867,** Courtesy of the Arizona Historical Society, Tuscon. #97329; **pp. 868, 869,** © Corbis; **p. 872,** © California Historical Society, San Francisco (FN-23115 [OV]); **p. 874,** © Yann Arthus-Bertand/Corbis.

CHAPTER 32

Photo Credits p. 878, © Carousel/Laurie Platt Winfrey, Inc.; **p. 884,** © W. & D. Downey/Getty Images; **p. 885,** © Culver Pictures; **p. 889,** Library of Congress; **p. 890,** © Hulton Archive/Getty Images; **p. 891,** © Chris Hellier/Corbis; **p. 893,** © Corbis; **p. 897,** © Collection Roger-Viollet/Getty Images; **p. 898,** © MacQuitty International Collection; **p. 900,** © Leonard deSelva/Corbis; **p. 901,** © The Art Archive/Private Collection/Laurie Platt Winfrey; **p. 904,** © Réunion des Musées Nationaux/Art Resource, NY.

CHAPTER 33

Photo Credits p. 908, © The Art Archive; **p. 912,** © Baldwin H. Ward/Corbis; **p. 915,** © Mary Evans Picture Library; **p. 917,** National Army Museum, London; **p. 919,** © The British Library (P1003); **p. 920,** © Hulton Archive/Getty Images; **p. 921,** © Anti-Slavery International/Panos; **p. 927,** © Mary Evans Picture Library; **p. 929,** © Brown Brothers; **p. 932,** © Mary Evans Picture Library; **p. 935,** Illustration of comparative physiognomy. From Indigenous Races of the Earth by J.C. Nott and G.R. Glidden, 1868; **p. 937,** © Royal Geographic Society.

CHAPTER 34

Text Credits p. 965, V.I. Lenin, *The State and Revolution.* Peking: Foreign Languages Press, 1973. Reprinted with permission of Foreign Language Press. **Photo Credits p. 944,** © Imperial War Museum, London; **p. 949,** © Christel Gersetenberg/Corbis; **pp. 951, 952, 954,** © Imperial War Museum, London; **p. 955,** © Bettmann/Corbis; **p. 956,** © AKG London; **p. 958,** © Imperial War Museum, London; **pp. 959, 960,** National Archives; **p. 962,** Fairstreet Pictures; **p. 964,** © Hulton-Deutsches Collection/Corbis; **p. 966,** © Bettmann/Corbis; **p. 967,** © Imperial War Museum, London; **p. 969,** © National Portrait Gallery, Smithsonian Institution/Art Resource, NY.

CHAPTER 35

Text Credits p. 998, From *Mein Kampf* by Adolf Hitler, translated by Ralph Manheim. Copyright © 1939, 1943 by Houghton Mifflin Company. Reprinted by permission of Houghton Mifflin Company. All rights reserved; **p. 998,** From *Mein Kampf* by Adolf Hitler, published by Pimlico. Reprinted by permission of The Random House Group Ltd. **Photo Credits p. 976,** Photo © Erich Lessing/Art

Index

Note: The date ranges after names of people refer to life spans, unless otherwise stated. The italicized word "*(map)*" following page numbers identifies maps. The italicized abbreviation "*(illus.)*" following page numbers identifies illustrations and tables. The italicized word "*(source document)*" identifies source documents.

Abdül Hamid, Ottoman sultan (reigned 1876–1909), 884 *(illus.)*, 885
abolition of slavery, 801–2, 851–53
abortion, 1000, 1080
"Abyss of Human Horror," 1050 *(illus.)*
Adwa, battle of (1896), 922
Afghanistan: prior to World War I, 948; refugees from, 1162, 1164 *(illus.)*; Soviet intervention in, 1081, 1082–83; Taliban in, 1083, 1152; United States invasion of, 1153
Africa: Back to Africa movement, 1019 *(source document)*, 1020; British colonies, 1011 *(illus.)*, 1015–16, 1110–12; colonial economy in, 1016–18, 1017 *(illus.)*, 1020 *(illus.)*; developing economies in, 1126–27; French colonies, 923 *(map)*, 948, 1015, 1106–8, 1107 *(illus.)*; German colonies, 923 *(map)*, 960–61, 1014–15; imperialism in, 919–25, 923 *(map)*, 924 *(source document)*; independence movements in, 1108–9, 1109 *(map)*; influenza pandemic (1918), 968; Italian colonies, 922, 923 *(map)*; migration from, as laborers, 934; nationalism in, 1014, 1018–20, 1019 *(source document)*; Pan-Africanism, 1019 *(source document)*, 1020, 1124; Portuguese colonies, 919, 923 *(map)*; railroads in, 1018; Spanish colonies, 923 *(map)*; in World War I, 960–61, 1014–16, 1015 *(illus.)*. See also north Africa; sub-Saharan Africa; *specific countries, kingdoms, and peoples*
African Americans: black nationalism, 1073; civil rights movement, 1073, 1075; freed slaves, 860, 869, 871 *(source document)*; segregation and,

1073; voting rights of, 802, 869, 869 *(illus.)*
African Economic Community (AEC), 1127
African National Congress (ANC), 1125–26
African Union (AU), 1127
Afrikaner National Party, 1125
Afrikaners, 921–22
agriculture: in Africa, 1017; in the Great Depression, 985–86; in India, 1114; in North America, 988, 1027; in People's Republic of China, 1079–80, 1113; in the Soviet Union, 993–94, 993 *(illus.)*; sugar plantations (*See* sugar plantations). *See also* peasants
Aguinaldo, Emilio, 929
ahimsa, 1007
Ahmadinejad, Mahmoud, President of Iran (1956–), 1117
AIDS (acquired immunodeficiency syndrome), 1144, 1149–51, 1150 *(map)*
airplanes: in World War I, 955–56, 956 *(illus.)*; in World War II, 1034, 1038–39, 1044
air pollution, 829, 1145, 1145 *(illus.)*, 1147
Alaska, 928, 1042
Albania, 1035
Alegre, Pedro Damian, 874 *(illus.)*
Alexander II, Tsar of Russia (reigned 1855–1881), 888–89, 889 *(illus.)*, 891
Algeria, 919, 1106–8, 1107 *(illus.)*, 1109
Alianza Popular Revolucionaria Americana, 1022
Allied powers, 1032, 1037–47, 1043 *(map)*, 1046 *(map)*. *See also* World War II
Allies (Triple Entente), 950, 952–56, 953 *(map)*, 960–63, 966–67, 971 *(map)*. *See also* World War I
All-India Muslim League, 937
All Quiet on the Western Front (Remarque), 979

al-Qaeda, 1152
American Express Train (Palmer), 864 *(illus.)*
American revolution, 784–86, 785 *(illus.)*, 787 *(map)*, 795
Amnesty International, 1156
Amritsar (Punjab), 1008, 1115
anarchism, 890
ANC (African National Congress), 1125–26
ancien régime, 787–88, 808
Anderson, Jourdan, 871
Angola, 919
Antietam, battle of (1862), 853 *(illus.)*
anti-Semitism: in fascist Germany, 998, 998 *(source document)*, 1000–1001; in fascist Italy, 996; Holocaust, 1050–53, 1050 *(illus.)*, 1051 *(source document)*, 1052 *(map)*, 1055; nationalism and, 806–7; in Russia, 806, 831, 891
Anzac Day, 961
Apache people, 849, 868 *(illus.)*
apartheid, in South Africa, 1124–26
Apollo space mission, 1075
appeasement policy, 1036–37
Aprismo, 1022
Apristas, 1022
Arabia: as mandate after World War I, 972; pan-Arab nationalism, 1104, 1115–16; in World War I, 962
Arab-Israeli wars, 1104, 1105 *(map)*, 1116, 1137
Arafat, Yasser (1929–2004), 1116
Arbenz Guzmán, Jacobo, President of Guatemala (1913–1971), 1120–21
architecture, 984–85, 984 *(illus.)*
Argentina: conflicts with indigenous peoples, 856–57; foreign capital in, 866; immigrant labor in, 862, 873; independence of, 799, 856 *(map)*; industrialization of, 841; under Perón, 1119–20, 1120 *(illus.)*; population growth in, 827; under Rosas, 857

Arias Sánchez, Oscar, President of Costa Rica (1940–), 1122
aristocracy and nobility: in French revolution, 787; in Japan, Meiji, 902; in Latin America, 796–800, 866. *See also* social classes
armaments. *See* weapons
Armenian genocide, 961–62
arms control, 1077, 1081
arms race, 1062 *(illus.)*, 1066–68, 1084, 1086
Arriaga, Ponciano (nineteenth century), 859 *(source document)*
art. *See* painting
Association of Southeast Asian Nations (SEATO), 1138–39
Astell, Mary (1666–1731), 802
Aswan, Egypt, 1105
Atatürk (Mustafa Kemal, 1881–1938), 961, 969
Aurangzeb, Mughal emperor (reigned 1659–1707), 916
Auschwitz concentration camp, 1052, 1052 *(map)*
Australia: aboriginal peoples in, 925–26; British colonies in, 925–26, 926 *(map)*; industrialization of, 841; in World War I, 960, 961, 962 *(illus.)*; in World War II, 1037
Austria: German annexation of, 1036; under Napoleon, 793; national consciousness in, 807; after World War II, 1056. *See also* Austria-Hungary
Austria-Hungary: anti-Semitism in, 806; in Central Powers, 949–50; declaration of war on Serbia, 951; nationalist aspirations within, 808, 947; unequal treaty with China, 896; women's rights in, 959; in World War I, 951, 953 *(map)*, 954, 967, 969, 971 *(map)*. *See also* Austria; Hungary
automobile production, 824
Axis powers, 1032, 1035–47, 1043 *(map)*, 1046 *(map)*. *See also* World War II

Back to Africa movement, 1019
(source document), 1020
Baedeker, Karl (1801–1859), 1163
bakufu, 899
balance-of-power diplomacy, 808
Balfour Declaration (1917), 1103
Balkans: Balkan wars, 948; nationalist uprisings in, 881; in World War I, 945–46, 951, 953 (map), 955, 969; in World War II, 1039, 1048. See also specific countries
Balkan wars (1912–1913), 948
Baltics: independence from Soviet Union, 1088, 1089 (map); opposition to Russian tsar in, 891–92; in World War I, 964; in World War II, 1043 (map)
bananas, 1025, 1027–28, 1027 (illus.), 1121
Bandaranaike, Sirimavo (1916–), 1159
Bandung Conference (1955), 1101
Bangladesh, 1100 (map)
banks and banking, 986
Barbarossa, Operation (1941), 1039–40, 1041 (illus.)
barbed wire, in wars, 954
Barbie dolls, 1140
Barth, Karl (1886–1968), 980
Bastille, storming of the (1789), 788, 790 (illus.)
Batista y Zaldívar, Fulgencio (1901–1973), 1069
Bauhaus, 984, 984 (illus.)
Bay of Pigs invasion (1961), 1069–70
Beatles, 1084
Beauvoir, Simone de (1908–1986), 1072
bedouin peoples, 962
Beijing, China, 897, 1033
Belgian Congo, 920, 921 (illus.), 923 (map), 1016, 1126
Belgium: in central Africa, 920, 921 (illus.), 923 (map), 1016, 1126; in the European Economic Community, 1137; independence from Netherlands, 808, 947; industrialization of, 822; unequal treaty with China, 896; in World War I, 952, 953 (map); in World War II, 1038, 1049
Berdiaev, Nikolai (1874–1948), 980
Berlin, Germany: Allied occupation of, 1056; Berlin Wall, 1066, 1066 (map), 1067 (illus.), 1087, 1087 (illus.), 1131; blockade and airlift in, 1065–66
Berlin Wall, 1066, 1066 (illus.), 1067 (illus.), 1087, 1087 (illus.), 1131
Berlin West Africa Conference (1884–1885), 922, 927
Bessemer, Henry (nineteenth century), 819

Beyond the Limits (Club of Rome), 1145
Bhagavad Gita, 1007
Bhuto, Benazir, Prime Minister of Pakistan (1953–), 1159
bin Laden, Osama (1957–), 1152–53
biodiversity, 1145–47
birth control: abortion, 1000, 1080; in China, 1147 (illus.), 1148, 1158; compulsory sterilization, 1000, 1114; condoms, 828; feminism and, 1157; in India, 1114; infanticide, 1158; in Nazi Germany, 999–1000; population control and, 1147–48; voluntary, 828
birthrates, industrialization and, 828
Bismarck, Otto von (1815–1898), 810–11, 810 (illus.), 822, 837, 911–12
bison, 869
Black Hand, 951
black nationalism, 1073
Blackshirts, 995
blast furnaces, 819
Blitzkrieg, 1037–39, 1038 (illus.)
bloodletting, World War I compared to, 955–56
Bloody Sunday massacre (Russia), 891
boats. See ships
Boers (Afrikaners), 921–22
Boer War (1899–1902), 921
Bolívar, Simón (1783–1830), 799, 799 (illus.), 802, 854–55
Bolshevik Party, 964, 965 (source document), 991
Bolshevik revolution (1917), 964, 965 (source document)
bombing of cities: in World War I, 955–56, 956 (illus.); in World War II, 1031, 1033–34, 1038–39, 1044, 1045 (source document), 1047, 1054
Borneo, 1042, 1048
Boston Tea Party (1773), 784
Botswana (Bechuanaland), 909
Boukman (Haitian Vodou priest; eighteenth century), 795
Boxer Rebellion (1898–1901), 895 (map), 899, 900 (illus.)
Brandenburg Gate (Berlin), 1067 (illus.)
Brazil: abolition of slavery in, 802; current economic growth in, 1137; independence of, 799 (map); industrialization of, 1024–25; sugar plantations in, 862
Brest-Litovsk, Treaty of (1918), 964
Brezhnev, Leonid Ilyich, Soviet premier (1906–1982), 1079
Brezhnev doctrine, 1079, 1086
Britain: abolition of slave trade by, 801–2; American revolution

against, 784–86, 785 (illus.), 787 (map), 795; appeasement policy towards Germany, 1036–37; battle of Britain, 1038–39, 1040 (illus.), 1054 (illus.); Berlin blockade and, 1065, 1066 (map); child labor laws in, 833–34, 837; coal mining in, 815, 817, 819 (illus.); East India Company, 892–93, 893 (illus.), 915–16; "Great Game," 917–18; industrialization in, 814 (illus.), 817–21, 819 (illus.), 947–48; in Opium War, 892–96, 893 (illus.), 894 (source document); on Palestine as Jewish homeland, 1103; population growth in, 828; Seven Years' War, 853; as sphere of influence in China, 896, 899; transportation networks in, 819–20, 820 (illus.), 823 (map); urbanization of, 829, 831, 831 (illus.); War of 1812, 854; women's rights in, 802–3, 958; World War I campaigns of, 952, 954–56, 960–62, 966–67; World War I causes and, 947–48, 950; World War I home front, 956–59, 957 (source document), 958 (illus.), 959 (illus.); World War I settlements, 968–69, 969 (illus.); in World War II, 1038–39, 1040 (illus.), 1041, 1043–44, 1053, 1055–56. See also British empire
Britain, battle of (1940-1941), 1039, 1040 (illus.), 1054 (illus.)
British Cape Colony, 909, 921
British East India Company, 892–93, 893 (illus.), 915–16
British empire: in Africa, 909, 920–22, 923 (map), 1011 (illus.), 1015–16, 1110–12; American revolution, 784–86, 785 (illus.), 787 (map), 795; English language legacy of, 1142; India in, 915–17, 917 (illus.); Indian self-rule, 1006–8, 1009 (source document), 1097–1101, 1098 (illus.); Ireland and, 967; in the Pacific, 925–27, 926 (map); racist attitudes in, 936; in southeast Asia, 918–19, 918 (map), 919 (illus.)
British Isles. See Britain
British North America Act (1867), 854
Brown v. Board of Education, 1073
bubonic plague, 937
Buenos Aires, Argentina, 873
buffalo, 869

Bulgaria: Soviet occupation of, 1056, 1086; in World War I, 967, 969, 971 (map)
burkas, 1152
Burke, Edmund (1729–1797), 800
Burma (Myanmar): in British empire, 898, 918, 918 (map), 919 (illus.); Suu Kyi imprisonment in, 1159–60, 1160 (illus.); in World War II, 1042, 1048
Burton, Richard, 920
Bush, George W., President of the United States (1946–), 1118, 1152
business organization: concessionary companies, 922; corporations, 816, 824–25, 996, 1133–34; economic imperialism, 1023–25, 1024 (map); factory system, 816, 820–21, 824; globalization and, 1133–34; international division of labor, 839–42, 841 (illus.); putting-out system, 820. See also banks and banking
Byron, Lord (1788–1824), 808

Calderón Hinojosa, Felipe de Jesús, President of Mexico (1942–), 1119
Calico Acts of 1720 and 1721, 818
California, 850, 850 (illus.), 861
California gold rush (1849), 861
Cambodia, 919, 1041, 1082, 1084. See also southeast Asia
Cameroon, 960, 1015
Canada: Dominion of, 854, 854 (map); ethnic diversity in, 870–71; foreign investment in, 865; French and English settlements in, 853; gold rushes in, 861, 870; independence of, 853–54; indigenous peoples in, 865, 870–72 (See also native Americans); industrialization of, 824, 841; National Policy, 865; population growth in, 865; railroads in, 854, 855 (map), 865, 872; War of 1812, 854; in World War I, 961; in World War II, 1037
canals: Grand Canal (China), 894; imperialism and, 914; Panama, 914, 929, 1024 (map), 1121; Suez, 914, 915 (illus.), 920, 1105
cancer, in chimney sweeps, 829
Cape Town, 921
Capital (Marx), 835
capitalism: British investment in United States, 862–63; Great Depression and, 986–87, 989; industrial, 824–25; Latin America and, 1021; Marx and Engels on, 835–37, 836 (source document); social

classes and, 821. *See also* foreign investment capital

capitulation treaties, 882

Caporetto, battle of (1917), 954

"captive nations" resolution, 1063

carbon dioxide emissions, 1147

Cárdenas, Cuauhtemoc, 1119

Cárdenas, Lázaro, President of Mexico (1895–1970), 1026, 1118

Caribbean Islands, United States possessions in, 928. *See also specific countries*

Caroline islands, 960

carrying capacity, 1144–45

Carson, Rachel (1907–1964), 1146 *(source document)*

cartels, 816, 825, 839

Carter, Jimmy, President of the United States (1924–), 1121

Cartwright, Edmund (eighteenth century), 818

Castillo Armas, Carlos (1914–1957), 1121

Castro, Fidel (1926–), 1021, 1069 *(illus.)*

caudillos, 800, 857, 873

Cavour, Count Camillo di (1810–1861), 810

Cawnpore, sepoy rebellion at, 916, 917 *(illus.)*, 934

CCP (Chinese Communist Party), 1010–12, 1011 *(map)*, 1034

Ceau_escu, Nicolae, Romanian dictator, 1087

central Africa. *See* Congo River basin

Central America. *See* Latin America; *specific countries*

central Asia, 917–18, 918 *(map)*, 1089 *(map)*

Central Intelligence Agency (CIA, United States): in Afghanistan, 1083; in Cuba, 1070; in Guatemala, 1121; in Iran, 1117; in Nicaragua, 1121, 1122; in Zaire, 1126

Central Powers (Triple Alliance), 949–50, 952–56, 953 *(map)*, 960–63, 966–67, 971 *(map)*. *See also* World War I

Ceylon (Sri Lanka), 916, 918 *(map)*, 931

Chamberlain, Neville (1869–1940), 1037

Chandigarh (Punjab), 985

Charles X, King of France, 808

chemical warfare, 954, 954 *(illus.)*, 1046

Cherokee people, 849

Chiang Kai-shek (Jiang Jieshi, 1887–1975), 1010–12, 1012 *(illus.)*, 1079

children: child labor, 833–34, 837, 1148–49; HIV/AIDS epidemic and, 1150; industrialization and, 833–34, 834 *(illus.)*, 837; native American, 869

Chile, 799, 856–57, 856 *(map)*

chimney sweeps, scrotum cancer in, 829

China: in Allied powers, 1032; Boxer Rebellion, 895 *(map)*, 899, 900 *(illus.)*; civil war, 1010–12, 1011 *(map)*; Communist revolution in, 959, 1079; industrialization of, 817, 898–99, 1079, 1113; Japanese imperialism in, 1013–14; Japanese invasion of (1937), 1033–35, 1033 *(illus.)*, 1034 *(illus.)*, 1048–49, 1053, 1055; Korean War and, 1068, 1080; migration from, as laborers, 933–34, 933 *(map)*; Opium War, 892–96, 893 *(illus.)*, 894 *(source document)*; Qing dynasty (*See* Qing dynasty of China); Republic, under Sun Yatsen, 1009–10; spheres of influence in, 895 *(map)*, 898–99; Taiping rebellion, 879, 896–98, 897 *(illus.)*; in World War I, 960, 1010. *See also* People's Republic of China

Chinese Communist Party (CCP), 1010–12, 1011 *(map)*, 1034

Chiquita Banana, 1027 *(illus.)*

cholera, 829

Christianity. *See* Roman Catholic church

Churchill, Winston, British prime minister (1874–1965), 961, 1042, 1055–56, 1074, 1097

CIA. *See* Central Intelligence Agency

Cinco de Mayo, 858

cities: aerial bombing of, 1031, 1034, 1038–39, 1044, 1045 *(source document)*, 1047; in Europe, industrialized, 823 *(map)*, 829, 831, 831 *(illus.)*; largest, 1161 *(illus.)*. *See also* urbanization

Civil Code of Napoleon, 793

civil codes. *See* legal codes

Civil Disobedience Movement of 1930, 1008

civil rights: for African Americans, 1073, 1075, 1157; for freed slaves, 869, 871 *(source document)*; for women, 869–70, 1157

civil service examinations, Chinese, 879

Civil War (Soviet Union, 1918–1920), 991

Civil War (Spain, 1936–1939), 1035, 1036

Civil War (United States, 1861–1865), 852–853, 852 *(illus.)*, 853 *(illus.)*, 954

Cixi, Empress of China (1835–1908), 898–99, 898 *(illus.)*

Clark, William, 849

class struggles, Marx and Engels on, 835–37, 836 *(source document)*

Clemenceau, Georges (1841–1929), 968

Cleveland, Grover, President of the United States (in office 1885–1899), 928

climate change, 1147

clocks, railroad, 863–64

Club of Rome, 1144–45

coal mining, 815, 817, 819 *(illus.)*, 823 *(map)*

Cody, Buffalo Bill, 869

cohongs, 892

coitus interruptus, 828

coke, 819

Cold War (1947–1991), 1063–92; Afghanistan in, 1082–83; alliances in, 1057, 1067, 1071 *(map)*; Arab-Muslim world and, 1115–16; China in, 1079–81; consumerism in, 1075; countercultural protests, 1083–84; decline of, 1084–85; *détente* policy and, 1081; in Europe, 1056, 1064–67, 1065 *(illus.)*, 1066 *(map)*, 1067 *(illus.)*, 1077–79, 1085–86; impact on independence movements, 1096, 1100–1103, 1104–5, 1120–22, 1126; Khrushchev on, 1074 *(source document)*; "kitchen debate" during, 1063, 1065 *(illus.)*, 1075, 1076; Korean War, 1067–68, 1068 *(illus.)*, 1080; nuclear arms race, 1062 *(illus.)*, 1066–68, 1086; peaceful co-existence in, 1075–76; Soviet Union collapse and, 1087–88, 1089 *(map)*; space race, 1075; Truman Doctrine, 1056–57

collectivized agriculture, 993–94, 993 *(illus.)*

Colombia, 799, 855, 856 *(map)*, 929

colonies and colonialization. *See* imperialism

Comanche people, 849

communalism, 1097

communication: globalization of, 1141–43; imperialism and, 914–15; steamships and, 914; telegraph, 914–15; television, 1143, 1143 *(illus.)*

communism: in China, 1010, 1011 *(map)*, 1080–81, 1112–14; after collapse of Soviet Union, 1089–90; containment policy, 1056–57, 1068; "domestic containment" of, 1072; in eastern Europe, 1056, 1078–79, 1078 *(illus.)*; in Latin America, 1021–22; Marx and Engels on, 835–37, 836 *(source document)*; in the Soviet Union, 991–94, 993

(illus.), 1080; in Vietnam, 1102; women and, 1157–58; in Yugoslavia, 1077

concessionary companies, 922

Concordat (1801), 792

condoms, 828

Congo Free State, 920, 921 *(illus.)*

Congo River basin: Belgian Congo, 920, 923 *(map)*, 1016, 1126; Congo Free State, 920, 921 *(illus.)*; Democratic Republic of the Congo, 1126; Zaire, 1126, 1143

Congress of Vienna (1814–1815), 807–8

conservatism, 800

constitutional states: constitutional monarchies, 788; Meiji Japan, 903; Mexico, 860, 1118–19; Ottoman empire, 885, 886 *(source document)*; United States, 786

Constitution of the United States, 786

consumerism, 1075, 1140–42

containment policy, 1056–57, 1068

Continental Congress (1774), 785

Contras, in Nicaragua, 1122

"Convention on the Rights and Duties of States" (1933), 1026

Cook, Capt. James (1728–1779), 925

Cook, Thomas (1808–1892), 1163

copper, 911

copra, 927

Le Corbusier (Charles Édouard Jeanneret, 1887–1965), 985

corporations, 816, 824–25, 996, 1133–34

corporatism, 996

cossacks, 917

Costa Rica, 799

cotton: Indian, 931; mechanization of industry, 814 *(illus.)*, 818, 823, 824; United States, 823, 851–52

cotton gin, 824

Council for Mutual Economic Assistance (COMECON), 1057

countercultural protests, 1083–84

crash of 1929, 986

creoles (*criollos*), 796–800, 855–57

Crimean War (1853–1856), 888

criollos (creoles), 796–800, 855–57

Crompton, Samuel (eighteenth century), 818

Crystal Palace exhibition (1851), 826, 826 *(illus.)*

Cuba: abolition of slavery in, 802; immigrant labor in, 862; missile crisis (1962), 1068–69, 1070; rise of Castro in, 1069, 1069 *(illus.)*; Spanish-Cuban-American War, 928; United States invasion (1961), 1069–70

cultural nationalism, 805–6

Cultural Revolution (China, 1966–1976), 1113, 1113 *(illus.)*, 1136
culture: Cold War, 1063, 1065 *(illus.)*, 1072, 1073, 1075–76, 1083–84; globalization and, 1063–65, 1139–43, 1143 *(illus.)*; labor migrations and, 934; mass tourism and, 1163–65; Pan-American, 1141–42; United States, nineteenth-century, 867–70; between the world wars, 982–85, 982 *(illus.)*, 983 *(illus.)*. See also literature; music; painting; religions
Custer, Col. George Armstrong, 849
Czechoslovakia: division of, 1087; German occupation of, 1036, 1037, 1049; independence from Soviet Union, 1086–87; self-determination and, 971–72; Soviet intervention (1968), 1078–79, 1078 *(illus.)*, 1085
Czech Republic, 1087

Dadié, Bernard, 1108
daimyo, 900–901
Darwin, Charles (1809–1882), 935
David, Jacques-Louis, 792 *(illus.)*
Dawes Severalty Act (1887), 869
D-Day (1944), 1044
debt peonage, 860, 1149
Declaration of Independence (United States), 785, 786 *(illus.)*, 849
Declaration of Independence (Vietnam), 1101
Declaration of the Rights of Man and the Citizen, 781, 788, 789 *(source document)*
Declaration of the Rights of Woman and the Female Citizen (Gouges), 781, 804 *(source document)*
The Decline of the West (Spengler), 979
decolonialization. *See* independence movements
Degas, Edgar (1834–1917), 983
de Gaulle, Charles (1890–1970), 1076–77
de Klerk, F. W., President of South Africa (1936–), 1125–26
Delacroix, Eugène, 780 *(illus.)*
democracy: Chinese prodemocracy demonstrations, 1114, 1115 *(illus.)*; fascist hostility to, 995; in India, postcolonial, 1114–15; liberalism and, 800; pessimism of interwar era, 980, 998. *See also* political organization
Democratic Republic of the Congo, 1126. *See also* Belgian Congo

demographic transition, 828–29
Les Demoiselles d'Avignon (Picasso), 983 *(illus.)*
Deng Xiaoping (1904–1997), 1113–14
Denmark, 896, 1038, 1048–49
dependency theory of economic development, 1123
descamisados, 1119, 1120 *(illus.)*
détente policy, 1081
diamond mining, 909, 921
Díaz, Porfirio, President of Mexico (1830–1915), 858, 866
Diem, Ngo Dinh, President of Vietnam (1901–1963), 1102
Diet, Japanese, 903
diets, globalization of, 1141
diplomacy, dollar, 1023, 1025
Directory (France, 1795–1799), 790–91, 792
dirigibles, 956
diseases: bubonic plague, 937; cholera, 829; dysentery, 829; globalization and, 1149; HIV/AIDS, 1144, 1149–51, 1150 *(map)*; polluted water and, 829; scrotum cancer in chimney sweeps, 829; smallpox, 925; syphilis, 828; tuberculosis, 829; typhus, 829; yellow fever, 796. *See also* epidemics
dissent. *See* protest
divine right of kings, 783
Dix, Otto, 976 *(illus.)*
Doctrine of Limited Sovereignty, 1079
dollar diplomacy, 1023, 1025
domestic abuse, 1159
domestic servants, 833
Dominican Republic, 928, 1025
"domino theory," 1068, 1102
Doré, Gustave (nineteenth century), 831 *(illus.)*
Down Argentine Way (film), 1027
dowry deaths, 1159
Dr. Strangelove (film, 1964), 1083–84
Dr. Zhivago (Pasternak), 1076
dreadnoughts, 948
Dresden, firebombing of (1945), 1044
Dreyfus, Alfred (1859–1935), 806-7
"Dry Your Tears, Africa!" (Dadié), 1108
Dual Alliance, 949
The Dual Mandate in British Tropical Africa (Lugard), 925
Dubček, Alexander (1921–1992), 1078
DuBois, W. E. B. (1868–1963), 1020
Duma (Russia), 891–92
Dunant, Jean Henri (1828–1910), 1154
Durham Report (1839), 854
Dutch. *See* Netherlands

Dutch East Indies, 918, 918 *(map)*, 1041, 1048
dysentery, 829

east Africa, in World War I, 960–61. *See also specific countries*
eastern Europe: German-Soviet planned division of, 1037; revolutions in, 1085–88, 1086 *(illus.)*, 1087 *(illus.)*, 1089 *(map)*; Soviet occupation of, 1056, 1064–67, 1076–79. *See also* Europe; *specific countries*
East Germany, 1065, 1086, 1087, 1087 *(illus.)*. *See also* Germany
East India companies: Dutch (VOC), 918; English, 892–93, 893 *(illus.)*, 915–16
Echeverria, Luis, 1147
economic systems: capitalism (*See* capitalism); communism (*See* communism); evolutionary socialism, 837; fascism, 994–1001, 997 *(illus.)*, 998 *(source document)*, 1000 *(illus.)*, 1001 *(illus.)*; Great Depression and, 988–89; imperialism (*See* imperialism); industrial capitalism, 824–25; socialism (*See* socialism); utopian socialism, 834; war communism, 991–92
economy: of African societies, 1016–18, 1017 *(illus.)*; of Canada, 865; corporations in, 816, 824–25, 996, 1133–34; globalization of, 1132–35, 1134 *(illus.)*; in the Great Depression, 985–89, 987 *(illus.)*, 988 *(illus.)*, 989 *(illus.)*, 990 *(source document)*; imperialism and, 931; industrial division of labor and, 839–42, 841 *(illus.)*; of Japan, 1135; of Latin America, 866–67, 1123; of the Soviet Union, 991–92; of western *vs.* eastern Europe, 1075; after World War II, 1057
Ecuador, 799, 855, 856 *(map)*, 1122–23
education: government schools for native Americans, 868 *(illus.)*, 869; in India, 1007; in Meiji Japan, 903; in Ottoman empire, 883–84; segregated, in the United States, 1073; of women, 803, 1155, 1158 *(illus.)*, 1159
Egypt: Arab-Israeli wars and, 1104, 1105 *(map)*, 1116; British occupation of, 920, 973; independence from Britain, 1103; under Muhammad Ali, 881; Napoleon's invasion of, 881; under Nasser, 1104–6, 1106 *(illus.)*; under Ottoman rule, 881
Einsatzgruppen, 1050

Einstein, Albert (1879–1955), 980–81, 980 *(illus.)*
Eisenhower, Dwight D., President of the United States (1890–1969), 1068–69, 1081, 1102, 1121
Elizabeth II, Queen of England (1926–), 1110, 1110 *(illus.)*
El Salvador, 799, 1122
Emancipation Proclamation (1863), 852
emigration. *See* migrations
Enfield rifles, 916
Engels, Friedrich (1820–1895), 835–37, 836 *(source document)*
England. *See* Britain
English East India Company, 892–93, 893 *(illus.)*, 915–16
English language, 1142
Enlightenment: on equality, 783; influence on American revolution, 785, 786; influence on French revolution, 787; influence on Latin American revolutions, 797, 799, 873; liberalism and, 800; Ottomans and, 884; on popular sovereignty, 783; slavery and, 801–2; socialism and, 834; on voting rights, 801; women's rights and, 802–5, 804 *(source document)*
entertainment, 832–33, 834 *(illus.)*, 1163–64
environmental issues: air pollution, 829, 1145, 1145 *(illus.)*, 1147; biodiversity reduction, 1145–47; carrying capacity, 1144–45; deforestation, 819; extinction, 1145–47; global warming, 1147; international organizations and, 1155; pesticides, 1146 *(source document)*; railroad impact on, 863; water pollution, 829
epidemics: in Australia and New Zealand, 925; bubonic plague, 937; globalization and, 1149; HIV/AIDS, 1144, 1149–51, 1150 *(map)*; in India, 937; influenza pandemic of 1918, 968, 1149; vaccinations and, 827 *(illus.)*, 828. *See also* diseases
Epistle to the Romans (Barth), 980
equality, 783, 788
Equiano, Olaudah (1745–1797), 801
Essay on the Inequality of the Human Races (Gobineau), 935
Essay on the Principle of Population (Malthus), 830 *(source document)*
Estates General, 787–88
Estonia, 1088. *See also* Baltics
Ethiopia, 922, 1014, 1035, 1036 *(illus.)*

eugenics, 1000
Europe: African colonies, 922, 923
    (map), 948, 960–61,
    1014–18, 1106–8, 1107
    (illus.); Balkan wars, 948;
    Christianity in (See Roman
    Catholic church); cold war in,
    1056, 1064–67, 1065 (illus.),
    1066 (map), 1067 (illus.),
    1071 (map); after the collapse
    of the Soviet Union, 1089
    (map); Congress of Vienna,
    807–8; countercultural
    protests, 1083–84; economic
    recovery after World War II,
    1057, 1075; Enlightenment in
    (See Enlightenment); European
    Union formation, 1137, 1138
    (map); Great Depression in,
    985–89; guest workers in,
    1162; Holocaust in, 1050–53,
    1050 (illus.), 1051 (source
    document), 1052 (map), 1055;
    industrialization of, 822, 823
    (map); labor migrations to
    colonies, 932, 933 (map);
    migration to Americas,
    861–62, 861 (illus.); Napoleon
    Bonaparte in, 792–93, 792
    (illus.), 794 (map), 799, 921;
    Opium War, 892–96, 893
    (illus.), 894 (source document);
    Ottoman empire and, 808,
    950; in Pacific islands, 925–27,
    926 (map); railroads in,
    819–20, 820 (illus.), 823
    (map); Seven Years' War, 784,
    853; in southeast Asia, 918–19,
    918 (map), 919 (illus.); Soviet
    occupation in, 1056, 1064–67,
    1076–79; World War I (See
    World War I); World War I
    settlements, 968–72, 969
    (illus.), 971 (map); World War
    II (See World War II); World
    War II settlements, 1055–56.
    See also eastern Europe;
    Europe; specific countries
European Union, 1137,
    1138 (map)
Euros, 1138 (map)
euthanasia, 1000
Evita (play and film), 1141–42
evolution, theory of, 935
evolutionary socialists, 837
Explorer I, 1075
external migration, 1161–62. See
    also migrations
extinction, 1145–47

factories: children in, 833–34;
    factory system, 816, 820–21,
    824; mass production in, 824,
    826; protoindustrial, 820
Facundo: Civilization and
    Barbarism (Sarmiento), 873
families, 832–33, 999–1000,
    1000 (illus.)

famines: in India, 937, 937 (illus.);
    in Ireland, 831; in Japan, 900;
    malnutrition from economic
    inequities, 1148
fanghuo qiang, 1143
Fanon, Frantz (1925–1961), 1107
A Farewell to Arms
    (Hemingway), 979
fascism: in Germany, 997–1001,
    997 (illus.), 998 (source docu-
    ment), 1000 (illus.), 1001
    (illus.); in Italy, 995–96;
    overview of, 994–95
les fauves, 982
Federal Republic of Germany
    (West Germany), 1065, 1137.
    See also Germany
The Feminine Mystique
    (Friedan), 1072
feminism, 1072–73, 1157. See also
    women's rights
Fiji, 926 (map), 927
"final solution" (Holocaust),
    1050–53, 1050 (illus.), 1051
    (source document), 1052
    (map), 1055
financial institutions. See banks
    and banking
Finland, 964
firearms: machine guns, 850, 914,
    954; Maxim guns, 914; muni-
    tions factories, 958, 958 (illus.);
    muskets, 914; rifles, 916
First Five-Year Plan (Soviet
    Union), 992–94
Five-Year Plan (China), 1079
flying shuttle, 818
food, globalization of, 1141
Ford, Henry, 824
foreign investment capital: British
    investment in the U.S. and
    Canada, 862–63, 865; in
    China, 1136; in Egypt, 920; in
    the Great Depression, 986; in
    Latin America, 866–67, 867
    (illus.), 1023–24; in Ottoman
    empire, 882; in Russia, 889
foreign policy: appeasement
    policy toward Nazi Germany,
    1036–37; Brezhnev doctrine,
    1079, 1086; containment
    policy of the United States,
    1056–57, 1068; détente and
    Soviet Union, 1081; dollar
    diplomacy, 1023, 1025;
    "domino theory" in United
    States, 1068, 1102; Good
    Neighbor Policy, 1025–26;
    Japan, Tokugawa, 900–901;
    Monroe Doctrine, 928, 929,
    1026, 1120; nonalignment
    policy, 1100–1101, 1104;
    peaceful coexistence, 1075–76;
    preemptive war, United States,
    1153; Roosevelt Corollary to
    the Monroe Doctrine, 929,
    1026; Truman Doctrine,
    1056–57

Fourier, Charles (1772–1837), 834
"four little tigers," 1135–36
Fourteen Points (Wilson),
    968–69, 973–74, 1007
Fox Quesada, Vincente, President
    of Mexico (1942–), 1119
France: abolition of slavery, 802;
    abolition of slave trade by,
    801; African colonies, 923
    (map), 948, 1015, 1106–8,
    1107 (illus.); anti-Semitism in,
    806–7; appeasement policy
    towards Germany, 1036–37;
    Berlin blockade and, 1065,
    1066 (map); under de Gaulle,
    1076–77; in the European
    Economic Community, 1137;
    Franco-Prussian War, 950;
    French Indochina, 919, 1041,
    1048, 1102–3; French revolu-
    tion, 787–92, 789 (source
    document), 790 (illus.), 791
    (illus.), 803–4, 804 (source
    document), 807; industriali-
    zation of, 822; Mexico, inter-
    vention in, 857–58, 858
    (illus.); under Napoleon Bona-
    parte, 792–93, 792 (illus.),
    794 (map); national identity
    in, 807; Pacific colonies of,
    926 (map), 927; Prussian
    victory over, 810 (illus.), 811;
    unequal treaty with China,
    896, 898; women's rights
    movements in, 803; World
    War I campaigns, 948,
    952–56, 953 (map), 967;
    World War I home front,
    956–59, 957 (source docu-
    ment), 958 (illus.), 959
    (illus.); World War I settle-
    ments, 968–69, 969 (illus.);
    World War II campaigns,
    1032, 1038–39, 1041, 1043
    (map), 1044, 1048–49; World
    War II settlements, 1056
Francis Ferdinand, Archduke
    of Austria (1863–1914),
    945–46, 951
Franco, Francisco
    (1892–1975), 1035
Franco-Prussian War
    (1870–1871), 950
Free Speech Movement, 1083
free trade, globalization and, 1133
French and Indian War
    (1754–1763), 784
French Indochina, 919, 1041,
    1048, 1102–3. See also south-
    east Asia; Vietnam
French revolution, 787–91; Con-
    vention, 788–90, 791 (illus.);
    Declaration of the Rights of
    Man and the Citizen, 781,
    788, 789 (source document);
    the Directory, 790–91, 792;
    Estates General, 787–88;
    National Assembly, 788;

national identity in, 807;
    Robespierre and the Jacobins,
    790–91; storming of the
    Bastille, 788, 790 (illus.);
    taxation and, 787–88; war
    with other European coun-
    tries, 788; women in, 781,
    803, 803 (illus.), 804 (source
    document)
Freud, Sigmund (1856–1939),
    981–82, 981 (illus.)
Friedan, Betty (1921–), 1072
Fukuzawa Yukichi
    (1835–1901), 902
Fulton, Robert, 841 (illus.)

Gadsden Purchase (1853),
    850 (map)
Gallipoli, 961
Gallipoli, battle of (1915), 961
Gandhi, Indira, Prime Minister of
    India (1917–1984), 1114–15,
    1116 (illus.), 1159
Gandhi, Mohandas Karamchand
    (1869–1948), 1007–8, 1073,
    1094 (illus.), 1095–96,
    1098–99
Gandhi, Rajiv, Prime Minister of
    India (1944–1991), 1115
Garibaldi, Giuseppe
    (1807–1882), 810
Garvey, Marcus (1887–1940),
    1019 (source document),
    1020, 1073
Gatling guns, 850
GATT (General Agreement on
    Tariffs and Trade), 1133
The Gaucho Martín Fierro
    (Hernandez), 873
gauchos, 857, 873, 874 (illus.)
Gauguin, Paul (1848–1903), 982
    (illus.), 983
Gaulle, Charles de (1890–1970),
    1076–77
General Agreement on Tariffs and
    Trade (GATT), 1133
The General Theory of Employment,
    Interest, and Money
    (Keynes), 989
Geneva Convention (1864), 1154
Geneva peace conference on
    Vietnam (1954), 1102
genocide, Armenian, 961–62
gens de couleur, 795
George, Lloyd, 968
Georgia, opposition to tsar in,
    891–92
German Democratic Republic
    (East Germany), 1065, 1086,
    1087, 1087 (illus.)
Germany: African colonies of, 923
    (map), 960–61, 1014–15;
    anti-Semitism in, 806, 998,
    998 (source document),
    1000–1001; in Axis powers,
    1032, 1035; in Central
    Powers, 949–50; division of,
    after World War II, 1056,

Germany *(continued)*
1064–66, 1065 *(map)*; East
Germany, 1065, 1086, 1087,
1087 *(illus.)*; fascism in, 994,
997–1001, 997 *(illus.)*, 998
(source document), 1000
(illus.); Great Depression in,
986; industrialization of, 822,
947–48; nationalism in, 805,
811; naval race with Britain,
948; Pacific colonies of, 926
(map), 927; population
growth in, 828; remilitarization under Hitler, 1036–37;
Second Reich, 811; social
reform in, 837; unequal treaty
with China, 896, 898; unification of (1815), 809, 809
(map), 810–11; unification of
(1989), 1087, 1087 *(illus.)*;
West Germany, 1065, 1137;
women's rights in, 959; World
War I campaigns, 952–56, 953
(map), 960, 966–67, 967
(illus.); World War I causes,
947–48, 952; World War I
home front, 956–59, 957
(source document), 958 *(illus.)*,
959 *(illus.)*; World War I
settlements, 968–69, 969
(illus.), 971 *(map)*, 985; in
World War II (*See* Nazi Germany). *See also* Nazi Germany
Gettysburg, battle of (1863), 852
Ghana (nation), 1108, 1109
(map), 1110, 1124
glasnost, 1088
Glenn, John (1921–), 1075
globalization: Asian growth and,
1135–37; of communication,
1141–43; cultural differences
in, 1140; cultural integration
and, 1132; economic,
1132–35, 1134 *(illus.)*; economic inequities in, 1148–49;
environmental degradation
from, 1145–47, 1146 *(source
document)*; HIV/AIDS and,
1149–51, 1150 *(map)*; international organizations and,
1153–56; migration of peoples
during, 1160–62; perils of,
1136; population pressures,
1143–45, 1144 *(illus.)*,
1147–48; terrorism and,
1151–53; tourism, 1163–65;
trading blocs in, 1137–39,
1138 *(map)*; women and,
1156–60, 1157 *(illus.)*, 1158
(illus.), 1160 *(illus.)*.
global warming, 1147
Gobineau, Count Joseph Arthur
de (1816–1882), 935
Golden Temple (Amritsar), 1115
gold mining: in Australia, 925; in
California, 846 *(illus.)*, 847,
861; in Canada, 861, 870; in
south Africa, 921

golondrinas, 862
Good Neighbor Policy, 1025–26
Gorbachev, Mikhail S., Premier of
the Soviet Union (1931–),
1084–88, 1086 *(illus.)*
Gouges, Olympe de (1748–1793),
781, 790, 804 *(source
document)*
government, 783–84. *See also*
political organization
Government of India Act
(1937), 1008
Gran Colombia, 799, 802, 855
Grand Canal (China), 894
The Grapes of Wrath
(Steinbeck), 988
Great Britain. *See* Britain
Great Depression, 985–89, 987
(illus.), 988 *(illus.)*, 989
(illus.), 990 *(source document)*
Great Easter Rebellion (Ireland,
1916), 967
Greater East Asia Co-Prosperity
Sphere, 1043
"Great Game," 917–18
Great Leap Forward (China,
1958–1961), 1113, 1136
Great Proletarian Cultural Revolu-
tion (China, 1966–1976),
1113, 1113 *(illus.)*
Great War. *See* World War I
Greece, 808, 881, 947, 953 *(map)*
greenhouse gases, 1147
Greenpeace, 1155
"green revolution," 1114
Grimm, Jakob and Wilhelm, 806
Gropius, Walter (1883–1969),
984, 984 *(illus.)*
Guadalupe Hidalgo, Treaty of
(1848), 850
Guam, 928, 1042
Guangzhou (China), 892
guano, 927
Guard Nacional (Nicaragua), 1025
Guatemala, 799, 1120–21
guerrilla warfare, 858, 1034,
1102, 1121
guillotine, 789, 790–91,
791 *(illus.)*
Gulf War (1990-1991), 1118
gunboats, 914
Guomindang (China), 1010–12,
1011 *(map)*, 1013, 1034, 1049
gypsies, in World War II, 1050

Haiti: abolition of slavery in,
801–2; Republic of, 796;
revolution by slaves in,
795–96, 796 *(illus.)*, 797
(illus.), 798 *(map)*; United
States financial control of,
1025; United States
occupation of, 928
Hanaoka, Japan, 1049
harijans, 1008
Harris, Betty (nineteenth century),
815, 819 *(illus.)*, 837
Harris, Townsend, 901

Hawai'ian Islands, 862, 928,
1041–42, 1042 *(illus.)*
Haya del la Torre, Victor Raúl
(1895–1979), 1022
health care, industrialization
and, 837
Heisenberg, Werner
(1901–1976), 981
Hemingway, Ernest
(1899–1961), 979
Herder, Johann Gottfried von
(1744–1803), 805–6
Hernandez, José (nineteenth
century), 873
Herzl, Theodor (1860–1904),
807, 807 *(illus.)*
Heydrich, Reinhard, 1049
Hezbollah, 1116
Hidalgo y Costilla, Miguel
(1753–1811), 798–99
Himmler, Heinrich, 1051
(source document)
Hindenburg, Paul von
(1847–1934), 999
Hirohito, Emperor of Japan
(1901–1989), 1047
Hiroshima, atomic bombing of,
1030 *(illus.)*, 1031, 1045
(source document), 1047
Hispaniola, 795–96, 796 *(illus.)*,
797 *(illus.)*, 798 *(map)*
Hitler, Adolf (1889–1945): assassination attempt on, 1049; early
life of, 977–78, 978 *(illus.)*;
Mein Kampf, 998 *(source
document)*; Nazi Party and,
997, 997 *(illus.)*, 998 *(source
document)*; remilitarization of
Germany, 1035–36; rise to
power, 999, 1035; suicide of,
1044. *See also* Nazi Germany
HIV/AIDS (epidemic), 1144,
1149–51, 1150 *(map)*
Ho Chi Minh (Vietnamese leader,
1890–1969), 1101–2,
1102 *(illus.)*
Hokkaido, Japanese annexation
of, 930
Holocaust, 1050–53, 1050 *(illus.)*,
1051 *(source document)*, 1052
(map), 1055
homosexuality, 1050
Honduras, 799, 928
Honecker, Erich
(1912–1994), 1087
Hong Kong, 896, 1042, 1048,
1135–36
Hong Xiuquan (nineteenth
century), 879, 896–98
Honor Cross of the German
Mother, 999
horsepower, 818
housing, for urban workers, 829,
831, 831 *(illus.)*
Huguenots, 921
Hull, Cordell, 1026
human rights, 1121, 1155–56
Human Rights Watch, 1156

Hundred Days reforms of 1898
(China), 899
Hungary: independence from
Soviet Union, 1086; rebellion
against Soviet Union (1956),
1076, 1078, 1085; in World
War I, 953 *(map)*, 967, 969,
971 *(map)*; in World War II,
1044, 1056. *See also* Austria-
Hungary
Hussein, Saddam, President of
Iraq (1937–2006), 1117–18,
1153, 1154 *(illus.)*

Iberia. *See* Portugal; Spain
Ibn Ali Hussain (1856–1931), 962
ICBM (intercontinental ballistic
missiles), 1075
IG Farben, 825
IMF (International Monetary
Fund), 1133
immigration. *See* migrations
imperialism: in Africa, 919–25,
923 *(map)*, 924 *(source
document)*, 1014–18, 1020
(illus.); Algerian independence, 1106–8, 1107 *(illus.)*;
in Brazil, 862; definition of
colonialism, 910–11; dependency theory of economic
development, 1123; disputes
among imperial countries,
948; economic, 1023–25,
1024 *(map)*; economic impact
of, 817, 931; "Great Game,"
917–18; India in British
empire, 915–17, 917 *(illus.)*,
918 *(map)*; Indian self-rule,
1006–8, 1009 *(source document)*, 1097–1101, 1098
(illus.); by Japan, 929–30,
1013–14; labor migrations
and, 932–34, 933 *(map)*;
League of Nation mandates
and, 972; motives of, 910–12;
nationalism and, 936–38 (*See
also* nationalism); in the
Pacific, 925–27, 926 *(map)*;
political organization in, 920,
922, 924–25, 924 *(source
document)*; poverty as legacy
of, 1148; in southeast Asia,
918–19, 918 *(map)*, 1041,
1048, 1102–3; technological
tools of, 912–15, 915 *(illus.)*;
by the United States, 928–29;
Vietnamese independence,
1101–3, 1102 *(illus.)*; World
War I and, 1014–16. *See also*
independence movements
Imperialism (Rivera), 1022
(illus.), 1023
indentured laborers, 860, 872,
932–34
independence movements: in
Algeria, 1106–8, 1107 *(illus.)*;
in the Baltics, 1088, 1089
(map); in Belgium, 808, 947;

in Canada, 853–54; in
Czechoslovakia, 1078–79,
1078 *(illus.)*, 1085, 1086–87;
in Egypt, 1103; in Greece,
808, 881, 947; in Haiti,
795–96, 796 *(illus.)*, 797
(illus.), 798 *(map)*; in
Hungary, 1076, 1078, 1085,
1086; impact of Cold War on,
1096, 1100–1103, 1104–5,
1120–22, 1126; in India,
1006–8, 1009 *(source document)*, 1097–1101, 1098
(illus.); in Iraq, 1103; in
Jordan, 1103; in Kenya, 1018,
1109 *(map)*, 1110–12, 1112
(illus.); in Korea, 898; in Latin
America, 796–99, 798 *(map)*,
799 *(illus.)*, 856 *(map)*; in
Lebanon, 1103; in Mexico,
798–99, 798 *(map)*, 856
(map); in Morocco, 948,
1106; in Pakistan, 1008, 1098,
1099 *(source document)*, 1162;
in Poland, 1085–86, 1086
(illus.); in southeast Asia, 1100
(map); in Spanish colonies,
798–99, 798 *(map)*; in sub-
Saharan Africa, 1108–9, 1109
(map); in Syria, 1103; in Taiwan, 898; in Tunisia, 1106; in
the United States, 784–86,
785, 785 *(illus.)*, 786 *(illus.)*,
787 *(map)*, 795, 849; in
Venezuela, 799, 855, 856
(map); in Vietnam, 1100
(map), 1101–3, 1102 *(illus.)*
India: agriculture in, 1114; in the
British empire, 915–17, 917
(illus.), 918 *(map)*; bubonic
plague in, 937; child-labor
servitude in, 1148–49; China
and, 1080; cotton industry
under colonization, 931; current economic growth in, 1137;
emigration as indentured laborers, 932–33, 933 *(map)*; under
Indira Gandhi, 1114–15, 1116
(illus.); Great Depression in,
1008; industrialization in, 839,
841; influenza pandemic
(1918), 968; Mughal empire in,
916; Muslim–Hindu conflict,
1007, 1008, 1097–1100, 1099
(source document); nationalism
in, 936–39, 937 *(illus.)*; under
Nehru, 985, 1097–98, 1098
(illus.), 1100–1101, 1114;
Pakistan formation from, 1008,
1098, 1099 *(source document)*,
1162; railroads in, 932 *(illus.)*,
1006; self-rule in, 1006–8,
1009 *(source document)*,
1097–1101, 1098 *(illus.)*; in
World War I, 960, 960 *(illus.)*,
1007; in World War II, 1037
Indian National Congress, 937,
1007–8

Indian Removal Act (1830), 849
Indian Territory, 849
Indigenous Races of the Earth (Nott
and Glidden), 935 *(illus.)*
Indochina, French, 919, 1041,
1048, 1102–3. *See also* southeast Asia; Vietnam
Indonesia, 918, 1041, 1101, 1136
industrialization: in Brazil,
1024–25; British investment in
United States, 862–63; of
Canada, 824, 841; child labor
in, 833–34, 837; in China,
817, 898–99, 1079, 1113; coal
in, 817; definition of, 816; in
England, 817–21, 819 *(illus.)*,
947–48; factory system, 816,
820–21, 824; international
division of labor, 839–42, 841
(illus.); of Japan, 838–39, 840
(illus.), 903; Marx and Engels
on, 835–37, 836 *(source document)*; mass production in,
824; migrations and, 827, 829,
831, 1160–61; population
growth and, 827–28; primary
products from colonies, 817;
protests against, 821; putting-
out system, 820; of Russia,
838–39, 889–90, 890 *(illus.)*;
social impact of, 821, 829,
832–34, 834 *(illus.)*; social
reform and, 837; spread of,
821–24; textile mills, 814
(illus.), 818, 820–21, 833,
839–40, 840 *(illus.)*, 862;
trade unions, 837, 838 *(illus.)*,
864–65, 904; urbanization
and, 829, 831, 831 *(illus.)*;
utopian socialists and, 834;
working conditions in, 814
(illus.), 815–16, 819 *(illus.)*,
820–21
infanticide, 1158
influenza pandemic (1918),
968, 1149
intercontinental ballistic missiles
(ICBM), 1075
internal migration, 1160–61. *See
also* migrations
International Monetary Fund
(IMF), 1133
Internet, 1142–43
Inukai Tsuyoshi, Prime Minister of
Japan (1855–1932), 1013
Iran: Barbie and Sara dolls in,
1140; Iranian revolution
(1979), 1117–18; Iran-Iraq
War, 1117–18; prior to World
War I, 948
Iran-Contra scandal, 1122
Iran-Iraq War (1980-1988),
1117–18
Iraq: as British mandate, 973
(map); Gulf War (1991), 1118;
under Hussein, 1117–18,
1153, 1154 *(illus.)*; indepen-
dence of, 1103; Iran-Iraq War,

1117–18; under Ottoman
rule, 882 *(map)*, 885; United
States invasion of (2003–),
1118, 1153
Iraq War (2003–), 1118, 1153
Ireland, Great Easter Rebellion
in, 967
"iron curtain," 1056, 1064
iron metallurgy, 818–19, 823–24
Islam: in Iran, 1117; Islamism,
1116–17; Shia and Sunni,
1117; Sufi brotherhood, 1016;
women in, 1152, 1159, 1160
Islamic realms: Muslim-Hindu
conflict in India, 1007, 1008,
1097–1100, 1099 *(source
document)*; Ottoman empire
(*See* Ottoman empire);
Pakistan formation, 1008,
1098–1101, 1099 *(source
document)*, 1159, 1162
Islamism, 1116–17
Israel (modern): Arab-Israeli wars,
1104, 1105 *(map)*, 1116;
conflict with Lebanon, 1116;
creation of, 1104, 1105 *(map)*;
Zionism and, 806–7, 807
(illus.), 1103. *See also* Palestine
Italy: African colonies, 922, 923
(map); in Axis powers, 1032,
1035; conquest of Ethiopia and
Libya, 1035, 1036 *(illus.)*; in
the European Economic Community, 1137; fascism in,
995–96, 996 *(illus.)*; under
Napoleon, 793; in the Triple
Alliance, 949–50; unification of,
806, 808, 809–10, 809 *(map)*;
in World War I, 953 *(map)*,
954, 1035; in World War II,
1038, 1042, 1044, 1048
Ito Hirobumi (1841–1909),
902–3
Iturbide, Augustín de, Emperor of
Mexico (1783–1824), 799
Iwo Jima, in World War II, 1044

Jacobin party (France), 790
Jamaica, black nationalism in,
1019 *(source document)*, 1073
Janissaries, 881, 883
Japan: atomic bombing of, 1030
(illus.), 1031, 1045 *(source
document)*, 1047; in Axis
powers, 1032, 1035; "comfort
women," 1053; Great Depression in, 986–87; industrialization of, 838–39, 840 *(illus.)*,
903; invasion of China (1937),
1033–35, 1033 *(illus.)*, 1034
(illus.); invasion of Manchuria,
1013–14; in Korea, 918
(map); in the League of Nations, 1012, 1013; Meiji, 878
(illus.), 901–4, 929–30, 936;
migration from, as laborers,
934; modern economic
growth in, 1135; Russo-

Japanese war, 891, 892 *(illus.)*,
930; Sino-Japanese War, 930;
sphere of influence in China,
896, 898–99; Tokugawa
shogunate, 839, 899–901,
901 *(illus.)*; United States
occupation of, 1056, 1135; in
World War I, 960; in World
War II, 1041–44, 1042
(illus.), 1046–47, 1046
(map), 1048–49, 1055
Jefferson, Thomas, 789 *(source
document)*
Jehovah's Witnesses, 1050
Jenner, Edward, 828
Jews: Holocaust in World War II,
1050–53, 1050 *(illus.)*, 1051
(source document), 1052
(map), 1055; Zionism, 806–7,
807 *(illus.)*, 1103. *See also*
anti-Semitism
Jiang Jieshi (Chiang Kai-shek,
1887–1975), 1010–12, 1012
(illus.), 1079
jihad, 1117
Jinnah, Muhammad Ali
(1876–1948), 1008, 1097,
1099 *(source document)*
Johnson, Lyndon B., President of
the United States (1908–1973),
1081, 1102
Jordan, independence of, 1103
Juárez, Benito, President of
Mexico (1806–1872), 857
Judenstaat (Herzl), 807

Kabila, Joseph (1971–), 1126
Kabila, Laurent, 1126
Kádár, János (1912–1989), 1078
kamikaze pilots, 1044
Kang Youwei (1858–1927), 899
Karmal, Babrak, President of
Afghanistan, 1082
Kashmir province, 1100
Kay, John (eighteenth
century), 818
Kellogg-Briand Pact (1928),
1012–13
Kemal, Mustafa (Atatürk,
1881–1938), 961, 969
Kennedy, John F., President of the
United States (1917–1963),
1069–70, 1075, 1081
Kenya: independence of, 1018,
1109 *(map)*, 1110–12, 1112
(illus.); Mumbo cult, 1016;
white ownership of land
in, 1017
Kenyatta, Jomo (1895–1978),
1018, 1112
Keynes, John Maynard
(1883–1946), 989
Khamenei, Ayatollah (1939–),
1117
Khoikhoi people (Hottentots), 921
Khomeini, Ayatollah Ruhollah
(1900–1989), 1117, 1118
(illus.)

Khrushchev, Nikita S., Premier of the Soviet Union (1894–1971), 1063, 1065 *(illus.)*, 1074 *(source document)*, 1076–78

Kikuyu people, 1110–12

Kimbangu, Simon, 1108

Kim Il Sung, Korean ruler, (1912–1995), 1067

King, Martin Luther, Jr. (1929–1968), 1073

Kipling, Rudyard (1864–1936), 912, 913 *(source document)*

"kitchen debate" (1959), 1063, 1065 *(illus.)*, 1075, 1076

Koehler, Robert, 838 *(illus.)*

Kolakowski, Leszek, 1085–86

Korea: independence from China, 898; under Japanese rule, 918 *(map)*, 930, 1048; Korean War, 1067–68, 1068 *(illus.)*, 1080; North Korea, 1067; postwar division of, 1056; South Korea, 1135–36

Korean War (1950–1953), 1067–68, 1068 *(illus.)*, 1080

Kristallnacht, 1001

Kubrick, Stanley, 1083

kulaks, 993

Kumaratunga, Chandrika Banda-ranaike, President of Sri Lanka (1945–), 1159

Kurile Islands, 930

Kyoto conference on global warming (1997), 1147

laborers. *See* workers

labor unions, 837, 838 *(illus.)*, 864–65, 904

Lakota Sioux, 849

Lambton, John George (1782–1840), 854

Land and Freedom Party (Russia), 891

land ownership and distribution: in colonial Africa, 1017; in Latin American republics, 856; Marx and Engels on, 835; in Mexico, 857, 858–60, 859 *(source document)*, 1119; in People's Republic of China, 1079; in the Soviet Union, 991

Lange, Dorothea, 988 *(illus.)*

Laos, 919, 1041, 1048. *See also* southeast Asia

Latin America: conflicts with indigenous peoples, 856–57; cultural diversity in, 872–74, 874 *(illus.)*; economic imperialism in, 1023–25, 1024 *(map)*; emigration to United States, 861; foreign investment in, 866–67, 867 *(illus.)*, 1023–24; gauchos, 857, 873, 874 *(illus.)*; Good Neighbor Policy, 1025–26; Great Depression in, 986, 1023–24; immigration to, 872–73; instability in early republics,

855–56; Mexican revolution, 858, 860, 860 *(illus.)*, 874, 1021; military leaders in, 857; Monroe Doctrine, 928, 929, 1026, 1120; slow pace of industrialization in, 841, 866–67; student activism in, 1021–23, 1022 *(illus.)*; United States interventions in, 1024 *(map)*; wars of independence in, 796–99, 798 *(map)*, 799 *(illus.)*, 856 *(map)*; women's rights in, 1122–23; World War I and, 1021–23, 1022 *(illus.)*. *See also specific countries*

Latvia, 1088. *See also* Baltics

Lausanne, Treaty of (1923), 969

law codes. *See* legal codes

League of Nations (1920–1946), 970, 1013–14, 1033, 1036

Lebanon, 1103, 1116. *See also* southwest Asia

Lebensraum, 1039

Le Corbusier (Charles Édouard Jeanneret, 1887–1965), 985

legal codes: of Napoleon, 793; in the Ottoman empire, 884; in Russia, 888–89

leisure activities. *See* entertainment

lend-lease program, 1041

Lenin, Vladimir Ilyich (1870–1924), 963–64, 964 *(illus.)*, 965 *(source document)*, 991–92

Leningrad, German invasion of (1941), 1039

Leopold II, King of Belgium (reigned 1865–1909), 920, 921 *(illus.)*

levée en masse, 789

Lewis, Meriwether, 849

Liang Qichao (1873–1929), 899

Liaodong Peninsula, 898, 918 *(map)*, 930

liberalism, 800

liberation theology, 1122

Liberia, 922, 923 *(map)*, 1014

Libya, 1016, 1035

Lidice, German massacre at (1942), 1049

Lij Iyasu, Emperor of Ethiopia (reigned 1913–1916), 1014

Lili'uokalani, Hawai'ian queen (reigned 1891–1893), 928, 929 *(illus.)*

Lincoln, Abraham, President of the United States (1809–1865), 851–52

Lin Zexu (nineteenth century), 893, 894 *(source document)*

literature, Soviet, 1076, 1078

Lithuania, 1088. *See also* Baltics

Little Big Horn, battle of (1876), 849

Livingstone, Dr. David, 920

Locke, John (1632–1704), 783, 785, 802

London, German bombing of (1940–1941), 1039, 1040 *(illus.)*

Long March (China), 1011 *(map)*, 1012

Lopez Obrador, Andres Manuel (1942–), 1119

"lost generation," 979

Louisiana Territory, purchase of, 849, 850 *(map)*

Louis XVI, King of France (reigned 1774–1793), 787–89, 791 *(illus.)*

Louverture (François-Dominique Toussaint, 1744–1803), 795–96, 796 *(illus.)*

Luddites, 821

Lugard, Frederick D. (1858–1945), 924 *(source document)*, 925

Luisa Amanda Espinoza Association of Nicaraguan Women (AMNLAE), 1122

Lumumba, Patrice (1925–1961), 1126

Lusitania (British liner), 966

Luxembourg, 1137

Maastricht Treaty (1993), 1137

Macdonald, John A. (1815–1891), 854

machine guns, 850, 914, 954

machismo, 874

Magic (code-breaking operation), 1044

Mahmud II, Ottoman sultan (reigned 1808–1839), 883

Maine (U.S. battleship), 928

Maji Maji rebellion (1905–1906), 934

Malaysia (Malaya): British conquest of, 918–19, 918 *(map)*; financial crisis in, 1136; Singapore, 918, 1042, 1048, 1135–36; in World War II, 1042, 1048

malnutrition, from economic inequities, 1148. *See also* famines

Malthus, Thomas R. (1766–1834), 830 *(source document)*

Manchukuo, 1013

Manchuria: Japanese rule in, 930, 1013–14, 1031; Mukden incident, 1013–14; in Russian empire, 888

"the mandate of heaven," 783

Mandela, Nelson (1918–), 1125–26

Manet, Edouard, 858 *(illus.)*

manifest destiny, 849

Manifesto of the Communist Party (Marx and Engels), 835–37, 836 *(source document)*

manufacturing, standardized parts in, 824, 826. *See also* industrialization

Maori King Movement *(Kingitanga),* 926

Maori people, 925–26, 927 *(illus.)*

Mao Zedong (1893–1976), 1010–13, 1012 *(illus.)*, 1079, 1113 *(illus.)*

March Revolution (1917), 963–64

Mariana Islands, 960, 1044

Mariátegui, José Carlos (1895–1930), 1021–22

Marie Antoinette, Queen of France (1755–1793), 789–90

Marley, Bob (1945–1981), 1073

maroon communities, 795

Marquesas, 926 *(map)*, 927

marriage, 916–17, 1158, 1159

"Marseillaise," 807

Marshall, George C. (1880–1959), 1057

Marshall islands, 926 *(map)*, 927, 960

Marshall Plan (1948–1952), 1057, 1075

Marx, Karl (1818–1883), 835–37, 836 *(source document)*

Marxism, 963–64, 965 *(source document)*, 1073

mass tourism, 1163–65

Matschat, Kristina, 1131

Maxim guns, 914

Maximilian, Mexican emperor (1832–1867), 858, 858 *(illus.)*

May Fourth Movement (China), 1010

Mazzini, Guiseppe (1805–1872), 806, 806 *(illus.)*, 809

Mbeki, Thabo, President of South Africa (1942–), 1126

McCarthy, Joseph (1909–1957), 1072

McCarthyism, 1072, 1076

McKinley, William, President of the United States (1897–1901), 929, 936

medicine, 827 *(illus.)*, 828, 837

Mehmed V Rashid, Ottoman sultan (reigned 1909–1918), 885

Meiji, Emperor of Japan (1852–1912), 901, 904 *(illus.)*

Meiji Japan (1868–1912), 878 *(illus.)*, 901–4, 902–30, 936

Mein Kampf (Hitler), 998 *(source document)*

men, industrialization and, 832–33

mestizos, 797–98

metallurgy, 818–19, 823–24, 839

métis, 871–72

Metternich, Prince Klemens von (1773–1859), 808–9, 808 *(illus.)*

Mexican-American War (1846–1848), 850–51, 857

Mexico: abolition of slavery in, 802; Constitution of, 860, 1118–19; current economic growth in, 1137; foreign capital in, 867 *(illus.)*; industrialization in, 866; Mexican-American War, 850–51, 857; Mexico City,

866; migration to United States, 1026–27; modern reforms in, 1118–19; monarchy in, 858, 858 *(illus.)*; nationalism in, 851; oil production nationalization in, 1026, 1119; painting in, 1022–23, 1022 *(illus.)*; *La Reforma* (1850s), 857, 859 *(source document)*; revolution in, 858, 860, 860 *(illus.)*, 874, 1021; war of independence in, 798–99, 798 *(map)*, 856 *(map)*

Mexico City, 866

middle class, 832, 833, 857. *See also* social classes

Middle Kingdom of China, 899

Midway Island, in World War II, 1042, 1044

Mies von der Rohe, Ludwig (1886–1969), 984

Migrant Mother, Nipomo California (Lange), 988 *(illus.)*

migrations: into the Americas, 827, 831, 861–62; "guest workers," 1162; under imperialism, 932–34, 933 *(map)*; between India and Pakistan, 1098, 1162; industrialization and, 827, 829, 831, 1160–61; internal *vs.* external, 1160–62; of Jews from Nazi Germany, 1001, 1050; of Jews to Palestine, 1103; of laborers to sugar plantations, 862, 933, 933 *(map)*; from Oklahoma, 988; United States immigration, 831; war refugees, 1162

militarism, 995

military: Indian colonial, 916; Japan, Meiji, 902; Ottoman, 881, 883

Mill, John Stuart (1806–1873), 800–801, 802

mining: of coal, 815, 817, 819 *(illus.)*, 823 *(map)*; in colonial Africa, 1017; of diamonds, 909, 921; of gold (*See* gold mining)

Miranda, Carmen (1909–1955), 1027, 1027 *(illus.)*

Missouri, U.S.S., 1047 *(illus.)*

Missouri Compromise (1820), 851

Mitsui combine, 839

Mizuno Tadakuni (nineteenth century), 900

Mobutu Sese Seko (1930–1997), 1126, 1143

Mohammed Reza Pahlavi, Shah of Iran (1919–1980), 1117

Mohammed VI, Ottoman sultan, 969

Moltke, Kelmuth Karl von (1800–1891), 956

monarchy, 783, 788

monopolies, 825

Monroe, James, President of the United States (in office 1817–1825), 928

Monroe Doctrine, 928, 929, 1026, 1120

moon landings, 1075

Morocco, independence of, 948, 1106

Moscow, Russia, 1039–40, 1044

Mozambique, Portuguese rule in, 919

MTV Latino, 1142

Mughal empire, 916

Muhammad Ali, ruler of Egypt (1805–1848), 881, 920

mujahideen, in Afghanistan, 1083, 1152

Mukden incident (Manchuria), 1013–14

mulattoes, 797

mullahs, 1152

multinational corporations, 1133

Mumbo cult (Kenya), 1016

Munich Conference (1938), 1036–37

munitions factories, 958, 958 *(illus.)*

music: African-American, 1073; globalization of, 1141; reggae, 1073; rock and roll, 1084

muskets, 914

Muslim League, 1007, 1008, 1097, 1099 *(source document)*

Muslim rebellion (China, 1855–1873), 896

Mussolini, Benito (Il Duce), Italian dictator (1883–1945), 994, 995–96, 996 *(illus.)*, 1035, 1038, 1042

mustard gas, 954, 954 *(illus.)*

Mutsuhito (Meiji), Emperor of Japan (1852–1912), 901, 904 *(illus.)*

mutually assured destruction (MAD), 1067

Myanmar. *See* Burma

Nafea Fan Ipoipo (Gauguin), 982 *(illus.)*

NAFTA (North American Free Trade Agreement), 1139

Nagasaki, Japan: atomic bombing of, 1031, 1047; trading at, 901

Nagy, Imre (1896–1989), 1078

Najibullah, Muhammad, 1083

Nam Viet. *See* Vietnam

Nanjing, China: under Guomindang, 1011, 1011 *(map)*; Japanese bombing of, 1033–34, 1054; under Taipings, 897–98

Nanjing, Treaty of (1842), 896

napalm firebombs, in World War II, 1046

Napoleon Bonaparte, Emperor of France (1769–1821): empire of, 793, 794 *(map)*, 799; fall

of, 793; invasion of Egypt, 881; rise to power, 792–93, 792 *(illus.)*; Saint-Domingue slave rebellion and, 796, 796 *(illus.)*; sale of Louisiana Territory, 849

Napoleonic Wars (1799–1815), 793, 794 *(map)*, 799, 921

Napoleon III, Mexico and, 858

Napoleon on Horseback at the St. Bernard Pass (David), 792 *(illus.)*

Nasser, Gamal Abdel, President of Egypt (1918–1970), 1104–6, 1106 *(illus.)*, 1115

Natal, Republic of, 921

nation, definition of, 805

National Aeronautics and Space Administration (NASA), 1075

nationalism, 805–11; in Africa, 1014, 1018–20, 1019 *(source document)*, 1108–9, 1109 *(map)*; anti-Semitism and, 806–7; Arab, 1115–16; black, 1073; in China during war with Japan, 1034; Congress of Vienna and, 807–8, 808 *(illus.)*; cultural, 805–6; definition of, 805; fascism and, 995; Fourteen Points and, 968–69, 973–74, 1007; political, 806; as a result of imperialism, 936–38; World War I and, 947, 961; Zionism, 806–7, 807 *(illus.)*, 1103. *See also* independence movements

National Organization for Women (NOW), 1157 *(illus.)*

National Socialism, 994, 997, 997 *(illus.)*. *See also* Nazi Germany; Nazi Party

native Americans: Apache people, 849, 868 *(illus.)*; in Canada, 865, 870–72; Cherokee people, 849; Comanche people, 849; government schools for, 868 *(illus.)*, 869; in Latin America, 856–57; Pawnee people, 849; Seminole people, 849; Sioux people, 849–50; westward expansion of the United States and, 849–50, 851 *(illus.)*, 868–69

NATO (North Atlantic Treaty Organization), 1057, 1067, 1071 *(map)*, 1077

natural resources: carrying capacity of the planet, 1144–45; colonial exploitation of, 817, 911, 930–31, 1017; economic imperialism and, 1023–25, 1024 *(map)*; Great Depression and demand for, 985–86; industrialization and global trade, 840–42; shortage of nonrenewable, 1145, 1147; in the United States, 863

naval blockade, in World War I, 956, 966–67, 968

Nazi Germany: Allied victory over, 1044; casualties in, 1055; conquest of Europe, 1037–39, 1038 *(illus.)*, 1039 *(illus.)*, 1043 *(map)*; Holocaust, 1050–53, 1050 *(illus.)*, 1051 *(source document)*, 1052 *(map)*, 1055; invasion of Soviet Union, 1039–40, 1041 *(illus.)*, 1044; nonaggression pact with Soviet Union, 1037; Nuremberg war crimes trials, 1155; occupation policies, 1048–49; postwar settlements and, 1055–56; pre-war expansion of, 1036–37; resistance in, 1049, 1052–53. *See also* Germany

Nazi Party, 998–1001, 998 *(source document)*, 1001 *(illus.)*. *See also* Nazi Germany

Ndebele, 921

Near East. *See* southwest Asia

Négritude, 1108

Nehru, Jawaharlal, Prime Minister of India (1889–1964), 985, 1097–98, 1098 *(illus.)*, 1100–1101, 1114

neocolonialism, 1021–23, 1022 *(illus.)*

Netherlands: abolition of slave trade by, 801; in the European Economic Community, 1137; under Napoleon, 793; national consciousness in, 807; Pacific colonies of, 926 *(map)*; in southeast Asia, 918, 918 *(map)*; unequal treaty with China, 896; in World War II, 1038, 1048–49

Neuilly, Treaty of (1919), 969

New Caledonia, 926 *(map)*, 927

New Deal (United States), 989

New Economic Policy (NEP; Soviet Union), 992

New Guinea, 960, 1048

New International Economic Order, 1127

New Lanark community (Scotland), 834

New Mexico, annexation of, 850, 850 *(map)*

New York, 1152

New York City terrorist attacks (2001), 1152

New Zealand: British colonies in, 925, 926 *(map)*, 927 *(illus.)*; industrialization of, 841; Maori people, 925–26, 927 *(illus.)*; in World War I, 960, 961; in World War II, 1037

New Zealand Wars (nineteenth century), 926

Ngo Dinh Diem, President of Vietnam (1901–1963), 1102

Nguyen Giap, Vo, 1102

Nian rebellion (China, 1851–1868), 895 *(map)*, 896

Nicaragua, 799, 928, 1024 *(map)*, 1025–27, 1121–22
Nicholas II, Tsar of Russia (reigned 1894–1917), 891, 952, 963, 991
nickel, 927
Nixon, Richard M., President of the United States (1913–1994), 1063, 1065 *(illus.)*, 1082, 1084
Nkrumah, Kwame (1909–1972), 1073, 1109–10, 1110 *(illus.)*, 1111 *(source document)*, 1124
nomadic peoples, 925–26, 962
"no-man's-land," 954, 955
nonalignment policy, 1100–1101, 1104
Non-Cooperation Movement (1920–1922), 1008
nongovernmental organizations (NGOs), 1154
Norris, George W., 966–67
north Africa: Algerian independence, 1106–8, 1107 *(illus.)*; Arab nationalism in, 1115–16; Moroccan independence, 948, 1106; Tunisian independence, 1106. *See also* Egypt
North America: agriculture in, 988, 1027; British colonies in, 784–85; French and Indian War, 784; indigenous peoples (*See* native Americans); industrialization of, 821, 822–24, 831, 862–63; population growth in, 827–28; slavery in, 851. *See also* native Americans; *specific countries*
North American Free Trade Agreement (NAFTA), 1139
North Atlantic Treaty Organization (NATO), 1057, 1067, 1071 *(map)*, 1077
Northern Alliance, 1153
North Korea, 1067. *See also* Korea
Northwest Rebellion, 872
Norway, in World War II, 1038, 1048–49
November Revolution (1917), 964, 965 *(source document)*
nuclear weapons: arms control, 1081; *Dr. Strangelove* (film, 1964), 1083; of France, 1077; intercontinental ballistic missiles, 1075; nuclear arms race, 1062 *(illus.)*, 1066–68, 1086; nuclear test ban treaties, 1077; Strategic Defense Initiative (Star Wars), 1084; use in World War II, by United States, 1030 *(illus.)*, 1031, 1045 *(source document)*, 1047
Nuremberg Laws (1935), 1000
Nuremberg war crimes trials, 1155

Oceania. *See* Pacific islands; *specific countries*
Oedipus complex, 982

O'Higgins, Bernardo (1778–1842), 799
oil embargoes, 1041, 1137
oil production: Great Depression and, 985; imperialism and, 911; Mexican nationalization of, 1026, 1119; Organization of Petroleum Exporting Countries, 1137–38; in Russia, 839, 889; in the United States, 825, 911
Okinawa, 930, 1044, 1046, 1046 *(map)*
Omdurman, battle of (1898), 908 *(illus.)*, 914, 922
"Omnipotent Technology" (photograph), 1130 *(illus.)*
One Day in the Life of Ivan Denisovich (Solzhenitsyn), 1078
OPEC (Organization of Petroleum Exporting Countries), 1137–38
Operation Barbarossa (1941), 1039–40, 1041 *(illus.)*
Operation Mongoose, 1070
Opium War (1839–1842), 892–96, 893 *(illus.)*, 894 *(source document)*
Orange Free State, 921
Oregon Territory, 850 *(map)*
Organization of African Unity (OAU), 1124, 1127
Organization of Petroleum Exporting Countries (OPEC), 1137–38
The Origin of Species (Darwin), 935
Orozco, José Clemente (1883–1949), 1022
Ortega y Gasset, José (1883–1955), 980
Ottoman empire: Armenian genocide, 961–62; capitulation treaties, 882; constitution in, 885, 886 *(source document)*; decline of, 880–83, 882 *(map)*, 947; Greek independence from, 808; Italian war on, 950; nationalism in, 961; reforms in, 883–84; Tanzimat era, 883–84; in World War I, 953 *(map)*, 961–62, 967, 969; Young Turk era, 884 *(illus.)*, 885, 885 *(illus.)*, 886 *(source document)*
Owen, Robert (1771–1858), 834
Owen, Wilfred (1893–1918), 957 *(source document)*

Pacific islands: European imperialism in, 925–27, 926 *(map)*; influenza pandemic (1918), 968; in World War I, 959–60; in World War II, 1041–42, 1042 *(illus.)*, 1044, 1048. *See also specific countries*
Pact of Steel (1939), 996
painting: Mexican, 1022–23, 1022 *(illus.)*; between the world

wars, 982–85, 982 *(illus.)*, 983 *(illus.)*
Pakistan, 1008, 1098–1101, 1099 *(source document)*, 1159, 1162
Palau, 960
Palestine: Balfour Declaration, 1103; as British mandate, 972, 973 *(map)*, 1103; creation of Israel from, 1104, 1105 *(map)*; Jews in, 1103; Palestinian Liberation Organization, 1116; Zionism and, 806–7, 807 *(illus.)*, 1103. *See also* Israel (modern)
Palestinian Liberation Organization (PLO), 1116
Palmer, Frances F., 864 *(illus.)*
Pan-Africanism, 1019 *(source document)*, 1020, 1124
Panama Canal (constructed 1904–1914), 914, 929, 1121
Panama Canal Zone, 1024 *(map)*, 1121
Pan-American culture, 1141–42
pan-Arab nationalism, 1104, 1115–16
Pan-Slavism, 947
Panzer columns, 1038
paper money, 1138 *(map)*
Paraguay, 1123
Paris, Treaty of (1856), 889 *(illus.)*
Paris Peace Accords (1973), 1082
Paris Peace Conference (1918), 968–69, 969 *(illus.)*, 1010, 1103
Parks, Rosa, 1073
Pashtuns, 1152
Pasternak, Boris (1890–1960), 1076
patriarchal societies, 793, 874
Pawnee people, 849
Peace of Paris (1783), 786
Pearl Harbor, Japanese attack on, 1041–42, 1042 *(illus.)*
peasants: in Meiji Japan, 903–4; in People's Republic of China, 1113; in Russia, 888; in the Soviet Union, 993
Pedro I, Emperor of Brazil (reigned 1822–1834), 799
PEMEX (*Petróleos Mexicanos*), 1119
peninsulares, 796, 797
People's Republic of China: agriculture in, 1113; Cultural Revolution, 1113, 1113 *(illus.)*, 1136; under Deng Xiaoping, 1113–14; economic growth of, 1136, 1137; formation of, 1079; Internet in, 1142–43; relationship with Soviet Union, 1080; social and economic transformations, 1079–80; Tiananmen Square demonstrations, 1114, 1115 *(illus.)*; women in, 1080, 1157–58
People's Will (Russia), 891

perestroika, 1088
Perón, Eva (1919–1952), 1119–20, 1120 *(illus.)*, 1141–42
Perón, Juan, President of Argentina (1895–1952), 1119–20
Perry, Matthew C., 901
Persian Gulf War (1990-1991), 1118
Peru, 799, 856 *(map)*, 862, 1021–22
Pescadores Islands, 930
Petróleos Mexicanos (PEMEX), 1119
Philippine Islands: in the Cold War, 1101; financial crisis in, 1136; Manila galleons, 935; Spanish conquest of, 918; under United States control, 928–29, 936; in World War II, 1042, 1044, 1046 *(map)*, 1048–49
philosophes, 783, 802
physics, 980–81, 980 *(illus.)*
Picasso, Pablo (1881–1973), 983, 983 *(illus.)*
plagues. *See* epidemics
PLO (Palestinian Liberation Organization), 1116
poetry, 867, 957 *(source document)*
pogroms, 1001
poisonous gas, 954, 954 *(illus.)*
Poland: German concentration camps in, 1051–52, 1052 *(map)*; German conquest of, 1037, 1038; independence from Soviet Union, 1085–86, 1086 *(illus.)*; nationalism in, 808; opposition to tsar in, 891–92; self-determination and, 971; Soviet occupation of, 1056; in World War I, 955, 964, 1043 *(map)*; in World War II, 1044, 1048, 1055
political ideologies: anarchism, 890; communism (*See* communism); conservatism, 800; definition of, 800; fascism, 994–1001, 997 *(illus.)*, 998 *(source document)*, 1000 *(illus.)*, 1001 *(illus.)*; liberalism, 800; Marxism, 963–64, 965 *(source document)*, 1073; monarchy, 783, 788; socialism (*See* socialism); utopian socialism, 834
political nationalism, 806
political organization: of African colonies, 920, 922; of Canada, 854; of France, Napoleonic, 793; of Germany in the Second Reich, 811; of India, 916, 1008; of Japan, Meiji, 903; of Russia, 888, 891–92, 963; of Turkish Republic, 970; of the United States, 786
popular culture: during the cold war, 1063, 1065 *(illus.)*, 1072, 1073, 1075–76, 1083–84; globalization and, 1139–43, 1143 *(illus.)*; portrayal of

Latin America in, 1026–28, 1027 (illus.); Taliban opposition to, 1152. See also culture; entertainment; music
popular sovereignty, 783
population growth: in Canada, 854; carrying capacity and, 1144–45; control of, 1147–48 (See also birth control); demographic transition and, 828–29; industrialization and, 827–28; Malthus on, 830 (source document); recent, 1143–44, 1144 (illus.); in sub-Saharan Africa, 1126–27; in the United States, 827–28
Portrait of America (Rivera), 1023
Portugal: African colonies of, 919, 923 (map); American colonies of, 799; government in exile, 799; under Napoleon, 793; nationalism in, 808; revolutions in colonies of, 798, 798 (map)
Potsdam Conference (1945), 1056
poverty, 1148. See also social classes; wealth
power looms, 818
"Prague Spring," 1078, 1078 (illus.)
Prebisch, Raul (1901–1985), 1123
Presley, Elvis (1935–1977), 1084
Princip, Gavrilo (1894–1918), 945
proletariat, 835–37, 836 (source document), 963. See also workers
propaganda: in Nazi Germany, 999, 1000 (illus.); in World War I, 959, 959 (illus.), 966
protest: African, during World War I, 1016; Chinese prodemocracy demonstrations, 1114, 1115 (illus.); countercultural, 1083–84; during the Great Depression, 987 (illus.); industrialization and, 821; labor strikes, 837, 838 (illus.), 864–65; in Latin America, 1021–22; in the Russian empire, 890–92; against South African apartheid, 1125–26; against the Vietnam War, 1083–84. See also resistance; revolutions and rebellions
protoindustrial factories, 820
Prussia: Franco-Prussian War, 950; under Napoleon, 793; national consciousness in, 807; in unification of Germany, 809 (map), 811; in World War I, 955. See also Germany
psychoanalysis, 982
psychology, 981–82
public opinion, before World War I, 948–49, 950–51
Puerto Rico, 928
Punjab, 985, 1115. See also India; Pakistan
putting-out system, 820

Pyongyang, Democratic Republic of Korea, 1067

al-Qaeda, 1152
Qing dynasty of China (1644–1911): Boxer Rebellion, 895 (map), 899, 900 (illus.); fall of, 1008–9; Hundred Days reforms, 899; Opium War, 892–96, 893 (illus.), 894 (source document); Self-Strengthening Movement, 898; Sino-Japanese War (1894), 930; Society of God Worshipers and, 879; spheres of influence in, 895 (map), 898–99; Taiping rebellion, 879, 896–98, 897 (illus.)
Quartering Act (1765), 784

Rabin, Yitzhak (1922–1995), 1116
racial relationships: apartheid in South Africa, 1124–26; in German fascism, 998–99, 998 (source document), 1000–1001; Holocaust, 1050–53, 1050 (illus.), 1051 (source document), 1052 (map), 1055; in Latin American colonies, 796–97; popular racism, 936; population control and, 1147; scientific racism, 935, 935 (illus.), 999, 1001 (illus.); in the United States, 1073, 1075, 1157. See also anti-Semitism; slavery
Raffles, Thomas Stamford, 918
railroads: in Africa, 1018; in Britain, 819–20, 820 (illus.), 823 (map); in Canada, 854, 855 (map), 865, 872; in Europe, 823 (map); immigrant labor on, 862; in India, 932 (illus.), 1006; invention of, 819–20, 820 (illus.); labor strikes against, 864–65; in Manchuria, 1013–14; in Mexico, 866; in Russia, 839, 887 (illus.); time measurement and, 863–64; in the United States, 863–65
"railroad time," 863–64
Rape of Nanjing (1937), 1034, 1054
Reagan, Ronald, President of the United States (1911–2004), 1084, 1085 (illus.), 1086, 1122
Realpolitik, 810
Reconstruction (United States, 1867–1877), 869
Red Cross, 1154
Red Terror campaign (1918–1920), 991
Reed, John (1887–1920), 964
La Reforma (1850s), 857
refugees, from wars, 1162, 1164 (illus.)
reggae music, 1073

religions: Christianity (See Roman Catholic church); imperialism and, 912; Islam (See Islam); native American, 850; as "opiate of the masses," 835; Sikhism, 1115; between the world wars, 979–80; Zoroastrianism
religious tolerance, 783, 793
Remarque, Erich Maria, 979
resistance: Chinese, to Japanese occupation, 1034–35; in Ethiopia, to colonization, 922; to industrialization, 821, 833; of Jews to Holocaust, 1052–53; in Kenyan independence movement, 1111–12; by native Americans, 849–50, 869; in Nazi Germany, 1049, 1052–53; reggae music as, 1073; to South African expansion, 921; during World War II, 1048–50, 1052–53. See also protest; revolutions and rebellions
retirement pensions, 837
reverse migration, 1161
"Revolt of the Masses" (Ortega y Gasset), 980
revolutions and rebellions: American civil war, 852–853, 852 (illus.), 853 (illus.), 954; American revolution, 784–86, 785 (illus.), 787 (map), 795; Boxer Rebellion (China), 895 (map), 899, 900 (illus.); Chinese revolution of 1911, 1008–9; Cultural Revolution (China), 1113, 1113 (illus.), 1136; in eastern Europe, 1085–88, 1086 (illus.), 1087 (illus.), 1089 (map); French revolution, 787–91, 789 (source document), 790 (illus.), 791 (illus.); Great Easter Rebellion (Ireland), 967; Greek revolution, 808; Haitian revolution, 795–96, 796 (illus.), 797 (illus.), 798 (map); Indian sepoys, against the British, 916, 917 (illus.), 934; Iranian revolution, 1117–18; Italy, unification of, 806, 808, 809–10, 809 (map); Latin American, 796–800, 798 (map), 799 (illus.); Luddite rebellion, 821; Maji Maji rebellion, 934; Marx and Engels on, 835–37, 836 (source document); Mexican revolution, 858, 860, 860 (illus.), 874, 1021; Muslim rebellion (China, 1855–1873), 896; Nian rebellion, 895 (map), 896; Northwest Rebellion (Canada), 872; Russian revolution of 1905, 891–92; Russian revolution of 1917, 963–64; Society of God

Worshipers, 879, 897; Soviet civil war, 991; Spanish civil war, 1035, 1036; Taiping rebellion, 879, 896–98, 897 (illus.); Tungan rebellion, 896; Warsaw ghetto uprising (1943), 1053; women's roles in, 803. See also resistance
Rhee, Syngman, Korean president (1875–1965), 1067
Rhodes, Cecil John (1853–1902), 909, 911, 912 (illus.)
Rhodesia, 909
Richet, Charles (1850–1935), 987
Riel, Louis (1844–1885), 872
rifles, 916
Rivera, Diego, 1022–23, 1022 (illus.)
Robespierre, Maximilien (1758–1794), 790–91
Rockefeller, John D., 825
Rolling Stones, 1084
Roman Catholic church: in Canada, 853; in France, 788, 790, 792; imperialism and, 912; liberation theology, 1122; Society of God Worshipers, 879, 897; in southeast Asia, 919; between the world wars, 980
Romania, 1044, 1056, 1086
Romanov dynasty of Russia (1613–1917), 887, 892, 963
Rome, Treaty of (1957), 1137
Rommel, Erwin, 1038
Roosevelt, Franklin Delano, President of the United States (1882–1945): Good Neighbor Policy, 1025; on the Great Depression, 990 (source document); New Deal policies, 989; in World War II, 1037, 1040–41, 1055–57
Roosevelt, Theodore, President of the United States (in office 1901–1909), 929, 1026
Roosevelt Corollary to the Monroe Doctrine, 929, 1026
Rosas, Juan Manuel de (reigned 1829–1852), 857
Rousseau, Jean-Jacques (1712–1778), 783, 802
Roy, Ram Mohan (1772–1833), 936
rubber, 841, 911, 920, 931, 985
Russell, Bertrand, 951
Russia: anti-Semitism in, 806, 831, 891; Crimean War, 888; current economic growth in, 1137; empire expansion, 887 (map); "Great Game," 917–18; industrialization of, 838–39, 889–90, 890 (illus.); invasion by Napoleon, 793; Moscow, 1039–40, 1044; national consciousness in, 807; Pan-Slavism and, 947; protests and repression in the nineteenth century, 890–91; railroads in, 839, 887 (illus.);

Russia *(continued)*
　revolution of 1905, 891–92;
　revolutions of 1917, 963–64,
　964 *(illus.)*; Russo-Japanese
　war, 891, 892 *(illus.)*, 930;
　serfdom in, 888, 889 *(illus.)*;
　trafficking of persons, 1149; in
　Triple Entente, 950; in World
　War I, 952, 953 *(map)*, 955,
　959, 962, 971 *(map)*. *See also*
　Soviet Union
Russian-German Treaty of
　Nonaggression (1939), 1037
Russian Revolution, 963–64,
　964 *(illus.)*
Russo-Japanese war (1904–1905),
　891, 892 *(illus.)*, 930
Ryukyu Islands, 930

Sacasa, Juan Batista, President
　of Nicaragua
　(1932–1936), 1025
Sadat, Anwar (1918–1981), 1116
Saint-Domingue slave revolt
　(1793), 795–96, 796 *(illus.)*,
　797 *(illus.)*, 798 *(map)*
Saipan, in World War II, 1046
Sakhalin island, 930
SALT (Strategic Arms Limitations
　Talks), 1081
Samoa, 960
samurai, 900–901, 902
Sandford, Mrs. John, 833
Sandinistas, 1121–22
Sandino, Augusto César
　(1893–1934), 1023, 1025–26,
　1026 *(illus.)*, 1121
San Martín, José de
　(1778–1850), 799
Santa Anna, Antonio López de
　(1797–1876), 857
Santo Domingo (Saint-Domingue)
　slave revolt (1793), 795–96,
　796 *(illus.)*, 797 *(illus.)*,
　798 *(illus.)*
Sara dolls, 1140
Sarajevo, assassination of Archduke
　Ferdinand in, 945
Sarmiento, Domingo Faustino,
　President of Argentina
　(1811–1888), 873
sati (suttee), 916–17
satyagraha, 1007, 1095
Scandinavia, in World War II,
　1038, 1048–49
Schlieffen, Alfred von
　(1833–1913), 950
Schlieffen plan, 950, 953 *(map)*
science: evolution, 935; medicine,
　827 *(illus.)*, 828, 837; physics,
　980–81, 980 *(illus.)*;
　psychology, 981–82
scientific racism, 935, 935 *(illus.)*,
　999, 1001 *(illus.)*
SEATO (Southeast Asian Treaty
　Organization), 1068
Second Reich (Germany), 811
The Second Sex (Beauvoir), 1072

*Second Treatise of Civil
　Government* (Locke), 783
segregation, 1073, 1124–26
self-determination concept, 947,
　969–73, 1006–7, 1018. *See
　also* nationalism
Self-Strengthening Movement
　(China), 898
Selim III, Ottoman emperor
　(reigned 1789–1807), 883
Seminole people, 849
Seneca Falls Convention (1848),
　803, 869–70
sepoys, 916, 917 *(illus.)*, 934
September 11, 2001 terrorist
　attacks, 1152
Serbia, 881, 951, 953 *(map)*
Serb people, 947
Seven Deadly Sins (Dix), 976 *(illus.)*
Seven Years' War (1756–1763),
　784, 853
Sèvres, Treaty of (1920), 969
sex trafficking, 1149
Shanghai, China, 897, 1033–34
sharecroppers, 869
Shia Muslims, 1117
ships: dreadnoughts, 948; gun-
　boats, 914; steamships,
　819–20, 841 *(illus.)*, 914;
　submarines, 955, 966, 966
　(illus.), 1038; *Unterseeboote*
　(U-boats), 1038
Sikhism, 1115
Silent Spring (Carson), 1146
　(source document)
silk, Japanese, 839, 840 *(illus.)*
Sinai Peninsula, 1105 *(map)*
Singapore, 918, 1042, 1048,
　1135–36
Sino-Japanese War (1894), 930
Sioux people, 849–50
Siqueiros, David Alfaro
　(1896–1974), 1022
slave rebellions, Haitian, 795–96,
　796 *(illus.)*, 797 *(illus.)*,
　798 *(map)*
slavery: abolition of, 801–2,
　851–53; in Brazilian agri-
　culture, 862; in Canada, 870;
　Enlightenment ideals and,
　801–2; Haitian revolution and,
　795–96, 796 *(illus.)*, 797
　(illus.), 798 *(map)*; industriali-
　zation and, 832; maroon
　communities, 795; in North
　America, 801–2, 851; run-
　aways, 795; in sub-Saharan
　Africa, 921; trafficking of
　persons as, 1149; in the United
　States, 801–2, 851; in World
　War II occupied lands, 1048
Slavic peoples, 947, 1050
Slovakia, 1087
slums, 1161, 1163 *(illus.)*
smallpox, 925
Smith, Adam (1723–1790), 820
Smoot-Hawley Tariff (United
　States, 1930), 987

social classes: in Africa, 1018; capi-
　talism and, 821, 835; French
　revolution and, 787–88;
　industrialization and, 821,
　829, 832–34, 834 *(illus.)*; in
　Latin America, 796–97, 800,
　872–73, 1123; in Mexico,
　866; poverty and, 1148; in
　Saint-Domingue, 795. *See also*
　aristocracy and nobility;
　peasants; workers
The Social Contract
　(Rousseau), 783
social Darwinism, 935
socialism: evolutionary, 837; in
　Latin America, 1021–22; Marx
　and Engels on, 835–37, 836
　(source document); Marxism,
　963–64, 965 *(source docu-
　ment)*; national (*See* fascism);
　utopian, 834; war commu-
　nism, 991–92. *See also*
　communism
Society Islands, 926 *(map)*, 927
Society of God Worshipers,
　879, 897
Society of Righteous and
　Harmonious Fists, 899
soldaderas, 874
Solzhenitsyn, Alexandr
　(1919–), 1078
Somme, battle of (1916), 956,
　960 *(illus.)*
Somoza Debayle, Anastacio, 1121
Somoza Debayle, Luis, 1121
Somoza Garcia, Anastacio
　(1896–1956), 1025–26, 1121
"Song of Myself" (Whitman), 867
South Africa: Afrikaners in,
　921–22; apartheid in,
　1124–26; Boer War, 921; in
　British empire, 921–22;
　industrialization of, 841; white
　land ownership in, 1017
South African Republic, 921
South African War
　(1899–1902), 921
South America: abolition of slavery
　in, 802; conflicts with indige-
　nous peoples in, 856–57; pop-
　ulation growth in, 827–28;
　slave labor in, 862; slow pace
　of industrialization in, 841,
　866–67; wars of independence
　in, 798 *(map)*, 799, 799
　(illus.), 856 *(map)*. *See also*
　Latin America; *specific countries*
southeast Asia: Association of
　Southeast Asian Nations,
　1138–39; child-labor servitude
　in, 1148–49; European impe-
　rialism in, 918–19, 918 *(map)*,
　919 *(illus.)*; French Indochina,
　919, 1041, 1048, 1102–3;
　HIV/AIDS epidemic in,
　1150, 1150 *(map)*; indepen-
　dence of colonies in, 1100
　(map); industrialization of,

841; as vassal states of Qing
　dynasty China, 896; in World
　War II, 1041, 1042, 1048.
　See also specific countries
Southeast Asian Treaty Organiza-
　tion (SEATO), 1068
South Korea, 1135–36. *See
　also* Korea
southwest Asia: Arab nationalism
　in, 1115–16; independence in,
　1103; Israel (modern), 806–7,
　807 *(illus.)*, 1103, 1104, 1105
　(map), 1116; Lebanon, 1103,
　1116; Palestine (*See* Palestine);
　Syria, 885, 973 *(map)*, 1103;
　Transjordan, 973 *(map)*; in
　World War I, 953 *(map)*,
　960–62
sovereignty, 783
Soviet Union: in Afghanistan,
　1081, 1082–83; agriculture in,
　993–94, 993 *(illus.)*; Berlin
　blockade and, 1056, 1064–67,
　1065 *(illus.)*, 1066 *(map)*,
　1067 *(illus.)*; Berlin Wall,
　1066, 1066 *(map)*, 1067
　(illus.), 1087, 1087 *(illus.)*,
　1131; Bulgaria and, 1056,
　1086; civil war, 991; in the
　Cold War (*See* Cold War);
　collapse of, 1087–88, 1089
　(map); communism in,
　991–94, 993 *(illus.)*, 1080;
　Council for Mutual Economic
　Assistance, 1057; Cuba and,
　1068–70, 1069 *(illus.)*;
　Czechoslovakia and, 1078–79,
　1078 *(illus.)*, 1085, 1086–87;
　decline of, 1084–85; de-
　Stalinization in, 1077; *détente*
　policy, 1081; East Germany
　and, 1056, 1064–67, 1086,
　1087, 1087 *(illus.)*, 1131;
　formation of, 990; German
　invasion of, 1039–40, 1041
　(illus.); Great Purge in, 994;
　Hungary and, 1076, 1078,
　1085, 1086; Korean War and,
　1067–68, 1068 *(illus.)*; New
　Economic Policy, 992; non-
　aggression pact with Germany,
　1037; pact with Japan, 1035;
　People's Republic of China
　and, 1080; Poland and,
　891–92, 1056, 1085–86, 1086
　(illus.); space race in, 1075;
　under Stalin, 992–94, 992
　(illus.), 993 *(illus.)*; Ukraine,
　891–92, 955, 964, 1149; war
　communism in, 991–92;
　women in, 1053; in World War
　II, 1032, 1039–40, 1041
　(illus.), 1043–44, 1046–49,
　1055. *See also* Russia
space race, 1075
Spain: abolition of slave trade by,
　801; African colonies of, 923
　(map); Civil War in, 1035,

1036; under Napoleon, 793; national consciousness in, 807; in Oceania, 928–29; revolutions in colonies of, 798–99, 798 *(map)*; Spanish-Cuban-American War, 928; unequal treaty with China, 896

Spanish Civil War (1936–1939), 1035, 1036

Spanish-Cuban-American War (1898–1899), 928

Speke, John, 920

Spencer, Herbert (1820–1903), 935

Spengler, Oswald (1880–1936), 979

spinning machines, 818

sports, 833

Sputnik, 1075

Sri Lanka, 916, 918 *(map),* 931

St. Germain, Treaty of (1919), 969

Stalin, Joseph (1879–1953): de-Stalinization of the Soviet Union, 1078; economic development plans of, 992–94, 992 *(illus.);* Great Purge of, 994; nonaggression pact with Germany, 1037; in World War II, 1039–40, 1055–56

Stalingrad, in World War II, 1040, 1044

Stamp Act (1765), 784

Standard Oil Company and Trust, 825

Stanley, Henry Morton, 920, 920 *(illus.)*

Stanton, Elizabeth Cady (1815–1902), 803

The State and Revolution (Lenin), 965 *(source document)*

steam engines, 818

steamships, 819–20, 841 *(illus.),* 914

steel, 818–19, 823–24, 839

Stein, Gertrude (1874–1946), 979

Steinbeck, John (1902–1968), 988

Stephenson, George, 819, 820 *(illus.)*

sterilization, compulsory, 1000, 1114

Stinger missiles, 1083

stock exchanges, 986

Stower, Willy, 966 *(illus.)*

Strategic Arms Limitations Talks (SALT), 1081

Strategic Defense Initiative (Star Wars), 1084

The Strike (Koehler), 838 *(illus.)*

strikes, labor, 837, 838 *(illus.),* 864–65

student activism, 1083–84

A Study of History (Toynbee), 979–80

submarines, 955, 966, 966 *(illus.),* 1038

sub-Saharan Africa: Belgian Congo, 920, 921 *(illus.),* 923 *(map),* 1016, 1126; British

rule in south Africa, 921–22; decolonialization effects, 1124; HIV/AIDS epidemic in, 1150, 1150 *(map);* independence in, 1108–9, 1109 *(map);* industrialization in, 841; population growth in, 1126–27; Portuguese colonies in, 919, 923 *(map);* in World War I, 960–61

Sudan, British rule in, 908 *(illus.),* 914, 922

Sudentenland, 1036

Suez Canal (constructed 1859–1869), 914, 915 *(illus.),* 920, 1105

Sufi brotherhood, 1016

Sugar Act (1764), 784

sugar plantations: in Brazil, 862; in Cuba, 1069; in Hawai'ian islands, 928; industrialization and, 817; labor migrations to, 862, 933, 933 *(map);* in Pacific islands, 927

Sukarno, Achmad, President of Indonesia (1901–1970), 1101

Sun Yatsen, President of China (1866–1925), 1009, 1010

Suu Kyi, Daw Aung San (1945–), 1159–60, 1160 *(illus.)*

Svinin, Pavel Petrovich, 841 *(illus.)*

syphilis, 828

Syria, 885, 973 *(map),* 1103

Taft, William Howard, American president (1857–1931), 1023

Tahiti, French rule in, 926 *(map),* 927

Taiping rebellion (China, 1850–1864), 879, 896–98, 897 *(illus.)*

Taiping tianguo, 879

Taiwan: Chinese government refuge on, 1079; economic growth in, 1135–36; independence from China, 898; Japanese rule in, 918 *(map),* 930

Taliban, 1083, 1152

Tanganyika, Maji Maji rebellion in, 934

tanks, 954

Tanzimat era (1839–1876), 883–84

taxation: in Africa, colonial, 1017; American revolution and, 784; French revolution and, 787–88; global corporations and, 1134–35; in Japan, Meiji, 902; Mill on, 800

Tea Act (1773), 784

tea production, 931

technology: electronic, 1142–43, 1143 *(illus.);* guillotine, 789, 790–91, 791 *(illus.);* in imperialism, 912–15, 915 *(illus.);* in industrialization, 817–20; power looms, 818; space race, 1075; steam power, 818–20,

841 *(illus.),* 914; steel, 818–19, 823–24, 839; telegraph, 914–15. See also weapons

telegraph, 914–15

television, 1143, 1143 *(illus.)*

terrorism, global, 1151–53

Texas, annexation of, 850–51, 850 *(map)*

textile mills: in Britain, 814 *(illus.),* 818, 820–21, 833; child labor in, 833; immigrant labor in, 862; international division of labor and, 840; in Japan, 839, 840 *(illus.)*

textiles: cotton, 814 *(illus.),* 818, 823–24, 824, 851–52, 931; in Europe, putting-out system, 820; silk, 839, 840 *(illus.);* woolens, 818. See also textile mills

Thailand, 919, 948, 1042, 1048, 1136. See also southeast Asia

Third Reich. See Nazi Germany

Three Principles of the People (Sun Yatsen), 1010

Tiananmen Square (China), 1114, 1115 *(illus.)*

Tibet, 1080

Tilak, Bal Gangadhar (1856–1920), 1009 *(source document)*

time zones, 864

tin, 911

Tito, Marshal (1892–1980), 1077

TNT poisoning, 958

Togoland, 960–61

Tojo Hideki (1884–1948), 1041

Tokugawa shogunate of Japan (1600–1867), 839, 899–901, 900–901, 901 *(illus.)*

Tokyo, firebombing of (1945), 1046

Tolley, Victor, 1031, 1047

Tonga, 927

tourism, 1163–65

Toussaint, François-Dominique (1744–1803), 795–96, 796 *(illus.)*

Townshend Act (1767), 784

Toynbee, Arnold J. (1889–1975), 979–80

trade: Chinese, in Qing dynasty, 892, 896; Dutch United East India Company, 918; English East India Company, 892–93, 893 *(illus.),* 915–16; globalization of, 1133, 1137–39, 1138 *(map);* Great Depression and, 986–87; international division of labor and, 839–42, 841 *(illus.);* in Islamic empires, 882; opium, 892–96, 893 *(illus.),* 894 *(source document)*

trade unions, 837, 838 *(illus.),* 864–65, 904

trafficking of persons, 1149

Trail of Tears (1838–1839), 849

Transjordan, 973 *(map)*

transportation: automobile production, 824; imperialism and, 914; steam power in, 818, 819–20, 841 *(illus.),* 914. *See also* railroads

trench warfare, 953–54

Trianon, Treaty of (1920), 969

Tripartite Pact (1940), 1035, 1041

Triple Alliance (Central Powers), 949–50, 952–56, 953 *(map),* 960–63, 966–67, 971 *(map). See also* World War I

Triple Entente (Allies), 950, 952–56, 953 *(map),* 960–63, 966–67, 971 *(map). See also* World War I

Truman, Harry S, President of the United States (1884–1972), 1055–57

Truman Doctrine, 1056–57

Trumbull, John, 786 *(illus.)*

trusts, 816, 825, 839

tuberculosis, 829

Tungan rebellion (China, 1862–1878), 896

Tunisia, independence of, 1106

Turkey, Republic of, 961–62, 969

Twenty-One Demands (Japan), 960, 1013

Two Sicilies, Kingdom of, 809, 809 *(map)*

typhus, 829

U-boats, 1038

Ukraine, 891–92, 955, 964, 1149. *See also* Soviet Union

ulama, 883, 884

uncertainty principle, 981

Underground Railroad, 870

unequal treaties: in China, 896, 930; in Japan, 899, 901, 929; in Korea, 930

Union of South Africa. *See* South Africa

Union of Soviet Socialist Republics (USSR). *See* Soviet Union

unions, 837, 838 *(illus.),* 864–65, 904

United East India Company (VOC), 918

United Fruit Company, 1027–28, 1027 *(illus.),* 1121

United Kingdom. *See* Britain

United Nations (UN): charter of, 1155; China's seat in, 1080; Decade for Women, 1160; formation of, 1057–58; Korean War and, 1067; Palestine and, 1104; World Health Organization, 1148, 1155

United States: abolition of slavery and slave trade in, 801, 802, 851; Afghanistan invasion by, 1153; agriculture in, 988, 1027; American revolution, 784–86, 785 *(illus.),* 787

United States *(continued)*
(map), 795; anticommunism in, 1072, 1076; atomic bomb use by, 1030 *(illus.)*, 1031, 1045 *(source document)*, 1047; Berlin airlift, 1065–66, 1066 *(illus.)*; British investment capital in, 862–63; California gold rush, 846 *(illus.)*, 847, 861; Chinese immigrants, 846 *(illus.)*, 847, 862, 870; civil rights movement, 1073, 1075, 1157; Civil War, 852–853, 852 *(illus.)*, 853 *(illus.)*, 954; Cold War (See Cold War); Constitution of, 786; consumerism in, 1075, 1141–42; counter-cultural protests in, 1083–84; Cuba and, 1068–70, 1069 *(illus.)*; Declaration of Independence, 785, 786 *(illus.)*, 849; *détente* policy, 1081; European immigrants, 831, 861–62, 861 *(illus.)*, 932, 933 *(map)*; French and Indian War, 784; Good Neighbor Policy, 1025–26; Great Depression in, 986–89, 987 *(illus.)*, 989 *(illus.)*, 990 *(source document)*; Gulf War, 1118; imperialism in Latin America, 928–29, 1024 *(map)*, 1025–26, 1056–57; indigenous peoples in (See native Americans); industrialization of, 822–24, 841; influenza pandemic (1918), 968; Iran-Contra scandal, 1122; Iraq War (2003–), 1118, 1153; Korean War, 1067–68, 1068 *(illus.)*, 1080; Marshall Plan, 1057, 1075; Mexican-American War, 850–51, 857; Mexican immigrants, 1026–27; military interventions in Latin America, 1024 *(map)*, 1120–21; Monroe Doctrine, 928, 929, 1026, 1120; multicultural society in, 867–70; New Deal policies, 989; oil embargo on, 1137; Pacific colonies of, 926 *(map)*, 927, 928–29, 936; Persian Gulf War, 1118; population growth in, 827–28; racial relationships in, 936, 1073, 1075, 1157; railroads in, 863–65; Reconstruction, 869; space race, 1075; Spanish-Cuban-American War, 928; strength after World War I, 972; Truman Doctrine, 1056–57; unequal treaty with China, 896; urbanization of, 829; Vietnam War, 1081–82, 1082 *(illus.)*, 1084, 1102–3; voting rights in, 786, 801, 849, 869–70; War of 1812, 854; Watergate scandal, 1084; westward expansion, 849–51,

850 *(map)*; women's rights movement in, 803–5, 869–70; in World War I, 963, 964–67, 968–69, 969 *(illus.)*; in World War II, 1032, 1041–42, 1042 *(illus.)*, 1043–47, 1046 *(map)*, 1053, 1055
Universal Declaration of Human Rights (1948), 1155–56
universities, student activism in, 1021, 1083–84
Unterseeboote (U-boats), 1038
urbanization: globalization and, 1160–62, 1161 *(illus.)*; industrialization and, 829, 831, 831 *(illus.)*. See also cities
Uruguay, 841
USSR. *See* Soviet Union
Utah Territory, 850 *(map)*
utopian socialists, 834

vaccinations, 827 *(illus.)*, 828
Vargas, Getúlio Dornelles, President of Brazil (1883–1954), 1024–25
"velvet revolution," 1086–87
Venezuela, independence of, 799, 855, 856 *(map)*
Verdun, battle of (1916), 955–56
Versailles, palace at, 788, 810 *(illus.)*
Versailles, Treaty of (1919), 969, 969 *(illus.)*, 998, 1035–36
viceroys, 916
Vichy France, 1043 *(map)*, 1048
Victor Emmanuel III, King of Italy, 996
Victoria, Queen of the United Kingdom (reigned 1837–1901), 916
Vietnam: American war in, 1081–82, 1082 *(illus.)*, 1084, 1102–3; division of, 1102; as French Indochina, 898, 919, 1041, 1048, 1101–3; Japanese conquest of, 1101; nationalist struggles of, 1101–3, 1102 *(illus.)*; in World War II, 1041
Vietnamization, 1082
Vietnam War, 1081–82, 1082 *(illus.)*, 1084, 1102–3
Villa, Francisco "Pancho" (1878–1923), 858, 860
A Vindication of the Rights of Woman (Wollstonecraft), 803
Virgin of Guadalupe, 798
Vittore Emanuele II, King of Italy (1820–1878), 810
VOC (Vereenigde Oost-Indische Compagnie), 918
Volks, German concept of, 805–6
Volksgeist, 806
Voltaire (François-Marie Arouet, 1694–1778), 783
voortrekkers, 921
voting rights: for African Americans, 802, 869, 869 *(illus.)*; American revolution and, 786,

801, 849; French revolution and, 788, 801; idea of universal suffrage, 800–801; for male workers, 837; in Meiji Japan, 903; in Mexico, 860; for women, 801, 869–70, 874, 958–59, 1122–23

Waitangi, Treaty of (1840), 926, 927 *(illus.)*
Wake Island, 1042
wangguan, 1143
Wannsee Conference (1942), 1051
war communism, 991–92
war criminals, 1056
warfare: airplanes in, 955–56, 956 *(illus.)*; *Blitzkrieg*, 1037–39, 1038 *(illus.)*; bombing of cities (See bombing of cities); chemical, 954, 954 *(illus.)*, 1046; against civilians, 956; gas, 954, 954 *(illus.)*; guerrilla, 858, 1034, 1102, 1121; kamikaze pilots, 1044; mutually assured destruction, 1067; napalm firebombs in, 1046; poisonous gas, 954, 954 *(illus.)*; propaganda in, 959, 959 *(illus.)*; submarines in, 955, 966, 966 *(illus.)*; tank, 954; trench, 953–55
"Warning to Humanity," 1144
War of 1812, 854
Warsaw ghetto uprising (1943), 1053
Warsaw Pact, 1057, 1067, 1071 *(map)*
Washington, George, President of the United States (1732–1799), 786
Watergate scandal (1972–1974), 1084
water supply, 829
Watt, James (eighteenth century), 818
WAVES (Women Appointed for Volunteer Emergency Service), 1053, 1053 *(illus.)*
wealth, unequal distribution of, 1148
Wealth of Nations (Smith), 820
weapons: firearms manufacture, 824; imperialism and, 914; intercontinental ballistic missiles, 1075; machine guns, 850, 914, 954; of mass destruction, 1153; Maxim guns, 914; muskets, 914; napalm, 1046; nuclear (See nuclear weapons); poisonous gas, 954, 954 *(illus.)*; rifles, 916; Stinger missiles, 1083; tanks, 954; zeppelins, 956. *See also* bombing of cities; nuclear weapons
weapons of mass destruction, 1153
Wedgwood, Josiah (1730–1795), 820

West Germany, 1065, 1137
The White Man's Burden (Kipling), 912, 913 *(source document)*
Whitman, Walt (1819–1892), 867, 868
Whitney, Eli (1765–1825), 824
WHO (World Health Organization), 1148, 1155
Wilberforce, William (1759–1833), 801–2
Wilhelm I, King of Prussia (1797–1888), 810, 810 *(illus.)*
Wilson, Woodrow, President of the United States (1856–1924), 964, 966, 968, 970, 1007
Witte, Sergei (served 1892–1903), 839, 889, 891
Witte system, 889
Wollstonecraft, Mary (1759–1797), 802–3
Woman in Her Social and Domestic Character (Sandford), 833
women: in China, between the world wars, 1004 *(illus.)*, 1005, 1010; in China, People's Republic of, 1080, 1157–58; in coal mines, 815, 819 *(illus.)*; during the Cold War, 1063, 1072; domestic abuse of, 1159; dowry deaths of, 1159; Enlightenment ideals and, 802–3; in France, 781, 790, 793; globalization and, 1156–60, 1157 *(illus.)*, 1158 *(illus.)*, 1160 *(illus.)*; in the Great Depression, 987; in India under British rule, 916–17; industrialization and, 814 *(illus.)*, 815, 833, 837; under Islamic rule, 1152, 1159, 1160; in Latin America, 874, 1122–23; in Nazi Germany, 999–1000, 1000 *(illus.)*; as political leaders, 1159–60, 1160 *(illus.)*; trafficking of, 1149; in World War I, 951, 958, 958 *(illus.)*; in World War II, 1053–54, 1053 *(illus.)*, 1054 *(illus.)*. See also women's rights
women's rights: to education, 803, 1155, 1158 *(illus.)*, 1159; Enlightenment ideals and, 802–3; feminism, 1072–73; French Revolution and, 781, 803, 803 *(illus.)*, 804 *(source document)*; globalization and, 1156–60, 1157 *(illus.)*, 1158 *(illus.)*, 1160 *(illus.)*; in Latin America, 874, 1122–23; in Pakistan, 1159; Taiping rebellion (China) and, 897; in the United States, 803, 869–70; voting rights, 801, 869–70, 874, 958–59, 1122–23
woolens, 818
workers: in Africa, colonial, 1018; children as, 833–34, 837, 1148–49; as consumers, 827;

in debt peonage, 860, 1149; "guest workers," 1162; immigrant, 861–62, 1162; as indentured laborers, 860, 872, 932–34; industrialization and, 815–16, 819 *(illus.)*, 820–21, 832–33; labor migrations under imperialism, 932–34, 933 *(map)*; Marx and Engels on, 835–37, 836 *(source document)*; proletariat, 835–37, 836 *(source document)*, 963; in Russia, 889–90, 993; social reform for, 837; trade unions, 837, 838 *(illus.)*, 864–65, 904; urban living conditions of, 829, 831, 831 *(illus.)*. *See also* peasants; slavery

work ethic, 832–33

World Health Organization (WHO), 1148, 1155

World Trade Organization (WTO), 1133, 1136

World War I (1914–1917), 945–75; in Africa, 960–61, 1014–16, 1015 *(illus.)*; alliances prior to, 949–50; assassination of Archduke Ferdinand, 945–46, 951; casualties in, 956, 967–68; civilians as targets in, 956; in east Asia and the Pacific, 959–60; in Europe, 953–56, 953 *(map)*, 956 *(illus.)*; German reparations after, 969, 985; in the home front, 956–59, 957 *(source document)*, 958 *(illus.)*, 959 *(illus.)*; influenza pandemic after, 968, 1149; Latin America and, 1021–23, 1022 *(illus.)*; mutinies in, 967; public opinion prior to, 948–49, 950–51; Russian revolution and, 963–64; settlements after, 968–72, 969 *(illus.)*, 971 *(map)*; in southwest Asia, 953 *(map)*, 961–62; as total war, 946, 951; underlying causes of, 946–50; United States entry into, 963, 964–67

World War II (1939–1945), 1030–60; Allied victory in Europe, 1044; appeasement policy towards Germany, 1036–37; atomic bombs in, 1030 *(illus.)*, 1031, 1045 *(source document)*, 1047; battle of the Atlantic, 1038; casualties in, 1055; collaboration and resistance during, 1048–50,

1052–53; German conquest of Europe, 1037–39, 1038 *(illus.)*, 1039 *(illus.)*, 1043 *(map)*; German expansion prior to, 1035–37; Italian expansion in Africa and, 1035, 1036 *(illus.)*; Japan's war with China, 1032–35, 1033 *(illus.)*, 1034 *(illus.)*; neutral nations in, 1043 *(map)*; Nuremberg war crimes trials, 1155; in the Pacific, 1041–42, 1042 *(illus.)*, 1044; peace settlements, 1055–56; women in, 1053–54, 1053 *(illus.)*, 1054 *(illus.)*

World Zionist Organization, 807

Wounded Knee Creek, battle of (1890), 850

The Wretched of the Earth (Fanon), 1107–8

WTO (World Trade Organization), 1133, 1136

Xhosa people, 921

Yalta Conference (1945), 1055–56

Yamaoka Michiko, 1045 *(source document)*

yellow fever, 796

Yeltsin, Boris N., President of Russia (1931–), 1088

Yom Kippur War (1973), 1116

Younghusband, Francis, 936

Young Italy, 806, 809

Young Ottomans, 884

Young Turks (Ottoman Society for Union and Progress), 884 *(illus.)*, 885, 885 *(illus.)*, 886 *(source document)*

Yugoslavia, 1076, 1077. *See also* Balkans

zaibatsu, 839, 903

Zaire, 1126, 1143. *See also* Belgian Congo

Zamudio, Adela, 874

Zapata, Emiliano (1879–1919), 858, 860, 860 *(illus.)*, 874

Zapatistas, 874

zemstvos, 888

zeppelins, 956

Zimbabwe, 1109, 1109 *(map)*

Zionism, 806–7, 807 *(illus.)*, 1103

Zulu people, 921